The Circular Economy and Its Implications on Sustainability and the Green Supply Chain

Ulas Akkucuk
Bogazici University, Turkey

A volume in the Advances in Finance, Accounting, and Economics (AFAE) Book Series

IGI Global
DISSEMINATOR OF KNOWLEDGE

Published in the United States of America by
IGI Global
Business Science Reference (an imprint of IGI Global)
701 E. Chocolate Avenue
Hershey PA, USA 17033
Tel: 717-533-8845
Fax: 717-533-8661
E-mail: cust@igi-global.com
Web site: http://www.igi-global.com

Library of Congress Cataloging-in-Publication Data

Names: Akkucuk, Ulas, 1975- editor.
Title: The circular economy and its implications on sustainability and the green supply chain / Ulas Akkucuk, editor.
Description: Hershey, PA : Business Science Reference, [2019]
Identifiers: LCCN 2018047032| ISBN 9781522581093 (hardcover) | ISBN 9781522581109 (ebook)
Subjects: LCSH: Sustainable development.
Classification: LCC HC79.E5 C53 2019 | DDC 338.9/27--dc23 LC record available at https://lccn.loc.gov/2018047032

This book is published in the IGI Global book series Advances in Finance, Accounting, and Economics (AFAE) (ISSN: 2327-5677; eISSN: 2327-5685)

British Cataloguing in Publication Data
A Cataloguing in Publication record for this book is available from the British Library.

For electronic access to this publication, please contact: eresources@igi-global.com.

Advances in Finance, Accounting, and Economics (AFAE) Book Series

Ahmed Driouchi
Al Akhawayn University, Morocco

ISSN:2327-5677
EISSN:2327-5685

Mission

In our changing economic and business environment, it is important to consider the financial changes occurring internationally as well as within individual organizations and business environments. Understanding these changes as well as the factors that influence them is crucial in preparing for our financial future and ensuring economic sustainability and growth.

The **Advances in Finance, Accounting, and Economics (AFAE)** book series aims to publish comprehensive and informative titles in all areas of economics and economic theory, finance, and accounting to assist in advancing the available knowledge and providing for further research development in these dynamic fields.

Coverage

- Fiscal Policy
- Economic Downturn
- Evidence-Based Studies
- Economics of Agriculture and Biotechnology
- Statistical Analysis
- Managerial Accounting
- Public Finance
- Auditing
- Behavioral Economics
- Economics of Migration and Spatial Mobility

IGI Global is currently accepting manuscripts for publication within this series. To submit a proposal for a volume in this series, please contact our Acquisition Editors at Acquisitions@igi-global.com or visit: http://www.igi-global.com/publish/.

The Advances in Finance, Accounting, and Economics (AFAE) Book Series (ISSN 2327-5677) is published by IGI Global, 701 E. Chocolate Avenue, Hershey, PA 17033-1240, USA, www.igi-global.com. This series is composed of titles available for purchase individually; each title is edited to be contextually exclusive from any other title within the series. For pricing and ordering information please visit http://www.igi-global.com/book-series/advances-finance-accounting-economics/73685. Postmaster: Send all address changes to above address.

Titles in this Series

For a list of additional titles in this series, please visit: www.igi-global.com/book-series

Corporate Insolvency Law and Bankruptcy Reforms in the Global Economy
Amit Kashyap (Nirma University, India)
Business Science Reference • copyright 2019 • 261pp • H/C (ISBN: 9781522555414) • US $185.00 (our price)

Time Bank as a Complementary Economic System Emerging Research and Opportunities
Lukas Valek (University of Hradec Kralove, Czech Republic) and Vladimir Bures (University of Hradec Kralove, Czech Republic)
Business Science Reference • copyright 2019 • 208pp • H/C (ISBN: 9781522569749) • US $175.00 (our price)

Economic Dynamics of Global Energy Geopolitics
Ahmet Salih Ikiz (Muğla Sıtkı Koçman University, Turkey)
Engineering Science Reference • copyright 2019 • 305pp • H/C (ISBN: 9781522542032) • US $195.00 (our price)

Co-Manufacturing and New Economic Paradigms
Giulio Focardi (Osun WES, Italy) and Lorenza Salati (Osun WES, Italy)
Business Science Reference • copyright 2019 • 217pp • H/C (ISBN: 9781522570899) • US $185.00 (our price)

Handbook of Research on Microfinancial Impacts on Women Empowerment, Poverty, and Inequality
Ramesh Chandra Das (Katwa College, India)
Business Science Reference • copyright 2019 • 452pp • H/C (ISBN: 9781522552406) • US $275.00 (our price)

Emerging Economic Models for Global Sustainability and Social Development
Bryan Christiansen (Global Research Society, LLC, USA) Irina Sysoeva (Independent Researcher, Russia) Alexandra Udovikina (Independent Researcher, Russia) and Anna Ketova (Khabarovsk State Academy of Economics and Law, Russia)
Business Science Reference • copyright 2019 • 430pp • H/C (ISBN: 9781522557876) • US $225.00 (our price)

Techno-Social Systems for Modern Economical and Governmental Infrastructures
Alexander Troussov (The Russian Presidential Academy of National Economy and Public Administration, Russia) and Sergey Maruev (The Russian Presidential Academy of National Economy and Public Administration, Russia)
Business Science Reference • copyright 2019 • 351pp • H/C (ISBN: 9781522555865) • US $205.00 (our price)

Perspectives, Trends, and Applications in Corporate Finance and Accounting
Constantin Zopounidis (Technical University of Crete, Greece) Apostolos G. Christopoulos (National and Kapodistrian University of Athens, Greece) and Petros Kalantonis (Technological Education Institute (TEI) of Piraeus, Greece)
Business Science Reference • copyright 2018 • 354pp • H/C (ISBN: 9781522561149) • US $215.00 (our price)

IGI Global
DISSEMINATOR OF KNOWLEDGE

701 East Chocolate Avenue, Hershey, PA 17033, USA
Tel: 717-533-8845 x100 • Fax: 717-533-8661
E-Mail: cust@igi-global.com • www.igi-global.com

Table of Contents

Detailed Table of Contents

This chapter presents a methodology to evaluate the benefit of using sensors in closed-loop supply chains. Sensors can be embedded into products to collect helpful information during their use and end-of-life (EOL) phases. This information can subsequently be employed to estimate the remaining lives of components and products and to ensure that proper maintenance is provided to avoid premature failures. The information is also useful in determining the quality of the components and products when planning EOL operations such as disassembly, inspection, and remanufacturing. To statistically illustrate these benefits, discrete event simulation is employed to a case study consisting of regular and sensor-embedded refrigerator systems. A design of experiments study is then employed where experiments are run to compare the two systems. The results reveal that the sensor-embedded systems perform much better than the regular systems in terms of disassembly costs, inspection costs, and EOL profits generated by selling the remanufactured products and components.

Brazil's national solid waste policy (PNRS) took nearly two decades to pass through legislative houses until it was approved as a law protecting the environment. During this period and after its approval, pro-environmental factors led to the right to transform and create protocols, agreements, and new companies in the sense of a reverse logistics or of a reversibility in the environmental effects of the supply chain. This chapter has aimed to present aspects of the Brazilian business reality in the process of implementation of the PNRS as a reflection on the perspective of product recycling and solid waste control and reverse logistics. The PNRS is in the phase of corporate expansion, taking stock of eight years since the creation of the law (2010). As some branches of Brazilian business activity have not yet had reverse logistics regulated, in the coming years there should be a much higher demand for this type of reverse business.

The research is aimed at assessing the benefits of compliance for corporate sustainability and sustainable development. The main achievement of the research is the outcome of the survey on companies' public reports to identify the trends and measure the progress achieved in disclosing information on compliance. There are both business and public drivers for disclosure of compliance information in non-financial reporting. Best practices in disclosing information on compliance by the company-leaders were revealed. There is a positive trend in the expansion of information on compliance in sustainability reports in recent years. Some problematic areas in reporting on compliance were identified. The outcomes of the research call for companies to disclose information on compliance in a more explicit way. The results may be valid for the improvement of corporate reporting practices.

Today, companies are trying to move from an existing linear business model of production to a circular one. This transition is not easy and demands contextual changes beyond the control of the company. Circular economy (CE) pursues closing material flows in productive systems to maximize the utilization of available resources. Thus, different circles to reduce, reuse, recycle, re-manufacture, recover, and recycle are produced along supply chain during the cycle of life of a product. Despite an innovative apparel, little is known about the companies with disruptive business models and supply chain structures that have emerged in the recent years.

Blue economy refers to economic sectors that are either directly or indirectly linked with the oceans. However, the blue economy does not only have an economic dimension. Environmental health is also an area that blue economy takes into account. This chapter draws attention to both social and economic potential to be created by blue economy and to consider and evaluate how to increase this potential through public policies in today's century, when the resources are gradually depleted and population growth continues. In order for the blue economy to be a driving force for sustainable growth, public-private partnerships emerge as a recipe for opportunities. In addition, the growth of the blue economy can be stimulated by conventional financial instruments (such as taxes and subsidies). Since the blue economy is at an intersection of environmental health and economic benefits, positive externalities that environmental health can have on generations should not be overlooked.

Preface

In an age of rising environmental concerns, it has become necessary for businesses to pay special attention the resources they are consuming and the long-term effects of the products they are creating. These concerns, coupled with the current global economic crisis, demand a solution that includes not only business, but politics, ecology, and culture as well.

This is the way I started out writing the preface of four of the volumes I edited with IGI Global on sustainability related issues. It is still valid and explains the gist of the sustainability issue so I will repeat it at the start of the new volume. I gave the first book proposal to IGI Global in the summer of 2013. This first book was finalized towards fall 2014 and published as hard copy in January 2015. This gave me the idea for the second book and this came out as a hard copy by 2016 March. Both of the books included a total of 47 papers from eminent authors worldwide. The third book which came out in 2017 included 14 contributions and was readily indexed by Web of Science. The last book entitled *Handbook of Research on Supply Chain Management for Sustainable Development* was published recently in 2018. This title was also indexed in SCOPUS. The last title includes 19 contributions. This brings the sum of the chapters to 80 and with the book you are about to read nearly 100 chapters have been sent by authors worldwide on many different aspects of sustainability touching the areas of Finance, Marketing, Operations, Waste Management and Economics. The number of authors has also reached near a figure of 150 with countries of the participants ranging from Turkey, USA, Bulgaria, Russia, Netherlands, Spain, Portugal, Zimbabwe, Saudi Arabia, Greece, Egypt, India, Canada, Malaysia, Thailand, Mexico and many others.

The books enjoy indexation by prestigious indices and citations by eminent authors. The book you are about to read is a follow up with an approach that encompasses a holistic view relating the most important elements of the concepts of circular economy. A circular economy is a regenerative system in which resource input and waste, emission, and energy leakage are minimized by slowing, closing, and narrowing material and energy loops. This can be achieved through long-lasting design, maintenance, repair, reuse, remanufacturing, refurbishing, and recycling. This is in contrast to a linear economy which is a 'take, make, dispose' model of production.

Following the research line, I developed in the previous volumes the main topic of this book is aptly chosen as "Circular Economy and its Implications on Sustainability and the Green Supply Chain". Circular Economy is an idea that extends the biological cycle found in nature to a technological cycle where goods when disposed properly are converted into new products in an environmentally efficient way. GSCM as it can be abbreviated focuses on delivering value along the Supply Chain in a way that also ensures fair labor practices, lower emissions and a cleaner environment. Principles of GSCM are practiced by many global companies with production and distribution operations around the world. Supply Chain Management and Reverse Logistics are particularly important areas of sustainability. Both solid and liquid wastes are growing with increasing population and wealth. How to deal with the waste resulting from human activities is a matter of concern for developing countries. The 4 R's consisting of Reduction, Reuse, Recycling, and Recovery deserve a lot of multidisciplinary research. The book extends on this idea and focuses on the Circular Economy.

Chapter 1 starts the discussion with a paper entitled "Design for a Closed-Loop Supply Chain System with Sensor-Embedded Refrigerators". This chapter presents a methodology to evaluate the benefit of using sensors in closed loop supply chains. Sensors can be embedded into products to collect helpful information during their use and end-of-life (EOL) phases. This information can subsequently be employed to estimate the remaining lives of components and products and to ensure that proper maintenance is provided to avoid premature failures. The information is also useful in determining the quality of the components and products when planning EOL operations such as disassembly, inspection and remanufacturing. To statistically illustrate these benefits, discrete event simulation is employed to a case study consisting of regular and sensor-embedded refrigerator systems. A design of experiments study is then employed where experiments are run to compare the two systems. The results reveal that the sensor-embedded systems perform much better than the regular systems in terms of disassembly costs, inspection costs, and EOL profits generated by selling the remanufactured products and components.

Chapters 2 is about "Brazilian Solid Waste Policy (PNRS)". Brazil's national solid waste policy (PNRS) took nearly two decades to pass through legislative houses until it was approved as a law protecting the environment. During this period and after its approval, pro-environmental factors led to the right to transform and create protocols, agreements and new companies in the sense of a reverse logistics or of a reversibility in the environmental effects of the supply chain. This study has aimed to present aspects of the Brazilian business reality in the process of implementation of the PNRS as a reflection on the perspective of product recycling and solid waste control and reverse logistics. The PNRS is in the phase of corporate expansion, taking stock of eight years since the creation of the law (2010). As some branches of Brazilian business activity have not yet had reverse logistics regulated, in the coming years there should be a much higher demand for this type of reverse business.

Chapter 3 investigates "Compliance in Sustainability Reporting". The research is aimed at assessing the benefits of compliance for corporate sustainability and sustainable development. The main achievement of the research is the outcome of the survey on companies' public reports to identify the trends and measure the progress achieved in disclosing information on compliance. There are both business and public drivers for disclosure of compliance information in non-financial reporting. Best practices in disclosing information on compliance by the company-leaders were revealed. There is a positive trend in the expansion of information on compliance in sustainability reports in recent years. Some problematic areas in reporting on compliance were identified. The outcomes of the research call for companies to disclose information on compliance in a more explicit way. The results may be valid for the improvement of corporate reporting practices.

Chapter 4 is a discussion "Circular Supply Chain and Business Model in Apparel Industry". Today, companies are trying to move from an existing linear business model of production to a circular one. This transition could be not be easy and demand contextual changes beyond the control of the company. Circular Economy (CE) pursues closing material flows in productive systems to maximize the utilization of available resources. Thus, different circles in order to reduce, reuse, recycle, re-manufacture, recover and recycle are produced along supply chain during the cycle of life of a product. Despite an innovative apparel companies with disruptive business models and supply chain structures have emerged in the last years in the industry little has knowledge yet.

Chapter 5 focuses on "An Assessment and Policy Proposals Within the Framework of the Blue Economy and Public Policies". Blue economy refers to economic sectors that are either directly or indirectly linked with the oceans. However, the blue economy does not only have an economic dimension. Environmental health is also an area that blue economy takes into account. In this article, it is aimed to draw attention to both social and economic potential to be created by blue economy and to consider and evaluate how to increase this potential through public policies in today's century, where the resources are gradually depleted and population growth continues. In order for the blue economy to be a driving force for sustainable growth, public-private partnerships emerge as a recipe for opportunities. In addition, the growth of the blue economy can be stimulated by conventional financial instruments (such as taxes and subsidies). Since the blue economy is at an intersection of environmental health and economic benefits, positive externalities that environmental health can have on generations should not be overlooked.

Chapter 6 is another look at the "Economic Impacts of Closed-Loop Supply Chains". Closed loop supply chain management has begun to gain more importance in recent years due to increased environmental concerns, reduced natural resources and legal regulations. In addition, with the shortening of product life cycles, the rate of returning products is increasing day by day. Therefore, businesses are trying to find ways to get more value from these returning products. Here, the Closed Loop Supply Chain (CLSC), which comes into effect at this point, refers to the design, operation and control of the system to ensure maximum value from returning products of different breeds and quantities. Recycling these returned products by different methods will provide significant savings in terms of both the production costs by providing return of the economically valuable materials to the economy as an input and the waste disposal costs by reducing the amount of waste. In this study, it is aimed to investigate the concept of closed loop supply chain and its benefits to the businesses.

Chapter 7 examines the "Influence of the EU Circular Economy Action Plan on Turkey's Energy Policy and Investments in Renewables". The European Union Circular Economy Action Plan is a new enactment but rapidly growing to transform EU economies into more sustainable sources and surroundings adopting measures that include renewable energy investments and low carbon strategy. As the world still faces huge environmental changes and climate problems, energy remains the major issue for both economic and ecological sustainability. Low carbon energy strategy is the main target for EU circular economy enforcing renewable energy sources which are healthy, clean and cheap. In this study, circular energy act and its development in Turkey are explored and questioned. The study emphasizes the great potential of renewables in Turkey and shows that there is still much to be done to transform the energy market in order to adopt circular economy in the future. Barriers of economic risks and lack of cultural awareness strongly challenge the progress of Turkey in energy solutions. And more than that, those problems trigger off the financial concerns limiting the future energy projects.

Chapter 8 focuses on "SERVQUAL-Based Evaluation of Service Quality of Energy Companies in Turkey". The aim of this study is to measure the service quality of energy companies. Within this context, 7 different energy companies that are listed on İstanbul Stock Exchange are considered. For this purpose, 5 dimensions and 14 criteria are identified by considering the details of SERVQUAL methodology. In the analysis process, fuzzy DEMATEL method is used to weight these dimensions and criteria and the performance of the energy companies are ranked by using fuzzy MOORA approach. The findings show that feedback is the most significant dimension and data security and physical security are the most important criteria. Another important conclusion is that the companies, which have high profitability, have better performance regarding service quality. Thus, it is recommended that the companies should mainly focus on the ways of getting necessary feedback from their customers, such as conducting a survey.

Chapter 9 illustrates "The Case of Turkish Companies in 3PL and 4PL Logistics Applications". The global supply chain applications are evolving and changing globally. In order to increase success some processes are now transferred to other firms. By such implementations, it is aimed to focus on the core business and to be successful. 3PL is the use of an external entity to perform some or all of the operations. Whereas, the 4PL approach is a revolutionary approach to supply chain management. This chapter aims to inform about the modernization processes in Turkey by examining successful examples.

Chapter 10 is a study on "The Effect of Health and Education Expenditures on Poverty". Poverty is a phenomenon which influences and complicates the living conditions of individuals. Along with the poverty, individuals experience health problems and educational and income levels of individuals may also be low. Countries are generally able to fight against poverty by increasing public expenditures and making some economic progresses. For that reason, analyzing the effect of health and education expenditures with a significant place in public expenditures and economic growth on poverty is highly important. In this study the effect of health and education expenditures and economic growth on poverty in 2005 and 2016 period in 8 Central and Eastern European countries has been analyzed using panel data analysis. As a result of the study, it has been determined that health and education expenditures and economic growth have a negative effect on poverty. In addition, a one-way causality from health and education expenditures to poverty and a two-way causality between economic growth and poverty have been detected.

Chapter 11 provides examples on the discussion of "Liability or Ethics? The Real Value of Compliance". The purpose of this paper is to reconsider a traditional approach to compliance function of the firms from a modern perspective, which broadens its concept as a company's liability only to secure its adherence to applicable laws and avoid regulatory sanctions in serving company's interests. The observation of issues regulated by the compliance function in the contest of managing situations of conflict of interest (COI) in different spheres concludes that, in fact, those issues, to a greater extent, relate to sustaining ethical behavior in business rather than stem from regulatory norms. Based on the findings of this analysis as well as other different sources, a new definition for effective compliance has been developed with the focus on adherence to ethical principles in respect to third parties, which addresses compliance function in terms of corporate social responsibility (CSR) and its sustainability role setting a vector for a further research.

Chapter 12 performs an analysis of "Green Marketing and Branding: Combining Micro and Macro Perspectives to Achieve a Circular Economy". Green products and services have become an important part of consumption, as consumers' knowledge and concern towards environmental sustainability has increased and they have started to concentrate on their environmental impact. Nonetheless, green marketing still constitutes a small portion of the overall consumer spending. This chapter aims to highlight the importance of marketing activities in the adoption and social normalization of green consumption by the consumers generating public support and economic benefits for the companies as well as environmental and social gains for the society in return. Combining both micro and macro level determinants and consequences, a conceptual framework is suggested which aims to contribute to literature both theoretically and practically.

Chapter 13 explores the relationship between "Financial Flexibility and Corporate Investment". The aim of this study is to investigate the impact of financial flexibility (FF) on investments, which constitutes the basis for sustainable corporate development. Using a large database of 1,205 firms from three emerging countries in Europe; Poland, Russia and Turkey, for the time period between 2000 and 2016; we provide evidence that financial flexibility, achieved through conservative leverage policies, enhances companies' investments and therefore positively contributes to corporate sustainability. Moreover, as the number of years of low leverage kept by firms increase, so does the impact of financial flexibility on corporate investment. Besides financial flexibility, internal cash generation capacity of firms and sales growth also prosper investment capability of firms, improving corporate sustainability. Our results support the hypothesis that financial flexibility enhances companies' investment capability, which is an extremely essential tool for firms to have sustainable development in their businesses.

Chapter 14 explains "Evaluation of Young Consumers' Remanufactured Products Purchase Intention Within Context of Extended Planned Behavior Theory". In this study, the remanufactured products which have an important place in the closed-loop supply chain are examined. The study aimed to evaluate the motivation of young consumers who are in close contact with technology within context of extended planned behavior theory. The theoretical model of the research was developed on the basis of the planned behavior theory and the developed model was tested by an empirical study on Ondokuz Mayis University students. As a result of the research, the environmental concerns of young consumers, the environmental knowledge of remanufactured products, and the awareness of remanufactured products positively and significantly affect the attitude towards remanufactured products. The study indicates that attitude and subjective norm related to remanufactured products are positively and significantly affect remanufactured products purchase intention and perceived behavioral control has no significant effect on intent to purchase remanufactured products.

Chapter 15 is on "Effects of Sustainable Medical Waste Management on Environment and Human Health". The increase in the number of health institutions, developments in technology, and the use of devices and materials utilized in diagnosis and treatment have increased the types and amount of medical waste. Therefore, it has become a necessity to reduce the health problems, remove the risks that may arise for human health, and protect the environment by effectively managing the medical wastes that are the results of the activities of health institutions. Hazardous medical wastes that harm human and environmental health are a risk factor for the whole society and the environment. For this reason, removal, collection, temporary storage, recycling, transportation, and disposal of medical wastes without harming people and the environment includes technical, administrative, and legal processes. This study summarizes the current literature for sustainable waste management, its relationship to environmental and human health, and international legislation on waste management.

Preface

During the first decade of the 21st century the world has witnessed corporate scandals, global economic crises and rising environmental concerns. As a result of these developments, there has been growing pressure on businesses to pay more attention to the environmental and resource consequences of the products they produce and services they deliver. The concept of sustainable development has gained more importance as a solution to these problems. Sustainable development has a number of facets related to politics, ecology, economics, business, supply chain management and waste management. Researchers and practitioners face increasing challenges in terms of integrating issues of sustainability with the traditional areas of management such as marketing, operations, finance, accounting and organizations management. In order to fully understand the Circular Economy and how it impacts global business this book tried to shed light on aspects related to green supply chains and reverse logistics.

Ulas Akkucuk
Bogazici University, Turkey
October 2018

Chapter 1
Design for a Closed-Loop Supply Chain System With Sensor-Embedded Refrigerators

Mehmet Talha Dulman
Northeastern University, USA

Surendra M. Gupta
Northeastern University, USA

ABSTRACT

This chapter presents a methodology to evaluate the benefit of using sensors in closed-loop supply chains. Sensors can be embedded into products to collect helpful information during their use and end-of-life (EOL) phases. This information can subsequently be employed to estimate the remaining lives of components and products and to ensure that proper maintenance is provided to avoid premature failures. The information is also useful in determining the quality of the components and products when planning EOL operations such as disassembly, inspection, and remanufacturing. To statistically illustrate these benefits, discrete event simulation is employed to a case study consisting of regular and sensor-embedded refrigerator systems. A design of experiments study is then employed where experiments are run to compare the two systems. The results reveal that the sensor-embedded systems perform much better than the regular systems in terms of disassembly costs, inspection costs, and EOL profits generated by selling the remanufactured products and components.

INTRODUCTION

For many years, manufacturing processes predominantly focused on profitably producing and selling products. However, strong competition in the market has forced businesses to offer value-added services with their products as a means of attracting more sales. One such service is that of competitive warranties through which manufacturers guarantee they will maintain products for a given period of time. While these warranties do appeal to customers, they also increase manufacturers' costs.

DOI: 10.4018/978-1-5225-8109-3.ch001

One of the purposes of this study is to identify methods by which manufacturers can reduce the costs associated with performing maintenance on refrigerators while also enhancing customer satisfaction. It proposes the use of embedded sensors to monitor the performance of the appliance during their use phases, provide information on the condition and use of the components, and help predict possible catastrophic failures. The availability of this information could result in shorter downtimes for the refrigerators in the event of failure and could reduce manufacturers' maintenance costs.

In addition to being beneficial to maintenance processes, sensors can also improve the performance of the refrigerators' end-of-life (EOL) processes. By retrieving critical condition information about the components, manufacturers could enhance the disassembly and inspection processes and, thereby, make EOL processing more profitable (Ilgin & Gupta, 2010b).

Our study introduces a closed-loop supply chain system that aims to enhance the system by which refrigerators are maintained during their life cycle and returned refrigerators are processed for EOL use. The goal of the study is to determine the economic benefit of incorporating sensors into new refrigerators. The study compares regular-refrigerator (RR) and sensor-embedded-refrigerator (SER) systems and tests these systems using discrete-event-simulation models and appropriate design of experiments. The results are compared for their performance measures, and pairwise t-tests are performed to determine the statistical significance of the differences between them.

LITERATURE REVIEW

This section presents a literature review of the studies conducted on remanufacturing, maintenance and sensor-embedded products. Several survey papers (Gungor & Gupta, 1999; Ilgin & Gupta, 2010a; Ilgin et al. 2015) were consulted during the literature review to acquire an in-depth understanding of environmentally conscious manufacturing and product recovery. Gupta and Ilgin (2018) published a book to cover multi-criteria decision making application in environmentally conscious manufacturing and product recovery.

Remanufacturing

Capacity Planning

Capacity planning decisions are essential within remanufacturing processes because attaining profitable utilization levels in remanufacturing systems can be challenging due to uncertainty and variation. Guide and Spencer (1997) suggested the use of rough cut capacity planning for remanufacturing. This planning method employs a bill-of-resources approach and involves the consideration of probabilistic material replacement and routing files. Guide et al. (1997) adapted five different rough cut capacity planning techniques to solve remanufacturing capacity planning problems. These techniques were bill of resources, capacity planning using overall factors, modified bill of resources, bill of resources with variance, and modified bill of resources with variance. They applied these techniques to solve a case study problem and compared the results by simulating the systems.

Georgiadis et al. (2006) and Vlachos et al. (2007) introduced system dynamics models to solve capacity planning problems in remanufacturing. The models considered the demand patterns of the product while it was in use, distribution of the residence time, and changes in remanufacturing capacity.

Georgiadis and Athanasiou (2010) modified the system dynamics model presented in Georgiadis et al.'s (2006) paper to assess the effectiveness of capacity planning with two-product joint lifecycles. Franke et al. (2006) presented a study to support the capacity planning decisions of a cell phone remanufacturing system. They used linear programming and discrete event simulation to recommend capacity planning strategies to the system executives.

Remanufacturing-to-Order Systems

Remanufacturing-to-order (RTO) systems operate according to a pull strategy. In these systems, the requirements for remanufacturing components is determined when there is a demand for remanufactured products. This supply is procured by either using disassembled components or purchasing the components from external vendors. These RTO systems were assessed in a series of studies by Ondemir and Gupta (2013a,b; 2014b). The main purpose of the RTO systems is to fulfill customer demands while also minimizing the overall cost of the systems. Moreover, the systems are designed to reduce disposed materials, increase material sales revenues and enhance recycling of non-operable components. The quality and quantity of the returned products represent uncertainties within RTO systems. To eliminate this uncertainty, the researchers proposed embedding sensors into the products as these sensors would help to estimate the remaining lifespan of the components, thereby allowing accurate material planning for remanufacturing. To solve the problems associated with RTO systems, the researchers adapted several mathematical models such as Internet of Things, fuzzy goal programming, and integer programming.

Maintenance

This chapter introduces the use of embedded sensors to improve the maintenance activities of products. The condition information that is provided by the sensors can be used to help predict failures. This type of maintenance strategy is known as predictive maintenance. Thus, papers that specifically described predictive maintenance were of particular interest in this study.

Rodriguez and Perez (2002) used sensors to detect the structural deformation of the blades within wind turbines, and they assessed how the condition information collated by the sensors can be processed to generate meaningful insights. Vijay Kumar et al. (2009) developed fuzzy modelling to process this information. Hashemian (2011) presented a study in which the use of sensors for the predictive maintenance of rotating equipment in research reactors was evaluated. The researchers found that, since these sensors continuously monitor the reactors, deformation and risk of failure can be detected before they cause an issue and the required maintenance can be provided to prevent failures. Efthymiou et al. (2012) demonstrated the use of sensors that have multiple sensing abilities to estimate the remaining life spans of the products and subsequently predict failures. Based on the study conducted by De Faria et al. (2015), sensors have the ability to monitor products on an ongoing basis to detect the density, flow, pressure, vibration, temperature, voltage, current, electrical resistance, capacitance, and inductance that they are exposed to. This facilitates the execution of predictive maintenance for the products.

Embedding Sensors Into Products

Product recovery can be executed in three ways: reuse, recycle or remanufacturing. To determine which product recovery option is best for the product, it is important to gain insights into the conditions of the components of the product before a decision is made. Embedding sensors into products can be useful in this context because they can provide the required information about the conditions of the components. Collating the condition information about the components is crucial to estimate the remaining life spans of the components (Vadde et al., 2008). Si et al. (2011) published a review paper that included previous research papers that had employed statistical approaches to identify the remaining life of the product. Data-driven approaches have been commonly used to produce a remaining life estimate. When these methods are employed, stored data is interpreted using statistical methods, such as regression, Brownian motion with drift, gamma processes, Markovian-based models, stochastic-filtering based models, and covariate-based hazard models, to forecast the estimated remaining life. Byington et al. (2004) proposed a data-driven neural network methodology to estimate the remaining life of the components in an aircraft actuator. They concluded that this data-driven methodology could be used in many industries for either product recovery or maintenance. Kara et al. (2005) studied neural networks to assess the remaining life of the components and proposed a two-step methodology. Herzog et al. (2009) experimented with neural networks to generate failure predictions for machines and components and found that data collection enhanced the accuracy of the results.

Ilgin and Gupta (2010b) published a sensor-embedded product study that simulated models to determine the best product recovery option for EOL products by using the remaining life information provided by the sensors. This information helped to reduce the costs associated with product recovery, such as disassembly, inspection, inventory, stock-out, and disposal costs, because the operations are planned prior to disassembly by means of sensors. The authors published a series of papers (Ilgin & Gupta, 2011a,b,c; Ilgin et al., 2011; Ilgin et al., 2014) that compared several simulation models developed for different products and product combinations to explore the benefits of sensors when they are used for product recovery. Sensor-embedded products were also studied in a series of papers (Ondemir & Gupta, 2012; Ondemir et al., 2012; Ondemir & Gupta, 2013a,b; Ondemir & Gupta, 2014a,b). The authors developed a range of systems including remanufacture-to-order, refurbish-to-order and repair-to-order. In these systems, different demands in terms of quality and prices were fulfilled by disassembling EOL products. The authors suggested the use of sensors to determine the quality of the returned products.

Dulman and Gupta (2015) conducted a study to analyze the economic impact embedded sensors have on closed-loop supply chain systems for cell phones. Dulman and Gupta (2016) extended previous studies by considering the use of sensors within the operations by which the products are maintained. They found that the condition information provided by the sensors could effectively predict the failures of the products. Dulman and Gupta (2018a,b) combined the idea of using sensors both for maintenance phase of the products and EOL phase. Dulman and Gupta (2018b) assessed the benefits of these sensors when they are embedded in wind turbines. Alqahtani and Gupta (2017a,b) proposed the use of the remaining life information collated by the sensors to determine the optimal warranty period that should be offered with remanufactured products.

SYSTEM DESCRIPTION

This section provides insights into the maintenance activities that are often required during the use phase of refrigerators and the EOL processes that are employed after they complete their life cycles. Once a manufacturer produces and sells a refrigerator, the customer or manufacturer maintains the refrigerator until it can no longer provide reasonable service to the customer. If the refrigerator is no longer usable, the customer returns it to the manufacturer, which processes it for EOL use. The manufacturer can either remanufacture or refurbish the unit, if feasible, and a second life cycle begins. Otherwise, the manufacturer recycles the materials contained in the refrigerator. The refrigerator will only be disposed of if none of the options outlined above is feasible. Figure 1 outlines the overall life cycle and processes of refrigerators.

Maintenance of Refrigerators

The life cycle of refrigerators starts with their arrival at the customer's location. The expected life span of the refrigerators is ten years. Like any other product, refrigerators might fail during their life cycle, and, if they fail, they require service to repair or replace failed components. At the end of their life cycle, the manufacturer collects the refrigerators and transfers them to an EOL facility. Figure 2 presents an overview of the life cycle of a refrigerator.

Maintenance of RR Systems

Once a refrigerator fails, the customer notifies the service facility and requests a maintenance service for the failed refrigerator. Repair personnel arrives at the customer's location and inspects the appliance to identify which of the components have failed. These operations are represented in Figure 3 by the recognition of failure and service activation process. If necessary, the manufacturer transfers the refrigerator to a service facility, replaces the failed components, and then delivers the repaired unit back to the customer. Otherwise, replacement is performed on site.

Figure 1. Maintenance and EOL Life-Cycle Scheme of Refrigerators

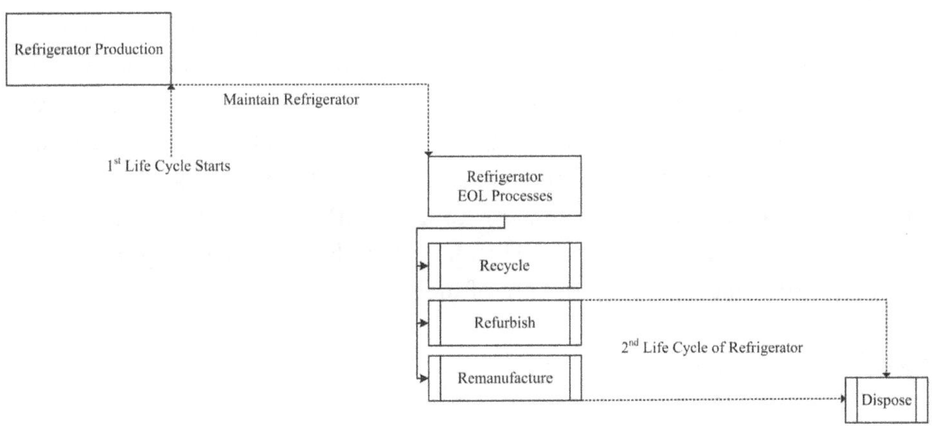

Figure 2. Life Cycle of Refrigerators

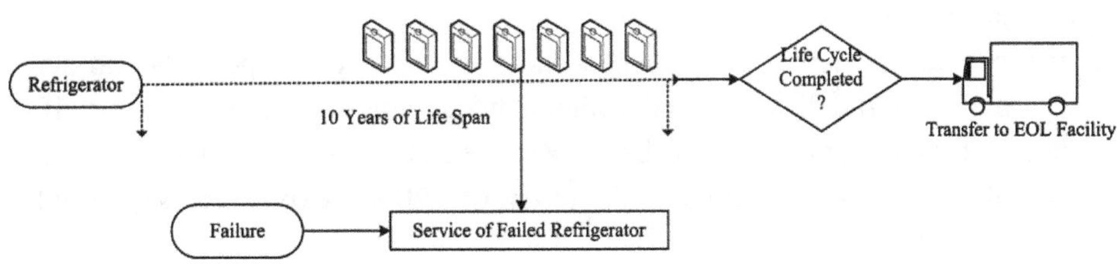

Figure 3. Maintenance Operations of RR Systems

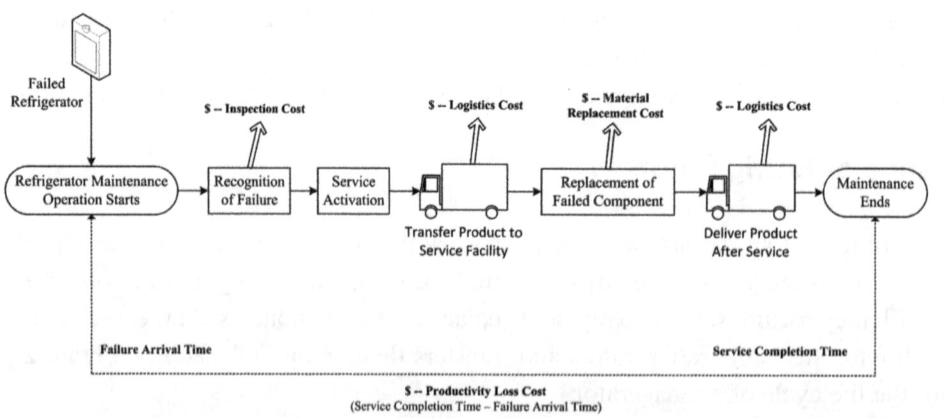

Failures cause productivity loss because customers cannot use the failed refrigerators during the failure and service period. Productivity loss is a function of the expected life span of the refrigerator and its purchase price. Calculating the productivity loss involves determining the time taken from initial failure to service completion.

In addition to productivity loss cost, manufacturers must also consider the cost of the inspection that service personnel must perform to determine the cause of the refrigerator failure, the cost of material that is purchased to replace the failed component or components, and the cost of transportation and delivery.

Maintenance of SER Systems

The sensors in SER systems can provide information about the conditions of the refrigerator's internal components. By processing this information, sensors estimate when a refrigerator will fail and send signals to the service facility so that the manufacturer can take appropriate action before such failure occurs. The use of sensors, therefore, eliminates the need for an inspection operation. Figure 4 provides a flow chart of the maintenance operations that are associated with the SER systems.

The failure and service period takes less time within an SER system than it does for an RR system, resulting in a shorter productivity loss period. This, in turn, reduces productivity loss cost. In addition, inspection costs are also reduced through the use of the sensors.

Refrigerator EOL Processes

Once a refrigerator completes its life cycle, the manufacturer collects it and sends it to a facility at which the EOL processes are performed. The manufacturer disassembles the EOL refrigerators on a disassembly line that consists of five stations. Figure 5 and Figure 6 show the sequence by which the components are disassembled.

Operators or robots at the EOL facility inspect the disassembled components and determine their conditions. They categorize the disassembled components as reusable or not reusable. If they are not reusable, the manufacturer either recycles or disposes of them. Otherwise, the manufacturer can sell the components or use them to remanufacture based on their conditions, expressed as quality levels, which

Figure 4. Maintenance Operations of SER Systems

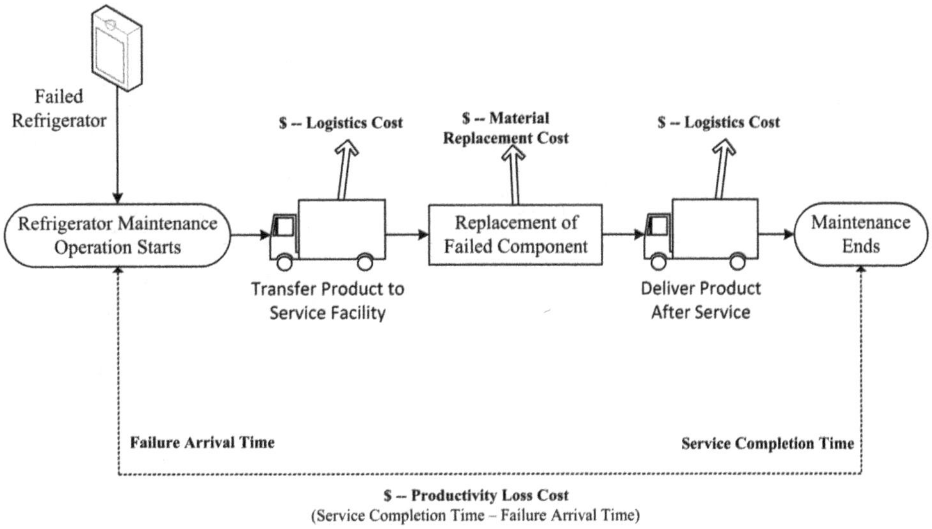

provide an estimation of their expected lifetime for reuse. In SER systems, the inspection process is unnecessary because sensors provide the condition information about the components. The manufacturer sends disassembled components directly to recycling, remanufacturing, or resale locations.

EOL Processes of RR Systems

Manufacturers of RR systems disassemble each component of the refrigerator unless the component is missing. If a component is missing, the manufacturer sends the refrigerator to the next station. For each component, the disassembly time and labor costs translate to disassembly costs. Inspection follows disassembly, during which the manufacturer inspects the disassembled components. Inspections involve two main activities: Determining the reusability of the components and determining the condition of the component. Based on these determinations, the appropriate reprocessing operations are performed. Figure 5 shows the disassembly and inspection processes of RR systems.

EOL Processes of SER Systems

SER systems have more complicated disassembly and inspection structures than RR systems because sensors provide condition information before the refrigerator is disassembled. The manufacturer can use this information to better plan the disassembly and inspection processes. Figure 6 details the disassembly and inspection processes involved in SER systems.

If the components are missing, the manufacturer sends the refrigerator directly to the next station. Otherwise, the operators check the reusability information that is available for each component and use that information to determine the flow. If the units are not reusable, they are not disassembled. Instead, they proceed to the next station. If another component in the next station requires disassembly, both units undergo disassembly together due to the precedence relationship. Disassembling them together can save costs because it will reduce the time taken to process the components separately. If the units are reusable,

Figure 5. RR Systems Disassembly and Inspection Processes

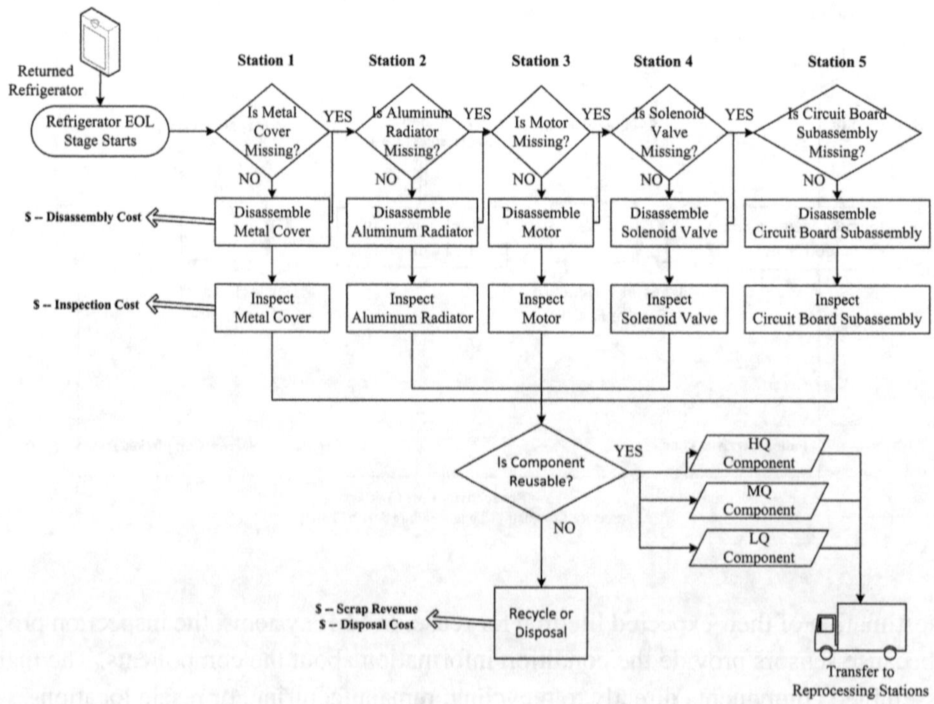

they are labeled with information that describes the quality level of the components as determined by the data provided by the sensors. These labels are subsequently used to check inventory levels of each quality level component. If the maximum inventory levels are not reached, operators disassemble them, and the units are relocated to the reprocessing area. Otherwise, the refrigerators proceed to the next station without undergoing disassembly. If another component at the next station requires disassembly, both units undergo disassembly together. The upfront inventory check and reduction in inventory reduces costs.

Reprocessing Operations of RR and SER Systems

Both systems have high-quality (HQ), medium-quality (MQ), and low-quality (LQ) level components, each of which has different flows through the systems. LQ components should last approximately one to two years. MQ components should last approximately two to three years, and HQ components should last three to four years. The manufacturer sends disassembled components to a reprocessing area.

Figure 7 outlines the HQ-component flow. If the maximum HQ-remanufactured-refrigerator inventory level is not reached in the system, the manufacturer sends the HQ component to the HQ-remanufacturing buffer area. Otherwise, the manufacturer checks the maximum HQ-component inventory for component sales. If the maximum HQ-component inventory level is met, the manufacturer sends the component for use in MQ processes instead of recycling it because using the HQ component in lower-level processes can increase the quality of that level. Similar flow also occurs at the MQ level. The manufacturer can repurpose any unnecessary MQ components at the LQ level. If none of the options are available, the manufacturer can recycle or dispose of the components.

Figure 6. SER Systems Disassembly and Inspection Processes

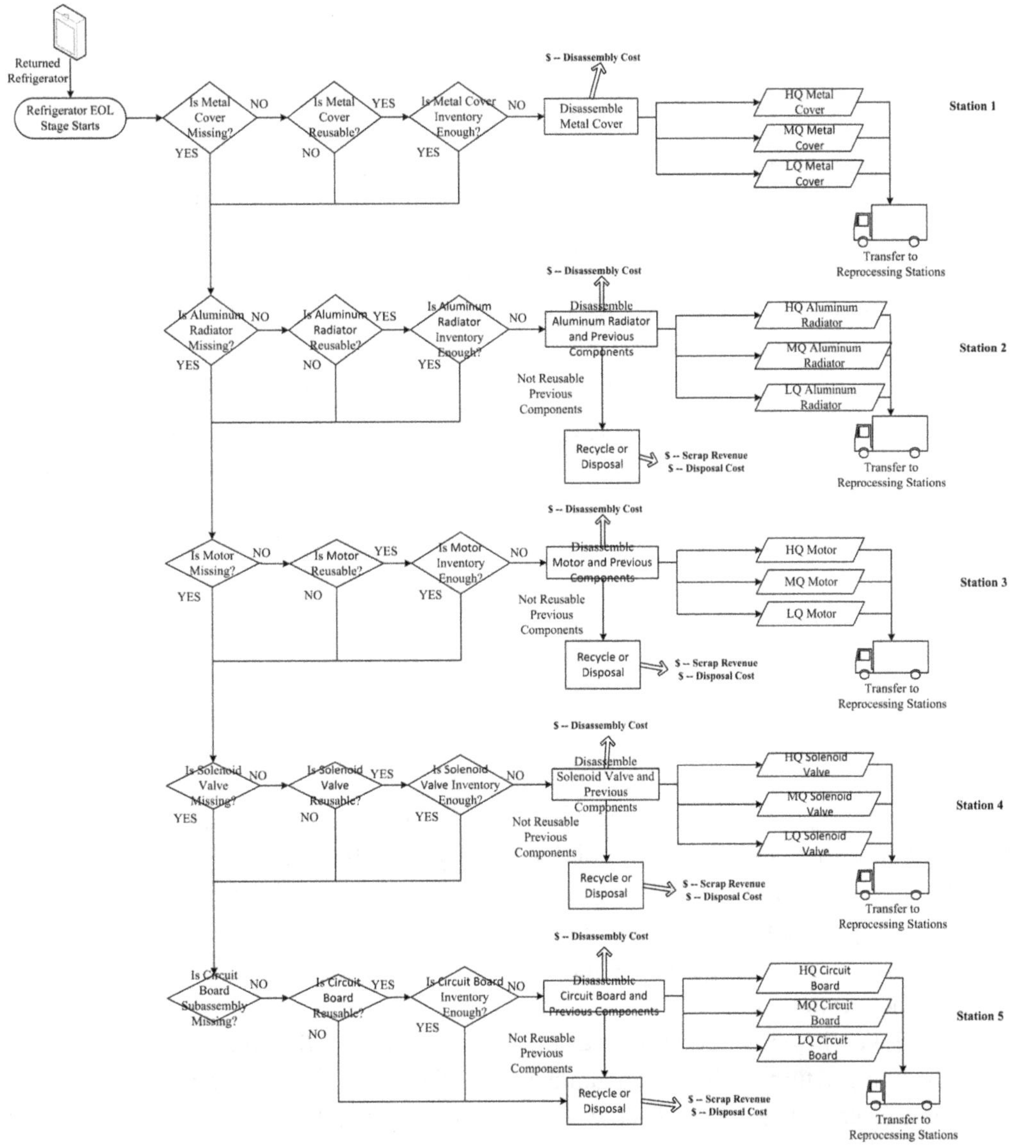

If the manufacturer chooses the resale option, the components are sold to generate sales revenue. These components can also generate revenue if they are sold as scrap. Disposing of them, on the other hand, adds cost to the systems.

Maintenance operations affect the quality levels of the returned products, and this effect determines the quality level probabilities. These probabilities are determined according to whether these components require replacement during their life cycle, how much time they were in use, and the condition information that is captured by inspecting them during the RR systems or as compiled by the sensors in the SER systems. The quality levels of the components are expected to be better if they have been in use for less than four years.

Figure 7. HQ-Component Flow for Recycle, Resale and Remanufacturing

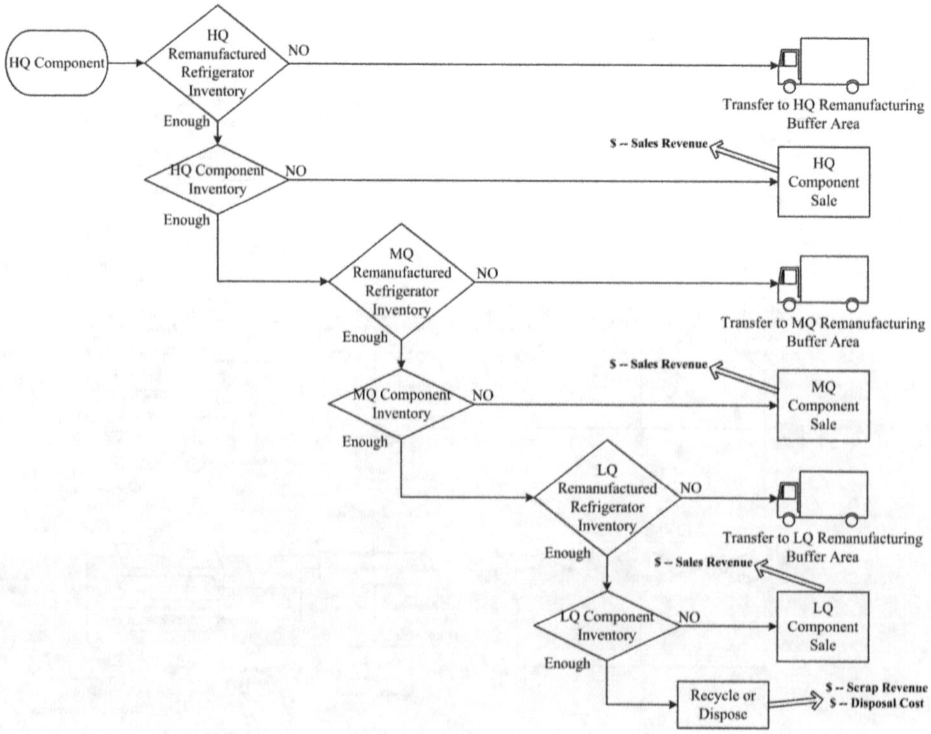

If the manufacturer opts to use components for remanufacturing, the components are stored in the remanufacturing buffer area for their corresponding quality level. If there is one of each component type, the manufacturer assembles them. These remanufactured refrigerators then join the remanufactured-refrigerator inventory. When there is a demand for them, the manufacturer sells them. If demand is lacking, they remain in inventory, and this increases the holding cost. The remanufacturing assembly process adds to the assembly cost.

The demands for each quality level follow a Poisson distribution. If the inventory is sufficient to fulfill the demand, the manufacturer sells the remanufactured refrigerators and generates revenue. Otherwise, the manufacturer places the units in a backordered status, incurring backordering costs. Figure 8 highlights the process of remanufacturing the refrigerators, demand flows, and the effect of remanufacturing and demands on revenue and costs.

DESIGN OF EXPERIMENTS STUDY

The purpose of the design of experiments study was to determine the impact the sensors have on the performance of the system. A total of 63 factors were identified that can affect the performance measures of the system. Full factorial design requires an excessive number of experiments; as such, previous studies have employed orthogonal arrays method to reduce the number of experiments to a reasonable size. The orthogonal arrays method suggests that 64 experiments can accommodate 63 factors with two levels each. The factorial design employed in this study used the $L_{64}(2^{63})$ orthogonal array (Phadke,

Figure 8. Remanufacturing Flow of Refrigerators

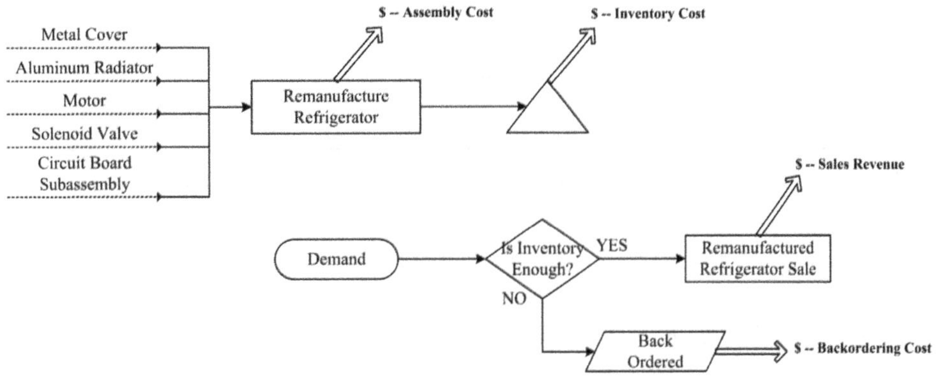

1989). The data used to determine the levels of the factors in the study was referenced from a previous study by Ilgin and Gupta (2010b).

Table 1 shows the price factors. The factorial design included the HQ- and MQ-level remanufactured refrigerator and component prices. The experiment considered the effect of LQ-level prices on the performance measures as insignificant; as such, they were not included in the factorial design.

The factorial design included the disassembly cost and disassembly times of the components, as shown in Table 2.

The factorial design also included the inspection cost and inspection times of the components, as shown in Table 3.

Table 4 presents the probability of retrieving refrigerators with missing components, the reusability of the components and their quality levels. LQ-level probabilities were excluded from the total number of factors because once HQ- and MQ-level probabilities were identified, LQ-level probabilities could be determined. Table 5 depicts the LQ-level probabilities.

Table 1. Remanufactured Refrigerator, Subassembly & Component Prices

Factor	Level 1	Level 2
HQ Refrigerator ($)	384	320
HQ Metal Cover ($)	24	20
HQ Aluminum Radiator ($)	72	60
HQ Motor ($)	120	100
HQ Solenoid Valve ($)	36	30
HQ Circuit Board ($)	84	70
MQ Refrigerator ($)	270	225
MQ Metal Cover ($)	12	10
MQ Aluminum Radiator ($)	48	40
MQ Motor ($)	90	75
MQ Solenoid Valve ($)	24	20
MQ Circuit Board ($)	60	50

Table 2. Disassembly Cost & Time Factors

Factor	Level 1	Level 2
Disassembly Cost ($/min)	3	2
Metal Cover Disassembly Time (min)	1	0.5
Aluminum Radiator Disassembly Time (min)	2	1
Motor Disassembly Time (min)	2	1
Solenoid Valve Disassembly Time (min)	2	1
Circuit Board Disassembly Time(min)	2	1

Table 3. Inspection Cost & Time Factors

Factor	Level 1	Level 2
Inspection Cost ($/min)	0.6	0.5
Metal Cover Inspection Time (min)	1.5	1
Aluminum Radiator Inspection Time (min)	6	5
Motor Inspection Time (min)	12	10
Solenoid Valve Inspection Time (min)	3	2
Circuit Board Inspection Time(min)	6	5

Table 4. Probability Factors

Probability Factors (%)		
Factor	Level 1	Level 2
Missing Metal Cover	10	20
Missing Aluminum Radiator	10	20
Missing Motor	10	20
Missing Solenoid Valve	10	20
Missing Circuit Board	10	20
Usable Metal Cover	90	80
Usable Aluminum Radiator	90	80
Usable Motor	90	80
Usable Solenoid Valve	90	80
Usable Circuit Board	90	80
HQ Metal Cover Return	55	50
MQ Metal Cover Return	30	30
HQ Aluminum Radiator Return	55	50
MQ Aluminum Radiator Return	30	30
HQ Motor Return	55	50
MQ Motor Return	30	30
HQ Solenoid Valve Return	55	50
MQ Solenoid Valve Return	30	30
HQ Circuit Board Return	55	50
MQ Circuit Board Return	30	30

Table 5. Low Quality Subassembly & Component Probabilities (%)

LQ Metal Cover Return	15	20
LQ Aluminum Radiator Return	15	20
LQ Motor Return	15	20
LQ Solenoid Valve Return	15	20
LQ Circuit Board Return	15	20

The probability levels when renewal-time threshold is exceeded are shown in Table 6.

Table 7 shows additional factors that are relevant to the maintenance operations of the systems. The first factor in Table 7 comprises both the recognition of failure and the service activation; that is, the time it takes for a customer to inform a service team about the failure, the service team to arrive at the user's location, and any further services to be activated. Inspection time, labor cost and productivity loss cost factors with their levels are also depicted in Table 7.

The factorial design also took the demand for remanufactured refrigerators and components into consideration. As noted before, the design excluded LQ-level demands and prices because they were deemed to have little or no significant effect. Table 8 illustrates the demand factors. The demand followed a Poisson distribution. For example, there was an average demand of 100 HQ remanufactured refrigerators per day based on poison distribution.

The factorial design considered the remanufacturing process, which requires assembly to remanufacture the refrigerators. The relevant factors, such as time and cost, were included in the factorial design. In addition, scrap revenue was considered to represent an important factor. Table 9 shows these factors together with their levels.

In the study, Arena 14.7 discrete event simulation software (Kelton et al., 2007) was used to model RR and SER systems. Various validation and verification techniques were used, such as plotting the measurements and evaluating the outcomes associated with extreme conditions, to determine whether the models represent the systems. The models were operated for 4,200 days, or approximately 11.5 years. The simulation run was deemed to be long enough to accommodate the completion of the maintenance activities, the refrigerators' ten-year life cycle and the EOL processing of the refrigerators. The models for both systems were run 64 times. Additional data that was required to perform the experiments is shown in the Appendix.

With the experiments, we collected and compared several performance measures as the output of the simulation models. The systems included both maintenance processes and EOL processes. Maintenance measures outline the maintenance costs that the sensors save, while the profits of the EOL processes help us observe whether refrigerators with sensors increase manufacturers' profits. These performance measures with their formulas are revealed below;

$$\text{Maintenance cost} = \text{Labor Cost} + \text{Productivity Loss Cost} + \text{Logistics Cost} + \text{Material Replacement Cost} \quad (1)$$

$$\text{Total Profit} = \text{Total Revenue} - \text{Total Cost} \quad (2)$$

Table 6. Quality Level Probabilities When Renewal-Time Threshold is Exceeded (%)

Factor	Level 1	Level 2
HQ Metal Cover Return	25	20
MQ Metal Cover Return	30	30
LQ Metal Cover Return	45	50
HQ Aluminum Radiator Return	25	20
MQ Aluminum Radiator Return	30	30
LQ Aluminum Radiator Return	45	50
HQ Motor Return	25	20
MQ Motor Return	30	30
LQ Motor Return	45	50
HQ Solenoid Valve Return	25	20
MQ Solenoid Valve Return	30	30
LQ Solenoid Valve Return	45	50
HQ Circuit Board Return	25	20
MQ Circuit Board Return	30	30
LQ Circuit Board Return	45	50

Table 7. Maintenance Factors

Factor	Level 1	Level 2
Recognition of Failure and Service Activation	3 days	1 day
Inspection Time of Failure (min) (Normally Distributed)	(20,1.2)	(15,1.2)
Labor Cost	$30/hour	$20/hour
Productivity-Loss Cost	$1.2/day	$0.5/day

Table 8. Remanufactured Refrigerator, Subassembly, & Component Demands

(Follows Poisson Distribution)		
Factor	**Level 1**	**Level 2**
HQ Refrigerator (/day)	100	80
MQ Refrigerator (/day)	80	60
HQ Metal Cover (/day)	100	80
MQ Metal Cover (/day)	80	60
HQ Aluminum Radiator (/day)	100	80
MQ Aluminum Radiator (/day)	80	60
HQ Motor (/day)	100	80
MQ Motor (/day)	80	60
HQ Solenoid Valve (/day)	100	80
MQ Solenoid Valve (/day)	80	60
HQ Circuit Board (/day)	100	80
MQ Circuit Board (/day)	80	60

Table 9. Remanufacturing Assembly & Scrap Revenue Factors

Remanufacturing Assembly and Scrap Revenue Factors		
Factor	**Level 1**	**Level 2**
Refrigerator Assembly Time (min)	6	5
Assembly Cost($/min)	4	3
Scrap Revenue ($/lbs.)	0.9	0.6

Total Revenue = Sales Revenue + Scrap Revenue (3)

Total Cost = Collection Cost + Disassembly Cost + Inspection Cost + Remanufacturing Cost + Holding Cost + Backordering Cost + Disposal Cost (4)

Sensor Value = (Maintenance Cost Savings + Total Profit Improvement) / Total Number of Sensors (5)

RESULTS AND ANALYSIS

Table 10 illustrates the mean values of the performance measures that were the output of the experiments. EOL profits for SER and RR systems were $105.59 and $92.99 respectively. Refrigerators can provide this much profit when they are processed after they complete their life cycles. Another measure that was determined to be indicative of the value of the sensor was maintenance cost. The maintenance costs per refrigerator were $161.59 and $92.39 for SER and RR systems respectively. These figures represent how much it would cost to maintain the refrigerators during their life cycles.

The disassembly costs for the SER and RR systems were $176,403.60 and $189,374.90 respectively. The inspection costs were $1,869.31 and $158,759.50 respectively. Table 10 presents the total profits for both systems.

To determine the statistical significance of the results presented in Table 10, a pairwise t-test was performed. The paired experiments for the RR and SER systems enabled us to conduct unbiased statistical tests because each experiment had its unique factor levels. Table 11 presents the t-test results, which include the mean differences between SER and RR systems and the p-values for each performance measure.

The mean difference in EOL profit per refrigerator between the SER and RR systems was $13.20. The p-value was less than 0.0001, meaning that the true difference between the two systems was not equal to 0 and, as such, this figure was of extreme statistical significance. The mean difference in the maintenance costs per refrigerator was minus $34.57, meaning that the manufacturers could save $34.57 as a result of using the SER system. This figure was also found to be of statistical significance. The total profit, disassembly cost, and inspection costs were also statistically significant. Table 11 presents these statistics.

Table 10. Experiment Results for SER & RR Systems

Measure	SER System ($)	RR System ($)
EOL Profit / Refrigerator	105.59	92.39
Maintenance Cost / Refrigerator	161.59	196.16
Total Profit	1393780.00	1219628.00
Disassembly Cost	176403.60	189374.90
Inspection Cost	1869.31	158759.50

Combining two determinant measures, such as EOL profit and maintenance cost per refrigerator, enabled the calculation of the value of the sensors, which was an average of $47.77. In other words, the use of embedded sensors could be profitable for manufacturers if they are able to purchase them for less than $47.77. Table 12 shows the confidence intervals of the performance measurements and t-tests.

Other factors may be of interest in further analysis. Factorial design does not include failure interarrival rate as a factor because the inclusion of this figure can result in biased experiment results. In the research, the effect the interarrival rate on maintenance costs was tested by running experiments in which all factors were kept the same excluding interarrival time, which was increased. This change should decrease the failure rate of the components. Figure 9 presents the maintenance cost per refrigerator for each scenario for both the SER and RR systems. The maintenance costs decreased when the interarrival times increased. Figure 10 shows the difference in the maintenance costs between the systems and reveals that an increase in the failure interarrival times resulted in an exponential decrease in the maintenance costs.

Figure 11 illustrates the behavior of the sensor value depending on failure interarrival times. The sensor value decreased in every scenario except the one with 0.235 days. This reduction was expected because the maintenance cost differences between the two systems decreased. However, in the case of failure interarrival time of 0.235 days, the sensor value increased. As such, the EOL profit, in this case, was higher than that of the other cases, resulting in an increase in sensor value. This can be explained by considering the impact that the sensors have on the performance of the EOL processes. In this case, the failure rate was lower than the others, which entailed that the EOL refrigerators were retrieved in better conditions. Since sensors provide this condition information about the products, the EOL operations for the refrigerators were planned prior to disassembly so that the profit acquired at this stage increased. In RR systems, all the components are disassembled in the absence of any information about the condi-

Table 11. Pairwise T-Test Results for Mean Difference

Measure	Mean Difference (SER-RR) ($)	P-Value
Sensor Value	47.77	N/A
EOL Profit / Refrigerator	13.20	<0.0001
Maintenance Cost / Refrigerator	-34.57	<0.0001
Total Profit	174152.10	<0.0001
Disassembly Cost	-12971.33	<0.0001
Inspection Cost	-156890.20	<0.0001

Table 12. 95% Confidence Interval of Mean Difference

Measure	95% Confidence Interval of Mean Difference (SER-RR)	
	Lower Limit ($)	Upper Limit ($)
Sensor Value	46.96	48.58
EOL Profit / Refrigerator	12.57	13.83
Maintenance Cost / Refrigerator	-35.04	-34.11
Total Profit	165781.60	182522.60
Disassembly Cost	-14149.87	-11792.79
Inspection Cost	-161250.40	-152530.00

Figure 9. Maintenance Cost of the Systems

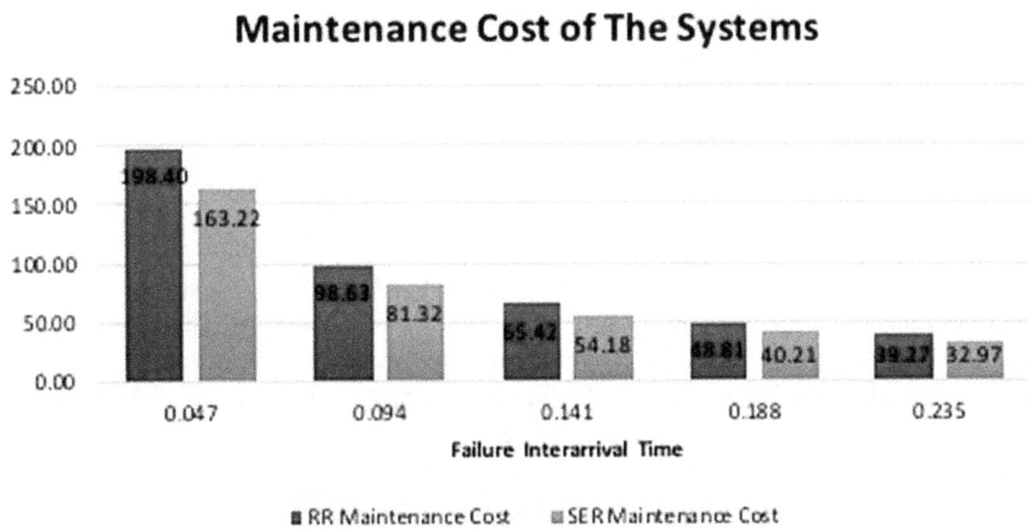

Figure 10. Maintenance Cost Difference Between Two Systems

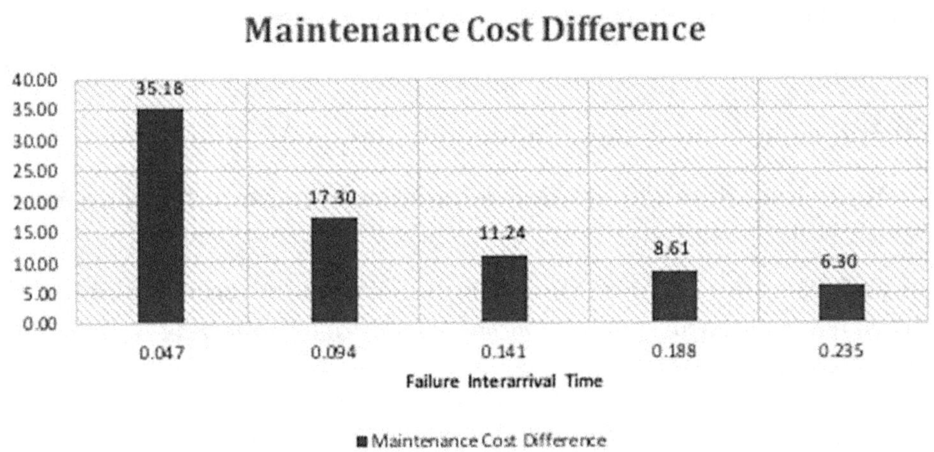

Figure 11. Sensor Value

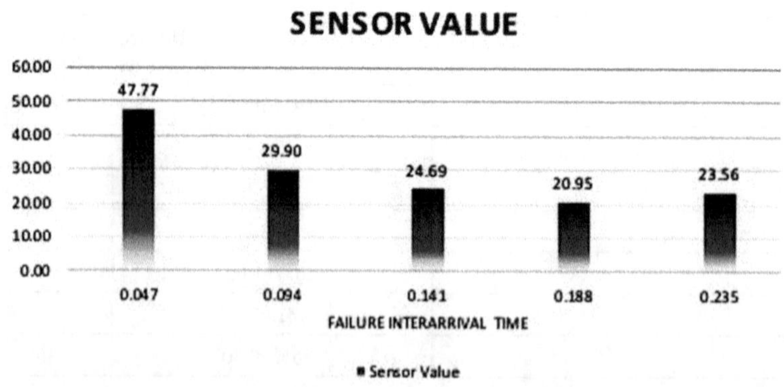

tion of the components. The sensors provide valuable information that can be crucial within planning activities because the EOL refrigerators are in better condition and they can produce higher value when they are remanufactured, or their components are sold.

CONCLUSION

This study reveals that SER systems are superior to RR systems because sensors help manufacturers maintain SER systems at a lower cost and generate a higher EOL profit. The maintenance cost saving associated with the use of sensors was an average of $34.57 per refrigerator. The disassembly cost of the SER systems was $12,971.33 lower than that of the RR systems. The inspection cost savings for the SER systems was $156,890.20. As a result of these cost savings, manufacturers can increase profit by an estimated $174,152.10, or $13.20 per refrigerator.

This research has a contribution by providing financial benefits of sensors when they are embedded into products. The assumption of using sensors is that they will provide accurate information during the products are in use. However, reliability of the sensors should also be considered and its impact should be investigated. This could be a good extension to this research. In addition, the use of sensors can be enhanced towards inventory control part of supply chains. It could be an interesting research idea by taking into account the implications that has been stated in this chapter.

REFERENCES

Alqahtani, A. Y., & Gupta, S. M. (2017a). One-dimensional renewable warranty management within sustainable supply chain. *Resources*, *6*(2), 16, 1-26. doi:10.3390/resources6020016

Alqahtani, A. Y., & Gupta, S. M. (2017b). Optimizing two-dimensional renewable warranty policies for sensor embedded remanufactured products. *Journal of Industrial Engineering & Management*, *10*(2), 145-187. doi:10.3926/jiem.2187

Byington, C. S., Watson, M., & Edwards, D. (2004). Data-driven neural network methodology to remaining life predictions for aircraft actuator components. In *Aerospace Conference* (vol. 6, pp. 3581-3589). IEEE. 10.1109/AERO.2004.1368175

De Faria, H. Jr, Costa, J. G. S., & Olivas, J. L. M. (2015). A review of monitoring methods for predictive maintenance of electric power transformers based on dissolved gas analysis. *Renewable & Sustainable Energy Reviews*, *46*, 201–209. doi:10.1016/j.rser.2015.02.052

Dulman, M. T., & Gupta, S. M. (2015). Disassembling and Remanufacturing End-of-Life Sensor Embedded Cell Phones. *Innovation and Supply Chain Management*, *9*(4), 111–117. doi:10.14327/iscm.9.111

Dulman, M. T., & Gupta, S. M. (2016). *Use of sensors for collection of end-of-life products. In Proceedings for the Northeast Region Decision Sciences Institute* (pp. 577–582). NEDSI.

Dulman, M. T., & Gupta, S. M. (2018a). Evaluation of Maintenance and EOL Operation Performance of Sensor-Embedded Laptops. *Logistics*, *2*(1), 3. doi:10.3390/logistics2010003

Dulman, M. T., & Gupta, S. M. (2018b). Maintenance and Remanufacturing Strategy: Using Sensors to Predict the Status of Wind Turbines. *Journal of Remanufacturing*. 8(3), 131-152.

Efthymiou, K., Papakostas, N., Mourtzis, D., & Chryssolouris, G. (2012). On a predictive maintenance platform for production systems. *Procedia CIRP*, *3*, 221–226. doi:10.1016/j.procir.2012.07.039

Franke, C., Basdere, B., Ciupek, M., & Seliger, S. (2006). Remanufacturing of mobile phones—capacity, program and facility adaptation planning. *Omega*, *34*(6), 562–570. doi:10.1016/j.omega.2005.01.016

Georgiadis, P., & Athanasiou, E. (2010). The impact of two-product joint lifecycles on capacity planning of remanufacturing networks. *European Journal of Operational Research*, *202*(2), 420–433. doi:10.1016/j.ejor.2009.05.022

Georgiadis, P., Vlachos, D., & Tagaras, G. (2006). The impact of product lifecycle on capacity planning of closed-loop supply chains with remanufacturing. *Production and Operations Management*, *15*(4), 514–527. doi:10.1111/j.1937-5956.2006.tb00160.x

Guide, V. D. R. Jr, & Spencer, M. S. (1997). Rough-cut capacity planning for remanufacturing firms. *Production Planning and Control*, *8*(3), 237–244. doi:10.1080/095372897235299

Guide, V. D. R. Jr, Srivastava, R., & Spencer, M. S. (1997). An evaluation of capacity planning techniques in a remanufacturing environment. *International Journal of Production Research*, *35*(1), 67–82. doi:10.1080/002075497195984

Gungor, A., & Gupta, S. M. (1999). Issues in environmentally conscious manufacturing and product recovery: A survey. *Computers & Industrial Engineering*, *36*(4), 811–853. doi:10.1016/S0360-8352(99)00167-9

Gupta, S. M., & Ilgin, M. A. (2018). *Multiple Criteria Decision Making Applications in Environmentally Conscious Manufacturing and Product Recovery*. Boca Raton, FL: CRC Press.

Hashemian, H. M. (2011). Wireless sensors for predictive maintenance of rotating equipment in research reactors. *Annals of Nuclear Energy*, *38*(2), 665–680. doi:10.1016/j.anucene.2010.09.012

Herzog, M. A., Marwala, T., & Heyns, P. S. (2009). Machine and component residual life estimation through the application of neural networks. *Reliability Engineering & System Safety*, *94*(2), 479–489. doi:10.1016/j.ress.2008.05.008

Ilgin, M. A., & Gupta, S. M. (2010a). Environmentally conscious manufacturing and product recovery (ECMPRO): A review of the state of the art. *Journal of Environmental Management*, *91*(3), 563–591. doi:10.1016/j.jenvman.2009.09.037 PMID:19853369

Ilgin, M. A., & Gupta, S. M. (2010b). Comparison of economic benefits of sensor embedded products and conventional products in a multi-product disassembly line. *Computers & Industrial Engineering*, *59*(4), 748–763. doi:10.1016/j.cie.2010.07.031

Ilgin, M. A., & Gupta, S. M. (2011a). Evaluating the impact of sensor-embedded products on the performance of an air conditioner disassembly line. *International Journal of Advanced Manufacturing Technology*, *53*(9-12), 1199–1216. doi:10.100700170-010-2891-0

Ilgin, M. A., & Gupta, S. M. (2011b). Performance improvement potential of sensor embedded products in environmental supply chains. *Resources, Conservation and Recycling*, *55*(6), 580–592. doi:10.1016/j.resconrec.2010.05.001

Ilgin, M. A., & Gupta, S. M. (2011c). Recovery of sensor embedded washing machines using a multi-kanban controlled disassembly line. *Robotics and Computer-integrated Manufacturing*, *27*(2), 318–334. doi:10.1016/j.rcim.2010.07.016

Ilgin, M. A., Gupta, S. M., & Battaïa, O. (2015). Use of MCDM techniques in environmentally conscious manufacturing and product recovery: State of the art. *Journal of Manufacturing Systems*, *37*, 746–758. doi:10.1016/j.jmsy.2015.04.010

Ilgin, M. A., Gupta, S. M., & Nakashima, K. (2011). Coping with disassembly yield uncertainty in remanufacturing using sensor embedded products. *Journal of Remanufacturing*, *1*(1), 1–14. doi:10.1186/2210-4690-1-7

Ilgin, M. A., Ondemir, O., & Gupta, S. M. (2014). An approach to quantify the financial benefit of embedding sensors into products for end-of-life management: A case study. *Production Planning and Control*, *25*(1), 26–43. doi:10.1080/09537287.2012.655801

Kara, S., Mazhar, M., Kaebernick, H., & Ahmed, A. (2005). Determining the reuse potential of components based on life cycle data. *CIRP Annals-Manufacturing Technology*, *54*(1), 1–4. doi:10.1016/S0007-8506(07)60036-5

Kelton, D. W., Sadowski, R. P., & Sadowski, D. A. (2007). *Simulation with arena*. New York: McGraw-Hill.

Ondemir, O., & Gupta, S. M. (2012). Optimal management of reverse supply chains with sensor-embedded end-of-life products. In K. D. Lawrence & G. Kleinman (Eds.), *Applications of Management Science* (pp. 109–129). Emerald Group Publishing Limited. doi:10.1108/S0276-8976(2012)0000015009

Ondemir, O., & Gupta, S. M. (2013a). Advanced remanufacturing-to-order and disassembly-to-order system under demand/decision uncertainty. In S. M. Gupta (Ed.), *Reverse supply chains: Issues and analysis* (pp. 203–228). Boca Raton, FL: CRC Press. doi:10.1201/b13749-9

Ondemir, O., & Gupta, S. M. (2013b). Quality assurance in remanufacturing with sensor embedded products. In Y. Nikolaidis (Ed.), *Quality Management in Reverse Logistics* (pp. 95–112). London: Springer. doi:10.1007/978-1-4471-4537-0_6

Ondemir, O., & Gupta, S. M. (2014a). A multi-criteria decision making model for advanced repair-to-order and disassembly-to-order system. *European Journal of Operational Research, 233*(2), 408–419. doi:10.1016/j.ejor.2013.09.003

Ondemir, O., & Gupta, S. M. (2014b). Quality management in product recovery using the Internet of Things: An optimization approach. *Computers in Industry, 65*(3), 491–504. doi:10.1016/j.compind.2013.11.006

Ondemir, O., Ilgin, M. A., & Gupta, S. M. (2012). Optimal end-of-life management in closed-loop supply chains using RFID and sensors. *IEEE Transactions on Industrial Informatics, 8*(3), 719–728. doi:10.1109/TII.2011.2166767

Phadke, M. S. (1989). *Quality engineering robust design*. Upper Saddle River, NJ: Prentice Hall.

Rodriguez, J. P., & Perez, C. R. (2002). Advanced sensor for optimal orientation and predictive maintenance of high power wind generators. In *Industrial Electronics Society, IEEE 2002 28th Annual Conference of the* (Vol. 3, pp. 2167-2172). IEEE.

Si, X. S., Wang, W., Hu, C. H., & Zhou, D. H. (2011). Remaining useful life estimation–A review on the statistical data driven approaches. *European Journal of Operational Research, 213*(1), 1–14. doi:10.1016/j.ejor.2010.11.018

Vadde, S., Kamarthi, S., Gupta, S. M., & Zeid, I. (2008). Product life cycle monitoring via embedded sensors. In S. M. Gupta & A. J. D. Lambert (Eds.), *Environment conscious manufacturing* (pp. 91–103). Boca Raton, FL: CRC Press.

Vijay Kumar, E., Chaturvedi, S. K., & Deshpandé, A. W. (2009). Maintenance of industrial equipment: Degree of certainty with fuzzy modelling using predictive maintenance. *International Journal of Quality & Reliability Management, 26*(2), 196–211. doi:10.1108/02656710910928824

Vlachos, D., Georgiadis, P., & Iakovou, E. (2007). A system dynamics model for dynamic capacity planning of remanufacturing in closed-loop supply chains. *Computers & Operations Research, 34*(2), 367–394. doi:10.1016/j.cor.2005.03.005

KEY TERMS AND DEFINITIONS

Closed-Loop Supply Chain: Covering all of the supply chain operations including both forward and reverse supply chain.

Disassembly: Deconstructing a product into its components.

End-of-Life: Stage that product is not being used by customer.

Inspection: Process of determining product's condition.

Maintenance: Providing service to ensure that product is working during its life cycle.

Remanufacturing: Building products by using their used components.

Sensor-Embedded Products: Products that have sensors embedded into them while they are being manufactured.

APPENDIX

Table 13. LQ Remanufactured Refrigerator, Subassembly & Component Prices

LQ Refrigerator ($)	130
LQ Metal Cover ($)	5
LQ Aluminum Radiator ($)	20
LQ Motor ($)	50
LQ Solenoid Valve ($)	10
LQ Circuit Board ($)	30

Table 14. LQ Remanufactured Refrigerator, Subassembly & Component Demands

(Follows Poisson Distribution)	
LQ Refrigerator (/day)	50
LQ Metal Cover (/day)	50
LQ Aluminum Radiator (/day)	50
LQ Motor (/day)	50
LQ Solenoid Valve (/day)	50
LQ Circuit Board (/day)	50

Table 15. Maintenance Data

Failure Interarrival Time (day) (Exponential)	0.047
Expected Lifetime (year)	10
Transportation Before Service (day)	1
Delivery After Service (day) (Triangular Distribution)	Min (1), Mean (2), Max (3)
Transportation Cost ($)	10
Delivery Cost ($)	60

Table 16. Subassembly & Component Replacement Times for Maintenance

(Normally Distributed) (Mean, Standard Deviation)	
Metal Cover (min)	(1,0.1)
Aluminum Radiator (min)	(1,0.1)
Motor (min)	(2,0.3)
Solenoid Valve (min)	(3,0.4)
Circuit Board (min)	(5,1)

Table 17. Subassembly & Component Replacement Costs for Maintenance

Metal Cover ($)	40
Aluminum Radiator ($)	120
Motor ($)	200
Solenoid Valve ($)	60
Circuit Board ($)	140

Table 18. Subassembly & Component Failure Probabilities (%)

Metal Cover Failure	5
Aluminum Radiator Failure	30
Motor Failure	25
Solenoid Valve Failure	10
Circuit Board Failure	30

Table 19. Production & Cost Data

Refrigerator Interarrival Time (min) (Exponentially Distributed)	1.5
Disposal Cost ($/lbs.)	0.4
Metal-Recycle Rate	0.3
Holding Cost Rate	0.2
Backordering Cost Rate	0.6

Chapter 2
Brazilian Solid Waste Policy (PNRS):
Some Aspects of Business Recycling in Reverse Logistics (RL)

Hermes de Andrade Júnior
https://orcid.org/0000-0002-3667-1354
Catholic University, Portugal

ABSTRACT

Brazil's national solid waste policy (PNRS) took nearly two decades to pass through legislative houses until it was approved as a law protecting the environment. During this period and after its approval, pro-environmental factors led to the right to transform and create protocols, agreements, and new companies in the sense of a reverse logistics or of a reversibility in the environmental effects of the supply chain. This chapter has aimed to present aspects of the Brazilian business reality in the process of implementation of the PNRS as a reflection on the perspective of product recycling and solid waste control and reverse logistics. The PNRS is in the phase of corporate expansion, taking stock of eight years since the creation of the law (2010). As some branches of Brazilian business activity have not yet had reverse logistics regulated, in the coming years there should be a much higher demand for this type of reverse business.

INTRODUCTION

Government pressures, stemming from stricter environmental laws, society's growing concern about the environment, scarcity of natural resources, increased pollution, and strengthening non-governmental environmental advocacy organizations (Gonçalves-Dias & Teodosio, 2011, Sellito et al., 2013) have forced companies to generate sustainable products and services (Macagno, 2013).

Several organizations already consider sustainability as one of the main factors to be discussed in their business strategies (Przychodzen & Przychodzen, 2013) and seek to implement environmental management tools, such as reverse logistics, defined as a service innovation that complements the chain

DOI: 10.4018/978-1-5225-8109-3.ch002

of distribution. With this logistics it is possible to efficiently control and operationalize the return to the productive cycle of the products that have lost their usefulness, which guarantees a lower impact of the disposal of products in the environment and a production model that uses, on a smaller scale, raw materials from nature (Miller & Sarder, 2012; Tenorio, Silva & Dacorso, 2014).

Brazil's national solid waste policy (PNRS) took nearly two decades to pass through legislative houses until it was approved as a law protecting the environment. During this period and after its approval, several pro-environmental movements led to the right to transform and create new companies in the sense of a reverse logistics or a reversibility in the environmental effects of the supply chain. Reverse logistics is a concept of sustainability that has reformed the supply chain in several solid examples in Brazil (Andrade Júnior, 2018) and it is perceived that the National Solid Waste Policy of Brazil encourages environmental education for the non-generation of waste and to reduce consumption, which is the basis for improving solid waste management (PNRS, 2010).

Logistics has positioned itself as a tool for business management for its contribution to obtaining economic benefits without disregarding environmental aspects (Rogers & Tibben-Lembke, 1998). Because the legislation that attributes greater responsibility to the producer becomes increasingly popular around the world, it tends to pass on to the manufacturer responsibility for the product from its manufacture to the end of its useful life. Although the final destination of these products is a major problem for the environment, it presents opportunities for recycling or reuse that can encourage several other operations that can bring positive results.

As alternative logistics and with a clearly environmental purpose, reverse logistics is linked at the same time to legal, environmental and economic issues, which makes it stand out and makes it indispensable in the organizational context, since it is the process through from which companies can become more environmentally efficient by recycling, reusing and reducing the amount of materials used (Carter & Ellram, 1998).

In addition, the factors of business cost reduction and good organizational image obtained through the use of secondary raw materials and the fight against waste tend to affirm the company as an environmental friend to the clients and stakeholders (Hu, Sheu & Haung, 2002). This can provide competitive advantages that, according to a survey of 93% of global CEOs, are essential conditions for company success (Przychodzen & Przychodzen, 2013, Tenorio, Silva & Dacorso, 2014). Therefore, the valuation and appropriate management of these solid wastes can promote a series of economic, environmental and even social benefits.

In this chapter, aspects of the Brazilian business reality in the process of implementation of the PNRS will be presented as a reflection on the perspective of product recycling and solid waste control and reverse logistics in Brazil.

SOLID WASTE AND REVERSE LOGISTICS (RL)

Solid waste is all material, substance, object, or well disposed resulting from human activities in society, whose final destination is carried, it is proposed to proceed or is obliged to carry, in solid or semi-solid and gases in containers and liquids whose peculiarities make it infeasible to be placed in the public sewage system or water bodies, or require technical or economically unviable solutions in view of the best available technology (Article 3 of Law 12,305/10).

Thus, solid waste is waste generated after the production or use of consumer goods. Although they can no longer have any utility for that purpose from which they were generated, these materials can be reused for other destinations or planned for a more sustainable porposes.

On the side of Brazilian public agencies, new laws and measures have focused on regulating and encouraging practice. In Brazil, the Solid Waste Policy (PNRS) was instituted by Law No. 12,305, of August 2, 2010, regulated by Decree No. 7404 of December 23, 2010. It is the responsibility of the companies to implement the actions established by the legislation, which results not only in reducing damages to the environment but also reductions in inputs and production.

According to Article 3 of Law 12.305 / 10 (PNRS), integrated solid waste management is set of actions aimed at finding solutions to the solid waste in order to consider the political, economic, environmental, cultural and social, with social control and under the premise of sustainable development. These actions are related to the steps of collection, transportation, handling, treatment, final destination and environmental impacts achieved and presupposes a systemic analysis with the purpose of guaranteeing maximum reuse to save energy and to discard the generated waste in a more appropriate way.

The management of solid waste is of extreme relevance for all companies that generate significant amounts of investable products. Through characterization and identification of the materials we can recognize the physicochemical properties of solid wastes. In this way, greater accuracy in the development of materials is possible to guide which actions should be addressed. This reduces the negative impact of some products. One example is the use of ecodesign[1] in production. In this case, reverse logistics can be applied to the solid waste management of the ecodesign project to enhance the results of reuse and reduction of waste.

Reverse logistics has been historically associated with product recycling activities and environmental aspects (Kopicki, Berg & Legg, 1993; Kroon & Vrijens, 1995; Stock, 1992), having become important in business due to the pressure exerted by stakeholders on environmental issues (Hu, Sheu & Haung, 2002) that could not be ignored.

Reverse logistics is a rather generic term that portrays one of the major commitments that companies and governments have made in recent years in favor of the planet and covers, in its broadest sense, all operations related to the reuse of products and materials, encompassing all logistic activities of collecting, dismantling and processing products and / or materials and used parts to ensure a sustainable recovery (Leite, 2009).

The potential benefits of reverse logistics can be grouped into three distinct levels: a) environmental demands that have led companies to worry about the final destination of products and packaging generated by them (Hu, Sheu & Haung, 2002); b) economic efficiency, because it allows the generation of financial gains by the economy in the use of resources (Minahan, 1998) and c) gain of image before its shareholders, besides raising the prestige of the brand (Rogers & Tibben-Lembke, 1998).

Leite (2009), one of the greatest supporters and pioneers who published on Brazilian reverse logistics, divides RL into two areas of activity, which is post-consumption and post-sale, where they can be distinguished according to the life cycle in which a particular product has returned.

Reverse after-sales logistics can be distinguished from post-consumer logistics by involving the return of products from links in the logistics distribution chain or even by the end consumer, which had little or no use, while post-consumer products that have already been consumed and can be recycled, reused or at least have an environmentally correct destination (Leite, 2009).

PNRS strategy makes all stakeholders liable, internalizing environmental costs and stimulating innovation. RL is the process of introducing recycled material after consumption on the supply chain. RL is one main instrument of the PNRS (see figure 1).

PNRS is essential for the correct implementation and operation of reverse logistics systems in Brazil, since through this law regulatory actions were intensified by the public authorities on the manufacturers, importers, distributors and merchants of the products covered by Law No. 12,305: I - Agrochemicals, their residues and packaging, as well as other products whose packaging, after use, constitutes hazardous waste, observing the hazardous waste management rules provided for by law or regulation [..] or technical standards; II - Batteries; III - Tires; IV - Lubricating oils, their residues and packaging; V - Fluorescent, sodium and mercury vapor and mixed light lamps; VI - Electrical and electronic products and their components. (BRAZIL, 2010, article 33).

DEVELOPING PNRS

In the text of the PNRS, reverse logistics is defined as an instrument of economic and social development characterized by a set of actions, procedures and means to enable the collection and restitution of solid waste to the business sector, for reuse, in cycle or in other productive cycles, or other environmentally appropriate final destination. (BRAZIL, 2010, article 3).

While it may seem otherwise, there are economic and reputational advantages of reverse logistics companies, such as (1) mitigating waste through increased recycling and reuse of solid waste, which promote better disposal of waste already generated; (2) disposal according to environmental norms and laws, providing adequate disposal for those wastes without restorative functionality; (3) feasibility to generate a solid image regarding the company's widespread environmental policy; (4) reduction of taxes, through compliance with legislation that influences various tax incentives, such as exemption from income tax and part of the Tax on the Circulation of Goods and Services (ICMS) and even with the ecological version of this tax[2] and (5) reducing costs, avoiding unnecessary expenses and allowing higher revenues through the reintegration of solid waste into the production cycle, which enhances a new market opportunity bias.

In 2010, in the year of the law that instituted the PNRS, the Institute of Applied Economic Research (IPEA) published a report stating that in Brazil there was low structural efficiency and installed capacity for waste management and that the potential for the recycling sector was around US$ 2 million annually (IPEA, 2010). Table 1[3] shows that some materials such as steel, aluminum, paper and cardboard, plastics

Figure 1. Forward and reverse logistics flow

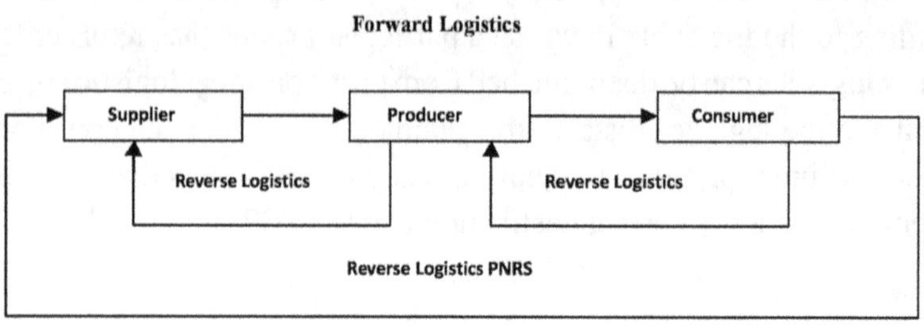

Table 1. The economic and environmental benefits of recycling at the time of publication of the PNRS

Materials	Benefits Generated by Recycling (R$ / t)	Current Benefit (R$ 1,000 / Year)	Potential Benefits (R $ 1,000 / Year)
Steel	88	387.200 – 387.200	89.232
Aluminum	2.941	473.501 – 952.884	488.206
Paper and Cardboard	241	148.215 – 877.963	1.671.094
Plastic Products	1.107	357.561 – 1.064.934	5.826.141
Glass	18	1.404 – 8.460	19.980
Total		1.367.881 – 3.291.441	**8.094.653**

Source: IPEA, 2010

and glass are already a promising market, considering the size of Brazil, its level of industrialization and its consuming population of more than 200 million people.

Two years later (2012) there was the 18th International Logistics Forum in Rio de Janeiro. In the event, it was reported that 60 of the 100 largest companies in the country were already developing some activity related to the reverse logistics operation (it foresees the collection and disposal by the manufacturer of the post consumer waste), but according to the survey, 40% of companies did not yet have programs for this purpose. The research was done by the Institute of Logistics and Supply Chain in Brazil. The institution is dedicated to the generation of knowledge and solutions in logistics (ILOS, 2012)[4].

Table 2 shows aspects about the implementation of RL in different business activities. It is important to note the existence of differences in the maturity level of the reverse chain of the several product classes described as mandatory in the PNRS. It is observed that there are structured processes for packaging and waste of pesticides and tires, both coordinated by management entities - National Institute of Empty Packaging Processing (INPEV) and Reciclanip[5], respectively. It is worth mentioning that both classes were regulated about 15 years ago, based on resolutions of the National Environment Council (CONAMA), undergoing a differentiated process of implementation (see ILOS, 2012). It can also be seen in Table 2 that representative associations of recyclable items of production[6] and trade unions occupy a prominent role in the conduct of sectorial agreements, which march with different speeds of regulation.

The cases of agrochemical packages and tires follow similar models for the operation of reverse logistics. In both, the collection takes place through receiving points, from which the waste that will be properly destined (reuse, incineration, generation of energy and new inputs, among others) is sorted.

For the tire sector, the main success factors in implementing this initiative were: the existence of a regulatory framework, the development of a solution by the National Pneumatic Industry Association (ANIP), the establishment of an independent management entity (Reciclanip) and the recognition by consumers of the importance of work in a context of sustainability.

Inpev started its activities in 2002, investing more than R$ 450 million and collecting about 220 million tons of empty packaging. Currently, the institute's operation collects and destines about 80% of the total of commercialized packaging, reaching 94% for plastic packaging, constituting a worldwide reference (ILOS, 2012).

With the exception of pesticide and tire packages, the other classes of products are still in the stage of discussing alternatives with the government, through class associations, on the regulation (goals, penalties) of the PNRS, and there is therefore no unified and national process.

Table 2. Discussion stage on the itemized reverse logistics implementation plan

Items with mandatory LR PNRS (2010)	Legality By the PNRS	Technical feasibility study	Agreements[1]	Implementation	Sector associations / managing entities
Packaging and waste from agrochemicals	CONAMA	✓	NO NEED	✓	INPEV
Tires	✓	✓	✓	✓	ANIP/RECICLANIP
Packaging and waste oils	✓	✓	✓	✓	SINDICOM
Electronic products and components	✓	✓	X	X	ABINEE
Batteries					ABINEE
Fluorescent, sodium vapor, mercury and mixed lamps	✓	✓	X	X	ABILUMI, ABILUX
Packaging	✓	✓	X	X	ABIPHEC, ABIOVE, ABIPLA; ABIVIDRO, etc.

Source: ILOS, 2012

The Brazilian Electrical and Electronic Industry Association (ABINEE) is the association that is leading the government with the discussions regarding batteries and electronic products and components. These sectors have found difficulties in the discussion with the government to define the goal of representativeness of the total volume to be collected. This difficulty is mainly due to the fact that there is a significant volume of pirated products on the Brazilian market. The alignment between the associated companies to design a joint operation is also a difficulty, since there is a view that a single operation will reduce the customer's perception of the environmental advantages related to the product, and may impact on the change in market share. In parallel to the discussions with the government, companies and groups of companies are working on independent initiatives for the reverse logistics of post consumer waste (ILOS, 2012).

Five years after (2010-2015), the organization called Corporate Commitment for Recycling (CEMPRE) published a report stating that the PNRS goal established for the five-year period was met in terms of capacity building, structuring and affirmation of activities of recycling in regulation (CEMPRE, 2015).

According to the goal of the implementation of the PNRS established by the Ministry of the Environment (MMA) for the Packaging Sector Agreement (ASE) (SINIR, 2015)[8], the actions of the companies should cover at least 258 Brazilian municipalities until the end of 2014, based on the twelve capitals of the World Cup and the cities of their respective metropolitan regions. However, a larger number of municipalities were included in the period: 371 in total, including some located outside the target region of Phase 1, corresponding to an estimated generation of 36.8 million tonnes of waste per year or 60.3% of all urban waste produced in Brazil (CEMPRE, 2015).

In these regions, the waste law mobilized numerous initiatives to support waste sorting, absorbing materials from municipal selective waste collection and increasing recycling productivity. However, there are still many landfills to be erected in Brazil, distributed by more than 2,000 municipalities, which still constitute barriers to the implementation of PNRS.

But the good trend was reflected in the number of coalition actions. Packagings together with waste pickers' organizations, with business investments in warehouses for separation of recyclables, capacity building, improvements in the structure and purchase of vehicles and equipment, increased dramatically from 80 to 956 between 2012 and 2014, according to data reported in the Cempre report (2015).

The Demajorovic & Massote study (2017) analyzes that the Sectorial Packaging Agreement (ASE) tends to positively impact the recycling chain, especially considering the more structured chains, such as paper, cardboard, glass, rigid plastics and aluminum. For these materials, an increase in the collection is expected, with diversion of increasing parcels of landfill waste and positive results for the collectors cooperatives. In this case, if the commitments to improve its infrastructure are also ensured, the consolidation of large volumes of waste and direct sales to large recyclers, not just intermediaries, should expand.

However, the same study states that the ASE covers many facets not discussed so far in the literature. First, the implementation of ASE enables manufacturers and users of packaging to be free-riders of structures already financed by municipal authorities, without a counterpart to this investment already made. The resources that are invested in cooperatives by the city, such as making the shed available and payments of operating expenses, will remain the responsibility of the public sector. Meanwhile, the question of the remuneration of the activities of the collectors cooperative, an important flag of the national collectors movement, was disregarded by the ASE (Demajorovic & Massote, 2017).

Also in terms of packaging, Tetra Pak has invested in education aimed at selective collection through educational leaflets and the Recycling Route site[9], as well as the training of cooperatives and the installation of collection points. But ILOS (2012) confirms that some companies have found it difficult to include in the waste disposal process some agents, such as collector cooperatives (which form only 26% of current operations) and retail (which is present in 53% of cases).

The difficulty of including collectors' cooperatives in the post-consumer waste disposal process is strongly related to the fact that they are not recognized by the companies as independent operating agents and need support for the implementation of physical structure and management. In the case of retail, the main difficulty lies in the organization of the secondary waste market in Brazil, recognized as a low performance market (ILOS, 2012).

INDICATORS OF BUSINESS SUCCESS IN RL PRACTICE

Adapting the work of Epelbaum (2004) that presents the indicators of business success linked to environmental management actions, it is possible to consider an affinity of these success indicators also for the implementation of reverse logistics systems (Callefi, Barbosa & Ramos, 2017). Epelbaum environmental management success indicators adapted to RL are: (1) Shareholder value, (2) Revenue, (3) Market share, (4) Attraction and customer retention, (5) Brand value and reputation, (6) Operational efficiency, (7) Intellectual and human capital and (8) Innovation (Epelbaum, 2004).

The analysis of the study by Tenorio, Silva & Dacorso, 2014 showed that of 43 articles with the title of reverse logistics presented at congresses or symposia in Brazil from 2007 to 2012, only in four articles did reverse logistics not be considered an innovation

Three of these four articles were not considered an innovation indicator because they had the branch of a large multinational company, such as Mcdonald's (Mei, Christiani & Leite, 2011), Tetra Pak (Pereira, Pavanelli & Souza, 2008), Coca-Cola (Oliveira, Santana & Silva, 2009) and an appliance factory in Japan (Giovine & Sacomano, 2007), which already adopted reverse logistics. The other studies considered reverse logistics as a service innovation related to their environmental practices, since this process was something new for the companies that implemented it.

In terms of obtaining competitive advantages from this innovative process, there seems to be unanimity, since 74.5% of the analyzed cases affirm that reverse logistics brings financial or image advantages, as seen in Braga Junior, Merlo & Nagano (2008). These authors affirm that the adoption of reverse logistics represented an increase of 9.6% in relation to the net profit of the company studied by them.

Batista & Martins (2009) studying the case of reverse logistics of PET bottles, show that the adoption of the reverse process contributed positively to the corporate image and its customers.

These empirical results confirm what has been seen in the literature, such as those of Silva, Pimenta & Campos (2013) and Miguez, Mendonça & Valle (2007), where reverse logistics can bring cost reduction and a differentiated image of company, both related to obtaining a competitive advantage (see Tenorio, Silva & Dacorso, 2014).

Taking advantage of this opportunity of international competitive advantage and image gain from the promising PNRS, TerraCycle, a multinational of the recycling sector and present in more than 21 countries, recognized the value of the trash in Brazil and dedicated itself to transform waste in matter for new products. Thus, TerraCycle has advanced and won the Amcham ECO 2016 Award[10], which chooses the best cases of sustainability in the market. Hard-to-recycle objects (cleaning sponges, toothbrushes, tubes and make-up jars, pens and pencils) made up a market that was still under-exploited and very lucrative. Since 2001 TerraCycle has been working in this segment and today it is one of the world leaders in the field.

Another aspect of this business is the "Prêmio Fecomercio de Sustentabilidade "[11] with access to an online platform of the Federation of Commerce of the State of São Paulo in which individuals and companies can register as volunteers in recycling programs. The programs are maintained by manufacturers who contract TerraCycle. The model is "sponsored waste", that is, companies need to pay for the programs.

Five international companies stood out in the "Sustainability Award": Colgate, Faber-Castell, 3M (Scotch-Brite), Avon and L'Occitane. The amount paid for them keeps the six TerraCycle programs in effect, which are separated by products - sponges, oral health (toothpaste brushes and tubes), writing instruments (pencil and pen, for example), cream packs and lotions, makeup, enamels and perfumes. Items are received from both the sponsoring corporations and from other manufacturers (except the L'Occitane product program, in which only branded cosmetic packaging is accepted).

Terracycle itself has already been one of the award winners and uses this information as advertising on its website. Terracycle leaves open free call and in contests for other prizes, where they appear the marks cited, the diapers and disposable products for babies and cartons of coffee capsules[12].

FINAL

In the present context where poor waste management leads to a series of environmental disruptions and harms the quality of life of people in various regions of the planet, reverse logistics proves to be an excellent opportunity to analyze and manage the ways in which byproducts of a production procedure will be discarded or reintroduced into the process.

Companies that use reverse logistics in their production chain have the capacity to add a greater value to their image before society, precisely because of their commitment to provide a greater benefit to the environment.

In addition, they provide unprecedented business opportunities, resulting in more employment opportunities and income generation. In this sense, companies that have an efficient logistics system can obtain a significant sustainable competitive advantage over those that do not, including reducing costs and improving their relationship with the consumer.

Companies operating in Brazil have different degrees of implementation of waste management actions, but they already see RL as a competitive advantage. There are differences in the maturity level of the reverse chain of the various classes of products described as mandatory in the PNRS. In general, most Brazilian companies in Brazil are aware of the new legislation and have already started some post-consumer waste management activity.

The business motivation would be to increase brand prestige, increase sales volumes, reduce costs and meet the demand of environmentalists. In addition, by examining the sites of the entities that act in the recycling in Brazil and through the documents processed it is verified that some of the indicators of success of the RL are being accompanied by new adherents to the PNRS.

The PNRS is in the phase of corporate expansion, taking stock of eight years since the creation of the law. As some branches of Brazilian business activity have not yet had reverse logistics regulated, in the coming years there should be a much higher demand for this type of reverse business. This will coincide with the time when new companies from other sectors not reached by sector agreements are required to give a correct destination for their products after use.

REFERENCES

Batista, M. V., & Martins, E. F. (2009). Identification and evaluation of reverse logistics channels: A study on the revaluation of pet bottles. *Proceedings of National Meeting of Production Engineering*.

Braga, S. Jr, Merlo, E. M., & Nagano, M. S. (2008). A comparative study of reverse logistics practices in midsize retail. *Proceedings of Symposium on Production, Logistics and International Operations Management*.

Brazil. (2010). *Federal Law 12,305, of August 2, 2010. Institutes the National Policy on Solid Waste. Official Gazette*. Brasília, DF: Federative Republic of Brazil, Executive Branch.

Business Commitment to Recycling (CEMPRE). (2015). *Cempre review 2015: An Overview of Recycling in Brazil*. Retrieved from http://cempre.org.br/artigo-publicacao/artigos

Callefi, M., Barbosa, W. P., & Ramos, D. V. (2017). The role of reverse logistics for companies: Fundamentals and importance. *R. Gest. Industr, 13*(4), 171–187.

Carter, C. R., & Ellram, L. M. (1998). Reverse Logistics: A review of the literature and framework for future research. *International Journal of Business Logistics, 19*(3), 85–103.

Demajorovic, J., & Massote, B. (2017). Packaging Sector Agreement: Evaluation In Light Of Extended Producer Responsibility. *Journal of Business Administration, 57*(5), 470–482. doi:10.15900034-759020170505

Epelbaum, M. (2004). *The influence of environmental management on competitiveness and business success* (Unpublished master dissertation). Polytechnic School, University of São Paulo, SP.

Giovine, H., & Sacomano, J. B. (2007). Reverse logistics as an instrument for improving the environment: A case study on the recycling plant for household appliances of matsushita. *Proceeding of National Meeting of Production Engineering.*

Gonçalves-Dias, S., & Teodósio, A. (2011). Perspectives of analysis of corporate environmentalism beyond demonization and sanctification. *Journal of Social and Environmental Management, 5*(2), 3-17.

Hu, T. L., Sheu, J. B., & Haung, K. H. (2002). A reverse logistics cost minimization model for the treatment of hazardous wastes. *Transportation Research Part E, Logistics and Transportation Review, 38*(6), 457–473. doi:10.1016/S1366-5545(02)00020-0

ILOS. (2012). *Brazilian Panorama of Reverse Logistics of Post-Consumer Waste.* Paper presentation by Gisela Sousa, Mega Session: XVIII International Logistics Forum. Available at http://www.ilos.com.br/web/tag/residuos/

IPEA. (2010). *Research Report on Payment for Urban Environmental Services for Solid Waste Management.* IPEA. Available at: http://www.ipea.gov.br/portal/images/stories/PDFs/100514_relatpsau.pdf

Júnior, A. H. (2018). Reverse Logistics and Solid Waste: Challenges for the National Waste Policy (PNRS) in Brazil. In Handbook of Research on Supply Chain Management for Sustainable Development. IGI Global. DOI: 10.4018 / 978-1-5225-5757-9.ch015

Kopicki, R., Berg, M., & Legg, L. L. (1993). *Reuse and recycling: reverse logistics opportunities.* Oak Brook, IL: Council of Logistics Management.

Kroon, L., & Vrijens, G. (1995). Returnable containers: An example of reverse logistics. *International Journal of Physical Distribution & Logistics Management, 25*(2), 56–68. doi:10.1108/09600039510083934

Leite, P. R. (2009). *Reverse logistics: environment and competitiveness* (2nd ed.). São Paulo: Prentice Hall.

Macagno, T. (2013). A Model for Managing Corporate Sustainability. *Business and Society Review, 118*(2), 223–252. doi:10.1111/basr.12009

Mei, L. B., Christiani, V. S., & Leite, P. R. (2011). The reverse logistics in the return of used cooking oil. *Proceedings of Anpad National Meeting.*

Miguez, E. C., Mendonça, F. M., & Valle, R. (2007). *Environmental, social and financial impacts of a reverse logistics policy adopted by a television factory - a case study* (Special Edition). Produção Online. doi:10.14488/1676-1901.v7i4.54

Miller, C. R., & Sarder, M. D. (2012). Public Works Policy Implications of Sustainable Reverse Logistics Operations. *Public Works Management & Policy, 17*(1), 68–82. doi:10.1177/1087724X11429044

Minahan, T. (1998). Manufactures take aim at the end of the supply chain. *Purchasing, 124*(6), 111–112.

Oliveira, A. D., Santana, E. M., & Silva, S. C. (2009). Reverse Logistics of Returnable Packaging: An alternative for reducing costs for sustainable development. *Proceedings of National Meeting of Production Engineering.*

Pereira, R. D. A., Pavanelli, G., & Souza, M. T. S. (2008). A Study of the Reverse Channels in a Cardboard Packaging Company. *Proceedings of National Meeting of Production Engineering.*

Przychodzen, J., & Przychodzen, W. (2013). Corporate sustainability and shareholder wealth. *Journal of Environmental Planning and Management, 56*(4), 474–493. doi:10.1080/09640568.2012.685927

Rogers, D. S., & Tibben-Lembke, R. (1998). *Going Backwards: Reverse Logistics Trends and Practices.* Reno: Reverse Logistics Executive Council.

Sellitto, M. A. (2013). Coprocessing of rice husks and waste tires and reverse logistics in the manufacture of cement. *Environment and Society, 16*(1), 141–162. doi:10.1590/S1414-753X2013000100009

Silva, L. A., Pimenta, H., & Campos, L. (2013). Reverse logistics of electronic waste in the IT sector: Reality, perspectives and challenges of the city of Natal-RN. *Produção. Online (Bergheim), 13*(2), 544–576.

SINIR. (2015). *Sectoral agreement on packaging in general.* Retrieved from http://www.sinir.gov.br/web/guest/packages-in-general

Stock, J. R. (1992). *Reverse logistics.* Oak Brook, IL: Council of Logistics Management.

Tenório, F., Silva, D., & Dacorso, E. (2014). Innovation And Decision-Making Process In Reverse Logistics: A Bibliometric Analysis. *Produção Online, Florianópolis, 14*(2), 593–616.

ENDNOTES

1 Ecodesign is a competitiveness tool used by companies in the areas of architecture, engineering and design, both in the domestic and foreign markets, attending new models of production and consumption, contributing to sustainable development through the substitution of products and processes for others less harmful to the environment.

2 ICMS is a type of tax that guarantees the states of the federation to settle their accounts with most of the productive activities that pass through its territory. There is also the ecological variant of ICMS, the ecological ICMS, which is a tax mechanism that allows municipalities access to larger parcels than those already entitled to these financial resources collected by the states through the Tax on Circulation of Goods and Services. It is not a new tax, but rather the introduction of new

criteria for the redistribution of ICMS resources, which reflects the level of economic activity in municipalities together with the preservation of the environment.

3 At the end of 2010, the parity of the American currency (US$) against the Brazilian real (R$) was 1: 1.75.

4 The authorities that attended the mega session were Fernando Von Zuben, director of the Environment (Latin America) of Tetra Pak; Fabio Neiva, Logistics Manager (Latin America), Goodyear; André Cordeiro, Director of Supply Chain (Latin America) of the FMC Corporation; André Saraiva, director of the Socio-Environmental Responsibility Area of the Brazilian Electrical and Electronics Industry Association (Abinee) and executive director of the Shared Environmental Responsibility Program (PRAC); Edgar Blanco, Director of Research at the Massachusetts Institute of Technology (MIT) Transportation and Logistics Center, USA; moderated by Dale Rogers, leader of Practices in Sustainability and Reverse Logistics at ILOS and a professor at Rutgers University.

5 Reciclanip is considered one of the largest initiatives of the Brazilian industry in the area of post-consumer responsibility, also known as reverse logistics. The entity's collection and disposal of waste tires is comparable to the largest recycling programs developed in the country, especially aluminum cans and agricultural pesticide packaging.

6 Brazilian Association of the Electrical and Electronic Industry (ABINEE), Brazilian Association of the Aluminum Industry (ABILUMI), Brazilian Association of Lighting Industry (ABILUX). The others are national associations for cleaning products, glass, hygiene, perfumery and cosmetics and vegetable oils, all involved in reducing the environmental impact with the collection or recycling of packaging. In addition to the sectors mentioned in the PNRS, others are being called on to participate in the process in the coming years, as is already the case with the drug industry.

7 Packaging and waste from pesticides and tires had no obligation to sign a sectoral agreement.

8 The sectoral agreement on packaging is a commitment of the business sector, through the coalition, to expand recycling in the country and meet the goals created by the PNRS. In the document, signed on November 25, 2015, the "Coalition" is committed to ensuring that packaging that comes to the market is correctly discarded and recycled, with a 22% increase in post-consumer packaging recycling by the end of 2017.

9 The Recycle Route application, site finder for recyclable delivery is now also available for the Android system. The new feature, now available for iPhones and iPads, is derived from a digital platform developed by Tetra Pak in 2008. Users can download it on their cell phone and / or tablets for free from the Play Store. See https://www.tetrapak.com/br/about/newsarchive/rota-da-reciclagem-para-android.

The app launch is yet another way to help consumers find places to properly dispose of post-consumer long-life packaging and other waste for recycling.

10 Launched by the US Chamber of Commerce in Brazil (Amcham) in 1982, the ECO® Award was a pioneer in the recognition of companies that adopt socially responsible practices and generated a rich reflection on sustainable business development in Brazil. The name ECO, merger of the words enterprise and community, translates the interest of its creators in making it an instrument of corporate commitment to social development. Over the years the ECO Award has gained recognition for the anticipation of trends and for its positive influence on the commitment of companies to the theme of sustainability. It has already mobilized 2,064 Brazilian and multinational companies, which registered 2,563 projects, of which 225 were awarded. See https://safe.amcham.com.br/premioeco/history.

11 In 2018, the 6th edition of the sustainability award took place. The website in the sustainability section also gives information and business orientations, characterizing Reverse Logistics (Information) and the fecomercio sustainability premium as special projects. See http://www.fecomercio.com.br/premio/sustentabilidade.

12 See https://www.terracycle.com.br/en/brigades, searching for free national recycling programs.

Chapter 3
Compliance in Sustainability Reporting

Svetlana Snezhko
M. V. Lomonosov Moscow State University, Russia

Ali Coskun
Boğaziçi University, Turkey

ABSTRACT

The research is aimed at assessing the benefits of compliance for corporate sustainability and sustainable development. The main achievement of the research is the outcome of the survey on companies' public reports to identify the trends and measure the progress achieved in disclosing information on compliance. There are both business and public drivers for disclosure of compliance information in non-financial reporting. Best practices in disclosing information on compliance by the company-leaders were revealed. There is a positive trend in the expansion of information on compliance in sustainability reports in recent years. Some problematic areas in reporting on compliance were identified. The outcomes of the research call for companies to disclose information on compliance in a more explicit way. The results may be valid for the improvement of corporate reporting practices.

INTRODUCTION

Compliance today is expected to address the interests of the third parties affected by the activities of companies. That's why compliance is no more an internal function of an organization but is becoming a public function and an integral part of corporate social responsibility (CSR), based on the CSR concept provided by ISO 26000 (2010).

Let's have a little deeper insight into CSR to assess its correlation with the compliance function of an organization. CSR is defined in different ways but in general the concept comes down to responsible behavior and its impact on social well-being. Different interpretations of CSR clarify responsibility through behavior in accordance with international norms and compliance with laws but, in particular, focus on ethical standards, for example: "corporate social responsibility is the continuing commitment by business to behave ethically and contribute to economic development while improving the quality of

DOI: 10.4018/978-1-5225-8109-3.ch003

life of the workforce and their families as well as of the local community and society at large" (Holme & Watts, 2000, p. 8). Such an approach implies that companies are expected to do some social good beyond their own interests and regulators requirements (McWilliams, Siegel, & Wright, 2006), in other words, through CSR the companies demonstrate how their business decisions and operations contribute to economic and social development and an environment that favors sustainable development and corporate sustainability.

CSR and corporate sustainability are often identified as one, however if differentiating them, corporate sustainability is reflecting the sustainable development of the company in terms of its CSR activity and thusly CSR aims at corporate sustainability. Corporate sustainability is achieved through long-term positive customer and stakeholder relations supported by following high ethical standards in social responsibility. "Corporate sustainability starts with a company's value system and a principled approach to doing business… By establishing a culture of integrity, companies are not only upholding their basic responsibilities to people and planet, but also setting the stage for long-term success" (UNGC, n.d.).

As is stated above compliance is integrated into companies CSR activities. This is particularly accurate when compliance relies on the promotion and support of ethical values and principles to secure responsible behavior towards stakeholders. If the company considers compliance only in terms of risk-management and strives only to meet the requirements of regulators then it may fail to meet ethical obligations to stakeholders and conduct responsible business. However, compliance based on an ethical approach to doing business encourages efforts that go beyond behavior required by legal obligations and thus engages in sustainable development. Sustainable companies are those that engage not only their legal responsibility but also their social responsibility:

Social responsibility involves an understanding of the broader expectations of society. A fundamental principle of social responsibility is respect for the rule of law and compliance with legally binding obligations. Social responsibility, however, also entails actions beyond legal compliance and the recognition of obligations to others that are not legally binding. These obligations arise out of widely shared ethical and other values. (International Organization for Standardization [ISO], 2010, p.6).

This research aims to consider the role of compliance function in CSR, prove its merit as a sustainability factor and provide findings for its significance in non-financial reporting.

THE ROLE OF COMPLIANCE IN SUSTAINABLE DEVELOPMENT

Progressive compliance systems aim not only to demonstrate that companies have made their maximum effort to abide by the law and avoid prosecution by regulators but also to optimize their input into the prevention of practices that harm sound economic relations, undermine confidence of market players, investors and stakeholders, and potentiate criminal activity. Organization and Economic Co-operation Development [OECD] Guidelines for multinational enterprises (2011) clarify how compliance programs contribute to the goals of sustainable development. For instance, by implementing and supporting anti-corruption compliance, companies contribute to counteract against corruption globally. OECD guidelines encourage enterprises to develop and adopt adequate internal controls, ethics and compliance programs or measures for the purpose of preventing and detecting foreign bribery.

United Nations Global Compact [UNDP] Guide to corporate sustainability states: *Corruption has considerable impacts on business: impeding growth, escalating costs and posing serious legal and reputational risks. It is also a major hindrance to advancing societies, with a disproportionate impact on poor communities. Corruption raises transaction costs, undermines fair competition, distorts development priorities, and impedes long-term foreign and domestic investment... Additionally, we are mobilizing business to provide a united voice against corruption, as collective action is essential for bringing an end to a systemic issue that is too complex for any company to tackle alone.*

Corruption is a global issue and many international public organizations make efforts to counteract its proliferation all over the world. Commercial organizations being the most exposed to corrupt payments have a direct influence on bribery and corruption practices. Certain business processes in any company carry an inherent risk of corruption. The way the companies address this risk influences their impact (positive or negative) on the prevention of corruption as a social evil.

In respect to antitrust compliance programs OECD guidelines (2011) stress the importance of abiding by competition policy and laws and regulations for domestic and multinational enterprises *to contribute to overall welfare and economic growth by promoting market conditions in which the nature, quality, and price of goods and services are determined by competitive market forces. In addition to benefiting consumers and a jurisdiction's economy as a whole, such a competitive environment rewards enterprises that respond efficiently to consumer demand, ...enterprises can contribute to this process by providing information and advice when governments are considering laws and policies that might reduce efficiency or otherwise reduce the competitiveness of markets.*

So, by maintaining and developing a solid compliance competition policy companies do not only support a competitive environment but can also participate in regulation of antitrust laws. In this way, an antitrust compliance program is also a significant component of CSR activity.

An undeniable role in CSR belongs to anti-money laundering and terrorist financing (AML/TF) compliance programs of companies subject to AML legislation. As defined by Financial Action Task Force [FATF] money laundering is "the processing of criminal proceeds to disguise their illegal origin. This process is of critical importance, as it enables the criminal to enjoy these profits without jeopardizing their source". Profits sent for laundering are obtained from a diversity of criminal activities: illegal arms sales, smuggling, drug trafficking, prostitution rings, bribery, FATF includes even insider trading and computer fraud schemes. For an understanding of the extent of money laundering, the study of United Nations Office for Drugs and Crime [UNODC] (2011) is usually referred to. This research estimated the amounts of money laundered at about US$1.6 trillion or 2.7% of GDP in 2009 and the largest income for transnational organized crime comes from illicit drugs, which account for some 20% (17%-25%) of all crime proceeds, about half of transnational organized crime proceeds and 0.6% to 0.9% of global GDP (UNODC, 2011).

Further research has found that through money laundering from corruption proceeds of about US$1 trillion leave developing countries each year that could have gone to public services and economic development and that as many as 3.6 million deaths could be prevented each year in developing countries if these illicit flows were invested in health systems (Transparency International [TI], 2015). Laundered criminal flows, besides that they contribute to crime flourishing, may also cause a number of negative socio-economic consequences if invested into the legal sector, for example, distortion of consumption and impact on imports, distortion of exports and potential problems with investment and economic growth, distortion of economic statistics and thus potential errors in economic policy decision taking and undermining of the credibility of legal institutions (UNODC, 2011).

The main counteraction to money-laundering can be made by companies identifying and reporting suspicions of money laundering. TI UK names them a **frontline of defense** against corrupt money and money received from criminal activity (TI, 2015). That's why anti-money laundering compliance is so important for sound economic development and prosperity all over the world.

Foremost, this relates to the financial services companies as well as other companies dealing with large payments and subject to AML legislation. However, according to TI UK and other experts they are not very effective in combating money-laundering today (Barrington, 2015; Hanning & Connett, 2015). It has been revealed that billions of pounds of suspected proceeds of corruption are laundered through the UK each year. While the UK has been considered the leading country on AML legislation and rules, there is a concern that the inefficiency of anti-money laundering compliance systems of UK companies may cause damage to the reputation and success of the City of London as an international financial centre and the wider UK economy (TI, 2015). The surveys find that the weakness of AML in the UK is caused by a number of gaps in companies' compliance systems[1] but the key factor is named as the lack of a presumption of personal responsibility by senior managers for money laundering failings that is compounded by low penalties in comparison to enforcement against banks in the US (TI, 2015). While money laundering is considered to be the main risk for the business of companies engaged in financial services, through a risk-based approach, the finding above leads to the conclusion that legal liability and even financial losses may not be such a convincing reason for companies to support a strong AML compliance. However, the consequences of inadequate AML controls can be much more threatening to the economic stability of the country(s) and international financial relations. Unawareness of companies of their responsibility for preventing money laundering as a global criminal activity will result in vulnerable AML compliance.

Compliance programs of goods and services providers regulating customer relationships and diligent customer care, in terms of CSR, serve consumer protection and sustainable consumption. Ethical principles followed by companies in customer relations provide for fair marketing and prevent malpractice that affects the economic interests of customers and distorts markets.

Taking into account that consumption levels of populations considerably vary among different countries depending on the economic advancement, development of production and supply, and educational levels, it is essential to support such a consumption environment that will enable consumers to obtain optimum benefit from their economic resources, consumers should be instructed in the proper use of goods and should be informed of the risks involved in intended or normally foreseeable use (United Nations [UN], 2003). "Enterprises should provide accurate, verifiable and clear information that is sufficient to enable consumers to make informed decisions, including information on the prices and, where appropriate, content, safe use, environmental attributes, maintenance, storage and disposal of goods and services". (OECD, 2011). The issues related to responsible behavior towards customers like mindful marketing, socially responsible marketing and customer-centric approach are broadly considered by Akkucuk (2015) in different works.

An organization's role in sustainable consumption arises from the products and services it offers, their life cycles and value chains, and the nature of the information it provides to consumers. Consumers play an important role in sustainable development by taking ethical, social, economic and environmental factors into account based on accurate information in making their choices and purchasing decisions ("ISO 26000", 2010).

Different international public organizations stress the importance of preventing unfair commercial and promotional practices. They also call for companies to make joint efforts with other authorities against deceptive marketing practices to secure public health and safety and the environment: "enterprises should co-operate fully with public authorities to prevent and combat deceptive marketing practices (including misleading advertising and commercial fraud) and to diminish or prevent serious threats to public health and safety or to the environment deriving from the consumption, use or disposal of their goods and services" ("ISO 26000", 2010). UN Guidelines for Consumer Protection appeal to consumer organizations, manufacturers and distributors in close collaboration with governments to take measures regarding misleading environmental claims or information in advertising and other marketing activities ("UN Guidelines", 2003).

Compliance in pharmaceutical companies is aimed at healthcare and the well-being of patients. Respect for ethical promotional standards in pharma business contributes to people's health and improves medical practice. Fair information disclosure on medications by manufactures enables healthcare professionals to get new information on pharmaceutical products as well as information for scientific and educational purposes and supports scientific and clinical research. "Ethical promotion helps to ensure that healthcare professionals globally have access to information they need, that patients have access to the medicines they need and that medicines are prescribed and used in a manner that provides the maximum healthcare benefit to patients" (International Federation of Pharmaceutical Manufacturers & Associations [IFPMA], 2012).

A data privacy compliance program is of great concern for many companies due to legislation tightening in this respect. The relevance of a data privacy program is determined to a considerable extent by the increased risk of financial losses. Global statistics on data breaches are outrageous[2]. Leaks of personal data cause serious damage to the reputation of a company and undermine the confidence of customers, partners and other stakeholders. A worrying phenomenon is "stolen or altered data can result in financial effects that are not known to the company until much later" (Petrocelli, 2005). These are strong arguments that determine the need to build effective compliance through data protection program. Furthermore, some experts consider data privacy not only as an integral part of the compliance system and a business issue but also as a component of a company's CSR. By obtaining customers or employees' personal information companies take responsibility for securing their most valuable possessions and negligent processing and storage of private information make people vulnerable to various forms of fraud. "Protecting customer's information is aligned with the social and economic aspects, 2 of the essential elements of CSR" (McPherson, 2014a). Going further, data protection is considered as an ethical issue and "governed by the organization's ethical stance and its goals for CSR" where smart and responsible companies go beyond regulations and implement their own initiatives or follow industry self-regulations (McPherson, 2014b). "In today's age of the customer, data protection really needs to be thought of as a corporate social responsibility. Companies following this approach have listed data protection in the CSR sections of their annual reports and other public communications" (Stilgherrian, 2014).

Diligent protection of people's data is a measure against cybercriminals who profit from selling different types of personal information. "Today, a global market for stolen data exists across various countries" ("Data Privacy Day", 2015). Information of about 110 million people in the USA has been hacked and was exposed in 2014 ("Data Privacy Day", 2016). Data which are the main target for scammers are tel. numbers, e-mails, details of banking cards and any other information relating to a particular individual that can be used for fraudulent transactions. However, there is also a special category of personal data concerning the private lives of individuals. The leakage of such information may jeopardize the constitutional rights of people to freedom and independence. So, data privacy concerns, first and foremost, the protection of people's personalities, private life and social security over business interests.

A recent case with Apple versus the FBI, perhaps, is an outstanding example of a company's CSR in respect of data privacy of its customers even in opposition to government. The company withstood a court order to assist the FBI and hack an iPhone of a particular terrorist as this precedent can be applied for any other device in the future and endanger the privacy of all users.

We built the iPhone for you, our customers. And we know that it is a deeply personal device. For many of us, the iPhone is an extension of our lives". "We didn't expect to be in this position, at odds with our government. We believe strongly that we have a responsibility to help protect your data and protect your privacy. We owe it to our customers and owe it to our country" (Tim Cook, CEO of Apple, Apple press conference, 2016, March).

The company published a letter on its site explaining to the customers its position and what is at stake: "While we believe the FBI's intentions are good, it would be wrong for the government to force us to build a backdoor into our products. And ultimately, we fear that this demand would undermine the very freedoms and liberty our government is meant to protect" (Apple letter, 2016). There is a dispute whether the company has higher moral obligations to assist government in fighting terrorism or protect customer's privacy but the position of Apple in respect to customer's privacy is firm and unyielding and it is determined to continue its resistance in this issue (Greenwald & McLaughlin, 2016).

COMPLIANCE IN REPORTING PRACTICES

Having considered the role of several compliance programs in regulating a range of global issues, it is apparent that compliance supported by companies is essential for efficient CSR and has a significant impact on corporate sustainability and sustainable development. At this stage this research has revealed an uncontestable correlation between companies' compliance outcomes and sustainability progress. To this end, the relevance and scope of information disclosure on compliance function in sustainability reporting[3] is becoming an issue for consideration.

Sustainability reporting is a topical issue today for many countries and international organizations. The significance of sustainability reporting for companies' business success and for global prosperity is now widely accepted. According to Global Reporting Initiative [GRI], sustainability reporting brings a number of external and internal benefits for companies, in particular, enabling external stakeholders to understand the organization's true value and gain their trust. "The value of the sustainability reporting process is that it ensures organizations consider their impacts on the sustainability issues, and enables them to be transparent about the risks and opportunities they face" (GRI, n.d.).

Ernst & Young [EY] (2013) claim that "sustainability disclosure can serve as a differentiator in competitive industries and fosters investor confidence, trust and employee loyalty". They distinguish the following benefits of sustainability reporting according to surveys: better reputation and public trust in business; meeting the expectations of employees and increased employee loyalty; improved access to capital and increased efficiency in decision-making processes.

Though the importance of sustainability reporting has been admitted by governments, businesses and public interest associations, there are global discussions and concerns about the content and materiality of issues included in sustainability reports. In fact, this problem is caused due to the absence, on a world-wide scale, of a generally accepted framework for writing a report that would benefit both society and the companies themselves.

The obligation to issue a sustainability report usually refers to large public and state-owned companies. However, a review of requirements existing in different countries in respect of sustainability reporting revealed that even mandatory requirements issued by governments and stock-exchanges overall are general and stress on environmental issues, some mention risks and corporate strategy, interests of employees and stakeholders, human rights, internal controls and other general references to CSR (Lingán &Wyman, 2013). Such ambiguity of requirements leaves companies to decide at their own discretion what kind of material information, and to what extent, to include in their report.

Currently different requirements on sustainability report information do not include statements on disclosing information about companies' compliance function and so there is no such mandatory rule. In preparing sustainability reports companies are usually referred to the several internationally-accepted guides: the OECD Guidelines, UNGC principles, ISO 26000 and GRI (Standards) – which has been considered as a universal standard for approaching sustainability report information, far exceeding the use of national standards and other guidelines (KPMG, 2013, 2015). Let's now analyze their approach to compliance information disclosure.

GRI provides detailed guidelines and recommendations for companies in sustainability report preparation[4]. Within General Standard Disclosures previous GRIG4 dictated for companies as a minimum to provide a general overview of company ethics and integrity by disclosing their values, principles, standards and norms and it detailed recommendations on the disclosure of compliance issues within Specific Standards Disclosures. Specific Standard Disclosures in a detailed way discovered information on different aspects that reflect significant economic, environmental and social performances or impacts of an organization.

Compliance was included in environmental and social aspect categories. Within the social category, compliance issues were considered in a more precise way under different sub-categories and some compliance issues were even separately distinguished. In particular, the sub-category "society" included a general "compliance" aspect and "anti-corruption" and "anti-competitive behavior" as stand-alone aspects. The "product responsibility" sub-category covered compliance in "customer health and safety" aspect, compliance in "product and service labeling" aspect, compliance in "marketing communications" aspect, "customer privacy" aspect and also a general "compliance" aspect.

For all compliance aspects guidelines provided recommendations for rather explicit information disclosure on the monetary value of significant fines and total number of non-monetary sanctions for non-compliance with applicable laws and regulation or the number of incidents of non-compliance with regulations. In case organizations had not identified any non-compliance with laws or regulations, it's recommended to provide a brief statement of this fact as sufficient[5].

Specified compliance aspects were and still required to be reported in a more detailed way. For example, in respect to anti-corruption compliance programs it is recommended to include information on the risk-assessment of operations and business processes exposed to corruption (G4-SO3; D 205-1), statistics on trainings conducted and policies communicated (G4-SO4; D 205-2) and statistics on incidents of corruption and actions taken (G4-SO5; D 205-3).

In disclosing information on anti-competitive behavior aspect companies are required to report on the number of legal actions pending or completed during the reporting period regarding anti-competitive behavior and violations of antitrust and monopoly practices and outcomes (G4-SO7; D 206-1).

Disclosing customer privacy aspect companies are expected to report the total number of substantiated complaints concerning breaches of customer privacy received from outside parties and from regulatory bodies and report the total number of identified leaks, thefts, or losses of customer data (G4-PR8; D 418-1).

As a matter of fact, guidelines provide recommendations to report the impact of compliance programs supported by companies on the environment, society and customers. However, specific standard disclosures should reflect information (indicators) only relevant to material aspects identified by companies. Materiality is the threshold at which aspects become sufficiently important that they should be reported. Thus, the selection of aspects and their indicators depend on the range of material topics identified by companies.

The companies preparing reports in accordance with GRIG4 guidelines usually publish a GRI summary table or GRI G4 content index that can provide some evidence for the information included in the report. As for material aspects, they are identified on the basis of material or key responsibility topics determined by the companies. These topics are usually selected with the involvement of stakeholders, discussed at special councils or committees, approved by the Board of Directors. While the material topics are provided, there is no clear justification for the aspects and indicators chosen relevant to these topics as well as for the extent of the information provided[6]. KPMG (2013) also make a point that there is a lack of transparency in the process of identifying material issues and a lack of consistency in how the GRI is used that is reflected in reporting quality: "Alignment between companies on how they apply the GRI framework, and how they focus reporting on material issues in line with the latest G4 Guidelines, is the next step", says Wim Bartels, KPMG's Global Head of Sustainability Reporting&Assurance.

Though the ex-version of GRIG4 includes recommendations on disclosing information on compliance aspects relevant to different compliance programs, they remain to the most part about declaring non-compliance issues and not about the compliance programs. So, whether or not reports contain information on violations this may not be enough and provides insignificant information about compliance practices and their input into sustainable development until a more detailed description of the compliance system is rendered. At the same time besides disclosing information on compliance aspects within Specific Standards Disclosures, some companies when following the General Standard Disclosures on providing information about Ethics and Integrity include rather substantial information about compliance systems in the reports. As a result, the information about compliance can be unstructured and dispersed throughout a report[7].

Analysis of several sustainability reports shows that companies following GRIG4 standards disclose different amounts and varying quality of information on compliance aspects even if identifying the same aspects as material and following the same indicators. Thus, companies are free to choose the content and explicitness of information about compliance programs to be included into reports. From such a perspective, the question of content and materiality in sustainability reports is certainly of no less, and arguably of more relevance to information on compliance to be reflected.

GRI G4 Guidelines recently have undergone a process of transformation into GRI Sustainability Reporting Standards (GRI Standards). Establishing standards instead of guidelines will allow them to be referenced even more broadly in policy initiatives around the world, supporting a greater uptake of credible sustainability reporting. Most changes focus on the format and presentation.

It is notable within the changes that the Ethics and Integrity standard has been raised from the bottom of the standards and placed in the third position. Also the "aspects" (that were renamed into "topics") Anti-corruption and Anti-competitive behavior have been moved from social sub-categories to the economic category emphasizing the impact of these compliance programs on the world economy.

It should be noted that within the topic Anti-corruption which, in comparison to other GRI compliance topics, includes more indicators for disclosure, in a new version, one can observe the expansion of these indicators. For instance, reporting recommendations contain more details about risk assessment procedure for disclosure (like criteria used in the assessment, location, activity and sector); information on managing conflict of interest, procedures and controls in respect to charitable donations and sponsorships; delivery of communications and training on anti-corruption to different third parties; information on a company's participation in collective actions against corruption.

There is a new topic introduced – Socioeconomic compliance which will combine Compliance aspects from Society and Product responsibility sub-categories. "This topic addresses an organization's overall compliance record" (GRI 419, 2016) and may include compliance with specific laws, and regulations and standards that are not distinguished as separate compliance topics. The Standard also requires organizations to provide a narrative description of how they manage a certain material topic and the related impacts.

It should also be mentioned that within the Environmental series of topics the aspect "Compliance" has been changed to "Environmental compliance" emphasizing its formation as a separate compliance area.

GRI performed transition in an open format that one could leave feedback on the draft of the standards. Presented changes evidence that compliance issues are gaining more weight and relevance. New standards apply since 2018.

Let's now consider information relative to compliance issues disclosure in other guidelines on sustainability reports.

OECD Guidelines for Multinational Enterprises (2008) are not heavily detailed and provide more general recommendations on non-financial reporting. If GRI G4 and now SRS is actually a guide for preparing reports, OECD Guidelines are, foremost, a set of recommendations (principles and standards, providing extended recommendations on compliance system) committed by OECD governments for responsible business conduct in a global context consistent with applicable laws and internationally recognized standards that benefit sustainable development. The Guidelines point out that, enterprises following principles of business conduct contribute to sustainable development. And this recommendation to operation is first on the list.

GRI G4 and OECD Guidelines correlate to the effect that the latter contains the majority of standards which are reflected in GRI as aspects (topics) of sustainable development to be reported on. GRI Guidelines also indicate linkage to OECD Guidelines for Multinational Enterprises towards the aspects.

OECD Guidelines (2008) assign a separate chapter for disclosure principles. It advises the enterprises to perform a report in two areas: in the first set of disclosures it is recommended to include basic material information like financial results, corporate governance, and structure of corporate holdings. In the second set of disclosures the enterprises are encouraged to provide additional information. Within this part of disclosure the guidelines recommend to include expanded information on compliance issues:

1. Value statements or statements of business conduct intended for public disclosure including, depending on its relevance for the enterprise's activities, information on the enterprise's policies relating to matters covered by the Guidelines;

2. Policies and other codes of conduct to which the enterprise subscribes, their date of adoption and the countries and entities to which such statements apply;
3. Its performance in relation to these statements and codes;
4. Information on internal audit, risk management **and legal compliance systems** (OECD, 2008).

Such a more comprehensive report is compared to "communication with the public and with other parties directly affected by the enterprise's activities", by which the companies "can demonstrate a commitment to socially acceptable practices" (OECD, 2008).

United Nations Global Compact promotes 10 principles of responsible business aimed at supporting sustainable development. UNGC signatories are required to issue a Communication on Progress (COP), a public disclosure to stakeholders on progress made in implementing the ten principles. GRI G4 disclosures also provided linkage and correlation between aspects and UNGC principles.

As for the COP content, UNGP does not provide any specific standards. The COP can be provided in a flexible format, in any language but must meet minimum requirements, which are: a statement by the chief executive expressing continued support for the UN Global Compact and renewing the participant's ongoing commitment to the initiative; a description of practical actions the company has taken or plans to take to implement the Ten Principles in each of the four areas (human rights, labour, environment, anti-corruption) and a measurement of outcomes (UNGP, n.d.). Aside from disclosures on anti-corruption practices and measures, there are not any recommendations for information on compliance issues. COP is not even required to be a separate document. UNGP assesses all reports submitted by companies and verifies whether there is information reflected in accordance with the ten principles and defines the level of COP.

ISO 26000 is an international standard which contains basic principles and core subjects of social responsibility (some of which have already been mentioned above) as well as directions on how to integrate them into companies strategies. It should be mentioned that compliance and ethics are rooted in the concept of social responsibility as one of its basic principles is Ethical behavior. ISO clarifies what organizations should do to support and promote ethical behavior. Another principle is transparency meaning "openness about decisions and activities that affect society, the economy and the environment, and willingness to communicate these in a clear, accurate, timely, honest and complete manner" ("ISO 26000", 2010). This implies that compliance based on ethics, and reporting constitute social responsibility.

The standards propose companies at appropriate intervals report about their performance on social responsibility to the stakeholders affected, notably, in various ways such as meetings with stakeholders, letters describing the organization's activities related to social responsibility for a defined period, website information and periodic social responsibility reports. Recommendations provide a few broad characteristics of the report content that companies should consider. Though, the standard gives detailed recommendations to sustain social responsibility for companies, as for reporting, there are just brief guidelines. Companies are expected to report on the core subjects of social responsibility included in the ISO Standard, namely, how they address them applying the principles and practices of social responsibility. *An organization should disclose in a clear, accurate and complete manner, and to a reasonable and sufficient degree, the policies, decisions and activities for which it is responsible, including their known and likely impacts on society and the environment. This information should be readily available, directly accessible and understandable to those who have been, or may be, affected in significant ways by the organization... and including achievements and shortfalls and the ways in which the shortfalls will be addressed ("ISO 26000", 2010).* This also covers a number of compliance issues relevant to fair operating practices that concern ethical conduct in an organization's dealings with other organizations partners, suppliers, contractors, customers, competitors, and the associations of which they are members. Particular topics include anti-corruption, antitrust, and consumer issues.

The standards that have been analyzed, in fact, are inter-related as they (OECD, UNGP and ISO 26000) promote similar standards for CSR and GRI provides guidelines for reporting on them. The standards cover to some extent compliance matters, though they are of a non-biding nature, but still they provide a niche for compliance disclosure in the reports.

There are a few more standards on reporting. Another standard that is widely used by companies in preparing sustainability reports is the Assurance standard series AA1000 [AA1000 Standards] issued by the Institute of Social and Ethical Accountability – "AccountAbility". Unlike GRI Guidelines the series of standards does not provide exact guidelines as to what information or what topics are to be disclosed, in particular, the guidelines given do not provide any recommendations about disclosing information on compliance. However, they lay down the principles for organizations to understand, manage and improve their sustainability performance and thus stay accountable in front of their stakeholders, while evaluating their adherence to these principles. These principles are: inclusivity, materiality and responsiveness which serve the accountability of the company.

Inclusivity is considered as a foundation principle and determines materiality and responsiveness[8]. This encompasses stakeholder's engagement in the company's activity and taking into account their interests, opinions and expectations to communicate appropriately on how the company considers their attitudes, concerns and trust.

Another principle is materiality. Information is material if it or its absence or misrepresentation in the report may influence the decisions and behavior of stakeholders or decisions, actions and performance of an organization. The criteria of materiality requires non-financial aspects that may cause considerable legal, regulatory or financial implications to be included in the report as well as norms and commitments established and supported by the business community ("AA1000 Standards", 2008).

The issue of materiality, as has already been mentioned, has been a matter of dispute for a lengthy period of time and currently remains a pressing issue in terms of non-financial reporting. Yet in 2006 AccountAbility issued "The Materiality Report" devoted to the problem of materiality determination. The report puts forward a shift away from the traditional approach (narrow focus on materiality) to a sustainability approach (a long-term focus on issues and stakeholders that could affect organizational performance). The main idea of the report about distinguishing materiality aspects yields with the approach that such aspects should be aligned with the strategy of the company, and this should be obvious and clear to the stakeholders.

It is noteworthy, that in the report issued 10 years ago compliance was already mentioned as a topic for disclosure reflecting the role of stakeholders in raising the significance of compliance issues:

Stakeholders are not just passive observers of business practice, they are actively engaged in trying to change what is material to the businesses bottom line. For example, advocates of anti-corruption have advanced the law, policies and practices in ways that have turned 'acceptable ways of doing business' involving illegal transactions into a growing liability. Environmentalists, increasingly working with business, have turned the spectre of climate change into material risks and opportunities across markets (AccountAbility & LRQA, 2006).

However, at that time, compliance was still not as much considered as a strategically material issue but relevant to the report as an issue of interest to some stakeholders.

Since the debate fails to demonstrate how business performance can make the biggest difference in addressing social and environmental issues, most external stakeholders remain focused on compliance, while mainstream investors ignore these issues altogether because the business fails to demonstrate why they are important to business success… Businesses will still need to disclose their performance with respect to laws, commitments and voluntary initiatives where they have identified a compliance responsibility or an area of information demand. But they should put clear emphasis on the issues that are critical to their strategic goals. (AccountAbility & LRQA, 2006). The report clarifies the criteria to be used to determine if the issue is material. It should be aligned to long-term business success; be important to stakeholders and business; align with the strategy.

As the authors have considered compliance from the CSR perspective, characterized it as an integral component of CSR, revealed the role of different compliance programs in sustainability, economic development (ex. anti-corruption, antitrust, AML) and impact for stakeholders (ex. data privacy), there should not be any doubt that the issue of compliance is material for a company's performance and sustainability in contemporary business. Since compliance offers a potential for a successful and sustainable organization and community, its importance for business and stakeholders is undeniable and if it is treated as a component of CSR, it should be also integrated into company strategy. CSR is taken seriously only in a mature organization with extensive compliance culture, says Brian Fahey (2016), CEO at "MyComplianceOffice"[9]. Integration of CSR issues into the system of corporate governance and the total management system is also taken into consideration for assurance of a company's reports.

The third principle set by AccountAbility is responsiveness. This is about how an organization responds to the issues of stakeholders that affect its sustainability performance and are addressed through decisions, actions and performance, as well as communication with stakeholders. The standard specifies this as: establishing policies, objectives and targets, governance structure, management systems and processes, action plans, stakeholder engagement, measurement and monitoring of performance or assurance. This means that the company is expected to disclose to the interested public considerable information including issues related to corporate governance, risk management and compliance (as a part of these aspects of company performance).

Based on the AA1000 Standards it can be concluded that a sustainable organization is one that not only admits and bears responsibility towards stakeholders, but also integrates the principles of responsible behavior into its strategy and reports on that. Therefore, compliance is a matter for disclosure.

The next reporting standard that is becoming popular nowadays is Integrated Reporting (IR). This is an initiative of the International Integrated Reporting Council [IIRC]. IR is about demonstrating how organizations' resources create value including in the social sphere (social capital). An IR approach is specifically focusing on a "creating value" aspect as it provides information not only about financial highlights but also about a company's strategy, performance and decision-making process thus giving investors insights in a broader context enabling them to see the correlation between sustainable development and financial performance (IIRC, 2015). According to IR approach, sustainable development is also becoming a mainstream concern on a par with financial stability. That is why organizations are demanded of to disclose non-financial results on their performance as well to provide investors with overall feedback on the management of their investments. The perspective is that investors also have responsibility for companies' performances: "Investors are the owners of the companies and they have to become more proactive in demanding more from the management of those companies, not only in terms of financial returns but also social responsibility etc., given that that will have an increasing value for investors as the public and the customers value more and more the way that companies behave themselves", says R. M. Guedes, Head of European Equity Strategy, MainFirst Bank (IIRC, 2015). The supporters of IR suppose that IR benefits both investors and companies: investors using non-financial information can improve their decision-making processes on investment and companies can enhance corporate transparency and encourage sustainable investment.

The IR framework does not contain particular compliance issues to be disclosed, however, the general issues about the organization include culture, ethical principles and values; the aspect "Governance" covers issues relevant to value creation including "specific processes used to make strategic decisions and to establish and monitor the culture of the organization, including its attitude to risk and mechanisms for addressing integrity and ethical issues" (IIRC, 2013). The growing role of compliance in sustainable development increases the attention and requirements of investors and other stakeholders to its disclosure and within the IR approach can be considered as a material issue as well.

Finally, is the The International Standard on Assurance Engagement 3000 (ISAE3000) issued by the International Federation of Accountants [IFAC] as the standard that sets the procedure to collect/select reliable information for assurance of non-financial reporting. The standard provides basic principles and a general framework for the practitioner[10] rather than certain topics for disclosure. It does include categorization of the range of possible underlying subject matters and information on them. In particular, "Aspects of behavior" contains "Compliance" – information on the entity's compliance with specific legal or regulatory requirements, an internally developed code of conduct or an agreed level of performance (such as the number of times a particular committee is expected to meet in a year). Since "compliance" is separately distinguished as a subject matter for reporting the authors place it among essential issues of non-financial reporting.

Through analysis of acknowledged and reliable guidelines and standards in non-financial reporting the researchers conclude that: there are recommendations on disclosing certain compliance issues, the topic on compliance is becoming an integral component of companies' responsible behavior and a material aspect of sustainable development.

Let's consider further grounds for and driving factors of compliance issues' expansion in sustainability reports. D. Kennedy-Glans and Dr. Bob Schulz over 10 years ago signified corporate reporting on companies' integrity commitments and actions, independent measurement and verification of alignment between corporate intention and corporate actions, and corporate management's response to deficiencies. "Without an ability to effectively judge corporate business integrity, public opinion and media reporting by corporate critics predictably sway stakeholders" (Kennedy-Glans & Dr. Bob Schulz, 2005, pp. 26-27). As they write, even at that time stakeholders had been challenging corporations to address less tangible non-financial indicators in reporting like stakeholder and government relations and impacts of investment on communities. They provide statistics that in 2003 about 100 of Europe's top corporations surged in ethical reporting in their annual reports. Though there were some companies issuing social accountability or sustainability reports then, there was not a standardized practice for reporting on non-financial objectives or outcomes. Even then, however, the authors emphasized the importance of companies' communication to stakeholders on business integrity and what is more – the companies had ought to assess their practices against their commitments on integrity (Kennedy-Glans & Dr. Bob Schulz, 2005, p. 141). Since then, though the standards of non-financial reporting have been developed, including guidelines and more clarity on compliance and ethics issues reporting, still for now, reporting on integrity practices and compliance remain outside of mandatory requirements. Let us next understand changes in social requests regarding disclosing this information in sustainability reports.

Recent surveys reveal that there is an increase in stakeholders' inquiries for sustainability reporting driven by the divergent needs and interests of an increasing number of stakeholders: "In today's economy there's a whole range of changing expectations from stakeholders — be they investors, employees or wider society. Different users look at sustainability information from different perspectives, and therefore accrue different benefits and insights", says Ernst Ligteringen, Chief Executive of GRI (EY &GRI survey, 2014, p. 6). EY point out that the approach to sustainability reporting has shifted to risk reduction and mitigation (i.e. how companies operate with regard to inherent risks to their business). According to EY, compliance and operational performance are becoming more influential in sustainability strategy (EY & GrinBeez Group, 2013).

Yet another survey of practices in preparing reports on CSR issues (sustainability reports) worldwide was conducted by KPMG in 2013. In general, the survey demonstrated an incremental increase of reporting globally (of 7 percent since 2011) what is becoming "a mainstream business practice worldwide" and among the world's largest 250 companies the CR reporting rate remained more or less stable at 93 percent. They provide an assessment of report quality in accordance with several criteria (7 quality criteria: strategy, risk and opportunity, materiality, target setting and indicators, suppliers and the value chain, stakeholder engagement, governance of CR, transparency and balance) which correlate with the principles of preparing sustainability reports in accordance with GRI G4. Based on these criteria KPMG conclude that one quarter of surveyed companies (G250[11]) achieved an overall quality score of 80 (out of 100) or above. These companies demonstrated a superior understanding of the impact of social and environmental issues on their business and reported on their strategy, performance and interaction with stakeholders more than others. Relying on the overall results of the survey, they conclude that there is room for improvement in the quality of reporting on CR issues. They do not provide a more detailed analysis of the topics included in reports or assessment of materiality aspects considered by the companies. Likewise, the research does not bring to attention compliance issues disclosure in the reports, however, the research revealed that among sustainability-related risks a large number of companies distinguish components of compliance risk: reputational risk is the most commonly cited type of business risk, as well as regulatory risk and legal risks ("KPMG survey", 2013) [12]. Consequently, management of compliance risk aspects is becoming a vital issue for sustainability and reporting on it.

On the same point, recent research by Thomson Reuters emphasizes another component of compliance risk – a conduct risk – and finds that it is becoming of high significance within managing regulatory risk as its "biggest driver" (English & Hammond, 2015). A conduct risk relates to unethical behavior. For example, the Australian Securities and Investment Commission defines conduct risk as:

The risk of inappropriate, unethical or unlawful behavior on the part of an organization's management or employees. Such conduct can be caused by deliberate actions or may be inadvertent and caused by inadequacies in an organization's practices, frameworks or education programs. Conduct risk can have significant ramifications for an organization, its shareholders, clients, customers, counter-parties and the financial services industry.

"Conduct risk is the threat of financial loss to an organization that is caused by the actions of managers and employees. The term conduct risk is typically used in the financial sector to describe risks that involve a breakdown of corporate culture and ethics, and that do not fall under other risk categories, such as credit, liquidity, market and operational risks" (Rouse, 2016). So, the lack of ethics and compliance culture may put the company at risk on a par with other risks, and this particular risk is becoming increasingly important. This concern should not be regarded as a duty of the compliance manager alone, but the entire management. "Firms should also be aware that good compliance officers will not choose to stay at firms with poor cultures and attitudes to compliance. Anecdotally, experienced compliance officers are already voting with their feet and moving to firms with a strong, positive approach to conduct risk, compliance and good customer outcomes" (English, & Hammond, 2015).

It's remarkable that Citigroup in its 2015 Annual report stresses the point of conduct risk:

U.S. and non-U.S. regulators have been increasingly focused on "conduct risk," a term that is used to describe the risks associated with behavior by employees and agents, including third-party vendors utilized by Citi, that could harm consumers, investors or the markets, such as failures to safeguard consumers' and investors' personal information, failures to identify and manage conflicts of interest and improperly creating, selling and marketing products and services. In addition to increasing Citi's compliance risks, this focus on conduct risk could lead to more regulatory or other enforcement proceedings and litigation, including for practices which historically were acceptable but are now receiving greater scrutiny.

KPMG survey of 2015 does not provide essential new findings but worth mentioning are the continuing growing rate of CR reporting among the G250 – over 90 percent, and also inclusion of CR data in annual financial reports as a firmly established global trend. The issue of quality has remained opened since 2013 for many countries and the questions "what?" and "how?" to report are still relevant. Notably, in 2013 Asia Pacific countries demonstrated the most significant increase in CR reporting rates, in 2015 the companies "in this region tend to focus on demonstrating compliance and managing risks, particularly in relation to supply chain, community and human rights issues" ("KPMG survey", 2015).

So, observation of recent trends in sustainability reporting identifies the brewing need for reflecting compliance issues in the reports. And with time one can expect more explicit information disclosure on compliance among CSR issues. Some compliance issues are already rooted in reports on sustainability like ethics, integrity and anti-corruption. Counteracting corruption as a priority issue for civil society organizations also demands a high level of transparency from businesses (KPMG, GRI, UNEP & Centre for Corporate Governance in Africa, 2013). Anti-corruption has become such a global issue that companies are expected to disclose their actions against bribery and corruption not so much in the interests of shareholders as a measure to protect business from being penalized for breaking anti-corruption legislation but in the interests of the world economy and society. All the guidelines considered above relied on by companies in preparing sustainability reports include a topic on anti-corruption measures. Even GRI G4 and now GRI Standards in comparison to other aspects provide more detailed issues to be disclosed on the measures taken against corruption such as risk assessment, training and communication, confirmed incidents of corruption, measures against employees including disciplinary sanctions or dismissals and cases of terminated contracts with business partners due to revealed incidents of corruption. So, while companies are expected to report on their anti-corruption measures, they decide at their own discretion how explicitly to present information about their anti-corruption programs in public reports, and the outcomes of these decisions reflect their transparency as the cornerstone of the fight against corruption and accountability to their stakeholders.

Assessment of anti-corruption programs disclosure is already available to society. Since 2012 Transparency International (TI) has been evaluating the transparency of corporate reporting among the largest publicly-listed and traded companies and of leading emerging market companies. Companies are being assessed on three criteria including anti-corruption programs, and examination of reporting on anti-corruption programs, together with further transparency practices, TI has been evaluating since 2008.

The TI report for 2014 revealed that 97% of companies committed to comply with laws. In particular, the report provides an overview of companies declaring prohibition of facilitation payments, their transparency in political contributions and consistency of anti-corruption policies with criteria used to assess the anti-corruption programs dimension in the report including geographical criteria.

Based on the results of corporate reporting transparency, TI annually ranks companies. It also calls for governments and regulatory bodies, investors and even civil society organizations to demand greater transparency from multinational companies. The main finding of the report is that, according to the three parameters, market-leading companies continue to achieve the best results in anti-corruption transparency, indicating that such companies strive to disclose their anti-corruption programs. Overall ratings show that the best performers are European companies and the worst performing are Asian companies, while there were only three large corporations from Russia included in the report.

In 2015 TI issued a report on the transparency of the world's telecommunications companies. The telecommunications sector, which is defined for the purposes of this report as the information and communication technologies (ICT) sector, plays a critical role in today's social, cultural and business life. The total market value of the major publicly listed companies in the sector is approximately US$2 trillion (TI report, 2015).The telecommunications sector in particular is affected by the risks of corruption inherent in its business transactions. For telecom companies, as for other companies, the first line of defence against the risk of bribery and corruption is a comprehensive anti-corruption program that is fully implemented and monitored on a continuing basis (TI report, 2015).

The survey revealed that 35 telecommunications companies assessed in this study achieved an average of 65 percent, out of a possible 100 percent, in regard to reporting on their anti-corruption programs. The average result in this dimension was the best among the three dimensions that were evaluated: commitment to comply with laws, confidential reporting channel and leadership support. Three leading companies that achieved a perfect score of 100 percent were Germany's Deutsche Telekom, France's Orange and Alcatel-Lucent. A group of Nordic companies: Telenor, Ericsson and TeliaSonera, followed closely behind with a result of 96 percent. Overall ratings demonstrated that as in the 2014 report the best performers for reporting on anti-corruption programs are European companies with the highest average score achieved at 85 percent. The worst scoring companies were Asian companies, with an average result of 37 percent.

The publication of elements of anti-corruption compliance demonstrates a company's commitment to fighting corruption as well as its adherence to fair business conduct and integrity, and increases its responsibility and accountability to stakeholders and the public.

At this stage of the research it can be concluded that companies are expected to report on their transparency practices and certain compliance programs, most of all, anti-corruption which is becoming more an obligation than a voluntary disclosure. This tendency can be already evidenced by EU Directive 2014/95/EU which mentions that the public-interest entities are expected to report on anti-corruption and bribery matters.

This research revealed the real value of compliance to sustainable development and this becomes a strong argument for information on compliance to be reflected in sustainability reporting. Moreover, there are studies proving the real financial value of compliance to the companies. For instance, prof. Curtis C. Verschoor of DePaul University and others analyzed the company's financial growth by measuring

Market Value Added (MVA) of the Standard & Poor's 500 and revealed that companies classified as having superior corporate governance substantially outperformed their less ethically focused competitors, to the tune of an average of $9.4 billion in 2004 (Verschoor, 2004). Another study, by the Aspen Institute and management consulting firm Booz Allen Hamilton, similarly found a financial benefit from strong corporate values: they found a strong correlation between financial performance and a focus on ethics and core values. There are studies that also prove that ethics and corporate culture aid hiring and retaining top quality employees and ensure productivity among U.S. employees: "Unethical behavior has a strongly deleterious effect on employee morale and distracts employees from the company's business at hand" (Biegelman, 2008).

Therefore, based on the results of these surveys compliance can be considered as an asset, and as it is an asset, it must be reported! Then, the questions that are of most concern about the quality of sustainability reports –"what?" and "how?" to report – are of primary relevance for compliance information disclosure as there is uncertainty on the range of issues, structure and volume of information to be included since there is not any framework or explicit recommendations in this regard. Disclosure of compliance information in the reports is an emerging practice and there are business and public drivers to make it a regular practice in time. The next stage of this investigation will be devoted to the survey of information disclosure on compliance in the sustainability reports of the world's leading companies to assess the trend and progress achieved in this respect.

Disclosure of Compliance in Sustainability Reporting

Data and Methodology

The practical part of the research is devoted to the analysis of a review of companies' public reports (annual, sustainability, integrated, etc.). The main achievement of the research will be the outcome of companies' reports surveyed to identify the trends and measure the advancements in disclosing information on compliance in the public reports. In reviewing corporate reporting documents the approach of KPMG was followed to studying corporate sustainability reporting and the reports of G250 (250 leading world companies of Global Fortune 500 list) were analyzed. The rating of G500 for 2015[13] was used – the latest available rating at the moment of the beginning of the project. GRI sustainability reports database[14] was accessed in addition to company websites to obtain company reports. To compare information on compliance disclosure in a timeline perspective the reports for two different years were taken: reports published in 2016 for 2015 or the most recent available reports alongside the reports for 2011 mainly. However, besides sustainability reports the research also covers annual reports for 2 years in accordance with the latest KPMG surveyed global trend to include information on CSR in annual reports. Thus, results and findings of this research are based on the review of approximately 1000 public reports in the sample (Table 1).

Since there aren't any strict requirements on providing information on compliance in public reports, to bring the assessment to a common standard the following table was developed (see Table 3). The table includes basic criteria to appraise the compliance system in a company and thus to assess what aspects of compliance a company discloses. The Table 2 comprises 4 main criteria:

Table 1. Sample

G250 companies (KPMG approach)
GRI sustainability reports database
Non-financial and Annual reports
Reports over a 4 year period for 2015/14 and 2011/2010
In total: around 1000 reports

Table 2. Criteria for assessment

<table>
<tr><td rowspan="2">Company</td><td rowspan="2">Year</td><td colspan="3">General information on compliance</td><td rowspan="2">General information on compliance and ethics: information on the Code of Conduct, ethical principles and values, information on compliance function, other general information</td></tr>
<tr><td>Code of conduct and values</td><td>Compliance function</td><td>Other</td></tr>
<tr><td colspan="5">Elements of compliance system</td><td rowspan="2">Elements of compliance system: these include the most essential and commonly described integral components of a compliance system: tone from the top, training and communications, whistleblowing system and other elements, for example, risk-assessment, due diligence, etc.</td></tr>
<tr><td>Tone from the top</td><td>Communications and training</td><td>Hotline (reports on violations)</td><td colspan="2">Others</td></tr>
<tr><td colspan="5">Compliance programs</td><td rowspan="2">Information about compliance programs: anti-corruption, data privacy (most disclosed in the reports) and any others (antitrust, AML, etc.)</td></tr>
<tr><td colspan="2">Anti-corruption</td><td colspan="2">Data privacy</td><td>Others</td></tr>
<tr><td colspan="2">Total number of pages devoted to compliance</td><td colspan="2">Separate paragraph "Compliance"</td><td>Type of report</td><td>Number of pages devoted to compliance (approximation varying on the font, format and style of the text allows to estimate the volume of information allotted to compliance); a separate section devoted to compliance and ethical issues; type of report reviewed (sustainability, annual, integrated, etc.).</td></tr>
</table>

FINDINGS

A review of the latest reports published mainly in 2016 revealed that the information on the companies' Code of Conduct, anti-corruption practices, training and hotlines is commonly reported by the companies in the public reports (over 50% of the companies in the scope – see table below for the statistics). A lower % of the companies on the list (just over 30%) provide information on their compliance function (composition, place in organization's structure, competences and roles) among which about 15% mention a collegial body – (Committee) to define strategy and coordinate activities to manage compliance risk and other issues of ethics and compliance (see Table 4).

Less often one can find information on elements of compliance systems (Table 5). For instance, few companies declare on their "tone from the top" practices. A good example of such initiative is implemented and declared by BMW where managers sign a declaration on implementing this principle. More frequently the companies declare on their responsible interaction with third parties and their compliance requirements for suppliers and service providers. Rarely reports contain information on other elements of compliance system like risk-assessment, due diligence, compliance audits and compliance system

Table 3. Assessment table

Company	Year	General Information on Compliance			Elements of Compliance System				Compliance Programs			Total Number of Pages Devoted to Compliance	Separate Paragraph "Compliance"	Type of Report
		Code of conduct and values	Compliance function	Other	Tone from the top	Communications and training	Hotline (reports on violations)	Others	Anti-corruption	Data privacy	Others		Yes/No	Sustainability, annual, Integrated, etc.

Table 4. Most disclosed information

Code of Conduct and values	65%*
Anti-bribery & corruption	52%
Communications & training	54%
Hotline	55%

* % calculated from the sample (250 companies)

Table 5. Other disclosed issues

Tone from the top
Other compliance programs: Antitrust, AML, Insider compliance
Human rights
Other elements of compliance system: risk assessment, due diligence, compliance audits, compliance system effectiveness assessment
Compliance requirements for suppliers and service providers

effectiveness assessments. A small number of companies like BMW, JP Morgan Chase, Deutsche Telecom, Deutsche Post, McKesson provide expanded information on their compliance systems components.

More regularly the companies include information on compliance programs in the reports. Data privacy compliance program is in second place after anti-corruption among disclosed compliance programs. Other compliance programs described in the reports are antitrust, AML, insider compliance, with fewer environmental compliance and product stewardship (typically for food industry, pharmaceuticals and oil companies). Human rights programs while topical elsewhere in reporting are however, regularly omitted from compliance section. There is an apparent tendency to distinguish a separate paragraph for compliance issues which is often named "Ethics" or "Business Integrity" (over 40% of the companies which reports were examined) (Table 7).

The majority of companies demonstrate stable disclosure of unchanged quantity of information on compliance from year to year. This is evidence that compliance issues have become conventional to disclose. 20% of companies (most of which are Chinese) demonstrate no progress on disclosure and provide no information on compliance in the reports (Table 6).

It is worth mentioning that among all companies of which reports were analyzed during the survey Walmart is the leader in publicly disclosing information on compliance. Since 2014 the company has been issuing A Global Compliance Program Report in line with enhancing anti-corruption programs as a consequence of corruption practices revealed in Mexico for obtaining licenses and permits for opening new stores. In their report Walmart declares what they have done since the violations were revealed and investigations started in cooperation with DOJ and SEC to improve the company's compliance program. The first report issued in 2014 is the most expansive and contains information on the development of Walmart's compliance program, in particular: how the compliance function has been reorganized, description of its structure, whom they have hired and how the compliance staff has been enlarged; review of compliance trainings, update of policies and procedures, enhancement of compliance-related systems; overview of all (14) compliance areas within the compliance program with brief information on the main changes and improvements in each area. The main attention is given to anti-corruption practices as the priority activity in light of the investigation. There is a separate Global Anti-corruption compliance officer for a group of companies.

Subsequent reports for 2015 and 2016 include information on consequent measures and steps the company took for the reported year in improving its compliance system, making reports informative and dynamic. Notably, the title of the report for 2016 has been changed to global Ethics and Compliance Program Report.

The companies that provide the most informative and qualitative reports include details that demonstrate the dynamics of compliance in their organizations, progress, and success or failure to reflect an objective overview of compliance outcomes for a reporting period. They do not only refer to aspects evidencing the presence of compliance function but provide broader details to assess its functioning and

Table 6. The progress in a 4-year timeline

Obvious expansion of information devoted to compliance in reports	20%
Stable disclosure	60%
No progress on disclosure	20%
No info on compliance in reports	Chinese companies

Table 7. Other results on disclosure

Data privacy	36%
Compliance function	33%
Compliance or Ethics Committee	15%
Separate paragraph on compliance and Ethics	Over 40%

effectiveness, in particular: inform on performed results, number of trained employees and their input or contribution into external projects in collaboration with other organizations (e.g. Siemens integrity initiative against corruption; Annual compliance seminar by Diamler Compliance Academy; the Hitachi Group Compliance Conference; International collaboration on compliance ("International Compliance Days") by Deutsche Telecom); Participation in collective actions initiatives on business ethics and anti-corruption by BHP Billiton; IBM collaborates with universities to deliver ethics and integrity seminars). Best practices describe plans and strategy on compliance; disclose information on legal proceedings, fines or investigations and assigned monitor; write on achievements and awards; share different activities to promote compliance e.g. surveys of employees awareness on ethics and compliance, promotion of compliance days, distribution of compliance materials (Table 8).

Analysis of public reports has also shed light on certain problems in the disclosure of information on compliance (Table 8). The main and most recurring drawback is the disparity of the information provided on compliance in the reports; information is not always structured to the principle of inclusion, information in the report is not always clear, making it difficult to perceive and to understand the compliance system in the company as a whole.

A further observation of the research is that information on the topic of ethics and compliance is often duplicated from the contents of the Code of Ethics, is not always updated and is a repeat of the reports of previous years. Therefore the content of the compliance sections is not always informative, often presented only in the form of general abstractions and statements of abidance with the requirements of the law. There is much less information about achievements, innovations, changes, successes or plans, that are a description of any progress of the company (implying a public report) including in the field of compliance. These observations raise the issue of the quality of information disclosed, which also remains relevant in general for non-financial reports. These issues require further consideration.

A notable fact is that through the reports of certain companies one can observe their approach to compliance and ethics as an integral component of CSR. The following findings evidence that a number of companies correlate compliance with the interests of third parties and CSR. The Trafigura Group (commodity trading) conducts a Materiality assessment among its stakeholders both internal and external to reveal and prioritise their objectives and interests. Their research finds that compliance is among the 3 greatest materiality issues for stakeholders next to transparency and social license to operate. Cisco considers ethical conduct within its CSR priorities, Toshiba declares that it places the highest priority on compliance as a part of CSR. Metro Group refers compliance and combating corruption to good corporate governance and social engagement and identifies these issues as of high relevance both for stakeholders and for the group.

Table 8. Analysis of information disclosed about compliance

Best Practices in Disclosing Information on Compliance	Revealed Negative Aspects/ Shortcomings
✓ Highlights in reported period	✗ Information on compliance is dispersed throughout the reports, not structured
✓ Plans and strategy on compliance	✗ Information repeats from year to year
✓ Participation in external activities and initiatives	✗ Information duplicates Ethics code or Code of Conduct
✓ Detailed statistics on training and messages or incidents reported to a hotline	✗ The content is not informative, often just statements about compliance with the law and legal requirements or mentioning of particular compliance aspects without details.
✓ Litigations, investigations, information on assigned monitor	
✓ Activities in compliance: Corporate Ethics week, Compliance/ Integrity week, Ethical surveys, Compliance Handbook or Manual	
✓ Awards	

CONCLUSION

So far, based on the outcomes of conducted analysis, it can be concluded that disclosing information on compliance is a developing practice and there are business and public drivers to make it a regular practice in a while. The reports that were analyzed confirm that companies in a varying degree include information on compliance and it is expected to observe a positive trend further during the recent years.

In general, the observation of companies' reports revealed an obvious trend to disclose information on compliance issues. The survey distinguishes a range of leading companies that set a benchmark in disclosing information on compliance and underlines its role in CSR. The reports of approximately 50 companies (20% of sample) demonstrate obvious expansion or greater inclusion of information devoted to compliance in reports. Among these companies there are company-leaders who explicitly provide information on compliance. These are: Walmart, Volkswagen, Siemens, Bayer, Samsung Electronics, Citigroup, BMW, Societe General, HP, JP Morgan Chase, Bank of America, Hitachi, Deutsche Telecom, Deutsche Post, Sony, Vodafone, BHP Billiton, Toshiba, Deutsche Bank, Intesa Sanpaolo, Renault, Lockheed Martin Corporation, Sanofi. The reports of these companies can be an example of best practices in disclosing information on compliance. These companies not only provide the maximum information on compliance in their organizations but also demonstrate its development, highlights and progress. Certain companies demonstrate considerable increases in the amount of information provided, for instance, Samsung Electronics (increase from 4 to 20+ pages on compliance issues); Sony (from 1 to 8 pages); Toshiba (from 4 to 14 pages).

A review of current trends and the findings of the study can serve as an incentive for companies to disclose information on compliance in a more detailed, structured and explicit way. The results of the survey offer a valid input into the advancement of corporate reporting practices and benefit the improvement of reporting quality. The research is particularly relevant for further progression and strengthening of focus on compliance as a supportive factor of CSR and sustainable development.

A considerable achievement of the research is in revealing both best practices and shortcomings in disclosing information on compliance in public reports that can be considered and used as recommendations by companies.

REFERENCES

AccountAbility. (2008). *AA1000 Assurance Standard.*

AccountAbility & LRQA. (2006). *The Materiality report. Aligning strategy, performance and reporting.* Retrieved from https://hiyamaya.files.wordpress.com/2009/12/the-materiality-report.pdf

Akkucuk, U. (2015). *Handbook of Research on Developing Sustainable Value in Economics, Finance and Marketing.* Hershey, PA: Business Science Reference. doi:10.4018/978-1-4666-6635-1

Apple. (2016, February 16). *A Message to Our Customers.* Retrieved from https://www.apple.com/customer-letter/

Barrington, L. (2015, November 23). *Inadequate dirty money regulation 'leaves UK open to terror funds': report.* Retrieved from reuters.com http://www.reuters.com/article/2015/11/23/us-britain-moneylaundering-idUSKBN0TC00520151123#pDBJT cbu5AoZk8hO.97

Biegelman, M. T. (2008). *Building a world-class compliance program: Best practices and strategies for success.* John Wiley & Sons. doi:10.1002/9781118268193

Conduct risk. (n.d.). In *Market supervision update, 57.* Australian Securities and Investment Commission. Retrieved from https://asic.gov.au/about-asic/corporate-publications/newsletters/asic-market-supervision-update/asic-market-supervision-update-previous-issues/market-supervison-update-issue-57/

Data Privacy Day: A call for better privacy practices. (2016). Retrieved from https://www.trendmicro.com/vinfo/us/security/news/online-privacy/data-privacy-day-a-call-for-better-privacy-practices

Data Privacy Day: Why data privacy awareness is important. (2015). Retrieved from https://www.trendmicro.com/vinfo/us/security/news/online-privacy/data-privacy-day-why-data-privacy-is-important

Global Reporting Initiative. (n.d.). *About Sustainability Reporting.* Retrieved from https://www.globalreporting.org/information/sustainability-reporting/Pages/default.aspx

Global Reporting Initiative. (n.d.). *Benefits of reporting.* Retrieved from https://www.globalreporting.org/information/sustainability-reporting/Pages/reporting-benefits.aspx

English, S., & Hammond, S. (2015). *The Cost of compliance.* Thomson Reuters. Retrieved from https://thegrcbluebook.com/wp-content/uploads/2015/05/Cost-of-Compliance-2015-Thomson-Reuters.pdf

Ernst&Young & Boston College Center for Corporate Citizenship. (2016). *Value of Sustainability Reporting.* Retrieved from https://www.ey.com/Publication/vwLUAssets/EY_-_Value_of_sustainability_reporting/%24FILE/EY-Value-of-Sustainability-Reporting.pdf

Ernst&Young & Global Reporting Initiative. (2014). *Sustainability reporting – the time is now.* Retrieved from https://www.ey.com/Publication/vwLUAssets/EY-Sustainability-reporting-the-time-is-now/$FILE/EY-Sustainability-reporting-the-time-is-now.pdf

Ernst&Young & GreenBiz. (2013). *2013 Six growing trends in corporate sustainability.* Retrieved from http://www.ey.com/Publication/vwLUAssets/Six_growing_trends_in_corporate_sustainability_2013/$FILE/Six_growing_trends_in_corporate_sustainability_2013.pdf

EU Directive 2014/95/EU of 22 October, 2014.

Fahey, B. (2016, August 24). *Culture of compliance: progress to the next level?* Educational seminar at MTS, Moscow, Russia.

Financial Actions Task Force. (n.d.). *What is money laundering?* Retrieved from http://www.fatf-gafi.org/faq/moneylaundering/

Greenwald, G., & McLaughlin, J. (2016, March 1). Apple Wins Major Court Victory Against FBI in a Case Similar to San Bernardino. *The Intercept*. Retrieved from https://theintercept.com/2016/02/29/apple-wins-major-court-victory-in-its-battle-against-fbi-in-a-case-similar-to-san-bernardino/

Hanning, J., & Connett, D. (2015, July 4). London is now the global money-laundering centre for the drug trade, says crime expert. *Independent*. Retrieved from http://www.independent.co.uk

Holme, R., & Watts, P. (2000, January). *Corporate Social Responsibility: making good business sense*. Retrieved from http://www.ceads.org.ar/downloads/Making%20good%20business%20sense.pdf

International Federation of Accountants. (2013). *ISAE 3000 (Revised), Assurance Engagements Other than Audits or Reviews of Historical Financial Information*. Author.

International Federation of Pharmaceutical Manufacturers & Associations. (2012). *Code of Practice*. Retrieved from http://www.ifpma.org/wp-content/uploads/2016/01/IFPMA_Code_of_Practice_2012_new_logo.pdf

International Organization for Standardization (2010). *ISO 26000:2010. Guidance to social responsibility*. ISO.

Kennedy-Glans, D., & Dr. Schulz, B. (2005). *Corporate Integrity: a toolkit for managing beyond compliance*. Mississauga, Ontario: John Wiley & Sons, Canada, Ltd.

KPMG. (2013). *The KPMG Survey on Corporate Social Responsibility report*. Retrieved from https://assets.kpmg.com/content/dam/kpmg/pdf/2015/08/kpmg-survey-of-corporate-responsibility-reporting-2013.pdf

KPMG. (2015). *Current of change. The KPMG Survey on Corporate Social Responsibility report*. Retrieved from https://home.kpmg.com/content/dam/kpmg/pdf/2015/12/KPMG-survey-of-CR-reporting-2015.pdf

KPMG Advisory N.V., Global Reporting Initiative, The Centre for Corporate Governance in Africa and United Nations Environment Programme. (2013). *Carrots and Sticks. Sustainability reporting policies worldwide – today's best practice, tomorrow's trends*. Retrieved from https://www.globalreporting.org/resourcelibrary/Carrots-and-Sticks.pdf

Lingân, J., & Wyman, L. (2013). *Exploring Civil Society Perspectives on Sustainability Reporting and Sustainability Reporting Policies, Working Paper*. Retrieved from http://citeseerx.ist.psu.edu/viewdoc/download?doi=10.1.1.737.1793&rep=rep1&type=pdf

Mansell, W. (2016, March 21). *Tim Cook On Apple Vs. FBI: We Did Not Expect To Be 'At Odds With Our Own Government*. Retrieved from https://www.player.one/tim-cook-apple-vs-fbi-we-did-not-expect-be-odds-our-own-government-521018

McPherson, H. (2014a, September 6). *Data Privacy—Essential for Corporate Social Responsibility.* https://www.isaca.org/Journal/Blog/Lists/Posts/Post.aspx?ID=237

McPherson, H. (2014b). Data Privacy—Protecting This Asset Is a Priority. *ISACA Journal, 3.* Retrieved from https://www.isaca.org/Journal/archives/2014/Volume-3/Pages/JOnline-Data-Privacy-Protecting-This-Asset-Is-a-Priority.aspx

McWilliams, A., Siegel, D. S., & Wright, P. M. (2006, March). *Corporate Social Responsibility: International Perspectives.* Rensselaer Working papers in economics, 0604. Rensselaer Polytechnic Institute, Department of Economics. Retrieved from http://www.economics.rpi.edu/workingpapers/rpi0604.pdf

Organization for Economic and Co-operation Development. (2011). *OECD Guidelines for multinational enterprises.* Retrieved from OECD Library. doi:10.1787/9789264115415-

Petrocelli, T. (2005, December 9). *The changing face of data protection.* Retrieved from http://www.informit.com/articles/article.aspx?p=422303&seqNum=3

Rouse, M. (n.d.). *Definition of a conduct risk.* Retrieved from http://searchcompliance.techtarget.com/definition/conduct-risk

Stilgherrian. (2014, November 7). *Customer data protection is a corporate social responsibility.* Retrieved from https://www.zdnet.com/article/customer-data-protection-is-a-corporate-social-responsibility/

The International Integrated Reporting Council. (2013). *The International <IR> framework.* Retrieved from http://integratedreporting.org/wp-content/uploads/2015/03/13-12-08-THE-INTERNATIONAL-IR-FRAMEWORK-2-1.pdf

The International Integrated Reporting Council. (2015). *Creating value. Value to investors.* Retrieved from http://integratedreporting.org/wp-content/uploads/2015/04/Creating-Value-Investors.pdf

Transparency International. (2014). *Transparency in corporate reporting: Assessing the World's Largest Companies.* Retrieved from https://www.transparency.org/whatwedo/publication/transparency_in_corporate_reporting_assessing_worlds_largest_companies_2014

Transparency International. (2015). *Transparency in corporate reporting: Assessing the World's Largest Telecommunications Companies.* Retrieved from http://www.transparency.org/whatwedo/publication/transparency_in_corporate_reporting_assessing_the_worlds_largest_telecommun

Transparency International UK. (2015). *Don't look, won't find: weaknesses in the supervision of the UK's anti-money laundering rules.* Retrieved from http://www.transparency.org.uk/publications/dont-look-wont-find-weaknesses-in-the-supervision-of-the-uks-anti-money-laundering-rules/

United Nations. (2003). *UN Guidelines for Consumer Protection.* Retrieved from http://www.un.org/esa/sustdev/publications/consumption_en.pdf

United Nations Global Compact. (n.d.). *The Communication on progress in brief.* Retrieved from https://www.unglobalcompact.org/participation/report/cop

United Nations Global Compact. (n.d.). *Guide to corporate sustainability. Shaping a sustainable future.* Retrieved from https://www.unglobalcompact.org/docs/publications/UN_Global_Compact_Guide_to_Corporate_Sustainability.pdf

United Nations Office on Drugs and Crime. (2011). *Estimating illicit financial flows resulting from drug trafficking and other transnational organized crime.* Retrieved from http://www.unodc.org/documents/data-and-analysis/Studies/Illicit_financial_flows_2011_web.pdf

Verschoor, C. C. (2004, October 1). Does Superior Governance Still Lead to Better Financial Performance? *Strategic Finance, 86*, 13–14.

ADDITIONAL READING

Akkucuk, U. (2017). *Ethics and Sustainability in Global Supply Change Management.* Hershey, PA: IGI Global. doi:10.4018/978-1-5225-2036-8

KEY TERMS AND DEFINITIONS

AML (Anti-Money Laundering): A compliance program aimed at prevention of money laundering through its operations and transaction.

Anti-Corruption: A compliance program aimed at prevention of corruption practices within a company and promotion of anti-bribery and corruption principles and measures into the society.

Compliance Program: A developed by a company a system of controls and ethical standards to mitigate risks in a certain business processes.

Conduct Risk: A risk of damage to stakeholders or a company as a result of unethical behavior of management or employees of the company.

CSR (Corporate Social Responsibility): Business responsibility of organizations to contribute to social, economic, and environmental development of the community to ensure its sustainability.

Data Privacy: A compliance program aimed at protection of personal information about any individual the company may poses.

GRI Standards: International guidelines on preparing sustainability reporting.

ISO 26000: International standard on developing and implementing principles of corporate social responsibility into company's strategy and business processes.

Sustainability Reporting: Any type of non-financial report of an organization which provides information on its CSR performance, including, its contribution into economic, social, and environmental spheres of a community life.

ENDNOTES

1 Low quality and quantity of SARs (suspicious activity reports) submitted to law enforcement agencies, the level of awareness in the relevant private sector institutions about money laundering

responsibilities, ignorance of KYC (know your customer) rules, persistent problems with compliance and awareness of how to make effective AML decisions, ineffective supervision by respective authorities due to their diversity and different standards (based on Weaknesses in the Supervision of the UK's Anti-Money Laundering Rules and the above mentioned researches).

2 See information on World's Biggest Data Breaches at http://informationisbeautiful.net/visualizations/worlds-biggest-data-breaches-hacks/

3 Sustainability reporting can be considered as synonymous with other terms for non-financial reporting: triple-bottom -line reporting, corporate social responsibility (CSR) reporting, and more. It is also an intrinsic element of integrated reporting – a more recent development that combines the analysis of financial and non-financial performance (globalreporting.org). According to KPMG survey of Corporate Responsibility Reporting of 2013 terminology used for reporting varies considerably between companies: Sustainability, Corporate social responsibility (CSR), Corporate responsibility (CR), Sustainable development, Corporate citizenship, Environmental and social report and others. However, the report also provides that the most commonly used term is still 'sustainability' report (43 percent). And in this research the term "sustainability report" will be mainly used. KPMG explains that they use the term 'corporate responsibility' also relatively to the term 'sustainability' and other similar terms. KPMG survey also revealed that the majority of companies (51 percent) include information on CR in their annual financial report. This figure has risen dramatically in comparison to 2008 (9 percent) and 2011 (20 percent), showing growing acceptance that CR issues are material for business. Retrieved from https://www.kpmg.com/Global/en/IssuesAndInsights/ArticlesPublications/corporate-responsibility/Documents/kpmg-survey-of-corporate-responsibility-reporting-2013.pdf

4 This research refers to GRI G4 Guidelines which were in effect at the time of research conduct. In 2016 the Guidelines were transformed into GRI Sustainability Reporting Standards (GRI Standards). A brief overview of changes in accordance with transition is given below, in particular, relevant to compliance issues.

5 Aspect "Compliance" in environmental category (G4-EN29), Aspect "Compliance" in social category, sub-category "Society" (G4-SO8), Aspect "Customer Health and Safety" (G4-PR2), Aspect "Product and Service Labeling" (G4-PR3), Aspect "Marketing Communications" (G4-PR7).

6 Many of G250 companies are unable, or choose not to explain the process used: 41 percent of the reporting companies do not explain the process they use and only a small minority (5percent) assess material issues on an ongoing basis.

7 Below is analysis of some compliance aspects disclosed in sustainability reports prepared in accordance with GRI G4 guidelines by different entities of one group – Ernst&Young group. For example, EY US in their Sustainability report for 2015 identify anti-corruption as a material aspect but specify only one indicator relevant to the aspect – about communication of policies and procedures (G4 -SO4) and general information on management approach to the aspect (DMA). However, in the comments they provide some overall statistics on all compliance trainings and include this information into the paragraph about Code of Conduct, while in the context of the report the paragraph "Anti-Corruption" contains very brief and general statement on anti-corruption approach. There is also no information nor comments on any reported incidents (if there were any and what actions were taken) and risk assessment procedure. The report contains a section about data protection which is considered as "an essential part of EY US' professional services to clients", providing statistics on training completion in information security and data protection by new employees,

however, the aspect "Customer privacy" is not defined as material and there is no information if there were any complaints about breaches of customer privacy or cases of data leaks. Report retrieved from http://www.ey.com/Publication/vwLUAssets/ey-us-sustainability-report-2015/$FILE/ey-us-sustainability-report-2015.pdf. EY NL (Netherlands) issue an Annual integral review which correlates with GRI G4 and the Transparency report. In reports for 2014/2015 EY NL identify anti-bribery and customer privacy as material aspects, but however, do not provide details in accordance with GRI G4 indicators. As for an anti-bribery aspect – only a general management statement without information on trainings conducted, risk assessment or incidents of non-compliance in the Transparency report. The same applies to the customer privacy aspect – a general statement, the report contains one complaint in relation to (probably) customer privacy, however, no details about the case. Reports retrieved from https://www.ey.com/Publication/vwLUAssets/EY-nederland-integrated-annual-review-2014-2015/$FILE/EY-nederland-integrated-annual-review-2014-2015.pdf ; https://www.ey.com/Publication/vwLUAssets/EY-gri-g4-content-index-2014-2015/$FILE/EY-gri-g4-content-index-2014-2015.pdf ; https://www.ey.com/Publication/vwLUAssets/EY-netherlands-transparency-report-2015-volume-2/$FILE/EY-netherlands-transparency-report-2015-volume-2.pdf EY Turkey issued its first Sustainability report for 2014. It identifies anti-corruption and customer privacy as material aspects based on GRI G4. In comparison to two previous reports there is also general information on anti-corruption, however, some statistics are given regarding trainings. As for customer privacy aspect – more extensive information is provided. Report retrieved from http://www.ey.com/Publication/vwLUAssets/EY-turkey-sustainability-report-2014/$FILE/EY-turkey-sustainability-report-2014.pdf. EY Russia issues Corporate responsibility report for a two-year-period. The last available report reflects information for 2013 and 2014. Like in Turkish and US reports there is a similar abstract on data protection, however, no information on breaches of customer privacy or trainings conducted (as in US). The information on anti-bribery is not explicit, but statistics on trainings is provided. Report retrieved from https://www.ey.com/ru/en/about-us/corporate-responsibility/ey-corporate-responsibility-report-2013-2014-foreword This overview of the reports by no means is either a critical review or a verification of information disclosure in accordance with GRI G4. It is presented as an example to demonstrate how companies disclose information relying on GRI G4 guidelines in their reports.

8 Inclusivity is the starting point for determining materiality. The materiality process determines the most relevant and significant issues for an organization and its stakeholders. Responsiveness is the decisions, actions and performance related to those material issues.

9 See https://mco.mycomplianceoffice.com/home

10 A person conducting the assurance engagement (usually the engagement partner or other members of the engagement team, or, as applicable, the firm (ISAE 3000 (Revised), Assurance Engagements Other than Audits or Reviews of Historical Financial Information).

11 250 companies from a Global Fortune List.

12 Reputational risk: damage to corporate reputation from being seen to do the wrong thing– mentioned by 53 percent of reporting G250; regulatory risk: complex and rapid changes to the regulatory landscape companies – mentioned by 48 percent, legal: exposure to potential legal action, for example, over non-disclosure of environmental, social and governance information – 21 percent (KPMG survey, 2013).

13 See the list here http://fortune.com/global500/2015

14 See GRI database here http://database.globalreporting.org/search

Chapter 4
Circular Supply Chain and Business Model in Apparel Industry:
An Exploratory Approach

María del Mar Alonso-Almeida
Universidad Autonoma de Madrid, Spain

José Miguel Rodriguez-Anton
Universidad Autonoma de Madrid, Spain

ABSTRACT

Today, companies are trying to move from an existing linear business model of production to a circular one. This transition is not easy and demands contextual changes beyond the control of the company. Circular economy (CE) pursues closing material flows in productive systems to maximize the utilization of available resources. Thus, different circles to reduce, reuse, recycle, re-manufacture, recover, and recycle are produced along supply chain during the cycle of life of a product. Despite an innovative apparel, little is known about the companies with disruptive business models and supply chain structures that have emerged in the recent years.

INTRODUCTION

Companies are currently trying to move from the existing linear business production model to a circular one. Van Loom et al. (2018) has advised that this transition will not be easy and will demand contextual changes beyond companies' control, such as changes in legislation, new modes of financing or changes in consumer behaviour, in addition to the needed changes inside the companies. The circular economy (CE) pursues the creation of closed material flow in productive systems to maximise the use of available resources. Along the supply chain different circles are therefore created to reduce, reuse, recycle, remanufacture, recover and redesign material during the life cycle of a product.

DOI: 10.4018/978-1-5225-8109-3.ch004

The life cycle of a product (including the circular production cycle) has three basic phases: pre-production, production and post-production (Turon & Czeech, 2017, quoted in Zielecki, 2006). During the pre-production phase, product design, market definition, materials and production processes are developed. In a CE, product design waste should be reduced in the pre-production phase by choosing appropriate materials that can decrease harmful substance emissions; so, for example, fossil energy resources could be replaced by renewable ones (Szita, 2017). Manufacturers will therefore look for ways to reduce consumption of raw materials by reusing products, components and materials (Van Loon et al., 2018). In a circular supply chain, a relevant driver could be to reuse an already used product or to use recycled ones; in other words, in a circular supply chain, 'a product gets a new life in a new form' (Turon & Czeech, 2017, quoted in Abec, 2014). This avoids the production of unnecessary waste and the use of most resources by pursuing a strategy of reduction and zero waste. Indeed, waste is considered a new input in the supply chain.

All the processes, activities and tasks to manufacture and distribute a product are included in the production phase. Thus, redesigning the production line, using clean sources of energy or new materials, producing more from less material and the consumption and reduction of losses and waste material can be added in the circular production phase (Szita, 2017).

Product sales, customer care, reverse logistics and recycling take place during the post-production phase. At this point, recycling becomes relevant so that most of the product can once again become raw material that enters the production process again to create a closed-loop supply chain.

Caniato et al. (2012) and De Brito et al. (2008) have explained that the fashion industry has had a very high environmental impact in a number of ways, including: 1) use of natural raw materials (e.g. cotton, wool or leather) that require large quantities of water or pesticides, and the use of synthetic products with a toxic production process; 2) some phases of production use toxic chemical products; and 3) the manufacture and distribution of clothing make intensive use of modes of transportation. Competitive pressures due to the increase in the number of competitors and the reduction of the life cycle of the product also lead to an increaser in pollution and waste (Chung & Wee, 2008).

Srivastava (2007, p. 55) defines Green Supply Chain Management as 'integrating environmental thinking into supply chain management, including product design, material sourcing and selection, manufacturing processes, delivery of the final product to the consumer as well as end-of-life management of the product after its useful life'. The adoption of a circular supply chain will thus include 'practices [that] have ranged from green purchasing to integrated supply chains flowing from suppliers, to manufacturers, to customers and reverse logistics, in order to "clos[e] the loop"', according the definition of green supply chain management given by Zhu and Sarkis (2006, p. 474).

A number of green practices have been adopted in supply chain management in the apparel industry in the last few years (Caniato et al., 2012; De Brito et al., 2008; Lakhal et al., 2008), but to the best of our knowledge, the circular supply chain aspects of this industry has not yet been analysed, although innovative apparel companies with disruptive business models and supply chain structures have recently emerged (Caniato et al., 2012).

This chapter explains how a circular supply chain could be developed in the apparel industry using case-based research. It is organised as follows: (1) the introduction provides a brief introduction to the topic and goals of the chapter; (2) the next section reviews the literature and defines key terms; (3) the section on the circular supply chain and circular business models in the fashion industry provides and case study; and (4) the final section offers conclusions and gives recommendations for the industry.

CIRCULAR SUPPLY CHAIN AND CIRCULAR BUSINESS MODELS: LITERATURE REVIEW AND DEFINITIONS

The concept of the circular economy is currently being built. The circular economy (CE) is considered a possible solution to problems such as the increasing global demand for resources, price volatility for raw materials, and the growing population and consumption worldwide, which are putting pressure on future access to resources (Whalen et al., 2018). CE is an approach to designing economic solutions according to ecological principles and includes the design for final business solutions that can satisfy the needs of both consumers and the environment without causing major imbalances. Kirchherr et al. (2017, p. 4) defined CE as:

an economic system that is based on business models which replace the 'end-of-life' concept with reducing, alternatively reusing, recycling and recovering materials in production/distribution and consumption processes, with the aim to accomplish sustainable development, which implies creating environmental quality, economic prosperity and social equity, to the benefit of current and future generations.

Considering the environment during the design and planning phases could save billions of euros. Changing to the CE model would also slow and prevent waste, the savings from which could reach 604 billion euros and a decrease in greenhouse gas (GHG) emissions of 2%–4% in the EU (Szita, 2017).

Although there appears to be a consensus about the value of CE during the whole life cycle of a product—pre-production, production and post-production (Turon & Czeech, 2017)—and in the generation of new resources, products and business (Anttonen et al., 2018), most of the current literature has concentrated on the reduction, reuse and recycling of waste (Anttonen et al., 2018; Bianchini et al., 2018). That is, the literature has focused mainly on the post-production phase and on the product end-on-life, with little research attention to the pre-production and production phases yet.

As already mentioned, the most developed aspect of the CE is currently recycling, that is, when 'a product gets a new life in a new form' (Turon & Czeech, 2017, quoted in Abec, 2014). The production of unnecessary waste and the excessive use of resources are avoided. Therefore, the CE introduces a new view on little-studied aspects of operations management related to reverse logistics and responsible packaging. To deploy the CE model in a properly sustainable way and totally close the loop, however, it is necessary to focus on the main aspects of reverse logistics. According to Turon and Czeech (2017), these key aspects are:

1. Finding ecological or economic motivation to adopt circular reverse logistics;
2. Using packaging with proven material composition (made of certified biodegradable materials);
3. Using packaging that can be reused after its first use by a customer;
4. Identifying the maximum quantity of parts, packages and goods that can be reused in the closed-loop supply chain;
5. Selecting the process and ways of reusing goods; and
6. Actively involving the stakeholders in the process.

THE CIRCULAR SUPPLY CHAIN AND CIRCULAR BUSINESS MODELS: LITERATURE REVIEW AND DEFINITIONS

Some researchers (e.g. Alonso-Almeida et al., 2016; Murray et al., 2017) have suggested that increased CE development requires a certain degree of creative thinking and innovation to make the required changes appealing to organisations. Anttonen et al. (2018) analysed a number of industrial reports and documents using the topic modelling methodology and found that, for most companies, the CE concept was focused primarily on waste and only secondarily on production. These results suggest that the CE concept is advancing slowly and that, as a consequence of this slow change, the European Union (EU) CE objectives for 2020 are not likely to be achieved.

These objectives, which were promulgated as part of the EU's Europe 2020 strategy, included a number of environmental objectives designed to ensure change in the current economic and production models regarding their impact on natural capital (Szita, 2017). More specifically, the 2020 Strategy aimed to do the following: (1) reduce GHG emissions by 20%; (2) increase the share of renewables in total energy consumption to 20%; and (3) increase total energy efficiency. The idea behind the 2020 Strategy is to change the current lineal production system into a circular one. At present, the Netherlands is the most advanced follower of the CE model in Europe, although the circular model is still in its infancy. To encourage the spread of CE as widely as possible, the attitudes of governments, manufacturers and people have to be changed. Anttonen et al. (2018) reinforced these ideas and asserted that materials, environmental and economic issues and organisational changes are required to advance to bring about a CE. They also found, as they looked deeper into the link among the government, university and industry spheres, a common concerned focus on 'resource efficiency, waste as resource, economic growth and business potential of recycling' (p. 2656).

The CE is a restorative and regenerative economic model. Indeed, a number of authors have noted that the CE combines the thoughts of the 3R (reduce, reuse and recycle) approach and moves beyond this to the 6R (reduce, reuse, recycle, redesign, remanufacture and recover) or even to more Rs such as replace, reinstate and rethink (Rodríguez-Antón & Alonso-Almeida, 2018) or with zero emissions (Szita, 2017; Mair & Stern, 2017). Camacho-Otero et al. (2017) noted that activities within CE are cascading and involve reuse, repair, maintain, remanufacturing and recycling.

This has led to a number of different strategies, but the transition from a linear economy to a CE involves incremental and radical changes that encounter barriers (shown in Table 1), which draw out these changes. Korhoner et al. (2018) classified CE barriers as either technical, financial and market or institutional issues. Camacho-Otero et al. (2017) also identified barriers for consumer acceptance.

As they looked at how companies could break down these barriers, especially inside the company and throughout the supply chain, Bianchini et al. (2018) proposed increasing the information and collaboration among members of the supply chain to share and develop sustainable capabilities and build competitive advantage. They suggested using advanced technologies to push CE on industries:

the emerging technologies in the Fourth Industrial Revolution context can contribute to the procurement of the missing information and, consequently, can drive the diffusion of CE strategies and the definition of new products and business models based on CE concepts. In fact, in Industry 4.0 context, intelligent products, assets, processes and services are able to communicate and cooperate with each other and with people through the availability of some tools, such as Internet of Things (IoT), Big Data, data analytics and cyber-physical systems (CPSs). (pp. 1–2)

Table 1. Main CE barriers

Technical	Inappropriate technology Lack of knowledge Lack of circular design Lack of technical support Lack of training Slow diffusion of CE principles
Financial and market	High upfront cost High transaction cost Increase supply-chain complexity Asymmetric supply-chain information Infrastructure failures Lack of cooperation Uncertainly on return and profit Rigidity of customer behaviour Businesses rigidity
Institutional	Legal and regulatory gaps Social and cultural limitations Misaligned incentives Lack of conducive legal system Poor institutional framework Slow legal framework in some countries
Customer acceptance	Beliefs that product performance worse than others Fear of the unknown. Risk aversion Animosity among lack of ownership Access problems Practice is tightly connected to other practices Price Mistrust until guaranteed Demographic issues Intrinsic motives. Lack of customer awareness Lack of benefits of CE

Source: Elaboration based on Korhoner et al. (2018) and Camacho-Otero et al. (2017).

A new framework for circular business models would be enhanced and enabled by a digital transformation.

Given that a CE involves all business functions, companies must redefine the whole supply chain, including product design, production processes, direct and reverse logistics and collection at the product at end-of-life 'to maintain resources in the loop and minimising residual waste' (Bianchini et al., 2018, p. 3). A key issue is 'to recapture value of post-production and post-consumption resources, products and packaging, realizing circularity through closed-loop production and consumption system, where a great part of waste is not disposed, but it is re-inserted in the same cycle' (Bianchini et al., 2018, p. 2).

Obviously, waste will have certain conditions, depending on its usage and age. Different strategies will have to be defined to give new life to that waste. As Bianchini et al. (2018, p. 7) noted:

monitoring the condition of an asset and its performance and degradation trends, due to wear and damages during its use, can be the basis for decision-making about the replacement or the refurbishment of old and unsustainable products with innovative and more effective products.

In some cases, material can be used again in a new production loop without changes, but in other cases material can be incorporated into other industries as raw material or into lower quality products or even to generate energy or be sold in second-hand markets. For example, Sweden uses 50% of the produced waste for energy supply (88% on district heating and 12% on electricity) and imports waste from Norway and United Kingdom to fulfil its energy needs (Szita, 2017).

In the recycling process, raw materials are recovered and are used as new inputs in the production process, reducing the need for new raw materials (Ruan et al., 2011). Some researchers (e.g. Van Weelden, et al., 2016; Wang and Hazen, 2016) have suggested the creation of outlets for secondary (recycled) raw materials, which would allow recovered resources to be the main source of new processes or products. In addition to the environmental benefits, the recycled of components for reuse have a very great economical potential (Elzinga & Boon, 2018).

The adoption of CE increases the necessity for information throughout the whole production cycle to optimise raw material use, energy consumption, reduce air emissions and minimise waste. CE deployment therefore requires collaboration among all stakeholders involved. That collaboration throughout the whole supply chain could identify ways and points to change following CE principles. The transition to a CE includes different levels (Bianchini et al., 2018) and involves: (1) the entire company; (2) the entire supply chain; (3) the entire industrial sector; and (4) the entire location where the company works.

The first step in the change to a CE model is to capture all core aspects of how companies engage in business, that is, their business model. A business model is a tool that gathers a company's competitive strategy throughout its value chain and value system (Rodriguez-Anton & Alonso-Almeida, 2018). A widely tool used to analyse company business models is the business model canvas (BMC) created by Osterwalder and Pigneur (2010), which contains the following nine dimensions:

1. Customer segment: This dimension identifies the target audience of the company; that is, for whom companies are running their value propositions.
2. Customer relations: This dimension describes what kind of relationship a company wishes to establish with its customers. Here the range could be from a punctual automatic transaction to a continuous communication.
3. Value proposition: This is the value created for the customer segment.
4. Revenue stream: This is the way in which a company makes money and contains the different general revenue schemes.
5. Cost structure: This dimension shows all costs related to the production processes that are needed to deliver the product or service to the customer.
6. Key resources: This dimension includes all of the resources—including tangibles, intangibles or human—required to deliver the product or service to the customer.
7. Key activities: This dimension is the core set of activities needed to deliver the value proposition.
8. Key partners: This dimension includes the alliances or collaborations developed with non-competitors and suppliers to deliver a company's value proposition.
9. Distribution channel: This includes all channels used to deliver the product or service to the customer.

Bocken et al. (2014) have categorised business models based on their technological, social or organisational nature, showing different circular business model archetypes. Business models based on technology are focused on innovation and efficiency, while business models based on social issues include innovations in their offerings that change customer behaviour and business models based on organisational issues apply business responsibility and changes in the supply chain through innovation. They developed the following archetypes, which will be considered in more detail below: (1) maximise material and energy efficiency; (2) create value from waste; (3) substitute renewables and natural processes; (4) deliver functionality rather than ownership; (5) adopt a stewardship role; (6) encourage sufficiency; (7) re-purpose the business for society or the environment; and (8) develop solutions for scaling up.

Maximising material and energy efficiency means 'do[ing] more with fewer resources, generating less waste, emissions and pollution' (Bocken et al., 2014, p. 48). This archetype seeks to reduce the consumption of energy, resources and waste to alleviate the industry's environmental impact. Some examples included in this archetype include low-carbon manufacturing solutions, lean manufacturing and additive manufacturing methods, dematerialisation schemes and increases in functionality with the same number of components or optimisation of functionality adapted to real customer use with fewer components.

Creating value from waste is defined as eliminating waste and transforming it into a useful and valuable input for other production process, as well as making better use of under-utilised capacity. Examples of this archetype include the CE closed loop, the cradle-to-cradle philosophy, industrial symbiosis, the 3R philosophy (reduce, reuse and recycle), the other R philosophies, taking back management, the use of excess capacity, sharing assets (e.g. sharing ownership and collaborative consumption) and extended producer responsibility.

Substitution with renewables and natural processes seeks to 'reduce environmental impacts and increase business resilience by addressing resource constraints "limits to growth" associated with non-renewable resources and current production systems' (Bocken et al., 2014, p. 50). Examples in this archetype could be moving from non-renewable to renewable energy sources; using solar and wind power energy solutions; zero emissions, blue, biomimicry and natural steps initiatives; slow manufacturing and green chemistry.

Delivering functionality, rather than ownership, substitutes consumer ownership with other ways of enjoying a product or service. This archetype is based on product service systems (PSS) and servitisation; that is, this involves how companies change their business model to offer experiences instead of the ownership of products or services or a mix of both. A review of how the economy of experience characteristics could push CE can be found in Alonso-Almeida (2018). Examples in this archetype are product-oriented PSS such as maintenance or extended warranties; use-oriented PSS such as rental, lease or shared; results-oriented PSS like pay per use; provided finance initiatives; the DBFO (design, build, finance and operate) philosophy and chemical management services (CMS).

Adopting a stewardship role supposes the achievement of an engaged role with all stakeholders involved with the company to ensure their long-term health and well-being. This archetype looks to maximise the positive societal and environmental impact caused by the company by emphasising health and well-being. Some examples are biodiversity protection, consumer-care promotion, fair trade, retailer choice editing, resource stewardship and radical transparency in societal and environmental issues.

Encouraging sufficiency involves solutions that actively diminish consumption and production. Such practices include consumer education, demand management, slow fashion, product longevity, premium branding, frugal business and responsible promotion and distribution.

Re-purposing the business for society and the environment involves rethinking the role of the company in society. In traditional business models, the customer is the focus of the company to maximise profits. However this archetype proposes prioritising social and environmental benefits, especially for local communities. The main drive is an organisational innovation that 'focuses on the changing fiduciary duty and structure of a firm for social and environmental (rather than economic and shareholder) benefits maximisation of an organisation and groups concepts that collectively see firms integrating more fully with their stakeholders' (Bocken et al., 2014, p. 53). Some examples linked to this archetype are the not-for-profit firm structure; hybrid businesses, such as social enterprises; alternative ownership structures, such as collectives or cooperative or mutual companies; social and biodiversity regeneration initiatives; base of pyramid solutions; localisation and home-based flexible working.

Developing scaled-up solutions supposes 'delivering sustainable solutions at a large scale to maximise benefits for society and the environment' (Bocken et al., 2014, p. 53). Some examples of this archetype include collaborative approaches, incubators and entrepreneur-support schemes, licencing and franchising, open innovation platforms, crowd-funding or patient or slow capital collaborations. The next section focuses on the apparel industry and analyses example business models and CE practices deployed in the supply chain.

CIRCULAR SUPPLY CHAIN AND CIRCULAR BUSINESS MODELS IN FASHION INDUSTRY: A CIRCULAR BUSINESS CASE.

The apparel industry currently is continuing with a traditional linear mode of production, where very large quantities of resources are consumed and enormous amounts of waste are generated (Bocken et al., 2018)

As has already been mentioned, Caniato et al. (2012) and De Brito et al. (2008) have explained that the fashion industry has a very high environmental impact in a number of ways, particularly regarding the use of natural raw materials that require large quantities of water and pesticides or use of polluting synthetic products, as well as the use of chemical products in some phases of production, manufacture and distribution that is not sustainable. The increase of competitive pressures have led to an increase in pollution and waste across the whole life cycle due to the fast fashion approach (Chung & Wee, 2008). There are also significant barriers to CE in the fashion industry, which have slowed down the development to sustainable practices; the most relevant of these barriers are shown in Table 2.

According to De Brito et al. (2008), the main environmental practices adopted in the apparel industry include the use of organic fibres (cotton, wool or silk) to reduce chemical products, use of raw natural materials and CO_2 emissions; reusing and recycling materials; the vintage and second-hand markets; green certifications such as Global Organic Textile Standard (GOTS); supply-chain traceability and resource-sharing solutions.

Caniato et al. (2012) have classified environmental practices according to whether they affect the product, process or supply chain. Main practices for products include the use of natural raw materials, sustainable packaging, recyclable products, low-chemical substances, and the use of organic cotton from local and fair-trade suppliers. Most of the adopted practices in production processes involve low-energy consumption facilities, collection and recycling of disposed products and clean production processes. Sustainable practices in the supply chain include the environmental certification of suppliers, codes of conduct, direct control of subcontractors, transport optimisation, green projects with suppliers, supplier selection based on green practices, fair-trade sources for raw materials and supplier education.

As in the other manufacturing and service industries, the first circular strategy adopted by the apparel industry has been the management of energy efficiency and attempts to adopt clean production processes (Bagur et al., 2013; Caniato et al., 2012; De Brito et al., 2008). This is the case even when the companies in question are very small and have limited resources (Alonso-Almeida et al., 2018).

Table 2. Main CE barriers in apparel industry

Institutional	Outdated waste legislation Lack of research and development support Lack of incentives Lack of promotion for slow fashion Need to adapt policy frameworks to CE business models
Internal	Unknown commercially viable recycling technology Lack of technological development Neglecting streams for more recovery solutions Economic risks Need for networks and business-to-business partnership Costly recovery process Lack of up-scaled processes Lack of know-how to sort and separate fibre types Quick money searching Internal resistance to change
Market	Lack of support for textile collectors Lack of collaborative innovation mechanisms Guarantees on resource supply Price stability of raw materials Scarce added value and commercially viable recycling options for low-grade textiles Low quality materials dominate the end-of-life material flow Low availability of textile recycling plants on local and regional levels Missing links between suppliers and recyclers Need for development and acceleration of markets for end-products made from recycled textiles
Customer acceptance	Poor consumer demand for recycled products Lack of knowledge about CE product benefits Fast fashion preferences Price

Source: elaboration based on Boiten et al. (2018) and Bocken et al. (2018).

INDITEX is a Spanish company and one of the largest fashion retail groups in the world. It is listed in different stock exchanges worldwide with brands including Zara, Massimo Duty or Pull and Bear, among others. It draws in 25.34 billion in revenue, has 171,839 employees, 1,824 suppliers, 7,210 factories and is currently a global presence worldwide in 96 markets with 7,448 stores (INDITEX, 2018). Regarding the adoption of efficiency practices, INDITEX has made public their commitment to clean energy. Thus, in 2016 they achieved the following numbers (INDITEX, 2017): clean energy sources supplying 30% of their worldwide energy consumption; 520 million KWh of electricity used at its facilities comes from renewable sources; 89% of the electricity consumed at their locations in Spain is renewable; and the use of clean electricity in its facilities has grown by a factor of ten since 2013. During 2017, INDITEX continued to reduce its electricity consumption in both its offices and stores, and also reduced water consumption per garment by 1%, reduced GHG emissions by 29% during the past four years, and stabilised plan for zero waste to landfills by 2025 (INDITEX, 2018). As this suggests, large companies have made relevant changes, but these changes are incremental in comparison to the changes introduced by small companies. While large companies are making changes over their traditional businesses, small companies have completely reshaped their supply chains.

To promote the CE model, Bocken et al. (2018) have suggested adopting strategies such as slowing, closing and narrow loops in the fashion industry. Slowing loops refers to the design of long-life goods and product-life extension. When the life of products is extended, this reduces the use of raw materials and the creation pollution and waste. Closing the loop refers to recycling and reuse, which achieves a circular flow of resources in the production process. Narrowing loops are about enhancing efficiency in manufacturing through the use of less material per manufactured product. Textiles should therefore be maintained in the best condition as long as possible with a focus on business models pursuing reuse.

Nevertheless, to change to a more circular production model, the apparel industry needs to innovate between and across supply chains (Boiten et al., 2018). A crucial driver is technological innovation in recycling by searching for new ways to sort, separate, decontaminate and recycle textile fibres. Recycling textile fibres can deploy two strategies: downcycling, where the materials obtained are of lower quality than the originals, and upcycling, which allows the creation of new fibres of the same quality as the originals (INDITEX, 2017). Technological innovation is also needed to look for new textiles.

INDITEX is engaged with the CE model in a number of ways, and Table 3 shows how the company is trying to use more sustainable raw materials.

It is worth mentioning that not only global brands such as INDITEX are making efforts to advance to a circular economy. Small alternative firms are developing eco innovations to create new fibres from non-traditional textile raw materials. An outstanding example of this is the Spanish firm ECOALF. In addition to recycled cotton and wool, this apparel company uses plastic bottles, used tyres, discarded fishing nets and post-consumer coffee grounds to create new fibres for its garments (see https://ecoalf.com/gb/recycled-fabrics/). As these examples suggest, strategic collaboration among supply-chain members is needed at each stage of the garment life cycle to promote a CE.

Recycling at the end-of-life stage has been, for some decades, the most adopted strategy, although this type of initiative has increased in the past twenty years (Ekström & Salomonson, 2014). Some manufac-

Table 3. INDITEX initiatives regarding sustainable raw materials

Organic cotton	'In 2016, INDITEX Group commercialised a total of 36.7 million garments made from organic cotton, which translates to the consumption of 5,000 tonnes of this material. As a consequence of this strong focus, the independent organisation Textile Exchange positioned us as the fourth company on a global scale in consumption of organic cotton by volume.'
TENCEL®Lyocell	'It is a fibre created from wood originating from sustainable forests, where the trees are cultivated in a controlled manner and with programmes that guarantee reforestation. The production process for this fibre is carried out in a closed circuit that allows the reuse of water and over 99% of chemicals used. 'INDITEX is the world leader in the consumption of this material, having sold 6.35 million garments made from it in 2016 according to Preferred Fibres Market Report 2016, Textile Exchange.'
Recycled materials	'REFIBRA™LYOCELL: In 2016, INDITEX and the Austrian company Lenzing jointly developed this new material, made from cotton waste and wood from sustainably managed forests.' SYNTHETIC FIBRES: 'For example, recycled polyester is produced from both synthetic textiles and plastic bottles that are shredded into small pieces. Through a process called polymerisation, they are transformed into a new synthetic fibre that allows us to create new garments.' RECYCLED WOOL AND COTTON: 'Materials such as cotton or wool can be easily reused to create new textiles through a conventional or mechanical recycling process.'

Source: INDITEX (2017). Annual Report 2016.

turers have shown hostility to second-hand markets because such markets could partially replace the sale of new products; for that reason, manufacturers have deployed strategies to control or turn second-hand markets to their advantage (Van Loon et al., 2017). Some of these strategies include developing high-value products for consumers (as luxury firms have done) or reduce the emotional durability of the product by frequently introducing new product styles (as global fast-fashion—so-called because there are a number of different clothing collections by season—brands have done; Chapman, 2015; De Brito et al., 2008).

Whether due to market pressure or based on their own convictions, the main apparel brand are currently launching programmes to gather the garments that consumers have decided to retire. One example of this is the C & A Company, which collects used garments and gives a small incentive for turning in used garments. INDITEX gathered 7,102 tonnes of garments, footwear and accessories at 596 stores in 2016 (INDITEX, 2017). This represents 100% of the Zara stores in Spain, Portugal, the United Kingdom, Ireland, the Netherlands and Denmark. In 2017, INDITEX gathered 12,229 tonnes of garments, footwear and accessories at 598 stores in 14 countries through the 'Closing the Loop Program'. INDITEX has also made the commitment to extend this program to 2,000 stores in 2020 (INDITEX, 2018). The rival firm, H&M, collected 18,000 tonnes of used apparel in 2016, for a total of 61,000 tonnes since 2013 (H&M, 2018).

The apparel industry often discards clothes when consumers decide they have finished their useful life, but often these garments still have nearly half of their useful life yet (Farrant et al., 2010; Woolridge et al., 2006). There has therefore been an increase in initiatives from global brands and other organisations to push second-hand apparel markets in places other than the traditional ones, like the United Kingdom (Ekström & Salomonson, 2014).

According to Bocken et al. (2018), once collected textiles are processed and sorted, they are separated between wearable and unwearable textiles and the garments are categorised for their new life. Collecting products for reuse involves many manual operations that increase the supply-chain cost (Van Loon et al., 2017). Farrant et al. (2010) have explained the route recollected garments take to the second-hand market. First, the best 3% of the collected garments are sold in the United Kingdom as premium or vintage clothing. These types of used garments have a re-sale value closer to that of new clothes. Second, the remaining high-quality best garments are resold in Western markets, while lower quality clothes are exported to Eastern Europe and Africa. Finally, the worst items are incinerated or thrown into a landfill to produce energy.

Given this situation, which is linked with barriers in the industry (see Table 2), some authors (e.g. Bocken et al. 2018) have promoted the claim for innovative approaches to recycling and the valorisation of specific fibre types such as cotton or polyester. As Table 3 suggests, initiatives are being developed by global brands, but they are still poorly developed in most textile companies.

It seems clear that collaboration is a key driver to push CE within the apparel industry. INDITEX has a strategic alliance with the Cáritas Confederation, for example, to recover clothing and footwear through reuse and recycling of collected garments. INDITEX has partnered with MIT (the Massachusetts Institute of Technology) and other universities in Spain and Europe with an investment of more than 3 million euro to develop new textile fibres (INDITEX, 2017, 2018). On a smaller scale, ECOALF also has strategic alliances to develop new fibres, such as with the fishing guilds of Valencia (ECOALF, 2018). These examples indicate that through collaboration, multiple players—without a natural relationship—can join forces to develop new products. A big challenge remains for the apparel industry in achieving a circular global supply chain, however, because most of its suppliers are located in developing countries and it is very difficult to engage them in a sustainable way (Faisal, 2010; Zhu et al., 2008).

INDITEX has deployed two significant CE initiatives in their fashion collections. The first is called 'Join Life', which includes sustainable garments manufactured to have a lower environmental impact. The second is called 'Wear the Change', which includes garments guaranteed to be environmentally responsible in terms of both materials and manufacturing processes (INDITEX, 2017). The company has also developed three types of sustainable labelling to identify sustainable products; these include:

1. Care for Fibre: identifies the products manufactured with sustainable raw materials such as organic or ecological cotton, TENCEL®Lyocell or recycled fibres such as recycled cotton, wool, polyester and polyamide; 2. Care for Water: this includes items that have been manufactured, in at least one stage of production, with technologies that reduce water consumption in comparison to the conventional process and 3. Care for Planet: accompanies garments that, during the manufacturing process, have consumed energy from renewable sources in at least one stage of their production or have been manufactured with materials that imply technological progress for the reduction of emissions. (INDITEX, 2017)

Regarding its supply chain, INDITEX is acting on factors such as packaging and shipment density. The packaging achievements for the 2016 fiscal year included: 10% thinner plastic bags used to transport clothing; boxes reused up to 5 times before being recycled; 101.8 million hangers reused; 1 billion security tags recycled; 100% of Zara Online orders shipped in recycled cardboard boxes; and 100% of boxes used in Spain are made from cardboard recycled from the company's own boxes. For shipping, meanwhile, the 2016 fiscal year achievements included: trucks carrying an average load of 58 cubic metres, which represents a year-on-year improvement of 16%, or 200 fewer truckloads per year; increase of the loads of trucks serving to an average of 65 cubic metres, eliminating 500 truckloads per year; and a 20% improvement in the volume of cargo in trucks with returns from Europe, with each truck transporting an average of 600 packages, a reverse logistics channel improvement that has saved 900,000 km of transport and associated emissions in Europe alone (INDITEX, 2017).

Such efforts continued in 2017, and this involved 'improving transport planning and optimising loads and reduced the number of vehicles that travel from our distribution centres in Spain to European destinations. Thanks to this and the measures put into place during previous years, an estimated saving of 2,000,000 km, a distance equivalent to 50 times around the Earth, has been achieved; (INDITEX, 2018). Packaging advances also continued in 2017, with notable figures including: 110 million recirculated hangers; 1,010 recycled security tags; 1,700 tonnes of virgin paper and 1,500 tonnes of plastic saved; and the company as a whole recycled 4.5 tonnes of its own cardboard boxes to make new shipping boxes (INDITEX, 2018).

ECOALF has also adopted sustainable practices in its supply chain, including the requirement that all of its provides 'have at least one Bluesign® certification, STANDARD 100 by OEKO-TEX®' (ECOALF, 2018). Obviously, the CE model is in its infancy in apparel industry, as has been pointed out by previous research (e.g. Boiten et al. 2018; Bocken et al. 2018). Even so, the apparel industry seems to be engaging with CE and further development along this line in the near future seems possible.

RECOMMENDATIONS FOR APPAREL INDUSTRY.

Given the environmental and economic problems derived from the past abusive, aggressive environmental practices and the finite character of natural resources, CE will become an unstoppable force in Europe for all industries and countries.

Its advance has been slow, however, and the high number of internal and external barriers to its implementation are significant reasons for this slow development. Larger companies with more visibility and resources have shown a commitment to the CE model to a greater or lesser extent, but this cannot be considered the general situation. Different levels of CE deployment have appeared across industries. The specific case of the apparel industry appears to be dichotomous: global brands and small alternative companies seem to have a commitment to circular practices, while the majority of the industry continues in a traditional production mode. It is therefore necessary to prioritise actions to make whole apparel industry more circular. Table 4 proposes three levels of priority actions.

The first priority includes a mix of actions for government, policy-makers and industry. For governments and policy-makers, the most urgent action is updating legislation to promote the CE model in a wide sense. The creation of innovation networks among different types of organisations would contribute to the creation of new products, services and research into new ways of exploiting technology. Such collaboration would reduce the economic and technological risks faced by individual companies and could reduced the barriers to entry into the CE for smaller companies. Private–public collaboration seems the best way to a speed up the advance of the CE.

The easiest step to accelerate circular markets relies on the collection of used textiles for second-hand markets or other uses. Garment collection is a key issue for reusing, recycling and resale in the apparel industry, but it requires infrastructure for recovery and reprocessing (Bocken et al. 2018). Convenience and accessibility have been pointed out as the main drivers for participating in recycling programs, and higher levels of participation have been recorded in communities where such programmes are convenient for people. Updating legislation to extend and promote clothes recycling programmes is essential. In some areas, charity shops are the most used method for clothing donation (Fletcher, 2013). In Spain, Humana is the best-known charity organisation for this kind of activity and has resold garments to develop social programmes, mainly in Africa (see https://www.humana-spain.org/). Consumer acceptance

Table 4. Priority actions

Priority one	Adapt legislation Accelerate circular markets Consumer involvement Redefine business models Network and collaboration for circular strategies Production process adaptation Financial and fiscal incentives to recycle
Priority two	Reverse logistics adaptation Supply-chain adaptation Business-to-business partnership Landfill tax
Priority three	Develop of quality standards Develop of certification systems Circular Corporate Social Responsability schemes

Source: elaboration based on Bocken et al. (2018) and analysed business cases is also relevant, because without demand, the CE would not be able to survive. It is therefore necessary to encourage the purchase of circular products through promotion and explanation of the benefits via communication campaigns and incentives based on the role of CE for the society and environment.

Companies will still need to redefine their business models. As Kant Hvass (2016) has asserted, the apparel industry should move from a product-centred approach to a material-centred approach that is focused on reusing and recycling materials and innovation. The hasten this transition, the establishment of networks and business-to-business partnerships for circular strategies and in all stages of supply chain are necessary. Accelerating a sustainable supply chain should therefore also be a priority (Akkucuk, 2017). Taxes should also be imposed to discourage disposal of clothing in landfills and other non-green practices. These initiatives will be part of priority two.

Finally, quality standards and certification systems for recycled products should be developed and labelled. Indeed, some of these certificates are already in the market, including the Cradle-to-Cradle certificate. Circular schemes involving corporate social responsibility should also be communicated, and sustainability and circular flow management should be included in organisations' quality management systems (Akkucuk & Gencer, 2017). Another recommendation for the apparel industry is the continued search for new business models. In a CE, reuse of products is often combined with servitisation, which means that products are leased instead of sold and product ownership remains with manufacturer or retailer (Sarkis & Zhu, 2017). The apparel industry might wish to consider this business model as part of its path to developing a CE.

In conclusion, it is possible to assert, following Van Loon et al. (2017, p.12), that 'The conditions under which a transition to a circular economy is economically beneficial for both consumer and manufacturer should be explored much more carefully. While the concept of a circular economy appears attractive and perhaps even necessary from a macroeconomic and societal perspective, it is insufficiently understood at a microeconomic level'. Thus, efforts to make CE familiar at the microeconomic level, especially among small business, consumers and families, should be considered a priority and specific plans at the European and country level should be made to familiarise CE among the citizens of the EU.

ACKNOWLEDGMENT

This study is part of a larger research project entitled "Ecoinnovation and Circular Economy in Services Industries" (ECO2016-79659-R), which is financed by the Ministry of Science, Innovation and Universities within its National Programme for Research Aimed at the Challenges of Society.

REFERENCES

Akkucuk, U. (2017). *Ethics and Sustainability in Global Supply Chain Management*. Hershey, PA: IGI Global. doi:10.4018/978-1-5225-2036-8

Akkucuk, U., & Gencer, Y. G. (2017). EFQM Model and Sustainability of Organizations. *DEStech Transactions on Computer Science and Engineering*. doi:10.12783/dtcse/ameit2017/12279

Alonso-Almeida, M. M. (2018). *El nuevo materialismo del siglo XXI: Luces y sombras*. Barcelona: Real Academia Europea de Doctores.

Alonso-Almeida, M. M., Bagur-Femenias, L., Llach, J., & Perramon, J. (2018). Sustainability in small tourist businesses: The link between initiatives and performance. *Current Issues in Tourism*, *21*(1), 1–20. doi:10.1080/13683500.2015.1066764

Alonso-Almeida, M. M., Rocafort, A., & Borrajo, F. (2016). Shedding light on eco-innovation in tourism: A critical analysis. *Sustainability*, *8*(12), 1262–1280. doi:10.3390u8121262

Anttonen, M., Lammi, M., Mykkänen, J., & Repo, P. (2018). Circular Economy in the Triple Helix of Innovation Systems. *Sustainability*, *10*(8), 2646–2660. doi:10.3390u10082646

Bagur-Femenias, L., Llach, J., & Alonso-Almeida, M. M. (2013). Is the adoption of environmental practices a strategical decision for small service companies? An empirical approach. *Management Decision*, *51*(1), 41–62. doi:10.1108/00251741311291300

Bianchini, A., Pellegrini, M., Rossi, J., & Saccani, C. (2018). *A new productive model of circular economy enhanced by digital transformation in the Fourth Industrial Revolution-An integrated framework and real case studies. XXIII Summer School "Francesco Turco"*. Industrial Systems Engineering.

Bocken, N., Miller, K., Weissbrod, I., Holgado, M., & Evans, S. (2018). *Slowing resource loops in the Circular Economy: an experimentation approach in fashion retail.* Available in https://www.researchgate.net/profile/Nancy_Bocken/publication/ 326587900_Slowing_resource_loops_in_the_Circular_Economy_an_experimentation_approach_in_fashion_retail/links/5b58270b0f7e9bc79a60aeeb/Slowing-resource-loops-in-the-Circular-Economy-an-experimentation-approach-in-fashion-retail.pdf

Bocken, N. M. P., Short, S. W., Rana, P., & Evans, S. (2014). A literature and practice review to develop sustainable business model archetypes. *Journal of Cleaner Production*, *65*, 42–56. doi:10.1016/j.jclepro.2013.11.039

Boiten, V. J., Han, L.-C. S., & Tyler, D. (n.d.). *Circular economy stakeholder perspectives: Textile collection strategies to support material circularity.* Available in http://resyntex.eu/images/downloads/ValrieJBoiten_Textile _collection_strategies.pdf

Camacho-Otero, J., Pettersen, I. N., & Boks, C. (2017). Consumer and user acceptance in the circular economy: what are researchers missing? In *PLATE: Product Lifetimes And The Environment*. TU Delft.

Caniato, F., Caridi, M., Crippa, L., & Moretto, A. (2012). Environmental sustainability in fashion supply chains: An exploratory case based research. *International Journal of Production Economics*, *135*(2), 659–670. doi:10.1016/j.ijpe.2011.06.001

Chapman, J. (2015). *Emotionally Durable Design: Objects, Experiences and Empathy*. London: Routledge. doi:10.4324/9781315738802

Chung, C. J., & Wee, H. M. (2008). Green-component life-cycle value on design and reverse manufacturing in some-closed supply chain. *International Journal of Production Economics*, *113*(2), 528–545. doi:10.1016/j.ijpe.2007.10.020

De Brito, M. P., Carbone, V., & Blanquart, C. M. (2008). Towards a sustainable fashion retail supply chain in Europe: Organisation and performance. *International Journal of Production Economics*, *114*(2), 534–553. doi:10.1016/j.ijpe.2007.06.012

ECOALF. (2018). *Re-Born Fabrics*. Available in: https://ecoalf.com/gb/recycled-fabrics/

Ekström, K. M., & Salomonson, N. (2014). Reuse and recycling of clothing and textiles—A network approach. *Journal of Macromarketing*, *34*(3), 383–399. doi:10.1177/0276146714529658

Elzinga, R., & Boon, W. (2018). *Consumer behaviour in a circular economy: Testing consumer willingness to participate in circular business models* (Master's thesis). Canon Europe and the University of Utrecht.

Faisal, M. N. (2010). Sustainable supply chains: A study of interaction among the enablers. *Business Process Management Journal*, *16*(3), 508–529. doi:10.1108/14637151011049476

Farrant, L., Olsen, S. I., & Wangel, A. (2010). Environmental benefits from reusing clothes. *The International Journal of Life Cycle Assessment*, *15*(7), 726–736. doi:10.100711367-010-0197-y

Fletcher, K. (2013). *Sustainable fashion and textiles: design journeys*. Routledge.

H & M. (2018). *Sustentability Report 2017 Summary*. Available in https://about.hm.com/content/dam/hmgroup/countrysites/es/documents/Executive%20Summary%20SPAIN%20FINAL.pdf

INDITEX. (2017). *Annual Report 2016*. Available in http://static.inditex.com/annual_report_2016/en/our-priorities/commitment-to-the-excellence-of-our-products/towards-a-circular-economy.php

INDITEX. (2018). *Annual Report 2017*. Retrieved from https://static.inditex.com/annual_report_2017/en

Kant Hvass, K. (2016). *Weaving a path from waste to value: Exploring fashion industry business models and the circular economy*. Copenhagen Business School.

Kirchherr, J., Reike, D., & Hekkert, M. (2017). Conceptualizing the circular economy: An analysis of 114 definitions. *Resources, Conservation and Recycling*, *127*, 221–232. doi:10.1016/j.resconrec.2017.09.005

Korhoner, J., Honkasalo, A., & Seppala, J. (2018). Circular Economy: The Concept and its Limitations. *Ecological Economics*, *143*, 37–46. doi:10.1016/j.ecolecon.2017.06.041

Lakhal, S. Y., Sidibe, H., & Mida, S. (2008). Comparing conventional and certified organic cotton supply chains: The case of Mali. *International Journal of Agricultural Resources, Governance and Ecology*, *7*(3), 243–255. doi:10.1504/IJARGE.2008.018328

Mair, C., & Stern, T. (2017). Cascading Utilization of Wood: A Matter of Circular Economy? *Current Forestry Reports*, *3*(4), 281–295. doi:10.100740725-017-0067-y

Murray, A., Skene, K., & Haynes, K. (2017). The circular economy: An interdisciplinary exploration of the concept and application in global context. *Journal of Business Ethics*, *140*(3), 369–380. doi:10.100710551-015-2693-2

Osterwalder, A., & Pigneur, Y. (2010). *Business model generation: a handbook for visionaries, game changers, and challengers*. John Wiley & Sons.

Rodriguez-Antón, J. M., & Alonso-Almeida, M. M. (2018). Organización y dirección de empresas hoteleras. Ed. Sintesis.

Rodríguez-Antón, J. M., & Alonso-Almeida, M. M. (2018). *La estrategia española de Economía circular y su adecuación al Plan de Acción de la UE para la Economía circular*. Comunicación presentada en el 25th APDR Congress, Lisboa, Portugal.

Ruan, J. J., Li, J., & Xu, Z. M. (2011). An environmentally friendly recovery production line of waste toner cartridges. *Journal of Hazardous Materials*, *185*(2–3), 696–702. doi:10.1016/j.jhazmat.2010.09.074 PMID:20956056

Sarkis, J., & Zhu, Q. (2017). Environmental Sustainability and Production: Taking the Road Less Travelled. *International Journal of Production Research*, *56*(1-2), 743–759. doi:10.1080/00207543.2017.1365182

Shih, D. H., Lu, C. M., Lee, C. H., Cai, S. Y., Wu, K. J., & Tseng, M. L. (2018). Eco-Innovation in Circular Agri-Business. *Sustainability*, *10*(4), 1140–1153. doi:10.3390u10041140

Srivastava, S. K. (2007). Green supply-chain management: A state-of-the-art literature review. *International Journal of Management Reviews*, *9*(1), 53–80. doi:10.1111/j.1468-2370.2007.00202.x

Szita, K. T. (2017). The application of life cycle assessment in circular economy. *Hungarian Agricultural Engineering*, *31*(31), 5–9. doi:10.17676/HAE.2017.31.5

Turoń, K., & Czech, P. (2017). Circular Economy in the Transport Industry in Terms of Corporate Social Responsibility Concept. *Journal of Corporate Responsibility and Leadership*, *3*(4), 83–94. doi:10.12775/JCRL.2016.025

Van Loon, P., Delagarde, C., & Van Wassenhove, L. N. (2017). The role of second-hand markets in circular business: A simple model for leasing versus selling consumer products. *International Journal of Production Research*, 1–14.

Van Weelden. (2016). Paving the way towards circular consumption: Exploring consumer acceptance of refurbished mobile phones in the Dutch market. *Journal of Cleaner Production*, *113*, 743–754.

Wang, Y., & Hazen, B. T. (2016). Consumer product knowledge and intention to purchase remanufactured products. *International Journal of Production Economics*, *181*, 460–469. doi:10.1016/j.ijpe.2015.08.031

Weelden, V. (2016). Paving the way towards circular consumption: Exploring consumer acceptance of refurbished mobile phones in the Dutch market. *Journal of Cleaner Production*, *113*, 743–754. doi:10.1016/j.jclepro.2015.11.065

Whalen, K. A., Berlin, C., Ekberg, J., Barletta, I., & Hammersberg, P. (2018). 'All they do is win': Lessons learned from use of a serious game for Circular Economy education. *Resources, Conservation and Recycling*, *135*, 335–345. doi:10.1016/j.resconrec.2017.06.021

Woolridge, A. C., Ward, G. D., Phillips, P. S., Collins, M., & Gandy, S. (2006). Life cycle assessment for reuse/recycling of donated waste textiles compared to use of virgin material: An UK energy saving perspective. *Resources, Conservation and Recycling*, *46*(1), 94–103. doi:10.1016/j.resconrec.2005.06.006

Zhu, Q., & Sarkis, J. (2006). An inter-sectoral comparison of green supply chain management in China: Drivers and practices. *Journal of Cleaner Production*, *14*(5), 472–486. doi:10.1016/j.jclepro.2005.01.003

Zhu, Q., Sarkis, J., & Lai, K. H. (2008). Confirmation of a measurement model for green supply chain management practices implementation. *International Journal of Production Economics*, *111*(2), 261–273. doi:10.1016/j.ijpe.2006.11.029

KEY TERMS AND DEFINITIONS

BMC: Business model canvas is a tool that allow identify the core business model of a company.

CE: Circular economy pursues closing material flows in productive systems to maximize the utilization of available resources.

Cradle-to-Cradle: It is a framework to explain how to achieve circular economy. It seeks to design products, production processes and post production processes efficient and waste free in circular flows where all is used.

Cradle-to-Cradle Certificate: The cradle-to-cradle certification is based on five criteria: material content, material reutilization/design for the environment, share of renewable energy, water stewardship during production, and socially responsible principles. The certification looks at the chemical components of ingredients used in the product to assess their effects on human and environmental health, as well as their ability to be recycled/composted.

Rs Philosophies: Strategies used to deploy CE such as reduce, reuse, and recycle.

Chapter 5
An Assessment and Policy Proposals Within the Framework of the Blue Economy and Public Policies

Gamze Yıldız Şeren
University of Namik Kemal, Turkey

ABSTRACT

Blue economy refers to economic sectors that are either directly or indirectly linked with the oceans. However, the blue economy does not only have an economic dimension. Environmental health is also an area that blue economy takes into account. This chapter draws attention to both social and economic potential to be created by blue economy and to consider and evaluate how to increase this potential through public policies in today's century, when the resources are gradually depleted and population growth continues. In order for the blue economy to be a driving force for sustainable growth, public-private partnerships emerge as a recipe for opportunities. In addition, the growth of the blue economy can be stimulated by conventional financial instruments (such as taxes and subsidies). Since the blue economy is at an intersection of environmental health and economic benefits, positive externalities that environmental health can have on generations should not be overlooked.

INTRODUCTION

Factors such as the rapidly growing population, industrialization and technology also bring about the risk of rapid depletion of natural resources. Public policies have also been used as a tool to inhibit the risks posed by the co-ownership of natural resources and the environment (negative externalities) and as an encouraging tool against the benefits of them (positive externalities). In this study, the role of public policies in the context of the opportunities and risks created by the blue economy was investigated. Accordingly, it was studied in what points and how public policies must be used to realize the opportunities and benefits offered by the blue economy or to reduce/eliminate the risks it faces. In this context,

DOI: 10.4018/978-1-5225-8109-3.ch005

the study aims to evaluate public policies from two dimensions. These two main dimensions are two fundamental elements of a sustainable blue economy. One of them is environmental health and the other is economic benefits. Considering the fact that the blue economy may be a driving force for growth, it was aimed to seek an answer the question whether or not careful monitoring of the ocean health and the benefits/hazards to be handed down to the next generations and ensuring both ocean health and gaining economic benefits can be achieved simultaneously by public policies. In this scope, the study consists of two main parts. The first part covers some definitions and evaluations regarding the concept of blue economy, while the second part contains a review of public policies regarding the connection between blue economy, sustainable growth and environmental health.

THE BLUE ECONOMOY APPROACH: A REVIEW ON THE BASIS OF CONCEPT AND SCOPE

Today's world is facing great challenges in terms of sustainable development. Durability against natural disasters, access to food and energy, management of natural resources, effects of climate change, security and sovereignty issues, and sustaining national development are among these challenges. When the world's population is thought to be an important factor that will magnify these challenges, the management of the world's resources manifests itself as a vital issue. At this point, the blue economy is seen as one of the main factors having a new point and growth potential with regard to the economic development of the sea and oceans. Thus, governments have begun to resort to the "blue economy" for a sustainable economy (Humayun & Zafar, 2014, p. 57).

The blue economy is a concept that has gained popularity recently. Through the blue economy, on the one hand, it is intended to extend means of living and business areas and, on the other hand, to protect the health of the ocean and coastal ecosystem by making use of ocean resources for economic growth. Blue economy, which encompasses a variety of economic activities such as ecotourism, marine energy, sustainable fishery, management of ocean wastes about oceans, is a great potential for coastal communities around the world, such as Caribbean (Kulkarni, 2018).

The blue economy; is an approach used to describe all economic sectors, directly or indirectly linked with the oceans. The true potential of the blue economy can be fulfilled only if the oceans are protected. (European Comission(a), 2018). The blue economy is also seen as a newly emerging development paradigm that covers ocean economy, green economy, coastal economy and marine economy. The blue economy, just like the green economy, stick to the reduction of environmental risks and ecological shortages in order to enhance human welfare and social equity (Attri, 2016, p.1 & Pauly, 2018, p.371).

There are two approaches addressing the blue economy in two main frameworks. One of them addresses the blue economy as a way to benefit from marine and coastal resources for the purpose of maximizing economic outputs as well as protecting the marine environment while the other approach adopts a sustainable and inclusive development perspective as the green economy does; and regards both protection and the link between socioeconomic outputs. (Norton, 2016). The blue economy is an extremely complex and interdependent economy, its qualities make it difficult to manage and monitor. As the individual sector activities of the ocean economy are interdependent, a sector activity can have various effects on other industries, the ocean ecosystem, and the food safety and lifestyle associated with this economy, creating adverse effects throughout the supply chain. When planning in this context, it is necessary to take a step by taking into account the whole ocean economy. For example, a poorly planned harbour has the power to influence habitats that are significant for fisheries. Unsustainable fisheries can disrupt ecosystems, such as coral reefs, and jeopardize their role in coastal protection. This can affect tourism and other job opportunities. Therefore, no ocean industry can operate independently from others (European Comission(a), 2018). Coasts and oceans are the most efficient ecosystems in the world. They directly or indirectly contribute to the quality of life of people, and they also provide services that support local coastal communities and national economies. For example, coral reefs provide a living space for fish. This constitutes the main food source for the 1 billion people in the developing countries that are dependent on the seafood as the main food resource. Mangroves, on the other hand, minimize the coastal erosion by acting as a barrier against climate change and assumes the role of barrier against floods (PEMSEA, 2015, p.11).

The World Bank defined the blue economy as an economy that ensures a sustainable use of ocean resources for economic growth, an improvement in business and living standards, and the health of the ocean ecosystem. Accordingly, the activities covered by the blue economy are (World Bank, 2017):

- Renewable energy
- Tourism
- Climate change
- Waste Management
- Sea transport
- Fishery

Coastal and sea ecosystem services are as follows (PEMSEA, 2015, p.11):

- Food obtained from wild hunting fish and aquaculture;
- Air conditioning and protection from natural hazards
- Coastal stabilization and erosion control
- Tourism and entertainment
- Carbon caption with mangroves, seaweed beds and salt marshes
- Energy from offshore oil, wind and waves
- Management and processing of food and waste in the environment
- Formation of sand, soil and other sediments
- Pharmaceutical and other biotechnology products
- Transportation and trading through ports

In the blue economy, ocean-based industries are divided into two as established and developing industries. Accordingly, developing industries are equally critical as established industries in order to see the economic and social benefits of the blue economy. It is necessary to state that the blended finance method, which will be explained in detail in the following sections, is significant due to the high investment costs in ocean-based developing industries.

Ocean resources have become an area that draws more attention to both investors and politicians for new opportunities and resources. According to the OECD projections, the performance of the blue economy until 2030 will be better than the growth of the global economy as a whole in terms of both added value and employment (European Comission(a), 2018). Ocean-based assets and economic activities offer opportunities for new growth, employment and innovation resources. However, they face risks due

Table 1. Ocean Based Industries in the Blue Economy

Ocean-Based Established Industries	Ocean-Based Developing Industries
Industrial capture fishery	Industrial sea fisheries
Industrial processing of aquatic products	Deep and ultra-deep water oil and gas
Shipping	Sea wind energy
Port activities	Ocean renewable energy
Ship Construction	Sea and sea-floor mining
Offshore oil and gas	Maritime safety and monitoring
Maritime manufacturing and construction	Marine biotechnology
Sea and coastal tourism	High-tech seafood and services
Maritime services	
Sea-floor screening	
Maritime research and development and education	

Source: OECD (a), 2016, p.8

to developed economic activities, demographic and environmental pressures (OECD (a), 2016, p.6). The foundations of the blue economy can be classified as good governance, blue management, monitoring, vision, and finally institutional and regulatory reforms (Attri, 2016, p.2). It is thought that public policies are of vital importance in realizing especially institutional and regulatory reforms.

Services provided by marine ecosystems mainly constitute the basis for much of the economic activity. For example, oceans play an important role in the global supply chain, and 90% of trade is carried out via sea transport. In addition, more than 30% of global oil and gas production is obtained from offshore areas. Worldwide income obtained from marine products exceeds US $ 190 billion, while marine and coastal tourism yield 161 billion US dollars per year. Fisheries, aquaculture, and tourism provide more than 300 million jobs worldwide (PEMSEA, 2015, p.11).

The blue economy covers both environmental health and economic benefits. In other words, it is the intersection of these two concepts. At this point, there is a policy agenda that improves ocean health and economic growth simultaneously, consistent with the social equality and participation principles of the blue economy (Patil and others, 2016, p.43).

PUBLIC POLICIES LINKED WITH BLUE ECONOMY, SUSTAINABLE GROWTH AND ENVIRONMENTAL HEALTH

Sustainable development has become a focal point from the 1960s to now and emerged as a concept referring to the difficulty of sustainable use of natural resources while safeguarding the economic and social goals. In this context, the environmental and resource dimension of the concept was defined at the first United Nations (UN) conference on sustainable development held in Stockholm in 1972, the economic dimension of the concept was defined in 1992 at the UN meeting held in Rio for the second time and finally the social dimension of the concept was defined at the UN meeting held in Johannesburg in 2002 (Eikeset and others, 2018, p.177). A new concept of "green growth" was coined at the meeting held on sustainable development in Rio in 2012. Accordingly, green growth stands for encouraging economic growth and development by safeguarding natural resources while fulfilling the resource and environmental services that ensure people's well-being. In this context, a group of small island nation states (SIDS) emphasized the importance of the blue economy and revealed the importance of blue growth. At the Rio+20 conference, the Food and Agriculture Organization (FAO) supported these views. Accordingly, the message is given that a healthy ocean ecosystem provided by a sustainable agricultural ecosystem is a prerequisite for the blue growth. After the conference, the concept of blue growth became a widespread concept used nationally, regionally and internationally (Eikeset and others, 2018, p. 178 & FAO, 2018). Akkucuk (2017) has pointed out that there is not a single dimension of sustainable development in his book, and there are many aspects such as politics, ecology, economy, business, supply chain management and waste management. Therefore, an integrated approach to other sectors needs to be developed to ensure a blue growth. For example, there are three principles in conducting the blue growth initiative through sustainable developed fisheries and aquaculture. These include maximizing economic benefits with blue growth and maximizing environmental sustainability and communal/social benefits. The aim here is to maximize the economic and social benefits while minimizing environmental degradation in sectors related to fisheries and aquaculture.

Taxes, subsidies and other economic instruments are influential on both producer and consumer behaviour. By the increase or decrease of the price of a product or service, the household or business sector can combine environmental costs and benefits in their budgets. They help to internalize the use of natural resources or emission of pollutants. Economic instruments for the control of pollution and the management of natural resources have gained an increasingly critical role since 1970s (OECD (b), 2017, p.3). In order for the blue economy to operate at a legal and economic level, this process must be supported with sufficient public incentives and rules. Economic instruments such as taxes, subsidies and wages should be used for the internalization of the environmental and social benefits, the risks and costs to be inflicted upon society, and so on. Furthermore, international and national laws and agreements, including special agreements, should be framed, implemented, and continuously ameliorated to support the sustainable blue economy (WWF).

Many actors are involved in a sustainable blue economy. These are governments (public sector), businesses (private sector), non-profit organizations, investors and consumers (WWF). This study aims to investigate the role of the public sector in this area. The purpose of this chapter is to examine public interventions aimed at the blue economy at the two main dimensions. Given the fact that the blue economy is at the intersection of environmental health and economic benefits, it is necessary to evaluate public policies around these two dimensions as well. Therefore, the sub-sections are examined with regard to the environmental health and economic benefits, and economic benefits are addressed focusing on the sustainable growth aspect.

Economy, Environmental Health, and Public Policies: Thoughts Regarding Opportunities and Threats

The necessity of safeguarding the blue economy through public policies (or intervention with public policies) can be better understood by revealing the threats it faces and the benefits it brings. Many public goods emerge in order to reduce or eliminate a risk, in case a risk has a negative benefit, in a broader sense, in case the public bad exists. For example, eliminating a global risk, such as infectious diseases, provides benefit to anyone and this is a global public benefit. Reducing this risk here is a public benefit, but in order to turn it into a public benefit at an international level, the benefit must affect everyone equally at this level. Reducing the risks causing pollution in a joint property source such as the ocean, lake, or forest is also a public benefit; however, there is a limited spatial range regarding who shares the source (Morrissey, Velde and Hewitt, 2002). The idea of internalizing environmental pollution through taxation was put forward by A.C. Pigou (Pigou, 1920), who developed the concept of externalities of Alfred Marshall. According to this, the existence of externalities for public intervention is a fundamental reason and he argued for the taxation for negative externalities such as environmental pollution and for subsidies for positive externalities. These are called Pigovian taxes and subsidies. Pigovian taxes are still seen today as an effective way to combat pollution (The Library of Economics and Liberty). For this reason, public policies are essential in ensuring that the environmental dimension of the blue economy achieves a sustainable quality through public policies.

The blue economy has a lot of economic and social benefits (positive externalities). Some of these benefits are that it produces 50% of the oxygen we inhale, absorbs 93% of the added heat, contains a great many genetic resources, absorbs 30% of global carbon dioxide emissions, and enables coral reefs and mangroves to protect the coasts. However, the blue economy confronts some threats (negative externalities) as a result of the misuse of resources in today's world and some other environmental factors. These are mainly the rapid decline of biodiversity, the rise in temperature and acidity, deterioration of habitats, accumulation of plastics and other wastes (European Comission (a), 2018). The biggest threat to the ocean economy in the long run is the health of the oceans, and this deterioration can continue if legal changes / technological innovations are not achieved. The four major factors that affect ocean health are climate change, acidification, pollution and overfishing (Morillo and Spalding, 2017). Marine biodiversity and ecosystems are facing risks such as climate change, overfishing (fisheries), habitat destruction and pollution, although the value of the ocean economy is expected to be more than two folds and support more than 40 billion jobs by 2030. Future innovations in science and technology are expected to play an important role in the development of economic activities based on environmental challenges and oceans in the years to come (OECD b, 2017, p.4).

By 2030, national governments have adopted 2015 sustainable development goals for a sustainable world. Accordingly, the 14th goal is related to the sustainable use of marine and marine resources, and the oceans. 60% of the world's marine ecosystem, which faces threats of overfishing, habitat destruction, pollution and climate change, has been used in an unsustainable manner. According to the estimations of 2016, 31% of fish stocks were over-hunted. The use and protection of the oceans for the economic development can be balanced by innovations that will take place in the established and developing ocean economies. Responsible business behaviour and the role of science and technology and availability of a national and international capacity for the ocean industry constitute some pillars of the solution (OECD b, 2017, p.3). In addition to these, marine areas protected by public policies can be created, and implementations such as taxation of marine pollution can be put into practice. Another major component of the solution is to encourage the recycling and reuse of plastic waste in line with the circular economy (OECD b, 2017, p.4). Every year an estimated 8 million tonnes of plastic is thrown into the oceans, and in case that the use of plastic and adequate waste management cannot be achieved, the figure is expected to rise to 60 tons per minute by 2050. This indicates that plastic pollution is today the world's fastest-growing environmental problem (Jensen, 2018). For example, in England disposable plastics are taxed against plastics, which is an important cause of ocean pollution (Walker, 2017).

Cooperation of all sectors is vital for a successful blue economy. Both the private sector, public and non-governmental organizations (NGOs) should take a collaborative approach and provide inter sectoral integration (Kilponen & Mosher, 2017). Akkucuk and Sekercıoglu (2016) have examined the sensitivity of a small NGO working for environmental protection to environmental sustainability. Accordingly, the study underlined that such environmental organizations play an important role in increasing public awareness of environmental problems, protecting habitats and enforcing environmental friendly laws. For a sustainable blue economy, NGOs with environmentally friendly activities in this area are very important. Businesses work in partnership with both the public sector and NGOs to build sustainable and inclusive economies. For example, the demand for seafood with sustainable certification now constitutes 14% of the global market. Therefore, businesses, investors and NGOs should continue to work together to promote consumer appetite for sustainable products. The role of the public sector is also changing. Governments exist in public-private partnerships and even tripartite partnerships that bring together public, private and civil societies. These comprehensive partnerships combine the existence of each industry with a common endeavor to solve specific problems, such as strengthening local and regional maritime economies (Kilponen & Mosher, 2017).

It should not be forgotten that a sustainable blue economy is a sea-based economy. Therefore, it offers social and economic benefits for the present and future generations, contributing to food security, elimination of poverty, sources of living, income, employment, health, safety, equality and political stability. Ensuring economic and social stability depends on clean technologies, renewable energy and circular material flows (WWF). At this point, public policies should also introduce a strategy to support these fields and prepare a roadmap. Additionally, actions should be taken in order to raise the awareness of citizens in this regard. For example, in China, the government distributes the blue economy book they prepared for schools, universities and libraries free of charge (MOSS). It is necessary to touch people's hearts and minds in order to overcome this situation, which the UN secretary-general Angel Gurría calls "*ocean blindness*" (OECD b, 2017, p.4).

Blue Economy, Sustainable Growth, and Public Policies

The emerging concepts of the blue economy and blue growth are important targets of public policy. Countries seeking to improve their ocean economies have acknowledged the need for a better balanced policy for future economic growth in the oceans by protecting and even restoring ocean health, which is the new focus of sustainable growth and global policy discourse. (Economist&Intelligence Unit, 2015, p.10). A sustainable ocean economy provides a way to assess economic development and ocean health. Properly planned and managed ocean areas should activate public and private sector investments and create strong returns and ecosystem benefits. By means of this approach, an ecosystem-based management perspective can bring a shift from traditional ocean sectors to new ocean-focused businesses. (Economist&Intelligence Unit, 2015, p.11). Sustainable Blue Economy includes industries and companies where ecological and environmental risks are reduced and slowed down. This is achieved only through the application of the principles of "cyclical economy" and can be developed with innovative technologies. (Morillo and Spalding, 2017, p.16). For example, the report published by European Commission stipulates the use of the plastic strategy to reduce marine litter by adopting the cyclical economy approach as one of the components of a strong European blue economy (European Comission (b), 2017, p.27) The principles of sustainable blue economy are as follows (WWF):

- The sustainable blue economy must be clearly defined. With this definition, it should be demonstrated that the only safe way is the growth of circular economy in order to ensure long-term welfare, respecting the integrity of the ecosystem of the blue economy.

- Sustainable blue economy vision must be implemented by the governments and all relevant stakeholders
- Actors in public and private sectors at all scales must express how a sustainable blue economy should be managed by providing guidance on governance, and it should be explained what each stakeholder should do if a sustainable blue economy is realized
- Awareness about the blue economy must be created
- Decision-making guidance on the blue economy should be given in both public and private sectors
- Progress should be monitored

Of course, the main principles and the things that must be done are not limited to what is listed above. As well as those mentioned, further efforts should be exerted internationally to ensure that the oceans have a sustainable future. To this end, an investment and development program framework needs to be prepared for the blue economy. For the sustainability of the blue economy, financial markets and institutions undertake very important roles. In a sustainable approach, both the public and private sectors play a key role in making investments in this field. (European Comission a, 2018). Increasing ocean-based activities contribute to the current pressures on the health of marine ecosystems. Innovation is one of the economic keys for the success of the ocean economy and will help reduce ocean health problems. (OECD (a), 2016, p.21).

The global economy is expected to expand moderately, in this context some industries related to the ocean have a great potential. However, not all of these are part of the Sustainable Blue Economy. For example, sectors that cause climate change, such as deep-sea oil and gas exploration or commercial fisheries, and sectors that contribute to environmental degradation are not included in this context since they are not sustainable (Morillo and Spalding, 2017, p.14).

The states are undoubtedly expected to undertake important duties regarding the blue economy, which will be the economic power of the century we live in. Gaining a strategic perspective on the development of ocean resources will be an important driving force for ocean economy. Both large and small ocean economies are working for the health of the oceans in order to support slow growth in the continental economies, to explore new opportunities for investment and employment, and to create competitive advantage in emerging industries such as deep sea mining and marine biotechnology. New strategic ocean development plans and policies, sometimes called "blue economy" plans, are prepared to encourage growth in and around the exclusive economic zones (EEZs) of countries. If this public policy become successful, the size and type of economic activity in the ocean will have a completely new scheme (The Economist & Intelligence Unit, 2015, p.9).

It is possible to illuminate the impact of public policies on the blue economy through the Irish example. Because of the tax regime applied, the Irish blue economy has achieved progress. Accordingly, the reasonable corporate taxation in effect in Ireland is creating an environment in which the blue economy can thrive. Moreover, maritime companies are also subject to the EU tonnage tax regime (Healy, 2018).

The blue economy can yield useful outputs for a country's economy. In order to make the best use of these outputs, it is necessary for countries to adopt a national maritime policy, which must comply with regional and international policies. Additionally, awareness of decision-makers should be raised in this regard and a capacity should be built through public-private partnerships. A significant growth transformation can be achieved by following these steps (Humayun and Zafar, 2014, p.57).

Potential investment opportunities have been created in the ocean-related industries by taking steps to prevent this situation through global agreements made in recent years. In addition, innovative technology and business models also aim to minimize / recover environmental damage. To this end, Sustainable Blue Economy offers investors new opportunities to benefit from the economic potential of the ocean. The idea of using the seas for economic gain is quite new. Although island countries have been benefiting from ocean resources for centuries and have contributed significantly to their economies, what is new is the understanding the share of new oceans in sustainable economic growth. (Commonwealth Secretariat, 2016, p.3). For example, the direct contribution of the Ocean Economy to the world economy in 2010 (Gross Value Added, GVA) = $ 1.5 trillion dollars; 3% of the world's GDP, 5-6% of the global "real economy"; direct employment contribution of the Ocean Economy to the world employment in 2010 (full-time equivalent jobs) = 31 million according to the OECD study. Each year, ocean economy has an estimated endorsement between 3 and 6 trillion US dollars, including cultural services, employment, and ocean-based ecosystem services. In addition, it is estimated that fisheries and aquaculture production is worth 100 billion US dollars per year and about 260 million business contributions to the global economy. (UN, 2017). According to estimates, 300 million people depend directly or indirectly on marine fisheries to ensure basic livelihoods. Our oceans and coasts are global public goods and critical resources that are vital for most of the planet's most vulnerable people. 'An inclusive blue economy' must consider both of these dimensions. (Norton, 2016).

Some steps can be recommended to achieve a sustainable blue economy without adding much to the problems encountered in the oceans (OECD (b), 2017, p.3):

- The development of a set of indicators in order to monitor progress during the process of achieving a sustainable blue economy
- Establishing specific statistics in order to analyse the contributions, needs and effects of maritime activities
- Providing a large environmental budget proposal/enlarging the environmental budget for the protection of marine resources
- Enlargement of maritime activities with various incentives

Inclusion of Public Policies Into the Blue Economy Along With Public Sector: Blended Finance

In order to protect the oceans, it is necessary to improve governance and change policies and lifestyles. Achieving this depends on the development of an effective multilateral and multidisciplinary cooperation (OECD (b), 2017, p.4). Investing in sectors linked with the blue economy (e.g. tourism, energy, transportation, fishery and food security, waste management) is a highly costly and complex process (PEMSEA, 2015, p.) The blended finance method, which is striking in the context of the blue economy and public policies in literature, will be discussed in this section. The OECD defines the blended finance as: "*Strategic use of development financing for the mobilization of additional financing towards a sustainable development in developing countries*" (OECD (c)). In this context, for a sustainable blue economy, stakeholders need to undertake responsibility with active and effective participation, and a roadmap including not only the public sector but also the private sector should be formed. Blended finance means a strategic combination of public and/or private development financing with other public or private sectors in order to improve resources in investments to be made in key areas in an economy like an infrastructure. The foundations of the blended finance, which can encompass public and public financial partnerships as well as public and private partnerships (Caribbean Development Bank, 2018, p. 67) are as follows:

- Increasing capital leverage, here aid and philanthropic funds are used in the meaning of attracting the capital of the public or private sector
- Increasing the impact of investments
- Managing gains in line with market expectations

Capital and expertise of the private sector are also significant for investments directed towards the blue economy. The investments in this area are beneficial to both the society and the companies, and private sector investments are required in order to increase these investments. Lack of consensus between local governments and the private sector regarding investment, shortcomings related to regulations, and lack of property rights are some of the obstacles to extending investments in the blue economy. At this point, governments and, therefore, public policies are of vital significance in terms of increasing investments in this area. For example, explicitly defined regulations can contribute to improving the risk-return profile of investments (PEMSEA, 2015, p.55).

Blended finance, which is one of the most dynamic areas in the financing of development, is a method of financing that has attracted interest in recent years. A number of actors, such as bilateral development agencies, multilateral development finance institutions and philanthropic foundations, are involved in the method of financing. This method of financing has often been used to support investments in infrastructure development where there is an expectation of an economic return and in other interventions. For example, green investments supported by blended financing can be listed as environment-friendly transport, renewable energy and environment-friendly buildings (Caribbean Development Bank, 2018).

The research areas to be supported by blended finance within the blue economy are as follows:

- Ocean renewable energy
- Sustainable marine fisheries
- Sustainable fisheries management and fish processing
- Responsible mining of sea and sea-floor

Blended finance model offers a couple of advantages to render it attractive to the private sector. Thus, it is aimed that the investments become reasonable and profitable for the private sector. Technical aids, insurance risk aiming investors to be fully or partially protected against various risk types, market incentives targeting future guarantees to the investors with the aim of promoting renovation for making preliminary investments in new markets or for new products/services, and top-up returns are among incentive tools that can be listed within this scope (Caribbean Development Bank, 2018). According to a survey conducted in East Asia, companies were asked how the government can help them grow the blue economy and the companies listed the reform policies, the clarity of the processes for investment, the implementation of sustainability practices in the political construction process, and the improved mechanisms for public-private partnership (PEMSEA, 2015, p.55).

Blended financing undoubtedly has the potential to significantly raise the resources of sustainable development. But that does not mean that there are no difficulties or constraints of the implementation.

For example, in the case of blended finance, since more than one financing agent, institution and organization are involved, completion might take time. Another constraint is that it is necessary to implement such regulations in such a way that public interest can be sought, while at the same time the social and environmental impacts of the project need to be taken into account. There is limited knowledge and technical capacity in such agents. Such restrictions exist not only in the supplier (financial institution) but also in the developing countries which are in the buyer position. In countries with debt sustainability problems, this type of financing management needs to be cautious about non-concessional finance (Caribbean Development Bank, 2018). In the Caribbean countries, for example, the tax base and the tight economy accompanied by the high public debt emerges as an important problem in the financing of investments (such as sustainable infrastructure and research and development) aimed at the growth of the blue economy. Moreover, the vulnerability of the region against climate change and environmental shocks calls for additional resources for aid and restructuring (Kulkarni, 2018).

Solution of Public Policy for the Blue Economy Problem: Reviews

The blue economy problem that can be categorized as effects of the unsustainable use of marine resources, such as unsustainable fisheries, physical changes and degradation of marine and coastal habitats and landscapes, marine pollution and climate change and unfair trade (World Bank Group & UN, 2017, pp.10-11) is a problem that should be examined under the theme of environmental problems. However, it is possible to seek solutions to this problem with the public policy remedy.

Environmental problems are caused by market failures, which can be divided into externalities and the public good quality of pollution. The negative externality mentioned here may have an impact area that can influence the whole world (Mutlu, 2002, p.19). The quality of public good refers to goods from which the whole public benefits and no party is excluded from the benefit, and in which consumption of the individual is not impeded by the consumption of another individual. In other words, the consumption is not competitive and additional cost is not required in case there is extra use (Samuelson, 1954, pp. 387-389). These qualities result in the failure of the prices of goods to be determined and it becomes impossible for the good to be produced in the market. Therefore, pricing and market solution cannot be realized (Mutlu, 2002, p.19). It is possible to take action through various means in case of this market failure specifically about the natural resources. For example, access to such services may be restricted by adding a fee, such as an entry fee to a service previously not priced. In this case, taxes and user fees are widely known price-oriented tools. Another way is the market-based incentive approach, which is directly compared to the regulatory approach (Davis and Gardside, 2001, p.225).

Various economic instruments have been designed against the externalities arising from the use of natural resources. These can be listed as taxes, fees, user fees, subsidies, payments for ecosystems, biodiversity offsets and individually transferable quotas. Undoubtedly, such economic instruments are useful tools to ensure a balance between the protection and the use of the marine area, coastal and ocean environments. However, the adequateness of data on economic and environmental parameters, irregular application of spatial management, and high data processing costs point to the insufficient use of economic instruments in the ocean environment (OECD (a), 2016, p.40). An international platform formed by representatives of environmental scientists, government agencies, regulators and users can be established for the dissemination of the use of economic instruments so that the right choice can be made by exchanging knowledge and experience (OECD, 2016, p.41).

The oceans, which have long been a source of living, are under great threat nowadays. Population growth, urbanization, the rise of the global middle class and the expansion of global trade lead to an increase in the risk of depletion of marine resources or irreversible damage. With global agreements made in recent years, steps have been taken to prevent this situation and potential investment opportunities have been created in the ocean-linked industries. Innovative technology and business models also aim to minimize/fix the environmental damage. Accordingly, the sustainable blue economy offers opportunities for investors to benefit from the economic potential of oceans (Rolando and Spalding, 2017). The public sector is undoubtedly a driving force with adequate regulatory frameworks and institutional arrangements in blue economy studies and in supporting sustainable ocean development. In this context, the public policies that could solve the blue economy problem should be implemented in cooperation with stakeholders. These policies should also support scientific and economic research, present effective regulatory policy frameworks, and provide sufficient incentives and financing sources (Kilponen, 2016).

For the effective management of oceans, economic analysis such as better use of science and technology innovations, stakeholder engagement and innovation in governance, benefit and cost analysis should be used more in this sector and, finally, economic instruments such as taxes, wages and tradable permits should be used (OECDa, 2016, p.227) The blended finance method for the blue economy constitutes one of the public policy proposals frequently found in the literature. Blended finance covers public-public good partnerships as well as public-private partnerships (Caribbean Development Bank, 2018). In the blue economy sector, where investments cost quiet a lot, this cooperation should operate with the goal of maximizing the economic and social benefits of the society.

Property rights is another problem in the sustainable management of resources. The fact that the blue economic resources (seas, coasts, oceans) are open to everyone also brings about waste of resources. Because many goods in this area cannot be priced and for this reason, they are excessively used. For example, the use of sea water for the disposal of wastewater has resulted in excessive use of water. Since environmental goods and services cannot be priced, markets cannot be used for an effective allocation here. This is inherent in many marine environment goods and is the characteristic of open access or public benefit. In the case of open access, there is no motivation in the individual for the exploited source. In other words, the user does not consider the costs. The environment is in everyone's ownership, but it is nobody's responsibility (Davis and Gardside, 2001, p.225). The state has options such as co-ownership, state ownership and privatization at this point. For example, unsustainability arising from overfishing was hindered via co-operative fisheries established in Brazil by means of co-ownership. Another means is the transfer of resources to state property for their protection. Finally, privatization is also a solution that is addressed within the context of the problems arising from property rights, which in turn hinders the overuse of natural resources but also causes other externalities to emerge (Mutlu, 2002, pp.193-194).

There is an incentive effect in the use of economic instruments. For example, when environmental costs are internalized within a product or service, consumers are encouraged to opt for lower priced and environment-friendly alternative products. In addition, economic instruments also have an income redistributing effect. For example, pollution can be reduced by environmental instruments such as environmental taxes, user fees and wages and the revenue to be obtained can be used to reduce a tax, such as personal income tax (OECDa, 2016, pp.229-230). It is evident that an effective government policy is essential for the strengthening and sustaining of the blue economy. It is required to put these policies into effect so as to activate maritime sector in various regions and countries although local or national conditions will have an impact on the policies to be formed (OECDa, 2016, p.36)

CONCLUSION AND REMARKS

Resources in the world are depleted in a swift manner, and the failure to pursue a sustainable policy results in the excessive use of resources. The blue economy faces threats such as pollution, habitat destruction, overfishing, climate change. 14th sustainable development goal set by the UN for a sustainable world is the *preservation and sustainable use of ocean, marine and marine resources for a sustainable development.* In this scope, for a sustainable blue economy, it should be prioritized to protect the health of these resources. To this end, economic policies can assume a deterrent role. The present study focuses on the idea that sustainable development through public policies can be achieved through both tax regulations and subsidies. It is necessary to attach particular importance to the fact that environmental pollution shouldn't be ignored for the sake of sustainable growth here. The growth promoted by the blue economy should not cause the resources and the environment to deteriorate.

- The main points to be addressed/intervened by public policies can be listed as follows:
- Protecting the health of the oceans and seas, taking necessary tax incentives or measures to avoid harming the environment
- Supporting the sectors that will increase the growth potential of the blue economy with various incentive mechanisms
- Creating corporate policies
- It is necessary to support public-private partnerships for blue economy and expand public-private partnership through blended financing method. Because investing in the blue economy brings along a costly and complex process.
- Creating a blue-sensitive budget
- Creation of specific statistics based on the blue economy
- Elaboration of the overall framework for investment and development
- Empowerment of NGO, public sector and private sector network
- The circular economy is a part of the solution for solving the blue economy problem. With cyclical economic principles, it is possible to decrease economic and environmental risks, which must be accompanied by innovative technologies. Taxation, for example, manifests itself an important public policy instrument, given that the use of plastics which is encouraged to be recycled by the cyclical economy is one of the greatest risks confronting the environment today

Public policies are one of the key tools in the protection of the environment, although they are seen as a barrier to the taxation in the solution of the problems that the blue economy brought due to the narrow tax base and high debt ratio in developing countries.

As the UN secretary general underlined, it is particularly important to raise the sensitivity of the society in this regard. Because everything starts with human beings, consciousness-raising activities should be carried out by eliminating the *ocean blindness* so that human beings do not put an end to everything. When economic benefits are ensured, all components of the blue economy should be shaped around the interests of future generations and the world's future, and public policies should undertake an active attitude by their tools during the management of the process.

REFERENCES

Akkucuk, U. (2017). *Ethics and sustainability in global supply chain management.* IGI Global. doi:10.4018/978-1-5225-2036-8

Akkucuk, U., & Sekercioglu, C. H. (2016). NGOs for environmental sustainability: The Case Of Kuzeydoga Foundation. *Fresenius Environmental Bulletin, 25*(12A), 6038–6044.

Attri, V. N. (2016). An emerging new development paradigm of the blue economy in IORA;A policy framework for the future. *IORA*. Retrieved August 8, 2018 from http://www.iora.int/media/23839/the-blue-economy-and-iora-2016.pdf

Caribbean Development Bank. (2018). Financing the blue economy. *A Caribbean Development Opportunity.* Retrieved August 13, 2018 from, http://issuu.com/caribank/docs/financing_the_blue_economy-_a_carib?e=21431045/61831833

Commonwealth Secretariat. (2016). The blue economy and small states. *Commonwealth Blue Economy Series.* Retrieved August 15, 2018 from http://www.cpahq.org/cpahq/Cpadocs/The%20Blue%20Economy%20and%20Small%20States.pdf

Davis, D., & Donald, F. (2001). Challenges for economic policy in sustainable management of marine natural resources. *Ecological Economics, 36*(2), 223–236. doi:10.1016/S0921-8009(00)00251-2

European Commission. (2017, June). Sustainable blue economy productive seas and oceans. *Research & Innovation Projects for Policy.* Retrieved August 15, 2018 from https://ec.europa.eu/info/sites/info/files/bluegrowth_p4p-report_2017.pdf

European Commission. (2018). *Introducing the sustainable blue economy finance principles.* Retrieved 16 August, 2018 from https://ec.europa.eu/maritimeaffairs/sites/maritimeaffairs/files/introducing-sustainable-blue-economy-finance-principles_en.pdf

FAO. (n.d.). *Blue growth initiative.* Retrieved August 18, 2018 from http://www.fao.org/3/a-i7862e.pdf

Healy, J. (n.d.). Why the blue economy matters? Ireland as a marine hub. *KPMG.* Retrieved from https://home.kpmg.com/ie/en/home/insights/2018/03/blue-economy.html

Humayun, A., & Zafar, N. (2014). Pakistan's 'blue economy' potential and prospects. *Polish Perspectives, 11*(1), 57–76. doi:10.13169/polipers.11.1.0057

Jensen, N. (2018). 8 steps to solve the ocean's plastic problem. *WEF.* Retrieved August 19, 2018 from https://www.weforum.org/agenda/2018/03/8-steps-to-solve-the-oceans-plastic-problem/

Kilponen, A. (2016). The blue economy and ocean health: part 2 - blue economy and decision-support frameworks. *OHI.* Retrieved August 6, 2018 from http://www.oceanhealthindex.org/news/blue-economy-and-decision-support-frameworks

Kilponen, A., & Mosher, L. (2017). The blue economy and ocean health: part 4: Working together for a successful blue economy. *Ocean Health Index.* Retrieved August 29, 2018 from http://www.oceanhealthindex.org/news/the-blue-economy-and-ocean-health-part-4

Kulkarni, R. (2018). Innovative financing and regional dialogue are central for a thriving 'blue economy'. *UNDP*. Retrieved August 15, 2018 from http://www.undp.org/content/undp/en/home/blog/2018/Innovative-financing-and-regional-dialogue-are-central-for-a-thriving-blue-economy.html

Maria, E. A., & ... (2018). What is blue growth? The semantics of "sustainable development" of marine environments. *Marine Policy*, *87*, 177–179. doi:10.1016/j.marpol.2017.10.019

Morillo, R., & Spalding, M. (2017). A sustainable blue economy. *Rockefeller & Co*. Retrieved August 14, 2018 from https://www.rockco.com/documents/FG/rockefeller/SI-docs/586666_RockCo-Blue_Economy_FINAL_WEB.pdf

Morrissey, O. (n.d.). *Dirk Willem te Velde and Adrian Hewitt, Defining International Public Goods: Conceptual Issues*. Retrieved from https://www.earthsummit2002.org/es/issues/

MOSS. (n.d.). *How does the Circular Economy differ to the Blue Economy?* Retrieved from http://www.moss.org.au/How-does-the-Circular-Economy-differ-to-the-Blue-Economy

Mutlu, A. (2002). *Çevre ekonomisi politikalari uygulamalar ve Türkiye*. Istanbul: Marmara university public finance research and administration publications.

Norton, A. (2016). Towards an inclusive blue economy. *IIED*. Retrieved August 10, 2018 from https://www.iied.org/towards-inclusive-blue-economy

OECD. (2016). *The Ocean Economy in 2030*. Paris: OECD Publishing. Retrieved August 5, 2018 from doi:10.1787/9789264251724-en

OECD. (2017a). Greening the ocean economy, summary report. *OECD*. Retrieved August 8, 2018 from http://www.oecd.org/greengrowth/GGSD_2017_Summary%20Report_WEB.pdf

OECD. (2017b). Policy instruments for the environment (PINE). Retrieved from http://www.oecd.org/environment/tools-evaluation/PINE_database_brochure.pdf

OECD. (n.d.). *OECD dac blended finance principles for unlocking commercial finance for the sustainable development goals*. Retrieved August 10, 2018 from http://www.oecd.org/dac/financing-sustainable-development/development-finance-topics/OECD-Blended-Finance-Principles.pdf

Patil, P. G., Virdin, J., Diez, S.M., Roberts, J., & Singh, A. (2016). *Toward a blue economy: a promise for sustainable growth in the Caribbean; An overview*. The World Bank. Retrieved April 17, 2018 from https://openknowledge.worldbank.org/bitstream/handle/10986/25061/Demystifying0t0the0Caribbean-0Region.pdf?sequence=4

Pauly, D. A. (2018). Vision for marine fisheries in a global blue economy. *Marine Policy*, *87*, 371–374. doi:10.1016/j.marpol.2017.11.010

PEMSEA. (2015). *Blue economy for business in east Asia towards an integrated understanding of blue economy.* Retrieved November 5, 2018 from http://www.pemsea.org/sites/default/files/PEMSEA%20Blue%20Economy%20Report%2011.10.15.pdf

Pigou, A. C. (1920). *The Economics of Welfare*. London: Macmillan.

Samuelson, P. A. (1954). The Pure Theory of Public Expenditure. *The Review of Economics and Statistics, 36*(4), 387–389. doi:10.2307/1925895

The Economist & Intelligence Unit. (2015). *The blue economy growth, opportunity and a sustainable ocean economy. An economist intelligence unit briefing paper for the World ocean summit 2015.* Retrieved March 27, 2018 from https://www.eiuperspectives.economist.com/sites/default/files/images/Blue%20Economy_briefing%20paper_WOS2015.pdf

The Library of Economics and Liberty. (n.d.). *Arthur Cecil Pigou.* Retrieved August 22, 2018 from http://www.econlib.org/library/Enc/bios/Pigou.html

UN. (2017, June). *Exploring the potential of the blue economy.* Retrieved August 22, 2018 from https://www.un.org/development/desa/en/news/sustainable/exploring-potential-of-blue-economy.html

Walker, P. (2017). *UK considers tax on single-use plastics to tackle ocean pollution.* Retrieved June 10, 2018 from https://www.theguardian.com/environment/2017/nov/18/uk-considers-tax-on-single-use-plastics-to-tackle-ocean-pollution

World Bank. (2017, June). *What is the blue economy?* Retrieved August 22, 2018 from http://www.worldbank.org/en/news/infographic/2017/06/06/blue-economy

World Bank Group & UN. (2017). *The potential of the blue economy.* Retrieved June 10, 2018 from, https://openknowledge.worldbank.org/bitstream/handle/10986/26843/115545.pdf?sequence=1&isAllowed=y

WWF. (n.d.). *Principles for a sustainable blue economy.* Retrieved August 10, 2018 from http://ocean.panda.org.s3.amazonaws.com/media/Principles+for+a+Blue+Economy+Brochure+LR.pdf

KEY TERMS AND DEFINITIONS

Blue Economy: Economic sectors directly or indirectly linked with the oceans.

Ecosystem: Interaction between living and non-living environment.

Externalities: The positive or negative effect (social costs or social benefits) arising from the production or consumption activity of a producer or consumer.

Ocean Economy: It is a part of the blue economy and it makes a significant contribution to the world economy with its developed and developing sectors and has a potential that needs to be grown.

Public Policies: Policies in which the state intervenes into the economy with various economic and social motives through the borrowing, taxes, and public expenditures.

Subsidies: Unreturned financial aids that the government make to support producers or consumer units.

Sustainable Blue Growth: Achieving growth with sustainable environment friendly policies to generate economic benefits from natural resources such as oceans, seas, costs that fall into the scope of blue economy.

Taxation: Taxation, a means of fiscal policy, is unreturned and state-based incomes for the financing of public expenditures or other economic/social/political goals.

User Fees: It is one of the economic instruments predominantly collected by the local governments, aiming at the elimination of environmental pollution, with the aim of generating income.

Chapter 6
Economic Impacts of Closed-Loop Supply Chains

Sibel Yıldız Çankaya
Bolu Abant Izzet Baysal University, Turkey

Bülent Sezen
Gebze Technical University, Turkey

ABSTRACT

Closed-loop supply chain management has begun to gain more importance in recent years due to increased environmental concerns, reduced natural resources, and legal regulations. In addition, with the shortening of product life cycles, the rate of returning products is increasing day by day. Therefore, businesses are trying to find ways to get more value from these returning products. Here, the closed-loop supply chain (CLSC), which comes into effect at this point, refers to the design, operation, and control of the system to ensure maximum value from returning products of different breeds and quantities. Recycling these returned products by different methods will provide significant savings in terms of both the production costs by providing return of the economically valuable materials to the economy as an input and the waste disposal costs by reducing the amount of waste. This chapter investigates the concept of closed-loop supply chain and its benefits to the businesses.

INTRODUCTION

With the tightening of environmental regulations, the increasing volume of waste, and the concentration of recycling of used products for the economy, the concept of a closed loop supply chain has begun to gain importance. Closed loop supply chain refers to the design, operation and control of the system to ensure maximum value from returning products of different breeds and quantities over time (Guide & Wassenhove, 2009). In short, this concept is expressed as systems in which forward and reverse supply chain structures work integrally (Talbot, Lefebvre, & Lefebvre, 2007; Guide, Jayaraman, & Linton, 2003a; Guide, Harrison, & Wassenhove, 2003b). Forward supply chain generally includes processes related to obtaining final products from raw materials and activities related to the delivery of these products to customers. Reverse supply chain includes the selection and implementation of the most appropriate

DOI: 10.4018/978-1-5225-8109-3.ch006

recycling (repair, reproduction, recycling) option or disposal methods by collecting products from the end user (Govindan, Soleimani, & Kannan, 2015).

In a closed-loop supply chain network that takes forward and reverse flows together, the raw materials, parts and components procured from the suppliers are processed at the production facilities to obtain new products and these products are delivered to the customers. If the products delivered to the customers are no longer able to fulfill their functions or if they are not required, they will be returned or discarded. In the later stages, for those products returned, the most appropriate recovery option is determined or these products are properly disposed of. With the products obtained after the recovery, the customer's demands are met again. The products which are decided to be disposed of are destroyed and leave this cycle between the producer and the customer. As a result, the two main tasks of a closed loop supply chain are: Creating processes that create value which meets the needs of the customer (as it used to be). The second task is to collect the scrap products from the customers and try to find the best way to evaluate these products (Govindan & Soleimani, 2017). However, it is no longer easy for manufacturers who routinely plan forward flow activities to plan reverse flow activities, including collection, recovery and disposal of used products. Because, by including reverse logistics activities in the system, the process becomes more complicated and some additional costs (e.g., acquiring, transporting, remanufacturing) arise (Kumar & Malegeant, 2006). One of the main problems that can be encountered in forward and reverse logistics (RL) is how to integrate these two different distributions (Fleischmann et al., 1997). There are some important differences between RL and forward logistics. The most important difference is, while in forward logistics the production and distribution of a new product is considered, in RL the post-stage distribution of products used in RL, such as sorting, inspection, recycling, recovery, etc. is considered. That is, producers need to integrate both production and reproduction activities using raw materials purchased from their suppliers and recovered items from returning products. The flow in the opposite direction is not as planned and regular as the forward flow due to uncertainties about the quality, quantity and timing of the returning product (Jindal & Sangwan, 2014). In addition, it is relatively difficult to transport, store, and handle products that are returned in the reverse flow. It is becoming increasingly difficult to apply reverse flow for certain product groups, especially non-durable products (Kumar & Malegeant, 2006). Due to these differences between RL and forward logistics, it is quite difficult for an organization to include RL operations into its existing logistics structure.

In addition to these difficulties, there are many benefits to returning used products to the market. It is known that a remanufactured product uses 20% less material and 16% less energy and releases only 35% of greenhouse gas emissions released during the process of producing a new product (Jindal & Sangwan, 2014). As can be seen, CLSC practices contribute to the combined development of the environment and the economy by reducing resource use and amount of waste. Many businesses, such as Hewlett-Packard and Kodak, have discovered that the collection of used products improves significantly their prestige as well as causes significant reductions in production costs (Zhang & Ren, 2016). However, many of the businesses are not aware of the benefits that the CLSC will provide them (Kumar & Malegeant, 2006). Therefore, in order for the use of CLSC to be widespread, it is necessary to discuss the benefits of this concept for the organization. With this in mind, it is aimed to examine the CLSC concept and its benefits in this study.

BACKGROUND

Forward Supply Chain and Reverse Supply Chain

Supply chain; is a network formed by producers and distributors who supply raw materials, convert these raw materials into intermediate goods and final products, and distribute final products to customers. In short, the supply chain focuses primarily on the movement of goods from the source to the final customer through the supply chain. Reverse supply chain takes the product from the end user to the starting point (Defee, Esper, & Mollenkopf, 2009).

The traditional supply chain, also called the forward supply chain, does not have any responsibility for end-of-life (EOL) products. But reverse supply chain or reverse logistics, tries to evaluate EOL products as environment friendly as possible (Govindan & Soleimani, 2017). Reverse supply chain management involves collecting from consumption points, inspecting, and adding value to these products to return to the economy that have been returned because of their completion of their lifetimes or returned due to poor quality, product recall, incorrect shipment and warranty / after-sales service.

Reverse supply chain begins by returning the products returned from the customers to a collection point. In the following stage, the collected products are examined, classified and separated. The most appropriate recovery option (repair, renewal, remanufacturing, recycling) is determined for these products or these products are destroyed. The products obtained after the recovery are delivered to the customer again, by including them in the forward supply chain process. The products that are decided to be disposed of are destroyed and leave this cycle between the producer and the customer (Kumar & Malegeant, 2006).

One of the five most important activities of the reverse supply chain is reverse logistics. Other activities can be listed as follows: It is collection, inspection / sorting, pre-processing and distribution network design (Srivastava, 2008). Similarly, Kumar and Malegeant (2006) also emphasize that phases of reverse supply chain (or closed loop) are; collection, inspection / separation, re-processing, disposal and re-distribution. Guide et al. (2003b) state the reverse supply chain phases as follows: Acquisition, reverse logistics, sorting, testing, disposition, remanufacturing and remarketing.

Reverse Logistics

Reverse logistics is often used to indicate recycling, waste disposal and hazardous waste management. When viewed from a broader perspective, it appears to include logistic activities during source reduction, recycling, material reuse and disposal (Jamshidi, 2011). Reverse Logistics European Working Group (Revlog) defined reverse logistics as a process involving the planning, implementation and control of transactions of raw materials, in-process inventories and final products from production, distribution and use points to the recovery or disposal point (Jamshidi, 2011). Similarly, in another definition, the concept of reverse logistics is described as the process of planning, implementing, and controlling the efficient flow of raw materials, work-in-process inventory, finished goods and all kinds of related information from the consumption point to the starting point for the purpose of recapturing value and/or proper disposal (Rogers & Tibben-Lembke, 1998). Dowlatshahi (2000), defined reverse logistics as the process of systematically accepting products or parts by the manufacturer sent from the point of consumption to recycle, reproduce, or dispose of. The common element in reverse logistics definitions is that a piece (like a used product, a scrap product, an out-of-fashion product) is moved to be evaluated from the end user to a place. But according to Reverse Logistics Association, reverse logistics should not be limited only by return transactions. This concept also includes repair, customer service, parts management, order fulfillment activities (Pinna & Carrus, 2012).

As can be seen, reverse logistics operations differ from forward logistics operations. One of the main problems that can be encountered in reverse logistics is how to integrate these two different distributions, namely forward and reverse logistics. The following questions should be answered in order to establish an effective distribution network (Fleischmann et al., 1997):

Who will be members of the reverse logistics channel?

Some of these members may be members in forward logistics, or they may be new members who perform RL specific tasks.

What functions should exist and should be performed on the reverse logistics channel?

The possible functions performed in reverse logistics are: collection, testing, sorting, moving and processing. A distribution network should be designed to determine in advance where these activities will be carried out.

What is the relationship between forward and reverse logistics channels?

Reverse logistics can also be performed directly on the original network through traditional intermediaries or specialist logistics providers. Even if the same actors are included in this process, problems may arise in the integration of these two distribution networks, since collection and delivery may require different processes.

COMPARISON OF FORWARD AND REVERSE LOGISTICS

Reverse logistics is not the symmetric of forward logistics. Reverse logistics involves more complex and different processes than forward logistics; it is therefore necessary to be more reactive (Srivastava, 2008). Risks and uncertainties in the reverse supply chain stem from the quantity, quality and timing of products returned from the customer to the producer (Srivastava, 2008). In RL, the amount of product returned and the return period is out of the control of the organization as the flow is initiated by the customer or by the lower-ranking members of the supply chain. So there is no standard time frame. For example; a toner cartridge can be used for an average of two months, a customer who uses the product frequently may change the cartridge once a week, or a customer who uses the product less frequently may replace the cartridge every six months. Also, the life cycle of each product is different. For example; the life span of a disposable camera is considerably shorter than that of a mobile phone. Therefore, all these uncertainties make forecasting, planning and inventory management more difficult in RL than in forward logistics (Guide et al., 2003a).

Krikke et al. (2001) stated that reverse supply chain is significantly different from forward logistics, and that these differences affect the process of designing the network. The authors stated that the following points should be considered in order to form an effective distribution network:

1. In addition to cost and service, the CLSC has environmental factors that make the goal function difficult.
2. In closed loop systems, the system complexity is greater due to both the increase in the number of parts flows and the increase in the relationships between flows. In these systems, uncertainties exist regarding the quality, quantity and timing of the returned product.

3. There is usually a mismatch between supply and demand.
4. In closed loop systems, there are a small number of customers against a large number of suppliers. Used products are the raw material for the reverse supply chain. Contrary to the forward chain, the raw material supply is excessive in these systems and the cost of the raw material is little or none. However, the value of the return flows is low.
5. Closed-loop systems have untapped market opportunities. Environmental requirements can lead to the creation of new markets or the reorganization of existing firms. By means of such a restructuring, the materials which are to come to an end as waste can be converted into useful products.

In Table 1, some features of forward and reverse logistics are given comparatively (Jamshidi, 2011).

As many authors have pointed out, in reverse logistics, planning is more difficult than forward logistics (e.g., Guide, Jayaraman, Srivastava, & Benton, 2000; Tibben-Lembke & Rogers, 2002), since uncertainty in logistics is evident. Because in reverse logistics it is not enough to estimate only the customer demand. At the same time, the usability/ availability of the product to be reproduced must also be estimated (Tibben-Lembke & Rogers, 2002).

The greatest difference between forward logistics and reverse logistics is due to the number of start and end points. In forward logistics, products move from a single starting point to many destination points. In reverse logistics, products move from a single point of arrival to many starting points (Tibben-Lembke & Rogers, 2002).

Another difference is due to the quality of product and packaging. Each new product from the dealer comes in a package that protects it during transport. New products that are transported in packages in a palette or a truck will not easily come out of the place and be damaged. These packages also enable the product to be easily transported and stacked at the same time. In reverse logistics, most of the products are not packaged. Some of the returned products, which are returned since they are not sold from

Table 1. Comparison of forward and reverse logistics

Forward Logistics	Reverse Logistics
Estimates are relatively obvious.	Estimates are more difficult.
Transport is from one point to multiple points.	Transport is from multiple point to one point.
Product quality, packaging and pricing are relatively standard.	Product quality and packaging are not standard. The price depends on many factors.
The place and route to which your product will be transferred is determined.	The place and route to which your product will be transferred is uncertain.
Channels are standard.	Channel is changeful.
The accounting system can be closely monitored for distribution costs.	It is often very difficult to measure reverse costs.
Product life cycle can be controlled.	It is more difficult to predict the product life cycle.
Transactions between the parties are obvious.	The operations are complex.
Concurrent information can be easily accessed to monitor the product.	Process monitoring is not very transparent.
Marketing methods are obvious.	Marketing activities are complex.
Inventory management is congruous.	Inventory management is not congruous.

Source: (Jamshidi, 2011)

retailers, are damaged during transport or while they wait on the shelf. On return from the customer, the product has already been unpacked for use. Often these products cannot be properly packaged later (Tibben-Lembke & Rogers, 2002). Even if the returned product is in a package, it is more difficult to transport this than to transport a new product. The new product, which travels to a certain target in large quantities, is transported using packages such as pallets, containers, etc., which minimize the space in the vehicle during transport and facilitate transportation. Besides, since the amount of the returned product is not as much as the amount of the new product going out, the packages (pallets, containers) that make the transportation easier cannot be used. This can cause the returning product to suffer further damage during transport (Tibben-Lembke & Rogers, 2002).

Flow monitoring in RL is more difficult compared to forward logistics. Because information systems of the most business systems are not designed to follow the returns. This makes it difficult to keep track of product arrivals, making even short-term operational plans difficult (Tibben-Lembke & Rogers, 2002).

Another difference is due to costs. In forward logistics, costs can be accurately determined. Accounting systems have been created to track the costs that will occur along the forward flow. There is no such thing as repackaging or renewing new products. In reverse logistics, products need to be processed in order to be able to operate again. Therefore, this renewed product will be sold at a much higher cost than the new product. However, it is worth noting that these additional costs will be less than the cost of producing a new product (Tibben-Lembke & Rogers, 2002). In reverse logistics, one of the most important costs is transport-related and higher than transport costs in forward logistics. The small amount of returned goods is a factor that increases the transportation costs. For example; a store might be picking up new products as much as a full truck every week, and then returning only one or two pallet of products at the same time period. This, in turn, increases the cost of transport (Tibben-Lembke & Rogers, 2002). In Table 2, RL costs and forward logistics costs are compared.

Most of the assumptions that apply to classical stock control methods cannot be applied in reverse logistics. The most important reason for not being able to apply is that the variables such as the amount of returned products, the selling price and the demand for these products are not fully known (Tibben-Lembke & Rogers, 2002). Finally, another difference that needs to be emphasized is the product pricing.

Table 2. Reverse logistics costs

Costs	Comparison With Forward Logistics Costs
Transport	Higher
Cost of stock	Lower
Shrinkage	Lower
Obsolescence	May be higher
Collection	Much higher – Less standardized
Classifying, quality identification	Much higher
Handling	Much higher
Refurbishing/Repackaging	Important for RL, non applicable for forward logistics
Change from book value	Important for RL, non applicable for forward logistics

Source: (Tibben-Lembke & Rogers, 2002)

The fact that product quality is not unique in RL, is also a factor that makes it difficult to price products (Tibben-Lembke & Rogers, 2002).

REASONS OF PRODUCT RETURN

The most common reasons for product return can be listed as errors, damage during transport, driving new model products to the market, replacing the product with another product, returning, repairing, recalling, and incorrect ordering (Min, Ko, & Ko, 2006).

However, the various reasons for return in the supply chain from the production stage to the delivery of the products to the customers can be grouped into three main groups as follows (Jamshidi, 2011):

- **Production Returns:** Production returns are the return of parts or products at the production stage. The returns at this stage can be classified as follows (Jamshidi, 2011).
    - Products with surplus raw materials
    - Quality control returns
    - Surplus products
    - Surplus raw materials and surplus products are shown in the category of products that are not needed; those who return from quality control are included in the category of faulty products (Pinna & Carrus, 2012).
- **Distribution Returns:** Returns that occur in distribution and whose reasons are listed as follows (Jamshidi, 2011):
    - Recalling the product; is collecting the product back due to security and health problems. It may be initiated by the supplier or manufacturer (Pinna & Carrus, 2012; Gencer & Akkucuk, 2016). This recall may be voluntary or it may be mandatory by law (Rogers, Lambert, Croxton, & Garcia-Dastugue, 2002).
    - Commercial returns; are inter-company returns due to damaged deliveries or non-sellable products.
    - Return of out-of-fashion products
    - Return of materials (e.g., pallets) used as carriers in the distribution of products
- **Customer Returns:** These returns occur for various reasons after the product reaches the consumer. These returns are as follows (Jamshidi, 2011):
    - Returns due to products' not meeting customer expectations
    - Returns in warranty period due to problems occurring during usage period
- **End-of-Use Returns:** End-of-use returns express the flow that occurs after the product has been used to remove the product from the hand. These products can also be sold in similar alternative markets such as those that can be reused in new products (e.g., Xerox's copiers). Some of the products in this category are in a position to be repaired and have high economic value (Krikke, Garcia-Dastugue, & van de Velde, 2004).
- **End-of-Life Returns:** These returns represent products that have completed their life span economically and physically.

- **Environmental Returns:** The reason for these returns is the destruction of hazardous substances or the regulation according to environmental legislation. Such returns are different from the other returns mentioned above because they are done in accordance with the legal restrictions. For example, the Environmental Protection Agency in the United States has banned computer monitors with lead since 1992 (Rogers et al., 2002).

CLOSED LOOP SUPPLY CHAIN

As mentioned earlier, reverse logistics is the process by which products are transported in order to re-value or dispose of them from where they were last used. This process includes activities such as remanufacturing and refurbishing. It also includes recycling programs, hazardous material programs, and activities for disposal of obsolete equipment. But reverse logistics does not include all activities involved in reflux management of the information in the supply chain and the material. If there is no returned goods or materials, we cannot talk about reverse logistics (Rogers et al., 2002).

Another concept that tries to define activities related to returned products is the closed loop supply chain management. Closed loop supply chain refers to the design, operation and control of the system to ensure maximum value from returning products of different breeds and quantities (Guide & Wassenhove, 2009). CLSC activities include reverse supply chain activities in addition to forward supply chain activities. These activities consist of the following steps (Guide et al., 2003b);

- Obtaining products from the end user
- Applying reverse logistics for the delivery of products from the point of use to the disposition point
- Testing and classifying to determine the current situation of the product and the reuse option
- Determination of the option that will provide the highest economic benefit such as direct reuse, repair, remanufacturing, recycling or disposal
- Performing remarketing and distribution of refurbished products.

In Figure 1, both forward supply chain processes (procurement, processing, assembly, distribution and procurement of raw materials) and reverse supply chain processes (repair, reconditioning, remanufacturing, recycling and disposal) are seen simultaneously (Khor & Udin, 2012).

As can be observed in Figure 1, in a closed loop supply chain network, which deals with forward and reverse flows, the raw materials, parts and components provided by the suppliers are processed in the production facilities to obtain new products and these products are transmitted to the customers. If the products delivered to the customer no longer fulfills their functions, or if they are not needed, they are either returned or disposed of. In the next stage, the most appropriate recovery option (repair, recondition, remanufacturing, recycling) is determined for these returned products or they are disposed of. Remanufactured products obtained after the recovery are marketed / distributed and delivered to the customer.

Recovery management involves the management of all used and / or discarded products, parts and materials. Product recovery aims to utilize as economically (and ecologically) as possible the amount of used products and to reduce the amount of waste (Thierry, Salomon, Nunen, Wasenhove, 1995; Sasikumar & Kanna, 2008). Product recovery is performed mainly due to three reasons: Legal regulations,

Figure 1. A general illustration of a closed-loop supply chains
Source: Khor & Udin, 2012

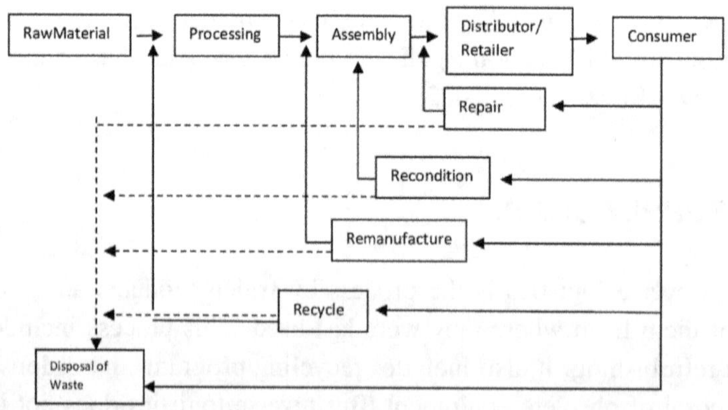

market requirements and the hidden economic value of solid waste (Sasikumar & Kanna, 2008). The following recovery procedures used for the used materials or the end-of-life materials are as follows:

- **Repair:** The goal here is to repair the returned product and include it back into the system. The quality of repaired products may be lower than the quality of new products (Kumar & Malegeant, 2006; Thierry et al., 1995). This stage involves the repair and / or replacement of broken parts. Other parts are not affected by this process. Repairs usually require only limited product disassembly and reassembly. These operations can be done either on site or at manufacturer-controlled repair centers. A large number of durable product manufacturers (e.g., IBM, DEC, and Philips) are performing repairs (Thierry et al., 1995).
- **Reuse:** Reuse refers to cases where returned products are of good quality to be used immediately on the same or an alternative market (Pinna & Carrus, 2012). In short, this practice indicates that the product is reused for a similar purpose with design purposes. Some products can be reused after cleaning or a small maintenance (Sasikumar & Kumar, 2008). Examples include bottles (Torres, Gil, Puente, Pomares, & Aracil, 2004), pallets and containers (Kroon & Vrijens, 1995). These products can be used again or sold to another customer.
- **Refurbishing/ Recondition:** This practice refers to operations carried out to raise the quality of the product used to a certain level. During the product renewal process, broken / damaged parts are replaced with new ones after they are separated from the product by the disassembly process. This process can also improve the quality and life of the product. Refurbishing can also involve activities to upgrade the technology by replacing outdated modules or components with technologically superior ones. Refurbishment on airplanes can be given as an example (Kumar & Malegeant, 2006; Thierry et al., 1995).
- **Remanufacturing:** The aim here is to tailor the used product to the quality standards applied for the new product. The used product is completely demounted and all modules / parts are checked. Broken or old parts and modules are replaced with new ones (Kumar & Malegeant, 2006). Remanufacturing can be combined with technological update. For example, a new machine can be obtained at a cost of 50% to 60% less by replacing a used piece of equipment with a new piece of equipment. Over the years BMW has been remanufacturing high-value parts such as engines,

starter motors and alternators. Remanufactured parts are being tested to stringent quality standards to become BMW replacement parts (Thierry et al., 1995).Remanufacturing centers require high-budget investments (Srivastava, 2008).

- **Cannibalization:** In other recovery options (remanufacturing, refurbishing, repair), most of the parts of the used products are reused. In cannibalization, only a small part of the product is reused. The aim here is to retrieve a limited set of available products or components. These parts are reused for repairs, refurbishment or remanufacturing of other products or components. Cannibalization processes require the separation of used parts and the testing of potentially reusable parts. The remaining parts or modules are not used. For example, Aurora, which is a US-based company, is dealing with cannibalizing of integrated circuits. The company receives, tests, repairs, and sells the parts it desires from used computers. The profits of the company between 1988 and 1993 exceeded $ 40 million (Thierry et al., 1995).
- **Recycling:** It refers to the use of various separation methods to obtain materials from used products and the evaluation of these materials for the production of original products (Kumar & Malegeant, 2006). The purpose in other product recovery options is to protect the functions and features of used products and components as much as possible. In recycling, the features and functions of the products and components are lost. The purpose of recycling is to reuse the materials in used products and parts. If these materials are of high quality, they can be involved in the production of original parts. The recycling starts with the separation of used products and parts. These pieces are then divided into different material classes. These separated materials are then used in the production of new parts. In countries such as Germany, the United Kingdom and the United States, almost all metals in cars discarded are subjected to recycling. Recycling is applied to a wide variety and large number of used products. Paper, glass, plastic products are some of the products that are widely recycled (Fleischman et al., 1997; Modak, Modak, Panda, & Sana, 2018).

The choice of recovery method varied depending on the technical feasibility, the availability of used products and components through suitable methods, the existence of demand for recycled products / components / materials, and the benefits that can be gained and costs involved (Thierry et al., 1995).

The different qualities of the product recovery options and the main differences between them are shown in the Table 3 (Thierry et al., 1995).

Kumar and Malegeant (2006) emphasized that reverse (or closed loop) supply chain stages are; collection, inspection / separation, re-processing, disposal and redistribution.

1. Collection

The collection activity is the physical transfer of used products from one location to another for processing. Collection operations include; product acquisition, transportation and storage (Kumar & Malegeant, 2006). Collection of used carpets from carpet sellers and used copiers from customers is an example for this stage (Fleischmann et al., 2000).The used product can be collected either directly from the customer or through retailer or third party logistics companies (Kumar & Putnam, 2008).

Collection constitutes a significant part of the total cost of any closed loop supply chain. Businesses can follow three methods to get over this highly costly phase. First of all, some costly transactions can be shifted to the consumer. That is, businesses can create waste collection points at various locations instead of collecting products from customers. Consumers can thus dump these at collection points.

Table 3. Comparison of recovery options

	Level of Disassembly	Quality Requirements	Resulting Product
Repair	To product level	Restore product to working order	Some parts are repaired or replaced with spare parts.
Refurbishing	To module level	All critical modules are tested and updated at the specified quality level.	Some modules are repaired / replaced and updated
Remanufacturing	To part level	All modules and parts are tested and updated to the new product quality level.	Used and new module / parts are included in the new product and updated
Cannibalization	Selective retrieval of parts.	It depends on the process in which the parts will be re-used.	Some parts are used again, the remaining product is recycled or discarded
Recycling	To material level	It is high for the production of original parts, and low for other parts.	The materials are used again to produce new parts.

Source: (Thierry et al., 1995)

An example is waste glass and paper collection boxes. This strategy requires additional storage space while reducing transportation costs. In addition, this method is limited to small and low value consumer products. The other method is to create a synergy by combining distribution and collection channels. The most typical examples that can be given for this are; "bring old- take new" campaigns with the collection of refillable bottles of beverages. The last method is to mail some products (such as blank print cartridges and reusable cameras) (Kumar & Malegeant, 2006).

Another method that can be used to collect used products is to establish a strategic business partnership between the manufacturer and eco-non-profit organizations. With this method, the business can have a green image, increase its profits and transfer the collection activity to external sources and focus on its own business/ skills (Kumar & Malegeant, 2006).

2. Inspection/Separation

It is the phase in which various recovery and disposal processes are performed. It is decided whether the products used in the process will be reused or not, and if so, what treatment will be performed (Kumar & Malegeant, 2006; Fleischmann et al., 2000). For example, photocopy machines can be divided into subgroups as "repair" or "recycle" (Sasikumar & Kannan, 2008). Testing, disassembly, shredding, sorting, storage processes are performed at this stage (Kumar & Malegeant, 2006; Fleischmann et al., 2000).

3. Re-Processing

It includes some operations in which the products that can be reused are made reusable by applying some processes. Depending on the appropriate recovery option, activities such as disassembly, shredding, replacement and repair are also included (Kumar & Malegant, 2006).

4. Disposal

It consists of applications for the disposal of products which cannot be reused due to technical or economic reasons. For example, products that do not have market potential since they require excessive repair and / or finished life spans are disposed by appropriate methods Transportation, landfill and incineration can be performed at this stage (Fleischmann et al., 2000).

5. Re-Distribution and Selling

It is the process of transporting reusable products to new markets to reach potential new users. This phase includes selling, transportation and storage activities (Kumar & Malegant, 2006).

This process can be carried out together with distribution and sales activities carried out in the forward chain. But in this process additional marketing efforts may be needed to convince the customer of the quality of the product. Therefore, for these products, it may be necessary to establish separate channels and to develop new markets (Krikke et al., 2004).

ADVANTAGES AND BENEFITS OF CLOSED LOOP SUPPLY CHAIN

Well-managed closed-loop supply chain operations do not only save costs, but they also make it easier to retain customers (Srivastava, 2008). Moreover, since reverse logistics practices are more complex and difficult than forward logistics practices, successful businesses who overcome these difficulties will gain a competitive advantage that cannot easily be imitated by their rivals (Srivastava, 2008).

Closed loop supply chain not only provides environmental and economic benefits, but also leads to new opportunities / new market areas for businesses. Kumar and Malegeant (2006) expressed the benefits and opportunities provided by the CLSC as follows (Kumar & Malegeant, 2006).

- Service/Market
  - Customer satisfaction increases
  - Research and development time is reduced
  - Availability of replacement parts increases
  - Early feedbacks allow the desired improvements to be made on time
  - Product quality is improved through re-engineering
  - Proactive repairs are possible
  - Green image increases
- Opportunities for Value Creation
  - Reduced liability risk
  - Reuse of materials and components is increased
  - Disposal costs are reduced
  - Reduced risk of aging due to timely returns
  - Spare part production is reduced

Businesses can use CLSC applications to recover parts and components that are available on return. Thus, these recycled products can be reused in new products. For example, Xerox is saving hundreds of millions of dollars a year by repairing, cleaning, and recycling returning copiers (Toffel, 2004).

- Environment / Safety
    - Environmental effects caused by the organization are reduced
    - Legal compliance rate increases

The management of returning products attracts the attention of producers because of the economic benefits they provide. Two other important reasons for producers to deal with this issue are: legislative regulations and change in the consumer's view of environmental issues (Talbot et al., 2007). In recent years, new environmental laws in Europe and Asia have taken the principle of expanding the responsibility of producers (Krikke et al., 2004). According to these legal regulations, companies are obliged to recover their products and dispose of them properly. For example, the European Directive on Waste Electrical and Electronic Equipment (WEEE) addresses issues such as recycling rates, level of recycled content, and take-back percentages (Talbot et al., 2007).

Faulty products are recalled more reliably

The economic impact of a closed loop supply chain can be examined under two headings: Direct benefits and indirect benefits

Direct Benefits

Remanufacturing and marketing of used products does not only benefit the environment and customers, but also reduces production costs (Jindal & Sangwan, 2014). Waste recovery will provide significant savings in both the production costs by providing return of the economically valuable materials to the economy as an input and the waste disposal costs by reducing the amount of waste. In recent years, the cost of disposing of the product has been significantly increased with the depletion of storage and burning capacities (Thierry et al., 1995). In short, CLSC can provide direct benefits to businesses by reducing raw material, energy and disposal costs (Rogers & Tibben-Lembke, 2001; De Brito & Dekker, 2003). The recovery of the returning product seems to save about 40-60% of the cost compared to normal production. It is known that a remanufactured product uses 20% less material and 16% less energy and releases only 35% of greenhouse gas emissions released during the process of producing a new product (Jindal & Sangwan, 2014). For example, Dell implemented a take-back program in 2014 to recycle 10% of the plastics used in the production process. This recycled plastic was then used in new computers to reduce the operator's need for raw materials (Kazemi, Modak, & Govindan, 2018). Another example is Kodak's single-use camera program. In 1990, Kodak configured this program to facilitate the reuse of parts and components. This closed-loop structure that Kodak has built consists of two phases. In the first stage, there are new designs that facilitate the reuse of parts and components. Thus, the reuse rate per camera is planned to be between 77 and 80 percent. In the second phase, agreements were signed with the photofinishers to return used cameras to Kodak. Through these practices, Kodak has reported that the rate of return was the United States is higher than 70 percent and around the world was about 60 percent (Guide et al., 2003a). Another example is the establishment of an organization called Auto Recycling Nederland by the Dutch automotive industry in 1995 (ARN), which was responsible for the recycling of end-of life vehicles. Car owners can return their vehicles to this organization regardless of their brand (Talbot et al., 2007). In 2016, ARN succeeded in recycling more than 90% of car content (ARN, 2018), Similarly, in 1991, Xerox set out a program to achieve a waste-free structure. Thanks to this program, the company saved over $ 76 million in 1999. In addition, the reuse of parts has also reduced the use of raw materials and energy to produce new parts (Guide et al., 2003a).

Thanks to the reverse chain it had established for valuable and critical Printed Wiring Assemblies, Honeywell recycled about 500 parts each year and had repaired two thirds of them. The company's total reverse chain cost is about 360 Euros per product, while the re-use value is 700 Euros (Krikke et al., 2004).

Indirect Benefits

The CLSC is in the triggering position in improving the market conditions of the companies. Management activities for the return of products improve customer loyalty, increase the profit of the company and improve the corporate image (Rogers et al., 2002). Customers are becoming more conscious every day and becoming more sensitive about the environment. Therefore, "environmentalist" image shows itself as an important marketing tool for businesses. Businesses can attract environmentally conscious customers and employees by offering green products (Thierry et al., 1995). In a survey, it was researched how various management practices influenced customers' purchase intentions and it was found out that environmental factors (such as increasing the use of recyclable materials) had the greatest positive effect on purchasing intentions (Toffel, 2004). For example, after customers reported concerns about the waste caused by Kodak's disposable cameras, Kodak initiated a take-back program that returned more than 90% of these cameras. Thus, the firm had succeeded in reversing the poor environmental image of the product. Similarly, IBM Europe and Xerox companies have indicated that their recovery activities strengthened their brand images. In fact, such gains are based on improvements in environmental performance. For example, remanufactured photocopiers consume 20-70% less material, water and energy and produce 35-50% less waste than traditional production (Toffel, 2004).

Similarly, return policies can also increase customer loyalty by reducing the risk for the customer. If a buyer knows that he can easily return the product, he or she will be more likely to buy a new product (Rogers et al., 2002). Especially in e-commerce, the likelihood of goods being returned is higher than in normal commerce. For this reason, establishing an effective return and return policy system for companies that implement e-commerce is extra important. This system, which the company has established, will be able to increase both customer satisfaction and competitive advantage.

Another impact of CLSC activities is to facilitate compliance with the new legislation in the future. Companies that are pro-active in the environment can influence the formation of new legislation and may be prepared for new laws in advance. (Thierry et al., 1995). Some companies are also trying to reduce the pressure that new laws will create by improving their environmental performance or by putting more stringent environmental requirements on their supply chain members. For example, in the middle of the 1980s, after accidents at some chemical plants, the chemical industry has initiated the Responsible Care program to reduce pressures about additional environmental regulations. This approach was followed by several voluntary take-back programs. For example, some electrical appliance manufacturers in Germany have decided to voluntarily purchase EOL products from customers (Toffel, 2004).

From a competitive standpoint, the company can prevent its competitors from imitating themselves or entering the market, thanks to effective recovery policies. One of IBM's reasons for recycling is the desire to prevent its products from being handed over to intermediaries (Pinna & Carrus, 2012). Similarly, Ford and Mercedes' close ties to the EOL vehicles can be seen as a strategy to prevent spare parts from falling into the hands of their competitors. Lexmark also offers discounts to customers who agree to return their print cartridges for remanufacture. In addition, the company forbade to its customers the sale of its cartridges to other businesses that would refill, reuse, or reproduce their cartridges, in accordance with the sales conditions that it established. The company states that the print quality is low when using the cartridges of other companies in its product, and that Lexmark's printers are accused by customers. That is why the firm is trying to preserve its brand image by creating a sales condition in this way. According to Lexmark, this application increased cartridge return rates. Similarly, Hewlett-Packard wants customers to return their used cartridges (Toffel, 2004).

Another reason for the implementation of RL by businesses is the development of supplier or customer relationships. For this application, the example of a car tire manufacturer extending the life cycle of the tire by offering new threading options for the tires that the customers have used, to reduce their costs can be given (Pinna & Carrus, 2012).

Finally, the economic effects of a closed-loop supply chain can be summarized as follows (Pinna & Carrus, 2012).

- Direct Benefits
- Input Materials
- Cost Reduction
- Value Added Recovery
- Indirect Benefits
- Anticipating/Impeding Legislation
- Market Protection
- Green Image
- Improved Customer/Supplier Relations

CONCLUSION

Closed loop supply chain management has begun to gain more importance in recent years due to increased environmental concerns, reduced natural resources and legal regulations. This concept is described as a system in which forward and reverse supply chain structures operate in an integrated manner (Talbot et al., 2007; Guide et al., 2003a; Guide et al., 2003b). In many industries, original equipment manufacturers (OEMs) are trying to integrate reverse logistics activities into their supply chains, seeking efficient ways to economize on returned products and reduce waste costs. For these reasons, it is very important for the used products to be collected from the customers and to add those that are qualified enough into the system for re-use. A large majority of unused, end-of-life or consumer-dissatisfying products and materials still have a value. These materials are in the form of waste, but they can become reusable by processes such as refurbishment, recycling, reuse, reproduction. Waste recovery will provide significant savings in both the production costs by providing return of the economically valuable materials to the economy as an input and the waste disposal costs by reducing the amount of waste. In short, CLSC can provide direct benefits to businesses by reducing raw material, energy and disposal costs (Rogers & Tibben-Lembke, 2001; De Brito, & Dekker, 2003). CLSC provides direct economic benefits to businesses in many respects as well as providing economic benefits from indirect ways such as improving the image of the business, preparing for new legislation in advance, or providing competitive advantage.

Another important cause of CLSC is its assistance in the reduction of environmental pollution and the protection of scarce natural resources. Used products that still have a value; they are stacked in garbage dumps, burned or buried in soil and disposed of, which causes environmental pollution. However, product recycling activities that are carried out effectively can reduce both the environmental pollution and the waste disposal costs, since it reduces the amount of waste. CLSC are particularly attractive in industrialized countries due to the depletion of landfills and increased emissions of harmful gases as a result of the proliferation of waste volumes (Talbot, 2007). In England, for example, 275,000 tons of plastic is used every year. Recycling of each toned plastic reduces energy use by 84% and greenhouse gas emissions by 71% (Modak et al., 2018). As a result, in addition to the direct and indirect gains that the closed-loop supply chain provides to the operations, there is also a significant contribution to the protection of the environment.

REFERENCES

Auto Recycing Nederland. (2018). Retrieved July 2, 2018, from https://arn.nl/en/over-arn/

De Brito, M. P., & Dekker, R. (2003). *A Framework for Reverse Logistics*. Retrieved July 18, 2018, from https://repub.eur.nl/pub/354/ERS-2003-045-LIS.pdf

Defee, C. C., Esper, T., & Mollenkopf, D. (2009). Leveraging closed-loop orientation and leadership for environmental sustainaibility. *Supply Chain Management*, *14*(2), 87–98. doi:10.1108/13598540910941957

Dowlatshahi, S. (2000). Developing a theory of reverse logistics. *Interfaces*, *30*(3), 143–155. doi:10.1287/inte.30.3.143.11670

Fleischmann, M., Bloemhof-Ruwaard, J. M., Dekker, R., Van Der Laan, E., Van Nunen, J. A., & Van Wassenhove, L. N. (1997). *Quantitative models for reverse Logistics: A review* (pp. 1–21). Fontainebleau, France: INSEAD.

Fleischmann, M., Krikke, H. R., Dekker, R., & Flapper, S. D. P. (2000). A characterisation of logistics networks for product recovery. *Omega*, *28*(6), 653–666. doi:10.1016/S0305-0483(00)00022-0

Gencer, Y. G., & Akkucuk, U. (2016). Reverse Logistics: Automobile Recalls and Other Conditions. In U. Akkucuk (Ed.), *Handbook of Research on Waste Management Techniques for Sustainability* (pp. 125–154). IGI Global. doi:10.4018/978-1-4666-9723-2.ch007

Govindan, K., & Soleimani, H. (2017). A review of reverse logistics and closed-loop supply chains: A Journal of Cleaner Production focus. *Journal of Cleaner Production*, *142*, 371–384. doi:10.1016/j.jclepro.2016.03.126

Govindan, K., Soleimani, H., & Kannan, D. (2015). Reverse logistics and closed-loop supply chain: A comprehensive review to explore the future. *European Journal of Operational Research*, *240*(3), 603–626. doi:10.1016/j.ejor.2014.07.012

Guide, V. D. R., Harrison, T. P., & Wassenhove, L. (2003b). The challenge of closed-loop supply chains. *Interfaces*, *33*(6), 3–6. doi:10.1287/inte.33.6.3.25182

Guide, V. D. R., Jayaraman, V., & Linton, J. (2003a). Building contingency planning for closed-loop supply chains with product recovery. *Journal of Operations Management*, *21*(3), 259–279. doi:10.1016/S0272-6963(02)00110-9

Guide, V. D. R. Jr, Jayaraman, V., Srivastava, R., & Benton, W. C. (2000). Supply-chain management for recoverable manufacturing systems. *Interfaces, 30*(3), 125–142. doi:10.1287/inte.30.3.125.11656

Guide, V. D. R. Jr, & Van Wassenhove, L. N. (2009). The evolution of closed-loop supply chain research. *Operations Research, 57*(1), 10–18. doi:10.1287/opre.1080.0628

Jamshidi, M. (2011). Reverse Logistics. In R. Z. Farahani, S. Rezapour, & L. Karder (Eds.), *Logistics Operations and management: Concepts and Models* (pp. 247–256). Elsevier. doi:10.1016/B978-0-12-385202-1.00013-X

Jindal, A., & Sangwan, K. S. (2014). Closed loop supply chain network design and optimisation using fuzzy mixed integer linear programming model. *International Journal of Production Research, 52*(14), 4156–4173. doi:10.1080/00207543.2013.861948

Kazemi, N., Modak, N. M., & Govindan, K. (2018). A review of reverse logistics and closed loop supply chain management studies published in IJPR: A bibliometric and content analysis. *International Journal of Production Research*, 1–24. doi:10.1080/00207543.2018.1471244

Khor, K.S., & Udin, Z.M. (2012). Impact of reverse logistics product disposition towards business performance in Malaysian E&E companies. *Journal of Supply Chain and Customer Relationship Management*. doi:10.5171/2012.699469

Krikke, H., Blanc, L., & van de Velde, S. (2004). Product modularity and the design of closed-loop supply chains. *California Management Review, 46*(2), 23–39. doi:10.2307/41166208

Krikke, H.R., Tsoulfas, G., Pappis, C., & Bloemhof-Ruwaard, J. (2001). *Design principles for closed loop supply chains:Optimizing economic, logistic and environmental performance.* Erasmus Research Institute of Management (ERIM).

Kroon, L., & Vrijens, G. (1995). Returnable containers: An example of reverse logistics. *International Journal of Physical Distribution & Logistics Management, 25*(2), 56–68. doi:10.1108/09600039510083934

Kumar, S., & Malegeant, P. (2006). Strategic alliance in a closed-loop supply Chain, a case of manufacturer and Eco-Non-Profit Organization. *Technovation, 26*(10), 1127–1135. doi:10.1016/j.technovation.2005.08.002

Kumar, S., & Putnam, V. (2008). Cradle to cradle: Reverse logistics strategies and opportunities across three industry sectors. *International Journal of Production Economics, 115*(2), 305–315. doi:10.1016/j.ijpe.2007.11.015

Min, H., Ko, H. J., & Ko, C. S. (2006). A genetic algorithm approach to developing the multi-echelon reverse logistics network for product returns. *Omega, 34*(1), 56–69. doi:10.1016/j.omega.2004.07.025

Modak, N. M., Modak, N., Panda, S., & Sana, S. S. (2018). Analyzing structure of two-echelon closed-loop supply chain for pricing, quality and recycling management. *Journal of Cleaner Production, 171*, 512–528. doi:10.1016/j.jclepro.2017.10.033

Pinna, R., & Carrus, P. P. (2012). Reverse Logistics and the Role of Fourth Party Logistics Provider. In A. Groznik (Ed.), Path ways to Supply Chain Excellence (pp. 90-114). In Tech.

Rogers, D., & Tibben-Lembke, R. S. (1999). *Going Backwards: Reverse logistics Trends and practices*. Pittsburgh, PA: RLEC Press.

Rogers, D. S., Lambert, D. M., Croxton, K. L., & Garcia-Dastugue, S. (2002). The Returns management process. *International Journal of Logistics Management*, *13*(2), 1–18. doi:10.1108/09574090210806397

Rogers, D. S., & Tibben-Lembke, R. S. (2001). An examination of reverse logistics practices. *Journal of Business Logistics*, *22*(2), 29–148. doi:10.1002/j.2158-1592.2001.tb00007.x

Sasikumar, P., & Kannan, G. (2008). Issues in reverse supply chains, part I: End-of-life product recovery and inventory management-an overview. *International Journal of Sustainable Engineering*, *1*(3), 154–172. doi:10.1080/19397030802433860

Srivastava, S. K. (2008). Network design for reverse logistics. *Omega*, *36*(4), 535–548. doi:10.1016/j.omega.2006.11.012

Talbot, S., Lefebvre, E., & Lefebvre, L.-A. (2007). Closed-loop supply chain activities and derived benefits in manufacturing SMEs. *Journal of Manufacturing Technology Management*, *18*(6), 627–658. doi:10.1108/17410380710763831

Thierry, M., Salomon, M., Nunen, V. J., & Wasenhove, L. V. (1995). Strategic issues in product recovery management. *California Management Review*, *37*(2), 114–135. doi:10.2307/41165792

Tibben-Lembke, R. S., & Rogers, D. S. (2002). Differences between forward and reverse logistics in a retail environment. *Supply Chain Management*, *7*(5), 271–282. doi:10.1108/13598540210447719

Toffel, M. W. (2004). Strategic management of product recovery. *California Management Review*, *46*(2), 120–141. doi:10.2307/41166214

Torres, F., Gil, P., Puente, S. T., Pomares, J., & Aracil, R. (2004). Automatic PC disassembly for component recovery. *International Journal of Advanced Manufacturing Technology*, *23*(1-2), 39–46. doi:10.100700170-003-1590-5

Zhang, C. T., & Ren, M. L. (2006). Closed-loop supply chain coordination strategy for the remanufacture of patented products under competitive demand. *Applied Mathematical Modelling*, *40*(13-14), 6243–6255. doi:10.1016/j.apm.2016.02.006

KEY TERMS AND DEFINITIONS

Cannibalization: Cannibalization is the retrieval of a limited set of available products or components from the used product or component.

Closed-Loop Supply Chain: CLSC refers to the design, operation, and control of the system to ensure maximum value from returning products of different breeds and quantities.

Recycling: Recycling refers to the use of a variety of separation methods to obtain materials from used products and the use of these materials for the production of original products.

Refurbishing: Refurbishing are the processes of upgrading the quality of the used product to a certain level.

Remanufacturing: Remanufacturing is to make the used product conform to the quality standards applied for the new product.

Reverse Logistics: RL is a process that includes moving used goods from the last user back to producer.

Supply Chain: The supply chain is a network that procures raw materials, converts these raw materials into intermediate goods and final products, and distributes final products to customers.

Chapter 7
Influence of the EU Circular Economy Action Plan on Turkey's Energy Policy and Investments in Renewables

Esin Okay
Istanbul Commerce University, Turkey

ABSTRACT

The European Union Circular Economy Action Plan is a new enactment but rapidly growing to transform EU economies into more sustainable sources and surroundings adopting measures that include renewable energy investments and low carbon strategy. As the world still faces huge environmental changes and climate problems, energy remains the major issue for both economic and ecological sustainability. Low carbon energy strategy is the main target for EU circular economy enforcing renewable energy sources which are healthy, clean, and cheap. In this chapter, circular energy act and its development in Turkey are explored and questioned. The study emphasizes the great potential of renewables in Turkey and shows that there is still much to be done to transform the energy market in order to adopt circular economy in the future. Barriers of economic risks and lack of cultural awareness strongly challenge the progress of Turkey in energy solutions. And more than that, those problems trigger the financial concerns limiting the future energy projects.

INTRODUCTION

The growing concerns in EU led to many environmental legislations and programmes since the start of the millenium. The latest one binding the economy and energy within the scope of low-carbon world is the EU Circular Economy. In December 2015 the European Commission published its Circular Economy Package that will enhance the strategy to protect environment.

DOI: 10.4018/978-1-5225-8109-3.ch007

The European Commission adopted an ambitious Circular Economy Package, which includes measures that will help stimulate Europe's transition towards a circular economy, boost global competitiveness, foster sustainable economic growth and generate new jobs. The Circular Economy Package consists of an EU Action Plan for the Circular Economy that establishes a concrete and ambitious programme of action, with measures covering the whole cycle: from production and consumption to waste management and the market for secondary raw materials and a revised legislative proposal on waste (EU, 2018a).

Regarding energy, measures aiming at promoting circular economy and using resources in a more efficient way also contribute to reducing energy demand: this is in particular the case when products are re-used, materials recycled, when all production and consumption chains are organised in a more efficient way (EU, 2018b). Energy is a hot issue central to social and economic well-being. For instance, it is assumed that more than 1 billion people have no access to electricity. Unfortunately, energy is the dominant contributor to climate change (Okay, 2018).

Circular Economy aims to scale up low-carbon and efficiency solutions that will fulfill the Paris Agreement and the Sustainable Development Goals (SDGs). It is a crucial act for policies that are consistent with ambitious plans on climate and enable business-led solutions to scale up and speed up the implementation of the Paris Agreement. Combating climate change and transforming the energy system are core challenges on the path to a sustainable future. The system planned to facilitate cutting-edge climate and energy solutions and worked with business, government and society to address critical climate and industry issues are for building a sustainable world. (World Business Council for Sustaibale Development, 2018)

Acting according to the United Nations Framework Convention on Climate Change and mainly the Kyoto Protocol, cities benefit from becoming smart cities through energy service company (ESCO) model (Okay, Akman, Okay, 2008) as energy consumption decrease to a great extent but creating a safer and more comfortable environment for the people (Andretta, 2014). The integrated goals of energy security and poverty alleviation are inextricably linked with the need to reduce harmful air pollution and address climate change (Okay, 2016).

Under the programme that was put into action in 2012 to diagnose Green Economy In Action (United Nations 2012) United Nations is leading a forum with the World Bank named as Sustainable Energy for All. The three objectives of the Forum firstly announced in 2015, are for improving energy efficiency that has the clearest impact on *saving money*, especially buildings that require less energy to heat and cool improving business results, and delivering more services for consumers that cost the same but use less energy (Sustainable Energy for All, 2017).

Furthermore, natural sources of energy in creative ways (solar, wind, hydro, biomass, biofuel and geothermal) is cheap and clean for protecting environment and acquiring sustainable clean cities. In the last decade, energy shortages grew fast as global demand increases enormously (Renewable Energy Policy Network for 21st Century, 2017). Understanding the benefits of natural energy sources, countries are forced to work on legislature to provide incentives for renewable energy. The cost of renewable energy derived from nature is decreasing continuously as countries ambitiously adopted national strategic targets like providing energy efficiency enhanced (Okay, 2016) by the implementations of ESCOs all around the World (Okay, Akman, Okay, 2008).

At the same time, the World Health Organization (WHO) declared key facts about air pollution which is associated with unhealthy practices. According to WHO, over 4 million people die prematurely from illness attributable to the air pollution, more than 50% of premature deaths among children under 5 are due to pneumonia caused by particulate matter (soot) inhaled from air pollution and 3.8 million premature deaths annually from noncommunicable diseases including stroke, ischaemic heart disease, chronic obstructive pulmonary disease and lung cancer are attributed to exposure to air pollution (World Health Organization, 2014).

This study has four main objectives. The first objective is to emphasize the global concerns and the going on so far about the world economy and energy problems. The second section is to explore and point out the importance of circular economy, and low- carbon energy solutions with renewable energy sources protecting ecology and lowering costs. In this context, EU's circular economy package and energy strategy are presented as the reference point of the paper. The third part is to extend the circular economy and circular energy act in Turkey. The next objective of the chapter focuses on the challenges regarding energy and financial problems in the middle of an emerging economic crise in Turkey aside the high potential of renewables. The study concludes with the recommendations for a revision of both economic and energy strategy in Turkey, whilst an adoption of circular economy programme that may provide a blood exchange giving a rise to the economy.

BACKGROUND

Energy and Global Concerns

In 1992, at the Rio Earth Summit 184 countries pronounced their commitment to sustainable development, i.e. 'to meet the needs of the present without compromising the ability of future generations to meet their own needs' (Okay, 2018). Many countries are already adopting efficient energy technologies and practices since United Nations Framework Convention on Climate Change entered into force on 21 March 1994 (United Nations, 2017).

Between 1990 and 2006, increased energy efficiency in the manufacturing sectors of 21 member countries of the International Energy Agency resulted in a 21% reduction of energy use per unit of output. Sharing and adopting these practices more widely among nations and industrial sectors can make energy more reliable and less expensive to homes and businesses. The opportunities are greater still:

- Economic growth
- New markets
- Sustainable and equitable development
- A cleaner planet. These are within the world's reach by 2030. Those who act now to improve energy efficiency are creating the future we want (Sustainable Energy for All, 2014).

Next, in 1994, United Nations Framework Convention on Climate Change was taken into account which is an international agreement named as "Kyoto Protocol" was adopted in Kyoto, Japan, on 11 December 1997 and entered into force on 16 February 2005 recognized by 194 countries (+ the EU) as of 2017. In Doha, Qatar, on 8 December 2012, the "Doha Amendment to the Kyoto Protocol" was adopted (United Nations, 2017).

At the same time, United Nations carries Sustainable Energy for All Forums. The Sustainable Energy for All Forum plays a core role in putting universal access to modern energy services at the heart of the Sustainable Development Goals and Paris Agreement. In September 2015, the world's leaders came together to agree on 17 SDGs. In 2015 (Paris Climate Conference), 195 nations negotiated an historic climate agreement—one that declared that not only do we need to hold the increase in the global average temperature to "well below 2°C above pre-industrial levels" but we also need to pursue efforts to limit the increase to 1.5°C (United Nations Sustainable Energy for All Forum, 2017).

As of July 2017, 79 states have accepted the Doha amendment that offers three market based mechanisms additional to the Kyoto Protocol. But the Doha amendment has not entered into force. The amendment includes:

- New commitments for Annex I Parties to the Kyoto Protocol who agreed to take on commitments in a second commitment period from 1 January 2013 to 31 December 2020
- A revised list of greenhouse gases (GHG) to be reported on by Parties in the second commitment period; and
- Amendments to several articles of the Kyoto Protocol which specifically referenced issues pertaining to the first commitment period and which needed to be updated for the second commitment period.

The last Forum took place in Lisbon, Portugal from May 2 – 3, 2018. The Forum examined the latest data on progress — or lack of — in achieving Sustainable Development Goal 7 (SDG7) goals from the 3rd forum in 2017. Under the Forum theme "Leaving No One Behind", countries came together to enhance the progress towards achieving universal access to modern energy services, doubling renewable energy and improving energy efficiency by 2030 (United Nations Sustainable Energy for All Forum, 2018).

There is an increasing understanding to low crbon investments for developing green economy and smart cities. According to British Petrolium (BP) it is projected that by 2035 global energy consumption increases by 37% from today's levels with virtually all (96%) the growth in non-OECD countries and more than half coming from India and China. Renewables account for 40% of the growth in power generation, causing their share of global power to increase from 7% in 2015 to nearly 20% by 2035. The European Union (EU) continues to lead the way in terms of the penetration of renewables, with the share of renewables within the EU power sector doubling over the Outlook to reach almost 40% by 2035 (BP, 2015).

The huge need of energy and the rise of the global awakening in low carbon economies push countries economies towards renewable energy solutions. For instance, EU has set the target of making the transition to a competitive low-carbon economy within the next 40 years. This means that the EU needs to reduce its domestic emissions by at least 80% by 2050 compared to 1990. With the urban proportion of the world's population forecast to increase to 70% by 2050, cities will have to make a substantial contribution to achieving this ambitious goal (Okay, 2018). Maybe, the world needs to change the model of sustainability with the help of a new one named as the circular economy. In the near future, it should be tested somehow especially by the green economies.

Circular Economy

The world economy is up to heavy struggle with never ending financial burdens and demands only to end up with ecological risks. Therefore, global authorities do never stop searching and making strategies for ways to provide sustainable development in the world. There is growing optimism about the potential of the circular economy as a new model for sustainable growth in developing countries. The latest effort to solve sustainability development (Geissdoerfer, Savaget, Bocken, Hultink, 2017) seems to be pertained by circular economy model.

The concept of circular economy has been first raised by two British environmental economists Pearce and Turner (1990). In their book "Economics of Natural Resources and the Environment", they pointed that traditional economy was developed with no in-build tendency to recycle and it treated environment as a reservoir of wastes (Su, Heshmati, Geng, 2013). A circular economy model is one in which products are recycled, repaired or reused rather than thrown away, and in which waste from one process becomes an input into other processes (Preston, Lehne, 2017). Circular economy can be defined as a system designed to be restorative and regenerative (Charonis 2012).

The starting point of circular economy's implementation is in Germany 1996, accompanied with an enactment of a law: "Closed Substance Cycle and Waste Management Act". This law provided for managing waste in a closed cycle and ensuring environmentally compatible waste disposal. Then, in 2000, Japan became the second country that issued a law to promote circular economy nationally. The Japanese government tried to transform the society featured with high production, high consumption and high waste into a "recycle-oriented society". One common feature of both countries' Circular economy policy is to prevent further environmental deterioration and to conserve scarce resources through effective waste management, especially the solid-waste management (Su, Heshmati, Geng, 2013).

A successful sustainability example is China providing reference in circular economy (Shen, Price, Wang, Li, 2012). China (Su, Heshmati, Geng, 2013) has already adopted a law for the implementation of the circular economy in 2008 (Korhonen, Nuur, Feldman, Birkie, 2018). In the meantime, EU followed up as the next candidate to implement circular economy as economic and environmental pressures to use natural resources or materials more efficiently are felt all across Europe. Nowadays, EU is trying to enhance the world gather into a wider circle -the so called circular economy- in which products are recycled, repaired or reused rather than thrown away, and in which waste from one process becomes an input into other processes (EU, 2015).

The circular economy is seen as a logical alternative to a linear economy. In a linear economy, natural resources are extracted for producing materials that are manufactured in products to be incinerated or landfilled after use. The essence of a circular economy is to preserve natural resources by retaining the quality and value of products and their parts, and the materials as shown in Figure 1 (PBL Netherlands Environmental Assessment Agency, 2017).

Figure 1. From a linear to a circular economy
Source: PBL Netherlands Environmental Assessment Agency, 2017

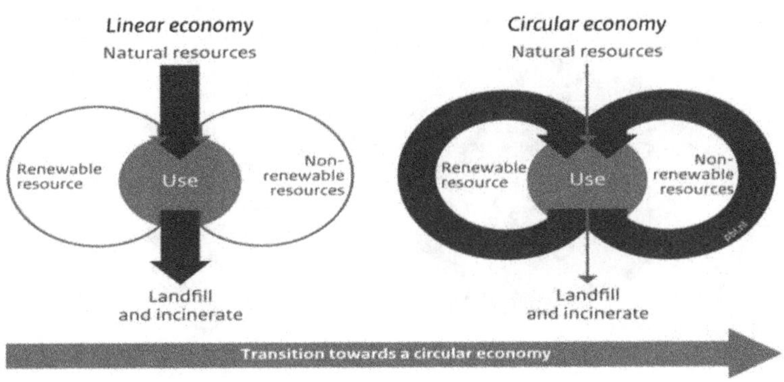

Circular Economy Package published by EU in December 2015, seeks to establish a programme of action, with measures covering the whole cycle: from production and consumption to waste management and the market for secondary raw materials. Under the Commission's proposals, the Circular Economy Package will aim to reduce waste to a minimum so that, when a product reaches the end of its life, its materials are kept within the economy wherever possible. Hence, what was previously considered to be 'waste' is transformed into a valuable resource (Hughes, 2017).

Circular economy and sustainability are increasingly gaining traction with academia, industry, and policymakers, the similarities and differences between both concepts remain ambiguous. The relationship between the concepts is not made explicit in literature, which is blurring their conceptual contours and constrains the efficacy of using the approaches in research and practice (Geissdoerfer, Savaget, Bocken, Hultink, 2017). While some of the approaches and models behind the circular economy discourse have made important contributions to sustainability science in the past, the theoretical connection is not that clear. The research using solid theoretical foundations is rather scanty, therefore it needs further scientific research. As there are severe limitations and challenges in the practical application of the concept, an improved definition is required (Korhonen, Nuur, Feldman, Birkie, 2018).

EU Circular Economy Action Plan

The European Commission adopted an ambitious Circular Economy Package on 2 December 2015, in line with EU commitments under the 2030 Agenda for Sustainable Development. EU recognized a model for improving waste management that could deliver positive effects for the environment, climate, human health and the economy. The Package consists of an EU Action Plan with measures covering the whole product life cycle: from design, sourcing, production and consumption to waste management and the market for secondary raw materials (see Figure 2). As part of a shift towards a circular economy, the European Commission made four legislative proposals introducing new waste-management targets regarding reuse, recycling and landfilling, strengthening provisions on waste prevention and extended producer responsibility, and streamlining definitions, reporting obligations and calculation methods for targets (European Parliament, 2018).

The 4 legislative proposals amending the following legal acts:

Figure 2. Circular economy and resource efficiency
Source: Pratt K., Lenaghan M., Mitchard E. (2016).

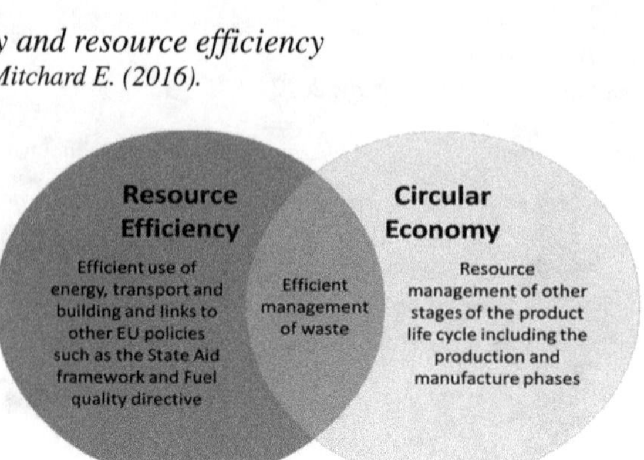

- Waste Framework Directive;
- Landfilling Directive;
- Packaging Waste Directive;
- Directives on end-of-life vehicles, on batteries and accumulators and waste batteries and accumulators, and on waste electrical and electronic equipment (European Parliament, 2016).

Key elements of the EU's new waste proposal include:

- A common EU target for recycling 65% of municipal waste by 2030;
- A common EU target for recycling 75% of packaging waste by 2030;
- A binding landfill target to reduce landfill to maximum of 10% of municipal waste by 2030;
- A ban on landfilling of separately collected waste;
- Promotion of economic instruments to discourage landfilling;
- Simplified and improved definitions and harmonised calculation methods for recycling rates throughout the EU;
- Concrete measures to promote re-use and stimulate industrial symbiosis –turning one industry's by-product into another industry's raw material;
- Economic incentives for producers to put greener products on the market and support recovery and recycling schemes (eg for packaging, batteries, electric and electronic equipment, vehicles) (EU, 2017e).

The transition towards a more circular economy brings great opportunities for Europe and its citizens. It is an important part of our efforts to modernise and transform the European economy, shifting it towards a more sustainable direction. There is a strong business case behind it which enables companies to make substantial economic gains and become more competitive. It delivers important energy savings and environmental benefits. It creates local jobs and opportunities for social integration. It is closely interlinked with key EU priorities on jobs and growth, investments, the social agenda and industrial innovation (EU, 2017a1).

The Circular Economy Action Plan can be certainly accepted as a climate action programme committed to deliver further progress in many issues like plastics, a monitoring framework for the circular economy and a proposal for promoting water re-use etc. The Package consists of an action plan with measures covering the whole product life cycle: from design, sourcing, production and consumption to waste management and the market for secondary raw materials (EU, 2017a2). Especially, the 'waste to energy' underlines the challenges and the opportunities linked to waste incineration, particularly in relation to recycling. This recognises the role of energy recovery (European Parliament, 2018).

The transition towards a more circular economy brings great opportunities for Europe and its citizens. It is an important part of our efforts to modernise and transform the European economy, shifting it towards a more sustainable direction. There is a strong business case behind it which enables companies to make substantial economic gains and become more competitive. It delivers important energy savings and environmental benefits. It creates local jobs and opportunities for social integration. It is closely interlinked with key EU priorities on jobs and growth, investments, the social agenda and industrial innovation. (EU, 2017a1).

The European Commission is in the process of setting up an informal expert group "Support to Circular Economy Financing", which will operate under Circular Economy Finance Support Platform. The expert group work will have the objectives of analysing the characteristics of circular economy projects and their financing needs, of providing general recommendations on structuring and improving the bankability of circular economy projects, of coordinating activities regarding the financing of the circular economy, and of sharing best practices. The group will bring together representatives of the Commission, the European Investment Bank, National Promotional Banks and other key circular economy stakeholders (EU, 2017b) by a call for applications on the behalf of Horizon 2020 which is the biggest EU Research and Innovation programme ever with nearly €80 billion of funding available over 7 years (2014 to 2020) (EU, 2014).

It has been launched on October 2017 for research and innovation work on 2018-2020 that represents a major investment of €30 billion offering an extraordinary occasion for scientific communities and innovators in third countries to tap on the opportunities provided by counterparts from the EU and countries associated to Horizon 2020 in areas of mutual interest (EU, 2017c).

The proposals are expected to deliver economic and environmental benefits. According to the Commission, the four legislative proposals put forward would create over 170,000 direct jobs in the EU by 2035; avoid greenhouse gases emissions (over 600 million tonnes of CO_2 equivalent between 2015 and 2035); increase the competitiveness of the EU waste management, recycling and manufacturing sectors; reduce the dependency of the EU on raw material imports; and reduce the administrative burden. In addition, the proposals would reduce the impacts on environment and human health described earlier. The proposals would also generate costs, which would most likely fall on public authorities, businesses and ultimately consumers (EU, 2016).

Circular Energy

The Circular Economy Package by EU stresses the important role of energy and renewables to improve the efficiency and environmental performance of energy-related products (Hughes, 2017). Charonis (2012) mentions energy while defining circular economy that denotes the materials and energy a society extracts, processes, transports and distributes, to consume and return back to the environment as waste.

Exclusively, circular economy may mean restructuring an industrial or agricultural system so that waste from one process becomes the feedstock for another or replacing non-renewable materials with renewable and biological materials. Overall, circular economy approaches could significantly reduce the need for extraction of primary resources and use of energy inputs (Preston, Lehne, 2017). Circular economy model can create an eco-mind and perception that can be called as circular energy. Thus, it has the potential to understand and implement radically new patterns and help society reach increased sustainability and well-being at energy and environmental costs (Ghisellini, Cialani, Ulgiati, 2016).

Circular economy is an industrial system that is restorative or regenerative by intention and design. It replaces the end-of-life concept with restoration, shifts towards the use of renewable energy, eliminates the use of toxic chemicals, which impair reuse, and aims for the elimination of waste through the superior design of materials, products, systems, and, within this, business models. Sustainable design is a design that aims at satisfying user's needs with the most efficient use of resources throughout the product's lifecycle (including manufacturing, use and end-of-life). Depending on the specific needs to be met (or services to be delivered) and the lifecycle assessment of resource use, the design may give a preference to the extension of life span of products (durability and reparability), using secondary materials, ensuring low-energy consumption during the use phase (EU, 2015).

For instance, the best effort in circular energy act of EU aims to ensure the recovery of energy from waste in the EU. The role of waste-to-energy processes (shown in Figure 3) is expected to be optimised play a part in meeting the objectives set out in the Energy Union Strategy and in the Paris Agreement. At the same time, by highlighting proven energy-efficient technology the approach to waste-to-energy set out meant to provide incentives for innovation and help create high-quality jobs (2017a2).

The EU modelling on the role of waste-to-energy processes in the circular economy will maximise the benefits of innovation of the national energy mix. It provides guidance for Member States to achieve the right balance of waste-to-energy capacity, highlighting the role of the waste hierarchy which ranks waste management options according to their sustainability and gives top priority to preventing and recycling of waste. It helps optimising their contribution to the Energy Union and exploiting the opportunities for cross-border partnerships where this is appropriate and in line with our environmental goals. The package adopted by the Commission also contains a proposal to update legislation to restrict the use of certain hazardous substances in electrical and electronic equipment. The proposal promotes substitution of hazardous materials to make the recycling of components more profitable. The proposed changes will further facilitate second-hand market operations (e.g. reselling) and repair of electrical and electronic equipment. It is estimated that the measures will prevent more than 3000 tonnes of hazardous waste per year in the EU and enable savings of energy and raw materials. In the health sector alone, an estimated EUR 170 million in healthcare costs could be saved. Finally, in its report on progress since last year, the Commission lists the key measures taken in areas such as waste, ecodesign, food waste, organic fertilisers, guarantees for consumer goods, and innovation and investment. Circular economy principles have been gradually integrated in industrial best practices, green public procurement, the use of cohesion policy funds, and through new initiatives in the construction and water sectors (EU, 2017a1).

Waste-to-energy processes can play a role in the transition to a circular economy provided that the EU waste hierarchy is used as a guiding principle and that choices made do not prevent higher levels of prevention, reuse and recycling. This is essential in order to ensure the full potential of a circular economy, both environmentally and economically and to reinforce the European leadership in green technology.

Figure 3. The role of waste to energy process in the circular economy
Source: European Commision

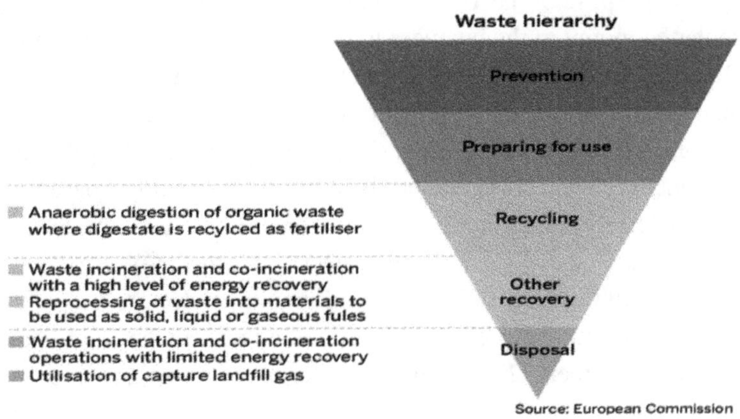

Moreover, it is only by respecting the waste hierarchy that waste-to-energy can maximise the circular economy's contribution to decarbonisation, in line with the Energy Union Strategy and the Paris agreement. As mentioned earlier, it is waste prevention and recycling that deliver the highest contribution in terms of energy savings and reductions in GHGs emissions (EU, 2017a2).

More circular economy programmes will widespread the consciousness of waste management and circular energy solutions in the world. For instance, the Horizon 2020 Energy info day will take place on 5 October 2018 in Brussels. It will present the upcoming funding opportunities offered by the EU's H2020 Programme to projects focusing on smart energy systems and smart cities and communities' concepts (EU, 2018c). It is expected that circular energy act in the world will be enhanced with these kinds of organizations held by global institutions and eco-minded economies.

CIRCULAR ECONOMY IN TURKEY

Circular economy is still a new concept in Turkey and government action is not enough for transition. There is a need of setting policies and providing guidelines of aim, role and scope of action by the government. NØW Turkey programme is the only action that the government is involved in. NØW is a strategic initiative EBRD programme to promote waste minimisation and pollution prevention projects in various sectors of the economy in Turkey (EBRD, 2015).

The Near Zero Waste NØW Programme consists of four main components:

1. Financing for waste minimisation projects, combining EBRD funds with concessional finance from the Clean Technology Fund (CTF), to support early movers in replicable investments currently hindered by market failures;
2. Free of charge technical support for project developers;
3. Policy dialogue to enable and mainstream the concept of waste minimisation in different economic sectors; and
4. Raising awareness and knowledge sharing to promote best global practices (NØW Turkey, 2016).

On the other hand, Turkey Business Council for Sustainable Development (Turkey BCSD) constitutes the circular economy and development work group in Turkey. The Council is targeting to pertain circular economy act within the framework of the UN's Sustainable Development Goals by the help of leader companies of Turkey. The purpose of the Turkey BCSD Circular Economy Working Group is to create awareness about circular economy in the business world, and to leverage collaboration and interaction in Turkey (Turkey Business Council for Sustainable Development, 2018).

To address this materials flow opportunity, the European Bank for Reconstruction & Development (EBRD) has engaged the United States Business Council for Sustainable Development (US BCSD) and the Turkey BCSD in launching the Turkey Materials Marketplace, a cloud-based platform designed to facilitate crossindustry materials reuse among Turkish companies and communities. The EBRD is providing funding support for the first two years of the project under the NØW Programme, which supports waste minimization projects in the Turkish industry and municipal sectors and aims to catalyze change in Turkey's waste management framework under the circular economy concept (United States Business Council for Sustainable Development, 2017). Turkey Materials Marketplace creates a new 'business-to-business' model, and thereby, it will radically change traditional recycling models, waste management systems and even the 'waste' concept.

Turkey BCSD focuses 4 principle goals to widespread sustainability and circular economy development in Turkey:

1. Transition to low carbon economy and efficiency
2. Sustainable agriculture and access to food
3. Sustainable industry and circular economy
4. Social inclusion (Turkey Business Council for Sustainable Development, 2018).

It is estimated that the circular economy in Turkey could be an opportunity with 15 to 27 billion $ (USD) of net value resulting a continuously evolving redesign of systems to establish higher value circular flows of materials (United States Business Council for Sustainable Development, 2017).

At the end of the efforts of BCSD and NØW Programme, Turkey can reach transition to circular economy by:

- Demonstrating best practices on material efficiency for different sectors of the economy;
- Reducing landfilling of 2 million tonnes of waste annually;
- Generating USD 50 millions per year in materials recovered;
- Saving, at least, 1 TWh of energy and 1.5 million tonnes of CO2-eq per year;
- Promoting cleaner, safer and more sustainable circular economy in Turkey (NØW Turkey, 2016).

Energy Act in Turkey: Towards the Circular Energy Model?

Turkey has increasingly aligned its energy efficiency targets and policies to the EU 2020 framework. Over the past decade, the government has progressively implemented EU energy efficiency rules and regulations. To date, Turkey has transposed most of the Eco-Design Directive 2009/129/EC, with a view to ensure access of Turkish products to the EU appliances market, a requirement of the customs union agreement. In the field of energy efficiency in buildings, Turkey has transposed the 2002 Energy Performance in Buildings Directive 2002/91/EC and recast as 2010/31/EU. *But Turkey has not yet transposed the* Directive on Energy End-Use Efficiency and Energy Services (2006/32/EC) or the Energy *Efficiency Directive (EED) 2012/27/EC* (IEA, 2016).

Turkey's energy sector reforms have attracted significant private investment and ensured, through a variety of interlinked measures, that capacity has kept pace with the economy's needs. But, the burdensome bureaucracy and concerns about rule of law in the country still hold investors back, according to surveys regularly conducted with foreign firms (World Bank, 2016). Although, Turkey is considered to have very large renewable energy resources that will reduce pollution and emissions of green house gases (World Bank, 2008), there are still problems of higher pre-investment costs, lack of medium-to-long term debt financing and primarily uncertainty regarding renewable energy solutions.

Nevertheless, it is impossible to declare that Turkey has neither reached the standards of a green economy nor the level of technologies for smart city solutions. Briefly, Turkey does not have a modern urban-city planning and zero-carbon city projects to develop smart cities with sustainable, cheap and affordable energy for economic development and low energy consumption (Okay, 2016). Actually, there are barriers like incompetent cultural awareness and level of education supressing the effect of enactments in Turkey. But more than that, the economical challenges strongly shape the energy profile of Turkey acting against the energy projects.

Turkey with inadequate solutions of low carbon or smart city planning must devise a set of objectives that will fulfill global requirements towards green economy, mainly the circular economy action plan. Some values will help to show the urgent notice about the green policy and poor transition period for eco-energy and related issues in Turkey.

For example, efforts to develop and catalyse private sector funding for energy efficiency improvements in buildings, industry and transport are being made, for example under small an medium sized enterprises (SME) support, tax incentives and energy audit companies. Indeed, there is a lack of familiarity with energy efficiency projects. Private sector investors often associate energy efficiency projects with high financial and technical risks and poor financial returns. In addition, upfront transaction costs which may arise from energy audits and feasibility studies can discourage investors. These costs can be increased by a lack of experience among the ESCOs that would develop such projects. Studies are under way on how to create an ESCO market. Turkey is not part of the EU emissions trading system (EU-ETS) and has no white certificates (IEA, 2016).

On the other hand, banks are not familiar with sustainable energy projects and have insufficient capacity to evaluate them. Most local banks have limited capacity and experience in identifying, evaluating, and processing energy efficiency and renewable energy projects. As a result, they offer few, if any, financial products designed specifically to finance sustainable energy projects, and require substantial technical assistance to develop such products. Financial resources and dedicated lending facilities are scarce. Sustainable energy measures require long-term funding. In recent years financial institutions have had limited access to long-term financing, and in Turkey banks have traditionally relied on short-term financial products (EBRD, 2014).

In a survey by EU considering all countries, it is observed that SMEs in Turkey are also amongst the most likely to be planning additional actions to save energy (71%). But planning is not enough of course, thus Turkey need to act seriously to pertain waste to energy management in EU Circular Economy Action Plan. Besides in the report regarding SMEs, resource efficiency and green markets, EU declared that Turkey is having a lack of specific environmental expertise and demand for resource efficient products or services, difficulty adapting environmental legislation to their company and complex administrative or legal procedures, cost of environmental actions and difficulty choosing the right resource efficiency actions (EU Directorate-General for Internal Market, Industry, Entrepreneurship and SMEs, 2017).

So, Turkey should start to enable circular energy act proceeding with the circular economy action plan in EU. Turkey BCSD focuses to widespread sustainability and circular economy in Turkey, mainly to transform the industry into a low carbon economy. For instance, BCSD's DO! (Be Sensitive) Project is launched in 2015, and it aims at promoting savings in work places by creating "Sensitive People". The savings can cover various materials and energy, such as electricity, water, fuel and paper. The Project is open for members of BCSD Turkey as well as non-members. The second version of the project is more comprehensive, covering measurement, assessment and reporting, and it is put into practice in 2017 (Turkey Business Council for Sustainable Development, 2018). But it is a new work group that needs more time to manage the establishment of a fully charged circular energy transition in Turkey.

At the same time, EBRD's NØW (EBRD, 2015) project aims to support efforts needed to unlock the resource and energy saving, at least, 1 TWh of energy and 1.5 million tonnes of CO2-eq per year in Turkey. Turkey only utilizes a fraction of its resource potential from waste. Energy efficiency approach could yield significant savings across sectors reducing 60 million tonnes of CO2 equivalent emission, saving energy equivalent to 10 million barrels of oil and producing biogas to meet electricity demand of 2 million households (NØW Turkey, 2015).

A circular market focus in Turkey can help removing barriers to improved waste and materials management and help industry achieve greater resource efficiency and subsequently lower GHG emissions (United States Business Council for Sustainable Development, 2017).

What Lies Behind the Economy Challenging Any Action Plan?

Nowadays, Turkey is facing a very serious economic situation different than previous years derived from various challenges but primarily provoked by high exchange rates. The other risks can be listed as uncertainty affecting economy, business environment, investment status and banking sector; huge dollar debts of enterprises alarming debt turnover rate and growing concerns; incredible delays in structural reform implementation; weak lira; credit rating firm's negative reports and ratings; and rising government debts.

Turkey's economy started to slow down since 2011. Although governing party continuously has the parliament majority, political environment is still incompetent to be helpful for an economic recovery. An erosion of institutions has already cost Turkey its investment status and business environment causing uncertainty. The economic slow-down worsened by 2017-2018, although the April 2017 constitutional referendum has stabilised Turkey's political landscape. Nevertheless, fiscal spending continued to rise and exports were subject to exchange rate fluctuations. Unfortunately, currency risk exposure flew high in 2018. The suppress on economy and finance still continues stressing the paybacks of enterprises that threatens the Turkish banks, ever (Okay, 2017).

At the same time, excessive weakness in Turkish lira continued to fly high by pushing up inflation. Inflation has a tremendous speed of rises reminding the crise years of Turkey. Turkey's economy has deteriorated dramatically during the summer of 2018 where it is headed very close to an economic contraction by the end of the year. The Turkish lira crashed by 33% in August, bringing the total depreciation for 2018 to around 70%. Inflation in August reached 17.9% year-on-year, and the central bank raised its key interest rate from 8% to 17.75% during the summer. Both consumer and business confidence have dropped sharply. In September, Turkey's central bank hiked interest rates once again to 24%. High inflation and a depreciating currency have caused the authorities to take drastic action, which could hinder credit expansion (Euromonitor, 2018b). Exchange rate volatility and geopolitical tensions pose risks. A heavy corporate debt burden, funded mainly by foreign financing, will be another problem (Euromonitor, 2018a). Increased global economic risks and trade wars can hurt Turkey's external sextor, hinder consumer income growth, as the country relies greatly on exports (Euromonitor, 2018c).

Credit ratings and expectations continued to fall since 2016. Rating institutions respectively announced negative reports about uncertainty and raising risks, downgraded ratings and revised the outlook of Turkey to negative (Okay, 2017). Then, the extreme weakening of Turkish lira in summer 2018, influenced the 3 rating institutions respectively to announce negative reports again. Forecasts show that Turkey is heading for a recession in 2019. The downgrade reflects that the extreme volatility of the Turkish lira and the resulting projected sharp balance of payments adjustment will undermine Turkey's economy (Standard and Poor's, 2018).

Hence, Moody's downgraded Turkey's ratings to Ba3 and assigns negative outlook (Moody's, 2018a). Moody's continued downgrading 20 financial institutions (18 of them are banks) in Turkey, again. It is expected that the solvency of Turkish banks will be weaker than reported figures suggest due to regulatory forbearance (Moody's, 2018b). Besides, while central bank has provided some breathing space to the domestic banks by lowering their reserve requirements, in Moody's view this is a short-term measure that does not address the underlying pressures the banking sector faces, nor does it address the mounting inflationary pressures. (Moody's, 2018a). Then again, lastly Moody's downgraded the foreign currency deposit ratings of 9 more banks which are expected as the solid institutions of the banking system in Turkey to B2 (means "very speculative") from B1 (means "speculative") B2 (Moody's 2018e).

Moody's declared that the New Economic Plan announced by Turkish Government (September 2018) falls short of addressing some of Turkey's key credit challenges despite credit-supportive objectives (Moody's, 2018d). Fitch shared the same view adding a note that the programme lacks detail, notably on the plans for the financial sector (Fitch, 2018c).

Lastly, Moody's lowered Turkey's country ceiling on foreign currency bank deposits to B2 from B1. Turkey's central bank reserves remain very low by comparison to currency debt payments falling due over the next year, in particular by the banks and non-financial private sector companies and continue to shrink. Moody's expects this negative trajectory to continue in the months ahead in view of the large external debt repayments coming due. (Moody's, 2018c).

On the other hand, Fithch ratings downgraded Turkey and assigned a negative outlook pointing out the absence of an orthodox monetary policy response to the Lira's fall, and the rhetoric of the Turkish authorities have increased the difficulty of restoring economic stability and sustainability. Fitch expects that Turkey will need IMF programme unless the situation worsens materially, as this would be politically unpalatable (Fitch, 2018a).

Turkey needs immediate structural reform implementations. Fitch emphasizes policy missteps that uncertainty and tougher external conditions will be immense next year (Fitch, 2018b). Nevertheless, future policy looks unknown and responses difficult to predict. Hence, the heightened political uncertainty will also likely put a brake on private investment and economic activity that threatens any action plan (Standard and Poor's, 2018).

SOLUTIONS AND RECOMMENDATIONS

Developing countries are facing a growing waste crisis, which has major consequences for environmental and health outcomes (Preston, Lehne, 2017). Therefore, countries like Turkey should adopt circular economy programme for their future welfare, sustainability and majorly the energy-related solutions. It is obvious that the future design of a smart city planning requires more research centers increasing discovery, invention, innovation and technology for eco-energy, eco-waste and eco-products. Smart systems and solutions will enable security to promote clean, safe and healthy environment in countries. Waste-to-energy processes can play a role in the transition to a circular economy (EU, 2017a2).

It must be noted that the ongoing problems in Turkish economy and huge energy demand the attention of the government, as it needs to reduce the environmental impacts of carbon emmissions within the help of circular energy act and low carbon economy activities securing and normalizing the standards of living in Turkey. In order to obtain a relatively high level low carbon economy (illustrated in Figure 4), Turkey should adopt programmes under the energy and circular economy action plans like EU programme stated above and United Nations SDGs only mentioned above.

Figure 4. Sustainable energy world under the circular economy
Source: Energy research Centre of the Netherlands (2017). https://www.ecn.nl

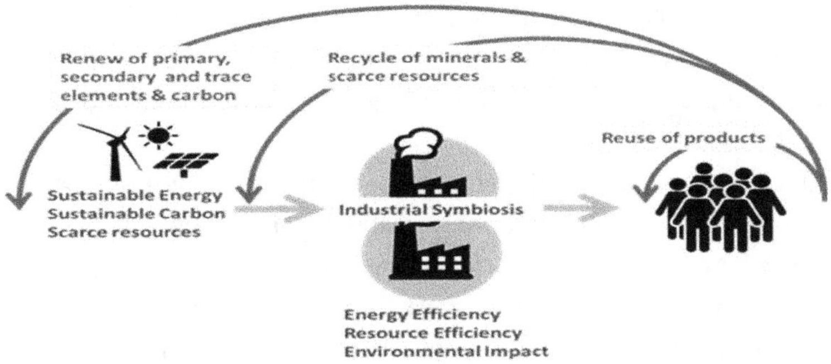

There are 17 goals in UN SDGs adopted by the world leaders in September 2015. They address the global challenges the economies face, including those related to poverty, inequality, climate, environmental degradation, prosperity, and peace and justice. The Goals interconnect and in order to leave no one behind, it ís important that each Goal and target will be achieved by 2030 (UN, 2015).

UN SDGs that should be the reference point for Turkey are listed as,

1. No poverty
2. Zero hunger
3. Good health and well-being
4. Quality education
5. Gender equality
6. Clean water and sanitation
7. Affordable and clean energy
8. Decent work and economic growth
9. Industry, innovation and infrastructure
10. Reduced inequalities
11. Sustainable cities and communities
12. Responsible production and consumption
13. Climate action
14. Life below water
15. Life on land
16. Peace, justice and strong institutions
17. *Partnerships for the Goals* (UN, 2015).

Therefore, Turkey should first of all support and practice UN *SDGs (especially the high lighted goals below reagarding energy, economy, health and environmental ones)* in order to be able to implement EU Circular Economy Action plan and apply the new waste management and transform the energy act into circular energy plan.

FUTURE RESEARCH DIRECTIONS

Circular economy is a relatively new topic for both Europe and the world. There is only limited evidence available regarding the focus and extend of circular economy activities across European regions. Regarding with the issue of circular energy, future design is to cross requirements of a low carbon economy and waste management.

The scientific and research content of the circular economy concept is superficial and unorganized. Circular economy seems to be a collection of vague and separate ideas from several fields and semi-scientific concepts. Circular economy is important for its power to attract both the business community and policy-making community to sustainability work, but it needs scientific research to secure that the actual environmental impacts of circular economy work toward sustainability (Korhonen, Honkasalo, Seppälä, 2018).

In the future, more consideration should be given to those processes, such as anaerobic digestion of biodegradable waste, where material recycling is combined with energy recovery. Conversely, the role of waste incineration – currently, the predominant waste-to-energy option - needs to be redefined to ensure that increases in recycling and reuse are not hampered and that overcapacities for residual waste treatment are averted (EU, 2017a2). Circular energy efficiency and environmental protection would become crucial

factors to orient policies for the transition to new production and consumption patterns, capable to delay the descent and allow a smoother transition to different and more environmentally sound lifestyles and socio-economic dynamics (Charonis, 2012).

The challenge of increasing the rate of improvement in energy efficiency is significant but achievable. The opportunities are greater still, mainly focusing economic growth and a cleaner planet (Okay 2018). EU -with the help of non-EU countries- aims to develop a world with a low carbon and climate resilient future. Therefore, all future programmes are designed to provide action on high research and innovation guided by technological development. Energy is the distinct key role of the future research directions targeting for clean, secure and efficient solutions.

The main items for future solutions of energy related technological developments can be listed as, a new generation of reliable, robust and cost-effective energy storage technologies, storage management systems, in particular batteries, able to provide high specific energy rates, large number of life cycles, fast response to the electrical network demands and low maintenance, power electronics for batteries and software to manage combined or hybridised decentralised energy systems, also combining several energy vectors: a key focus is on significant cost reduction of these key components for homes, districts and larger systems which have the potential to accelerate significantly the energy transition of the electricity network (EU, 2018c).

Benefits of circular energy action under circular economy:

1. Advanced modelling tools are expected to: increase the knowledge on how to design of price structure and magnitude in order to be able to finance e.g. infrastructure and research and innovation; enhance the accuracy of the prediction of electricity production from variable renewables and better qualify and quantity associated issues and remedies
2. Advanced tools are expected to develop new approaches to electricity grid planning, monitoring and maintenance that are better suited to today's future characteristics of the grid and enable savings on infrastructure costs.

3. The technological developments are expected to reduce costs of key technology components to allow European Industry to keep and extend its leadership in power electronics for stationary battery systems of all sizes (from home to utility scale) and the integration of battery systems with high shares of renewable electricity and eventually also heating and cooling.
4. Contribute to the objectives of mission innovation and provide efficient innovative small scale power to heat/cool flexibility measures that can be deployed in a large number of buildings so as to enable the grid to operate with large share of variable renewable energy (EU, 2017d).

CONCLUSION

Cultural awareness and level of education play an important role on developing sustainability and sensitivity to environment. Unfortunately, in Turkey cultural understanding is crucially low for the adoption of a green economy and smart city planning according to the requirements of EU circular economy action plan. But lately, the challenge in financial concerns and costs are against to policy stability, awareness and progress. The challenge is so immense that commitment to environmental quality and sustainability seem to halt in Turkey because of a growing economic and financial crise beyond the rapid growth of population, rural-urban migrants in search of jobs and slow training of public to raise awareness of green and circular economy. Therefore, Turkey is beyond developing eco-mind to build circular energy solutions and clean cities.

Although Turkey has a considerable potential for renewable energy sources and adopted sustainable energy action plan there is still a sign of incompetence in policy making which challenges renewable energy utilisation and adopting the eco-energy standards in Turkey. At the same time, Turkey has severe economic burdens nowadays and inability to provide reforms like EU transitional measures or azction plans for energy and sustainability. The major target is to fix the economic downturn and reverse it with sound monetary and fiscal policies and structural reforms supporting and redesigning institutional and administrative environments.

After regaining economic and financial stability, Turkey must and will need to promote policy stability for pertaining eco-mind and sustainable energy action plan to ensure future circular energy. A transition towards low carbon and waste to energy model with renewables lowering, decreasing energy burden will help Turkey to promote sustainability. Therefore, government in Turkey has to convince and help the public for a circular economy life to improve a better and healtier environment.

REFERENCES

Andretta, A. (2014). Key enablers for the future of Smart Cities. *Philips Lighting*. Retrieved from https://www.theclimategroup.org/sites/default/files/archive/files/Dubai-Philips---Business-Case-1.pdf

BP. (2015). *Energy Outlook Global Insights 2035*. Retrieved from https://www.bp.com/content/dam/bp/pdf/energy-economics/energy-outlook-2015/bp-energy-outlook-2035-booklet.pdf

Charonis, G. (2012). Degrowth, steady state economics and the circular economy: three distinct yet increasingly converging alternative discourses to economic growth for achieving environmental sustainability and social equity. *World Economic Association Sustainability Conference 2012*. Retrieved from http://sustainabilityconference2012.worldeconomicsassociation.org/wp-content/uploads/WEASustainabilityConference2012_Charonis_Alternative-Discoursesto-Economic-Growth.pdf

EBRD. (2014). *Turkish Sustainable Energy Finance Facility (TURSEFF)*. Retrieved from Retrieved from https://www-cif.climateinvestmentfunds.org/sites/default/files/knowledge-documents/turseff_case_study_jan_2014_0.pdf

EBRD. (2015). https://www.ebrd.com/work-with-us/procurement/pn-46442.html

Energy Research Centre of the Netherlands. (2017).Retrieved from https://www.ecn.nl

EU. (2014). *What is Horizon2020*. Retrieved from https://ec.europa.eu/programmes/horizon2020/what-horizon-2020

EU. (2015). *Framework conditions to support emerging industries and clusters in the area of circular economy, European Cluster Observatory Case Study*. Retrieved from http://ec.europa.eu/DocsRoom/documents/16266/attachments/1/translations/en/renditions/native

EU. (2017b). *Parliamentary Questions*. Retrieved from http://www.europarl.europa.eu/sides/getAllAnswers.do?reference=E-2017-002428&language=EN

EU. (2017c). *Launch of Horizon 2020 Work Programme for Research & Innovation 2018-2020*. EU.

EU. (2017d). *Research on advanced tools and technological development*. Retrieved from http://ec.europa.eu/research/participants/portal/desktop/en/opportunities/h2020/topics/lc-sc3-es-6-2019.html

EU. (2017e). *Review of Waste Policy and Legislation*. Retrieved from http://ec.europa.eu/environment/waste/target_review.htm

EU. (2018a). *Circular Economy, Implementation of the Circular Economy Action Plan*. Retrieved from http://ec.europa.eu/environment/circular-economy/index_en.htm

EU. (2018b). *Energy, Climate and Environment*. Retrieved from http://ec.europa.eu/environment/integration/energy/index_en.htm

EU. (2018c). *Horizon2020 Energy Info Day*. Retrieved from https://ec.europa.eu/inea/en/news-events/events/horizon-2020-energy-info-day

EU. (2017a). *Circular Economy: Commission delivers on its promises, offers guidance on recovery of energy from waste and works with EIB to boost investment*. Retrieved from http://europa.eu/rapid/press-release_IP-17-104_en.htm

EU Directorate-General for Internal Market, Industry, Entrepreneurship and SMEs. (2017). *SMEs, resource efficiency and green markets, FL456 Eurobarometer report*. Retrieved from http://ec.europa.eu/commfrontoffice/publicopinion/index.cfm/survey/getsurveydetail/instruments/flash/surveyky/2151

Euromonitor. (2018a). *Turkey: Country Profile*. Retrieved from https://www.euromonitor.com

Euromonitor. (2018b). *Turkey's Currency Crash Worsens Outlook for the Economy.* Retrieved from https://www.euromonitor.com

Euromonitor. (2018c). *Income and Expenditure: Turkey.* Retrieved from https://www.euromonitor.com

European Parliament. (2016). *Circular economy package: Four legislative proposals on waste.* Retrieved from http://www.europarl.europa.eu/EPRS/EPRS-Briefing-573936-Circular-economy-package-FINAL.pdf

European Parliament. (2018). *Circular economy package: Four legislative proposals on waste.* Retrieved from http://www.europarl.europa.eu/thinktank/en/document.html?reference=EPRS_BRI(2018)614766

Fitch Ratings. (2018a). *Turkey Moves Insufficient to Restore Policy Credibility.* Retrieved from https://www.fitchratings.com

Fitch Ratings. (2018b). *Turkey Faces Lower Growth, Lengthy Forced Adjustment.* Retrieved from https://www.fitchratings.com

Geissdoerfer, M., Savaget, P., Bocken, N., & Hultink, E. J. (2017). The Circular Economy – A new sustainability paradigm? *Journal of Cleaner Production, 143*, 757–768. doi:10.1016/j.jclepro.2016.12.048

Ghisellini, P., Cialani, C., & Ulgiati, S. (2016). A review on circular economy: the expected transition to a balanced interplay of environmental and economic systems. *Journal of Cleaner Production, 114*, 1-22. Retrieved from https://www.sciencedirect.com/science/article/pii/S0959652615012287

IEA. (2016). *Turkey 2016 Preview*. IEA.

Korhonen, J., Honkasalo, A., & Seppälä, J. (2018). Circular Economy: The Concept and its Limitations. *Ecological Economics, 143*, 37–46. doi:10.1016/j.ecolecon.2017.06.041

Korhonen, J., Nuur, C., Feldman, A., & Birkie, S. E. (2018, February). Circular economy as an essentially contested concept. *Journal of Cleaner Production, 175*, 20. doi:10.1016/j.jclepro.2017.12.111

Moody's. (2018a). *Moody's downgrades Turkey's ratings to Ba3 and assigns negative outlook.* Retrieved from https://www.moodys.com

Moody's. (2018b). *Moody's downgrades 20 financial institutions in Turkey.* Retrieved from https://www.moodys.com

Moody's. (2018c). *Moody's lowers Turkey's country ceiling on foreign currency bank deposits to B2.* Retrieved from https://www.moodys.com

Moody's. (2018d). *Government of Turkey: Despite credit-supportive objectives, New Economic Plan falls short of addressing some of Turkey's key credit challenges.* Retrieved from https://www.moodys.com

Moody's. (2018e). *Sector In-Depth: Sovereigns – G-20: Policy banks pose limited fiscal risk and provide upside from business cycle smoothing for those with fiscal space.* Retrieved from https://www.moodys.com

Okay, E. (2015). Creative Energy Alternatives: Cheap and Future Energy for Turkey. In Handbook of Research on Developing Sustainable Value in Economics, Finance, and Marketing (pp. 157-178). IGI Global.

Okay, E. (2016). Towards Smart Cities in Turkey? Transitioning from Waste to Creative, Clean and Cheap Eco-Energy. In Handbook of Research on Waste Management Techniques for Sustainability, (pp. 277-303). IGI Global. doi:10.4018/978-1-4666-9723-2.ch015

Okay, E. (2017). A New Barrier for the Future of Energy Market in Turkey: Internal Capital Adequacy Assessment Process (ICAAP). In Ethics and Sustainability in Global Supply Chain Management. (pp. 178-196). IGI Global.

Okay, E. (2018). Investment on Heat Pumps: Geothermal Green Solutions for Turkey Lowering Energy Costs. In Handbook of Research on Supply Chain Management for Sustainable Development, (pp. 194-217). IGI Global.

Okay, E., Okay, N., & Akman, U. (2008). Views on Turkey's impending ESCO market: Is it promising? *Energy Policy*, *36*, 1821–1824. doi:10.1016/j.enpol.2008.02.024

Okay, E., Okay, N., & Akman, U. (2012). Turkey chapter. In P. Langlois & S. J. Hansen (Eds.), *World ESCO Outlook* (pp. 396–403). The Fairmont Press.

Pratt, K., Lenaghan, M., & Mitchard, E. (2016). Material flows accounting for Scotland shows the merits of a circular economy and the folly of territorial carbon reporting. *Carbon Balance and Management*. Retrieved from https://link.springer.com/article/10.1186/s13021-016-0063-8

Preston, F., & Lehne, J. (2017). *A Wider Circle? The Circular Economy in Developing Countries*. Chatam House.

Renewable Energy Policy Network for 21st Century. (2017). *Renewables 2013 Global Status Report*. Retrieved from http://www.ren21.net/gsr

Shen, B., Price, L., Wang, J., & Li, M. (2012) *China's Approaches to Financing Sustainable Development: Policies, Practices, and Issues*. Ernest Orlando Lawrence Berkeley National Laboratory. Retrieved from http://china.lbl.gov/sites/all/files/lbl-5579e-green-finance-wiresjune-2012.pdf

Standards and Poor's Ratings. (2018). *Turkey Long-Term Foreign Currency Rating Lowered To 'B+' On Implications Of Extreme Lira Volatility; Outlook Stable*. Retrieved from http://www.standardandpoors.com

Su, B., Heshmati, A., & Geng, Y. (2012). A Review of the Circular Economy in China: Moving from Rhetoric to Implementation. *Journal of Cleaner Production*, *42*. Retrieved from https://www.sciencedirect.com/science/article/pii/S0959652612006117

Sustainable Energy for All. (2014). *Achieving Universal Energy Access*. Retrieved from http://www.se4all.org/sites/default/files/l/2014/12/fp_se4all_access.pdf

Sustainable Energy for All. (2017). *Energy Efficiency*. Retrieved from http://www.se4all.org/about-us_our-ambition_energy-efficiency

Sustainable Energy for All Forum. (2018). Retrieved from http://www.seforallforum.org/about

NØW Turkey, (2015). *Waste into resources: EBRD moving towards a Circular economy with the near zero waste – NØW*. Retrieved from http://www.now-turkey.org/uploads/Pdf/bb2_sTkki8cHZqBwjK-wRAtMvPxE23L9xHFnk.pdf

NØW Turkey. (2016). Retrieved from http://www.now-turkey.org

Turkey Business Council for Sustainable Development. (2018). Retrieved from http://www.skdturkiye.org

UN. (2012). *Green Economy In Action: Articles and Excerpts that Illustrate Green Economy and Sustainable Development Efforts (Development Programme).* Retrieved from http://www.undp.org/content/undp/en/home/librarypage/environment-energy/integrating_environmentintodevelopment/green-economy-in-action

UN. (2015). *The Sustainable Development Agenda: 17 Goals to Transform Our World.* Retrieved from https://www.un.org/sustainabledevelopment/development-agenda/

UN. (2017). *First steps to a safer future: Introducing The United Nations Framework Convention on Climate Change.* Retrieved from http://unfccc.int/essential_background/convention/items/6036.php

United States Business Council for Sustainable Development. (2017). *Circular Change: Turkey Materials Marketplace.* Retrieved from http://www.circularchange.com/wp-content/uploads/2017/05/Astrid-Motta-2.pdf

World Business Council for Sustainable Development. (2018). *Energy & Circular Economy.* Retrieved from https://www.wbcsd.org/Programs/Energy-Circular-Economy

World Health Organization. (2014). *Household air pollution and health, Fact sheet No. 292, March 2014.* Retrieved from http://www.who.int/mediacentre/factsheets/fs292/en/

ADDITIONAL READING

Agora Energiewende. (2014). Comparing the Cost of LowCarbon Technologies: What is the Cheapest Option? https://www.agora-energiewende.de/fileadmin/Projekte/2014/low-carbon-technologies/Agora_Analysis_Decarbonisationtechnologies_web_final.pdf

Agora Energiewende. (2016). Reducing the cost of financing renewables in Europe. https://www.agora-energiewende.de/fileadmin/Projekte/2016/De-Risking/Agora_RES-Derisking.pdf

Akkucuk, U. (2016). *Handbook of Research on Waste Management Techniques for Sustainability, SCOR Model and the Green Supply Chain, Hersey.* IGI Global. doi:10.4018/978-1-4666-9723-2

Akman, U., Okay, E., Okay, N. (2013). Current Snapshot of The Turkish ESCO Market. *Energy Policy, 60* (September), 106–115. doi:. enpol.2013.04.080. doi:10.1016/j

Babbitt, C. W., Gaustad, G., Fisher, A., Chen, W., & Liu, G. (2018). Closing the loop on circular economy research: From theory to practice and back again. *Resources, Conservation and Recycling, 135*, 1–2. https://www.sciencedirect.com/science/article/pii/S0921344918301496. doi:10.1016/j.resconrec.2018.04.012

BP. (2017). BP Energy Outlook 2017 Edition. http://www.bp.com/content/dam/bp/pdf/energy-economics/energy-outlook-2017/bp-energy-outlook-2017.pdf

Chandler, J. (2009). Trendy solutions: Why do states adopt sustainable energy portfolio standards. *Energy Policy*, *37*(8), 3274–3281. doi:10.1016/j.enpol.2009.04.032

Cobo, S., Dominguez-Ramos, A., & Irabien, A. (2018). From linear to circular integrated waste management systems: A review of methodological approaches. *Resources, Conservation and Recycling*, *135*, 279–295. https://www.sciencedirect.com/science/article/pii/S0921344917302422. doi:10.1016/j.resconrec.2017.08.003

EU. (2011). Energy Roadmap 2050. http://eur-lex.europa.eu/legal-content/EN/TXT/PDF/?uri=CELEX:52011DC0885&from=EN

EU. (2012). Turkey's Energy Strategy. http://ec.europa.eu/enlargement/pdf/european_energy_policy/turkeys_energy_strategy_en.pdf

Euromonitor (2018). *Business Dynamics: Turkey*. Report date: 20 July 2018. https://www.euromonitor.com

General Directorate of Renewable Energy. (2009). Energy Efficiency Strategy Paper 2012- 2023. Ankara. http://www.eie.gov.tr/verimlilik/document/Energy_Efficiency_Strategy_Paper.pdf

International Energy Agency. (2012). Tracking Clean Energy Progress. OECD/IEA, Paris. http://www.iea.org/media/etp/Tracking_Clean_Energy_Progress.pdf

International Energy Agency. (2012). A Policy Strategy for Carbon Capture and Storage, OECD/ IEA, Paris.

International Energy Agency. (2013). Redrawing The Energy-Climate Map, World Energy Outlook Special Report, OECD/IEA, Paris.

International Network for Sustainable Energy. (2010). Europe, Sustainable Energy Vision 2050: A Global Vision for 2050. http://www.inforse.org/europe/VisionWorld.htm

Kalmykova, Y., Sadagopan, M., & Rosado, L. (2018). Circular economy – From review of theories and practices to development of implementation tools. *Resources, Conservation and Recycling*, *135*, 190–201. https://www.sciencedirect.com/science/article/pii/S0921344917303701. doi:10.1016/j.resconrec.2017.10.034

Lu, B., Yang, J., Ijomah, W., Wu, W., & Zlamparet, G. (2018). Perspectives on reuse of WEEE in China: Lessons from the EU. *Resources, Conservation and Recycling*, *135*, 83–92. https://www.sciencedirect.com/science/article/pii/S092134491730191X. doi:10.1016/j.resconrec.2017.07.012

Okay, E. (2014). The Risks of Financing Energy in Turkey: Heading for a Rocky Road. *Open Journal of Energy Efficiency*, *3*(1), 1–13. doi:10.4236/ojee.2014.31001

Oliveira, F. R., França, S. L. B., & Rangel, L. A. D. (2018). Challenges and opportunities in a circular economy for a local productive arrangement of furniture in Brazil. *Resources, Conservation and Recycling*, *135*, 202–209. https://www.sciencedirect.com/science/article/pii/S092134491730191X. doi:10.1016/j.resconrec.2017.10.031

State of Green. (2014). CITIES: Center for IT-Intelligent Energy System in Cities. https://stateofgreen.com/en/profiles/technical-university-of-denmark/solutions/cities-center-for-it-intelligent-energy-system-in-cities

US Department of Energy. (2000). *Scenarios for a Clean Energy Future*. Retrieved from http://www.nrel.gov/docs/fy01osti/29379.pdf

Wellington (WGTN) 2040: A Green Economy. (n.d.). http://www.wgtn2040.govt.nz/node/162

World Bank. (2008). REToolKit Case, Turkey Renewable Energy Project. http://siteresources.worldbank.org/INTRENENERGYTK/Resources/5138237-1239828812934/Turkey0Renewable0Energy0Project.pdf

World Bank. (2009). Climate Resilient Cities: Dongtan. http://siteresources.worldbank.org/INTEAPREGTOPURBDEV/Resources/573631-1233613121646/dongtan_extop.pdf

World Bank. (2013). Turkey Green Growth Policy Paper: Towards a Greener Economy. Washington. http://documents.worldbank.org/curated/en/2013/04/17782290/turkey-green-growth-policy-paper-towards-greener-economy

World Bank. (2015). Turkey Partnership: Country Program Snapshot. http://pubdocs.worldbank.org/en/331611443694008785/Turkey-Snapshot.pdf

KEY TERMS AND DEFINITIONS

Circular Economy: A new economy model in which products are recycled, repaired, or reused rather than thrown away, and in which waste from one process becomes an input into other processes.

Circular Energy: Energy derived from waste process, the so-called waste to energy model.

Energy Finance: Financial solutions for renewable energy, efficient energy projects, and technologies in the energy market.

ESCOs: Energy service companies providing finance and consultancy for renewable energy solutions.

EU Circular Economy Action Plan: The new economy model of EU introducing new waste-management targets regarding reuse, recycling and landfilling, strengthening provisions on waste prevention and extended producer responsibility, and streamlining definitions, reporting obligations, and calculation methods for targets.

Low Carbon Strategy: Sustainable economy and society with low carbon emissions.

Renewable Energy Investment: Natural sources of energy projects derived from wind, sun, and biomass.

Sustainability: It is a multidisciplinary process of maintaining economic development, environmental protection, and social development by searching for ways of affordable solutions in sustainable usage of resources and environment mainly with the help of renewables reducing carbon emissions.

Turkey: Turkey is a developing country located between Europe and Asia.

Chapter 8
SERVQUAL-Based Evaluation of Service Quality of Energy Companies in Turkey:
Strategic Policies for Sustainable Economic Development

Hasan Dinçer
Istanbul Medipol University, Turkey

Serhat Yüksel
İstanbul Medipol University, Turkey

Fatih Pınarbaşı
Istanbul Medipol University, Turkey

ABSTRACT

The aim of this chapter is to measure the service quality of energy companies. Within this context, seven different energy companies that are listed on İstanbul Stock Exchange are considered. For this purpose, five dimensions and 14 criteria are identified by considering the details of SERVQUAL methodology. In the analysis process, fuzzy DEMATEL method is used to weight these dimensions and criteria and the performance of the energy companies are ranked by using fuzzy MOORA approach. The findings show that feedback is the most significant dimension and data security and physical security are the most important criteria. Another important conclusion is that the companies, which have high profitability, have better performance regarding service quality. Thus, it is recommended that the companies should mainly focus on the ways of getting necessary feedback from their customers, such as conducting a survey.

DOI: 10.4018/978-1-5225-8109-3.ch008

INTRODUCTION

Especially after the globalization, it is seen that competition increased in almost all different sectors (Greer and Hauptmeier, 2016). It can also be said that energy industry was affected for this situation significantly (Wesseler and Drabik, 2016). In order to survive such a competitive environment, energy companies should take some actions. Otherwise, it may be very difficult for these companies to survive in this market. For this purpose, energy companies can generate new products or services, focus on new investment areas or consider minimizing their costs

Focusing on service quality is another example to increase their competitive powers in comparison with their rivals (Dabholkar, 2015). In other words, energy companies can take actions to increase the quality of the services to their individual and corporate customers. If they achieve this objective, it can be possible to attract the attention of their customers. Hence, because they are preferred, it will have a positive influence on the financial performance of these companies. Therefore, it is obvious that these companies should take necessary actions to have higher service quality, such as considering customer expectations (Dhar, 2015; Aryee et. al, 2016).

SERVQUAL refers to the methodology that considers expectations of the customers. This method is very helpful to measure the service quality of the companies. Within this context, it focuses on 5 different dimensions. With respect to the reliability, performing the services in an accurate way plays a key role. Moreover, for the dimension of assurance, the quality of the employee is taken into the consideration. Furthermore, the physical facilities of the companies are analyzed for the dimension of the tangibles. Also, caring of the customers and the ability to solve their problems are considered regarding the dimensions of empathy and responsiveness (Parasuraman et al., 1988).

Parallel to the issues emphasized below, the main purpose of this study is to evaluate the service quality of energy companies in Turkey. Within this framework, SERVQUAL-based 5 dimensions and 14 criteria are identified by considering the similar studies in the literature. Furthermore, fuzzy DEMATEL methodology is used so as to weight these dimensions and criteria. In addition to this aspect, fuzzy MOORA method is taken into the consideration to rank the performance of the energy companies in Turkey.

According to the results of these analysis, it can be possible to understand which dimension and criterion are more important in comparison with the others. Therefore, it can be obvious for energy companies to focus on which areas in order to increase the service quality. Another important point is that it can be possible to identify which energy companies have higher performance. Hence, necessary recommendations can be presented to improve the performance in the energy industry so that strategic policies can be identified for sustainable economic development.

This study consists of 4 different sections. After giving general information about the study in the first part, the second section explains the similar studies in the literature. As a result, it can be possible to understand the missing part in the literature. The third section details the application in Turkish energy industry. Within this scope, first of all, fuzzy DEMATEL and fuzzy MOORA approaches are identified. After that, the details of the analysis are shared by considering these methodologies. In the final section, necessary recommendations are given according to the analysis results.

Literature Review

Service quality is a very old subject in the literature. It can be seen that the first context in service quality studies is related to hospitality and tourism studies. Wong Ooi Mei et al. (1999) studied service quality in hospitality context and found that there were three dimensions; employees, tangibles and reliability. After this general context, there were specific context studies in literature. Akbaba (2006) examined service quality in a business hotel context in Turkey. It is concluded that there were five dimensions of quality; tangibles, assurance, understanding and caring, convenience and adequacy in service supply. Wilkins et al. (2007) studied on structure and antecedents of service quality in a first-class and luxury hotels context. They presented three main types of service quality in hotels. These were physical product, service experience and quality food and beverage.

Beyond the general studies about service, Lee and Cheng (2018) studied green hotel industry and developed a scale measuring service quality of green hotels. The scale included six dimensions; reliability, empathy, environmental communication, green energy saving, assurance and tangible. Bastič and Gojčič (2012)'s study is another example of different perspective in hospitality studies. They studied eco-component of hotel service quality and found four dimensions; hotel staff's eco-behaviour, efficient use of energy and water, bio-food and environmentally friendly and healthy equipment. Additionally, Ye et al. (2014), Tsang et al. (2015), Taylan Dortyol et al. (2014), Lee and Severt (2017) and Wu and Liao (2016) are other studies which focused on the importance of the service quality in the tourism and hospitality sectors.

One of the contexts studied in service quality subject is related to transportation and airline industry. Deb and Ahmed (2018) studied on service quality of city bus service. This study was based on users' expectations and perceptions and they concluded four latent factors affecting service quality attributes. These factors were safety, comfort, timely performance and accessibility. Perçin (2018) studied service quality of airline by using combined fuzzy-decision making approach. Author used sixteen airline service quality criteria under five dimensions. Most important service quality dimension found in this study is the satisfaction. Employees, reliability, management and tangibles followed quality dimension in rankings.

In addition to these studies, Hapsari et al. (2016) also examined service quality by Indonesian airline passengers. They studied on customer side of service quality and investigated relationship between service quality and customer satisfaction. The study concluded that perceived value had a partial mediating role in this relationship. Moreover, Hussain et al. (2015) made an analysis to evaluate the service quality in airline industry of United Arab Emirates. By using a survey methodology, it is concluded that service quality is an essential subject in order to measure customer satisfaction effectively. Furthermore, Basfirinci and Mitra (2015), Ghorabaee et al. (2017) and Ford et al. (2015) are other examples which focused on the service quality subject in the airline industry.

On the other side, energy context in service quality has limited studies comparing to the hospitality and transportation contexts. For instance, Deng et al. (2018) studied on technical and service quality efficiency of electricity companies in China. This study underlined the importance of China's electricity reforms in 2002. Similarly, de Souza Barbosa et al. (2018) studied electricity distribution in their study by examining regulatory evaluation of electricity distribution service quality. Analytic Hierarchy Process (AHP) and Preference Ranking Organization Method for Enrichment Evaluations (PROMETHEE) methods are taken into the consideration in this study. In addition to these studies, it can also be seen that service quality is analyzed in many other industries as well. For example, there are some studies related to the service quality of internet of things (Shaoshuai et al, 2011), museums (Su & Teng, 2018), hospital (Untachai, 2013), e-commerce (Palese & Usai, 2018), and banking (Rod et al., 2009).

Moreover, for the consumer side of energy; Ibáñez et al. (2006) studied service quality variable with trust, satisfaction and switching cost variables in customer loyalty context. The study included three distinct dimensions of perceived service quality; technical quality of core services, service process quality and technical quality of peripheral services. It was concluded that service process quality had significant effect on satisfaction directly, while it affected customer loyalty indirectly. Additionally, Huang et al. (2017), Jernick et al. (2018) and Vigolo and Cassia (2015) are other studies which assessed the service quality in energy industry. As it can be understood that there are lots of different studies related to the service quality in the literature. However, it is seen that the number of these studies are very limited for the energy sector. Therefore, it is believed that there is a need for a new study which focuses on the service quality in energy sector with an original methodology.

METHODOLOGY

Fuzzy DEMATEL

The first letters of "The Decision-Making Trial and Evaluation Laboratory" generates the word of DEMATEL. Geneva Research Institute generated this word. With this methodology, it is aimed to make decisions among different alternatives (Wu and Lee, 2007). DEMATEL approach is very helpful under complex environment. In the analysis, alternatives are weighted, so it can be possible to see more significant ones. Additionally, cause and effect relationship between the alternatives can also be analyzed by using this approach. Moreover, it can also be seen that DEMATEL methodology is considered with fuzzy logic. The details of the steps in this approach are given below (Tzeng et al., 2007).

The purpose is determined in the first step. Moreover, the criteria are identified in the second step. For this situation, fuzzy linguistic scales are taken into the consideration which are named as "no", "low", "medium", "high", "very high". Additionally, these criteria are evaluated in the third step. Within this framework, evaluations of the decision makers are considered. Average fuzzy matrix is firstly developed in this process. The details of this matrix are given below.

$$= \frac{{}^{1} \oplus {}^{2} \oplus \ldots \oplus {}^{p}}{p} \tag{1}$$

$$= \begin{bmatrix} 0 & \cdots & {}_{1n} \\ \vdots & \ddots & \vdots \\ {}_{n1} & \cdots & 0 \end{bmatrix} \tag{2}$$

The number of decision makers is named as "p" in these equations. In addition to this issue, fuzzy matrixes are shown as Ž. These matrixes are generated by considering decision makers' evaluations. Moreover, the direct relation fuzzy matrix is normalized in the fourth step. The generation of normalized direct relation matrix and the calculation process are detailed on equations (3)-(5).

$$\bar{X} = \begin{bmatrix} \bar{X}_{11} & \cdots & \bar{X}_{1n} \\ \vdots & \ddots & \vdots \\ \bar{X}_{n1} & \cdots & \bar{X}_{nn} \end{bmatrix} \quad (3)$$

$$\bar{X}_{ij} = \frac{_{ij}}{r}\left(\frac{l_{ij}}{r}, \frac{m_{ij}}{r}, \frac{u_{ij}}{r}\right) \quad (4)$$

$$r = max_{1 \le i \le n}\left(\sum_{j=i}^{n} u_{ij}\right) \quad (5)$$

In step 5, total relation fuzzy matrix is developed. This process is demonstrated on the equations form (6) to (11).

$$d^{def} = \begin{bmatrix} \breve{t}_{11}^{def} & \cdots & \breve{t}_{in}^{def} \\ \vdots & \ddots & \vdots \\ \breve{t}_{n1}^{def} & \cdots & \breve{t}_{nn}^{def} \end{bmatrix} \quad (6)$$

$$\breve{t}_{ij} = (l''_{ij}, m''_{ij}, u''_{ij}) \quad (7)$$

$$l''_{ij} = X_l \times (1 - X_l)^{-1} \quad (8)$$

$$m''_{ij} = X_m \times (1 - X_m)^{-1} \quad (9)$$

$$u''_{ij} = X_u \times (1 - X_u)^{-1} \quad (10)$$

$$X_l = \begin{bmatrix} 0 & \cdots & l'_{1n} \\ \vdots & \ddots & \vdots \\ l'_{n1} & \cdots & 0 \end{bmatrix}, X_m = \begin{bmatrix} 0 & \cdots & m'_{1n} \\ \vdots & \ddots & \vdots \\ m'_{n1} & \cdots & 0 \end{bmatrix}, X_u = \begin{bmatrix} 0 & \cdots & u'_{1n} \\ \vdots & \ddots & \vdots \\ u'_{n1} & \cdots & 0 \end{bmatrix} \quad (11)$$

Table 1. Studies with Fuzzy DEMATEL Methodology

Subject	Authors
Supplier selection	Chang et al. (2011), Gharakhani (2012), Keskin (2015), Mehregan et al. (2014), Raut et al. (2011), Mirmousa and Dehnavi (2016), Mavi and Shahabi (2015)
Evaluation of green supply chain management	Lin (2013), Govindan et al. (2015), Irajpour et al. (2012), Vafadarnikjoo (2014), Kazancoglu et al. (2018), Malviya and Kant (2014)
Selection of the best location	Yeh and Huang (2014), Karaşan and Kahraman (2017), Jeong and Ramírez-Gómez (2018), Saracoglu (2017)
Performance management in the banking sector	Vafadarnikjoo et al. (2015), Nosratabadi et al. (2011), Dinçer et al. (2016)

In step 6, which is the last step, the values of $\left(\breve{D}_i + \breve{R}_i\right)^{def}$ and $\left(\breve{D}_i - \breve{R}_i\right)^{def}$ are calculated. For this purpose, the fuzzy numbers are defuzzificated. Consequently, a new matrix is created, and the details are given below.

$$d^{def} = \begin{bmatrix} \breve{t}_{11}^{def} & \cdots & \breve{t}_{in}^{def} \\ \vdots & \ddots & \vdots \\ \breve{t}_{n1}^{def} & \cdots & \breve{t}_{nn}^{def} \end{bmatrix} \quad (12)$$

Fuzzy DEMATEL methodology is very popular in the literature. Some studies, which used this method, are demonstrated on Table 1.

Fuzzy MOORA

The term "Multi-Objective Optimization on the basis of Ratio Analysis" generates the word of MOORA. Brauers and Zavadskas (2006) developed this methodology for decision making in complex environment. MOORA approach considers some limitation in the process of problem solving. It does not take too much time to make analysis with this methodology. In addition to this situation, implementation of this approach is very simple. It can be said that these conditions increase the preferability of this model. The details of MOORA methodology are given below (Chakraborty, 2011).

In the first step, fuzzy decision matrix is developed. For this purpose, different alternatives are taken into the consideration. The details of this matrix are demonstrated as following.

$$X_{ij} = \begin{bmatrix} \left(X_{11}^{\ l}, X_{11}^{\ m}, X_{11}^{\ n}\right) & \cdots & \left(X_{1n}^{\ l}, X_{1n}^{\ m}, X_{1n}^{\ n}\right) \\ \vdots & \ddots & \vdots \\ \left(X_{m1}^{\ l}, X_{m1}^{\ m}, X_{m1}^{\ n}\right) & \cdots & \left(X_{mn}^{\ l}, X_{mn}^{\ m}, X_{mn}^{\ n}\right) \end{bmatrix} \quad (13)$$

In equation (12), "X_{ij}" gives information about the value of the criterion i regarding alternative j. In addition to this aspect, lower, middle and upper values are shown as "$X_{ij}^{\ l}$", "$X_{ij}^{\ m}$", "$X_{ij}^{\ n}$". In the second step, there is a normalization of this matrix. In this process, equations (14) – (16) are taken into the consideration.

$$r_{ij}^{l} = \frac{X_{ij}^{\ l}}{\sqrt{\sum_{j=1}^{m}\left(X_{ij}^{\ l}\right)^{2} + \left(X_{ij}^{\ m}\right)^{2} + \left(X_{ij}^{\ n}\right)^{2}}} \tag{14}$$

$$r_{ij}^{m} = \frac{X_{ij}^{\ m}}{\sqrt{\sum_{j=1}^{m}\left(X_{ij}^{\ l}\right)^{2} + \left(X_{ij}^{\ m}\right)^{2} + \left(X_{ij}^{\ n}\right)^{2}}} \tag{15}$$

$$r_{ij}^{n} = \frac{X_{ij}^{\ n}}{\sqrt{\sum_{j=1}^{m}\left(X_{ij}^{\ l}\right)^{2} + \left(X_{ij}^{\ m}\right)^{2} + \left(X_{ij}^{\ n}\right)^{2}}} \tag{16}$$

In the third step, alternatives are weighted. Thus, the more important ones can be identified. This calculation process is stated in the equations (17) and (19).

$$v_{ij}^{l} = W_{j} r_{ij}^{\ l} \tag{17}$$

$$v_{ij}^{m} = W_{j} r_{ij}^{\ m} \tag{18}$$

$$v_{ij}^{n} = W_{j} r_{ij}^{\ n} \tag{19}$$

In addition to them, step 4 gives information about the identification of the beneficial and non-beneficial criteria. Equations (20) – (22) explain the beneficial criteria. On the other hand, non-beneficial criteria are given on the equations (23) – (25).

$$S_{i}^{+l} = \sum_{j=1}^{n} v_{ij}^{\ l} \tag{20}$$

$$S_{i}^{+m} = \sum_{j=1}^{n} v_{ij}^{\ m} \tag{21}$$

$$S_i^{+n} = \sum_{j=1}^{n} v_{ij}^{\ n} \tag{22}$$

$$S_i^{-l} = \sum_{j=1}^{n} v_{ij}^{\ l} \tag{23}$$

$$S_i^{-m} = \sum_{j=1}^{n} v_{ij}^{\ m} \tag{24}$$

$$S_i^{-n} = \sum_{j=1}^{n} v_{ij}^{\ n} \tag{25}$$

In the fifth step, there is the calculation of overall performance index (S_i). In this process, equation (26) is taken into the consideration.

$$S_i\left(S_i^{+},S_i^{-}\right) = \sqrt{\frac{1}{3}\left[\left(S_i^{+l} - S_i^{-l}\right)^2 + \left(S_i^{+m} - S_i^{-m}\right)^2 + \left(S_i^{+n} - S_i^{-n}\right)^2\right]} \tag{26}$$

In the final step, alternatives are ranked by looking at the results. Similar to the fuzzy DEMATEL approach, fuzzy MOORA methodology was also preferred in many different studies in the literature. Some of these studies are shown on Table 2.

AN APPLICATION ON THE TURKISH ENERGY INDUSTRY

In this section of the study, an application is performed on Turkish energy industry. Within this framework, first of all, dimensions and criteria are identified. After that, these dimensions and criteria are weighted with the help of fuzzy DEMATEL. In the last part, Turkish energy companies are ranked by considering fuzzy MOORA methodology.

Table 2. Studies with Fuzzy MOORA Methodology

Subject	Authors
Supplier selection	Mavi et al. (2017), Pérez-Domínguez et al. (2015), Matawale et al. (2016), Arabsheybani et al. (2018)
Performance evaluation of the companies	Stanujkić et al. (2013), Mandal and Sarkar (2012), Dinçer et al. (2017), Yüksel et al. (2017), Dinçer et al. (2018)

Selecting the Dimensions and Criteria

This study aims to evaluate the service quality of energy companies in Turkey. For this purpose, 5 dimensions and 14 criteria are identified. In this process, SERVQUAL methodology are taken into the consideration. The details of these dimensions and criteria are given on Table 3.

With respect to the dimension of physical conditions (D1), 3 different criteria are defined. Firstly, operating hours (C1) play a key role because customers give information to access the companies at any time (Curry and Sinclair, 2002; Kumar et al., 2009). Another important expectation of customer is also accessing this service (C2) in many different channels (Malhotra et al., 2005). Furthermore, effective information and communication infrastructure (C3) can also increase the service quality.

Regarding the dimension of functionality (D2), ease of using the services (C4), operating facilities (C5) and service experience (C6) are significant criteria that affect the service quality of energy companies (Zavareh et al., 2012; Adetayo and Apollos, 2013; Wilkins et al., 2007). As for the dimension of feedback (D3), first of all, there should be a customer support (C7) for any kind of problem (Sigala, 2009). Moreover, the speed of feedback on the problems (C8) also plays a key role in service quality (Chatterjee et al., 2009). Similarly, this service should also be provided by considering market needs (C9) (Marković et al., 2014).

Furthermore, for the dimension of security (D4), the security of data (C10) and physical security (C11) have a strong influence on service quality (Berezina et al., 2012; Sigala, 2004; Greenland et al., 2006). In addition to them, with respect to the last dimension of empathy (D5), there are 3 different criteria. Within this context, the cost of the service (C12) should be competitive (Liao and Cheung, 2008). Moreover,

Table 3. SERVQUAL-based dimensions and criteria of service quality

Dimensions	Criteria	Supported Literature
Physical Conditions (D1)	Operating hours (C1)	Curry and Sinclair (2002), Kumar et al. (2009), Yousapronpaiboon (2014)
	Access to the service (C2)	Youssef (1996), Fodness et al. (1993), Malhotra et al. (2005)
	Information and Communication Infrastructure (C3)	Delone and McLean (2003), Badri et al. (2005), Potgieter et al. (2005)
Functionality (D2)	Ease of use for services (C4)	Zavareh et al. (2012), Al-Momani et al. (2009), Li and Soumi (2009)
	Operational facilities (C5)	Mohammad et al. (2012), Adetayo and Apollos (2013)
	Service experience (C6)	O'Neill et al. (2002), Kouthouris and Alexandris (2005), Wilkins et al. (2007)
Feedback (D3)	Customer support (C7)	Negash et al. (2003), Sigala (2009)
	Speed of feedback on the problems (C8)	Jain and Gupta (2004), Chatterjee et al. (2009)
	Providing services considering the market needs (C9)	Gu and Ryan (2008), Marković et al. (2014)
Security (D4)	Data security (C10)	Berezina et al. (2012), Sigala (2004)
	Physical security (C11)	Greenland et al. (2006), Berezina et al. (2012)
Empathy (D5)	Costs (C12)	Newman (2001), Liao and Cheung (2008)
	Pricing (C13)	Hu and Zhang (2013), Koc (2006)
	Promotions (C14)	Hung et al. (2014), Naik et al. (2010)

pricing policy (C13) should be fair as well (Hu and Zhang (2013; Koc, 2006). Finally, promotions (C14) should also be effective with the aim of high service quality (Hung et al., 2014).

Weighting SERVQUAL-Based Dimensions and Criteria for the Energy Industry

The dimensions and the criteria are weighted in the second stage of the analysis. For this purpose, fuzzy DEMATEL methodology is considered. In this process, firstly, initial direct relation matrix is created. The details of this matrix for SERVQUAL dimensions are shown on Table 4.

Next, normalized matrix is created and the details for the dimensions are demonstrated on Table 5.

In addition to the normalized direct relation matrix, total relation fuzzy matrix is generated. For the dimensions of the study, this matrix is detailed on Table 6.

In the last stage of DEMATEL methodology, total impact relation degrees are calculated. The results for the dimensions are explained on Table 7.

Table 7 indicates that feedback (D3) is the most significant dimension because it has the highest weight (0.213). In addition to this issue, it is also determined that physical conditions (D1) and functionality (D2) are other important dimensions. Moreover, it is also found that feedback (D3) is the most influencing dimension with the highest impact relationship degree. On the other hand, empathy is the most influenced dimension because this value is the lowest. This situation gives information that energy companies mainly focus on the feedback dimension in order to increase their service quality. Within this scope, these companies can conduct a market survey to get the feedback of their customers. This situation gets a chance to these countries to improve themselves and it has a positive influence on the customer satisfaction. Marković et al. (2014), Chatterjee et al. (2009) and Sigala (2009) are some example studies in the literature that underlined the importance of this aspect. DEMATEL methodology is also used to weight all criteria under these dimensions. The details of the calculation process are stated on the appendix section. The summary results are explained on Table 8.

Table 4. The initial direct-relation fuzzy matrix for SERVQUAL Dimensions

Dimensions	D1			D2			D3			D4			D5		
Physical Conditions (D1)	0.000	0.000	0.000	0.250	0.500	0.750	0.500	0.750	1.000	0.250	0.500	0.750	0.250	0.500	0.750
Functionality (D2)	0.500	0.750	1.000	0.000	0.000	0.000	0.250	0.500	0.750	0.250	0.500	0.750	0.250	0.500	0.750
Feedback (D3)	0.500	0.750	1.000	0.500	0.750	1.000	0.000	0.000	0.000	0.250	0.500	0.750	0.500	0.750	1.000
Security (D4)	0.250	0.500	0.750	0.500	0.750	1.000	0.250	0.500	0.750	0.000	0.000	0.000	0.250	0.500	0.750
Empathy (D5)	0.250	0.500	0.750	0.250	0.500	0.750	0.250	0.500	0.750	0.250	0.500	0.750	0.000	0.000	0.000

Table 5. Normalized direct-relation fuzzy matrix for the dimensions

Dimensions	D1			D2			D3			D4			D5		
Physical Conditions (D1)	0.000	0.000	0.000	0.067	0.133	0.200	0.133	0.200	0.267	0.067	0.133	0.200	0.067	0.133	0.200
Functionality (D2)	0.133	0.200	0.267	0.000	0.000	0.000	0.067	0.133	0.200	0.067	0.133	0.200	0.067	0.133	0.200
Feedback (D3)	0.133	0.200	0.267	0.133	0.200	0.267	0.000	0.000	0.000	0.067	0.133	0.200	0.133	0.200	0.267
Security (D4)	0.067	0.133	0.200	0.133	0.200	0.267	0.067	0.133	0.200	0.000	0.000	0.000	0.067	0.133	0.200
Empathy (D5)	0.067	0.133	0.200	0.067	0.133	0.200	0.067	0.133	0.200	0.067	0.133	0.200	0.000	0.000	0.000

Table 6. The total-relation fuzzy matrix for the dimensions

Dimensions	D1			D2			D3			D4			D5		
Physical Conditions (D1)	0.050	0.227	1.383	0.111	0.342	1.541	0.161	0.375	1.512	0.095	0.302	1.380	0.105	0.324	1.464
Functionality (D2)	0.166	0.391	1.585	0.044	0.220	1.363	0.105	0.324	1.460	0.094	0.301	1.372	0.101	0.320	1.453
Feedback (D3)	0.183	0.433	1.753	0.178	0.428	1.741	0.055	0.243	1.451	0.106	0.335	1.520	0.172	0.408	1.657
Security (D4)	0.111	0.342	1.540	0.165	0.389	1.575	0.101	0.321	1.457	0.032	0.183	1.205	0.101	0.319	1.453
Empathy (D5)	0.101	0.319	1.452	0.100	0.317	1.444	0.095	0.302	1.376	0.088	0.283	1.296	0.032	0.183	1.205

Table 7. Total impact-relationship degrees and the weights for the dimensions

Dimensions	$\tilde{D}_i^{def}$	$\tilde{R}_i^{def}$	$\tilde{D}_i^{def} + \tilde{R}_i^{def}$	$\tilde{D}_i^{def} - \tilde{R}_i^{def}$	Weights
D1	2.499	2.676	5.175	-0.177	0.205
D2	2.486	2.655	5.141	-0.169	0.204
D3	2.868	2.495	5.363	0.373	0.213
D4	2.478	2.298	4.777	0.180	0.189
D5	2.277	2.485	4.762	-0.207	0.189

Table 8. Local and Global weights of the SERVQUAL-based factors

Dimensions	Local Weights	Criteria	Local Weights	Global Weights
D1	0.205	C1	0.345	0.071
		C2	0.328	0.067
		C3	0.327	0.067
D2	0.204	C4	0.327	0.067
		C5	0.328	0.067
		C6	0.345	0.070
D3	0.213	C7	0.332	0.071
		C8	0.335	0.071
		C9	0.333	0.071
D4	0.189	C10	0.503	0.095
		C11	0.497	0.094
D5	0.189	C12	0.354	0.067
		C13	0.335	0.063
		C14	0.311	0.059

Table 8 shows that data security (C10) and physical security (C11) are the most important criteria since they have the highest weights (0.095 and 0.094). Additionally, it is also identified that the criteria under the dimension of feedback are also significant. This situation indicates that energy companies should take necessary actions in order to have data and physical security. Within this context, an effective IT investment can be very helpful. In addition to this factor, energy companies should give importance to physical security measures. For example, materials must be checked against possible hazards before use. Moreover, it is also crucial that necessary precautions should be taken against a possible fire threat. The importance of this situation was also emphasized in various studies in the literature (Greenland et al., 2006; Berezina et al., 2012). In addition to the data and physical security, customer expectations should also be taken into the consideration, such as speed answer to the problems and providing services considering the market needs.

Ranking of Energy Firms Listed in Istanbul Stock Exchange

After defining the weights of the dimensions and criteria, Turkish energy companies are ranked according to the service quality. In this circumstance, all 7 energy companies listed in Istanbul Stock Exchange are taken into the consideration. The details of these energy companies are given on Table 9.

In order to rank these energy companies regarding the service quality, fuzzy MOORA approach is considered in the analysis process. In the first stage, fuzzy decision matrix is created, and it is detailed in Table 10.

After creating fuzzy decision matrix, Turkish energy companies are ranked according to the service quality performance. The results are demonstrated on Table 11.

Table 11 gives information that A5 is the energy company which has the highest performance with respect to the service quality because it has the highest S_i value. Similarly, A7 has the second-best performance. While combining these results with the information in Table 9, it can be understood that there is a positive relationship between total asset amount and service quality of the energy companies. Another important point is that these companies are in a profitable situation according to the financial results of the period March 2018. On the other side, it is seen that A3 and A6 are on the last ranks and these companies have loss in this period. Merkert and Assaf (2015), Singh et al. (2017), Chang et al. (2017) also stated in their studies that profitable companies have better performance in terms of service quality.

Table 9. The Details of Energy Companies Considered in the Analysis (2018-March)

Energy Companies	Alternative Number	Total Assets (TL)	Net Profit or Loss (TL)
Company 1	A1	5,727,159,398	-144,308,944
Company 2	A2	5,759,023,289	133,330,064
Company 3	A3	64,298,039	-3,990,585
Company 4	A4	2,206,343,722	6,582,982
Company 5	A5	20,388,355,000	498,972,000
Company 6	A6	1,842,838,086	-56,321,633
Company 7	A7	13,570,266,000	25,016,000

Source: Public Disclosure Platform of Turkey

Table 10. Fuzzy decision matrix

	A1			A2			A3			A4			A5			A6			A7		
C1	0.75	1	1	0.75	1	1	0.75	1	1	0.75	1	1	0.75	1	1	0.5	0.75	1	0.75	1	1
C2	0.75	1	1	0.75	1	1	0.5	0.75	1	0.5	0.75	1	0.75	1	1	0.5	0.75	1	0.5	0.75	1
C3	0.5	0.75	1	0.75	1	1	0.5	0.75	1	0.5	0.75	1	0.75	1	1	0.5	0.75	1	0.5	0.75	1
C4	0.5	0.75	1	0.75	1	1	0.5	0.75	1	0.5	0.75	1	0.75	1	1	0.5	0.75	1	0.75	1	1
C5	0.5	0.75	1	0.75	1	1	0.5	0.75	1	0.5	0.75	1	0.75	1	1	0.5	0.75	1	0.75	1	1
C6	0.5	0.75	1	0.25	0.5	0.75	0.5	0.75	1	0.5	0.75	1	0.5	0.75	1	0.25	0.5	0.75	0.5	0.75	1
C7	0.5	0.75	1	0.75	1	1	0.5	0.75	1	0.5	0.75	1	0.75	1	1	0.5	0.75	1	0.75	1	1
C8	0.5	0.75	1	0.75	1	1	0.5	0.75	1	0.5	0.75	1	0.5	0.75	1	0.5	0.75	1	0.5	0.75	1
C9	0.5	0.75	1	0.75	1	1	0.5	0.75	1	0.5	0.75	1	0.75	1	1	0.25	0.5	0.75	0.75	1	1
C10	0.5	0.75	1	0.25	0.5	0.75	0.25	0.5	0.75	0.25	0.5	0.75	0.25	0.5	0.75	0.25	0.5	0.75	0.25	0.5	0.75
C11	0.75	1	1	0.75	1	1	0.75	1	1	0.75	1	1	0.75	1	1	0.75	1	1	0.75	1	1
C12	0.5	0.75	1	0.25	0.5	0.75	0.5	0.75	1	0.5	0.75	1	0.25	0.5	0.75	0.25	0.5	0.75	0.25	0.5	0.75
C13	0.5	0.75	1	0.25	0.5	0.75	0.5	0.75	1	0.5	0.75	1	0.25	0.5	0.75	0.25	0.5	0.75	0.25	0.5	0.75
C14	0.5	0.75	1	0.25	0.5	0.75	0.5	0.75	1	0.5	0.75	1	0.5	0.75	1	0.25	0.5	0.75	0.5	0.75	1

Table 11. Ranking of energy firms

Alternatives	The Values of S_i	Ranking
A1	0.1612	4
A2	0.1696	3
A3	0.1500	6
A4	0.1500	5
A5	0.1763	1
A6	0.1442	7
A7	0.1710	2

SOLUTIONS AND RECOMMENDATIONS

As a result of fuzzy DEMATEL analysis, it is defined that feedback is the most important dimension regarding the service quality of energy companies. Therefore, it is recommended that energy companies mainly focus on the feedback dimension to have higher service quality. Within this framework, it can be very beneficial for these companies to conduct a market survey to get the feedback of their customers. Additionally, it is also defined that data security and physical security are the most significant criteria for this aspect. Thus, it is obvious that physical security measures should be implemented by energy companies, such as checking the materials against any possible treat before the use of the customers.

FUTURE RESEARCH DIRECTIONS

In this study, Turkish energy companies are evaluated with respect to the service quality. In the analysis process, fuzzy DEMATEL and fuzzy MOORA methods are considered to reach this objective. Also, it the future studies, an analysis can be made by covering energy companies in many different countries. For example, an evaluation related to the service quality of energy industry in developing countries can make significant contribution to the literature.

CONCLUSION

Evaluation of the service quality is a key issue for the companies. The main reason is that by making this kind of analysis, it can be possible to identify the ways to increase the quality of the services. With the help of this situation, companies can get a chance to increase their competitive powers. Thus, it is obvious that the quality of the methodology by evaluating the service quality has an importance. Within this framework, SERVQUAL methodology is very popular in the literature that focuses on 5 different dimensions at the same time to measure the service quality of the companies which are reliability, assurance, physical facilities, empathy and responsiveness.

In this study, it is aimed to measure the service quality in energy industry. Within this scope, 7 different energy companies, which are listed on İstanbul Stock Exchange, are taken into the consideration. By focusing on the SERVQUAL methodology, 5 dimensions and 14 criteria are identified. In the analysis process, fuzzy DEMATEL methodology is used in order to weight these dimensions and criteria. In addition to this issue, the performance of the energy companies in Turkey are ranked with respect to the service quality with the help of fuzzy MOORA approach.

According to the results of fuzzy DEMATEL, it is defined that feedback is the most significant dimension. Another important point is that feedback is the most influencing dimension with the highest impact relationship degree whereas empathy is the most influenced dimension. On the other side, it is also concluded that data security and physical security are the most important criteria. While considering these issues, it can be said that energy companies mainly focus on the feedback from the customers in order to increase their service quality. Moreover, an effective IT investment and necessary precautions should be taken against a possible threat play also an essential role.

As a result of fuzzy MOORA analysis, it is defined that A5 is the energy company that has the best performance with respect to the service quality and A7 has the second-best performance regarding this issue. By looking at the details of these companies, it is understood that there is a positive correlation between the profitability and service quality performance of the energy companies. In other words, it can be said that profitable companies have better performance in terms of service quality. Therefore, it is recommended that the companies with lower performance should focus on the necessary issues to improve service quality, such as getting feedback from the customers and taking precautions to have data and physical security.

REFERENCES

Adetayo, J. O., & Apollos, E. A. (2013). An Overview of Service Delivery and Customer Satisfaction in the Telecommunications Industry in Nigeria. *Indian Journal of Marketing*, *43*(8), 14–22. doi:10.17010/ijom/2013/v43/i8/36318

Akbaba, A. (2006). Measuring service quality in the hotel industry: A study in a business hotel in Turkey. *International Journal of Hospitality Management*, *25*(2), 170–192. doi:10.1016/j.ijhm.2005.08.006

Al-Momani, K., Noor, M., & Azila, N. (2009). E-service quality, ease of use, usability and enjoyment as antecedents of e-CRM performance: An empirical investigation in Jordan mobile phone services. *The Asian Journal of Technology Management*, *2*(2), 50–64.

Arabsheybani, A., Paydar, M. M., & Safaei, A. S. (2018). An integrated fuzzy MOORA method and FMEA technique for sustainable supplier selection considering quantity discounts and supplier's risk. *Journal of Cleaner Production*, *190*, 577–591. doi:10.1016/j.jclepro.2018.04.167

Aryee, S., Walumbwa, F. O., Seidu, E. Y., & Otaye, L. E. (2016). Developing and leveraging human capital resource to promote service quality: Testing a theory of performance. *Journal of Management*, *42*(2), 480–499. doi:10.1177/0149206312471394

Badri, M. A., Abdulla, M., & Al-Madani, A. (2005). Information technology center service quality: Assessment and application of SERVQUAL. *International Journal of Quality & Reliability Management*, *22*(8), 819–848. doi:10.1108/02656710510617247

Basfirinci, C., & Mitra, A. (2015). A cross cultural investigation of airlines service quality through integration of Servqual and the Kano model. *Journal of Air Transport Management*, *42*, 239–248. doi:10.1016/j.jairtraman.2014.11.005

Bastič, M., & Gojčič, S. (2012). Measurement scale for eco-component of hotel service quality. *International Journal of Hospitality Management*, *31*(3), 1012–1020. doi:10.1016/j.ijhm.2011.12.007

Berezina, K., Cobanoglu, C., Miller, B. L., & Kwansa, F. A. (2012). The impact of information security breach on hotel guest perception of service quality, satisfaction, revisit intentions and word-of-mouth. *International Journal of Contemporary Hospitality Management*, *24*(7), 991–1010. doi:10.1108/09596111211258883

Brauers, W. K., & Zavadskas, E. K. (2006). The MOORA method and its application to privatization in a transition economy. *Control and Cybernetics*, *35*, 445–469.

Chakraborty, S. (2011). Applications of the MOORA method for decision making in manufacturing environment. *International Journal of Advanced Manufacturing Technology*, *54*(9-12), 1155–1166. doi:10.100700170-010-2972-0

Chang, B., Chang, C. W., & Wu, C. H. (2011). Fuzzy DEMATEL method for developing supplier selection criteria. *Expert Systems with Applications*, *38*(3), 1850–1858. doi:10.1016/j.eswa.2010.07.114

Chang, M., Jang, H. B., Li, Y. M., & Kim, D. (2017). The relationship between the efficiency, service quality and customer satisfaction for state-owned commercial banks in China. *Sustainability*, *9*(12), 2163. doi:10.3390u9122163

Chatterjee, A., Ghosh, C., & Bandyopadhyay, S. (2009). Assessing students' rating in higher education: A SERVQUAL approach. *Total Quality Management*, *20*(10), 1095–1109. doi:10.1080/14783360903247114

Curry, A., & Sinclair, E. (2002). Assessing the quality of physiotherapy services using SERVQUAL. *International Journal of Health Care Quality Assurance*, *15*(5), 197–205. doi:10.1108/09526860210437412

Dabholkar, P. A. (2015). How to improve perceived service quality by increasing customer participation. In *Proceedings of the 1990 academy of marketing science (AMS) annual conference* (pp. 483-487). Springer. 10.1007/978-3-319-13254-9_97

de Souza Barbosa, A., Shayani, R. A., & de Oliveira, M. A. G. (2018). A multi-criteria decision analysis method for regulatory evaluation of electricity distribution service quality. *Utilities Policy*, *53*, 38–48. doi:10.1016/j.jup.2018.06.002

Deb, S., & Ahmed, M. A. (2018). Determining the service quality of the city bus service based on users' perceptions and expectations. *Travel Behaviour and Society*, *12*, 1–10. doi:10.1016/j.tbs.2018.02.008

Delone, W. H., & McLean, E. R. (2003). The DeLone and McLean model of information systems success: A ten-year update. *Journal of Management Information Systems*, *19*(4), 9–30. doi:10.1080/07421222.2003.11045748

Deng, N. Q., Liu, L. Q., & Deng, Y. Z. (2018). Estimating the effects of restructuring on the technical and service-quality efficiency of electricity companies in China. *Utilities Policy*, *50*, 91–100. doi:10.1016/j.jup.2017.11.002

Dhar, R. L. (2015). Service quality and the training of employees: The mediating role of organizational commitment. *Tourism Management*, *46*, 419–430. doi:10.1016/j.tourman.2014.08.001

Dincer, H., Hacioglu, U., & Yuksel, S. (2016). Balanced scorecard-based performance assessment of Turkish banking sector with analytic network process. *International Journal of Decision Sciences & Applications-IJDSA*, *1*(1), 1–21.

Dinçer, H., Hacıoğlu, Ü., & Yüksel, S. (2017). Balanced scorecard based performance measurement of European airlines using a hybrid multicriteria decision making approach under the fuzzy environment. *Journal of Air Transport Management*, *63*, 17–33. doi:10.1016/j.jairtraman.2017.05.005

Dinçer, H., Yuksel, S., & Bozaykut-Buk, T. (2018). Evaluation of Financial and Economic Effects on Green Supply Chain Management With Multi-Criteria Decision-Making Approach: Evidence From Companies Listed in BIST. In *Handbook of Research on Supply Chain Management for Sustainable Development* (pp. 144–175). IGI Global. doi:10.4018/978-1-5225-5757-9.ch009

Fodness, D., Pitegoff, B. E., & Truly Sautter, E. (1993). From customer to competitor: Consumer cooption in the service sector. *Journal of Services Marketing*, *7*(3), 18–25. doi:10.1108/08876049310044529

Ford, J. B., Paparoidamis, N., & Chumpitaz, R. (2015). Service quality, customer satisfaction, value and loyalty: An empirical investigation of the airline services industry. In *The Sustainable Global Marketplace* (pp. 187–187). Cham: Springer. doi:10.1007/978-3-319-10873-5_98

Gharakhani, D. (2012). The evaluation of supplier selection criteria by fuzzy DEMATEL method. *Journal of Basic and Applied Scientific Research*, *2*(4), 3215–3224.

Ghorabaee, M. K., Amiri, M., Zavadskas, E. K., Turskis, Z., & Antucheviciene, J. (2017). A new hybrid simulation-based assignment approach for evaluating airlines with multiple service quality criteria. *Journal of Air Transport Management*, *63*, 45–60. doi:10.1016/j.jairtraman.2017.05.008

Govindan, K., Khodaverdi, R., & Vafadarnikjoo, A. (2015). Intuitionistic fuzzy based DEMATEL method for developing green practices and performances in a green supply chain. *Expert Systems with Applications*, *42*(20), 7207–7220. doi:10.1016/j.eswa.2015.04.030

Greenland, S., Coshall, J., & Combe, I. (2006). Evaluating service quality and consumer satisfaction in emerging markets. *International Journal of Consumer Studies*, *30*(6), 582–590. doi:10.1111/j.1470-6431.2005.00484.x

Greer, I., & Hauptmeier, M. (2016). Management whipsawing: The staging of labor competition under globalization. *Industrial & Labor Relations Review*, *69*(1), 29–52. doi:10.1177/0019793915602254

Gu, H., & Ryan, C. (2008). Chinese clientele at Chinese hotels—preferences and satisfaction. *International Journal of Hospitality Management*, *27*(3), 337–345. doi:10.1016/j.ijhm.2007.10.005

Hapsari, R., Clemes, M., & Dean, D. (2016). The mediating role of perceived value on the relationship between service quality and customer satisfaction: Evidence from Indonesian airline passengers. *Procedia Economics and Finance*, *35*, 388–395. doi:10.1016/S2212-5671(16)00048-4

Hu, H., & Zhang, J. (2013). The evaluation system for cloud service quality based on servqual. In *Proceedings of the 2012 International Conference on Information Technology and Software Engineering* (pp. 577-584). Springer. 10.1007/978-3-642-34528-9_60

Huang, H. C., Chang, Y. T., Yeh, C. Y., & Liao, C. W. (2014). Promote the price promotion: The effects of price promotions on customer evaluations in coffee chain stores. *International Journal of Contemporary Hospitality Management*, *26*(7), 1065–1082. doi:10.1108/IJCHM-05-2013-0204

Huang, Y., Yang, L., Tang, T., Gao, Z., & Cao, F. (2017). Joint train scheduling optimization with service quality and energy efficiency in urban rail transit networks. *Energy*, *138*, 1124–1147. doi:10.1016/j.energy.2017.07.117

Hussain, R., Al Nasser, A., & Hussain, Y. K. (2015). Service quality and customer satisfaction of a UAE-based airline: An empirical investigation. *Journal of Air Transport Management*, *42*, 167–175. doi:10.1016/j.jairtraman.2014.10.001

Ibáñez, V. A., Hartmann, P., & Calvo, P. Z. (2006). Antecedents of customer loyalty in residential energy markets: Service quality, satisfaction, trust and switching costs. *Service Industries Journal*, *26*(6), 633–650. doi:10.1080/02642060600850717

Irajpour, A., Golsefid-Alavi, M., Hajimirza, M., & Soleimani-Nezhad, N. (2012). Evaluation of the most effective criteria in green supply chain management in automotive industries using the Fuzzy DEMATEL Method. *Journal of Basic and Applied Scientific Research, 2*(9), 8952–8961.

Jain, S. K., & Gupta, G. (2004). Measuring service quality: SERVQUAL vs. SERVPERF scales. *Vikalpa, 29*(2), 25–38. doi:10.1177/0256090920040203

Jeong, J. S., & Ramírez-Gómez, Á. (2018). Optimizing the location of a biomass plant with a fuzzy-DEcision-MAking Trial and Evaluation Laboratory (F-DEMATEL) and multi-criteria spatial decision assessment for renewable energy management and long-term sustainability. *Journal of Cleaner Production, 182*, 509–520. doi:10.1016/j.jclepro.2017.12.072

Jernick, G. A., Suganthi, L., & Iniyan, S. (2018). Development and validation of multi-dimensional wind turbine service quality scale for measuring operations and maintenance service quality in wind energy sector. *International Journal of Productivity and Quality Management, 23*(1), 31–54. doi:10.1504/IJPQM.2018.088607

Karaşan, A., & Kahraman, C. (2017). A novel intuitionistic fuzzy DEMATEL–ANP–TOPSIS integrated methodology for freight village location selection. *Journal of Intelligent & Fuzzy Systems*, 1-18.

Kazancoglu, Y., Kazancoglu, I., & Sagnak, M. (2018). Fuzzy DEMATEL-based green supply chain management performance: Application in cement industry. *Industrial Management & Data Systems, 118*(2), 412–431. doi:10.1108/IMDS-03-2017-0121

Keskin, G. A. (2015). Using integrated fuzzy DEMATEL and fuzzy C: Means algorithm for supplier evaluation and selection. *International Journal of Production Research, 53*(12), 3586–3602. doi:10.1080/00207543.2014.980461

Koc, E. (2006). Total quality management and business excellence in services: The implications of all-inclusive pricing system on internal and external customer satisfaction in the Turkish tourism market. *Total Quality Management & Business Excellence, 17*(7), 857–877. doi:10.1080/14783360600595252

Kouthouris, C., & Alexandris, K. (2005). Can service quality predict customer satisfaction and behavioral intentions in the sport tourism industry? An application of the SERVQUAL model in an outdoors setting. *Journal of Sport & Tourism, 10*(2), 101–111. doi:10.1080/14775080500223165

Kumar, M., Tat Kee, F., & Taap Manshor, A. (2009). Determining the relative importance of critical factors in delivering service quality of banks: An application of dominance analysis in SERVQUAL model. *Managing Service Quality: An International Journal, 19*(2), 211–228. doi:10.1108/09604520910943198

Lee, J. E., & Severt, D. (2017). The role of hospitality service quality in third places for the elderly: An exploratory study. *Cornell Hospitality Quarterly, 58*(2), 214–221. doi:10.1177/1938965516686110

Lee, W. H., & Cheng, C. C. (2018). Less is more: A new insight for measuring service quality of green hotels. *International Journal of Hospitality Management, 68*, 32–40. doi:10.1016/j.ijhm.2017.09.005

Li, H., & Suomi, R. (2009). A proposed scale for measuring e-service quality. *International Journal of u-and e-Service. Science and Technology, 2*(1), 1–10.

Liao, Z., & Cheung, M. T. (2008). Measuring consumer satisfaction in internet banking: A core framework. *Communications of the ACM*, *51*(4), 47–51. doi:10.1145/1330311.1330322

Lin, R. J. (2013). Using fuzzy DEMATEL to evaluate the green supply chain management practices. *Journal of Cleaner Production*, *40*, 32–39. doi:10.1016/j.jclepro.2011.06.010

Malhotra, N. K., Ulgado, F. M., Agarwal, J., Shainesh, G., & Wu, L. (2005). Dimensions of service quality in developed and developing economies: Multi-country cross-cultural comparisons. *International Marketing Review*, *22*(3), 256–278. doi:10.1108/02651330510602204

Malviya, R. K., & Kant, R. (2014, December). Identifying critical success factors for green supply chain management implementation using fuzzy DEMATEL method. In *Industrial Engineering and Engineering Management (IEEM), 2014 IEEE International Conference on* (pp. 214-218). IEEE.

Mandal, U. K., & Sarkar, B. (2012). Selection of best intelligent manufacturing system (ims) under fuzzy moora conflicting mcdm environment. *International Journal of Emerging Technology and Advanced Engineering*, *2*(9), 301–310.

Marković, S., Lončarić, D., & Lončarić, D. (2014). Service quality and customer satisfaction in the health care industry-towards health tourism market. *Tourism and Hospitality Management*, *20*(2), 155–170.

Matawale, C. R., Datta, S., & Mahapatra, S. S. (2016). Supplier selection in agile supply chain: Application potential of FMLMCDM approach in comparison with Fuzzy-TOPSIS and Fuzzy-MOORA. *Benchmarking: An International Journal*, *23*(7), 2027–2060. doi:10.1108/BIJ-07-2015-0067

Mavi, R. K., Goh, M., & Zarbakhshnia, N. (2017). Sustainable third-party reverse logistic provider selection with fuzzy SWARA and fuzzy MOORA in plastic industry. *International Journal of Advanced Manufacturing Technology*, *91*(5-8), 2401–2418. doi:10.100700170-016-9880-x

Mavi, R. K., & Shahabi, H. (2015). Using fuzzy DEMATEL for evaluating supplier selection criteria in manufacturing industries. *International Journal of Logistics Systems and Management*, *22*(1), 15–42. doi:10.1504/IJLSM.2015.070889

Mehregan, M. R., Hashemi, S. H., Karimi, A., & Merikhi, B. (2014). Analysis of interactions among sustainability supplier selection criteria using ISM and fuzzy DEMATEL. *International Journal of Applied Decision Sciences*, *7*(3), 270–294. doi:10.1504/IJADS.2014.063226

Merkert, R., & Assaf, A. G. (2015). Using DEA models to jointly estimate service quality perception and profitability–Evidence from international airports. *Transportation Research Part A, Policy and Practice*, *75*, 42–50. doi:10.1016/j.tra.2015.03.008

Mirmousa, S., & Dehnavi, H. D. (2016). Development of criteria of selecting the supplier by using the fuzzy DEMATEL method. *Procedia: Social and Behavioral Sciences*, *230*, 281–289. doi:10.1016/j.sbspro.2016.09.036

Mohammad, M. I., Gambo, Y. L., & Omirin, M. M. (2012). Assessing facilities management service in postgraduate hostel using servqual technique. *Journal of Emerging Trends in Economics and Management Science*, *3*(3), 252.

Naik, C. K., Gantasala, S. B., & Prabhakar, G. V. (2010). SERVQUAL, customer satisfaction and behavioural intentions in retailing. *European Journal of Soil Science*, *17*(2), 200–213.

Negash, S., Ryan, T., & Igbaria, M. (2003). Quality and effectiveness in web-based customer support systems. *Information & Management*, *40*(8), 757–768. doi:10.1016/S0378-7206(02)00101-5

Newman, K. (2001). Interrogating SERVQUAL: A critical assessment of service quality measurement in a high street retail bank. *International Journal of Bank Marketing*, *19*(3), 126–139. doi:10.1108/02652320110388559

Nosratabadi, H. E., Pourdarab, S., & Nadali, A. (2011). Credit Risk Assessment of Bank Customers using DEMATEL and Fuzzy Expert System. *Economics and Finance Research*, *4*, 255–259.

O'Neill, M., Palmer, A., & Charters, S. (2002). Wine production as a service experience–the effects of service quality on wine sales. *Journal of Services Marketing*, *16*(4), 342–362. doi:10.1108/08876040210433239

Palese, B., & Usai, A. (2018). The relative importance of service quality dimensions in e-commerce experiences. *International Journal of Information Management*, *40*, 132–140. doi:10.1016/j.ijinfomgt.2018.02.001

Parasuraman, A., Zeithaml, V. A., & Berry, L. L. (1988). Servqual: A multiple-item scale for measuring consumer perc. *Journal of Retailing*, *64*(1), 12.

Perçin, S. (2018). Evaluating airline service quality using a combined fuzzy decision-making approach. *Journal of Air Transport Management*, *68*, 48–60. doi:10.1016/j.jairtraman.2017.07.004

Pérez-Domínguez, L., Alvarado-Iniesta, A., Rodríguez-Borbón, I., & Vergara-Villegas, O. (2015). Intuitionistic fuzzy MOORA for supplier selection. *Dyna (Bilbao)*, *82*(191), 34–41. doi:10.15446/dyna.v82n191.51143

Potgieter, B. C., Botha, J. H., & Lew, C. (2005, July). Evidence that use of the ITIL framework is effective. *18th Annual conference of the national advisory committee on computing qualifications,* 160-167.

Raut, R. D., Bhasin, H. V., & Kamble, S. S. (2011). Evaluation of supplier selection criteria by combination of AHP and fuzzy DEMATEL method. *International Journal of Business Innovation and Research*, *5*(4), 359–392. doi:10.1504/IJBIR.2011.041056

Rod, M., Ashill, N. J., Shao, J., & Carruthers, J. (2009). An examination of the relationship between service quality dimensions, overall internet banking service quality and customer satisfaction: A New Zealand study. *Marketing Intelligence & Planning*, *27*(1), 103–126. doi:10.1108/02634500910928344

Saracoglu, B. O. (2017). Location selection factors of small hydropower plant investments powered by SAW, grey WPM and fuzzy DEMATEL based on human natural language perception. *International Journal of Renewable Energy Technology*, *8*(1), 1–23. doi:10.1504/IJRET.2017.10001528

Shaoshuai, F., Wenxiao, S., Nan, W., & Yan, L. (2011). MODM-based evaluation model of service quality in the Internet of Things. *Procedia Environmental Sciences*, *11*, 63–69. doi:10.1016/j.proenv.2011.12.011

Sigala, M. (2004). The ASP-Qual model: Measuring ASP service quality in Greece. *Managing Service Quality: An International Journal*, *14*(1), 103–114. doi:10.1108/09604520410513703

Sigala, M. (2009). E-service quality and Web 2.0: Expanding quality models to include customer participation and inter-customer support. *Service Industries Journal*, *29*(10), 1341–1358. doi:10.1080/02642060903026239

Singh, H., Saufi, R. A., Tasnim, R., & Hussin, M. (2017). The relationship between employee job satisfaction, perceived customer satisfaction, service quality, and profitability in luxury hotels in Kuala Lumpur. *Prabandhan: Indian Journal of Management*, *10*(1), 26–39. doi:10.17010/pijom/2017/v10i1/109101

Stanujkić, D., Đorđević, B., & Đorđević, M. (2013). Comparative analysis of some prominent MCDM methods: A case of ranking Serbian banks. *Serbian Journal of Management*, *8*(2), 213–241. doi:10.5937jm8-3774

Taylan Dortyol, I., Varinli, I., & Kitapci, O. (2014). How do international tourists perceive hotel quality? An exploratory study of service quality in Antalya tourism region. *International Journal of Contemporary Hospitality Management*, *26*(3), 470–495. doi:10.1108/IJCHM-11-2012-0211

Tsang, N. K., Lee, L. Y. S., & Qu, H. (2015). Service quality research on China's hospitality and tourism industry. *International Journal of Contemporary Hospitality Management*, *27*(3), 473–497. doi:10.1108/IJCHM-01-2014-0048

Tzeng, G. H., Chiang, C. H., & Li, C. W. (2007). Evaluating intertwined effects in e-learning programs: A novel hybrid MCDM model based on factor analysis and DEMATEL. *Expert Systems with Applications*, *32*(4), 1028–1044. doi:10.1016/j.eswa.2006.02.004

Untachai, S. (2013). Modeling service quality in hospital as a second order factor, Thailand. *Procedia: Social and Behavioral Sciences*, *88*, 118–133. doi:10.1016/j.sbspro.2013.08.487

Vafadarnikjoo, A. (2014). Corrigendum to "Using fuzzy DEMATEL to evaluate the green supply chain management practices. *Journal of Cleaner Production*, *82*, 232. doi:10.1016/j.jclepro.2014.06.065

Vafadarnikjoo, A., Mobin, M., Allahi, S., & Rastegari, A. (2015, January). A hybrid approach of intuitionistic fuzzy set theory and DEMATEL method to prioritize selection criteria of bank branches locations. In *Proceedings of the International Annual Conference of the American Society for Engineering Management*. (p. 1). American Society for Engineering Management (ASEM).

Vigolo, V., & Cassia, F. (2015, August). Brand Reputation and Service Quality in the Italian Energy Market: A business-to-Business Perspective. *Toulon-Verona Conference Excellence in Services*.

Wesseler, J., & Drabik, D. (2016). Prices matter: Analysis of food and energy competition relative to land resources in the European Union. *NJAS Wageningen Journal of Life Sciences*, *77*, 19–24. doi:10.1016/j.njas.2016.03.009

Wilkins, H., Merrilees, B., & Herington, C. (2007). Towards an understanding of total service quality in hotels. *International Journal of Hospitality Management*, *26*(4), 840–853. doi:10.1016/j.ijhm.2006.07.006

Wong Ooi Mei, A., Dean, A. M., & White, C. J. (1999). Analysing service quality in the hospitality industry. *Managing Service Quality: An International Journal*, *9*(2), 136–143. doi:10.1108/09604529910257920

Wu, P. H., & Liao, J. F. (2016). Service-oriented organizational citizenship behavior, perceived service quality and customer satisfaction in hospitality industry. *Journal of Applied Sciences (Faisalabad)*, *16*(1), 18–24. doi:10.3923/jas.2016.18.24

Wu, W. W., & Lee, Y. T. (2007). Developing global managers' competencies using the fuzzy DEMATEL method. *Expert Systems with Applications*, *32*(2), 499–507. doi:10.1016/j.eswa.2005.12.005

Ye, Q., Li, H., Wang, Z., & Law, R. (2014). The influence of hotel price on perceived service quality and value in e-tourism: An empirical investigation based on online traveler reviews. *Journal of Hospitality & Tourism Research (Washington, D.C.)*, *38*(1), 23–39. doi:10.1177/1096348012442540

Yeh, T. M., & Huang, Y. L. (2014). Factors in determining wind farm location: Integrating GQM, fuzzy DEMATEL, and ANP. *Renewable Energy*, *66*, 159–169. doi:10.1016/j.renene.2013.12.003

Yousapronpaiboon, K. (2014). SERVQUAL: Measuring higher education service quality in Thailand. *Procedia: Social and Behavioral Sciences*, *116*, 1088–1095. doi:10.1016/j.sbspro.2014.01.350

Youssef, F. N. (1996). Health care quality in NHS hospitals. *International Journal of Health Care Quality Assurance*, *9*(1), 15–28. doi:10.1108/09526869610109125 PMID:10156537

Yüksel, S., Dinçer, H., & Emir, Ş. (2017). Comparing the performance of Turkish deposit banks by using DEMATEL, Grey Relational Analysis (GRA) and MOORA approaches. *World Journal of Applied Economics*, *3*(2), 26–47. doi:10.22440/wjae.3.2.2

Zavareh, F. B., Ariff, M. S. M., Jusoh, A., Zakuan, N., Bahari, A. Z., & Ashourian, M. (2012). E-service quality dimensions and their effects on e-customer satisfaction in internet banking services. *Procedia: Social and Behavioral Sciences*, *40*, 441–445. doi:10.1016/j.sbspro.2012.03.213

KEY TERMS AND DEFINITIONS

DEMATEL: It refers to the first letters of the Decision-Making Trial and Evaluation Laboratory.

Fuzzy Logic: It is a type of methodology in which the evaluation of the decision makers is taken into the consideration.

IT: Information technology.

MOORA: It is an approach used to rank different alternatives.

Public Disclosure Platform: It is an institution which explains the financial tables of the companies which are open to public.

SERVQUAL: It is a methodology developed by Parasuraman to measure the service quality.

Stock Exchange: It is a platform where different types of the securities can be traded.

Tangibles: It refers to the real assets that can be touched.

APPENDIX

Table 12. The initial direct-relation fuzzy matrix for the criteria of D1

Criteria	C1			C2			C3		
Operating hours (C1)	0.000	0.000	0.000	0.250	0.500	0.750	0.500	0.750	1.000
Access to the service (C2)	0.500	0.750	1.000	0.000	0.000	0.000	0.250	0.500	0.750
Information and Communication Infrastructure (C3)	0.250	0.500	0.750	0.250	0.500	0.750	0.000	0.000	0.000

Table 13. Normalized direct-relation fuzzy matrix for the criteria of D1

Criteria	C1			C2			C3		
Operating hours (C1)	0.000	0.000	0.000	0.143	0.286	0.429	0.286	0.429	0.571
Access to the service (C2)	0.286	0.429	0.571	0.000	0.000	0.000	0.143	0.286	0.429
Information and Communication Infrastructure (C3)	0.143	0.286	0.429	0.143	0.286	0.429	0.000	0.000	0.000

Table 14. The total-relation fuzzy matrix for the criteria of D1

Criteria	C1			C2			C3		
Operating hours (C1)	0.109	0.537	6.568	0.208	0.683	6.243	0.347	0.854	7.000
Access to the service (C2)	0.347	0.854	7.000	0.086	0.468	6.000	0.254	0.785	7.000
Information and Communication Infrastructure (C3)	0.208	0.683	6.243	0.185	0.615	5.676	0.086	0.468	6.000

Table 15. Total impact-relationship degrees and the weights for the criteria of D1

Criteria	$\tilde{D}_i^{def}$	$\tilde{R}_i^{def}$	$\tilde{D}_i^{def} + \tilde{R}_i^{def}$	$\tilde{D}_i^{def} - \tilde{R}_i^{def}$	Weights
C1	5.102	5.083	10.184	0.019	0.345
C2	5.154	4.550	9.704	0.604	0.328
C3	4.515	5.138	9.654	-0.623	0.327

Table 16. The initial direct-relation fuzzy matrix for the criteria of D2

Criteria	C4			C5			C6		
Ease of use for services (C4)	0.000	0.000	0.000	0.250	0.500	0.750	0.250	0.500	0.750
Operational facilities (C5)	0.250	0.500	0.750	0.000	0.000	0.000	0.500	0.750	1.000
Service experience (C6)	0.500	0.750	1.000	0.250	0.500	0.750	0.000	0.000	0.000

Table 17. Normalized direct-relation fuzzy matrix for the criteria of D2

Criteria	C4			C5			C6		
Ease of use for services (C4)	0.000	0.000	0.000	0.143	0.286	0.429	0.143	0.286	0.429
Operational facilities (C5)	0.143	0.286	0.429	0.000	0.000	0.000	0.286	0.429	0.571
Service experience (C6)	0.286	0.429	0.571	0.143	0.286	0.429	0.000	0.000	0.000

Table 18. The total-relation fuzzy matrix for the criteria of D2

Criteria	C4			C5			C6		
Ease of use for services (C4)	0.086	0.468	6.000	0.185	0.615	5.676	0.208	0.683	6.243
Operational facilities (C5)	0.254	0.785	7.000	0.086	0.468	6.000	0.347	0.854	7.000
Service experience (C6)	0.347	0.854	7.000	0.208	0.683	6.243	0.109	0.537	6.568

Table 19. Total impact-relationship degrees and the weights for the criteria of D2

Criteria	$\tilde{D}_i^{def}$	$\tilde{R}_i^{def}$	$\tilde{D}_i^{def} + \tilde{R}_i^{def}$	$\tilde{D}_i^{def} - \tilde{R}_i^{def}$	Weights
C4	4.515	5.138	9.654	-0.623	0.327
C5	5.154	4.550	9.704	0.604	0.328
C6	5.102	5.083	10.184	0.019	0.345

Table 20. The initial direct-relation fuzzy matrix for the criteria of D3

Criteria	C7			C8			C9		
Customer support (C7)	0.000	0.000	0.000	0.250	0.500	0.750	0.250	0.500	0.750
Speed of feedback on the problems (C8)	0.500	0.750	1.000	0.000	0.000	0.000	0.500	0.750	1.000
Providing services considering the market needs (C9)	0.500	0.750	1.000	0.250	0.500	0.750	0.000	0.000	0.000

Table 21. Normalized direct-relation fuzzy matrix for the criteria of D3

Criteria	C7			C8			C9		
Customer support (C7)	0.000	0.000	0.000	0.125	0.250	0.375	0.125	0.250	0.375
Speed of feedback on the problems (C8)	0.250	0.375	0.500	0.000	0.000	0.000	0.250	0.375	0.500
Providing services considering the market needs (C9)	0.250	0.375	0.500	0.125	0.250	0.375	0.000	0.000	0.000

Table 22. The total-relation fuzzy matrix for the criteria of D3

Criteria	C7			C8			C9		
Customer support (C7)	0.083	0.373	1.971	0.157	0.473	1.886	0.175	0.521	2.057
Speed of feedback on the problems (C8)	0.349	0.781	2.743	0.083	0.373	1.971	0.314	0.710	2.514
Providing services considering the market needs (C9)	0.314	0.710	2.514	0.175	0.521	2.057	0.083	0.373	1.971

Table 23. Total impact-relationship degrees and the weights for the criteria of D3

Criteria	$\tilde{D}_i^{def}$	$\tilde{R}_i^{def}$	$\tilde{D}_i^{def} + \tilde{R}_i^{def}$	$\tilde{D}_i^{def} - \tilde{R}_i^{def}$	Weights
C7	2.090	2.700	4.790	-0.610	0.332
C8	2.723	2.119	4.842	0.604	0.335
C9	2.404	2.398	4.802	0.006	0.333

Table 24. The initial direct-relation fuzzy matrix for the criteria of D4

Criteria	C10			C11		
Data security (C10)	0.000	0.000	0.000	0.500	0.750	1.000
Physical security (C11)	0.250	0.500	0.750	0.000	0.000	0.000

Table 25. Normalized direct-relation fuzzy matrix for the criteria of D4

Criteria	C10			C11		
Data security (C10)	0.000	0.000	0.000	0.500	0.750	1.000
Physical security (C11)	0.250	0.500	0.750	0.000	0.000	0.000

Table 26. The total-relation fuzzy matrix for the criteria of D4

Criteria	C10			C11		
Data security (C10)	0.143	0.600	3.000	0.571	1.200	4.000
Physical security (C11)	0.286	0.800	3.000	0.143	0.600	3.000

Table 27. Total impact-relationship degrees and the weights for the criteria of D4

Criteria	$\tilde{D}_i^{def}$	$\tilde{R}_i^{def}$	$\tilde{D}_i^{def} + \tilde{R}_i^{def}$	$\tilde{D}_i^{def} - \tilde{R}_i^{def}$	Weights
C10	2.632	2.145	4.777	0.488	0.503
C11	2.121	2.609	4.729	-0.488	0.497

Table 28. The initial direct-relation fuzzy matrix for the criteria of D5

Criteria	C12			C13			C14		
Earnings (C12)	0.000	0.000	0.000	0.500	0.750	1.000	0.500	0.750	1.000
Competitive pricing (C13)	0.500	0.750	1.000	0.000	0.000	0.000	0.250	0.500	0.750
Promotions (C14)	0.250	0.500	0.750	0.250	0.500	0.750	0.000	0.000	0.000

Table 29. Normalized direct-relation fuzzy matrix for the criteria of D5

Criteria	C12			C13			C14		
Earnings (C12)	0.000	0.000	0.000	0.250	0.375	0.500	0.250	0.375	0.500
Competitive pricing (C13)	0.250	0.375	0.500	0.000	0.000	0.000	0.125	0.250	0.375
Promotions (C14)	0.125	0.250	0.375	0.125	0.250	0.375	0.000	0.000	0.000

Table 30. The total-relation fuzzy matrix for the criteria of D5

Criteria	C12			C13			C14		
Earnings (C12)	0.120	0.455	2.333	0.320	0.727	2.667	0.320	0.727	2.667
Competitive pricing (C13)	0.302	0.679	2.485	0.102	0.406	2.152	0.213	0.606	2.424
Promotions (C14)	0.178	0.533	2.182	0.178	0.533	2.182	0.067	0.333	1.909

Table 31. Total impact-relationship degrees and the weights for the criteria of D5

Criteria	$\tilde{D}_i^{def}$	$\tilde{R}_i^{def}$	$\tilde{D}_i^{def} + \tilde{R}_i^{def}$	$\tilde{D}_i^{def} - \tilde{R}_i^{def}$	Weights
C12	2.825	2.517	5.342	0.308	0.354
C13	2.550	2.517	5.066	0.033	0.335
C14	2.177	2.517	4.694	-0.341	0.311

Chapter 9
Supply Chain Modernization:
The Case of Turkish Companies in 3PL and 4PL Logistics Applications

Yasin Galip Gencer
Yalova University, Turkey

ABSTRACT

The global supply chain applications are evolving and changing globally. In order to increase success, some processes are now transferred to other firms. By such implementations, it is aimed to focus on the core business and to be successful. 3PL is the use of an external entity to perform some or all of the operations. The 4PL approach is a revolutionary approach to supply chain management. 3PL and 4PL activities are used for many purposes by multinational companies for increasing the productivity and efficiency and for decreasing the overall operational costs. Like all countries, Turkey also faces strategic organizational changes in terms of logistics activities. Modernization of logistic professes are widely examined in the literature. The scope of this chapter is the logistics modernization processes of Turkish companies, and it aims to inform about the modernization processes in Turkey by examining successful real-life examples.

INTRODUCTION

The total size of the logistics industry in Turkey is determined to be around 80 billion US dollars according to the Business Consulting Firms. The study was published by Brand Research with the name of Turkey Logistics Industry Survey 2011(Ozbek et al., 2013). This study was based on the logistics sector that has a share of 22% at Turkey's GDP with a great potential in terms of growth. On the other hand, the 3PL market was estimated to be nearly 22 billion US dollar. It is another fact that the logistics industry was seen to have grown by approximately 45% in past three years. In the same study, although the industry has grown steadily since 2002, the share of 3PL has increased by only 7%, which means that there is a growth potential not yet realized for 3PL companies. This data shows that 3PL logistics in Turkey will considerably increase. Businesses have focused on making improvements in their logistics activities in terms of customer satisfaction, together with reducing their costs (Gencer, 2016). While

DOI: 10.4018/978-1-5225-8109-3.ch009

some businesses are serviced by 3PL companies, others manage their own logistics networks themselves. Logistics activities have a great potential to increase (Yıldız et al., 2017).

The global supply chain applications are evolving and changing globally. In order to increase success some processes are now transferred to other firms (Ozcan, 2008). By such implementations, it is aimed to focus on the core business and to be successful. Logistics applications are also facing this reality (Gencer, 2017). Factors such as globalization, reduced supply times, customer harmonization and outsourcing have influenced the formation of third party logistics services. 3PL is the use of an external entity to perform some or all of the supply chain functions internally (Gencer et al., 2017). On the other hand, the 4PL approach is a revolutionary approach to supply chain management. Differences in 4PL approach from other outsourcing sources; to offer holistic supply chain solutions and to create values that will affect the entire supply chain (Kara, 2018).

CONCEPTUAL FRAMEWORK

Businesses, whether outsourcing or performing logistics activities on their own initiative, aim to keep operating costs at a minimum level and to maintain customer satisfaction by keeping service quality at the highest level (Akkucuk, 2009). For this reason, enterprises want to work with companies that want to have high quality among the 3PL enterprises in order to carry out their logistics activities, in addition to being the most suitable to their own corporate identity and having the lowest costs (Ozbek et al., 2013). The origin of the logistic word is Greek. Logistics is a science and it was used as an account bookmaking concept. Another meaning is economical resourcefulness (Akkucuk, 2011). Logistics is a word which was used in military terminology more recently. But recently it has become used mainly in businesses. In terms of logistics, many meanings are taken in many places. Things are put under the name of logistics. It is important to know that a logistical process is. It is an old idea that shipment is equivalent to logistics Shipping only should not come to mind. Today, however, logistics is now represented by more serious sectors with the addition of several sections and process; it has gained more serious meanings (Gencer et al., 2016). The most general one is that it is the process from the first point of a goods or service since reaching to the final buyer. If we think of a good or service as a product, for example, we can consume biscuits every day and this package comes as a package of biscuits. This biscuits can pass from a set of phases so that we can get to it in a certain way. Logistics is everywhere including customs, insurance, etc. these are things that are called processes.

It is thought that it is possible to sell every property that we can show to everywhere in the world. One of the most important points for buyers and sellers is price (Akkucuk et al., 2016). This factor naturally holds a great place in logistics companies including cost analysis or logistics information. Therefore it is possible to have a desired logistics at the desired time. In the case of military units, the meaning of transportation is the section about the transportation of the continents and the health needs in peace and voyage times. The logistics comes in the meaning of mathematical logic. When logistics is mentioned, as a consequence, we can describe logistics in three main sections. The first one is national logistics, the second is geo logistics and the last one is military logistics.

Furthermore, technology is one of the most important events of the world which has an important place in meeting and supplying human demands. Machines, devices, and methods, that are formed in order to collect, control, process and transmit information and power in the industry sector. On the other hand, technology is a Latin word. It means having knowledge to create and use devices such as the construction of an automobile. The technology is in fact being able to produce completely a device. When the technology produces and focuses its knowledge on the products, technology becomes very important in many directions (Kara, 2018). Technology usage in the businesses is almost the same with only slight differences. To find the methods to be used during the production of goods and services and to raise these methods is to make applications for solving the problems. Developing countries and/or developed countries are using technology to increase economic efficiency and achieve rapid growth. If developed countries cannot produce technology they have to buy them from developed countries.

SUPPLY CHAIN MODERNIZATION

Technology development never stops, thus, it is possible to face a different technological innovation every day. These developments affect human life at a great deal. Technological developments cannot be only a theorem idea as there is no benefit or benefit for all of them unless they are represented in the real life. There are many positive benefits for the lives of people. Technological changes have made a lot of improvements in the field of logistics and many things have become easier. For this reason, technology plays a very important role in logistics. As a result, it is obvious that the technology which is kept in this stage facilitates the work. All things in logistics are going on fast. The important thing is not to do it only faster and more, but more important is to improve the innovation and technology in this sector. Recalculation and pouring the work into computer data means a great speed development for logistics.

There is a noticeable rapid change in information technology in a global manner. In the logistics sector, customers are conscious, besides this, product variety increases and competition is getting hotter day by day. The importance of logistics software is increasing day by day. There are many software programs. Also there are companies established to produce and sell software in the logistics sector. Many times more than one software system is needed to be used in the logistics sector. This situation results by combinations of many different software solutions and the adopted versions needed to be developed for specific purposes. In other words, the software will be designed to correspond to the logistic needs of the companies. Companies using information technology are increasing their profits in their logistics efficiency. Customer satisfaction, increasing service quality, providing to pass ahead of competitors, reducing labor costs, and time decrease in service durations are the most important contributions of the technology in the logistics sector.

The logistics sector, which constitutes the main body of international trade in the world, is a big issue. It increases every passing day and this is why the limitations and problems of trade are left behind. The concept of logistics in the world has gained momentum after 1980s. It was the times when the functions of the companies were taken separately before the beginning. After the 1980s, the logistics companies started to stand out more and more and the market has emerged and divided by American, European and Asia-Pacific Market. Apart from this, there are natural markets but the most important 3 are these markets. Another element emerging in the markets is the Logistics Base. It is possible that a lot of logistics activities can be realized together and therefore the costs are reduced, which is beneficial for the enterprises.

Logistic in Turkey is a power that carries other sectors besides being a lone logistics sector. All sectors are almost over it. The reason for this is that production in Turkey is unlike all over the world. The logistics sector, which determines the winner of the competition, is strategic, but serious improvements have been achieved in the efficiency factor. Firms in Turkey want to leave behind each other by providing high efficiency in logistics and this is a prerequisite for searching 3PL and 4PL activities. Turkey's overall logistics costs are slightly behind when compared to developed countries. The reason for this is the inadequacy of the infrastructure. We can give examples of motorways and railways. The government of Turkey is making massive investments for highways nowadays. This is an unimaginable reality. But we can say that we are behind on the railways. For that reason, high logistics costs are also obvious. Logistics, by increasing its popularity in Turkey, will be a strategic core competence factor in the future.

Turkey, as a country experiences overall growth in exports, but making the events in the largely affect foreign trade. This is especially important in the transport sector. The political and economic events that are happening make exportation limited. We have a situation where we have an important place as a position to look at and exemplify logistics from the point of view of our country. The political crises that are happening in the west are reflected in the transportability, that is to say, logistics. These kinds of events, the reflection of crises on the logistics sector, are serious threats such as terrorism and sabotage, cargo security and cargo damage. In this case, the events caused by these crises cause companies that deal with the logistics company to be in a difficult situation and risk the transportation company. In this case, it results in serious dissatisfaction between the two sides. This is a serious shortcoming at a high level, especially in terms of branded logistics companies, because the companies doing this business should carry out the transport in an impartial and orderly manner, but unfortunately this type of political and economic crisis is causing serious shortcomings, and it is a situation that clearly explains that quality affects a great deal.

THIRD PARTY LOGISTICS (3PL)

Factors such as globalization, reduced supply times, customer harmonization and outsourcing have influenced the formation of third party logistics services. 3PL is the use of an external entity to perform some or all of the supply chain functions internally. Another definition is that it is an alliance in which a customer and service provider come together to establish a close and long-lasting relationship in order to meet the logistics needs of the system. (Skjoett Larsen et al., 1999) Instead of the concept of 3PL, "outsourcing" or "contract logistics" concepts are used in the literature. Firms may be able to enter into agreements for all logistics operations with other companies that provide 3PL service; they can receive services in part. Furthermore, in 3PL; the supplier is the first party, the buyer is the second party, and the intermediary company that carries out the logistics activities between these two parties is defined as the third party. Three parties cooperate to identify customers' logistics needs. All parties are responsible for the formation and structuring of logistics bases and determine performance measurement criteria. The main purpose is to bring a deal that both sides will profit. Multiple logistics services provided by a single service provider under a contract is the general definition of the 3PL. According to the Logistics Association, 3PL is defined as receiving services from several logistics companies in the supply chain (at least three different activities in succession, for example storage, transportation and inventory management). The traditional shipping approach, which was implemented before the introduction of 3PL, was an approach aimed at delivering only shipping services in a stereotyped way, where the customer could not offer any special services.

The development of new technologies and insights, and the increasing use of 3PL in scientific literature, has led to intense demand for 3PL companies. The most important factors in the emergence of 3PL companies are that; firms must realize that they have a lack of experience in reducing non-essential costs, and they should try to focus on core business and companies that are constantly improving in global markets. Companies needed to get services such as transportation, warehousing, stock, management and distribution within the supply and demand chain outside their core activities from other companies. Along with this, electronic commerce has spread rapidly and the understanding of transportation has changed and the logistics field has been improved. All these factors have contributed to the formation of 3PL companies.

The global supply chain applications are evolving and changing globally. In order to increase success some processes are now transferred to other firms. By such implementations, it is aimed to focus on the core business and to be successful. Logistics applications are also facing this reality. Factors such as globalization, reduced supply times, customer harmonization and outsourcing have influenced the formation of third party logistics services. 3PL is the use of an external entity to perform some or all of the supply chain functions internally. On the other hand, the 4PL approach is a revolutionary approach to supply chain management.

The services offered by 3PL companies have evolved over time as both information and technology. This development led to the formation of the first, second and third waves in the formation of the 3PLs. The first wave was in the 1980s when traditional shipping companies began to turn into 3PLs. During the second wave that began in the early 1990s, large logistics firms such as TNT and Fedex entered the sector. During the last and still ongoing third wave, companies that produce services in the field of auditing, finance and information technologies such as Anderson Consulting and General Electric, which inspect and supervise companies that enter the sector as new players. (Berglund, et al., 1999)

In addition, in practice, 3PL applications are far from strategically supporting operations throughout the supply chain. Most 3PL operators are focused on transport and storage. However, this situation is insufficient to meet the customers' integrated solution requests. Nowadays, a more comprehensive chain of supply management is beginning to be needed to meet the comprehensive needs of the companies and the demands of the customers. To address this shortcoming, a concept emerged that included a new relationship between suppliers and firms: "Fourth Party Logistics"

FOURTH PARTY LOGISTICS (4PL)

Factors such as globalization, reduced supply times, customer harmonization and outsourcing have influenced the formation of third party logistics services. 3PL is the use of an external entity to perform some or all of the supply chain functions internally. On the other hand, the 4PL approach is a revolutionary approach to supply chain management. Differences in 4PL approach from other outsourcing sources; to offer holistic supply chain solutions and to create values that will affect the entire supply chain. Most 3PL operators are focused on transport and storage. However, this situation is insufficient to meet the customers' integrated solution requests. Nowadays, a more comprehensive chain of supply management is beginning to be needed to meet the comprehensive needs of the companies and the demands of the customers. To overcome this shortage, 4PL concept is emerged. In this study, firstly the literature about the field was examined and then the concepts of 3PL and 4PL were explained, some important information about the status of these concepts are provided and the current situation related to the modernization of the Turkish logistics companies in the field of logistics is analyzed.

The success of companies implementing 4PL lies at the heart of their ability to provide customers with services that are best of breed. The 4PL approach is a revolutionary approach to supply chain management. Differences in 4PL approach from other outsourcing sources are; to offer holistic supply chain solutions and to create values that will affect the entire supply chain. A holistic 4PL supply chain solution has 4 different phases: (1) Rediscovery, (2) Conversion, (3) Application and (4) Action. For 4PL appliers to be successful; 3PL providers, IT providers, and providers of some other services should collaborate and provide various extra services such as call centers. At this point, the firm will provide a single intermediary firm instead of having to work with different providers. The concept and content of 4PL was first used by the Accenture Company and the company still holds its trademark. For this reason, other logistics firms that have been working on this subject are called "Leading Logistics Provider" 4PL; which provides services in its field of expertise by evaluating, designing, creating and operating the firm's supply chain solutions. Traditional approaches focus only on active transfer and cost reduction. 4PL practitioners face benefits such as income increase; operation cost decrease, working capital decrease and fixed value decrease.

Increase in revenue and in the product quality creates strategic advantage for companies and increased suitability will be achieved in customer service. The focus of the 4PL implementer on all supply chain management beyond transit or transportation activities contributes to a significant improvement in this regard. Synchronous management of supply chain operations reduces operational costs. In order for 4PL implementers to be able to effectively deliver successful and sustainable solutions, they must have certain criteria in terms of supply chains which should:

- Be effective in integration technologies and outsourcing opportunities
- Have the ability to access global resources
- Be active in the redesign of processes, technological integration and management
- Have experienced technical experts in business process management and outsourcing
- Have the ability to manage and organize multiple service providers in different areas
- Be able to meet organizational change needs.

In addition, companies may be hesitant to work with 4PL practitioners. One of the main reasons for this is that they do not want to share their secure data with another company at this scale. The reluctance of companies to share information and data about the entire supply chain with these providers is the most important reason for the mishaps in practice. In addition, it is difficult for retailers to see the 4PL approach as a cost priority. Logistics firms concentrate on creating value while reducing costs by moving out of transportation and transportation processes. This helps to create a different perspective for both companies. Fourth-party logistics companies have to make large-scale IT investments in order to meet customer demands and manage the full-time supply chain. For this reason, 4PL providers prefer to make long term contracts with customers. As a result, the concept of fourth-party logistics seems like a new concept, but it offers an effective way to manage the supply chains of the firm. This area is likely to experience much more development in the near future and its use will become more widespread.

COMPANIES USING 3PL AND 4PL APPLICATIONS

As explained above, traditional approaches focus only on active transfer and cost reduction. 4PL practitioners face benefits such as income increase; operation cost decrease, working capital decrease and fixed value decrease. Increase in revenue and in the product quality creates strategic advantage for companies and increased suitability will be achieved in customer service. The focus of the 4PL implementer on all supply chain management beyond transit or transportation activities contributes to a significant improvement in this regard. By the concept of fourth party logistics; information processing, consulting and financial services firms have also entered the third-party logistics market. These two companies can cooperate with each other. There are many examples in this regard in the world.

Reysaş Logistics

Reysaş; in 1990, started transportation business in Ankara with a limited number of trucks, cars, personnel and limited activity. Then, in 5 years, the company showed a great improvement and continued its activities rapidly and increased the number of customers. As of today, Reysaş is a large logistics company with a very large vehicle capacity, exceeding millions of car ownerships. Reysaş is a company that attaches importance to technological investment. It is the first company to use satellite system in the sector. It also provides warehouse management for its customers by using barcode and radio frequency systems in cold air and textile stores prepared using advanced technology. Reysaş, with its 6, 2 and 4 car transport vehicles, Cooled System transportation vehicles, Tilt, Hanging, Hydraulic Lift, and Seagull Wing technologies and; various volumes of vehicles provides services according to the customer demand. The average age of these machines is very low, and with other commercial vehicles, which can technologically be managed and are convenient to 4PL technologies it can provide a wide range of transportation services to enterprises by high customer satisfaction levels. The company has and uses hi-tech equipment that can manage and control themselves by smart artificial intelligence solutions and according to the company managers the prerequisite of successful and sustainable logistics processes is 4PL implementation. Thus, this implementation can only be provided by investment to such hi-tech vehicles. Also, according to Reysaş managers, besides the money spent for the investment, the staff should also be educated and should not avoid using this technology.

Aras Cargo

Aras Holding has established Aras Logistics in 2004 to carry out its activities in the field of logistics. Aras Logistics was established to undertake the entire logistics process and to be a professional support and solution partner for the holding. Aras Logistics provides customs clearance, warehousing, inventory control, packaging, labeling, invoicing, and distribution and transportation services for customers. Aras Logistics was established to provide distribution and transportation service for each and every specific product in the supply chain from the production to the stores and final users. In order to achieve this, the importer provides the services of importing, palletizing and/or packaging the goods from every corner of the world, making heavy intercity transport, stocking in the distribution centers in the regions and delivering the desired addresses in the fastest way according to the data coming from the digital environment. The managers of the company state that for a successful supply chain operations the collaboration is a must and can only be provided by the technology. 4PL implementation brings together these infrastructure producers or importers with; the entities in all other cities, exit ports or customs. Although Aras Logistics is a newly established company, it is assertive to provide 3PL and 4PL services according to the company managers. They emphasize the intention to capture all transportation of various companies from all sectors by their 4PL logistics solutions. According to them, it is enough for any company to make a phone call, and then they solve all logistics problems and provide sustainable and successful services by 4PL implementation. They also state that the 4PL implementation creates a competitive advantage for the companies that work by Aras Logistics, because they can use their efforts for their core businesses not logistics operations.

Yurtiçi Tibbett and Britten

Yurtiçi Logistics was founded in 2002 by Turkey's first domestic shipping company. They were still benefiting from this domestic courier experience. Yurtiçi Logistics opened an international market with the protocol signed between Arikanli Holding and Tibbett & Britten Group. Founded in Logistics on 30 July 2003, YTB Logistics brought a new impetus to the logistics sector, and to deal with Turkey's integration with the world. They tried to make benefit of this new dimension. With this partnership, the supply chain services provided to customers by Yurtiçi Lojistik exceeded the borders of the country and gained the advantage of competition with the international market for the Turkish business enterprises. According to the reviews done by the managers of the company speed and customer focus are the two most important elements for YTB Logistics. YTB Logistics supports its customers with consultancy services for efficient work in sectors such as fast consumption and textiles where expertise proposes strategic advantage. The company managers state that with project management approach, YTB Logistics offers sector specific solutions and correct cost proposals in all areas of the supply chain by 4PL implementation solutions. YTB Logistics has 540 branches across Turkey and carrying out their work with 18 regional offices. They also mention that in terms of 3PL and 4PL applications, YTB logistics is one of the most successful companies to implement. Especially they work on fast consumption and textile industries and their operations are planned and organized accordingly with the expectations of these businesses. YTB Logistics has many more branches than any other logistics company allover Turkey and this is the main advantage for companies that will outsource their 4PL logistics operations to them. Lastly the managers also state that they were very successful in the 3PL logistics solutions but now they do not hesitate from any investment regarding 4PL investments. They know that by these investments their customers will face higher satisfaction levels.

REFERENCES

Akküçük, U. (2009). İş Etiğinde Sarbanes-Oxley (SOX) Yasası'nın Etkisi ve Toplam Kalite Yönetimi Uygulamalarında Yansımaları. *İş Ahlakı Dergisi, 2*(3), 7-17.

Akkucuk, U. (2011). Combining Purchase Probabilities and Willingness to Pay Measures: A Case on Recycled Products. *European Journal of Soil Science, 23*(3), 353–361.

Akkucuk, U., & Esmaeili, J. (2016). The impact of brands on consumer buying behavior: An empirical study on smartphone buyers. *International Journal of Research in Business and Social Science, 5*(4), 1-16.

Berglund, M., Van Laarhoven, P., Sharman, G., & Wandel, S. (1999). Third-party logistics: Is there a future? *International Journal of Logistics Management, 10*(1), 59–70. doi:10.1108/09574099910805932

Gencer, Y. G. (2016). Mystery of recycling: Glass and aluminum examples. In *Handbook of research on waste management techniques for sustainability* (pp. 172–191). IGI Global. doi:10.4018/978-1-4666-9723-2.ch009

Gencer, Y. G. (2017). Supply chain management in retailing business. *Ethics and sustainability in global supply chain management*, 197-210.

Gencer, Y. G., & Akkucuk, U. (2016). Product Recalls as an Important Category of Reverse Logistics. *DEStech Transactions on Environment, Energy and Earth Sciences.*

Gencer, Y. G., & Akkucuk, U. (2017). Measuring Quality in Automobile Aftersales: AutoSERVQUAL Scale. *Amfiteatru Economic, 19*(44), 110.

Kara, A. (n.d.). Yeni İletişim Ortamlarinda Pazarlama Faaliyetlerinin Kullanimi İle İlgili İçerik Analizi: Türk Organik Tarim Sektörü Örnek Olayi. *İşletme Ekonomi ve Yönetim Araştırmaları Dergisi, 1*(1), 17-33.

Özbek, A. (2013). Analitik Ağ Süreci Yaklaşimiyla Üçüncü Parti Lojistik (3pl) Firma Seçimi. *Atatürk Üniversitesi İktisadi ve İdari Bilimler Dergisi, 27*(1).

Özcan, S. (2008). Küçük ve Orta Büyüklükteki İşletmelerde Lojistik Yönetiminin Önemi/The Importance of Logistics Management in Small And Medium Sized Enterprises. *Mustafa Kemal Üniversitesi Sosyal Bilimler Enstitüsü Dergisi, 5*(10).

Skjøtt-Larsen, T. (1999). Interorganisational relations from a supply chain management point of view. *Logistik management, 1*(2), 96-108.

Yıldız, M. S., & Aksoy, S. (2015). *Analitik Hiyerarşi Prosesi ile Personel Seçimi Üzerine Bir Çalışma.* Abant İzzet Baysal Üniversitesi Sosyal Bilimler Enstitüsü Dergisi.

Chapter 10
The Effect of Health and Education Expenditures on Poverty:
The Case of Central and Eastern European Countries

Mahmut Unsal Sasmaz
Usak University, Turkey

Omer Faruk Ozturk
Usak University, Turkey

Yunus Emre Yayla
Sakarya University, Turkey

ABSTRACT

Poverty is a phenomenon that influences and complicates the living conditions of individuals. Along with the poverty, individuals experience health problems, and educational and income levels of individuals may also be low. Countries are generally able to fight against poverty by increasing public expenditures and making some economic progresses. For that reason, analyzing the effect of health and education expenditures with a significant place in public expenditures and economic growth on poverty is highly important. In this chapter, the effect of health and education expenditures and economic growth on poverty in 2005 and 2016 period in eight Central and Eastern European countries has been analyzed using panel data analysis. As a result of the study, it has been determined that health and education expenditures and economic growth have a negative effect on poverty. In addition, a one-way causality from health and education expenditures to poverty and a two-way causality between economic growth and poverty have been detected.

DOI: 10.4018/978-1-5225-8109-3.ch010

INTRODUCTION

Poverty is an issue which complicates the lives of people and influences the life quality of people. In the countries in which poverty is experienced people are not able to meet their needs to sustain their lives. Poverty is generally experienced as the absence of essential materials such as food, clean drinking water, clothes and sheltering and therefore, the lack of health conditions. The lack or absence of basic food materials leads the health level to be low and endangers the lives of people.

Poverty is rather observed in the countries that have not been able to develop although it is rarely observed in all countries. Poverty in the countries that have not been able to develop generally refers to the absence of basic food and living materials. Poverty is less experienced in developing countries than in underdeveloped countries. However, poverty rate is minimum in developed countries. It is observed that the poverty rate has reduced as compared to previous years as a result of the policies against poverty both on the national and global basis. Thus, according to the World Bank data, while 44% of the world's population lives with or below $ 1,90 per day in 1981, this rate was 35% in 1990 and 10,7% in 2013 (World Bank, 2018a).

Although poverty level reduces globally, it is still one of the most important issues that countries fight against because it still exists. Countries develop various plans and programs in order to fight against poverty and provide better living conditions for individuals. Countries generally try to make economic progresses by increasing public expenditures qualitatively and quantitatively in the fight against poverty. For that reason, it is very important to research the effect of health and education expenditures with a significant and high share in public expenditures and economic growth on poverty.

Akkucuk (2017) states that "sustainable development has a number of facets related to politics, ecology, economics, business, supply chain management and waste management". In previous works related to sustainability, mainly the connection to supply chain management related issues have been discussed. The relationship between SCOR model and the green supply chain (Akkucuk, 2016), reverse logistics considerations (Gencer and Akkucuk, 2016), the relationship to quality management models (Akkucuk and Gencer, 2017) and the role of nongovernmental bodies (Akkucuk and Şekercioğlu, 2016) are examples to these. Elimination of poverty, however, is an integral element of the circular economy and relates to the sustainability of the world economy as poverty can lead to instability and chaos. Therefore the study of poverty should be included in a work covering issues on the circular economy and sustainability.

In this study the effect of health and education expenditures and economic growth on poverty in 2005 and 2016 period in 8 Central and Eastern European countries has been analyzed using panel data analysis. First of all, the theoretical information about poverty, health and education expenditures has been included in order to understand the issue better. In the next part, literature review, data, empirical analyses applied with methodology and the related information and analysis results have been included. The study has been concluded with conclusion and evaluation part.

THEORY

Theoretical information about poverty, health expenditures, education expenditures and economic growth will be presented in this part.

Poverty

A poor person as a word meaning is a person who does not have enough money and the necessary tools for a comfortable life. Poverty means being deprived of the opportunities that the life necessitates (Aktan and Vural, 2002). Poverty is a multi-dimensional problem which includes the factors such as finance, catering, health, dwellings, protection of health, politics, infrastructure, war and education (Walingo, 2006, p. 288).

Traditional definitions of poverty focus on income and wealth or lack of money and properties. However, the definition of poverty has recently expanded to other non-materialistic aspects of human welfare. Evolution of the concept of poverty generally reflects the changes in development theories and practices and especially the analysis of the causes of poverty (Angelsen and Sven, 2006).

When the living standards of people is compared both unconditionally or with the other people in society, whether people meet the basic needs of the life or not will reflect that they live in poverty (Weziak-Bialowolska and Dijkstra, 2014, p. 6). Since the needs of individuals to maintain their lives will change depending on their society, environment and conditions, the concept of poverty will bring up the comparison of the continuously observed situation and the standard situation (Aktan and Vural, 2002).

Poverty is a phenomenon which can be seen in all underdeveloped, developing and developed countries or regions in different rates and forms. While poverty is the failure to meet the basic food needs especially in the countries that are not able to develop, it is rather relative poverty in developed countries (Şantaş, 2017, p. 550). 44% of the world's population lived with or below $ 1.90 per day in 1980, this rate was 35% in 1990 and it was 10.7% in 2013 (World Bank, 2018a).

While income poverty criteria are usually in the forefront in measuring the poverty ($ 1 per day criterion by World Bank is often used), there are also compound indices to measure multidimensional human poverty. Poverty rate (head count rate), poverty gap rate, squared poverty gap rate and Sen index are especially used in measuring the income poverty. Human Poverty Index published by United Nations in 1997 and Multidimensional Poverty Index published in 2010 are generally used in measuring human poverty (Doğan, 2014, pp. 13-19).

Poverty and social exclusion risk indicators are the sum of those living in poverty and those with very low work intensity or at risk of serious financial deprivation. It includes the indicators about financial deprivation, economic stress and durability. People with heavy financial deprivation have severely limited living conditions due to the lack of sources. Besides the poverty, individuals experience at least 4 items of 9 items consisting of paying rent or utility bills, keeping the house warm enough, facing unexpected costs, eating meat and fish or protein equivalent of every two days, weekly holiday home, car, washing machine, color television and telephone (Eurostat, 2018a).

2016 poverty and social exclusion risk (%) data of the countries forming the sample group of the study are presented in Table 1. Poverty and social exclusion risk is published by Eurostat as percentage data and as the rate increases, poverty and social exclusion risk increases. When the data is analyzed, the country with the highest poverty and social exclusion risk among 8 countries is Lithuania and Latvia follows it. We can see that the country with the lowest poverty and social exclusion risk is Czechia and then Slovakia follows it. Poverty and social exclusion risk may vary depending on the factors such as difference in development among countries, economic size of countries, understanding of social state, population of country etc.

Table 1. 2016 Yearly Poverty and Social Exclusion Risk in the Countries of the Sample Group (%)

2016 Year Ranking	Country	Poverty and Social Exclusion Risk (%)
1	Lithuania	30,1
2	Latvia	28,5
3	Hungary	26,3
4	Estonia	24,4
5	Poland	21,9
6	Slovenia	18,4
7	Slovakia	18,1
8	Czechia	13,3

Source: (Eurostat, 2018a)

Health Expenditures

Health expenditures have significant effects on life span and life qualities of individuals. Hereby, healthcare sector is important for countries because it is a type of human investment. Along with the improvement in health conditions, providing better health services is one of the basic aspects of social and economic development. Hence, making investments on healthcare sector is considered as a model of the planned human resources development among the infrastructure investments just like other sectors (Razmi et al. 2012). We can see that health is emphasized more than ever in development process in terms of human development. The reason for this is that health points to the formation of human characteristics that reveal the primary dimension of human development (Mirahsani, 2016, p. 373).

World Health Organization (WHO), one of the international organizations in healthcare sector, is in the system of United Nations and it is an authority which works on, coordinates and manages health. The experts of WHO develop health rules and standards and help countries to handle the community health problems. In addition, WHO supports and promotes the health researches. Countries can fight against global healthcare problems together via WHO and increase the welfare of people (World Health Organization, 2007, p. 2).

Total health expenditures as a share of world Gross National Product (GNP) was 3% in 1948; however, this increased to 8%. In the world, more than US $ 600 per person was spent for health in 2001 and US $ 3.8 trillion was spent as health expenditure worldwide (World Health Organization, 2004, p. 1). We can see that global health expenditures were US $ 7.2 trillion in 2015. In other words, it was 10% of global GNP (World Health Organization, 2018).

The rate of 2016 health expenditures of 8 countries forming the sample of the study to GNP is presented in Table 2. When the data are analyzed, the country with the highest rate of health expenditures to GNP among the 8 countries is Slovenia and Hungary follows it. The country with the lowest rate of health expenditures to GDP among the countries is Latvia and Poland follows it. Health expenditures may vary depending on the factors such as economic development levels of countries, health systems of countries and development of health system in the country.

Table 2. 2016 Yearly Ratio of Health Expenditures to GDP in the Sample Group Countries (%)

2016 Year Ranking	Country	Ratio of Health Expenditures to GDP (%)
1	Slovenia	8,47
2	Hungary	7,37
3	Czechia	7,14
4	Slovakia	7,13
5	Estonia	6,68
6	Lithuania	6,67
7	Poland	6,51
8	Latvia	6,24

Source: (OECD, 2018)

Education

Education has significant effect in social life by contributing to the improvements in the lives of individuals and the reduction in poverty. Education promotes social development by helping people to become more productive and gain more, improving health and nutrition, enriching people's lives directly and strengthening social cohesion, and giving better opportunities to more people. A good education system is a necessary, but insufficient condition for development and its benefits are strong even if its public policy is managed equally as other fields (World Bank, 1999, p. 5)

Education is critically important for reducing poverty. As a result of changing technology and economic reforms, it is at the forefront of education that economies can meet increasing demands for adaptable workers who can gain new skills and support the continuous expansion of knowledge. Investment in education contributes the accumulation of human capital. Education leads to decrease the fertility and poverty by increasing especially the basic (primary- middle-lower) education-poor productivity and provides people with the skills that they join in the economy and the society thoroughly by improving the health. (World Bank, 1995, pp. 1-2).

Education is in Human Development Index which indicates the development level of countries. As a result of the development, poverty level in countries decreases obviously. For that reason, including education in the index indicates the importance of education in development process of countries. Human Development Index published since 1990 is calculated depending on health, education and income indices. Expected education period and average education period are in sub-components of education which is one of the components of Human Development Index (Human Development Report, 2016).

The data for the rate of 2016 education expenditures of the countries in the study to GNP are presented in Table 3. When we have a look at the data, we can see that Estonia is the country with the highest rate of education expenditures to GDP among 8 countries in the sample group and Slovenia follows it. Slovakia is the country with the lowest rate of education expenditures to GNP and Czechia follows it. Education expenditures in a country may vary depending on the factors such as the development level of the country, education system and development level of education system.

Table 3. Ratio of 2016 Annual Education Expenditures to GDP in the Sample Group Countries (%)

2016 Year Ranking	Country	Ratio of Education Expenditures to GDP (%)
1	Estonia	5,9
2	Slovenia	5,6
3	Latvia	5,5
4	Lithuania	5,2
5	Poland	5
6	Hungary	4,9
7	Czechia	4,5
8	Slovakia	3,8

Source: (Eurostat, 2018b)

Economic Growth

Economic growth is usually defined as an increase in overall Gross National Product (GNP) or GNP per capita (Angelsen and Sven, 2006). The value of GNP is used to compare the development levels of countries. In addition, GNP per capita can be used instead of GNP (Özsoy, 2012, p. 6).

Economic growth is the most powerful tool for decreasing poverty and increasing the life quality in developing countries. Growth may generate welfare and opportunity-virtuous environment. Strong growth and employment opportunities provide incentives for parents to make investments on education for their children by sending them to schools. This may lead to the occurrence of a strong and growing entrepreneur group which is obliged to make pressure for advanced governance. For that reason, a strong economic growth promotes the human development and this encourages the economic growth (Department for International Development, 2008)

The annual increase rate of 2016 income per capita of 8 sample group countries is presented in Table 4. When the data are analyzed, Lithuania is the country with the highest annual increase rate of income per capita among 8 countries and Slovakia follows it. Estonia is the country with the lowest annual increase rate of income per capita and Czechia follows it. Economic status, economic size, economic development levels of countries and global cyclical situation, etc. can be said among the main reasons for the differences in economic growth.

LITERATURE

There are several studies on the effect of health and education expenditures and economic growth on poverty in literature (See. Jha et al. (2001), Agrawal (2007), Nandori (2010), Widiastuti (2010), Kurita and Kurosaki (2011), Dahlquist (2014), Erkal et al. (2015)). In the conducted studies it was determined that health and education expenditures and economic growth had a negative on poverty ((See. Jha et al. (2001), Agrawal (2007), Widiastuti (2010), Afzal et al. (2012), Dahlquist (2014), Kiki et al. (2015)). However, there are a few studies that cannot identify a long term relationship among health and education expenditures, economic growth and poverty. (See. Ahmad and Batul (2013). The studies carried out to identify the effect of health and education expenditures and economic growth on poverty are outlined

Table 4. Annual Growth Rate of Per Capita Income in Sample Group Countries in 2016 (%)

2016 Year Ranking	Country	Annual Growth Rate of Per Capita Income (%)
1	Lithuania	3,607043093
2	Slovakia	3,191572522
3	Slovenia	3,0728814
4	Latvia	3,01276702
5	Poland	2,90855455
6	Hungary	2,515274973
7	Czechia	2,396486237
8	Estonia	2,033554222

Source: (World Bank, 2018b)

as the following: Riman et al. (2010) in their study analyzing the relationship for the effect of health expenditures on poverty researched the relationship among health expenditures, poverty and health status between 1980 and 2004 in Nigeria by using Granger causality test and Vector Error Correction Model (VECM). As a result of their study, they determined a long term relationship between poverty and health status. However, they could not find a significant long term relationship between health status and health expenditures of the government. In a similar study Jha et al. (2001) researched the effect of public expenditures about education, health and other development activities to reduce poverty between 1957-1958 and 1997 in 14 states of India by using panel data analysis method. As a result of their study they determined that the public expenditures about education, health and other development activities reduced the poverty. Njong (2010) in the study researching the effect of education expenditures on poverty analyzed the effect of education in reducing poverty using 2001 Cameroon Household Survey data by National Statistics Institute in Cameroon through logistic regression method. As a result of the study, it was found out that the educational success had a negative effect on poverty. In another study Bakırtaş and Kandemir (2012) analyzed the relationship between educational variables and poverty in eighty one province of Turkey using multilinear regression method. As a result of their study, they determined that illiteracy and primary and secondary education schooling rate expressed the poverty with 79% in provinces. In a similar study Ahmad and Batul (2013) analyzed the relationship among poverty, education expenditures and educational status in Pakistan between 1971 and 2011 using Johansen cointegration test, VECM, Wald Test and Granger causality test. As a result of their study, they found a two-way causality relationship poverty rate and educational status. However, they could not find a significant long term relationship between poverty rate and education expenditures. In another study Sarkaria and Shiwani (2016) analyzed the relationship between education and poverty using 1520 household survey data between 2008 and 2010 in Punjap using logistic regression method. As a result of the study, they determined that success in education had a negative effect on poverty. Agrawal (2007) in the study researching the effect of economic growth on poverty used the 2000-2012 period with the data of province level in Kazakhstan through panel data analysis. As a result of the study, it was determined that the provinces with higher growth rate experienced a faster decline in poverty. In a similar study Nandori (2010) researched the relationship among economic growth, income inequality and poverty through regression analysis method using household surveys and 39 observations which have been available since 1990 in 9 Eastern European countries. As a result of the study it was determined that economic growth had a significant effect on poverty. In another study Kurita and Kurosaki (2011) researched the relationship among growth, poverty and inequality through panel data analysis method using household spending micro data in Philippines in 1985-2003 period and in Thailand in 1988-2004 period. As a result of their study, it was determined that inequality reduced the growth and poverty decreasing rate in Thailand; however, this realized in Philippines indirectly. However, Açıkgöz (2015) analyzed the relationship among poverty, development and public expenditures in developed and developing countries using FMOLS method. As a result of the study, it was identified that the effect of public expenditures on development in developed countries was less than in developing countries. It was also found that public expenditures had significant effects on poverty and development in underdeveloped and developing countries. In another study Erkal et al. (2015) analyzed the relationship among poverty, income inequality and economic growth in 1998 and 2010 period in 11 countries selected in Eastern Europe and Latin America. They set two different models on growth and poverty. As a result of the study, they determined that along with the emergence of the poverty as a result of an increase in income inequality led to growth. In addition, they concluded that public expenditures, one of the variables they used in the model, reduced poverty; however, private health expenditures increased poverty.

Widiastuti (2010) in the study analyzing the effect of education expenditures and economic growth on poverty analyzed the factors affecting poverty in 2004 and 2008 period in 35 districts of Java using panel data analysis. As a result of the study, it was identified that economic growth and education variables had a negative and significant effect on poverty. In a similar study, Afzal et al. (2012) researched the relationship among education, poverty, real capital and economic growth between 1971-1972 and 2009-2010 years in Pakistan using ARDL and Toda Yamamoto Augmented Granger Causality (TYAGC) test. As a result of the study, they determined that there was an inverse significant relationship in long term between poverty and economic growth. In addition, they found a two-way causality relationship between education and economic growth, economic growth and poverty and poverty and education according to causality test results. In another study Dahlquist (2014) examined poverty and growth rate of income per capita, poverty level, income level per capita, average education period, employment in industry, public education expenditures relationships in 2000 and 2009 period in 123 countries using multivariable linear regression model. As a result of the study it was determined that growth reduced the poverty and public expenditures for education was for reducing the poverty. However, Kiki et al. (2015) analyzed the poverty causing factors in 2003 and 2013 period in Indonesia using multilinear regression analysis method. They used economic growth, unemployment and illiteracy as variables in the study. As a result of the study, they determined that there was a positive and significant relationship between unemployment and illiteracy and poverty level, but a negative and significant relationship between economic growth and poverty.

DATA

The long term relationship and causality between health expenditures, education expenditures, economic growth and poverty in 2005-2016 period in 8 Central and Eastern European countries were analyzed in this study. 8 Central and Eastern European countries forming the sample of the study are the countries which have left central planning since 1990's and passed on to market economy. Compared to the other countries in European Union known as EU transition economies, they later passed on to the market economy and had many reforms to catch the EU standards. For that reason, the countries with transition economies were preferred in order to benefit from transition economies and examine the effect of the reforms.

In the process of data selection target of the study and theoretical and empirical literature were taken into consideration. The data used in this study are presented in Table 5 and the related data were obtained from European Union Statistics Office (Eurostat), Organization of Economic Cooperation and Development (OECD) and World Bank. We used poverty as the dependent variable, health and education expenditures affecting the poverty as the independent variable and the annual increase rate of income per capita as a representative of economic growth as the control variable in the study.

METHODOLOGY

The long term relationship between health and education expenditures and economic growth and poverty in 8 Central and Eastern European countries and the causality relationship were examined in the study by using panel data analysis.

Firstly, cross-sectional dependence test was used in the study, and then panel CADF unit root test considering cross-sectional dependence was performed. After the unit root test, Peseran and Yamagata (2008) homogeneity test was performed. After that, through Westerlund and Edgerton (2007) test cointegration relationship and through FMOLS test long term relationship between the variables and the direction of the relationship were analyzed. Then, Kónya (2006) Panel Bootstrap Granger causality test and Emirmahmutoglu and Kose (2011) causality test were performed. First of all, the information about the tests performed in econometric analysis was given and then test results were evaluated.

The expected relationships between the variables are presented in Table 6 by considering the theoretical and empirical literature. Health expenditures, education expenditures and economic growth used in the study are expected to reduce the poverty. Because education expenditures affect the life quality of an individual since they are the investments on human and economic growth provide economic development, it can be said that they may reduce poverty.

EMPIRICAL RESULTS

Only one model was estimated in the study. As the dependent variable of the model in the study poverty (POV), as the independent variable health expenditures (HE) and education expenditures (EE), as the control variable economic growth (GRW) were used. The effect of health and education expenditures and economic growth on poverty was analyzed in the model. The model was given with the following equation:

Table 5. Variables and Definitions Used in Analysis

Variable	Symbol	Source
Poverty	POV	Eurostat (2018a)
Health Expenditure	HE	OECD (2018)
Education Expenditure	EE	Eurostat (2018b)
Economic Growth	GRW	World Bank (2018b)

Table 6. Variable, Variable Abbreviation and Possible Impact

Variable	Variable Abbreviation	The Estimated Effect
Health Expenditure	HE	(-)
Education Expenditure	EE	(-)
Economic Growth	GRW	(-)

Model: $POV2_{it} = \alpha_{it} + \beta_1 HE_{it} + \beta_2 EE_{it} + \beta_3 GRW_{it} + u_{it}$ (1)

Cross-Sectional Dependence Test

When there is a cross-sectional dependence between the variables to be used in econometric analysis, making the analysis without considering this situation remarkably affects the results. For that reason, cross-sectional dependence between variables has to be tested (Pesaran, 2004).

While performing the cross-sectional dependence test, Breusch and Pagan (1980) LM test (Equation 2) is used when it is stable and the section dimension is smaller than the time dimension (Baltagi et al., 2012, pp. 165-167). However, when the time dimension is smaller than the section dimension, Peseran CD_{LM} test is used in cross-sectional dependence test. Peseran (2004) developed a scaled version of LM_{BP} test data. That being said, when the time dimension is equal to the section dimension Peseran (2004) CD_{LM2} test is performed. In addition, Pesaran et al. (2008) developed a bias-adjusted LM test using finite sample approaches in a heterogeneous panel model.

$$LM_{BP} = T\sum_{i=1}^{n-1}\sum_{j=i+1}^{n} \rho_{ij}^{\varsigma 2} . \qquad (2)$$

Hypotheses of cross-sectional dependence test are as follows:

H_0: There is no cross-sectional dependence.
H_1: There is cross-sectional dependence.

Cross-sectional dependence test results are presented in Table 7:

When the probability value is under 0.05, the H_0 hypothesis of "There is no cross-sectional dependence between the series" is rejected at 5% of significance level in cross-sectional dependence test results and it is concluded that there is cross-sectional dependence between the series in the panel (Pesaran et al., 2008). When we look at the cross-sectional dependence test results, we can see that H_0 hypothesis is rejected at 5% of significance level across the panel. For that reason, a second generation unit root test considering the cross-sectional dependence was performed in the study.

Table 7. Horizontal Cross-Section Dependency Test Results

Horizontal Cross Section Dependence in Variables	POV		HE		EE		GRW		MODEL	
	Stat.	Prob.	Stat	Prob.	Stat.	Prob.	Stat.	Prob.	Stat.	Prob.
CD_{LM1} (BP,1980)	91.919	0.000	117.635	0.000	88.074	0.000	64.933	0.000	201.649	0.000
CD_{LM2} (Pesaran, 2004)	8.542	0.000	11.978	0.000	8.028	0.000	4.935	0.000	23.205	0.000
CD_{LM} (Pesaran, 2004)	-1.330	0.092	-1.586	0.056	-1.883	0.030	-1.315	0.094	14.052	0.000
Bias-Adjusted CD Test	5.273	0.000	2.280	0.011	8.540	0.000	-	-	23.621	0.000

CADF Unit Root Test

CADF unit root test (Cross-Sectionally Augmented Dickey-Fuller) was developed by Peseran (2007). It is unrealistic to assume that the cross-sectional units in the analysis are not affected by each other in case of a shock to the series. Unit root tests (second generation unit root tests) considering cross-sectional dependence should be used in order to get healthy econometric analysis results (Pesaran, 2007).

In CADF unit root test, the fact that unit root tests can be performed for each cross-section of the series used in the panel allows to test the stability of the series across the panel and the possibility to separately calculate the panel overall and each cross-section (Pesaran, 2007).

Peseran (2007) CADF regression equation is presented in Equation 3;

$$y_{it} = \left(1-\phi_i\right)\mu_i + \phi_i y_{i,t-1} + u_{it}, i = 1,\ldots,N; t = 1,\ldots,T \quad u_{it} = Y_i f_t + \varepsilon_{it} \tag{3}$$

CADF unit root test can be used when the section dimension is bigger than the time dimension and the time dimension is bigger than the section dimension. Hypotheses of CADF unit root test are presented in Equation 4 and 5 (Pesaran, 2007, p. 268).

$$H_0 : \beta_0 = 0 \text{ (The series is not stable.)} \tag{4}$$

$$H_1 : \beta_0 < 0, i = 1,2,\ldots,N_1, \beta_1 = 0, i = N_1 + 1, N_1 + 2,\ldots,N \text{ (The series is stable.)} \tag{5}$$

The CIPS value in CADF unit root test result (Equation 6) is obtained by calculating the average of t value calculated for each cross-section (Pesaran, 2007, p. 276).

$$\mathrm{CIPS}\left(\mathrm{N},\ \mathrm{T}\right) = \mathrm{t} - \mathrm{bar} = \mathrm{N}^{-1}\sum_{i=1}^{N} \mathrm{t}_i\left(\mathrm{N},\ \mathrm{T}\right) \tag{6}$$

CADF unit root test results are presented in Table 8;

Table 8. CADF Unit Root Test Results

LEVEL	POV	HE	EE	GRW
Constant Statistic	-2.222	-2.063	-1.893	-2.227
FIRST DIFFERENCE	**POV**	**HE**	**EE**	**GRW**
Constant Statistic	**-5.454*****	**-4.026*****	**-3.556*****	**-4.421*****

Note: * %10, ** %5, *** %1 it shows that zero hypothesis is rejected at the level of significance. A fixed model was used for the test model. Constant critical values are -2.97 (1%), -2.52 (5%), -2.31 (10%). Pesaran (2007) article was used for critical value calculations.

When we look at the CIPS values according to CADF unit root test results, the hypothesis of "there is unit root" cannot be rejected because the CIPS values are not stable at the levels of series in the panel. It was determined that they became stable when their first difference was taken, in other words they were I(1). As the series become stable, there is no objection to perform a panel cointegration test.

Westerlund and Edgerton (2007) Cointegration Test

Before the panel cointegration test, a homogeneity test is performed in order to identify whether the cointegration slope coefficients are homogeneous or heterogeneous. In addition, the homogeneity test is effective in identifying the stability of the series and determining the tests to be performed for testing whether there is cointegration relationship among series or not (Pesaran and Yamagata, 2008, p. 56). While the null hypothesis of Peseran and Yamagata (2008) homogeneity test is as "slope coefficients are homogeneous", the alternative hypothesis is as "slope coefficients are not homogenous".

As a result of homogeneity test, when the probability value is bigger than 0.10, the null hypothesis is accepted at 10% of significance level. If the null hypothesis is accepted, it can be said that the cointegration test results to be performed after the homogeneity test are valid and reliable (Pesaran and Yamagata, 2008). Homogeneity test results are presented in Table 9. The null hypothesis is accepted since the probability value of the tests calculated in Table 9 is bigger than 0.10. In other words, it was concluded that the constant term and slope coefficients are homogeneous in the cointegration equation.

After the homogeneity test, panel bootstrap cointegration test developed by Westerlund and Edgerton (2007) was performed in order to identify whether there is a cointegration relationship among variables or not. Westerlund and Edgerton cointegration test which is based on Lagrande test multiplier developed by McCoskey and Kao (1998) considers the dependence among cross section units. It was determined that Westerlund and Edgerton (2007) cointegration test gave good results when small samples were used (Westerlund and Edgerton, 2007).

The hypotheses used in Westerlund and Edgerton (2007) panel statistics are as follows:

Table 9. Homogeneity Test Results

	Test Statistic	Probability Value
$\tilde{\Delta}$	0.724	0.235
$\tilde{\Delta}_{adj}$	0.825	0.205

$H_0^p: \alpha_i = 0$ (There is a cointegration.)
$H_A^p: \alpha_i = \alpha < 0$ (There is no cointegration.)

Westerlund and Edgerton (2007) cointegration test results are presented in Table 10:

When we look at Westerlund and Edgerton (2007) cointegration test results, the basic hypothesis of "there is a cointegration" is accepted at 5% of significance level.

Panel FMOLS Test

After panel cointegration test, analysis methods were developed in order to determine the coefficients of the relationship among variables. FMOLS (Least Squares Estimation) method which was developed by Pedroni and which is one of these analysis methods allows correcting the deviations in fixed effect (standard) estimators.

Panel FMOLS method test results are presented in Table 11:

According to panel FMOLS test results, a negative relationship was found between health and education expenditures and economic growth and poverty. The relationship between education expenditures and economic growth was found significant at 1% level and the relationship between health expenditures and poverty was found significant at 5% level. It can be expressed that since health and education expenditures are types of human investments, individuals may have a negative effect on poverty as a result of the fact that their quality of life is affected although they are healthy and adult. It can also be said that since economic growth provides an economic development in countries, it may cause a negative effect on poverty.

Table 10. Westerlund and Edgerton (2007) Cointegration Test Results

Model	LM-Statistic	Asymptotic Probability Value	Bootsrap Probability Value
Constant Model	1.336	0.091	0.879

Note: Bootstrap probability values from 10,000 repetitive distributions; the asymptotic probability values are obtained from the standard normal distribution. The delay and premise were taken as one, and the fixed model was preferred.

Table 11. Panel FMOLS Test Results

Model: $POV2_{it} = \alpha_{it} + \beta_1 HE_{it} + \beta_2 EE_{it} + \beta_3 GRW_{it} + u_{it}$			
Variable	**Coefficient**	**t-Statistic**	**Prob.**
HE	-0.976794	1.069391	**0.0282****
EE	-0.315792	-10.47896	**0.0000*****
GRW	-0.145935	44.18575	**0.0000*****

Note: * %10, ** %5, *** %1 ıt makes sense at the level.

Causality Test Results

Kónya (2006) Panel Bootstrap Causality Test and Emirmahmutoglu and Kose (2011) causality test were performed in the study. Two causality tests were used because results of the countries were given due to the absence of panel average in Kónya panel bootstrap causality test and due to the fact that panel average was considered and the overall panel was included in Emirmahmutoglu and Kose causality test.

Kónya (2006) Panel Bootstrap Causality Test Results

Panel Bootstrap causality test was added to literature by Kónya (2006). Panel bootstrap causality test is based on the estimations of Seemingly Unrelated Regression (SUR) estimators developed by Zellner (1962). The critical values for the estimation are Bootstrap critical values generated for each cross-section. Thanks to the critical values and estimators, cross-sectional dependence assumption is relaxed. However, unstable and non-cointegrated series can be analyzed; in other words, bootstrap causality test can be performed without performing unit root test and cointegration test (Kónya, 2006, p. 991). Since SUR estimators give more effective results compared to EKK estimators in case of the existence of cross-sectional dependence, using Kónya (2006) causality test will lead to find more reliable results.

As a result of Kónya (2006) causality test results, the H_0 hypothesis of "there is no causality between the variables" is rejected and the H_1hypothesis of "there is causality between the variables" is accepted when Wald statistics value is bigger than Bootstrap critical value. Panel bootstrap causality results are presented in Table 12, 13 and 14.

When panel bootstrap causality results are analyzed in Table 12, causality is detected in Lithuania and Slovakia, but no causality cannot be found in other countries between health expenditures and poverty. The existence or absence of a causality relationship between health expenditures and causality in countries may vary depending on quantity and quality of health expenditures and poverty level.

When panel bootstrap causality results are analyzed in Table 13, causality is detected in Lithuania, but no causality cannot be found in other countries between education expenditures and poverty. The

Table 12. Kónya (2006) Panel Bootstrap Causality Test Results (The Causality Between Health Expenditures and Poverty)

H_0: Health Expenditures Are Not the Cause of Poverty.				
		Bootstrap Critical Values		
COUNTRIES	Wald Statistics	1%	5%	10%
Czechia	1.1366753	120.18282	48.76479	29.76388
Estonia	5.8274252	67.15000	28.41265	18.05103
Hungary	3.9575855	95.70065	40.17479	25.25641
Latvia	17.388439	126.85857	47.56073	28.95190
Lithuania	**89.368045****	105.34344	44.29664	27.98170
Poland	19.968794	113.18808	44.90775	27.30297
Slovakia	**39.883358***	152.19469	61.61969	38.13220
Slovenia	2.8204455	86.28199	38.12611	24.20995

existence of causality relationship between education expenditures and poverty may vary depending on education expenditures in the country, quality of the education expenditures and poverty level.

When panel bootstrap causality results are analyzed in Table 14, causality is detected in Hungary, Latvia and Lithuania, but no causality cannot be found between economic growth and poverty. It can be said that the causality relationship between economic growth and poverty may vary depending on economic growth rate, economic size and development and poverty rate of the country.

Emirmahmutoglu and Kose (2011) causality test considering the cross-sectional dependence can be used when series are stable in different levels, in other words some of the series are I(0) and some of them are I(I) and no cointegration relationship is detected between series. Emirmahmutoglu and Kose (2011) Granger causality test is based on Toda and Yamammoto (1995) causality test (Emirmahmutoglu and Kose, 2011, pp. 871-872).

Table 13. Kónya (2006) Panel Bootstrap Causality Test Results (The Causality Between Education Expenditures and Poverty)

H_0: Education Expenditures Are Not the Cause of Poverty.				
		Bootstrap Critical Values		
COUNTRIES	**Wald Statistics**	**1%**	**5%**	**10%**
Czechia	4.5512531	105.48556	42.65503	26.17533
Estonia	0.40092987E-02	88.04539	35.12307	21.24160
Hungary	2.6922574	120.27882	51.57789	30.74607
Latvia	15.748325	84.59219	38.10361	23.19403
Lithuania	**27.065091***	97.13638	39.83295	25.85581
Poland	1.5311443	127.53216	54.99873	36.46356
Slovakia	0.55210591	137.54997	54.15079	33.93624
Slovenia	0.15584212	98.52383	38.09697	23.27320

Table 14. Kónya (2006) Panel Bootstrap Causality Test Results (The Causality Between Economic Growth and Poverty)

H_0: Economic Growth Is Not the Cause of Poverty.				
		Bootstrap Critical Values		
COUNTRIES	**Wald Statistics**	**1%**	**5%**	**10%**
Czechia	0.57036308	64.04266	28.73404	18.93313
Estonia	2.5949029	69.48751	29.07754	17.61846
Hungary	**18.497850***	64.70646	28.27163	17.67158
Latvia	**39.785883****	64.94781	30.19007	19.28083
Lithuania	**27.123746***	84.29684	35.61308	22.64863
Poland	3.5048629	111.06414	44.36242	26.67294
Slovakia	10.812824	80.01581	37.30583	24.58823
Slovenia	2.3625411	52.16021	23.48142	14.46432

Emirmahmutoglu and Kose (2011) Causality Test

The VAR model (Equation 7 and 8) developed by Emirmahmutoglu and Kose (2011) is outlined as the following:

$$x_{i,t} = \mu_i^x + \sum_{j=1}^{k_i + d\max_i} A_{11,ij} x_{i,t-j} + \sum_{j=1}^{k_i + d\max_i} A_{12,ij} y_{i,t-j} + u_{i,t}^x \tag{7}$$

$$y_{i,t} = \mu_i^y + \sum_{j=1}^{k_i + d\max_i} A_{21,ij} x_{i,t-j} + \sum_{j=1}^{k_i + d\max_i} A_{22,ij} y_{i,t-j} + u_{i,t}^y \tag{8}$$

dmax$_i$, indicates the highest cointegration level in the system for each i.

Emirmahmutoglu and Kose (2011) causality test results are presented in Table 15;

When Emirmahmutoglu and Kose (2011) causality test results are analyzed, a one-way causality relationship from health expenditures and education expenditures to causality and a two-way causality relationship between economic growth and poverty are identified. The reason for the one-way causality relationship between health expenditures and education expenditures to poverty can be stated that with the increase in health and education expenditures, the standards of life of the individuals may cause a change in poverty along with improvement both in terms of health and education. The reason for the two-way causality relationship between economic growth and poverty can be stated that a change may occur in poverty with the economic growth and economic growth may happen as a result of the policies for fighting against poverty in the countries with poverty problem.

CONCLUSION

The concept of poverty as a humanistic issue refers to the lack or absence of essential materials that individuals need to sustain their lives. Health conditions are also influenced depending on the level of poverty and therefore, lives of individuals become difficult. The states in which poverty is experienced make various plans and programs to reduce poverty. In order to reduce poverty, states try to make economic developments and therefore, they increase public expenditures.

Table 15. Emirmahmutoglu and Kose (2011) Causality Test Results

EMPTY HYPOTHESIS	Fisher Stat.	p-Value
HE is not Granger reason POV	**31.711****	0.011
POV is not Granger reason HE	23.492	0.101
EE is not Granger reason POV	**25.740***	0.058
POV is not Granger reason EE	21.729	0.152
GRW is not Granger reason POV	**22.802*****	0.009
POV is not Granger reason GRW	**79.487*****	0.000

Note: * %10, ** %5, *** %1 ıt makes sense at the level.

For that reason, measuring the effect of health and education expenditures with a significant place in public expenditures and economic growth on poverty is a highly important issue. The effect of health and education expenditures and economic growth on poverty between 2005 and 2016 in 8 Central and Eastern European countries was analyzed in the study using panel data analysis. Since the effect of health and education expenditures and economic growth on poverty in 8 Central and Eastern European countries was analyzed in the study by using high quality and various econometrical tests, this study is thought to contribute to literature.

As a result of the study, it was determined that health and education expenditures and economic growth had a negative effect on poverty. In addition, a one-way causality relationship from health and education expenditures to poverty and two-way causality relationship between economic growth and poverty were identified. From this point of view, it can be said that countries can reduce poverty as a result of some regulations about health expenditures, education expenditures and economic growth. These regulations can be listed as follows:

- As a result of health expenditures, living conditions of individuals improve and life quality increases. The presence of healthy individuals leads to a healthy society to be established and play an important role in the development of countries as a human capital. From this point of view, it can be said that quantitative and qualitative increases to be made in health expenditures may reduce poverty when we consider that the presence of healthy individuals may develop countries.
- Education expenditures are important for individuals to be educated with fund of knowledge. Well-educated individuals play active roles in providing economic, social, cultural development of the countries. For that reason, it can be said that the education expenditures for the presence of educated individuals who have important missions in the development of countries would have an effect to reduce poverty.
- Economic growth is a concept which indicates that a country develops. As a result of economic growth, economic development of a country will be provided and welfare of individuals will increase. After the economic growth and the increase in individual welfare, the development in the country will accelerate. For that reason, it can be said that economic growth will reduce poverty because economic growth is an important step in the development of countries.

REFERENCES

Açıkgöz, B. (2015). Yoksulluk, Kalkınma ve Kamu Harcamaları İlişkisinin Ekonometrik Analizi. *Hukuk ve İktisat Araştırmaları Dergisi*, *7*(1), 37–49.

Afzal, M., Malik, M. E., Begum, I., Sarwar, K., & Fatima, H. (2012). Relationship Among Education, Poverty and Economic Growth in Pakistan: An Econometric Analysis. *Journal of Elementary Education*, *22*(1), 23–45.

Agrawal, P. (2007). Economic Growth and Poverty Reduction: Evidence from Kazakhstan. *Asian Development Review*, *24*(2), 90–115.

Ahmad, Z., & Batul, T. (2013). Relationship Among Poverty, Education Expenditure, and Education Status: Empirical Evidence from Pakistan. *Proceedings of the World Congress on Engineering*, 1, 3-5.

Akkucuk, U. (2016). SCOR Model and the Green Supply Chain. In U. Akkucuk (Ed.), *Handbook of Research on Waste Management Techniques for Sustainability* (pp. 108–124). Hershey, PA: IGI Global. doi:10.4018/978-1-4666-9723-2.ch006

Akkucuk, U. (2017). *Ethics and Sustainability in Global Supply Chain Management*. Hershey, PA: IGI Global. doi:10.4018/978-1-5225-2036-8

Akkucuk, U., & Gencer, Y. G. (2017). EFQM Model and Sustainability of Organizations. *DEStech Transactions on Computer Science and Engineering*. doi:10.12783/dtcse/ameit2017/12279

Akkucuk, U., & Sekercioglu, C. H. (2016). NGOs For Environmental Sustainability: The Case Of Kuzeydoga Foundation. *Fresenius Environmental Bulletin*, *25*(12A), 6038–6044.

Aktan, C. C., & Vural, İ. Y. (2002). *Yoksulluk: Terminoloji, Temel Kavramlar ve Ölçüm Yöntemleri, Yoksullukla Mücadele Stratejileri* (C. C. Aktan, Ed.). Ankara: Hak-İş Konfederasyonu Yayınları. Retrieved from http://www.canaktan.org/ekonomi/yoksulluk/birinci-bol/aktan-vural-yoksulluk.pdf

Angelsen, A., & Sven, W. (2006). Poverty and Inequality: Economic Growth is Better Than its Reputation. In D. Banik (Ed.), Poverty, Politics and Development: Interdisciplinary Perspectives. Fagbokforlaget.

Bakırtaş, T., & Kandemir, O. (2012). Türkiye'de Yetersiz Eğitim ve Yoksulluk İlişkisi: İller Bazında Ekonometrik Bir Analiz. Uluslararası İstanbul Finans Kongresi. Okan Üniversitesi.

Baltagi, B. H., Feng, Q., & Kao, C. (2012). A Lagrange Multiplier Test for Cross-Sectional Dependence in a Fixed Effects Panel Data Model. *Journal of Econometrics*, *170*(1), 164–177. doi:10.1016/j.jeconom.2012.04.004

Breusch, T. S., & Pagan, A. R. (1980). The Lagrange Multiplier Test and İts Applications to Model Specification in Econometrics. *The Review of Economic Studies*, *47*(1), 239–253. doi:10.2307/2297111

Dahlquist, M. (2014). *Does Economic Growth reduce Poverty? An Empirical Analysis of the Relationship between Poverty and Economic Growth across Low- and Middle-income Countries, illustrated by the Case of Brazil.* Södertörn University. Retrieved from http://www.diva-portal.org/smash/get/diva2:747531/FULLTEXT01.p

Dandume, M. Y. (2014). Financial Sector Development, Economic Growth and Poverty Reduction: New Evidence From Nigeria. Çankırı Karatekin University. *Journal of the Faculty of Economics and Administrative Sciences*, *4*(2), 2–22.

Department for International Development. (2008). Growth: Building Jobs and Prosperity in Developing Countries. London: Department for International Development.

Doğan, E. (2014). *Türkiye'de Yoksulluğun Ölçülmesi.* TC Kalkınma Bakanlığı Bölgesel Gelişme ve Yapısal Uyum Genel Müdürlüğü, Uzmanlık Tezi, Yayın.

Emirmahmutoglu, F., & Kose, N. (2011). Testing for Granger Causality in Heterogeneous Mixed Panels. *Economic Modelling*, *28*(3), 870–876. doi:10.1016/j.econmod.2010.10.018

Erkal, G., Akıncı, M., & Yılmaz, Ö. (2015). Yoksulluk, Gelir Eşitsizliği ve Ekonomik Büyüme İlişkisi: Seçilmiş Doğu Avrupa ve Latin Amerika Ülkeleri İçin Ampirik Bir Analiz. *TISK Academy/TISK Akademi, 10*(19), 66-87.

Eurostat. (2018a). *People at risk of poverty or social exclusion.* Retrieved from http://ec.europa.eu/eurostat/tgm/table.do?tab=table&init=1&plugin=1&language=en&pcode=tipslc10

Eurostat. (2018b). *Total General Government Expenditure, Percentage of GDP.* Retrieved from http://appsso.eurostat.ec.europa.eu/nui/submitViewTableAction.do

Gencer, Y. G., & Akkucuk, U. (2016). Reverse Logistics: Automobile Recalls and Other Conditions. In U. Akkucuk (Ed.), *Handbook of Research on Waste Management Techniques for Sustainability* (pp. 125–154). Hershey, PA: IGI Global. doi:10.4018/978-1-4666-9723-2.ch007

Granger, C. W. (1969). Investigating Causal Relations by Econometric Models and Cross-Spectral Methods. *Econometrica, 37*(3), 424–438. doi:10.2307/1912791

Human Development Report. (2016). United Nations Development Programme. Retrieved from http://hdr.undp.org/en/2016-report

Jha, R., Biswal, B., & Biswal, U. D. (2001). *An Empirical Analysis of the Impact of Public Expenditures on Education and Health on Poverty in Indian States.* Working Papers 998. Queen's University, Department of Economics.

Kiki, R. A., Subagiarta, I. W.& Viphindrartin, S. (2015). Determinan Kemiskinan Di Kabupaten Jember Tahun 2003-2013. *Artikel Ilmiah Mahasiswa.*

Kónya, L. (2006). Exports and Growth: Granger Causality Analysis on OECD Countries With a Panel Data Approach. *Economic Modelling, 23*(6), 978–992. doi:10.1016/j.econmod.2006.04.008

Kurita, K., & Kurosaki, T. (2011). Dynamics of Growth, Poverty and İnequality: A Panel Analysis of Regional Data From Thailand and the Philippines. *Asian Economic Journal, 25*(1), 3–33. doi:10.1111/j.1467-8381.2011.02046.x

McCoskey, S., & Kao, C. (1998). A Residual-Based Test of The Null of Cointegration in Panel Data. *Econometric Reviews, 17*(1), 57–84. doi:10.1080/07474939808800403

Mirahsani, Z. (2016). The Relationship Between Health Expenditures and Human Development İndex. *Journal of Research & Health, 6*(3), 373-377. DOI: . doi:10.7508/jrh.2016.03.011

Nándori, E. S. (2010). The Effect of Economic Growth on Poverty in Eastern Europe. *Zarządzanie Publiczne, 1-2*(9-10), 37-44.

Njong, A. M. (2010). The Effects of Educational Attainment on Poverty Reduction in Cameroon. *International Journal of Educational Administration and Policy Studies, 2*(1), 1-8.

OECD. (2018). *Health spending (indicator).* Retrieved from https://data.oecd.org/healthres/health-spending.htm

Özsoy, C. (2012). Kalkınma Ekonomisinin Anlam ve İçeriği. In İktisadi Kalkınma (pp. 2-26) Eskişehir: Anadolu Üniversitesi Yayınları.

Pedroni, P. (2000). Full Modified OLS for Heterogeneous Cointegrated Panels. *Advances in Econometrics*, *15*, 93–130. doi:10.1016/S0731-9053(00)15004-2

Pesaran, M. H. (2004). *General Diagnostic Tests for Cross Section Dependence in Panels.* CESifo Working Paper Series, 1229.

Pesaran, M. H. (2007). A Simple Panel Unit Root Test in the Presence of Cross-Section Dependence. *Journal of Applied Econometrics*, *22*(2), 265–312. doi:10.1002/jae.951

Pesaran, M. H., Ullah, A., & Yamagata, T. (2008). A Bias-Adjusted LM Test of Error Cross-Section İndependence. *The Econometrics Journal*, *11*(1), 105–127. doi:10.1111/j.1368-423X.2007.00227.x

Pesaran, M. H., & Yamagata, T. (2008). Testing Slope Homogeneity in Large Panels. *Journal of Econometrics*, *142*(1), 50–93. doi:10.1016/j.jeconom.2007.05.010

Razmi, S. M. J. & E. Abbasian & S. Mohammadi (2012). Investigating the Effect of Government Health Expenditure on HDI in Iran. *Journal of Knowledge Management, Economics and Information Technology*, (5).

Riman, H., Bassey, J., Ibi, E., & Edu, B. (2010). *Poverty, Health Expenditure, and Health Status: A Long Term Perspective with Evidence from Nigeria.* Retrieved from http://ssrn.com/abstract=1540303

Şantaş, F. (2017). Yoksulluğun Sağlık Statüsü ve Sağlık Hizmetleri Kullanımı İle İlişkisi. *Igdir University Journal of Social Sciences*, (13), 545-591.

Sarkaria, M. S., & Shiwani. (2016). Education and Poverty Relationship in Punjab. *IRA-International Journal of Management & Social Sciences*, *4*(2), 394-416. Retrieved from https://research-advances.org/index.php/RAJMSS/article/download/437/460

Toda, H. Y., & Yamamoto, T. (1995). Statistical İnference in Vector Autoregressions With Possibly İntegrated Processes. *Journal of Econometrics*, *66*(1-2), 225–250. doi:10.1016/0304-4076(94)01616-8

Walingo, M. K. (2006). The Role of Education in Agricultural Projects For Food Security and Poverty Reduction in Kenya. *Review of Education*, *52*, 287–304.

Westerlund, J., & Edgerton, D. L. (2007). A Panel Bootstrap Cointegration Test. *Economics Letters*, *97*(3), 185–190. doi:10.1016/j.econlet.2007.03.003

Weziak-Bialowolska, D., & Dijkstra, L. (2014). Regional Human Poverty Index Poverty in the regions of the European. *JRC Science and Policy Report*. doi:10.2788/10063

Widiastuti, A. (2010). *Analisis Faktor-Faktor Yang Mempengaruhi Kemiskinan Di Jawa Tengah Tahun 2004-2008* (Doctoral dissertation). Universitas Diponegoro.

World Bank. (1995). *Development in Practice: Priorities and Strategies for Education.* Washington, DC: World Bank. Retrieved from http://siteresources.worldbank.org/EDUCATION/Resources/278200-1099079877269/547664-1099080118171/Priorities_and_Strategies_for_Ed_WB_Review.pdf

World Bank. (1999). *Educatıon Sector Strategy*. The World Bank. Retrieved from http://siteresources.worldbank.org/EDUCATION/Resources/ESSU/education_strategy_1999.pdf

World Bank. (2018a). *Measurıng Poverty*. Retrieved from Retrieved from http://www.worldbank.org/en/topic/measuringpoverty#1

World Bank. (2018b). *GDP per capita growth (annual %)*. Retrieved from http://databank.worldbank.org/data/reports.aspx?source=2&series=NY.GDP.PCAP.KD.ZG&country=

World Health Organization. (2004). *The İmpact of Health Expenditure on Households and Options for Alternative Financing* (No. EM/RC51/R. 6). Retrieved from www.who.int/health_financing/documents/emrc51-4-healthexpenditureimpact.pdf

World Health Organization. (2007). *Working for Health. An İntroduction to the World Health Organization*. Retrieved from http://www.who.int/about/brochure_en.pdf

World Health Organization. (2018). *Global Health Observatory (GHO) Data*. Retrieved from http://www.who.int/gho/health_financing/health_expenditure/en/

Zellner, A. (1962). An Efficient Method of Estimating Seemingly Unrelated Regressions and Tests for Aggregation Bias. *Journal of the American Statistical Association*, *57*(298), 348–368. doi:10.1080/01621459.1962.10480664

KEY TERMS AND DEFINITIONS

Economic Growth: Represents the annual rate of increase in national income in a country. Foreign trade transactions are also included.

Education Expenditure: It involves expenditures made to the education sector for the presence of more knowledgeable individuals and thus the knowledgeable society.

Health Expenditure: It covers healthcare spending and aims to protect health.

Poverty: Poverty is a phenomenon that affects living conditions and complicates matters, and individuals do not have the tools they need to lead a good life.

Chapter 11
Liability or Ethics? The Real Value of Compliance

Svetlana Snezhko
M. V. Lomonosov Moscow State University, Russia

Ali Coskun
Boğaziçi University, Turkey

ABSTRACT

The purpose of this chapter is to reconsider a traditional approach to the compliance function of firms from a modern perspective, which broadens its concept as a company's liability to only secure its adherence to applicable laws and avoid regulatory sanctions in serving company's interests. The observation of issues regulated by the compliance function in the contest of managing situations of conflict of interest (COI) in different spheres concludes that, in fact, those issues, to a greater extent, relate to sustaining ethical behavior in business rather than stem from regulatory norms. Based on the findings of this analysis as well as other different sources, a new definition for effective compliance has been developed with the focus on adherence to ethical principles in respect to third parties, which addresses compliance function in terms of corporate social responsibility (CSR) and its sustainability role setting a vector for a further research.

INTRODUCTION

The term "compliance" goes hand in hand with corporate governance and risk management. It has come to be understood as an organization's function to protect business from adherent risks. Let's refer to two reliable and reputable sources for a widely accepted definition of a compliance function. One of the first definitions was introduced by The Basel Committee on Banking Supervision (2003) in its consultative document "The compliance function in banks" which defines a bank's compliance function as "an independent function that identifies, assesses, advises on, monitors and reports on the bank's compliance risk, that is, the risk of legal or regulatory sanctions, financial loss, or loss to reputation a bank may suffer as a result of its failure to comply with all applicable laws, regulations, codes of conduct and standards of good practice (together laws, rules and standards)."

DOI: 10.4018/978-1-5225-8109-3.ch011

The International Compliance Association (2016) provides the following explanation of compliance: "in the context of financial services businesses compliance operates at two levels: level 1 - compliance with the external rules that are imposed upon an organization as a whole; level 2 - compliance with internal systems of control that are imposed to achieve compliance with the externally imposed rules".

Traditional understanding of compliance function concludes its role in serving a company's interests mainly by securing its adherence to applicable laws to avoid regulatory sanctions. In this sense, the role of compliance is limited to the liability of a company created by external factors and the regulatory environment. And until recently this has been a widespread approach to its valuation, and its significance has been perceived by some as no more than a formality to meet the requirements of regulators and auditors. However, nowadays, the paradigm of compliance is shifting from merely a liability to its broader function which also impacts economic relations and may have additional value for companies and society. According to ISO 19600 Guidelines on Compliance management systems (2014) "organizations that aim to be successful in the long term need to maintain a culture of integrity and compliance, and to consider the needs and expectations of stakeholders. Integrity and compliance are therefore not only the basis, but also an opportunity, for a successful and sustainable organization".

This work provides a review of reports, researches, opinions, statistics, legal cases, company practices to examine the value of compliance function not only to organizations but to stakeholders, society and sustainable development.

THE SCOPE OF COMPLIANCE REGULATION

What is effective compliance today? Nowadays though compliance in its traditional meaning is still defined through adherence to laws and rules, more often it implies fair business practices, integrity and principles of business ethics. Director of ethics and professional standards, at CFA Institute (Chartered Financial Analysts), Mr. Michael McMillan clarifies the correlation between compliance and ethics:

Just because you have a good or great compliance program doesn't mean people are not going to be behaving unethically or not have an environment that encourages unethical behavior. Compliance really focuses upon rules and regulations. Are you following the rules, are you following the regulations and the laws of your company, or the laws and regulations of the country or environment in which you work? Ethics are about encouraging behavior that is above just following rules and regulations. It is requiring to get people to act more in consonance with the values of the company. Ethics should permeate the entire company. (McMillan in DiPietro, 2014).

Thus, it is logically to conclude that compliance without strong ethics will be not effective.

The general concept of "ethics" implies what actions are right or wrong in particular circumstances. "At its simplest, ethics is a system of moral principles. They affect how people make decisions and lead their lives. Ethics is concerned with what is good for individuals and society". (BBC Ethics guide, 2014). So the compliance system of an organization will function when employees are not only informed on forbidden and illegal practices but when they also understand and follow the ethical principles. "If you have a strong ethical culture then you don't really need to have a huge compliance department because people are going to do the right thing because that's what the values of the company are promoting. The stronger the ethical culture of the company the less you need a large or well-developed compliance program." (McMillan in DiPietro, 2014). The phrase "Everyone is responsible for compliance" has for a definite reason become established within good compliance system. Therefore, compliance is about ethical behavior which ensures following rules and regulations. Ethics sustain an effective compliance system. When a compliance system is based on ethical principles and values then there is a compliance culture in the company. And it is of more relevance to speak about compliance culture in a company because without it the compliance function may fail to manage the associated risk successfully. The notion of compliance culture is firmly rooted in "ISO 19600" (2014) principles and defined as: values, ethics and beliefs that exist throughout an organization and interact with the organization's structures and control systems to produce behavioral norms that are conducive to compliance outcomes. The standard emphasizes the leading role of governing bodies, top management and senior management in promoting and supporting strong compliance culture through a common commitment to the published standard of behavior. Thus, ethics are the key factor in securing compliant behavior of employees.

A further point on compliance is that it should not be limited primarily to abidance of laws and regulatory norms applicable to a company's business but also take into account the expectations and requirements of interested parties. And in this sense compliance serves in favor of commitments, which are not covered by regulatory requirements, which companies have accepted in respect to both the internal and external stakeholders of the company. Standard "ISO 19600" (2014) provides a number of sources out of which such commitments may arise: agreements with community groups or non-governmental organizations, agreements with public authorities and customers, organizational requirements, such as policies and procedures, voluntary principles or codes of practice, voluntary labelling or environmental commitments. For example, Intesa Sanpaolo Group rejecting war as a means of conflict resolution implements a policy curtailing involvement in the military weapons industry even if such activities are permitted by law. Exceptions to the policy consider only the interests of national defence. As commented upon in their sustainability report (Intesa Sanpaolo Group, 2014) on this point "in accordance with the values and principles in the Code of Ethics, the Bank has decided to take on its responsibility as financial intermediary" sharply limiting its participation in activities that involve the production and trade of military weapons.

If we consider the scope of compliance issues, they come down to far more than only the regulatory norms. Trevino and Nelson (2010) clarify: laws and legal regulation reflect society's minimum norms and standards of business conduct. However, many standards of conduct are agreed upon by society and not codified in law. Based on the vivid correlation between law and ethics in terms of a Venn diagram let's outline the scope of compliance regulation (Figure 1). In point of fact, in their book the authors describe efficient compliance as a function of managing and driving ethics and integrity within an organization (Trevino & Nelson, 2010, p. 314).

COI REGULATION: THE CORE OF ETHICAL BEHAVIOR IN BUSINESS

Whereas, for example, managing conflict of interest (COI) is more about sustaining ethical behavior in business. In fact, a diversity of conflict situations require regulation in order to secure fair market relations and maintain such global principles of market interaction as the protection of investors, ensuring transparency, as well as maintaining consumer confidence in the financial services markets, their trust of goods and services providers and even systems of public administration. So, ultimately, while COI

Figure 1. The scope of compliance regulation

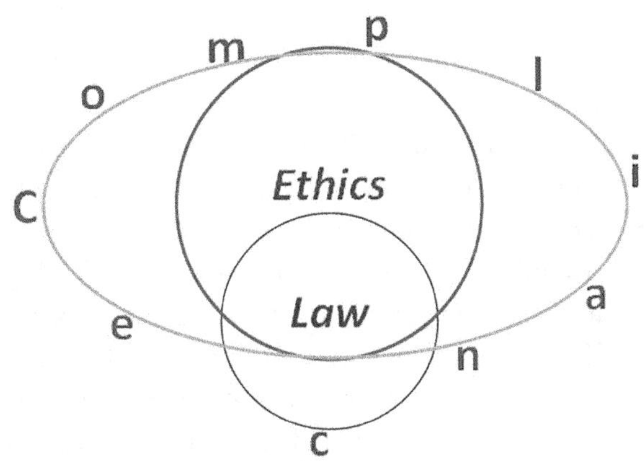

management aims to develop trust among business participants, not all aspects of COI are covered by legal regulation and there is a gap in regulating COI in different jurisdictions.

Insider Trading: Regulatory and Ethical Compliance

The problem of COI is huge when taking into account industries, businesses and consequences such as unfair business practices that it may lead to (Snezhko, 2015, pp. 26-28). Let's consider insider trading as such an outcome of COI. An insider trading compliance program is common in firms' compliance systems, especially in public companies. Prohibition of insider trading is one of the basic principles companies postulate in their codes of conduct either as a separate thesis or within a Conflict of interest section.

Insider trading regulation originates from USA and as defined by U.S. Securities and Exchange Commission [SEC] (n.d., para.1) "insider trading is buying or selling a security, in breach of a duty of trust or confidence owed directly or indirectly to the issuer, the issuer's stockholder or the source of information, while in possession of material, non-public information about the security".

The arguments for insider trading as an adverse practice are usually the following (Yevmenyeva, 2013):

- A breach of justice: it is considered unfair that people possessing information that is not available to other investors, as a result are able to receive profit;
- A loss of investor confidence: if the stock market has no public confidence then it will not attract investors that is highly destructive for a market since the more investors are in it, the greater its liquidity;
- A breach of fiduciary duties: if the person is in a relationship of trust with their employer or client and therefore has access to certain information, he does not have the right to abuse his position and personally profit from it.

Thus, the purpose of control and prevention of insider trading is to secure fair relations in financial markets and this is nothing but the ethical behavior of insiders that provides for a company's reputation and trust of stakeholders.

Though insider trading is forbidden in advanced and developing countries, a personal liability for insider trading is more severe and more toughly regulated (Thompson, 2013) than for corporations and legal entities. For instance, in USA regulation of insider trading is considered the most developed and besides individual liability presumes both civil and criminal liability of legal entities. However, in practice, the cases of civil litigations against individuals considerably exceed such cases against legal entities[1]. Employers are also rarely held criminally liable for their insider's acts and in contrast to the numerous individuals indicted for insider trading in recent years, the cases where business entities have been charged for the insider trading of their employees are estimated as a "handful" (Kaplan, 2014).

In comparison, in the UK where insider trading also comes under strong regulation with an emphasis on ethical principles (there is a Handbook issued by the regulator establishing high standards, principles for business and Code of Conduct) one can count few cases of penalizing companies for insider trading (e.g. Reckitt Benckiser case of 2015 and D. Enchorn and Greenlight Capital case of 2012, in contrast to individuals sentenced[2]). Though a number of countries, outside the UK, presume criminal liability for legal entities Overland (2015) observes the absence of statutory provisions within the relevant legislation prohibiting insider trading and, as a result, the general principles of corporate criminal liability, which are applicable in the relevant jurisdiction, must be relied upon to determine the manner in which corporations may be found liable for insider trading. Despite the fact, that regulators do have to find "good reasons" for a company to be subject to liability for insider trading, the number of individual's prosecutions for insider trading is evidence of the increase of regulator's attention to the issue all over the world and that enforcement is becoming stricter. Notably, in June 2014 The European Parliament and The Council of the European Union issued an updated Regulation (Regulation (EU) No 596/2014) on market abuse which establishes "a more uniform interpretation of the Union market abuse framework, which more clearly defines rules applicable in all Member States", as well as Directive on criminal sanctions for market abuse that tightens personal and legal entities criminal liability for market abuse and insider trading (Directive 2014/57/EU).

In fact, if an employee is held liable for insider trading this is not an immediate indictment of a company. The regulators, however, will always assess the possibility of the company's complicity in insider trading. Indeed, US regulators SEC and DOJ both in civil and criminal proceedings follow statutory norms providing penalties for companies which fail to develop and implement compliance procedures against insider trading. And even where the company manages to avoid liability for its employee insider trading activities the prosecution of an individual will cause no less damage to the company's reputation than in case it were penalized itself. "With the regulator looking at insider trading more closely, and with the scale of fines ramping up, it is important for companies and financial institutions to take this seriously", says Iain Coke, head of ICAEW's (Institute of Charted Accountants in England and Wales) Financial Services Faculty. "Insider trading is not a minor offence. It could inflict fatal damage to organizations, and people can go to jail!" (Biebuyck, 2014, para. 3).

Thus, the primary point is that the importance of a compliance insider trading program is not only determined by securing the company from being charged by regulators. Even if the company implements and practices all recommended measures to prevent insider dealing such as pre-clearance, information barriers (Chinese Walls), closed periods and disclosures it may avoid liability, while however, still being at risk of having reputational costs caused by an employee's violation. As even as it is stated in the U.S. Attorney Manual (1934) "...the Department recognizes that no compliance program can ever prevent all criminal activity by a corporation's employees, the critical factors in evaluating any program are whether the program is adequately designed for maximum effectiveness in preventing and detecting wrongdoing by employees and whether corporate management is enforcing the program or is tacitly encouraging or pressuring employees to engage in misconduct to achieve business objectives."

A second point is that effective regulation of insider trading relies considerably on ethics and ethical principles promoted by companies and incorporated into their compliance culture. And besides the companies' responsibility for maintaining a good compliance program, employees bare no less responsibility for proper dealing with insider information that strongly depends on their personal professional ethics and values and their conduct when experiencing a personal conflict of interest.

And thirdly, compliance culture (as in the example of insider trading prevention) ensures investor confidence. Luis A. Aguilar, a commissioner of SEC, in his speech of April 18, 2013 emphasizes the importance of building a culture of compliance that will result in a robust and effective compliance environment that works for investors. The following statement is best suited to support this point.

Building a strong culture of compliance is important, especially when the success of your business depends largely on investor trust and confidence. A compliance program that focuses on investor protection also protects your business. This is true because the potential costs of serious compliance failures and violations of the federal securities laws can be much higher than any sanctions imposed by regulators. In the end, the reputational harm to your business may be more severe...In the end, it's important to do what's right according to the letter of the law, but it's better to think in terms of doing what's right because it is in the best interest of the client — and that is the real foundation of a culture of compliance (Aguilar, 2013).

Corporate Conflicts

Corporate conflicts are another well-known and highly common aspect of COI. Corporate conflicts imply a contradiction of interests that may occur between the shareholders and top-managers. In particular, this involves situations where directors (this may refer to the boards and executive directors either) may experience conflicts between the company's and their own interests. The legislation of many countries from the USA to Australia stipulates the fiduciary duty of directors towards the company and its members and obliges corporate directors to avoid and declare any COI. Statutory and corporate code provisions assign directors certain duties based on an ethical approach to their managerial role like acting in "good faith", putting interests of the company above their own, act honestly, exercise reasonable care, skill and diligence, with duty of care and loyalty, to promote the success of the company for the benefit of its members as a whole[3].

Regulation of corporate conflicts is not as much about a company's liability towards the regulator as the fairness and business ethics of directors, where the ignorance or breach of which will have a negative reputational effect on companies even if directors are held liable for improper actions. Legislative acts establishing director's duties also provide for bearing liability on them in case of breaching these obligations, albeit in a concise way. In practice, this can be achieved through court decisions as a result of litigation initiated by a company or shareholders. However, such litigations are not commonplace nor always turn out in favor of companies, as they are cost-intensive and misconduct is not always easy to prove unless there is serious evidence of misappropriation of corporate assets or fraudulent misstatements. So, the liability for a director may be limited to a dismissal only, or in the worst case, disqualification[4], while the company, besides reputational losses, may be left without redress.

For example, in the EU, cases of breaches of director's duties usually do not lead to judicial enforcement of a company's claims against directors (Gerner-Beuerle, Paech & Schuster, 2013). According to the Study on Director's duty and liability there are several reasons for that: the organ authorized to act on behalf of the company may be conflicted, especially, when the board of directors has the authority to instigate proceedings on behalf of the company, as in a one-tier board structure, in this case the conflict is apparent; a further reason is that directors are not straightforward to accuse as in most jurisdictions important business decisions are taken by or with the preliminary approval of the controlling shareholders; and proceedings do not always give a clear outcome of enforcement and are lengthy, expensive, and fraught with uncertainties (Gerner-Beuerle at al., 2013). Due to these obstacles enforcement in most jurisdictions is initiated only in cases of grave breaches of directors' duties like fraudulent conduct, self-dealing or misappropriated corporate assets. Otherwise, shareholders may prefer to remove a director than appeal to court.

As for derivative suits (when a claim is made by the shareholders on behalf of a company against a director for damage compensation caused by wrongful acts towards the corporation and not by the company directly through the authorized members or organ) – they are also rare in Europe due to requirements the shareholders have to meet (stock amount), conditions to proceed with the claim and the cost rules (in most jurisdictions the shareholders pay and bear litigation risk). The most progressive derivative suits have been in the USA, though, the same difficulties refer to derivative actions there, as only shareholders who meet certain standing requirements may file derivative actions (Scarlett, 2011). Perhaps, it's a paradox, but despite that derivative suits are a common practice in the USA, at the same time shareholder derivative litigation in the United States presents many obstacles and hurdles (Scarlett, 2011) to have a successful outcome for a shareholder[5].

The incidents of possible breaching of fiduciary duties as the consequences of COI are not sufficiently regulated by either detailed statutory norms or by liability rules. Sarbanes-Oxley Act (2002) (SOX) is considered to be a US government measure to prevent the misconduct of unscrupulous managers and fraudulent practices, to protect shareholders and secure the confidence of investors and the public in the securities market. The law establishes certain provisions in order to ensure fiduciary duties fulfilment by directors, like setting restrictions on giving loans to directors and requires public companies to issue an ethics code for senior financial officers postulating standards that are "reasonably necessary to promote: honest and ethical conduct, including the ethical handling of actual or apparent conflicts of interest between personal and professional relationships" and to disclose this information in the periodic reports. The law also enhances the provisions regarding COI in different aspects and goes as far as to make COI situations unlawful.

Though, the law has expanded requirements and responsibility for all U.S. public company boards of directors and top-managers to enhance companies' financial accountability, still the legal provisions mainly refer to internal controls, rules on financial information disclosure and financial reporting. So, it does not expand or make changes in directors' liability and "it would be unrealistic to imagine that any board director could adequately monitor all of the compliance obligations of SOX Act" (Skinner, 2006, p. 31), in any case, many of the functions are taken by the committees.

Thus, directors' duties to act in good faith and avoid situations where their personal interests can contradict the interests of the company fully rest on the ethical standards, personal values and business principles of directors. Even while these duties are legislated, it is not enough to secure directors' total commitment to fulfill their duties in the best manner. Also, ambiguity of directors' liabilities for breaching fiduciary duties may waive the responsibility of directors in avoiding conflict situations. However, a directors' misconduct or wrongdoing will have a negative impact and consequences for a company and its reputation regardless. For example, if the conflict is not disclosed and regulated, at a minimum, the interests of the company will be infringed, and where the director is dismissed or the case goes to court (where director can be fined or imprisoned as a result of fraud) – these outcomes will cause a substantial damage to the company's reputation.

COI Between the Employee and Organization

The issue of COI concerns not only directors but all employees in an organization. And in respect to the rest of the employees the legal regulation is less developed. A number of employees may be placed in the situation of COI when, for example, owning shares and having significant financial interest in other companies that the employer-company is dealing with, serving as a director or senior manager in another company, work and occupying positions in other companies, consulting or providing other services to third parties, favoring business development of another company to the detriment of the current employer's interests.

The problem of COI is raised by the abuse of a dominant position by an employee as a result of access to some privileged resources or powers giving him\her opportunity to gain benefit in an unfair or unlawful way that may cause the company a loss of profit. Such situations cannot be treated as a breach of legal obligations by an employee to a company but as breach of faith and fidelity owed to the employer. The situation of COI by itself cannot be reason enough to fire an employee. In many countries regulation of personal COI is more advanced in public service. The prohibition of COI postulated in legislative norms usually refers to government and public officials[6]. Nevertheless, regulation of COI among employees is inherent to the compliance function of any commercial organization. The policy of COI is accepted as a fundamental company document that many companies make publicly available and a directive to avoid COI is one of the basic principles of any Ethics code. Thus, COI management by companies is rather more challenged by ethical insights than liability which, in fact, falls on employees to a greater extent, than on companies.

Conflicts of Interest in Pharmaceutical Industry

COI is indisputably an ethical issue and an essential aspect of doing business today. COI is a most urgent topic for the pharmaceutical industry where the ethical side of the issue is of the highest importance. Today, without ethics, pharmaceutical businesses would hardly survive! Pharma-business is highly regulated, while compliance in pharma-companies deals in great depth with ethics. The primary activity of pharmaceutical companies is producing safe medications to support people's health, but at the same time, it is business for profit. Business goals rather often make companies focus on sales results more than on real customers and patients' needs. Indeed, it is pharma that is one of the few industries (on a par with oil and gas) where companies have been fined so frequently as in no other. One can easily look up a list of the largest pharmaceutical settlements on Wikipedia. It would be logical to assume that penalties are a standard practice for pharma-companies, especially, given that the amounts for penalties are very low in comparison to companies' profits[7] (Almashat & Wolfe, 2012) and can be treated as a cost of doing business (Kessel, 2014). However, punishment for violations in the form of disgorgements is unlikely to be such a concern as reputation that has considerably fallen in recent years. Such reputational damage was brought about as a result of "a shift in ideology of corporations that the only social responsibility is to increase profits and enhance investor returns" (Kessel, 2014, para 8.), whereby the interests and needs of shareholders prevailed over patients. The consequence of such a strategy is unethical marketing practices to incentivize the customers and the physicians. That has caused unlawful promotions and bribery and corruption that have become the most common of violations in pharma business.

While pharmaceutical companies have responsibilities towards patients in addressing their health problems, indeed, they often neglect this ethical obligation and create a market for a drug. For example, there are companies being accused of malpractice for direct-to-customer advertising (DTC ads)[8], which are allowed in USA, because they focus more "on peddling elixirs for trivial human conditions rather than focusing on finding drugs that ameliorate or cure debilitating diseases" (Kessel, 2014). Other typical violations committed by pharmaceuticals are off-label promotions[9], withholding information on drug's risks and stimulating physicians to prescribe a medication. As a matter of fact, the pharmaceutical industry faces a wide variety of situations of ethical concerns (Haque at al., 2014).

So, as reviews, surveys and statistics of violations in pharma-business show, that breach of legal requirements as a result of disregard of ethical principles by companies has led to reputational costs and loss of trust from their shareholders and patients. Some improvement in overall pharmaceutical industry reputation ratings has been observed in 2014[10] but ethics in compliance remains a very pressing issues for pharmaceutical companies and to recover their reputation they are required to focus on patients and customers' needs.

Supporting and securing ethical behavior in pharma is of great concern for the healthcare community, in particular, the different international associations represented by many pharmaceutical companies, like EFPIA, AIPM and IFPMA. They issue Codes of Practice, focusing on COI regulation, standards of promotional practices and principles of interaction with healthcare representatives, which are required standards of behavior for members who in cases of non-compliance can be fined by associations. So, compliance in the pharmaceutical industry is required to make companies act in the best interests of patients.

"POLICIES AND CULTURE WILL WIN OVER RULES AND REGULATIONS" (SAWYER, 2004)

Taking the aforesaid into consideration, we can summarize, that the role of compliance today cannot be reduced to securing companies interests only while protecting from regulators prosecution. Financial penalties are not the main factor that should guide companies in their compliant behavior. As an example with insider trading when the companies are not so exposed to the risk of being penalized as insider-employees or with pharmaceutical business where amounts of penalties, perhaps, are not so significant to the companies' profits, the reputational damage due to irresponsible behavior to the interested parties is still unavoidable. It is insufficient to consider compliance mainly through the application of laws and regulatory norms and it should be understood as adherence to ethical principles in respect to third parties.

Back in 2005 the authors of "Corporate Integrity: a toolkit for managing beyond compliance" wrote that corporate managers in most organizations were increasingly focused on ensuring compliance with rules and regulations that they considered as necessary corporate motivators, but not a guarantee of business integrity, however. The authors approached compliance as adherence to laws and regulations only – a minimum standard of corporate performance – that might not anticipate stakeholders' expectations and reinforce corporate credibility and thereby cause managers to focus on observing third-party rules on a reactive basis rather than proactively managing business integrity (Kennedy-Glans & Schulz, 2005). A business culture of integrity was considered as proactive management beyond compliance that would foster a corporate "win" in the court of public opinion and in the marketplace (Kennedy-Glans & Schulz, 2005).

Prior to that research was conducted to estimate the outcome of compliance-oriented programs on employee's ethical behavior compared with values-oriented programs. The researchers identified the compliance-oriented program or legal compliance as based on the rule of law and sanctions for non-compliance, and the values-oriented program – as based on shared values with a focus on "respect" and "responsibility". The general approach to these two programs differentiated between them in the following way: though compliance-oriented programs support obedience by rules and laws through the fear of discipline for nonconformity heightening employees' awareness of circumstances that might present risks of ethical failure (Trevino & Weaver, 2003, p. 201), it is not enhancing organizational commitment that can be favored by values. Compliance programs impose rules on employees from "outside" rather than resulting from values with which all organizational members identify, it constitutes a "top-down" imposition, rather than identification and internalization processes (Trevino & Weaver, 2003, p. 200).

The results of the research revealed that both programs are significant for employees awareness of ethical issues, employee willingness to seek ethical advice within an organization and a decrease in unethical behavior, however, a value-based program greater benefits employees ethical behavior: towards commitment to the organization, for employee integrity, communicating "bad news" – about failures, mistakes and violations of rules, and better decision-making results. Thus, a value-orientation approach implies additional distinctive and desirable outcomes that are not achieved by a focus on behavioral compliance. "The values orientation program may frame the way employees understand the purpose of compliance activities. When a values orientation is strong, compliance activities can be perceived as part of an overall system of support for ethical behavior. Without a strong values orientation, however, compliance activities might be perceived to be part of system aimed only at detecting misconduct" (Trevino &Weaver, 2003, p. 212).

The authors appeal to US Sentencing Commission guidelines (1994) on building a legal compliance system but conclude that to be effective the employees should better receive a values orientation in ethics program than merely only compliance orientation. The results of their study suggest that it is not optimal to enforce "the rules" and managers are recommended to create a sense of shared values that can help define an ethical role identity for employees and set forth organizational support for employees as an ideal (Trevino & Weaver, 2003, p. 212). Instead of focusing solely on the detection and discipline of offences – suggesting perhaps that employees cannot be trusted or are in some other way ethically incompetent – a values-oriented program suggests that employees are already committed to ethical behavior. Thus, effective compliance programs can be maintained only based on promotion of values that constitute an ethical orientation for employees' behavior.

Another interesting finding of these researches is a positive correlation between employee's commitment and the perception by the employees that the ethics program is oriented toward serving the interests of external stakeholders (customers or community), while a perception by employees that the ethics program exists to protect top-management from blame and failures showed a negative correlation to employees commitment (Trevino & Weaver, 2003, p. 217). Figure 2 represents the outcomes of different compliance orientation programs basing on the research of these authors.

Figure 2. Ethics and compliance program orientation

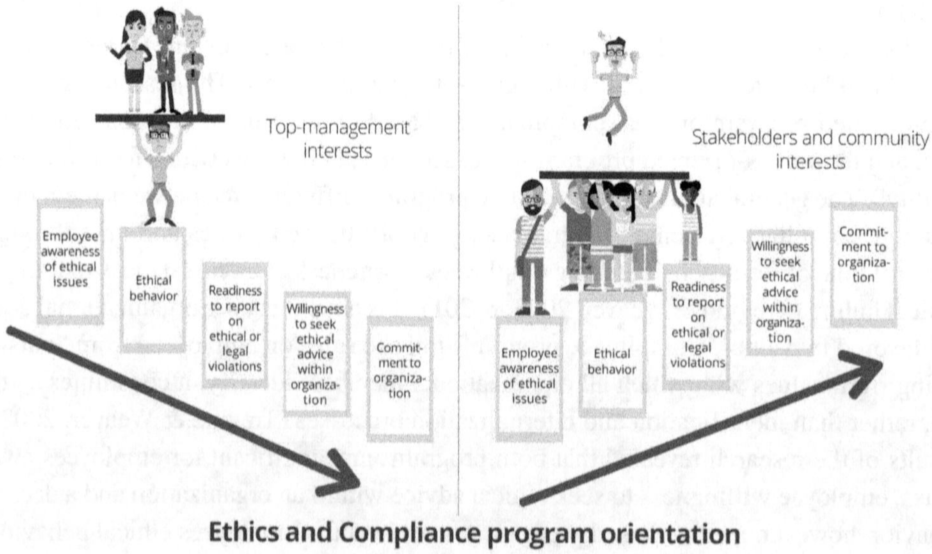

CONCLUSION

As it has been analyzed compliance today goes far beyond abidance of laws. Today, the principles of ethics and integrity are the basis for compliance culture. With the promotion of principles and values of ethical behavior it is easier to secure a functional and successful compliance system. Moreover, the diagram on pic.1 demonstrates that though compliance addresses legal issues, this regulation correlates more with ethics and is aimed at securing ethical behavior in business conduct. Thus, the integration of ethics into a compliance system is required to create a compliance culture within an organization that promotes the ethical business conduct of organizational representatives outside of the organization.

The authors of this research develop a definition of comprehensive compliance today as promotion and observance of the principles of integrity and business ethics to secure the interests of the third parties (interested parties/ stakeholders) that provide for a company's abidance of applicable legal norms and rules as well as good reputation. Whatever the compliance program is – anti-corruption, anti-trust, anti-money laundering, etc., eventually, it regulates economic and social relations and aims to prevent illegal practices, crime and dishonest business conduct, as in the end regulators develop laws and impose sanctions to secure "fair play" for the interests of market participants and stakeholders.

The role of ethics is becoming predominant in compliance framework. At a recent conference devoted to trends in Internal Audit Prof. Steve Goodson of University of Texas at Austin reported on the shift of focus in IA in 2016: from less emphasis on operational and compliance audits and internal controls investigations to corporate governance, Enterprise Risk Management and ethics audits (Goodson, 2016). An interesting fact is though compliance audits have always been an element of an effective compliance system, the audits of ethics and corporate values are becoming of more significance than simply compliance controls, apparently, as such controls won't be efficient if there is a lack of ethics supported by the tone from the top.

REFERENCES

Aguilar, L. A. (2013). Doing the right thing: compliance that works for investors. *Paper presented at Conference Regulation, Operations & Compliance (ROC) 2013*, New York, NY.

Basel Committee on Banking Supervision. (2003). *The compliance function in banks*. Bank for international settlements. Retrieved from https://www.bis.org/publ/bcbs103.pdf

Biebuyck, C. (2014). The risks of insider trading. *Economía, 16*(July). Retrieved from http://economia.icaew.com/finance/july-2014/the-risks-of-insider-trading

DiPietro, B. (2014). Difference Between Compliance, Ethics: interview with M. McMillan. *Risk & Compliance Journal*. Retrieved from: http://blogs.wsj.com/riskandcompliance/2014/06/30/the-difference-between-compliance-and-ethics/

Ethics (2014). In *BBC Ethics guide online*. Retrieved from http://www.bbc.co.uk/ethics/introduction/intro_1.shtml#h1

European Parliament. (2014). Directive 2014/57/EU of 16 April 2014 of the European Parliament and of the Council on criminal sanctions for market abuse (market abuse directive).

European Parliament. (2014). Regulation (EU) of 16 April 2014 No 596/2014 of the European Parliament and of the Council on market abuse (market abuse regulation).

Gerner-Beuerle, C., Paech, P., & Schuster, E. P. (2013). *Study on Director's duty and liability*. London School of Economics. Retrieved from http://ec.europa.eu/internal_market/company/docs/board/2013-study-analysis_en.pdf

Goodson, S. (2016, May 6). Stop acting like auditors! *Paper presented at International Academic Forum 2016: Professional and Academic Innovation in Internal Auditing*, Istanbul, Bogazici University.

Haque, O. S., Freitas, J. D., Bursztajn, H. J., Cosgrove, L., Gopal, A. A., & Paul, R. … Wolfman, S. (2013). *The ethics of pharmaceutical industry influence in medicine*. Ministry of Education, Israel. Retrieved from http://medlaw.haifa.ac.il/index/main/4/EthicsofPharmaceutical.pdf

International compliance Association. (n.d.). *What is compliance?* Retrieved from http://www.int-comp.org/careers/a-career-in-compliance/what-is-compliance/

ISO. (2014). ISO 19600 Compliance management systems – Guidelines.

Kaplan, H. J. (2014, December 4). Corporate Criminal Liability for Insider Trading. Retrieved from https://www.americanbar.org/content/dam/aba/administrative/litigation/materials/2014/2014_sac/2014_sac/corporate_criminal_liability.authcheckdam.pdf

Kennedy-Glans, D., & Dr. Schulz, B. (2005). *Corporate Integrity: a toolkit for managing beyond compliance*. Mississauga, Ontario: John Wiley & Sons, Canada, Ltd.

Kessel, M. (2014). Restoring the pharmaceutical industry's reputation. *Nature Biotechnology Journal, 32*, 983–990. Retrieved from http://www.nature.com/nbt/journal/v32/n10/full/nbt.3036.html

Overland, J. R. (2015). *The criminal liability of corporations for insider trading in Australia: Proposals for reform* [Doctoral dissertation]. Retrieved from http://hdl.handle.net/1885/96475

Patientview. (2015). The corporate reputation of pharma in 2014 — the patient perspective and how the corporate reputation of pharma companies has changed over the past four years. Retrieved from http://www.patient-view.com/uploads/6/5/7/9/6579846/patientview_11-2-2015_press_release_corp_rep_global.pdf

Sarbanes-Oxley Act of 2002, Pub. L. No. 107-204, 116 Stat. 745 (2002).

Sawyer, L. (2004). *Sawyer's words of wisdom*. The IIA Research Foundation.

Scarlett, A. M. (2011). Investors be aware: Assessing shareholder derivative litigation in India and China. *University of Pennsylvania Journal of International Law, 33*(1), 173–237. Retrieved from https://www.law.upenn.edu/journals/jil/articles/volume33/issue1/Scarlett33U.Pa.J.Int'lL.173(2011).pdf

Skinner, D. C. (2006). Director responsibilities and liability exposure in the era of Sarbanes-Oxley. *The Practical Lawyer, June*. Retrieved from https://files.apks.com/practica_lawyer_skinner.pdf

Snezhko, S. (2015). Time to step up… . *INCOMPLIANCE, 19*, 26-28.

The Securities and Exchange Act of 1934, Pub. L. No. 73-291, §1, 46 Stat. 881 (1934).

Thompson, J. H. (2013). A Global Comparison of Insider Trading Regulations. *International Journal of Accounting and Financial Reporting, 3*(1), 1. doi:10.5296/ijafr.v3i1.3269

Trevino, L. K., & Nelson, K. A. (2010). *Managing Business Ethics: straight talk about how to do right*. U.S.: J. Wiley & Sons Inc.

Trevino, L. K., & Weaver, G. R. (2003). *Managing ethics in business organizations: a social scientific perspective on business ethics*. Stanford University Press.

United States Department of Justice. (n.d.) *U.S. Attorney Manual.* Title 9: Criminal, 9-28.000 Principles of Federal Prosecution of Business Organizations, 9-28.800 Corporate Compliance Programs [Abstract]. Retrieved from https://www.justice.gov/usam/united-states-attorneys-manual

U.S. Securities and Exchange Commission site. (n.d.). Insider trading. Retrieved from https://www.sec.gov/answers/insider.htm

Yevmenyeva, A. (2013). Insider violations in EU. What can bring to justice. *Arbitration practice, 5*. Retrieved from http://pravorf.ru/upload/pravorf.ru-ins2.pdf

ADDITIONAL READING

F. C. A. (n.d.Handbook. Retrieved from https://www.handbook.fca.org.uk/handbook

Financial Conduct Authority. (2015). FCA fines Reckitt Benckiser £539,800 for listing rule failures. Retrieved from https://www.fca.org.uk/news/fca-fines-reckitt-benckiser-for-listing-rule-failuresand

Financial Services Authority. (2012). David Enhorn and Greenlight Capital Inc fined £7.2m for trading on inside information in Punch Taverns Plc. Retrieved from FSA Library http://www.fsa.gov.uk/library/communication/pr/2012/005.shtml

IFPMA. (2012). Code of Practice. Retrieved from https://www.ifpma.org/resource-centre/ifpma-code-of-practice/

Israelstam, I. (n.d.) Case law shows several important conditions must be satisfied. *Labour Guide*. Retrieved from http://www.labourguide.co.za/discipline-dismissal/211-complicated-cases-of-conflict-of-interest

LaCroix, K. (2014). Largest Derivative Lawsuit Settlements. *The D&O Diary Journal*. Retrieved from http://www.dandodiary.com/2014/12/articles/shareholders-derivative-litigation/largest-derivative-lawsuit-settlements/

KEY TERMS AND DEFINITIONS

Compliance: Abidance by the principles of business ethics to secure the interests of the company's stakeholders.

Conflict of Interest: A situation where the interests of two parties are incompatible (employee vs. company, employee vs. customer, company and senior manager/ director).

Corporate Conflict: A conflict between a company's and own director's interests.

Ethics: Moral obligations and principles of behavior.

Fiduciary Duties: Ethical obligations of directors to act in the company's interests.

Insider Trading: Trading of securities by a person who has non-public material information about the security.

Integrity: A culture of business conduct led by high ethical principles rather than formal obligations.

ISO 19600: An international standard on implementation of effective compliance system.

Stakeholders: All third parties that are influenced by the company's operations or activity (employees, customers, shareholders, business-partners, government, communities, etc.).

ENDNOTES

1 See SEC Enforcement Actions, Insider trading cases available at http://www.sec.gov/spotlight/insidertrading/cases.shtml

2 See Financial Conduct Authority Enforcement available at https://www.fca.org.uk/about/enforcement and Financial Services Authority Enforcement cases available at http://webarchive.nationalarchives.gov.uk/20130403023549/http:/www.fsa.gov.uk/about/press/facts/fines

3 See for example, U.S. Model Business Corporation Act; UK Companies Act of 2006; Australian Corporations Act of 2001; NZ Companies Act of 1993; German Corporate Governance Code; A guide for directors of subsidiary companies in Germany; OECD Principles of Corporate Governance; Russian Federal Laws "On Joint-stock companies" #208-FZ of 1995 and "On Limited liabilities companies" #14- FZ of 1998; Code of Corporate Governance issued by the letter of Central Bank of Russian Federation of 2012, # 06-52/2463; South Africa Companies Act of 2008.

4 Most jurisdictions provide for disqualification of the director as a sanction – as substitute for weak private enforcement, disqualification is particularly effective where the sanction is also available outside insolvency and for management mistakes that do not amount to a criminal offence (Gerner-Beuerle at al.., 2013).

5 This refers to a business judgment rule – the principle of a common law which serves in defense of directors for their business decisions. An interesting fact requires an excursus here into the practice of derivative litigations in Delaware Court, state of Delaware, USA. In fact, many large U.S. corporations, including publicly-traded US companies are incorporated in the state of Delaware. For this reason state courts have an extensive experience in corporation case law. So, a number of derivative suits have been brought through Delaware courts. Delaware courts apply to business judgement rule as a presumption that directors have acted consistently with their fiduciary duties making decisions in the interests of the corporation. And the plaintiff is required to provide serious evidence that directors in taking a decision has breached any one of their fiduciary duty — good faith, loyalty, or due care. If the plaintiff fails to prove the breach of fiduciary duties by a director, reference to a business judgement rule by Delaware judges in most shareholder derivative actions dismiss boards of directors from legal liability and hold directors liable only in case of fraudulent behavior [Based on public sources].

6 See, for example, National Conference of State Legislatures. *50 States table: Conflict of Interest definitions in US states*. Retrieved from http://www.ncsl.org/research/ethics/50-state-table-conflict-of-interest-definitions.aspx .

7 The settlements paid out by pharmaceutical companies since 1991 up to 2010 (`$30 billion) represent just over two-thirds of the profits made by the 10 largest companies in a single year (2010).

8 Advertising of a product through TV, radio or other social media directly to a customer, a form of promotion widely-used by pharmaceutical companies in USA.

9 Off-label promotion of a prescription drug is when a drug manufacturer markets or promotes a drug for a condition for which it has not received an approval of a regulating agency (Food and Drug Administration in U.S.).

10 39% of the 1150 patient groups respondent in 2014 say that pharma has either an "excellent" or a "good" corporate reputation in 2014 (compared with 35.4% which said the same in 2013) (Patientview, 2015), while there was an inverse tendency in 2013 (34% of respondents believed that multinational drug companies have an excellent or even good reputation – a 19% decline from the prior year), (Kessel, 2014).

Chapter 12
Green Marketing and Branding: Combining Micro and Macro Perspectives to Achieve a Circular Economy

Asli Kuscu
Yeditepe University, Turkey

ABSTRACT

Green products and services have become an important part of consumption, as consumers' knowledge and concern towards environmental sustainability has increased and they have started to concentrate on their environmental impact. Nonetheless, green marketing still constitutes a small portion of the overall consumer spending. This chapter aims to highlight the importance of marketing activities in the adoption and social normalization of green consumption by the consumers generating public support and economic benefits for the companies as well as environmental and social gains for the society in return. Combining both micro and macro-level determinants and consequences, a conceptual framework is suggested which aims to contribute to literature both theoretically and practically.

INTRODUCTION

The notion of the circular economy (CE) fosters "reduction, reuse and recycle" of all resources and materials and those three fundamental aims can be achieved through the interplay of both micro (single company and consumer) and macro (region and country) levels (Ghisellini, Cialani, & Ulgiati, 2015). A circular economy is defined as "an industrial economy that is restorative or regenerative by intention and design" (MacArthur, 2013, p. 14) and "...which aims to keep products, components and materials at their highest utility and value, at all times" (Webster, 2015, p. 16). More recently, Geissdoerfer et al. (2017) include that circular economy is "a regenerative system in which resource input and waste, emission, and energy leakage are minimized by slowing, closing, and narrowing material and energy loops" (p.763). They add that "this can be achieved through long-lasting design, maintenance, repair, reuse, remanufacturing, refurbishing, and recycling" (p. 763). Thereafter, more environmentally conscious and "cleaner" production and consumption models as well as regulations and laws that encourage such

DOI: 10.4018/978-1-5225-8109-3.ch012

models are among the antecedents and results of CE. Hence, not only recycling, which is the primary focus worldwide particularly in the early stages of CE, maintained through regional and national policies and legislations in most of the countries, but consumers' and companies' awareness and responsibility towards production, consumption and reuse of more environment-friendly thus greener products/services are also main and inevitable concerns of the CE (He, Lü, Zhang, & Shao, 2013).

Green products are products that are "typically durable, non-toxic, made of recycled materials, or minimally packaged" (Ottman, 1998, p. 89). More specifically, "a green product is a product whose design and/or attributes (and/or production and/or strategy) uses recycling (renewable/toxic-free/biodegradable) resources and which improves environmental impact or reduces environmental toxic damage throughout its entire life cycle" (Durif, Boivin, & Julien, 2010, p. 31). Hence; reduction, reuse and recycling as well as biodegradability are important terms for green production. On top of these, green products need to also be certified as such by a recognized organization (Gurău & Ranchhod, 2005) and should not employ animal testing (Durif et al., 2010). Consumers expect green products to be not harmful for the nature, themselves, their overall health and overall planet wellbeing (Durif et al., 2010). Green services, on the other hand, are defined as "services, in the offering or use of which the key target criterion is ecological sustainability" by Cocca and Ganz (2015, p. 181). Although some services such as laundry or cleaning services are concerned about their environmental footprint, most of the green services are more on the waste reduction aspect of green marketing. Hence, they focus on how to reduce energy and resources used during service encounters and on how to employ renewable energy supplies (Cocca and Ganz, 2015). With the dominant logic moving from products to services (Vargo and Lusch (2008), not only green products but also green services have become an important part of consumption since consumers' knowledge and concern towards environmental sustainability has increased and they have started to concentrate on their environmental impact. Though economically still not a huge market, as consumers have started to choose sustainable consumption over others, companies that advance in that aspect started to gain economic advantage over competitors. Accordingly, green consumption started to generate a non-negligible and important growing market. A recent international study reveals that brands' sustainability actions and intentions are shaping purchase decisions in more than 30% of consumers (Unilever, 2017). Moreover, consumers worldwide increase their green consumption and they are also willing to pay more for green products/services, particularly when they see a significant benefit and they are actively communicated by the brands about their sustainable acts as a differentiation point (BCG, 2009). Consequently, implementation of CE and green marketing at the micro level may create further opportunities generating high growth potential for sustainable brands; but obviously that requires continuous encouragement of the consumers' responsibility towards the environment (Zhijun & Nailing, 2007; Geng & Doberstein, 2008; Su, Heshmati, Geng, & Yu, 2013). Literature, more specifically scarce case studies, point out the fact that there is a beneficial cycle of interaction between macro and micro forces when it comes to CE and green consumption.

The aim of this chapter is to highlight the importance of marketing activities and branding, in the adoption of green marketing by generating public support and economic benefits for the companies. As stated in Ghisellini et al. (2015), companies' and consumers' awareness and knowledge worldwide are crucially important in the development of the CE. Nonetheless, there is scarce literature analyzing these issues from a micro level perspective, yet alone from a perspective combining both micro and macro levels, which will contribute both theoretically and practically. The chapter will initially discuss the role of consumers in the increased adoption of renewable technologies and materials at both micro and macro levels, as it will eventually generate economic growth and support for the implementation of CE.

Consequently, how companies and brands will benefit from a circular adoption viewpoint particularly from green marketing to generate a sustainable competitive financial and perception-based advantage and secure growth in the market will be examined from a branding perspective. And, finally, the chapter will cover how consumers' and society's attitude towards circular economy can be shaped by the green marketing mix. Deliberating over all these topics, a conceptual framework will be suggested taking a cycle of micro and macro level determinants and consequences into consideration.

BACKGROUND

Role of Green Consumers

There is no debate on the fact that consumer demand is running the world and has a dramatic impact on the business processes worldwide. Companies are competing against each other and try to convince the consumer that their products/services provide better solutions to their problems. Although demand for new products or services is initiated by the few market-driving companies, at the end of the day it is the consumers who make the final purchase as well as adoption decisions and who rule the marketplace and particularly influence market-driven businesses. Taking the circular economy's adoption at both micro and macro levels into consideration, this influence becomes more drastic, as the governmental interventions are not enough for businesses and consumers to adjust to the new business model and consumers' demand is a more significant contributor to the overall adoption from the industry side yet alone from the consumer side. When consumers are convinced to adopt green products/services at higher levels, they will generate a demand that will be unrecognizable by the companies. They will further prompt governmental action and force governments to pass along regulations and financial incentives (further than the ones already existing) so that other companies are not simply pushed through governments but willingly invest in green to eventually increase their sales and profits. Within this perspective, consumers' role in the adoption of the circular economy is inevitable.

Consumer Motivations for Green Purchase

Previous research on green consumption demonstrates that consumers purchase green brands due to intrinsic reasons such as their own self-interest and involvement towards environmental issues and sustainability and their concern about the welfare of the world (macro level) but also due to extrinsic reasons, such as enhancement of their own image through the purchase and usage of green products/services (micro level) (Gadenne, Sharma, Kerr, & Smith, 2011; Griskevicius, Tybur, & Van den Bergh, 2010; Kumar & Ghodeswar, 2015; Lee, 2009; Polonsky, 2011). Biswas and Roy (2015) further denote that consumers' major concerns are along financial and social values as well as along situational factors and believes, where information need and price perception dominate the influence on actual purchase act. Hence, green consumers actually do not buy green products/services unconsciously or out of habit, but they want to either support green companies and try to adopt long-term sustainable consumption practices to protect the environment (Gadenne et al., 2011) or to add value to their own selves and most likely to their self-image (Griskevicius et al., 2010; Kumar & Ghodeswar, 2015), while also looking for a financial and information gain.

Consumers' responsibility towards the environment is represented as their individual commitment and activities to protect it. When consumers believe that they personally can protect the environment by engaging in environmentally friendly actions such as purchase of green products or use of green services, they are intrinsically motivated to continue their activities (Lee, 2009). They believe that they are doing it for the world's wellbeing and for the up-coming generations and get joy out of it and feel proud of themselves. Kalafatis, Pollard, East, & Tsogas (1999) using the Ajzen's Theory of Planned Behavior (Ajzen, 1991), similarly point out that positive attitudes towards green products are formed through the development of culture-independent outcome belief systems among the consumers. Hence, when consumers worldwide believe in their contribution and gain an altruistic value, they start to develop more positive attitudes towards adoption of green products/services and thus thereafter towards the circular economy. Although some differences might exist among countries regarding green marketing adoption rate and demand on green products (Gurău & Ranchhod, 2005; Lazaro, 1993; Kalafatis et al., 1999; Ottman, 1992; Peattie & Ratnayaka, 1992) as well as on the approach being top down or bottom up (Gurău & Ranchhod, 2005) – meaning either regulated by the governments or demanded by the end-consumers -, attitude towards green brands have risen in the western as well as in the Asian countries (Kumar & Ghodeswar, 2015).

Nonetheless, previous research also shows that increased positive attitude towards green products does not always lead to more consumption (Kalafatis et al., 1999; Mintel, 1991) and it is in fact not always linear, so that it changes from one category to the other and it is affected by financial factors (Biswas & Roy, 2015; Kalafatis et al., 1999), which is also the case for green services (Cocca & Ganz, 2015). More specifically, consumers were found to switch to non-green products/services when they are faced with a financial struggle (Biswas & Roy, 2015; Cocca & Ganz, 2015; Corrado & Ross, 1990). Major gaps in prices or no perceived financial benefits in buying green products/services would also make them choose to buy regular substitutes. As stated by Polonsky (2011), "unfortunately, a value concept that is based on financial returns and discounts the natural environment will see the environment as a resource to exploit rather than a partner in existence" (p. 1314). In a similar vein, Camacho-Otero, Pettersen, & Boks (2017) performed a meta-analysis on the adoption of reused products and found that consumers' concerns for the performance, hygiene and value of the product are hindering consumers to adopt circular economy practices. Hence, consumers need to be re-assured about the functional benefits. Further, Wastling, Charnley, & Moreno (2018) add that behavioral change instead of intentional change is needed for a circular economy adoption, which was found to be culture specific by Kalafatis et al. (1999). Consumers' purchase intentions were found to differ for UK and Greek samples as societal influence is more important for the previous, whereas individual influence is prominent for the latter, which suggests that image-related aspects still play a role in green consumption even in developed countries and refers to the social benefits associated with consumption.

Consumption is an activity, where individuals reflect or enhance their own identities onto the society, while taking the society's and their norms and expectations into consideration (Sirgy, 1982). In other words, consumers' final purchase decisions are influenced by their and the society's perception of the products/services available in the market (Dholakia, Bagozzi, & Pearo, 2004; Kleine, Kleine, & Kernan, 1993; Ozaki & Sevastyanova, 2011; Sen, Gürhan-Canli, & Morwitz, 2001). Griskevicius et al. (2010) demonstrate that a conspicuous part of green consumption can be attributed to this, where consumers buy overpriced and, in some cases, even low-quality green products just to be accepted and perceived at a higher status by the society. In other worlds, as it is in almost all versions of consumption, they adjust to their either actual or idealized images regulated by the social norms so that this social appeal influences consumers' green purchase decisions (Kumar & Ghodeswar, 2015). Nonetheless, on the opposite direction, consumers can also generate an impact on the society's perceptions and norms by their choices (Arnould & Price, 2000; Schatzki, 1996) and this social influence is also quite significant in the product preferences (Lee, 2008) and adoption decisions (Kulviwat, Bruner & Al-Shuridah, 2009). Particularly, consumers were found to adjust themselves more easily to using green services (Cocca & Ganz, 2015). It is through consumption that individuals gain social status and recognition (Fisher & Price, 1992). Social influence is one of three main aspects – social, economic and environmental- of sustainability, reflecting not only society's well-being but also social gains achieved through sustainability (Murray, Skene, & Haynes, 2017). When it comes to green consumption, consumers either buy products that are in line with their own concerns or they want to position themselves more socially and environmentally conscious than they really are within the society they live in (Nyborg, Howarth, & Brekke, 2006). Particularly this is more evident in emerging countries and in some cultures than developed countries (Unilever, 2017). Rettie, Burchell, & Barnham (2014) when analyzing this process from a green marketing perspective referred to it as "social normalization" (p. 14), where green consumption becomes a standard and normal act that is highly accepted in the society rather than a so-called niche market targeting a small and environmentally friendly section of the consumers. Unfortunately, at the current situation, the "social normalization" process does not take place in most of the cases regarding green consumption. So, when defining values for the consumers to adopt a greener consumption and circular economy approach, image as well as social related recognition and its contagious nature should also be taken into consideration and be enhanced.

Table 1 provides a brief classification of the factors defined by previous research and discussed in this section. As can be seen from the table, the expectations of the consumers from green products/services are like the ones they do from conventional products/services. One thing that is also evident in the table is that most of the researchers working on the reasons why consumers choose green consumption concentrated on limited factors rather than on the whole. Taking this into consideration, all values consumers associate with green consumption and expect to be delivered by green products/services can be termed as the overall green value.

Table 1. Values consumers associate with green consumption: overall green value

Financial	Biswas & Roy (2015); Corrado & Ross (1990); Gadenne et al. (2011); Kalafatis et al. (1999); Polonsky (2011); Sauza (2004)
Information	Biswas and Roy (2015); Kalafatis et al. (1999); Polonsky (2011); Sauza (2004)
Utilitarian/ Performance	Kumar & Ghodeswar (2015; Lee (2009); Ottman et al. (2006); Polonsky (2011); Sauza (2004)
Environmental / Altruistic	Gadenne et al. (2011); Hartmann & Apaolaza-Ibáñez (2012); Hartmann et al., 2005; Kumar & Ghodeswar (2015); Lee (2009); Nyborg et al. (2006); Polonsky (2011); Sauza (2004); Schultz (2000); Wong et al. (1996)
Image / Social acceptance	Biswas & Roy (2015); Gadenne et al. (2011); Griskevicius et al. (2010); Hartmann & Apaolaza-Ibáñez (2012); Hartmann et al., 2005; Kalafatis et al. (1999); Kumar & Ghodeswar (2015); Lee (2009); Nyborg et al. (2006); Ottman et al. (2006); Polonsky (2011); Rettie et al. (2014); Sauza (2004); Schultz (2000)

GREEN MARKETING FROM A BRANDING PERSPECTIVE

Companies take on green marketing activities mainly due to the pressure generated by the governments, competitors or due to financial constraints such as the increasing costs of by-product disposal and product returns (Gencer & Akkucuk, 2016; Polonsky, 2011; Wong, Turner, & Stoneman, 1996). In some countries or regions, the adoption within a particular sector was initiated by the governmental regulations, whereas in others it was the environmental concern of individuals that made governments pass along some initiatives or laws for companies to adopt sustainable procedures and acts. For instance, Akkucuk (2016) demonstrated how some companies implemented green logistics and supply chain management to their overall operations by using the Supply Chain Operations Reference (SCOR) Model developed by the American Production and Inventory Control Society (APICS) and Supply Chain Council (SCC). Those are good examples where companies that took a "greener" supply chain logistics approach were able to gain financial as well as brand-related returns (Gencer & Akkucuk, 2016); nonetheless, it is obvious that there is a struggle in green market adoption as companies, consumers and governments lack the capacity to combine micro and macro perspectives (Polonsky, 2011).

The American Marketing Association (AMA) terms a brand as "a name, term, sign, symbol, or design, or the combination of them, intended to identify the goods or services of one seller or group of sellers and to differentiate them from those of a competitor". Alongside branding, viewed either from a customer-based (Aaker, 2009) or a financial-based (Farquar, 1989) viewpoint, brand equity is considered as the sum of consumers' value perceptions and knowledge of a brand (Baldauf, Cravens, & Binder, 2003), that are developed through marketing actions. Hence the stronger the perceived value that is communicated to the consumer, the higher is the brand equity. Brand equity is a major intangible asset to companies generating customer-value (long-lasting customer-company relationships) as well as company-value that is manifested in financial returns to companies in the form of profitability and market performance (Baldauf et al., 2003). Brand equity is believed to be formed through loyalty, awareness, associations, quality and market measures (Aaker, 2009) and consumers choose brands that they perceive to have higher brand equity due to their higher levels of loyalty, awareness, trust and quality perceptions among other factors and when they evaluate the values generated by all the substitutes in the market, they use brand equity as a shortcut to come up with the final purchase decision. Also, when the main promise of all available products is perceived almost the same by the consumers, their final decision will be based on their overall analysis of brand equity. Hence, they would choose the one that they show attitudinal as well as behavioral loyalty and the one that they trust and believe to reflect higher quality. Brand equity further justifies price premiums and provides consumers a higher value/price ratio (Anselmsson, Johansson, & Persson, 2007), which is also the case for green products (Biswas & Roy, 2015). Higher prices that are in most of the cases associated with green production and green products are thereafter rationalized by the consumers when they believe in the overall equity of the brand.

Although brand equity can be made measurable, it is really a perception. Hartmann and Apaolaza-Ibáñez (2012) state that consumers generally believe that green products provide added values and thus perceive green products as having higher brand equity. As suggested earlier, this is mainly either due to consumers' own believes or due to the impact of the society's norms (Rettie et al., 2014). Nonetheless, this implies that consumers possess a satisfactory level of awareness and attitudinal loyalty towards green products, justifying higher brand equity. But as green consumption still does not dominate the marketplace, which can be attributed to and thus be solved through the generation of higher levels of trust and quality perceptions, companies need still be concentrating on these factors. Marketing is all about the relationship between consumers and organizations. When a company and its products/services do not provide additional benefits to the consumers and are not viewed as reflecting high quality and trust, it is very unlikely that it will convince the consumer to continue the relationship and eventually activate a governmental reaction. Hence, when companies aim to increase consumers' overall engagement with green products/services, they need to be providing added perceived benefits to the consumers, which will make the consumer notice increased brand equity and warrants them higher prices. From an international and corporate perspective, Gurău and Ranchhod (2005) investigate attractiveness of the green-markets and suggest that markets, where there is only governmental pressure in the form of legislations and rules but no consumer awareness, can be termed as unfavorable as those investments would not be supported by the consumers and would eventually turn to be generating a low ROI (return on investment). Consequently, consumers need to be convinced by green marketing actions that green products/services possess a higher level of overall green value and thus higher brand equity than conventional products/services, so that their purchase/usage becomes the norm in the society. Even that justifies that there should be an adoption of green marketing at both micro and macro levels, where not only governments push and try to trigger consumer reaction; but governments, consumers and companies all see a benefit from green marketing.

The Green Marketing Mix

AMA defines marketing as "the activity, set of institutions, and processes for creating, communicating, delivering, and exchanging offerings that have value for customers, clients, partners, and society at large", which can be best performed through the use of a "mix of controllable marketing variables (4P's - marketing mix) that the firm uses to pursue the desired level of sales in the target market". As the definition of marketing by AMA suggests the scope of marketing has been enlarged to include societal concerns such as environment in the spectrum of marketing. Marketing mix further influences consumers' overall equity perceptions of the brands and creates value for consumers as well as for organizations (Yoo, Donthu, & Lee, 2000). The first step in building a strong and desirable perception is awareness that is followed by trust and quality. When those are established within the consumers, they start to favor the products over the others and develop loyal relationships. Hence, desired sales are achieved by using the marketing mix as a tool to generate a desirable and valuable perception among the consumers. Green marketing, in a similar vein as it is in conventional marketing, requires a strategic mix of marketing actions to be able to persuade consumers on the overall equity of the green brands and convince consumers and the society to adopt and socially normalize the usage of green products. That necessitates a targeted approach and thus an understanding of the target audience's expectations and needs, which is initially achieved through segmentation. Sauza (2004), using cognitive/non-cognitive perspectives and perceived product benefits/risks as the axes, developed a two-by-two matrix just to come up with a 4-group categorization of the green consumers, which are termed as (1) environmentally green, (2) emerging green, (3) price sensitive green and (4) conventional consumers. This segmentation provides more grounds on targeting than the one provided by Polonsky (1995), which classifies consumers as dark-green, semi-green, light-green, and non-green based on their propensity towards buying green products but lacks the underlying reasons of their purchase. Each group identified by Sauza (2004) reflects a different set of expectations of the values outlined in Table 1. For instance, environmentally green consumers are extremely environmentally conscious and seek tremendous amount of information, whereas conventional consumers are more concerned about the risks associated with buying green products over conventional ones. Emerging greens buy products not because of their environmental benefits but rather due to other benefits associated with green consumption, such as social aspects. And price sensitive greens can easily switch due to price concerns. As can be seen, all four groups have different expectations from green products and every group can be reached through a different mixture of benefits.

Following the identification of the market segments, companies need to select their target audiences and develop their marketing mix accordingly to be able to appeal to their target market. Thereafter, green products and services, prices and places to sell those products/services and particularly communication must be designed by the companies, to deliver a distinct identity and value proposition (positioning and differentiation as suggested by Aaker, 2009), while providing answers to what, how, why, and where questions that are commonly asked by marketers.

When green products are concerned, Peattie and Peattie (2009) and later Polonsky (2011) add that more extreme actions should be taken by the green companies to stand out in the competition and being chosen by the consumers, that are far beyond new products or substitutes of the current non-green products in the market. Brand positioning and generating a stronger and a more unique brand perception to create a high equity perception while using all marketing mix elements (but specifically communication) should be highly desirable at this stage. Regarding green products/services, one way to achieve this is through the functional positioning (Cocca and Ganz, 2015; Hartmann, Apaolaza Ibáñez, & Forcada Sainz, 2005). Obviously, there is an expectation from the consumer side, particularly from emerging greens that green products/services perform at least at the level of their competitors. Functional related requirements form the lowest level of values and luckily can easily be addressed by green companies, which is one of the main reasons they are less likely to be influential on consumer attitude when it comes to green products (Hartmann et al., 2005). Consumers also want to be informed by the product and service labels or packages and labeling has been gaining prevalence in most countries (Ghisellini et al., 2015). Specifically, environmentally green and conventional green consumers require additional information; one to be assured on the environmental benefits, the other on the functional, financial and social benefits and risks associated with green products. Labels/packages that provide additional information and certification make particularly those groups of consumers' evaluations of green over non-green products/services easier (Biswas & Roy, 2015; Cocca and Ganz, 2015; D'Souza, 2004). However, managers of green companies also point out the fact that in some cases differentiating the product only at the environmental level may be harmful (Wong et al., 1996). As stated in Hartmann et al. (2005) previous research also shows that emphasizing the green benefits of the products may backfire in some cases, particularly when consumers perceive "a trade-off between functional performance of the brand and its environmental impact" (p. 12). Rex and Baumann (2007) further add that consumers were afraid to be charged extra for a green product. There are examples where companies following this logic specifically did not position their products on the environmental value. For instance, some green products such as lamps or biodegradable paper products are widely accepted and bought by the consumers as they were not explicitly viewed or communicated as green products. One thing that those products do well is to inform the consumers about their benefits that are not just environmentally centered. Consumers evaluate them not only based on their effect on the environment; rather, those products are able to satisfy consumers' expectations at different levels suggested in Table 1. Particularly for the emerging green and price sensitive green consumers they are good options in the market communicating financial and image-related social benefits. Contrary to products though, services in general benefit from their "greenness". Green services are at the early stages of development, hence offering and communicating green services provides a differentiation point and competitive advantage to services companies (Cocca and

Ganz, 2015). Thus, communication in any form (whether it be on the labels/packages or on the owned/paid/earned media) directed towards the target audience is the most important aspect of the marketing mix. Within conventional marketing, communication serves as a tool to inform, educate and persuade the consumer and thus generate and increase demand. The same outcome can also be achieved through the communication of green products, which will be quite beneficial as their competitive advantage is usually regarded as suspicious (Rex & Baumann, 2007). Further, communication makes "social normalization" pass through easily specifically for the markets that are termed as "underdeveloped eco-markets" (Gurău & Ranchhod, 2005, p.555), where both consumer awareness and governmental intervention is lacking by increasing the overall awareness.

Green products as well as services are usually higher priced (Cocca and Ganz, 2015) and companies rarely use lower prices to penetrate the market (Wong et al., 1996) even though not only price sensitive green consumers but most consumers other than environmentally greens consider their finances when buying green products/services and they in most of the cases compete with non-green counterparts in the market. Communicating the extra benefits that are accrued through the purchase and usage of the product/service over regular and other green products/services influences consumers' overall value perceptions (Hartmann et al., 2005) that is termed as the overall green value and provides a justification for the price premium. As a result, communication becomes a very critical part of the marketing mix, as the overall perceived brand equity of the products/services relies largely on the signal the green marketing mix is sending to the target consumers.

Another important but neglected aspect and one of the significant challenges within the green marketing mix is the channel acceptance and support (Wong et al., 1996), which can be achieved through the anticipated consumer demand and market size. Once consumers start to find green products/services in more outlets, convenience expectations of most of the consumers will be fulfilled (Ottman, Stafford, & Hartman, 2006). It will further contribute to the "social normalization" process, reflecting again a mutual connection between consumers and companies.

SOLUTIONS AND RECOMMENDATIONS

So far, the chapter in general dealt with the company and consumer side of green marketing. The third factor namely the influence of the government, which has a more macro perspective than the other two needs to be also taken into consideration. As stated in Polonsky (2011) governments in general consider using either punishments or rewards to convince consumers and companies to act ecologically conscious. Further, governments also use zero waste or waste management programs (Ghisellini et al., 2015). However, as stated earlier governmental intervention without the interplay of consumers and companies neither generates the desirable profit level for the companies nor the attitudinal or behavioral change within consumers. Hence, those efforts are usually unsuccessful, giving that green marketing and environmental consumption still constitutes only a small proportion of the world trade. Figure 1 below displays a summary of the desired interaction between companies, consumers and governments with consumers still placed at the center and playing an important role in shaping companies and governments, while also being influenced by their actions. As such, the framework represented in Figure 1 displays a three-way interaction between the major actors of green marketing - company-consumer-government - combining micro and macro perspectives.

Figure 1. Desired interaction

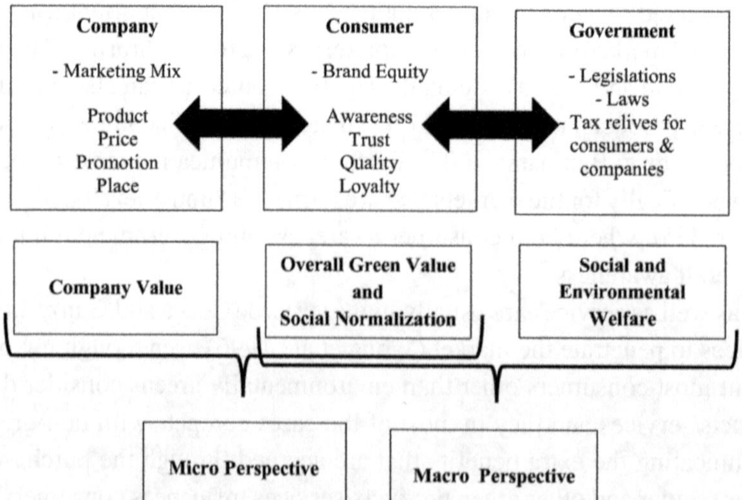

Putting the consumer at the center of these relationships does not mean that the full responsibility lies within the consumers. On the contrary, it means that the consumers are an important part of the interaction, formulating and combining micro and macro perspectives, but they are not the only ones accountable for the overall transition. Similar to a top down approach that must be proved unsuccessful a bottom up approach that is not supported by other actors would also fail. Hence, all economic actors need to work for greener production and consumption. As can be seen, it is highly useful for the companies and countries to focus on the values consumers associate with green consumption. By generating and emphasizing different values through their marketing actions for different groups of green consumers, other than just the hard-loyal green ones, companies can create higher overall green value for different segments, generate higher brand equity for their brands and reach a broader consumer base that eventually create higher levels of company value. Further, when consumers adopt green activities, they will require governments to act in favor of green production and consumption. On the other hand, governments also need to understand consumers' values so that green consumption is not just pushed through by regulations and laws but made normal to generate a long-lasting social change and environmental welfare.

Currently there are more and more companies that are trying the convince the consumers to make green product and service choices by offering the consumers several benefits and gaining reductions in costs and risks as well as trust and steady growth in return. Examples include hotel chains providing extra points or benefits such as free breakfasts for their guests when they choose to skip room cleaning services for a specific period. Also, banks waive some customer fees when customers choose their bank statements to be delivered by e-mail rather than by post. Some utility companies in Europe are using similar promotions for their customers' utility bills. Those are examples, where the consumers are provided a financial benefit when they choose the green option. When viewed from the overall green value perspective whether those promotions provide any value other than financial value is questionable. Nonetheless, those companies educate regular consumers who are initially not concerned about the environment on green consumption and help them to adopt a new behavior and make them regard green choices as normal. Also, they intensify their brand equity among the green consumers as they already expecting companies to act green. From this perspective, it can be said that they further add environmental/altruistic value and image/social value to the overall green value. And, they do it by educating the consumers and changing their everyday behavior without creating any risks, doubts or unpleasant memories for the consumers. On the other hand, there are also companies that force the consumer adopt environmental actions by making the consumer pay for the consequences. For instance, in most European countries supermarkets do not provide any free plastic bags and charge them for the bags they offer or make the consumers bring their own reusable bags to shop. In a similar way, in the UK an international coffee chain started to charge extra fees for the paper cups offered at its coffeeshops. Those type of reinforcements that push the consumer towards green choices do not generate any benefits for the consumers in general and therefore do not help to the "social normalization" of green marketing.

FUTURE RESEARCH DIRECTIONS

The framework presented in this chapter is fruitful in terms of both qualitative and quantitative future research directions. First of all, at the micro level the stated relationships between companies' marketing actions and consumers' value perceptions can be analyzed in depth while taking consumer segments' differences and perceptions of the current normal into consideration. This will provide useful information for green companies to position and promote their offerings. Also, green products and what type of values (intrinsic or extrinsic) they offer to make an influence in the form of awareness, trust, quality or loyalty can differ from one country to the other yet alone from one sector to the other. Understanding the contingency situations where and how emphasizing a benefit of the offering backfires is another rewarding research path. Second of all, at the macro level, understanding and following how these changes develop is enormously valuable. That requires longitudinal study settings which are quite difficult to achieve though it might generate interesting outcomes specifically for policy makers.

CONCLUSION

This chapter focuses on an area of circular economy namely green marketing and tries to discuss how green marketing can become the norm within the society to increase the adoption of a circular economy perspective. Obviously, there is a direction towards a more environmentally friendly consumption, where products are reused, recycled and waste is reduced. Nonetheless, green marketing to be regarded as the normal way of consumption still needs some improvement. All in all, the question asked is "how green consumption can become mainstream?". The challenges faced by companies, consumers and countries cannot be solved by the amplified usage of the current methods but necessitates a more comprehensive solution. Deliberating over all those aspects discussed in the chapter, consumers' responsibility regarding environmental (sustainable/recyclable/green) products needs to be nurtured (Geng & Doberstein, 2008; Su et al., 2013) and more importantly habits need to be changed (Mentink, 2014); so that green marketing becomes the new norm. Hence, taking the consumers into green consumption and thus into the circular economy bandwagon requires not only generating more positive attitudes towards environmental responsibility (which is tried to be done currently) but also more perceived overall green value for the consumers; so that there will be a continuous demand for and development towards more circular business models. When consumers see any value – intrinsic or extrinsic – they will turn into circular economy practices. This chapter aims to highlight the importance of marketing activities in the adoption and social normalization of green consumption by the consumers generating public support and economic benefits for the companies as well as environmental and social gains for the society in return. Combining both micro and macro level determinants and consequences, the conceptual framework suggested can be used as a starting point for new strategies.

REFERENCES

Aaker, D. A. (2009). *Managing brand equity*. NY: Simon and Schuster.

Ajzen, I. (1991). The theory of planned behavior. *Organizational Behavior and Human Decision Processes*, *50*(2), 179–211. doi:10.1016/0749-5978(91)90020-T

Akkucuk, U. (2016). SCOR model and the green supply chain. In U. Akkucuk (Ed.), *Handbook of research on waste management techniques for sustainability* (pp. 108–124). Hershey, PA: IGI Global. doi:10.4018/978-1-4666-9723-2.ch006

Anselmsson, J., Johansson, U., & Persson, N. (2007). Understanding price premium for grocery products: A conceptual model of customer-based brand equity. *Journal of Product and Brand Management*, *16*(6), 401–414. doi:10.1108/10610420710823762

Arnould, E. J., & Price, L. L. (2000). Authenticating acts and authoritative performances: Questing for self and community. in S. Ratneshwar, D. G. Mick, and C. Huffman (Eds.), The Why of Consumption: Contemporary Perspectives on Consumer Motives, Goals, and Desires pp. (140–163). London, UK: Routledge.

Baldauf, A., Cravens, K. S., & Binder, G. (2003). Performance consequences of brand equity management: Evidence from organizations in the value chain. *Journal of Product and Brand Management*, *12*(4), 220–236. doi:10.1108/10610420310485032

BCG. (2009, January). Capturing the green advantage for consumer companies. Retrieved from https://www.bcg.com/documents/file15407.pdf

Biswas, A., & Roy, M. (2015). Leveraging factors for sustained green consumption behavior based on consumption value perceptions: Testing the structural model. *Journal of Cleaner Production*, *95*, 332–340. doi:10.1016/j.jclepro.2015.02.042

Camacho-Otero, J., Pettersen, I. N., & Boks, C. (2017). Consumer and user acceptance in the circular economy: what are researchers missing? In C. A. Bakker & R. Mugge (Eds.), *PLATE: Product Lifetimes and The Environment – Research in Design Series* (Vol. 9, pp. 65–69). Netherlands: Delft University of Technology and IOS Press.

Cocca, S., & Ganz, W. (2015). Requirements for developing green services. *Service Industries Journal*, *35*(4), 179–196. doi:10.1080/02642069.2014.990002

Corrado, M., & Ross, M. (1990). Green Issues in Britain and the Value of Green Research Data. In *Esomar Annual Congress: Environmental Issues in the 90's* (pp. 347-369).

D'Souza, C. (2004). Ecolabel programmes: A stakeholder (consumer) perspective. *Corporate Communications, 9*(3), 179–188. doi:10.1108/13563280410551105

Dholakia, U. M., Bagozzi, R. P., & Pearo, L. K. (2004). A social influence model of consumer participation in network-and small-group-based virtual communities. *International Journal of Research in Marketing, 21*(3), 241–263. doi:10.1016/j.ijresmar.2003.12.004

Durif, F., Boivin, C., & Julien, C. (2010). In search of a green product definition. *Innovative Marketing, 6*(1), 25–33.

Farquhar, P. H. (1989). Managing brand equity. *Marketing research, 1*(3).

Fisher, R. J., & Price, L. L. (1992). An investigation into the social context of early adoption behavior. *The Journal of Consumer Research, 19*(3), 477–486. doi:10.1086/209317

Gadenne, D., Sharma, B., Kerr, D., & Smith, T. (2011). The influence of consumers' environmental beliefs and attitudes on energy saving behaviours. *Energy Policy, 39*(12), 7684–7694. doi:10.1016/j.enpol.2011.09.002

Geissdoerfer, M., Savaget, P., Bocken, N. M., & Hultink, E. J. (2017). The Circular Economy–A new sustainability paradigm? *Journal of Cleaner Production, 143*, 757–768. doi:10.1016/j.jclepro.2016.12.048

Gencer, Y. G., & Akkucuk, U. (2016). Reverse logistics: Automobile recalls and other conditions. In U. Akkucuk (Ed.), *Handbook of research on waste management techniques for sustainability* (pp. 125–154). Hershey, PA: IGI Global. doi:10.4018/978-1-4666-9723-2.ch007

Geng, Y., & Doberstein, B. (2008). Developing the circular economy in China: Challenges and opportunities for achieving'leapfrog development'. *International Journal of Sustainable Development and World Ecology, 15*(3), 231–239. doi:10.3843/SusDev.15.3:6

Ghisellini, P., Cialani, C., & Ulgiati, S. (2016). A review on circular economy: The expected transition to a balanced interplay of environmental and economic systems. *Journal of Cleaner Production, 114*, 11–32. doi:10.1016/j.jclepro.2015.09.007

Griskevicius, V., Tybur, J. M., & Van den Bergh, B. (2010). Going green to be seen: Status, reputation, and conspicuous conservation. *Journal of Personality and Social Psychology, 98*(3), 392–404. doi:10.1037/a0017346 PMID:20175620

Gurău, C., & Ranchhod, A. (2005). International green marketing: A comparative study of British and Romanian firms. *International Marketing Review, 22*(5), 547–561. doi:10.1108/02651330510624381

Hartmann, P., & Apaolaza-Ibáñez, V. (2012). Consumer attitude and purchase intention toward green energy brands: The roles of psychological benefits and environmental concern. *Journal of Business Research, 65*(9), 1254–1263. doi:10.1016/j.jbusres.2011.11.001

Hartmann, P., Apaolaza Ibáñez, V., & Forcada Sainz, F. J. (2005). Green branding effects on attitude: Functional versus emotional positioning strategies. *Marketing Intelligence & Planning, 23*(1), 9–29. doi:10.1108/02634500510577447

He, P., Lü, F., Zhang, H., & Shao, L. (2013). Recent developments in the area of waste as a resource, with particular reference to the circular economy as a guiding principle, in waste as a resource. In R. E. Hester & R. M. Harrison (Eds.), *Issues in Environmental Science and Technology No 37*. The Royal Society of Chemistry.

Kalafatis, S. P., Pollard, M., East, R., & Tsogas, M. H. (1999). Green marketing and Ajzen's theory of planned behaviour: A cross-market examination. *Journal of Consumer Marketing*, *16*(5), 441–460. doi:10.1108/07363769910289550

Kleine, R. E. III, Kleine, S. S., & Kernan, J. B. (1993). Mundane consumption and the self: A social-identity perspective. *Journal of Consumer Psychology*, *2*(3), 209–235. doi:10.1016/S1057-7408(08)80015-0

Kulviwat, S., Bruner, G. C. II, & Al-Shuridah, O. (2009). The role of social influence on adoption of high tech innovations: The moderating effect of public/private consumption. *Journal of Business Research*, *62*(7), 706–712. doi:10.1016/j.jbusres.2007.04.014

Kumar, P., & Ghodeswar, B. M. (2015). Factors affecting consumers' green product purchase decisions. *Marketing Intelligence & Planning*, *33*(3), 330–347. doi:10.1108/MIP-03-2014-0068

Lazaro, C. (1993). Green marketing: Looking beyond the quick fix. *Business Marketing Digest*, *18*(4), 67–74.

Lee, K. (2008). Opportunities for green marketing: Young consumers. *Marketing Intelligence & Planning*, *26*(6), 573–586. doi:10.1108/02634500810902839

Lee, K. (2009). Gender differences in Hong Kong adolescent consumers' green purchasing behavior. *Journal of Consumer Marketing*, *26*(2), 87–96. doi:10.1108/07363760910940456

MacArthur, E. (2013). Towards the Circular Economy Vol. 2: Opportunities for the Consumer Goods Sector. *Ellen MacArthur Foundation*. Retrieved from https://www.ellenmacarthurfoundation.org/publications/towards-the-circular-economy-vol-2-opportunities-for-the-consumer-goods-sector

Mentink, B. (2014). *Circular business model innovation: a process framework and a tool for business model innovation in a circular economy* [Master's Thesis]. Delft University of Technology & Leiden University, Leiden, The Netherlands.

Murray, A., Skene, K., & Haynes, K. (2017). The circular economy: An interdisciplinary exploration of the concept and application in a global context. *Journal of Business Ethics*, *140*(3), 369–380. doi:10.100710551-015-2693-2

Ng, P. F., Butt, M. M., Khong, K. W., & Ong, F. S. (2014). Antecedents of green brand equity: An integrated approach. *Journal of Business Ethics*, *121*(2), 203–215. doi:10.100710551-013-1689-z

Nyborg, K., Howarth, R. B., & Brekke, K. A. (2006). Green consumers and public policy: On socially contingent moral motivation. *Resource and Energy Economics*, *28*(4), 351–366. doi:10.1016/j.reseneeco.2006.03.001

Ottman, J. A. (1992). Sometimes consumers will pay more to go green. *Marketing news*, *26*(6), 16.

Ottman, J. A., Stafford, E. R., & Hartman, C. L. (2006). Avoiding green marketing myopia: Ways to improve consumer appeal for environmentally preferable products. *Environment, 48*(5), 22–36. doi:10.3200/ENVT.48.5.22-36

Ozaki, R., & Sevastyanova, K. (2011). Going hybrid: An analysis of consumer purchase motivations. *Energy Policy, 39*(5), 2217–2227. doi:10.1016/j.enpol.2010.04.024

Peattie, K., & Peattie, S. (2009). Social marketing: A pathway to consumption reduction? *Journal of Business Research, 62*(2), 260–268. doi:10.1016/j.jbusres.2008.01.033

Peattie, K., & Ratnayaka, M. (1992). Responding to the green movement. *Industrial Marketing Management, 21*(2), 103–110. doi:10.1016/0019-8501(92)90004-D

Polonsky, M. J. (1995). A stakeholder theory approach to designing environmental marketing strategy. *Journal of Business and Industrial Marketing, 10*(3), 29–46. doi:10.1108/08858629510096201

Polonsky, M. J. (2011). Transformative green marketing: Impediments and opportunities. *Journal of Business Research, 64*(12), 1311–1319. doi:10.1016/j.jbusres.2011.01.016

Rettie, R., Burchell, K., & Barnham, C. (2014). Social normalisation: Using marketing to make green normal. *Journal of Consumer Behaviour, 13*(1), 9–17. doi:10.1002/cb.1439

Rex, E., & Baumann, H. (2007). Beyond ecolabels: What green marketing can learn from conventional marketing. *Journal of Cleaner Production, 15*(6), 567–576. doi:10.1016/j.jclepro.2006.05.013

Schatzki, T. R. (1996). *Social practices: A Wittgensteinian approach to human activity and the social.* Cambridge University Press. doi:10.1017/CBO9780511527470

Schultz, P. W. (2000). New environmental theories: Empathizing with nature: The effects of perspective taking on concern for environmental issues. *The Journal of Social Issues, 56*(3), 391–406. doi:10.1111/0022-4537.00174

Sen, S., Gürhan-Canli, Z., & Morwitz, V. (2001). Withholding consumption: A social dilemma perspective on consumer boycotts. *The Journal of Consumer Research, 28*(3), 399–417. doi:10.1086/323729

Sirgy, M. J. (1982). Self-concept in consumer behavior: A critical review. *The Journal of Consumer Research, 9*(3), 287–300. doi:10.1086/208924

Su, B., Heshmati, A., Geng, Y., & Yu, X. (2013). A review of the circular economy in China: Moving from rhetoric to implementation. *Journal of Cleaner Production, 42*, 215–227. doi:10.1016/j.jclepro.2012.11.020

Unilever. (2017, January) Report shows a third of consumers prefer sustainable brands. Retrieved from https://www.unilever.com/news/Press-releases/2017/report-shows-a-third-of-consumers-prefer-sustainable-brands.html

Vargo, S. L., & Lusch, R. F. (2008). Service-dominant logic: Continuing the evolution. *Journal of the Academy of Marketing Science, 36*(1), 1–10. doi:10.100711747-007-0069-6

Wastling, T., Charnley, F., & Moreno, M. (2018). Design for Circular Behaviour: Considering Users in a Circular Economy. *Sustainability, 10*(6), 1743. doi:10.3390u10061743

Webster, K. (2017). *The circular economy: A wealth of flows*. Isle of Wight: Ellen MacArthur Foundation Publishing.

Wong, V., Turner, W., & Stoneman, P. (1996). Marketing Strategies and Market Prospects for Environmentally-Friendly Consumer Products 1. *British Journal of Management*, *7*(3), 263–281. doi:10.1111/j.1467-8551.1996.tb00119.x

Yoo, B., Donthu, N., & Lee, S. (2000). An examination of selected marketing mix elements and brand equity. *Journal of the Academy of Marketing Science*, *28*(2), 195–211. doi:10.1177/0092070300282002

Zhijun, F., & Nailing, Y. (2007). Putting a circular economy into practice in China. *Sustainability Science*, *2*(1), 95–101. doi:10.100711625-006-0018-1

ADDITIONAL READING

Aaker, D. A. (2004). Leveraging the corporate brand. *California Management Review*, *46*(3), 6–18. doi:10.1177/000812560404600301

Ginsberg, J. M., & Bloom, P. N. (2004). Choosing the right green marketing strategy. *MIT Sloan Management Review*, *46*(1), 79–84.

Kapferer, J. N. (2012). *The new strategic brand management: Advanced insights and strategic thinking*. Kogan page publishers.

Keller, K. L. (1993). Conceptualizing, measuring, and managing customer-based brand equity. *Journal of Marketing*, *57*(1), 1–22. doi:10.2307/1252054

Keller, K. L., Parameswaran, M. G., & Jacob, I. (2011). *Strategic brand management: Building, measuring, and managing brand equity*. Pearson Education.

Leonidou, C. N., Katsikeas, C. S., & Morgan, N. A. (2013). "Greening" the marketing mix: Do firms do it and does it pay off? *Journal of the Academy of Marketing Science*, *41*(2), 151–170. doi:10.100711747-012-0317-2

Ottman, J. (2017). *The new rules of green marketing: Strategies, tools, and inspiration for sustainable branding*. Routledge. doi:10.4324/9781351278683

Papista, E., Chrysochou, P., Krystallis, A., & Dimitriadis, S. (2018). Types of value and cost in consumer–green brands relationship and loyalty behaviour. *Journal of Consumer Behaviour*, *17*(1), 101–113. doi:10.1002/cb.1690

KEY TERMS AND DEFINITIONS

Brand Equity: Brand equity is the overall value accrued to a brand. It is a perception that is formed within the consumers' minds, but it can directly relate to the financial value and market success of a company. Consumers develop strong bonds with companies that have high brand equity. They believe that those companies' offerings are better in generating functional, hedonic and symbolic values for them and are also willing to pay more for their offerings.

Green Consumers: Consumers who choose environmentally friendly products/services over traditional ones are termed as green consumers.

Green Marketing: Green marketing refers to the marketing strategy and activities that are designed to promote and sell green, thus environmentally conscious products and services.

Green Products/Services: Green products and services are offerings that are environmentally friendly and are not only manufactured in a way that does not harm the environment, but their usage and disposal does not harm the environment, as well.

Green Value: Green value is the overall value consumers gain by using green products and services. Green value is the sum of the financial, environmental, social, information and functional benefits that a green product or service can provide to the consumers. Consumers evaluate offerings based on these benefits and form positive or negative attitudes.

Marketing Mix: The four p's of marketing – product, place, price and promotion – are referred as the marketing mix. The marketing mix is developed based on the overall strategy of the company.

Segmentation: Segmentation refers to the identification of groups of individuals that share some characteristic with each other but are different from the others. In marketing, those groups are defined as market segments and are further used for targeting and positioning.

Social Normalization: It is a process where a new social norm is established. In some cases, it might take place by destroying the old normal acts of the society whereas in some cases it might just generate a new pattern of behavior which is in general accepted by the society.

Chapter 13
Financial Flexibility and Corporate Investment:
Does Financial Flexibility Affect Sustainability of Firms?

Seda Bilyay Erdoğan
Boğaziçi University, Turkey

ABSTRACT

This chapter investigates the impact of financial flexibility (FF) on investments, which constitutes the basis for sustainable corporate development. Using a large database of 1,205 firms from three emerging countries in Europe—Poland, Russia and Turkey—for the time period between 2000 and 2016. The authors provide evidence that financial flexibility, achieved through conservative leverage policies, enhances companies' investments and positively contribute to corporate sustainability. Moreover, as the number of years of low leverage kept by firms increase so does the impact of financial flexibility on corporate investment. Besides financial flexibility, internal cash generation capacity of firms, and sales growth also improve the investment capability of firms, improving corporate sustainability. The results support the hypothesis that financial flexibility enhances companies' investment capability, which is an extremely essential tool for firms to have in their businesses.

INTRODUCTION

In perfect capital markets, companies are assumed to be able to invest in all profitable projects, and consequently they are able to capture all growth opportunities, hence there is no necessity for financial flexibility (FF). However, in real life scenarios, where the capital markets are imperfect, financial flexibility appears as a significant concept, because it becomes extremely crucial for companies to find necessary funding required for growth opportunities. Furthermore, empirical studies demonstrate that companies issue a lesser amount of bank borrowing when compared to what the main capital structure theories suggest, which constitutes a puzzle. It is claimed that the traditional capital structure theories do not take into account companies' requirement for financial flexibility. It is argued that companies

DOI: 10.4018/978-1-5225-8109-3.ch013

choose to preserve financial flexibility as spare borrowing capacity (Marchica & Mura, 2009; Graham & Harvey, 2001; Gamba & Triantis, 2008; DeAngelo & DeAngelo, 2007; De Jong, Verbeek & Verwijmeren, 2012; Denis & McKeon, 2012). Therefore, financial flexibility explains the gap between what the classical capital structure theories suggest and the empirical findings.

Financial Flexibility (FF) is the "ability of a firm to access and restructure its' financing at a low cost" (Gamba & Triantis, 2008). In line with this view, there are mainly two ways through which financial flexibility becomes significant for companies: avoiding financial distress costs in a negative shock situation and mitigating underinvestment complications.

Until recently, there are only a few studies conducted on financial flexibility; mainly because FF is not directly measurable and hard to quantify. Given the importance of the concept of financial flexibility which is expected to have a huge impact on corporate sustainability, the main purpose of this study is to fill this gap. Our objective is to classify the firms in our sample as flexible or not, based on their maintenance of low leverage for a minimum number of years, following which we aim to comprehend the impact of FF on corporate investment level, which constitutes the basis for sustainable development.

Our sample covers three emerging countries from Europe: Poland, Russia and Turkey; coinciding to 1,205 publicly quoted companies in total. Our sample includes market and accounting data for the time span between 2000 and 2016. For the calculation of the financial flexibility dummy used in the analysis, it is necessary that each company in our sample has a minimum of 4 years of observations in the 17-years' time frame.

Following the methodology adopted by Marchica and Mura (2010), we classify firms in our sample as financially flexible or not based on their possession of Spare Debt Capacity (SDC) for a minimum number of years. A leverage equation is estimated with several control variables included in the estimation. The residuals of the leverage estimation captures the systematic deviation between observed and predicted leverage. According to Ferrando, Marchica and Mura (2017), "the demand for financial flexibility is indirectly captured by the negative deviations from estimated target leverage" and in accordance with this we classify a company as financially flexible if low leverage policy is sustained for three successive years (two, four and five successive years of SDC is also calculated for robustness purposes). Our findings show that almost 19% of the companies in our sample have financial flexibility (FF calculated with three years of SDC).

Following the classification of the flexible companies in our sample, in the next step of our analysis, we examine whether financial flexibility has any effect on the companies' investment capability. In order to test this conjecture, we estimate an investment equation, with the inclusion of an FF dummy and also an interaction term between the FF dummy and the cash flow of the company. We hypothesize that the FF dummy will significantly and positively affect the investment level of companies. Consistent with our expectations, the impact of flexibility on investment is positive and significant for the three emerging countries in our sample.

The remainder of the study is arranged as follows. In the next section, we present the related literature on the topic, providing empirical findings on financial flexibility, following which we describe the empirical design used in the study encompassing the sample and dataset used; as well as the methodology that will be adopted throughout the study; and also identifying financially flexible firms. The results of the impact of FF on investment level will be analyzed in the following chapter, finalizing with the concluding remarks.

LITERATURE REVIEW

It is empirically demonstrated that firms tend to issue a lesser amount of debt as compared to what the leading capital structure theories suggest, which constitutes a puzzle in the finance literature. This puzzle is explained by the companies' preference to maintain financial flexibility, which is achieved through maintaining spare borrowing capacity (Marchica & Mura, 2009; Graham & Harvey, 2001; DeAngelo & DeAngelo, 2007; De Jong et al., 2012; Denis & McKeon, 2012; Gamba & Triantis, 2008). It is claimed by researchers that companies keep spare debt capacity intentionally with the ultimate purpose of being able to draw funds from low-cost sources of external financing in later periods, as a consequence to which they will not be obliged to issue shares at unattractive prices.

Despite the fact that all around the world managers perceive Financial Flexibility as the most significant contributing factor to financial policies (Graham & Harvey, 2001), "the capital structure literature has remained relatively distant to recognize and incorporate financial flexibility" (Byoun, 2007). In line with this, Killi, Rapp & Schmid (2011) also claim that financial flexibility has not obtained enough attention in the academic literature, which might provide an answer for the well-known debt conservatism puzzle.

The traditional capital structure theories take into consideration the asymmetric information framework and tend to concentrate on the advantages and disadvantages of financing through borrowing. Nevertheless, these theories miss an essential point: managers' desire to retain financial flexibility (Graham & Harvey, 2001; Brounen et al., 2004; Bancel & Mittoo, 2004). According to Fama and French (2005), the empirical corporate finance literature has focused on the pecking order and trade-off theories in the last decades; which cannot explain the capital structure choices of firms and as a consequent to this there is now no empirically sustainable capital structure theory (DeAngelo & DeAngelo, 2007).

Focusing on the importance of financial flexibility, DeAngelo and DeAngelo (2007) fill the gap in capital structure literature, through developing a theory on this topic. DeAngelo and DeAngelo (2007) presume that managers construct, keep and reconstruct their debt capacities in "normal" times in order to let themselves obtain debt in "abnormal" times to encounter unexpected capital requirements. The authors provide empirical evidence that the capital structure decisions of firms are taken with the intention of keeping financial flexibility. DeAngelo and DeAngelo (2007) claim that financial flexibility is the critical missing link in attaching observed behavior of companies with the capital structure theory.

Empirical studies demonstrate that Chief Financial Officers around the globe perceive financial flexibility as the single most significant determinant of financial policies. Graham and Harvey (2001), who conducted a survey with CFOs in US, are the first to consider financial flexibility as a capital structure determinant. They state that FF is acknowledged as the key constituent of companies' capital structure decisions by the corporate managers in US. In line with the findings of Graham and Harvey (2001), Brounen et al. (2004) and Bancel and Mittoo (2004) also confirm the same result in similar surveys conducted with managers from 16 countries in Europe. These surveys conducted all around the world imply that firms maintain low leverage in their balance sheets as a result of which they give up on their tax advantages and consequently maintain some borrowing capacity for future dates.

Despite its significance as stated above, empirical evidence on Financial Flexibility is limited, which is attributable to the fact that the value of financial flexibility for companies is not directly observable (Denis, 2011; Rapp, Schmid & Urban, 2014) and it is difficult to quantify. Therefore, empirical analysis on financial flexibility of companies is scarce (De Jong et al., 2012; Marchica & Mura, 2010; Rapp et al., 2014). The common point about the studies conducted on this topic is that financial flexibility plays a significant role in capital structure decisions and moreover it has a positive impact on the investment levels of companies.

Analyzing the impact of financial flexibility on capital structure choices, Byoun (2007) is one of the first researchers working on this topic and argues that companies that are in their development stages during their growth cycle need flexibility the most, as a consequent to which these companies tend to issue equity more, keeping their leverage levels low.

On the other hand, according to Killi et al. (2011), who propose a financial flexibility view, argues that optimal debt level of a company depends on a number of factors including the necessity for future financial flexibility, tax benefits and bankruptcy costs. The empirical findings of Killi et al. (2011), which are based on the data of 17 European countries reveal that the need to maintain FF in the form of borrowing capacity is a significant yet largely ignored capital structure determinant, concluding that debt conservatism can be observed as a firm's optimum reply to make sure that the firm is financially flexible rather than as having irrational behavior.

Furthermore, Denis and McKeon (2012) provide empirical evidence that financial flexibility, attained through unused borrowing capacity plays a significant role in the capital structure dynamics of the US firms. The analysis conducted by Denis and McKeon (2012) show that large increases in the levels of leverage represent proactive actions, which take the company away from target leverage ratios that are long-run in order to fund investment and operating necessities.

Conducting one of the milestone studies on the topic, Marchica and Mura (2010) argue that companies that are financially flexible show better investment capability for their sample selected from firms in UK. Marchica and Mura (2010) state that "a conservative leverage policy directed at maintaining financial flexibility can enhance investment ability". Furthermore, Marchica and Mura (2010) also argue that FF companies realize more and better investments than the non-flexible companies. For the first time, Marchica and Mura (2010) provide direct evidence on the value of FF to companies through investigating the effect this strategy has on firms' long-run performance and ability to invest. It is also concluded by Marchica and Mura (2010) that "financial flexibility in the form of untapped borrowing power is a crucial missing link in capital structure theory", demonstrating that the results obtained by Marchica and Mura (2010) are similar to the findings of DeAngelo, DeAngelo and Whited (2011).

The findings of Marchica and Mura (2010) are enlarged with the empirical study conducted by Ferrando et al. (2017) for nine European countries, who also obtained similar results. Ferrando et al. (2017) use a company's unused borrowing capacity to quantify financial flexibility of a firm. The findings of Ferrando et al. (2017) demonstrate that FF augments the investment capability of the firms in Europe.

Financial flexibility issues constitute a much bigger challenge for the companies in emerging countries as compared to those companies in developed countries. Capital markets are relatively less developed in emerging countries, which makes it even harder for companies to obtain external financing (Yung, Li and Jian, 2015). The primary reason that impacts companies looking for funding from external sources in developing countries is the existence of highly volatile capital flows (Agosin & Huaita, 2012; Bekaert & Harvey, 2003; Demir, 2009). Moreover, volatile capital flows result in bank debt to be unavailable in emerging markets (Guo & Stepanyan, 2011). Hence, the search for financial flexibility is extremely significant in decisions regarding corporate finance, especially for firms domiciled in emerging countries.

Despite its' significance, there are only a few empirical analyses studying corporate financial flexibility in emerging markets and all of these studies reveal that financial flexibility plays a significant role in the investment level of companies, the details of which can be found below.

One of the significant studies is conducted by Arslan-Ayaydın et al. (2014), who study 1,608 firms from five East Asian countries, over the period between 1994-2009, studying the effect of FF on investment of corporations and firm performance. Their results indicate that firms can be financially flexible mainly as a result of conservative financial policies including maintenance of low leverage and also through keeping high levels of cash and equivalents. Furthermore, Yung et al. (2015), took 33 emerging countries into their sample, analyzing whether FF is vital for companies in developing countries. Where relatively weaker capital markets present in developing economies are associated with a high instability in capital flows; the significance of acquiring FF in fast growing developing countries is emphasized in this study. Their results demonstrate that "corporate financial flexibility enhances investment ability and reduces the sensitivity of investment to cash flow" (Yung et al., 2015). In a nutshell, in agreement with the conclusions of Arslan-Ayaydin et al. (2014); Yung et al. (2015) also argue that FF improves investment capability of companies.

EMPIRICAL DESIGN

To start with, the entire universe of firms publicly quoted within the databases of three emerging countries in Europe; Poland, Russia and Turkey are taken into the empirical analysis. The data set is made up of 17 years of market and accounting data for the time span between 2000 and 2016. In order to calculate some of the variables (i.e. sales growth) used within the analysis, we lose a year of observations. We only take into consideration publicly quoted companies, because we also need to use the market values for the firms in the analysis and therefore private companies are excluded from this empirical study. Furthermore, some companies in specific sectors have different capital structures and they are under different regulations, therefore are excluded from the study, which are financial services companies (SIC codes between 6000 and 6999), insurance and real estate investment trusts.

We need to have at least four consecutive years of data for each company, in order to build the FF dummy variable. Hence, the firms which do not possess at least four consecutive years of market and accounting data are eliminated from the sample. Moreover, we exclude from the sample those companies, which are not quoted on the major stock exchanges of the respective countries, following which we exclude the observations, which have inputting faults, such as total assets being negative. All variables used in the analysis are winsorized at the top and bottom 1% of their own distribution. As a result of this data filtering procedure, we end up with an unbalanced panel data of 1,205 firms and 20,485 observations for the selected emerging countries in Europe; Poland, Russia and Turkey.

The sample construction procedure is provided in Table 1, where the number of firms at the beginning of the procedure and the number of firms that remain at the end of the application of the above-mentioned criteria is listed.

For the remaining 1,205 firms, yearly accounting and stock market data is collected from Thomson Reuters Eikon for the years between 2000 and 2016.

According to Ferrando et al., 2017, financial flexibility of a firm is an "unobservable factor that depends largely on managers' assessment of future growth options." Therefore, we will use "unused debt capacity" to measure financial flexibility (DeAngelo & DeAngelo, 2007; Marchica & Mura, 2010; DeAngelo et al., 2011; Denis & McKeon, 2012; Ferrando et al., 2017). A leverage equation will be estimated with the inclusion of various control variables, the details of which is provided below. The residual of the leverage estimation is expected to contain financial flexibility, wherein a systematic gap is

Table 1. Sample selection procedure

Sample Size	Number of Firms
List of all active equity firms in Turkey, Poland and Russia for the years 2000-2016	2,466
Less firms from specific industries (banking, financial services, insurance and real estate)	-516
Less firms with less than 4 years of accounting data	-681
Less firms that are not in the major securities	-34
Less firms with inputting mistakes or inconsistent data (Negative total assets, negative number of shares, etc.)	-30
Final Sample Size	**1,205**

anticipated to be produced in between predicted and observed leverage. The difference between predicted and actual level of leverage of firms indirectly contain financial flexibility of firms.

Model 1 stated below will be used to estimate the leverage status of firms.

$$Leverage_{it} = \beta_0 Leverage_{it\text{-}1} + \sum_{k=1}^{K} \beta_k X_{kict} + n_i + n_t + \nu_{ict} \quad (1)$$

Where $Leverage_{it}$ constitutes the "Leverage" of company *i* at time t and "$Leverage_{it\text{-}1}$" is the Leverage of company i at time t-1. $Leverage_{it\text{-}1}$ is included in the estimation as a regressor as required by the Generalized Method of Moments (GMM) technique, the details of which may be found in the next section. Following Flannery and Rangan (2006), the following control variables are added in the leverage model. Non-Debt Tax Shield (NDTS), Size, Profitability, Tangibility and Tax. These control variables are widely used in the literature and it is empirically proven that these control variables significantly affect leverage. Moreover, following Frank and Goyal (2008) and Flannery and Rangan (2006), MTB ratio is also added as a control variable in the regression analysis in order to capture the effect of growth opportunities on leverage. MTB ratio is also used as a control variable to capture the intangible side of the respective firm, i.e. as this ratio expresses how the company is perceived by the potential investors in the stock market (Erdogan, 2015). Finally, we have also used cash ratio as a control variable to capture the impact of other factors, which may let the firm to attain financial flexibility. A list of all the variables with their definitions may be found in Table 2.

We expect the effect of size, tangibility and MTB on leverage to be positive; while the anticipated effect of profitability, tax and cash ratio on leverage is negative. Depending on the controversial empirical studies on the topic, the impact of depreciation (NDTS) on leverage can be either positive or negative.

The descriptive statistics for the variables used in Model 1 may be found in Table 3.

As can be depicted from Table 3 above, the companies domiciled in the emerging countries in Europe have an average profitability of 11%. Another important item that needs special emphasis is about their mean leverage ratio, which stands at 22%, implying that companies in emerging countries in Europe tend to depend more on their own funds in financing their operations. Finally, average tangibility and average cash ratio stands at 0.35 and 0.05, respectively.

Table 2. Variable definitions: Leverage Model

Variable	Notation	Definition
Leverage	LEV	Total Debt / Total Assets Total Debt: Short term debt + current portion of long term debt + long term debt
Size	Size	Log of total assets
Tangibility	Tang	Fixed assets / total assets
Profitability	Prof	Earnings before extraordinary items / total assets
Non-Debt-Tax-Shield	Ndts	Depreciation / total assets
Tax	Tax	Total tax charge / total assets
Cash Ratio	Cash	Cash and cash equivalents / total assets
Market to Book Ratio	MTB	Market capitalization / Net Book Value Market capitalization: stock price x number of shares outstanding Net Book Value: Net asset value

Table 3. Summary statistics of Leverage Model

	Observations	Mean	Median	Standard Deviation	Min	Max
Leverage	12,974	0.22	0.18	0.21	0.00	1.05
Size	13,836	5.86	5.77	1.14	3.44	8.82
Tangibility	13,752	0.35	0.33	0.23	0.00	0.90
Profitability	12,414	0.11	0.10	0.14	-0.46	0.52
Non-Debt Tax Shield (Ndts)	12,805	0.04	0.03	0.03	0.00	0.17
Tax	13,736	0.01	0.01	0.02	-0.05	0.11
Cash Ratio	10,791	0.05	0.02	0.08	0.00	0.42
MTB	10,041	0.20	0.14	1.00	-2.30	3.28

METHODOLOGY

In order to capture the targeting behavior of firms, as a result of which the leverage status of companies will be identified, a dynamic partial adjustment leverage model is estimated, for which Generalized Method of Moments (GMM) is used for all the models in this empirical study.

We will follow Arellano and Bond's (1991) methodology, in which the first differences of the model is taken and appropriate lagged regressors are used as instruments in the system, with the purpose of controlling the endogeneity of the variables used in the regression and country fixed effects simultaneously, which might have a correlation with the explanatory variables (Lemmon, Roberts & Zender, 2008; Blundell & Bond, 1998). We have also included Country fixed effect (*ni*) in the estimations with the ultimate purpose of describing probable correlation in between characteristics special to the countries and regressors. Moreover, we have also included time effect in the analysis to account for any potential macro-economic factors, including economic crisis years. Following Ferrando et al. (2017), we have used System GMM in all estimations, mainly because System GMM appears to offer efficiency gain relative to Difference GMM.

With the estimations conducted using Generalized Method of Moments technique, Arellano-Bond (AR) test for autocorrelation is implemented in order to make sure that the instruments used in the estimations are valid and the model is correctly specified. Arellano-Bond tests for the autocorrelation of the residuals are obtained from the estimations. AR (1) examines whether the residuals are correlated; while AR (2) tests whether the first differences of the residuals are correlated. The null hypothesis of AR (2) is "no second order serial autocorrelation in differenced residuals". With the purpose of ensuring that the model is correctly specified, we expect AR (2) to be insignificant, indicating the model is properly structured and the instruments implemented in the model are valid.

RESULTS

The results of the leverage estimation, i.e. Model 1, conducted for the three emerging countries in Europe, Poland, Russia and Turkey may be found in Table 4.

As can be depicted from Table 4, the results obtained from the leverage estimation are consistent with the previous studies conducted on this topic (Rajan & Zingales, 1995; Wanzenried, 2006; Flannery & Rangan, 2006). For the three emerging countries in Europe, there is a size effect, demonstrated with the significantly positive impact size has on leverage. This indicates that as firm size is getting bigger, firms tend to issue debt easily at more advantageous costs. Moreover, larger companies tend to carry more debt on their balance sheets, because they are inclined to be more transparent and have lower asset volatility.

Moreover, tangibility also has a significant positive effect on leverage, which is as expected in line with the literature; since having fixed assets in their portfolios is a positive sign for the firms in obtaining external financing and moreover it eases the process of obtaining debt for companies. Profitability, on the other hand, negatively and significantly affects leverage, in line with the predictions, providing evidence for Pecking Order Theory, suggesting that companies would favor internally generated funds to outside financing and as the profit level of firms rises, the necessity for external finance drops. Similar to the result obtained from the profitability of firms, the cash level of firms also negatively and significantly effects the leverage of firms, such that firms use the cash-in-hand for their funding requirements instead of external borrowing.

Furthermore, our results show that the tax level of firms has a significant negative effect on leverage for firms in the selected emerging countries in Europe. Similarly, Non-Debt-Tax-Shield, which is defined as depreciation over total assets, also negatively affects leverage in our sample, stemming from the fact that for companies in emerging countries, more depreciation expense means less necessity for the interest deductions associated with debt financing, hence leading to an inverse relationship between depreciation and leverage. Finally, MTB ratio, which is used as a growth opportunity proxy, has a significant positive impact on leverage, implying that firms with high growth opportunities need more leverage to finance this growth.

In order to test for the validity of the instruments and correctness of the model used for leverage estimation, AR (2) statistic is analyzed, which stands at 34.2%, implying that both the model and the instruments are valid and correctly specified.

As we have indicated in Empirical Design section above, following Faulkender, Flannery, Hankins and Smith (2012), we take the fitted values from the leverage estimation, and compare fitted values

Table 4. Results of the Leverage Model

Dependent Variable: $Leverage_t$	
$Leverage_{t-1}$	0.720***
	[0.000]
Size	0.035***
	[0.000]
Tangibility	0.057***
	[0.002]
Profitability	-0.146***
	[0.000]
Non Debt Tax Shield (NDTS)	-0.751***
	[0.003]
Tax	-0.482***
	[0.000]
Cash Ratio	-0.059***
	[0.009]
MTB	0.021***
	[0.000]
Observations	5,930
No. Of firms	866
No. Of instruments	411
Country fixed effects	Yes
Year fixed effects	Yes
AR(1)	0.000
AR(2)	0.342

with the actual values of leverage for each separate observation. Please note that fitted values of leverage imply the amount of maximum leverage that the firm can carry given its financial standing; while the actual values of leverage represent what the company has actually carried in its balance sheet. If the difference between the actual and the fitted values is negative; we define the company as having Spare Debt Capacity (SDC); implying that the company could have received more debt given its financial standing, however has chosen to borrow less. It is anticipated that the systematic portion of the deviations between fitted and actual values in the leverage estimation result from the undetected impact of financial flexibility. In order to remove the impact of small deviations, we impose that the deviations have to be greater than 5% (Ferrando et al., 2017). Finally, we want to ensure that the negative deviation, which is at least 5%, is not just a temporary capital structure shock, but the policy of the firm. To reach this end, a firm is designated as financially flexible if the firm has Spare Debt Capacity for a minimum number of subsequent years, following Marchica and Mura (2010). In our baseline estimations, we built the FF dummy such that, FF dummy is equal to 1, when the firm has SDC for at least three consecutive periods and 0 otherwise (FF3). However as there is no theoretical rationale for taking three consecutive periods for baseline specifications, in order to comprehend whether the results change based on the time horizon picked up for the specification of FF firms, alternative proxies have been used throughout the analysis in the following sections, ranging from a period of two years to five years. We aim to observe whether the impact of financial flexibility changes when the number of consecutive years of spare debt capacity changes.

In Table 5, we provide the share of financially flexible firms in the total sample covering the firms domiciled in Poland, Russia and Turkey.

Within the selected emerging countries in Europe, while 27.6% of the sample can be categorized as FF2 (2 consecutive periods of SDC), this ratio drops to 18.9% when FF3 dummy is used. Furthermore, the share of financial flexibility firms over the entire sample drops to 11.6% and 7.5% for FF4 (4 consecutive years of SDC) and FF5 (5 consecutive years of SDC), respectively in the selected emerging countries. Please also note that as the number of consecutive years of SDC increases (from FF2 to FF5), the percentage of financially flexible firms in total sample gradually decreases in emerging countries, mainly because it is getting more difficult for companies to maintain flexibility for longer periods of time. Once the financially flexible firms within the sample are identified, the effect of financially flexibility on investment can be analyzed.

To the degree that financial flexibility permits companies to sidestep financial distress in case of unexpected events, we claim that FF companies have improved investment capability and in line with this reasoning, we hypothesize that:

Hypothesis 1: Financial Flexibility enhances the investment level of firms.

Moreover, maintaining spare debt capacity for a greater number of years implies that firms have more flexibility as compared to their previous years, which provides them with more funding opportunities and therefore we anticipate that the impact of financial flexibility on corporate investment will be higher for those firms, which have maintained spare debt capacity for longer time periods, leading us to our next hypothesis:

Hypothesis 2: As the number of years in which spare debt capacity is maintained increases, the impact of financial flexibility on corporate investment levels also increases.

In order to test the above stated hypothesis, while investment is taken as our dependent variable, cash flow at the beginning-of-year and sales growth are taken as our independent variables, following Cleary (1999), Alti (2003) and Brown and Petersen (2009). Furthermore, FF dummy and an interaction term multiplying cash flow and FF dummy is also added as independent variables into the estimation following Ferrando et al. (2017), Yung et al. (2015) and Marchica and Mura (2010); with the ultimate aim of testing if FF companies have superior investment capabilities and moreover if the sensitivity of

Table 5. Financially flexible firms

	FF2	FF3	FF4	FF5
Emerging Countries	27.6%	18.9%	11.6%	7.5%

capital expenditures to cash flow gets lower for FF firms. Please note that four different estimations are conducted, with each estimation taking a different version of the FF dummy, i.e. FF2, FF3, FF4 and FF5. We want to analyze whether the impact of financial flexibility on investment changes when financial flexibility dummy is calculated with different time spans.

Accordingly, Model 2 presented below will be estimated for the sample:

$$Investment_{i,t} = y_1 Investment_{i,t\text{-}1} + y_2 Cash\,Flow_{i,t\text{-}1} + y_3 Sales\,Growth_{i,t} + y_4 FF_{i,t} + y_5 FF_{i,t} \times Cash\,Flow_{i,t\text{-}1} + n_c + n_t + \nu_{it} \quad (2)$$

Where $\text{Investment}_{i,t}$ is the capital expenditure divided by Total Assets i at time t. In order to proxy for growth opportunities Sales Growth is used as a regressor and in order to proxy for internal funds generated by companies Cash Flow is used, which is calculated as Earnings before interest, tax, depreciation and amortization (EBITDA) divided by total assets at the beginning-of-year.

Detailed descriptions of the definitions for the variables used in the investment analysis may be found in Table 6.

Table 7 below presents the descriptive statistics for the additional variables used in the investment model. It is essential to note that while the companies in emerging countries have an average growth rate of 19% over the 17 years' time horizon, the average investment and cash flow constitute 9% and 11% of their total assets, respectively.

The results of the estimations conducted for the investment level of selected emerging countries in Europe may be found in Table 8.

Both Sales Growth and Cash Flow positively and significantly affect the Investment level of firms. A firm gives more importance to its investments if it wants to grow its business. Therefore, growth opportunities have a significant place when a firm is deciding on its investments and consequently sales growth positively affects investment levels. On the other hand, cash flow positively affecting the capital expenditure level of firms also demonstrates that firms continue to rely on their own internal funds in addition to external capital markets when deciding on their investment decisions.

Table 6. Variable definitions – Investment Model

Variable	Notation	Definition
Investment	Inv	Capex / Total Assets Capex: Annual change in (net) fixed assets plus depreciation
Financial Flexibility	FF2 FF3 FF4 FF5	FF is a dummy variable: - Gets a value of 1 if the company is Financially Flexible - 0 otherwise. - **FF2**: Financial flexibility attained through following 2 consecutive periods of SDC - **FF3**: Financial flexibility attained through following 3 consecutive periods of SDC - **FF4**: Financial flexibility attained through following 4 consecutive periods of SDC - **FF5**: Financial flexibility attained through following 5 consecutive periods of SDC
Cash Flow	CF	EBITDA / Total Assets Total Assets calculated at the beginning of year
Sales growth	SG	$(Sales_t – Sales_{t\text{-}1}) / Sales_{t\text{-}1}$

Table 7. Summary statistics of Investment Model

	Observations	Mean	Median	Standard Deviation	Min	Max
Investment	13,836	0.09	0.05	0.15	-0.31	0.72
Cash Flow	12,414	0.11	0.10	0.14	-0.46	0.52
Sales Growth	12,478	0.19	0.11	0.56	-0.87	3.68

Table 8. Results of the Investment Model

Dep Var: $Investment_t$	FF2	FF3	FF4	FF5
$Investment_{t-1}$	0.106***	0.121***	0.120***	0.129***
	[0.000]	[0.000]	[0.000]	[0.000]
$Cash\ Flow_{t-1}$	0.324***	0.312***	0.315***	0.284***
	[0.000]	[0.000]	[0.000]	[0.000]
Sales Growth	0.056***	0.057***	0.057***	0.058***
	[0.000]	[0.000]	[0.000]	[0.000]
FF Dummy	0.049***	0.057***	0.091***	0.092***
	[0.000]	[0.000]	[0.000]	[0.000]
$Cash\ Flow_{t-1}$ x FF Dummy	-0.307***	-0.396***	-0.686***	-0.740***
	[0.000]	[0.000]	[0.000]	[0.000]
Observations	9,940	9,785	9,611	9,385
No. Of firms	1,024	1,024	1,024	1,024
No. Of instruments	423	419	409	396
AR(1)	0.000	0.000	0.000	0.000
AR(2)	0.387	0.324	0.529	0.457

*, ** and *** indicate statistical significance levels of 10%, 5% and 1%, respectively.

The coefficients of the financial flexibility dummy variables are positive and significant for all four specifications of investment, proposing that if companies have Spare Debt Capacity for a certain period of time, they tend to invest more, which validates our expectation set forth in Hypothesis 1. It is also essential to note that while the effect of FF on investment is 4.9% following conservative leverage of two years; the effect increases to 5.7%, 9.1% and 9.2% following conservative leverage of three, four and finally five years. This finding suggests that the impact of financial flexibility on Investment dramatically increases as the number of consecutive years with Spare Debt Capacity increases, validating Hypothesis 2. Finally, the interaction term between Cash Flow and FF is significantly negative in all investment estimations, suggesting that financially flexible firms in selected emerging markets are less exposed to the imperfections in capital markets. It is easier for financially flexible firms to issue debt from external sources in order to finance their investments thanks to the availability of financial flexibility; which results for them being less dependent on internally generated funds.

All in all, investment analysis conducted for the selected emerging countries in Europe demonstrate that, sales growth, cash flow and most importantly financial flexibility positively and significantly affects investment level of firms, supporting Hypothesis 1. The positive impact of financial flexibility on investment increases as the number of conservative leverage policy maintained by the company increases, supporting Hypothesis 2. The interaction term between FF and cash flow negatively affects investment in the selected emerging countries in Europe, suggesting that financially flexible firms do not fully rely on their internal funds in their investment decisions and their ability to invest is not risked by asymmetry problems. The results clearly demonstrate that financial flexibility is very valuable for firms in emerging countries, since for some of them keeping low leverage may be the only option of realizing their investments.

It is also essential to note that AR(2) statistics of all the baseline estimations conducted for the emerging countries are greater than 10%, implying that the instruments used in the dynamic modelling are valid and the models are correctly specified.

CONCLUSION

Empirical studies show that companies get less bank borrowing as compared to what the classical capital structure theories suggest. By many researchers, this gap is explained by the financial flexibility concept and it is perceived as the critical missing link in the capital structure literature (DeAngelo & DeAngelo, 2007, Marchica & Mura, 2010, Byoun, 2011).

Until recent times, the concept of financial flexibility were not taken into consideration by managers when giving decisions on their financial policies, mainly stemming from the fact that financial flexibility is not directly measurable and hard to quantify. Since this concept is extremely important proven with the surveys conducted all around the globe, the main purpose of this study is to fill this gap.

In this study, we aim to investigate the relationship between financial flexibility and companies' capability to invest, which constitutes the basis for sustainable development for firms. Initially, using a broad sample from 3 emerging countries between 2000 and 2016; we categorize companies as flexible or not based on the condition that low leverage status is maintained for a number of successive years, ranging from two to five years. Based on the information that each firm is designated as flexible or not, we examine whether financial flexibility has any influence on companies' investment capabilities, which is expected to positively contribute to corporate sustainability.

Our empirical findings demonstrate that financial flexibility obtained through maintaining conservative leverage policies results in improved investment levels, in line with the results of Marchica and Mura (2010), De Jong et al. (2012), Yung et al. (2015) and Ferrando et al. (2017). Moreover, we also empirically demonstrate that as the number of years with low leverage increases, so does its positive impact on investment and therefore so does its positive impact on corporate sustainability.

To sum up, our findings present strong empirical evidence that financial flexibility achieved through preserving spare borrowing capacity, is an extremely important missing link in capital structure theory and financial flexibility is appreciated by companies mainly because financial flexibility mitigates underinvestment born from absence of financial opportunities and furthermore circumvents financial distress and hence helping firms improve their corporate sustainability.

REFERENCES

Agosin, M. R., & Huaita, F. (2012). Overreaction in capital flows to emerging markets: Booms and sudden stops. *Journal of International Money and Finance*, *31*(5), 1140–1155. doi:10.1016/j.jimonfin.2011.12.015

Alti, A. (2003). How Sensitive Is Investment to Cash Flow When Financing Is Frictionless? *The Journal of Finance*, *58*(2), 707–722. doi:10.1111/1540-6261.00542

Arellano, M., & Bond, S. (1991). Some Tests of Specification for Panel Data: Monte Carlo Evidence and an Application to Employment Equations. *The Review of Economic Studies*, *58*(2), 277. doi:10.2307/2297968

Arslan-Ayaydin, Ö., Florackis, C., & Ozkan, A. (2014). Financial flexibility, corporate investment and performance: Evidence from financial crises. *Review of Quantitative Finance and Accounting*, *42*(2), 211–250. doi:10.100711156-012-0340-x

Bancel, F., & Mittoo, U. R. (2004). Cross-country determinants of capital structure choice: A survey of European firms. *Financial Management*, 103–132.

Bekaert, G., & Harvey, C. R. (2003). Emerging markets finance. *Journal of Empirical Finance*, *10*(1–2), 3–55. doi:10.1016/S0927-5398(02)00054-3

Blundell, R., & Bond, S. (1998). Initial conditions and moment restrictions in dynamic panel data models. *Journal of Econometrics*, *87*(1), 115–143. doi:10.1016/S0304-4076(98)00009-8

Brounen, D., de Jong, A., & Koedijk, K. C. G. (2004). *Corporate Finance in Europe Confronting Theory with Practice*. doi:10.2139srn.559415

Brown, J. R., & Petersen, B. C. (2009). Why has the investment-cash flow sensitivity declined so sharply? Rising R&D and equity market developments. *Journal of Banking & Finance*, *33*(5), 971–984. doi:10.1016/j.jbankfin.2008.10.009

Byoun, S. (2007). *Financial Flexibility, Leverage, and Firm Size*. Hankamer School of Business: Baylor University.

Byoun, S. (2011). *Financial Flexibility and Capital Structure Decision*. SSRN Electronic Journal; doi:10.2139srn.1108850

Cleary, S. (1999). The Relationship between Firm Investment and Financial Status. *The Journal of Finance*, *54*(2), 673–692. doi:10.1111/0022-1082.00121

De Jong, A., Verbeek, M., & Verwijmeren, P. (2012). Des Financial Flexibility Reduce Investment Distortions? *Journal of Financial Research*, *35*(2), 243–259. doi:10.1111/j.1475-6803.2012.01316.x

DeAngelo, H., & DeAngelo, L. (2007). *Capital Structure, Payout Policy, and Financial Flexibility*. SSRN Electronic Journal; doi:10.2139srn.916093

DeAngelo, H., DeAngelo, L., & Whited, T. M. (2011). Capital structure dynamics and transitory debt. *Journal of Financial Economics*, *99*(2), 235–261. doi:10.1016/j.jfineco.2010.09.005

Demir, F. (2009). Volatility of Short-term Capital Flows and Private Investment in Emerging Markets. *The Journal of Development Studies*, *45*(5), 672–692. doi:10.1080/00220380802582379

Denis, D. J. (2011). Financial flexibility and corporate liquidity. *Journal of Corporate Finance*, *17*(3), 667–674. doi:10.1016/j.jcorpfin.2011.03.006

Denis, D. J., & McKeon, S. B. (2012). Debt Financing and Financial Flexibility Evidence from Proactive Leverage Increases. *Review of Financial Studies*, *25*(6), 1897–1929. doi:10.1093/rfs/hhs005

Erdoğan, S. (2015). The effect of capital structure on profitability: an empirical analysis. In Handbook of Research on Developing Sustainable Value in Economics, Finance, and Marketing (pp. 307-323). Hershey, PA: IGI Global.

Fama, E. F., & French, K. R. (2005). Financing decisions: Who issues stock? *Journal of Financial Economics*, *76*(3), 549–582. doi:10.1016/j.jfineco.2004.10.003

Faulkender, M., Flannery, M. J., Hankins, K. W., & Smith, J. M. (2012). Cash flows and leverage adjustments. *Journal of Financial Economics*, *103*(3), 632–646. doi:10.1016/j.jfineco.2011.10.013

Ferrando, A., Marchica, M.-T., & Mura, R. (2017). Financial Flexibility and Investment Ability Across the Euro Area and the UK: Financial Flexibility and Investment Ability. *European Financial Management*, *23*(1), 87–126. doi:10.1111/eufm.12091

Flannery, M. J., & Rangan, K. P. (2006). Partial adjustment toward target capital structures. *Journal of Financial Economics*, *79*(3), 469–506. doi:10.1016/j.jfineco.2005.03.004

Frank, M. Z., & Goyal, V. K. (2008). *Profits and Capital Structure*. SSRN Electronic Journal; doi:10.2139srn.1104886

Gamba, A., & Triantis, A. (2008). The Value of Financial Flexibility. *The Journal of Finance*, *63*(5), 2263–2296. doi:10.1111/j.1540-6261.2008.01397.x

Graham, J. R., & Harvey, C. R. (2001). The theory and practice of corporate finance: Evidence from the field. *Journal of Financial Economics*, *60*(2–3), 187–243. doi:10.1016/S0304-405X(01)00044-7

Guo, K., & Stepanyan, V. (2011). Determinants of bank credit in emerging market economies. *International Monetary Fund.*

Killi, A., Rapp, M. S., & Schmid, T. (2011). *Can Financial Flexibility Explain the Debt Conservatism Puzzle? Cross-Country Evidence from Listed Firms*. doi:10.2139srn.1814182

Lemmon, M. L., Roberts, M. R., & Zender, J. F. (2008). Back to the Beginning: Persistence and the Cross-Section of Corporate Capital Structure. *The Journal of Finance*, *63*(4), 1575–1608. doi:10.1111/j.1540-6261.2008.01369.x

Marchica, M.-T., & Mura, R. (2010). Financial Flexibility, Investment Ability, and Firm Value: Evidence from Firms with Spare Debt Capacity. *Financial Management*, *39*(4), 1339–1365. doi:10.1111/j.1755-053X.2010.01115.x

Rajan, R. G., & Zingales, L. (1995). What Do We Know about Capital Structure? Some Evidence from International Data. *The Journal of Finance*, *50*(5), 1421–1460. doi:10.1111/j.1540-6261.1995.tb05184.x

Rapp, M. S., Schmid, T., & Urban, D. (2014). The value of financial flexibility and corporate financial policy. *Journal of Corporate Finance*, *29*, 288–302. doi:10.1016/j.jcorpfin.2014.08.004

Wanzenried, G. (2006). Capital Structure Dynamics in the UK and Continental Europe. *European Journal of Finance*, *12*(8), 693–716. doi:10.1080/13518470500460178

Yung, K., Li, D. D., & Jian, Y. (2015). The value of corporate financial flexibility in emerging countries. *Journal of Multinational Financial Management*, *32–33*, 25–41. doi:10.1016/j.mulfin.2015.07.001

Chapter 14
Evaluation of Young Consumers' Remanufactured Products Purchase Intention Within Context of Extended Planned Behavior Theory

Murat Burucuoglu
Ondokuz Mayis University, Turkey

Evrim Erdogan
https://orcid.org/0000-0001-8689-4137
Ondokuz Mayis University, Turkey

ABSTRACT

In this chapter, remanufactured products which have an important place in closed-loop supply chains are examined. The study evaluates the motivation of young consumers who are in close contact with technology within context of extended planned behavior theory. The theoretical model of the research was developed on the basis of the planned behavior theory and the developed model was tested by an empirical study on Ondokuz Mayis University students. As a result of the research, the environmental concerns of young consumers, the environmental knowledge of remanufactured products, and the awareness of remanufactured products positively and significantly affect the attitude towards remanufactured products. The study indicates that attitude and subjective norm related to remanufactured products are positively and significantly affect remanufactured products purchase intention and perceived behavioral control has no significant effect on intent to purchase remanufactured products.

DOI: 10.4018/978-1-5225-8109-3.ch014

INTRODUCTION

From the 1970's to the present, sensitivity to environmental issues has continued to increase both in marketing literature and in business literature. From the point of view of marketing, from manufacture to distribution and sales activities, there is the increasing number of consumers who care about changing climate, environmental issues and sustainability of the resources. In developed societies, concerns about environmental awareness and the sustainability of the world have led to the emergence of current marketing concepts such as sustainable marketing, green marketing, and increased ecological awareness. Even later in the developing societies, the amount of the consumers who has environmental sensitivities have reached a quantity that businesses cannot ignore. More conscious of the consumer than ever, businesses have been pushed to increase their green marketing activities to influence consumers as well as the various practices they make to comply with the obligatory regulations imposed by providing sustainability globally. Even though business practices such as green marketing and green logistics on the business front come to the forefront within the scope of sustainability, it has become more important to transform the macro-scale supply chain into a sustainable structure. One of the activities that will enable both production and consumption in the supply chains to become sustainable is the closed-loop supply chains (Khor & Hazen, 2017). In the closed-loop supply chains, the process of product (forward supply chain) starting from the producer and ending with the consumer (customer) is included in the processes that involve the reverse flow of the products used (Lieder & Rashid, 2016, p. 45). The closed-loop supply chain also includes activities such as repairing, remanufacturing, recycling and disposal, as opposed to forward supply chain operations (Yilmaz & Belbag, 2016, p. 2). Remanufacturing from these activities is as an ultimate form of recycling and an engine of the closed-loop supply chain (CLSC) process (Hazen, Boone, Wang & Khor, 2017, p. 716). The purchase of remanufactured products, which are the output of reproduction, is considered a pro-environmental consumer behavior (Vafadarnikjoo, Mishra, Govindan & Chalvatzis, 2018, p. 231). In this direction, closed-loop supply chain practices and remanufactured products which can be considered as the common field of green marketing have emerged as a remarkable research area. Remanufactured products are notable for their businesses, especially in various sectors operating on a global scale (tire, mobile phone, computer, etc.), and for certain characteristic consumers, both in terms of ensuring sustainability and in terms of providing profitability to enterprises with cost advantage. Although the concept of remanufactured products in developing countries such as Turkey is exactly unknown, it is observed that young consumers' information in the environmental issues has increased the purchasing trends towards environmentally friendly products (Oflac & Gocer, 2015) and that environmental-friendly consumption behavior appears to be moderate, though. This case increases the likelihood that the young people market in Turkey could create the potential, for remanufactured products. On the other hand, the ability of sellers to offer remanufactured products at lower quality and price (Guide & Wassenhove, 2001, p. 149) could be an option for consumers who have low purchasing power and price sensitivity to these products, especially in developing countries. Sustainable consumption requires structural changes for both producers and consumers. There is a need for producers to evolve to technologies that reduce resource use and to manage the perceptions of consumers (Tseng, Han, Geng & Govindan, 2016).

Although research on consumer behavior against remanufactured products is increasing day by day, the relatively late practice of green consumption, green logistics and reverse logistics activities in developing countries has led to the late start of the research in these countries. As a result, there is not much information on consumer attitudes towards remanufactured products in developed countries. Moreover, studies of the attitudes of young consumers towards such products as consumers of the future have been examined more in the context of eco-friendly behavior, sustainable marketing and green marketing. In this study, young consumers' behavior of purchasing remanufactured products within the framework of the Theory of Planned Behavior was examined and tried to fill the gap in the literature. It is seen that young consumers are much more active in environmental issues than other groups (Kanchanapibul, Lacka, Wang & Chan, 2014, p. 533). Vicente-Molina, Fernández-Sáinz and Izagirre-Olaizola (2013) showed that environmental knowledge of young people positively influenced pro-environmental intention and behavior. For this reason, young consumers create a good potential market for green products (Lee, 2008, p. 538).

The purpose of this study is to examine the intentions of young consumers to purchase remanufactured products on the basis of the Theory of Planned Behavior, which is often used to explain consumer behaviors. In the study, the model of planned behavior theory was expanded by adding environmental variables of environmental concern, remanufactured products' environmental knowledge, and awareness variables of remanufactured products, which are frequently included in studies that study environmentally friendly product and remanufactured product purchasing behavior. At the same time, remanufactured laptop computers were used as a product group in the research.

CONSUMER BEHAVIORS REGARDING REMANUFACTURING AND REMANUFACTURED PRODUCTS

Remanufacturing is a production strategy that is carried out using still well-functioning parts of used products. The aim of remanufacturing is to regain the remaining values of used products. Remanufactured products are obtained by collecting used products and replacing worn components with new ones (Thierry, Salomon, Nunen & Wassenhove, 1995). Remanufacturing is a concept that is included in the reverse logistics definition (Rogers & Tibben-Lembke, 1998, p. 3). Moreover, remanufacturing is one of the common areas of logistics as opposed to green logistics (Rogers & Tibben-Lembke, 2001, p. 131). Thierry, et al. (1995) in the context of reverse logistics in a supply chain, defines recovery in five categories. These are repair, refurbishing, remanufacturing, cannibalization, and recycling. However, remanufacturing is different from repair, refurbishment and recycling. The first three categories include product renewal and upgrade (Rogers & Tibben-Lembke, 1998, p. 3). The defects identified in the repair are corrected and the product is brought into working order (King & Burgess, 2005). Refurbishment is the process of bringing the used product to a desired quality. However, this quality standard is lower than the quality standards of new products (Thierry et al., 1995). On recycling, the functionality of the components and products and the identity disappear. The product may have new physical and chemical properties (Sarkis, 2003).

Atasu et al. (2010) describes the remanufacturing process as taking used products, bringing them back to a new state, and usually reselling them with the same warranty as a new product (p. 56). As one of the remanufacturing sustainable supply chain applications; it has the benefits of protecting natural resources, reducing raw material use by up to 85% and energy use by 55% compared to new units, protecting the environment by reducing CO_2 equivalent emissions of millions of tons of potential worldwide, and providing a reasonable price for the end user (Automotive Parts Remanufacturers Association, [APRA], 2018). In addition to its environmental benefits, remanufactured products have a low rate of 30% to 40% compared to new products (Hazen et al., 2017, p. 716). Moreover, the cost of producing a completely new product for a firm is about 40% to 60% of its total cost, while the cost of a remanufactured product is around 20% (Dowlatshahi, 2000, p. 144). In other words, the remanufactured products have many benefits for the environment, producers and consumers. The European Remanufacturing Network lists the benefits of remanufactured products for consumers as the ease of purchase at low price, ease of purchase, accessibility and flexibility of purchase; for environmental benefits as reducing raw materials, reducing energy consumption, reducing CO_2 emissions, reducing waste material sent to storage sites; for producers as creating local jobs, increasing profit margins, improving business skills, developing new production techniques, and establishing better relations with customers (European Remanufacturing Network [ERN], 2018).

Although a remanufactured product is similar to a low-quality product that is produced as a low-cost, it is quite different from an ordinary low-quality new product. First, a remanufactured product is actually the same as the new product in terms of functional quality. However, there may be a difference in quality perception for consumers. Consumers cannot act voluntarily in purchasing with the idea that these products are of lower quality. The second issue is due to supply constraints. The supply of remanufactured products naturally depends on new product sales. For this reason, the production and consumption of new products largely determine the amount of product used and the timing of production. The cannibalization of new product sales will reduce the need for re-production in the future. This is not valid for poor quality products. Furthermore, a new product can determine the production capacity or market availability of a low-quality product; but this is not possible for remanufactured products that are produced due to external conditions such as product durability, use intensity and return conditions (Atasu, Guide & Van Wassenhove, 2010, p. 58).

According to Atasu et al. (2008), there is a green consumer segment that prefers remanufactured products. Accordingly, remanufactured products have a green image as they reduce the amount of waste and allow for the reuse of old materials and thereby they create a green image for producers. Thus, there are green consumers who prefer these products. On the other hand, it cannot be said that the remanufactured goods markets have a homogeneous structure. Atasu et al. (2010) divides the remanufactured product market into two customer types: newness-conscious and functionality-oriented. Innovation and quality for newness-conscious customers are equivalent. Therefore, they do not find remanufactured goods as functional as new products, and they have a lower perception of value about these products. They do not prefer to buy these products unless they offer very low prices compared to new products. Functionality-oriented customers are more concerned with the functionality of the product and do not equal functionality with quality. They compare new products with remanufactured products in terms of functionality. If they do not see any difference in terms of functionality, they prefer the remanufactured product if offered at a lower price (p. 63).

According to Abbey et al. (2015), 20-40% of consumers do not consider purchasing a remanufactured product at any price level and 60-80% of them are indifferent to these products (p. 32). In support of this research, Guide and Li (2010) concluded that consumers' willing to pay remanufactured products was relatively low compared to new products. Michaud and Llerena (2006) and Hazen et al. (2012; 2017) define consumers' reluctance to purchase remanufactured products as a low quality perception resulting from uncertainty in the remanufacturing process. They found that cost, quality and green product information about the products positively affected the perceived value of the products, while reducing the perceived risk. The high-risk perceptions of the consumers against the remanufactured products and the low value perceptions cause them to become suspicious to these products. For this reason, in order to build trust between remanufacturers, their own products and consumers, firms need to set high quality standards for remanufactured goods and to provide them with documentation to guarantee these standards. In this way, the perception of value that is affected by consumers' perception of quality, cost and green products increases (Wang & Hazen, 2016).

On the other hand, Michaud and Llerena (2011) stated that consumers tend to valued more than traditional products when they inform consumers that remanufactured products are green products. Hazen et al. (2017) identifies the factors that determine the quality of remanufactured products that will encourage consumers to purchase lifespan, specifications, serviceability as performance. Gaur et al. (2015) states that factors that encourage consumers' intention to purchase remanufactured products are environmental consciousness, individual values, post-use perception, nature of purchase, and socio-cultural norms. Wang et al. (2013) determined that intent to purchase remanufactured products was directly influenced by the purchasing stance and perceived behavioral control, and indirectly from perceived risk, perceived benefit and product knowledge. Liao et al. (2015) states that manufacturers offer opportunities to give higher price proposals for their products' remedies for remanufactured products. Similarly, Jimenez-Parra et al. (2014) found that attitudes toward buying, subjective norms, price and social environment increase the consumers' willingness to buy remanufactured products while marketing-related factors such as technological environment and distribution, design and brand reputation decrease it.

RESEARCH MODEL

The Theory of Planned Behavior and Extended Model Variables

In this study, young consumers' purchasing behaviors of remanufactured laptops were examined based on Planned Behavior Theory. The Planned Behavior Theory (Ajzen, 1985, 1991) is based on the Theory of Reasoned Action developed by Fishbein and Ajzen (1975). According to the Planned Behavior Theory, there are three factors that guide human behavior. The first is the behavioral beliefs about the possible consequences of the behavior or other characteristics of the behavior. Second; normative beliefs about other people's beliefs about normative expectations and third; beliefs about the existence of factors that can improve or prevent the performance of the behavior. Behavioral beliefs produce positive or negative attitudes towards behavior, normative beliefs result in perceived social pressure or subjective norm, and control beliefs result in perceived behavioral control related to the difficulty or ease of performing behavior (Ajzen, 2002, p. 665). According to the Planned Behavior Theory, attitude toward behavior, subjective norm and perceived behavioral control constitute three independent determinants of intention to behavior (Ajzen, 1991).

Attitude towards behavior is identified as refers to "the degree to which a person has a favorable or unfavorable evaluation or appraisal of the behavior in question" (Ajzen, 1991, p. 188). In other words, the positive attitude towards the behavior increases the possibility of the behavior, reducing the negative attitude. Attitude is an important determinant of intention toward behavior or behavior (Kotchen & Reiling, 2000). It has been conducted that the attitude affects the intention towards behavior positively and significantly in the studies on purchasing behavior of eco-friendly products (Paul, Modi & Patel, 2016; Suki, 2016; Maichum, Parichatnon & Peng, 2016; Yadav & Pathak, 2017; Hsu, Chang & Yansritakul, 2017; Nguyen, Lobo & Nguyen, 2017; Jaiswal & Kant, 2018) and remanufactured products (Jiménez-Parra, Rubio & Vicente-Molina, 2014; Wang, Wiegerinck, Krikke & Zhang, 2013) in different countries and cultures. Based on the discussions in the literature, the following hypothesis has been formulated.

Figure 1. Proposed Research Model

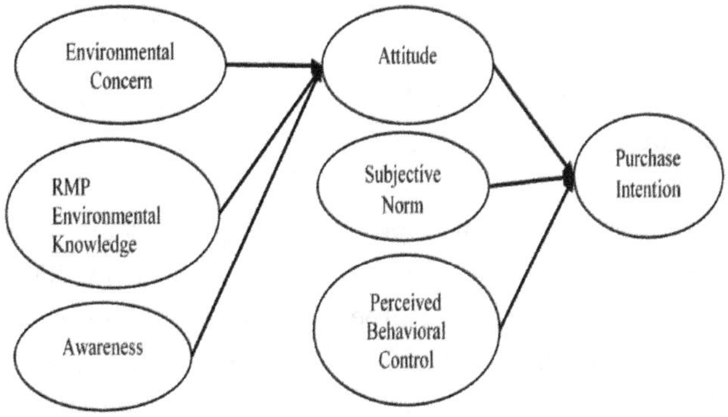

Hypothesis One: Consumers' attitude toward remanufactured products affects positively and significantly their intention to purchase remanufactured products.

Subjective norm refers to "the perceived social pressure to perform or not to perform the behavior" (Ajzen, 1991, p. 188). Subjective norm includes perceived behavioral expectations of various reference groups such as family, friends, peers, colleagues. The individual tends to meet the expectations of these references when he/she decides to perform the behavior or not (Han & Kim, 2010). Although some studies (Paul et al., 2016; Chaudhary & Bisai, 2018) in the literature did not find any relationship between subjective norm and the intention to purchase eco-friendly products, some studies (Maichum et al., 2016; Hsu et al., 2017; Yadav & Pathak, 2017; Setyawan, Noermijati, Sunaryo & Aisjah, 2018) showed that the subjective norm has a positive and significant impact on the intention to purchase eco-friendly products. According to studies that examine the relationship between the subjective norm variable and remanufactured products, the subjective norm positively and significantly affects the intention to purchase remanufactured products (Wang et al., 2013; Jimenez-Parra, 2014; Khor & Hazen, 2017). Based on research in the literature, the following hypothesis has been developed.

Hypothesis Two: The subjective norm influences consumers' intention to purchase remanufactured products positively and significantly.

Perceived Behavioral Control is defined as "the perceived ease or difficulty of performing the behavior" (Ajzen, 1991, p. 188). Perceived behavioral control has an important role in the Theory of Planned Behavior. Perceived behavioral control is a result of the perceived power of control beliefs. Control belief is related to the difficulty or ease of performing behavior. Perceived power includes the assessment of the effects of factors related to difficulty or ease of performing the behavior (Ajzen, 1991; Yadav & Pathak, 2017). The researches on environmentally friendly products showed that the perceived behavioral control has a positive and significant effect on the intention to purchase environmentally friendly products (Maichum et al., 2016; Paul et al., 2016; Hsu et al., 2017; Yadav & Pathak, 2017; Chaudhary & Bisai, 2018; Setyawan et al., 2018). There is a little research on the relationship between perceived behavioral control and the intention to buy remanufactured products. While Khor and Hazen (2017) was found no significant relation between the perceived behavioral control and the intention to purchase remanufactured products, Wang et al. (2013) found out that the perceived behavioral control has a positive and significant effect on the intention to purchase remanufactured products. Based on the discussions in the literature, the following hypothesis has been developed.

Hypothesis Three: Perceived behavioral control (PBC) positively and significantly affects the willingness of consumers to purchase remanufactured products.

Environmental concern is a concept used to express "the degree of belief, posture, and concern that an individual has against the environment" (Said, Ahmadun, Paim & Masud, 2003, p. 307). Environmental concern can be expressed more broadly as "consumers are aware of environmental problems and these problems can be expressed as assisting struggles to solve or signify the readiness to contribute personally to their solution" (Dunlap & Jones, 2002, p. 485). Environmental concern constitutes the basis of environmental research and its consumers are seen as one of the key determinants of the decision-making process (Yadav & Pathak, 2016). In the studies conducted on environmentally friendly products, it has been found that environmental concern has a positive and significant effect on the attitude toward environmentally friendly products (Aman, Harun & Hussein, 2012; Maichum et al., 2016; Chaudhary & Bisai, 2018). Based on the findings in the literature, it can be said that consumers with high environmental concerns have a more positive attitude towards environmentally friendly products. Therefore, the following hypothesis is submitted:

Hypothesis Four: Consumers' environmental concern positively and significantly affect their attitudes towards remanufactured products.

The concept of environmental knowledge on remanufactured products is a newly emerging concept in the literature and is used by consumers to describe the level of knowledge about the economic benefits of remanufactured products (Wang & Kuah, 2018). The environmental knowledge of remanufactured products refers to the fact that significant resource and energy savings as well as solid waste reductions are achievable through the recovery of used components and their subsequent remanufacturing (Wang & Hazen, 2016). Suki (2016) found that green brand knowledge of environmentally friendly products positively and significantly affects the attitude towards environmentally friendly products. In Wang and Hazen's (2016) study, it is concluded that the environmental knowledge of the remanufactured products positively and significantly affects the perceived value of the remanufactured products. Increasing the level of knowledge of consumers about the environmental, social and economic benefits of remanufactured products will lead to improved attitudes towards remanufactured products. The following hypothesis has been proposed from the researches.

Hypothesis Five: Environmental knowledge on consumers' remanufactured products positively and significantly affects attitudes towards remanufactured products.

Consumer awareness is one of the key concepts that guide consumers in purchasing environmentally friendly products in the product market (Suki, 2013). Wang and Kuah (2018) found that the possibility of purchasing remanufactured products increases as the level of awareness for remanufactured products increases. In Suki's (2013) study, it has been found that the price awareness of the eco-friendly products and the awareness of the brand image have a positive effect on the purchasing eco-friendly products, and that the awareness of eco-friendly products has no significant effect. It is also assumed that consumers will develop more positive attitudes towards remanufactured products if their awareness of remanufactured products increases. In the light of the discussions in the literature, the following hypothesis is proposed.

Hypothesis Six: Consumers' awareness of remanufactured products positively and significantly affects attitudes towards remanufactured products.

Methodology

The research population is composed of Ondokuz Mayis University students. Convenience sampling method was used as a sampling method. The data collected by using a survey from the students who volunteered to participate in the study. The data were collected by face-to-face interviews with participants in the university campus. 400 interviews were carried out. A number of 394 usable data were analyzed after the faulty survey form was removed. In Table 1, given the demographic characteristic of the participants.

A survey consisting of seven different scales has been used to gather empirical data in this study. The survey has been formed and adapted by using given studies and items in Table 2. The scales of the Environmental Concern, Environmental Knowledge of Remanufactured Products and Perceived Behavioral Control consist of four items. The scales of the Attitude, Subjective Norm and Intention to Purchase have three items and the scale of the Awareness has two items. All measurement items in the scales were assessed using five-point Likert scales, ranging from 1 (Strongly Disagree) to 5 (Strongly Agree).

Table 1. Sample demographics

(N:394)	n	%
Gender		
Female	238	60.4
Male	156	39.6
Class		
Freshmen	72	18.3
2nd Class	59	15.0
3rd Class	119	30.2
4th Class	144	36.5
Age		
17-20	74	18.8
21-23	258	65.5
24-27	48	12.2
28 and over	14	3.5
Income		
0-65 USD	85	21.6
66-162 USD	185	47.0
163-243 USD	55	13.9
244 USD and over	69	17.5

Table 2. Measures

Constructions and Measurement Items	Resources
Environmental Concern The balance of nature is very fragile and can easily be upside down. When people intervene in nature, this usually results in disaster. People have to live in harmony with nature to survive. People are abusing the environment seriously.	Yadav & Pathak (2016)
Environmental Knowledge of Remanufactured Products Remanufactured products are environmentally friendly products. Remanufactured products help to conserve resources. Remanufactured products reduce the amount of waste. Remanufactured products reduce the amount of pollution.	Wang & Kuah (2018)
Awareness I understand very well what a remanufactured product is. I know very well how a product is remanufactured.	Wang & Kuah (2018)
Attitude I like the idea of buying remanufactured products. I have a positive attitude to buy remanufactured products. Buying remanufactured products is a good idea.	Khor & Hazen (2017)
Subjective Norm People I care about their ideas (family, friends, and colleagues) support me to buy remanufactured products. People who value my opinion and who are important to me (friends, family, and colleagues) agree with me about buying a remanufactured laptop because its low priced. Most people (friends, family, colleagues) that I care about their ideas think that I should not buy remanufactured laptops because they think I will stay away from significant improvements (cutting edge technology, performance, etc.).	Jimenez-Parra et al. (2014), Khor & Hazen (2017)
Perceived Behavioral Control I know where to buy remanufactured products. I have the resources (such as time and money) to buy remanufactured products. It is entirely up to me to buy remanufactured products. The decision to buy remanufactured products is entirely under my control.	Khor & Hazen (2017)
Intention to Purchase I intend to buy remanufactured products as remanufactured products are beneficial to the environment. Since remanufactured products are environmental protection features, I hope to receive remanufactured products in the future. Overall, I am happy to buy remanufactured products because they are environmentally friendly.	Wang et al. (2018)

Partial least squares path analysis (PLS-SEM) was used in the analysis of data in the study (Ringle, Wende & Becker, 2015). Partial least squares path analysis is a variance based method used to predict the structural equation model. The purpose of partial least squares path analysis is to maximize the explanatory variance of endogenous latent variables (Hair, Hult, Ringle & Sarstedt, 2014a: p. 30). Partial least squares path analysis includes a two-step assessment. The measurement model is assessed in the first stage and the structural model in the second stage (Sarstedt, Ringle, Smith, Reams & Hair, 2014: p. 108). In this study, the results of the factor loadings, composite reliability, Crobach's alpha coefficient, average variance extracted and discriminant validity results were evaluated in the evaluation of the measurement model. In the evaluation of the model, the R^2 values, the effect and significance of the path analysis, and the SRMR goodness of fit results were evaluated. In the literature, it is expected that the threshold values of the criteria used in the evaluation of the measurement model must be above 0.50, if possible above 0.70, for factor loadings, C.Alfa and Composite Reliability (CR), the values must be above 0.70 and for Average Variance Extracted (AVE), the values must be above 0.50 (Hair, Black, Babin, Abderson & Tatham, 2006; Hair et al., 2014a; Hair, Sarstedt, Hopkins & Kuppelwieser, 2014b; Sarstedt et al., 2014). The Table 3 below shows the statistics of the measurement model.

As seen from Table 3, factor loadings are higher than 0.50; Crobach's Alpha and Composite Reliability (C.R.) values are higher than 0.70 and the average variance extracted values are higher than 0.50. According to measurement model modification two statements are removed due to fact that factor loading is lower than 0.50. Removed statements are *PBC1* and *SN3.*

The Fornell and Larcker criterion was used to evaluate discriminant validity. According to the Fornell and Larcker criteria, in order for the model to be valid for discriminant, the square root of the average variance extracted (AVE) must be higher than the correlation between all structures and each expression (Fornell and Larcker, 1981).

When the values in the table are examined, it is seen that the research model provides the discriminant validity. When the results of the measurement model are evaluated, it is seen that the research model is a valid and reliable model. As the measurement model criteria are provided, the second step of evaluation of the structural model is partial least squares path analysis. One of the commonly used measures in evaluating the structural model is R^2. The R^2 coefficient expresses the combined effects of exogenous

Table 3. Statistics on the Measurement Model

Variable	Items	Factor Load	C.Alpha	C.R.	AVE
Attitude	ATT1	0.915	0.899	0.937	0.832
	ATT2	0.920			
	ATT3	0.901			
Awareness	AW1	0.917	0.718	0.874	0.777
	AW2	0.845			
Environmental Concern	EC1	0.744	0.827	0.885	0.658
	EC2	0.782			
	EC3	0.858			
	EC4	0.855			
Intention	INT1	0.921	0.745	0.857	0.669
	INT2	0.921			
	INT3	0.899			
Perceived Behavioral Control	PBC2	0.695	0.901	0.938	0.835
	PBC3	0.874			
	PBC4	0.872			
Environmental Knowledge of Remanufactured Products	RP3	0.889	0.898	0.929	0.766
	RP4	0.846			
	RP1	0.861			
	RP2	0.904			
Subjective Norm	SN1	0.910	0.795	0.907	0.830
	SN2	0.911			

Table 4. Results of Discriminant Validity of the Research Model according to Fornell-Larcker Criteria

	1	2	3	4	5	6	7
Attitude (1)	**0.912***						
Awareness (2)	0.399	**0.881***					
Environmental Concern (3)	0.441	0.235	**0.811***				
Perceived Behavioral Control (4)	0.390	0.561	0.426	**0.818***			
Intention to Purchase (5)	0.785	0.437	0.435	0.407	**0.914***		
Environmental knowledge of Remanufactured Products (6)	0.575	0.359	0.533	0.451	0.536	**0.875***	
Subjective Norm (7)	0.504	0.541	0.357	0.474	0.558	0.456	**0.911***

* Bold elements placed on the diagonal line represent the square root of AVE

latent variables on endogenous latent variables. R^2 has a value of 0 to 1. It is expected that this value will be above 0.20 in consumer researches while it is expected to be over 0.25, 0.50 and 0.75 in marketing researches (Hair et al., 2014a; Hair, Ringle, & Sarstedt, 2011). In this study, R^2 value of attitude variable is 0.395 and R^2 value of intention variable is 0.654. In other words, environmental concern, awareness and environmental knowledge variables of remanufactured products explain approximately 40% of the attitude toward remanufactured products and attitude, subjective norm, and perceived behavioral control variables represent about 65% of the intention to purchase. SRMR value is 0.061, which is acceptable.

According to the results of the research model path analysis, the strongest relationship is between attitudes towards remanufactured products and intention to purchase for remanufactured products. The attitude towards remanufactured products positively and significantly affects the intention to purchase. The subjective norm variable affects the intention to purchase remanufactured products positively and significantly. It has been reached the result that perceived behavioral control, another variant of planned behavior theory, has no effect on the intention to purchase remanufactured products. The environmental knowledge of remanufactured products, awareness, and environmental concern variables of remanufactured products positively and significantly affect the attitude toward remanufactured products, respectively.

Table 5. Results of the Research Model Path Analysis

	Path Coefficient	t Statistics	p Value	Result
Environmental Concern -> Attitude	0.175	3.476	0.001	Supported
Environmental knowledge of Remanufactured Products -> Attitude	0.405	6.815	0.000	Supported
Awareness -> Attitude	0.212	4.450	0.000	Supported
Attitude -> Intention	0.665	17.212	0.000	Supported
Subjective Norm -> Intention	0.197	4.551	0.000	Supported
Perceived Behavioral Control -> Intention	0.054	1.381	0.168	Not Supported

FUTURE RESEARCH DIRECTIONS

The focus of the work carried out with closed loop supply chain and sustainable supply chain management practices are often seen as supply-oriented. Although the studies on the demand part of this topic have recently increased, it is still a limited number. For this reason, in the future, researchers' focus on the consumer-oriented research of the recovery activities within the closed loop supply chain will enable the development of the literature and application. The increase in studies examining consumer behavior will improve the identification of purchasing motivations and barriers for remanufactured products and will facilitate communication strategies and identification of remanufactured product markets. Although theories and practices related to remanufacturing are more preliminary in developed countries, they have also great potential for both consumers and producers for developing countries. The realization of studies on remanufacturing practices, especially in developing countries, will facilitate the spread and development of theory and practice.

CONCLUSION

Many strategies and practices are being developed in the economic, environmental and social dimensions of sustainability to ensure sustainable development. Supply chain management practices contribute to sustainable development by creating closed-loop supply chains. As one of the closed chain supply chain management recovery activities and the output of remanufacturing, remanufactured products have a key role in ensuring the sustainability of the supply chain. In this study, remanufacturing and remanufactured products, consumers who are one of the founders of the supply chain in both forward and reverse flow, have been examined in this study from the perspective of young consumers. In order for the closed-loop supply chain to be successful, every recovery activity must meet consumer expectations. Products and services that are not purchased by the consumer will mean that investments made for narrowly business and for the supply chain in a broader scope, labor and time are wasted. For this reason, businesses that are particularly interested in closed-chain supply chain practices need to understand consumer behavior and to know what motivations and barriers to purchasing products and services are that are the outcomes of recovery.

In this study, remanufactured products were examined from a young consumer perspective and purchasing behaviors were tried to be explained with a model. The model of planned behavior theory was expanded by including environmental concern, environmental knowledge of remanufactured products, and awareness as an antecedent of attitude variables. Variables in the research model explain approximately 40% of the attitude towards remanufactured products and about 65% of the intention to purchase. For consumer behavior studies these ratios seem to be at acceptable levels.

In the study, it has been found that environmental concern affects the attitude variable positively and significantly. As young consumers increase their sensitivity to environmental issues, they appear to have developed a positive attitude towards remanufactured products. It can be said that consumers who are conscious of nature's sensitivity to this sensitive balance and the influence of human beings can have a favorable attitude on remanufactured products. In the researches in the literature, it is stated that environmental concern is an important determinant of purchasing behavior towards environmentally friendly products (Kim & Choi, 2005; Paul et al., 2016; Yadav & Pathak, 2016).

The influence of the environmental knowledge of remanufactured products has been tested as another antecedent of the study. Environmental knowledge of remanufactured products positively and significantly affects attitude. Young consumers can develop a more positive attitude when they have knowledge of the environmentally friendly of remanufactured products. As Wang and Hazen (2016) stated in the study, environmental knowledge of remanufactured products positively influences the perceived value of remanufactured products.

It was concluded that the other variable that affected the attitude was awareness. It is seen that young consumers have developed a more positive attitude as the level of awareness for remanufactured products increases. Wang and Kuah (2018) found that the probability of purchasing increases as the level of awareness for remanufactured products increases.

While the attitude and subjective norm which two variables of planned behavior theory positively and significantly affect the intention to purchase for the remanufactured products, no significant effect on the intention to purchase of perceived behavioral control has been found. It is seen that attitude has a strong influence on the intention to purchase remanufactured products. The positive perceptions and feelings that young consumers have developed for remanufactured products strongly increase their intention to purchase. It has been reached the result in the Jimenez-Parra et al. (2014) and Wang et al. (2013) studies on remanufactured products that attitude similarly affects positively and significantly intention to purchase. The subjective norm variable that represents various reference groups like family, friends, and colleagues positively and significantly influence the intention to purchase. It can be said that thinking in the same way of various reference groups with individuals strengthen the intention to purchase. It has been found that the subjective norm variable influences the intention to purchase positively and significantly in studies conducted in the literature (Jimenez-Parra et al., 2014; Wang et al., 2013; Khor & Hazen, 2017). Perceived behavioral control was seen to have no significant effect on the intention to purchase. Perceived behavioral control represents beliefs that the individual has adequate resources to perform the behavior and that the control is in itself. Depending on the factors beyond the control of the individual like that remanufactured products are not widely available at the point of purchase, the need for special effort and labor to purchase may result in the emergence of such a result. Similarly, in the literature, it has been found that behavioral control perceived in the study of Khor and Hazen (2017) does not have a significant effect on the intention to overtake.

Based on the findings of this research; it can be said that remanufactured product producers primarily need to improve marketing activities in order to develop a positive attitude towards remanufactured products. So they could draw attention of the young consumers to remanufactured products. In developing a positive attitude, it can be useful to run various activities, events and advertising campaigns which contain briefing remanufactured products' solutions to environmental problems.

REFERENCES

Abbey, J. D., Meloy, M. G., Guide, V. D. R. Jr, & Atalay, S. (2015). Remanufactured products in closed-loop supply chains for consumer goods. *Production and Operations Management*, *24*(3), 488–503. doi:10.1111/poms.12238

Ajzen, I. (1985). From intentions to actions: A theory of planned behavior. In *Action control* (pp. 11–39). Springer. doi:10.1007/978-3-642-69746-3_2

Ajzen, I. (1991). The theory of planned behavior. *Organizational Behavior and Human Decision Processes, 50*(2), 179–211. doi:10.1016/0749-5978(91)90020-T

Ajzen, I. (2002). Perceived behavioral control, self-efficacy, locus of control, and the theory of planned behavior. *Journal of Applied Social Psychology, 32*(4), 665–683. doi:10.1111/j.1559-1816.2002.tb00236.x

Aman, A. L., Harun, A., & Hussein, Z. (2012). The influence of environmental knowledge and concern on green purchase intention the role of attitude as a mediating variable. *British Journal of Arts and Social Sciences, 7*(2), 145–167.

Atasu, A., Guide, V. D. R. Jr, & Van Wassenhove, L. N. (2010). So what if remanufacturing cannibalizes my new product sales? *California Management Review, 52*(2), 56–76. doi:10.1525/cmr.2010.52.2.56

Atasu, A., Sarvary, M., & Van Wassenhove, L. N. (2008). Remanufacturing as a marketing strategy. *Management Science, 54*(10), 1731–1746. doi:10.1287/mnsc.1080.0893

Automotive Parts Remanufacturers Association. (n.d.). Europe. Retrieved from https://apra.org/page/Europe

Chaudhary, R., & Bisai, S. (2018). Factors influencing green purchase behavior of millennials in India. *Management of Environmental Quality, 29*(5), 798–812. doi:10.1108/MEQ-02-2018-0023

Dowlatshahi, S. (2000). Developing a theory of reverse logistics. *Interfaces, 30*(3), 143–155. doi:10.1287/inte.30.3.143.11670

Dunlap, R., & Jones, R. (2002). Environmental concern: Conceptual and measurement issues. In R. Dunlap & W. Michelson (Eds.), *Handbook of Environmental Sociology*. London: Greenwood.

Fishbein, M., & Ajzen, I. (1975). *Belief, attitude, intention and behavior: an introduction to theory and research*. Reading, MA: Addison-Wesley.

Fornell, C., & Larcker, D. F. (1981). Evaluating structural equation models with unobservable variables and measurement error. *JMR, Journal of Marketing Research, 18*(1), 39–50. doi:10.2307/3151312

Gaur, J., Amini, M., Banerjee, P., & Gupta, R. (2015). Drivers of consumer purchase intentions for remanufactured products: A study of Indian consumers relocated to the USA. *Qualitative Market Research, 18*(1), 30–47. doi:10.1108/QMR-01-2014-0001

Guide, V. D. R. Jr, & Li, J. (2010). The potential for cannibalization of new products sales by remanufactured products. *Decision Sciences, 41*(3), 547–572. doi:10.1111/j.1540-5915.2010.00280.x

Guide, V. D. R. Jr, & Van Wassenhove, L. N. (2001). Managing product returns for remanufacturing. *Production and Operations Management, 10*(2), 142–155. doi:10.1111/j.1937-5956.2001.tb00075.x

Hair, J.F., Jr., Sarstedt, M., Hopkins, L., & Kuppelwieser, V.G. (2014b). Partial least squares structural equation modeling (PLS-SEM) An emerging tool in business research. *European Business Review, 26*(2), 106–121. doi:10.1108/EBR-10-2013-0128

Hair, F. J., Ringle, C. M., & Sarstedt, M. (2011). PLS-SEM: Indeed a silver bullet. *Journal of Marketing Theory and Practice, 19*(2), 139–152. doi:10.2753/MTP1069-6679190202

Hair, J. F., Black, W. C., Babin, B. J., Anderson, R. E., & Tatham, R. L. (2006). *Multivariate data analysis* (Vol. 6).

Hair, J. F. Jr, Hult, G. T. M., Ringle, C., & Sarstedt, M. (2014a). *A primer on partial least squares structural equation modeling (PLS-SEM)*. Sage Publications.

Han, H., & Kim, Y. (2010). An investigation of green hotel customers' decision formation: Developing an extended model of the theory of planned behavior. *International Journal of Hospitality Management*, *29*(4), 659–668. doi:10.1016/j.ijhm.2010.01.001

Hazen, B. T., Boone, C. A., Wang, Y., & Khor, K. S. (2017). Perceived quality of remanufactured products: Construct and measure development. *Journal of Cleaner Production*, *142*, 716–726. doi:10.1016/j.jclepro.2016.05.099

Hazen, B. T., Boone, C. A., Wang, Y., & Khor, K. S. (2017). Perceived quality of remanufactured products: Construct and measure development. *Journal of Cleaner Production*, *142*, 716–726. doi:10.1016/j.jclepro.2016.05.099

Hazen, B. T., Overstreet, R. E., Jones-Farmer, L. A., & Field, H. S. (2012). The role of ambiguity tolerance in consumer perception of remanufactured products. *International Journal of Production Economics*, *135*(2), 781–790. doi:10.1016/j.ijpe.2011.10.011

Hsu, C. L., Chang, C. Y., & Yansritakul, C. (2017). Exploring purchase intention of green skincare products using the theory of planned behavior: Testing the moderating effects of country of origin and price sensitivity. *Journal of Retailing and Consumer Services*, *34*, 145–152. doi:10.1016/j.jretconser.2016.10.006

Jaiswal, D., & Kant, R. (2018). Green purchasing behaviour: A conceptual framework and empirical investigation of Indian consumers. *Journal of Retailing and Consumer Services*, *41*, 60–69. doi:10.1016/j.jretconser.2017.11.008

Jiménez-Parra, B., Rubio, S., & Vicente-Molina, M. A. (2014). Key drivers in the behavior of potential consumers of remanufactured products: A study on laptops in Spain. *Journal of Cleaner Production*, *85*, 488–496. doi:10.1016/j.jclepro.2014.05.047

Kanchanapibul, M., Lacka, E., Wang, X., & Chan, H. K. (2014). An empirical investigation of green purchase behaviour among the young generation. *Journal of Cleaner Production*, *66*, 528–536. doi:10.1016/j.jclepro.2013.10.062

Khor, K. S., & Hazen, B. T. (2017). Remanufactured products purchase intentions and behaviour: Evidence from Malaysia. *International Journal of Production Research*, *55*(8), 2149–2162. doi:10.1080/00207543.2016.1194534

Kim, Y., & Choi, S. M. (2005). Antecedents of green purchase behavior: an examination of collectivism, environmental concern, and pce. In G. Menon & A. R. Rao (Eds.), *NA - Advances in Consumer Research* (Vol. 32, pp. 592–599). Duluth, MN: Association for Consumer Research.

King, A. M., & Burgess, S. C. (2005). The development of a remanufacturing platform design: A strategic response to the Directive on Waste Electrical and Electronic Equipment. *Proceedings of the Institution of Mechanical Engineers. Part B, Journal of Engineering Manufacture*, *219*(8), 623–631. doi:10.1243/095440505X32526

Kotchen, M. J., & Reiling, S. D. (2000). Environmental attitudes, motivations, and contingent valuation of nonuse values: A case study involving endangered species. *Ecological Economics*, *32*(1), 93–107. doi:10.1016/S0921-8009(99)00069-5

Lee, K. (2008). Opportunities for green marketing: Young consumers. *Marketing Intelligence & Planning*, *26*(6), 573–586. doi:10.1108/02634500810902839

Liao, B. F., Li, B. Y., & Cheng, J. S. (2015). A warranty model for remanufactured products. *Journal of Industrial and Production Engineering*, *32*(8), 551–558. doi:10.1080/21681015.2015.1090490

Lieder, M., & Rashid, A. (2016). Towards circular economy implementation: A comprehensive review in context of manufacturing industry. *Journal of Cleaner Production*, *115*, 36–51. doi:10.1016/j.jclepro.2015.12.042

Maichum, K., Parichatnon, S., & Peng, K. C. (2016). Application of the extended theory of planned behavior model to investigate purchase intention of green products among Thai consumers. *Sustainability*, *8*(10), 1077.

Maichum, K., Parichatnon, S., & Peng, K. C. (2017). Factors affecting on purchase intention towards green products: A case study of young consumers in Thailand. *International Journal of Social Science and Humanity*, *7*(5), 330–335.

Mat Said, A., Ahmadun, F. L. R., Hj. Paim, L., & Masud, J. (2003). Environmental concerns, knowledge and practices gap among Malaysian teachers. *International Journal of Sustainability in Higher Education*, *4*(4), 305–313. doi:10.1108/14676370310497534

Michaud, C., & Llerena, D. (2006). An economic perspective on remanufactured products: Industrial and consumption challenges for life cycle engineering. In *Proceedings of LCE2006* (pp. 543–548).

Michaud, C., & Llerena, D. (2011). Green consumer behaviour: An experimental analysis of willingness to pay for remanufactured products. *Business Strategy and the Environment*, *20*(6), 408–420.

Mohd Suki, N. (2016). Green product purchase intention: Impact of green brands, attitude, and knowledge. *British Food Journal*, *118*(12), 2893–2910. doi:10.1108/BFJ-06-2016-0295

Mostafa, M. M. (2009). Shades of green: A psychographic segmentation of the green consumer in Kuwait using self-organizing maps. *Expert Systems with Applications*, *36*(8), 11030–11038. doi:10.1016/j.eswa.2009.02.088

Nguyen, T. N., Lobo, A., & Nguyen, B. K. (2017). Young consumers' green purchase behaviour in an emerging market. *Journal of Strategic Marketing*, 1–18.

Oflac, B. S., & Gocer, A. (2015). A study on young consumers' perceived environmental knowledge levels and approach towards eco-labelled products. *Gazi University Journal of Faculty of Economics and Administrative Sciences*, *17*(2), 216–228.

Paul, J., Modi, A., & Patel, J. (2016). Predicting green product consumption using theory of planned behavior and reasoned action. *Journal of Retailing and Consumer Services, 29*, 123–134. doi:10.1016/j.jretconser.2015.11.006

Ringle, C. M., Wende, S., and Becker, J.-M. (2015). SmartPLS 3.

Rogers, D. S., & Tibben-Lembke, R. (2001). An examination of reverse logistics practices. *Journal of Business Logistics, 22*(2), 129–148. doi:10.1002/j.2158-1592.2001.tb00007.x

Rogers, D. S., & Tibben-Lembke, R. S. (1998). *Going backwards: reverse logistics trends and practices.* Pittsburgh, PA: Reverse Logistics Executive Council.

Sarkis, J. (2003). A strategic decision framework for green supply chain management. *Journal of Cleaner Production, 11*(4), 397–409. doi:10.1016/S0959-6526(02)00062-8

Sarstedt, M., Ringle, C. M., Smith, D., Reams, R., & Hair, J. F. Jr. (2014). Partial least squares structural equation modeling (PLS-SEM): A useful tool for family business researchers. *Journal of Family Business Strategy, 5*(1), 105–115. doi:10.1016/j.jfbs.2014.01.002

Setyawan, A., Noermijati, N., Sunaryo, S., & Aisjah, S. (2018). Green product buying intentions among young consumers: Extending the application of theory of planned behavior. *Problems and Perspectives in Management, 16*(2), 145–154. doi:10.21511/ppm.16(2).2018.13

Suki, N. M. (2013). Green awareness effects on consumers' purchasing decision: Some insights from Malaysia. *International Journal of Asia-Pacific Studies, 9*(2), 49–63.

The European Remanufacturing Network. http://www.remanufacturing.eu/about-remanufacturing.php

Thierry, M., Salomon, M., Van Nunen, J., & Van Wassenhove, L. (1995). Strategic issues in product recovery management. *California Management Review, 37*(2), 114–136. doi:10.2307/41165792

Tseng, M. L., Tan, K. H., Geng, Y., & Govindan, K. (2016). Sustainable consumption and production in emerging markets. *International Journal of Production Economics, 181*(2), 257–261. doi:10.1016/j.ijpe.2016.09.016

Vafadarnikjoo, A., Mishra, N., Govindan, K., & Chalvatzis, K. (2018). Assessment of Consumers' Motivations to Purchase a Remanufactured Product by Applying Fuzzy Delphi Method and Single Valued Neutrosophic Sets. *Journal of Cleaner Production, 196*, 230–244. doi:10.1016/j.jclepro.2018.06.037

Vicente-Molina, M. A., Fernández-Sáinz, A., & Izagirre-Olaizola, J. (2013). Environmental knowledge and other variables affecting pro-environmental behaviour: Comparison of university students from emerging and advanced countries. *Journal of Cleaner Production, 61*, 130–138. doi:10.1016/j.jclepro.2013.05.015

Wang, P., & Kuah, A. T. (2018). Green Marketing Cradle-to-Cradle: Remanufactured Products in Asian Markets. *Thunderbird International Business Review, 60*(5), 783–795. doi:10.1002/tie.21925

Wang, Y., & Hazen, B. T. (2016). Consumer product knowledge and intention to purchase remanufactured products. *International Journal of Production Economics, 181*, 460–469. doi:10.1016/j.ijpe.2015.08.031

Wang, Y., Hazen, B. T., & Mollenkopf, D. A. (2018). Consumer value considerations and adoption of remanufactured products in closed-loop supply chains. *Industrial Management & Data Systems*, *118*(2), 480–498. doi:10.1108/IMDS-10-2016-0437

Wang, Y., Huscroft, J. R., Hazen, B. T., & Zhang, M. (2018). Green information, green certification and consumer perceptions of remanufctured automobile parts. *Resources, Conservation and Recycling*, *128*, 187–196. doi:10.1016/j.resconrec.2016.07.015

Wang, Y., Wiegerinck, V., Krikke, H., & Zhang, H. (2013). Understanding the purchase intention towards remanufactured product in closed-loop supply chains: An empirical study in China. *International Journal of Physical Distribution & Logistics Management*, *43*(10), 866–888. doi:10.1108/IJPDLM-01-2013-0011

Yadav, R., & Pathak, G. S. (2016). Young consumers' intention towards buying green products in a developing nation: Extending the theory of planned behavior. *Journal of Cleaner Production*, *135*, 732–739. doi:10.1016/j.jclepro.2016.06.120

Yadav, R., & Pathak, G. S. (2017). Determinants of consumers' green purchase behavior in a developing nation: Applying and extending the theory of planned behavior. *Ecological Economics*, *134*, 114–122. doi:10.1016/j.ecolecon.2016.12.019

Yilmaz, K. G., & Belbag, S. (2016). Prediction of consumer behavior regarding purchasing remanufactured products: a logistics regression model. *International Journal of Business and Social Research*, 6(2), 01-10.

ADDITIONAL READING

Abbey, J. D., & Guide, V. D. R. Jr. (2018). A typology of remanufacturing in closed-loop supply chains. *International Journal of Production Research*, *56*(1-2), 374–384. doi:10.1080/00207543.2017.1384078

Abbey, J. D., Kleber, R., Souza, G. C., & Voigt, G. (2017). The role of perceived quality risk in pricing remanufactured products. *Production and Operations Management*, *26*(1), 100–115. doi:10.1111/poms.12628

Akkucuk, U. (2016). SCOR model and the green supply chain. In Handbook of research on waste management techniques for sustainability (pp. 108–124). Hershey, PA: IGI Global. doi:10.4018/978-1-4666-9723-2.ch006

Carter, C. R., & Rogers, D. S. (2008). A framework of sustainable supply chain management: Moving toward new theory. *International Journal of Physical Distribution & Logistics Management*, *38*(5), 360–387. doi:10.1108/09600030810882816

Gencer, Y. G., & Akkucuk, U. (2016). Reverse logistics: Automobile recalls and other conditions. In Handbook of research on waste management techniques for sustainability (pp. 125–154). Hershey, PA: IGI Global. doi:10.4018/978-1-4666-9723-2.ch007

Govindan, K., & Soleimani, H. (2017). A review of reverse logistics and closed-loop supply chains: A Journal of Cleaner Production focus. *Journal of Cleaner Production*, *142*, 371–384. doi:10.1016/j.jclepro.2016.03.126

Shaharudin, M. R., Govindan, K., Zailani, S., Tan, K. C., & Iranmanesh, M. (2017). Product return management: Linking product returns, closed-loop supply chain activities and the effectiveness of the reverse supply chains. *Journal of Cleaner Production*, *149*, 1144–1156. doi:10.1016/j.jclepro.2017.02.133

Yildizbaşi, A., Çalik, A., Paksoy, T., Farahani, R. Z., & Weber, G. W. (2018). Multi-level optimization of an automotive closed-loop supply chain network with interactive fuzzy programming approaches. *Technological and Economic Development of Economy*, *24*(3), 1004–1028. doi:10.3846/20294913.2016.1253044

KEY TERMS AND DEFINITIONS

Environmentally Friendly Product: Product that does not harm environment during production, consumption and disposing and has eco-label.

Forward Supply Chain: Flow of products, services and information from the supplier to the customer in the supply chain.

Green Marketing: As defined by the American Marketing Associations (AMA): "(environments definition) The efforts by organizations to produce, promote, package, and reclaim products in a manner that is sensitive or responsive to ecological concerns."

Recycling: Activities for recovering materials such as glass, wood, metal, plastic by various processing.

Remanufacturing: A production strategy that aims to produce new product from used products which considers reusing, refurbishing, replacing components manufacturing processes and production of new products in terms of technical specifications, warranty and performance.

Responsible Consumer: Consumers who do not harm the environment with natural resources and product consumption behaviors.

Reverse Logistics: The whole of the activities related to managing the product flow in the opposite direction from points such as customers, retailers, waste collection centers in the supply chain.

Chapter 15
Effects of Sustainable Medical Waste Management on the Environment and Human Health

İlknur Sayan
Istanbul Kent Üniversitesi, Turkey

ABSTRACT

The increase in the number of health institutions, developments in technology, and the use of devices and materials utilized in diagnosis and treatments have increased the types and amount of medical waste. Therefore, it has become a necessity to reduce the health problems, remove the risks that may arise for human health, and protect the environment by effectively managing the medical wastes that are the results of the activities of health institutions. Hazardous medical wastes that harm humans and environmental health are a risk factor for the whole society. For this reason, removal, collection, temporary storage, recycling, transportation, and disposal of medical wastes without harming people and the environment includes technical, administrative, and legal processes. This study summarizes the current literature for sustainable waste management, its relationship to environmental and human health, and international legislation on waste management.

INTRODUCTION

Medical waste management has become one of the complex and challenging processes humanity faces due to the rapid growth in global population and increased demand for health care. Waste coming from health institutions is called hospital waste and it causes environmental pollution. Such waste may create significant health risks for hospital workers, patients, and the community (Ozder, Teker, Eker, Altındis, Kocaakman, & Karabay, 2013, p. 1). For this reason, in terms of human and environmental health, it is very important that waste resources are used efficiently, and that medical waste is disposed of without harming human and environmental health. Medical waste is a particular type of waste that can create risks in this sense (Gao, Shi, Mo, Nie, Yang, Rozelle, & Sylvia, 2018, p. 2). Ineffective management of waste adversely affects the environment and human health (Abdulla, Qdais, & Rabi, 2008, p. 450).

DOI: 10.4018/978-1-5225-8109-3.ch015

Sustainable waste management is an important issue in terms of environmental and economic development, and protection of human and environmental health. (Cansaran, 2010, p. 1). Therefore, the aim in waste management is to provide an ecological and economic balance in a sustainable environment and to enforce policy and laws that will provide benefits to the individual and the society (Aydemir, 2017, p. 295; Akkucuk, 2017).

Medical waste may consist of infectious, radioactive, toxic, or genotoxic substances as a result of activities carried out by hospitals, clinics, laboratories, and veterinary clinics (Insa, Zamorano, & López, 2010, p. 1049). Such waste constitutes environmental and occupational health risks (Ali, Wang, Chaudhry, & Geng, 2017, p. 1). In addition, it is generated at health centers, dental clinics, acupuncture centers, patient care at home, and other institutions where medical care and treatment is provided (Insa et al., 2010, p. 1049).

Waste generated during health services carry more environmental and human health risks than other wastes. This situation requires the safe management of medical waste and the completion of related processes with reliable methods (Aydemir, 2017, p. 296). If such waste is not managed and destroyed using proper methods, it poses serious threats to human health and the environment. For this reason, it is necessary to separate the waste in the place where it is produced and to manage it in accordance with legal regulations (Ozder et al., 2013, p. 1).

The objective of this article is to evaluate the relationship between sustainable medical waste management and the environmental and human health and to monitor international legislation in the light of literature.

SUSTAINABLE MEDICAL WASTE MANAGEMENT

Definition of Medical Waste

The term 'medical waste' is defined as "the flow of waste collected from health institutions, research facilities, laboratories and from emergency aid donations, according to the World Health Organization (WHO) (Örgev & Utku, 2017; Gencer & Akkucuk, 2016). It also refers to residues resulting from health services and medical procedures performed in hospitals, clinics, laboratories, veterinary clinics, and research centers (Windfeld & Brooks, 2015, p. 99). Hospital waste is a specific type of waste that carries a high potential of infection and injury (Amin, Gul, & Mehrab, 2013, p. 2). The recent definition of medical waste by World Health Organization also includes the waste that is generated as a result of healthcare services given at home (Windfeld & Brooks, 2015, p. 99).

In addition, wastes from small or scattered sources such as wastes generated during home medical care (dialysis, insulin injections) are included in the scope of medical wastes (Örgev & Utku, 2017). The definition of medical waste varies from country to country. While medical waste is defined as "waste generated by research related to human and/or animal health" in Chapter 18 of the European Waste Catalog of European Union, it is defined as "waste generated by the diagnosis, treatment, or immunization of human beings or animals, and by the related research or production and testing of biological products" in the USA at the Medical Waste Tracking Act of 1988 (Windfeld & Brooks, 2015, p. 99).

Medical waste is all kinds of waste that cause infection when they come into contact with humans, generated by medical, nursing, patient care, dental, veterinary, pharmaceutical or similar applications and treatment, care, education, and research or blood collection (Güvez, Dege, & Eren, 2012, p. 42).

Hospital waste, regulated medical waste, and infectious medical waste are concepts that are universally accepted and that can be used in place of medical waste (Windfeld & Brooks, 2015, p. 99).

Medical Waste Generation

There are many studies on the amount of medical waste generated in health institutions (Windfeld & Brooks, 2015, p. 99). According to the data of World Health Organization, quantities of generated medical waste vary depending on the level of development of countries, level of income, and number and capacity of health institutions (Cesaro & Belgiorno, 2017, p. 1820). The amount of medical waste depends on many factors such as waste management techniques, the type of health facility, and the number of patients accepted in the health facility (Cesaro & Belgiorno, 2017, p. 1820). In developed countries, the average amount of waste per bed is 1.1 to 1.2 kg. Approximately 0.4 to 0.5 kg of this is hazardous waste. On an annual basis, 465,000 tons of medical waste in the USA, 150,000 tons in Italy, 200,000 tons in the UK, and 21,000 tons in Australia is generated (Akbolat, Işık, Dede, & Çimen, 2011, p. 133). It is generated in health-related research institutions, hospitals, health education and training institutions, clinics, laboratories, blood banks, and veterinary institutes. Waste from the health services provided at home can also be evaluated in this context (Aydemir, 2017, p. 299). Waste generation data, generation rates in different medical areas, and calculation of income from planning, budgeting, and recycling can be used to generate optimization of waste management systems and general data in the assessments of environmental impact (Chartier, Emmanuel, Pieper, Prüss, Rushbrook, Stringer, Townend, Wilburn, & Zghondi, 2014). Table 1 shows the approximate percentage of waste type per total waste in health care institutions (Meyer, 2007, p. 508; Örgev & Utku, 2017).

The most common measure that is used to measure the amount of medical waste produced in health-care facilities is dividing the total waste kilogram the hospital produces daily by the number of occupied beds (Windfeld & Brooks, 2015, p. 101). Gathering data for a month or more gives clearer results about waste. For waste minimization, an inventory of recyclable materials and their quantities is required. In addition to calculating average ratios, the data range or standard deviation information is also important for dissemination of data (Chartier et al., 2014).

The rate of medical waste production varies from country to country in accordance with the level of economic development, while also depending on the size and type of the institution. Table 2 shows the average medical waste generation rate in hospitals in different countries and cities (Hossain, Santhanam, Norulaini, & Omar, 2011, p. 757).

Table 1. Approximate percentage of waste type per total waste in health care institutions (Örgev & Utku, 2017)

Waste Type	Percentage (%)
Non-infectious waste	80
Pathological waste and infectious waste	15
Chemical or pharmaceutical waste	3
Sharps waste	1
Pressurized cylinders, broken thermometers, etc.	< 1

Table 2. Resource: Alagöz and Kocasoy (2008)

Country/City	Waste generation rate	Non-clinical waste, %	Clinical waste, %	Generation period	Number of sample	Region	References
Algeria	0.7-1.22 kg/ bed/day	75-90	10-25	16 September to 10 October, 2006	10	Africa	Bendjoudi et al. (2009)
Libya	1.3 kg/patient/ day	72	26	N/A	14	Africa	Sawalem et al. (2009)
South Africa	0.60 kg/ patient/day	60.74	39.26	April and July, 2003	2	Africa	Nemathaga et al. (2008)
Taiwan	2.41-3.26 kg/ bed/day	N/A	N/A	N/A	150	Asia	Cheng et al. (2009)
Brazil	2.63 kg/bed/ day	80-85	15-20	September 2001 to March 2002	N/A	South America	Da Silva et al. (2005)
Jordan	6.10 kg/ patient/day	N/A	N/A	March to September, 2004	14	Asia	Bdour et al. (2007)
Ulaanbaatar, Mongolia	1.4-3.0 kg/ patient/day	70.67	29.43	January and February 2005	56	Asia	Shinee et al. (2008)
Dhaka, Bangladesh	1.71 kg/bed/ day	79	21	Over 5 months in 2006	69	Asia	Patwary et al. (2009a, 2009b)
Croatia	2.4 kg per capita	86	14	N/A	151	Europe	Marincovic et al. (2008)
El-Beheira Governorate, Egypt	2.07 kg/bed/ day	60.10	38.9	6 months period in 2008	8	Africa	Abd El-Salam (2010)
Sylhet city Bangladesh	0.934 kg/bed/ day	63.97	36.03	July 2003 to June 2004	17	Asia	Kaisar Alam Sarkar et al. (2006)
Binzhou District, China	1.22 kg/bed/ day	N/A	N/A	December 2006 to January 2007	6	Asia	Ruoyan et al. (2010)
Greece	8.4 kg/bed/day	83.33	16.67	N/A	N/A	Europe	Tsakona et al. (2007)

Developed countries generate more medical waste than developing countries. The data of World Health Organization show that North America generates 7-10 kg of medical waste per day and bed, while South America generates 3 kg of waste per day and bed. This difference is also found in European and Asian countries. Western Europe produces 3-6 kg per bed and day, Eastern Europe 1.4-2 kg, rich countries in Asia 2.5 kg, and poor countries 1.8-2 kg. Present data shows that the amount of medical waste generation depends on the level of economic development of the region. It also draws attention to the fact that North America produces the most amount of waste due to its higher level of economic development. The reason for this is the lifestyle of people and higher consumption of goods and services in developed countries. In addition, the use of disposable equipment and packaging materials instead of reusable products in health centers in developed countries increases waste generation. (Hossain et al., 2011, p. 757).

Classification of Medical Waste

Medical waste "is waste generated during the processes of diagnosis, treatment, or vaccination of humans or animals" (Windfeld & Brooks, 2015, p. 99; Amin et al., 2013, p. 988). In Japan, they are categorized as contagious and non-contagious waste, while in Turkey, they are categorized as infectious, pathological, and sharp waste that may cause stab wounds (Cesaro & Belgiorno, 2017, p. 1019). An important part of the medical waste contains a wide variety of pathogenic substances and dangerous substances (Cesaro & Belgiorno, 2017, p. 1820). The infectious, harmful, cytotoxic, and chemical properties of medical waste make it dangerous. This creates a risk of infection for healthcare professionals and the whole community. Estimated mortality in the USA, including infections of healthcare workers, is 17-57 cases per one million workers (Meyer, 2007, p. 508; Örgev & Utku, 2017). Medical waste that is not properly used and not properly destroyed constitutes a high risk of infection. This threatens the healthcare personnel and human health through the dissemination of microorganisms from healthcare facilities (Windfeld & Brooks, 2015, p. 99; Amin et al., 2013, p. 988). According to the World Health Organization (WHO), 75% to 90% of the waste generated by healthcare providers is household waste. Household waste is often called 'non-hazardous' or 'healthcare waste.' It mainly includes packaging wastes. The remaining 10-25% of medical waste is waste that may be contagious, toxic, or radioactive. Hazardous waste is the type of waste that can create various environmental and health risks (Chartier et al., 2014; Ali et al., 2017, p. 1; Akkucuk & Gencer, 2017). Classification of hazardous medical waste is summarized in Table 3.

Table 3. Hazardous Medical Waste

Waste category	Description and examples
Hazardous Medical Waste	
Sharps waste	Used or not used cutter and piercer tools (e.g. hypodermic, intravenous, or other needles; auto-disable syringes; needle-syringes; infusion sets; scalpels; pipettes; knives; broken glass)
Infectious waste	Waste suspected of containing pathogens and bearing the risk of disease transmission (e.g. waste contaminated with blood and other body fluids, laboratory cultures and microbiological stocks; waste from patients infected with highly contagious diseases lying in isolation wards)
Pathological waste	Human tissues, organs, or fluids; body parts; fetuses; unused blood products
Pharmaceutical waste, cytotoxic waste	Drugs that are expired or are no longer needed; substances contaminated by or containing pharmaceuticals. Cytotoxic waste containing substances with genotoxic properties (e.g., waste containing cytostatic drugs frequently used in cancer therapy, genotoxic chemicals)
Chemical waste	Waste materials containing chemical substances (e.g. laboratory reagents; photographic developer; disinfectants that are expired or no longer needed; solvents; heavy metals such as batteries, broken thermometers, and blood pressure monitors)
Radioactive waste	Waste materials containing radioactive substances (e.g. liquid substances not used in radiotherapy or laboratory research, contaminated glassware, packages or absorbent papers; urine and feces taken from patients treated with radionuclides; leakproof resources)
Non-hazardous or general healthcare waste	Any biological, chemical, radioactive, or physically non-hazardous waste

Medical Waste Management

Medical waste management is considered a critical issue worldwide and an important step in improving general quality of health institutions (Cesaro & Belgiorno, 2017, p. 1820). The aim of waste management is to economically collect, separate, make reusable, and dispose of waste in a safe way without harming human and environmental health (Özerol, 2005, p. 436). Waste management is the process of generating, transporting, storing, separating, recycling, and disposing of wastes (Insa et al. 2010, p. 1055) and carrying out these processes in accordance with the legislation. (Tıbbi Atıkların Kontrolü Yönetmeliği, 2017). Waste that is originating from health institutions, that remains in the air, water, and soil permanently, and disrupts ecological balance are classified as hazardous waste (Cansaran, 2010, p. 18). Medical waste management is the prevention of potential environmental risks that hazardous waste creates and the elimination of risks it creates for public health (Örgev & Utku, 2017). Medical waste consists of hazardous and non-hazardous waste (Amin et al., 2013, p. 989).

Effective management of medical waste is possible with waste management plans at the national and local levels in order to accurately identify medical waste sources, separate reusable waste, minimize waste, ensure recycling processes at the lowest cost, and identify disposal methods. A waste management team is formed within this plan and the authorities and responsibilities of team members are established (Özerol, 2005, p. 436).

Separation at the source should always be the responsibility of the waste generator. The process of separation should be carried out as close as to the source of waste as possible and the waste should be transported to the storage areas after being separated. In addition, temporary storage and transportation should be done in a proper way. Separation, transportation, and final disposal of waste should be carried out by a properly trained team (Örgev & Utku, 2017). Waste management in health facilities is an important environmental and social obligation and therefore requires proper planning (Amin et al., 2013, p. 3). The basic planning steps of medical waste management are as follows:

- Increasing awareness of workers regarding medical waste and environmental health,
- The establishment of an environment commission in the health institution and the appointment of a chief coordinator,
- The environmental control of all areas in the hospital where waste is generated,
- Identifying all waste materials through a specific questionnaire,
- In order to reduce the amount of medical waste, reviewing the steps of production and consumption,
- Identification and classification of waste in accordance with governmental legislation and regulations,
- Training all employees on medical waste and management, and carrying out internal inspection
- Allocation of responsibilities to employees,
- Reuse, recycling, other rescue operations and, as a last resort, ensuring safe and environmentally friendly waste management,
- Ensuring that waste is processed or disposed of in an appropriate area,
- Initiation of documentation activities. In particular, ISO 14001 environmental management systems and standards (Meyer, 2007, p. 510; Insa et al., 2010, p. 1050).

Especially during waste processing, contact with shredders, contagious and dangerous substances through lacerations is the risk that most frequently occurs for environmental and human health (Cesaro

& Belgiorno, 2017, p. 1820). For these reasons, quantitative evaluation of medical waste generation data, determination of objectives, planning, increase of cooperation of personnel, equipment purchases (e.g. weighing scales, protective equipment), data collection, necessary analyses, and suggestions should be made. Managers responsible for medical waste should approximately determine the areas that generate waste, types and amounts of waste, and conduct on-site inspections with certain frequencies to ensure waste management. In waste assessment activities, control should be provided until the final stage of the process by monitoring existing practices, making necessary improvements, ensuring that health professionals are informed and sensitive about waste management, and providing recycling if possible (Chartier et al., 2014; Amin et al., 2013, p. 989).

Separation, Collection, Transportation, and Temporary Storage of Medical Waste

Appropriate separation, collection, temporary transportation, storage, and disposal rules and procedures must be applied in order to prevent the harmful effects of medical waste generated in health institutions. Separation of medical waste is the separation of infected waste from domestic and recyclable waste at the place where it is produced. Medical waste is collected separately at the source without mixing with other wastes and placed in separate plastic bags (Cansaran, 2010). The collecting team transports it to the temporary storage area in accordance with the type of the waste. Medical waste may in no way be mixed with municipal waste, packaging waste, hazardous waste, and other such waste. Biologically hazardous waste should be placed in red bags. The red bags must be marked in an attention-grabbing way with the label "Biohazardous Waste" or the international biological hazard symbol for biohazards. These bags must be made resistant to tearing, puncturing, explosion, and transportation (Shiffman, 1999, p. 321). In hospitals and other healthcare facilities, wastes are often separated in color-coded boxes or bags, and a different type of waste is stored in each storage. Separately colored bags or boxes are used for each type of waste (Windfeld & Brooks, 2015, p. 103; Tıbbi Atıkların Kontrolü Yönetmeliği, 2017).

Waste with cutting and piercing properties is collected in boxes or containers made of hard plastic with "SHARPS WASTE" label, that are puncture resistant, leakproof, or labeled with black international biological hazard symbol "BIOHAZARD." These containers are resistant to perforation, tearing, breakage, and explosion and watertight and leakproof, apart from other medical wastes, (Windfeld & Brooks, 2015, p. 103; Tıbbi Atıkların Kontrolü Yönetmeliği, 2017).

Pathological waste is separated from other medical waste by the black "International Biohazard" emblem and black writing "Attention! Pathological Medical Waste" in red plastic containers. These containers may never be opened, emptied, and recycled after being filled. Blood bags and body parts and organs that have not been treated with any chemical can be collected in medical waste bags. Liquid medical wastes, on the other hand, are thickened with appropriate absorbent materials and put in medical waste bags (Tıbbi Atıkların Kontrolü Yönetmeliği, 2017).

Temporary storage of medical waste is done in an area where medical waste containers with the Code §118310 are stored for collection or processing (Shiffman, 1999). These temporary storage areas must be secured to prevent access to unauthorized persons. They should be marked with warning signs that are easily readable from 25 meters. They must show warning signs in English and Spanish or other languages determined by the infection control staff or the local executive office (Shiffman, 1999, p. 321; Windfeld & Brooks, 2015, p. 103). In countries where medical waste transportation is developed, international regulations have been introduced for the transportation of dangerous substances on the highway known as ADR. Only a licensed carrier can transport the waste. Different methods are used to transport contaminated and clean waste of hospitals in these countries (Ali et al., 2017, p. 6).

Training staff on separation, collection, transportation, and temporary storage of medical waste constitutes the basis for ensuring proper waste management (Cesaro & Belgiorno, 2017).

Methods of Medical Waste Disposal

Since they can adversely affect human and environmental health in various ways, disposal or transformation of medical wastes into non-hazardous substances (Cesaro & Belgiorno, 2017, p. 1820) protects human and environmental health (Cansaran, 2010). It has been seen that depending on various factors (type of waste, capacity of disposal system, investment and application costs) the method of waste disposal can be selected from various methods (Özerol, 2005, p. 444; Windfeld, & Brooks, 2015, p. 103). Methods of medical waste disposal are burning, autoclaving, land filling, recycling, using electron beam technology, irradiating, thermal methods, biological and chemical sterilization, etc. Burying the waste is a common method. This method has negative effects on the environment and human health due to the atmospheric release of methane gas and other toxic gases that have explosive properties. However, in many European countries all waste materials are buried in the soil (Özerol, 2005, p. 444). Some countries such as Germany, Slovenia, Portugal, etc. have gradually removed medical waste incineration furnaces to avoid environmental pollution. On the other hand, some developed countries such as Korea have adopted other non-hospital waste disposal methods such as steam sterilization, landfilling, and incineration (Ali et al., 2017, p. 7). The most common methods of medical solid waste disposal, especially in developing countries, are dumping into a landfill, storage, or incineration. These disposal methods are cheaper. However, these methods are seen as a potential source of infection for human health and environmental pollution. The reason is that this uncontrolled medical waste transmits infectious pathogenic microorganisms to the environment by direct contact or indirect contact through inhalation, swallowing, food chain, or main pathogenic species (Hossain et al., 2011, p. 759). However, it has been seen that in many countries of the world medical waste is not disposed of under appropriate conditions. Optimal disposal of medical waste is very important in terms of protecting the health of healthcare workers and the society, protecting the economic benefits and protecting the environment. It also plays an important role in preventing environmental contamination and reducing injuries (Hassan, Ahmed, Rahman, & Biswas, 2008).

Impact of Medical Waste on Environment and Human Health

The proper handling, treatment, and disposal of waste will reduce costs and protect the environment and human health. The waste from the treatment of patients suffering from infectious diseases can be transmitted either directly through contact or indirectly through the environment. Contagion of infectious diseases is a serious issue. For this reason, an appropriate waste management system is essential (Örgev & Utku, 2017). Inadequate management of medical waste causes a risk of infection and injury to the personnel who is in contact with this waste due to improper treatment and disposal. It also increases the risk of environmental pollution. Especially during the processing of waste, contact with shredders, and contagious and dangerous substances through lacerations is the risk that most frequently occurs for environmental and human health (Cesaro & Belgiorno, 2017, p. 1820).

International Legislations and Basic Regulations on Medical Waste

Reducing risks to human health and environment associated with medical waste management is often controlled by specific national legislations or guidelines that result in different outcomes (Cesaro & Belgiorno, 2017, p. 1825). To do medical waste management with a certain system, many countries have prepared legislations and implementation guidelines to protect the environment and reduce the risks to human health (Insa et al., 2010, p. 1049). Directive 75/442/EEC on waste is the first regulation issued by the European Economic Community to protect human health and the environment against the harmful effects of waste collection, transportation, treatment, storage, and eventual disposal (Insa et al., 2010, p. 1050).

World Health Organization, 1983; US Environmental Protection Agency, 1986; US Environmental Protection Agency, 1991; The US Centers for Disease Control and Prevention, 1978 and many other countries have already set strict rules for the management of contagious waste substances from medical institutions (Örgev & Utku, 2017, p. 295). In this context, many European countries have defined medical wastes by categorizing them according to their characteristics in order to provide the most appropriate methods of packaging, storage, treatment, and disposal, and have enacted legal regulations (Cesaro & Belgiorno, 2017, p. 1820). In 1991, a European steering committee was set up to examine medical waste problems and this committee prepared a series of proposals submitted to the European Commission in 1997 (Insa et al., 2010, p. 1049). Because the United States (USA), Canada, the European Union (EU) and the United Kingdom (UK) are rich G7 member countries with developed economies, the European Union (including the UK) is a group of nations and some countries classified as upper middle income contains (Windfeld & Brooks, 2015, p. 101). Among the federal agencies involved in the control of medical waste, the most known are CDC (Centers for Disease Control), OSHA (Occupational Safety and Health Administration), and EPA (Environmental Protection Agency) (Erdoğan, 2018, p. 99).

The proportion of medical waste generated in the continents of Africa (South Africa, Algeria, Egypt, Libya) and Asia (Bangladesh, Mongolia) is much higher than in developing countries in the European continent (Croatia, Greece). The reason is that developed countries follow advanced legislation and guidelines during the collection of waste and apply various procedures to minimize the generation of medical waste in the process of disposal, storage, and transportation of waste. On the other hand, medical waste is not fully known in developing countries yet, and it is still taken up and disposed of with non-medical waste (Hossain et al., 2011, p. 757).

Since 1993, Environmental Impact Assessment (Çevresel Etki Değerlendirmesi -- ÇED) is being applied in Turkey. Within the scope of ÇED regulation, it is obligatory to take the ÇED document. The aim of the ÇED is to reduce the use of natural resources, to minimize waste generation, to improve waste disposal management, to prevent economic losses, and to enable people to live in a healthier environment by providing a sustainable environment. ÇED Regulation was enforced in 2013 (T.C. Çevre ve Orman Bakanlığı, 2005). In Turkey starting from 1991, regulations relating to general waste management, including medical waste, have been developed in line with waste diversity and European Union legislation, and this has continued with adjustments in legislation in accordance with the conditions of the country (T.C. Çevre ve Orman Bakanlığı, 2005; Aydemir, 2017, p. 297). With the "Medical Waste Control Regulation" (Tıbbi Atıkların Kontrolü Yönetmeliği -- TAKY) published in the Official Gazette with the date 22.07.2005 and number 25883, applications regarding medical waste were organized (Akbolat et al., 2011, p. 132). In general, inadequate medical waste management is a major problem in developing countries. In these countries, insufficient financial investment, lack of effective control, and lack of training of personnel in the context of waste management cause insufficient waste management. In addition, lack of a waste management manual and national legislation in health services is one of these reasons (Hossain et al., 2011, p. 755).

Legislations and basic regulations in developing countries are presented below in Table 4 (Ali et al., 2017, p. 3).

Sustainable Medical Waste Management

Environmental protection began in the 1970s as a result of protests of ecological groups and, at the same time, with the emergence of the concept of sustainable development. The most important goal of sustainable development is to protect the environment from potentially adverse effects, from the big increase in waste generation, and the rapid consumption of non-renewable resources (Insa et al., 2010, p. 1049). It can be defined as protecting the necessary elements for social, economic, and ecological systems, not wasting resources, ensuring recycling, and reusing resources in a way that they can be reproduced. Protecting the necessary elements for social, economic and ecological systems can be defined as not wasting resources, ensuring recycling, and reusing resources in a reproducible way.

Table 4. Hospital waste legislations and regulatory authorities

Country	Regulatory authority	Legislation	Reference
China	Ministry of Health, State Environmental Protection Administration	Medical Waste Control Act 380, Regulation 287	Yong et al. 2009
Jordon	Ministry of Health	Medical Waste Management Regulations, 2001	Abdulla et al., 2008
Iran	Ministry of Health	Medical Waste Management Regulations, 2008	Taghipour et al., 2014
Brazil	National Environmental Council of Brazil	CONAMA (2001) Resolution No. 283	Da Silva et al., 2005
Turkey	Ministry of Environment and Forestry	Medical Waste Control Regulation, 1993, 2005	Birpinar et al., 2009
Egypt	Ministry of Environment	Decree No. 338/1995 and No. 1741/2005 of Environmental Law No. 4 (1994)	Abd El-Salam, 2010
Cameroon	Ministry of Public Health	1964, Law on The Conservation of Public Health, 1996 Framework Health Law	Manga et al., 2011
Botswana	National Conservation Strategy Agency	Clinical Waste Management Code of Practice of 1996	Mbongwe et al., 2008
India	Ministry of Environment and Forests	Bio-Medical Waste (Management and Handling) Rules, 1998	Hanumantha Rao, 2009
Mauritius	Ministry of Health, Ministry of Environment	Public Health Act, 1925 and Standards for Hazardous Waste Regulations, 2001	Mohee, 2005
Laos	Ministry of Health	Healthcare Waste Management Regulation, 2004	Phengxay, 2005
Pakistan	Ministry of Environment	Hospital Waste Management Rules, 2005	Khattak, 2009
Serbia	Ministry of Health	National Guide for the Safe Management of HCW in Serbia, 2009	Stankovic et al., 2008
Vietnam	Ministry of Health	Regulation on Healthcare Waste Management	Visvanathan, 2006
Nepal	Ministry of Population and Environment	National Health Care Waste Management Guidelines, 2002	Chandra Shekhar Yadav, 2002

Resource consumption and minimizing emissions and negative environmental impacts, including all waste, is addressed in the context of environmental sustainability. One of the important aspects of sustainability is waste management. The necessity of removing wastes in a way sensitive to the environment and human health and destroying them in economical ways has introduced the concept of sustainable waste management. Effective use of resources that underlies sustainability is achieved through recycling, reusing, and producing energy and compost from incineration of waste (Örgev & Utku, 2017; Akkucuk & Sekercioglu, 2016). Various financial problems, the education and awareness of health professionals, and the lack of public awareness are the main problems in these issues. Similarly, it is important to educate all stakeholders, the municipal staff, patients, hospital personnel, visitors, and disposers of waste that are responsible for off-site transportation of hospital waste, and also the general public, about handling hazardous medical waste and dangers of managing it. For this reason, it is important to compare and monitor the goals of the trainings and the real results (Ali et al., 2017, p. 3). Research shows that appropriate management reduces the generation of infectious waste by up to 15%, resulting in less environmental and health problems in the storage, transportation, and disposal of hospital waste. In this context, regular trainings should be given to hospital personnel in order to make their behavior and attitudes about waste management sustainable (Alagöz & Kocasoy, 2008). In addition, managers need to ensure that medical waste is being disposed of in the most cost-effective way and with the least amount of health risk to employees and the community. For this reason, thorough and periodic health screening should be done to healthcare workers at regular intervals (Studnicki, 1992).

CONCLUSION AND RECOMMENDATIONS

In this study, literature on waste management was examined in order to evaluate the environment and human health relation, sustainable waste management, and regulations related to international legislation on waste management. The definition of medical waste and sustainable medical waste management systems, classification of waste, waste management, and implementation process were also presented. In addition, international regulations for the management of medical waste were examined.

Sustainable waste management will provide a sustainable environment for future generations, conservation of natural resources, and consequently economic success. More importantly, it will prevent the harm medical waste may cause to human health. For this purpose, awareness of the community should be increased starting with the of education of the medical staff in protecting the environmental and human health. In the field of medical waste management, regulations should be extended to standardize basic principles by taking into consideration the characteristics of the region to which international and local waste management will be applied. The examination of the relevant legislation in waste management constitutes the first step in the establishment of the waste management project through the evaluation of the region, institution, and area in which the applications will be managed in accordance with the legislation. Procedures and implementation instructions of medical waste management should be prepared, and training should be provided on management of the waste and protection of the environment to all personnel, patients, and their relatives. Close monitoring of internal supervision is recommended for sustainable waste management.

In health facilities, collection, separation, and recycling-repurposing plans of medical waste materials provides a safe environment for the protection of human and environmental health. Moreover, it will reduce the exposure of healthcare professionals and patients to infectious waste, reduce costs in healthcare facilities, and make a significant contribution to ensuring a viable environment and sustainable development for future generations.

REFERENCES

Abdulla, F., AbuQdais, H., & Rabi, A. (2008). Site investigation on medical waste management practices in northern Jordan. *Waste Management (New York, N.Y.)*, *28*(2), 450–458. doi:10.1016/j.wasman.2007.02.035 PMID:17507209

Akbolat, M., Işık, O., Dede, C., & Çimen, M. (2011). Sağlık çalışanlarının tıbbi atık bilgi düzeylerinin değerlendirilmesi. *Acıbadem Üniversitesi Sağlık Bilimleri Dergisi*, *2*(3), 131–140.

Akkucuk, U. (2016). SCOR Model and the Green Supply Chain. In U. Akkucuk (Ed.), Handbook of Research on Waste Management Techniques for Sustainability (pp. 108-124). Hershey, PA: IGI Global.

Akkucuk, U. (2017). *Ethics and Sustainability in Global Supply Chain Management*. Hershey, PA: IGI Global. doi:10.4018/978-1-5225-2036-8

Akkucuk, U., & Gencer, Y. G. (2017). EFQM Model and Sustainability of Organizations. In *2nd International Conference on Advances in Management Engineering and Information Technology (AMEIT 2017)*, Shangai, China. DEStech Publications. 10.12783/dtcse/ameit2017/12279

Akkucuk, U., & Sekercioglu, C. H. (2016). NGOs For Environmental Sustainability: The Case of Kuzeydoga Foundation. *Fresenius Environmental Bulletin*, *25*(12A), 6038–6044.

Alagöz, A. Z., & Kocasoy, G. (2008). Improvement and modification of the routing system for the health-care waste collection and transportation in Istanbul. *Waste Management*, *28*(8), 1461–1471. doi:10.1016/j.wasman.2007.08.024 PMID:17949966

Ali, M., Wang, W., Chaudhry, N., & Geng, Y. (2017). Hospital waste management in developing countries: A mini review. *Waste Management & Research*, *35*(6), 581–592. doi:10.1177/0734242X17691344 PMID:28566033

Amin, R., Gul, R., & Mehrab, A. (2013). Hospital waste management. *The Professional Medical Journal*, *20*(6), 988–994.

Aydemir, İ. (2017). Türkiye'de çevre bilinci kapsamında tıbbi atık üretim süreçleri ve yönetimi. *Bingöl Üniversitesi Sosyal Bilimler Enstitüsü Dergisi*, *7*(13), 295–311. doi:10.29029/busbed.310594

Cansaran, D. D. (2010). *Çevre-sağlık ilişkisi ekseninde tıbbi atık yönetimi (Yayınlanmamış doktora tezi)*. Ankara: Ankara Üniversitesi Sosyal Bilimler Enstitüsü.

Cesaro, A., & Belgiorno, V. (2017). Sustainability of medical waste management in different sized health care facilities. *Waste and Biomass Valorization*, *8*(5), 1819–1827. doi:10.100712649-016-9730-y

Chartier, Y., Emmanuel, J., Pieper, U., Prüss, A., Rushbrook, P., Stringer, R., ... Zghondi, R. (Eds.). (2014). *Safe management of wastes from health-care activities* (2nd ed.). Geneva: World Health Organization Press.

Erdoğan, Ö. (2018). Tıbbi atık yönetimi. In A. Başustaoğlu & A. Z. Avcı (Eds.), *Hemşirelik uygulamalarında klinik mikrobiyoloji ve enfeksiyon hastalıkları*. Ankara: Hipokrat Kitabevi.

Gao, Q., Shi, Y., Mo, D., Nie, J., Yang, M., Rozelle, S., & Sylvia, S. (2018). Medical waste management in three areas of rural China. *PLoS One*, *13*(7), 1–13. doi:10.1371/journal.pone.0200889 PMID:30028841

Gencer, Y. G., & Akkucuk, U. (2016). Reverse Logistics: Automobile Recalls and Other Conditions. In U. Akkucuk (Ed.), Handbook of Research on Waste Management Techniques for Sustainability (pp. 125-154). Hershey, PA: IGI Global.

Güvez, H., Dege, M., & Eren, T. (2012). Medical waste collection with vehicle routing problem in Kırıkkale. *Uluslararası Mühendislik Araştırma ve Geliştirme Dergisi*, *4*(1), 41–45.

Hassan, M. M., Ahmed, S. A., Rahman, K. A., & Biswas, T. K. (2008). Pattern of medical waste management: Existing scenario in Dhaka City, Bangladesh. *BMC Public Health*, *8*(36). PMID:18221548

Hossain, M. S., Santhanam, A., Norulaini, N. A. N., & Omar, A. K. M. (2011). Clinical solid waste management practices and its impact on human health and environment – A review. *Waste Management (New York, N.Y.)*, *31*(4), 754–766. doi:10.1016/j.wasman.2010.11.008 PMID:21186116

Insa, E., Zamorano, M., & López, R. (2010). Critical review of medical waste legislation in spain. *Resources, Conservation and Recycling*, *54*(12), 1048–1059. doi:10.1016/j.resconrec.2010.06.005

Meyer, R. (2007). Management of waste from health care institutions. *CLEAN – Soil, Air, Water (Basel)*, *35*(5), 508–510.

Örgev, C., & Utku, A. Ç. (2017). Sağlık kurumlarında atık kovalarının tıbbi atık yönetimine göre mikrobiyolojik değerlendirilmesi. *Sakarya Üniversitesi Fen Bilimleri Dergisi*, *21*(3), 294–301.

Ozder, A., Teker, B., Eker, H. H., Altındis, S., Kocaakman, M., & Karabay, O. (2013). Medical waste management training for healthcare managers - a necessity? *Journal of Environmental Health Science & Engineering*, *11*(1), 1–8. doi:10.1186/2052-336X-11-20 PMID:24499642

Özerol, İ. H. (2005). Tıbbi atık stratejileri nelerdir? EN/ISO normları nelerdir? Avrupa'da birlik? ABD'nin yaklaşımı? Ülkemizde durum? In *Ulusal Sterilizasyon Dezenfeksiyon Kongresi* (pp. 434-472).

Shiffman, M. A. (1999). Medical waste regulations. *The American Journal of Cosmetic Surgery*, *16*(4), 321–321. doi:10.1177/074880689901600408

Studnicki, J. (1992). The management of hospital medical waste: How to increase efficiency through a medical waste audit. *Hospital Topics*, *70*(2), 11–17. doi:10.1080/00185868.1992.10543687 PMID:10119174

T.C. Çevre ve Orman Bakanlığı. (2005). Tıbbi Atıkların Kontrolü Yönetmeliği.

T.C. Çevre ve Orman Bakanlığı Çevre Yönetimi Genel Müdürlüğü. (2008). Güvenli Atık Yönetimi.

Tıbbi Atıkların Kontrolü Yönetmeliği. (2017). 25.01.2017 tarih ve 29959 sayı ile Resmi Gazete.

Windfeld, E. S., & Brooks, M. S. L. (2015). Medical waste management – A review. *Journal of Environmental Management*, *163*, 98–108. doi:10.1016/j.jenvman.2015.08.013 PMID:26301686

ADDITIONAL READING

Curi, K., Ekinci, E., & Kocasoy, K. (1998). *Management of Solid and Healthcare Wastes – National Environmental Plan, Planning State of Turkey*. Ankara, Turkey: DPT Press.

Diaz, L. F., Savage, G. M., & Eggerth, L. L. (2005). Alternatives for the treatment and disposal of healthcare wastes in developing countries. *Waste Management (New York, N.Y.)*, *25*(6), 626–637.

Houng, H. 2003. Policies and measures of waste disposal and treatment in Taiwan. In G.D. Taine (Ed.), *Sustainable Urban Services-Shanghai Seminar. Pacific Economic Cooperation Council*, Taiwan (pp. 73-81).

Lakshmi, B.S. & Kumar, P. (2010). Awareness about bio-medical waste management among healthcare personnel of some important medical centers in Agra. *Int. J. Eng. Res. Tech.*, *1*(7), 1–5.

Mathur, V., Dwivedi, S., Hassan, M.A. & Misra, R.P. (2011). Knowledge, attitude, and practices about biomedical waste management among healthcare personnel: A cross-sectional study. *Indian J. Community Med.*, *36*, 143–145. 9.

Rushbrook, P., Chandra, C. & Gayton, S. (2000). Starting healthcare waste management in medical institutions – a practical approach. Copenhagen Practical Health care Waste Management, WHO Regional Office for Europe.

Sabour, M. R., Mohamedifard, A., & Kamalan, H. (2007). A mathematical model to predict the composition and generation of hospital wastes in Iran. *Waste Management*, *27*(4), 584–587. doi:10.1016/j.wasman.2006.05.010 PMID:17239577

Shirazinejad, A. (1996). Investigation of Collection and Disposal of Fars Province's Hospital Wastes.

Suwarna, M., & Ramesh, G. (2012). Study about awareness and practices about healthcare wastes management among hospital staff in a medical college hospital, Bangalore. Int J Basic Med Sci 2012, 3(1):7–11. 10.

UNEP. (1996). International Source Book on Environmentally Sound Technologies for Municipal Solid Waste Management. International Environmental Technology Centre.

Vishal, B., Swarn, L., Mahesh, M., Arvind, A., Sanjay, A., & Uma, S. (2012). Knowledge Assessment of Hospital Staff Regarding Biomedical Waste Management in A Tertiary Care Hospital. *National Journal of Community Medicine*, *3*(2), 197–200.

WHO. (1999). *Safe Management of Wastes from Health-Care Activities*. Geneva: World Health Organization.

KEY TERMS AND DEFINITIONS

Disposal: Destroying waste by various methods when waste generation is inevitable.

Environmental Health: The external factors that affect living beings in a certain environment and the precautions taken to protect them.

Hazardous Waste: All waste that is harmful to the environment and human health.

Medical Waste: Includes all the waste generated during the procedures performed at health institutions, research facilities, and laboratories, and during medical services provided at home.

Medical Waste Management: Taking the necessary precautions to prevent potential environmental hazards that hazardous waste creates and to remove the risks it poses for community health.

Sustainability: Taking precautions to ensure that the needs of future generations can be met while currently meeting the needs of people, and to maintain this situation.

Compilation of References

Aaker, D. A. (2009). *Managing brand equity*. NY: Simon and Schuster.

Abbey, J. D., Meloy, M. G., Guide, V. D. R. Jr, & Atalay, S. (2015). Remanufactured products in closed-loop supply chains for consumer goods. *Production and Operations Management*, *24*(3), 488–503. doi:10.1111/poms.12238

Abdulla, F., AbuQdais, H., & Rabi, A. (2008). Site investigation on medical waste management practices in northern Jordan. *Waste Management (New York, N.Y.)*, *28*(2), 450–458. doi:10.1016/j.wasman.2007.02.035 PMID:17507209

AccountAbility & LRQA. (2006). *The Materiality report. Aligning strategy, performance and reporting*. Retrieved from https://hiyamaya.files.wordpress.com/2009/12/the-materiality-report.pdf

AccountAbility. (2008). *AA1000 Assurance Standard*.

Açıkgöz, B. (2015). Yoksulluk, Kalkınma ve Kamu Harcamaları İlişkisinin Ekonometrik Analizi. *Hukuk ve İktisat Araştırmaları Dergisi*, *7*(1), 37–49.

Adetayo, J. O., & Apollos, E. A. (2013). An Overview of Service Delivery and Customer Satisfaction in the Telecommunications Industry in Nigeria. *Indian Journal of Marketing*, *43*(8), 14–22. doi:10.17010/ijom/2013/v43/i8/36318

Afzal, M., Malik, M. E., Begum, I., Sarwar, K., & Fatima, H. (2012). Relationship Among Education, Poverty and Economic Growth in Pakistan: An Econometric Analysis. *Journal of Elementary Education*, *22*(1), 23–45.

Agosin, M. R., & Huaita, F. (2012). Overreaction in capital flows to emerging markets: Booms and sudden stops. *Journal of International Money and Finance*, *31*(5), 1140–1155. doi:10.1016/j.jimonfin.2011.12.015

Agrawal, P. (2007). Economic Growth and Poverty Reduction: Evidence from Kazakhstan. *Asian Development Review*, *24*(2), 90–115.

Aguilar, L. A. (2013). Doing the right thing: compliance that works for investors. *Paper presented at Conference Regulation, Operations & Compliance (ROC) 2013*, New York, NY.

Ahmad, Z., & Batul, T. (2013). Relationship Among Poverty, Education Expenditure, and Education Status: Empirical Evidence from Pakistan. *Proceedings of the World Congress on Engineering*, 1, 3-5.

Ajzen, I. (1985). From intentions to actions: A theory of planned behavior. In *Action control* (pp. 11–39). Springer. doi:10.1007/978-3-642-69746-3_2

Ajzen, I. (1991). The theory of planned behavior. *Organizational Behavior and Human Decision Processes*, *50*(2), 179–211. doi:10.1016/0749-5978(91)90020-T

Ajzen, I. (2002). Perceived behavioral control, self-efficacy, locus of control, and the theory of planned behavior. *Journal of Applied Social Psychology*, *32*(4), 665–683. doi:10.1111/j.1559-1816.2002.tb00236.x

Akbaba, A. (2006). Measuring service quality in the hotel industry: A study in a business hotel in Turkey. *International Journal of Hospitality Management, 25*(2), 170–192. doi:10.1016/j.ijhm.2005.08.006

Akbolat, M., Işık, O., Dede, C., & Çimen, M. (2011). Sağlık çalışanlarının tıbbi atık bilgi düzeylerinin değerlendirilmesi. *Acıbadem Üniversitesi Sağlık Bilimleri Dergisi, 2*(3), 131–140.

Akküçük, U. (2009). İş Etiğinde Sarbanes-Oxley (SOX) Yasası'nın Etkisi ve Toplam Kalite Yönetimi Uygulamalarında Yansımaları. *İş Ahlakı Dergisi, 2*(3), 7-17.

Akkucuk, U. (2016). SCOR Model and the Green Supply Chain. In U. Akkucuk (Ed.), Handbook of Research on Waste Management Techniques for Sustainability (pp. 108-124). Hershey, PA: IGI Global.

Akkucuk, U., & Esmaeili, J. (2016). The impact of brands on consumer buying behavior: An empirical study on smartphone buyers. *International Journal of Research in Business and Social Science, 5*(4), 1-16.

Akkucuk, U., & Gencer, Y. G. (2017). EFQM Model and Sustainability of Organizations. *DEStech Transactions on Computer Science and Engineering.* doi:10.12783/dtcse/ameit2017/12279

Akkucuk, U. (2011). Combining Purchase Probabilities and Willingness to Pay Measures: A Case on Recycled Products. *European Journal of Soil Science, 23*(3), 353–361.

Akkucuk, U. (2015). *Handbook of Research on Developing Sustainable Value in Economics, Finance and Marketing.* Hershey, PA: Business Science Reference. doi:10.4018/978-1-4666-6635-1

Akkucuk, U. (2016). SCOR Model and the Green Supply Chain. In U. Akkucuk (Ed.), *Handbook of Research on Waste Management Techniques for Sustainability* (pp. 108–124). Hershey, PA: IGI Global. doi:10.4018/978-1-4666-9723-2.ch006

Akkucuk, U. (2017). *Ethics and Sustainability in Global Supply Chain Management.* Hershey, PA: IGI Global. doi:10.4018/978-1-5225-2036-8

Akkucuk, U., & Sekercioglu, C. H. (2016). NGOs for environmental sustainability: The Case Of Kuzeydoga Foundation. *Fresenius Environmental Bulletin, 25*(12A), 6038–6044.

Akkucuk, U., & Sekercioglu, C. H. (2016). NGOs For Environmental Sustainability: The Case of Kuzeydoga Foundation. *Fresenius Environmental Bulletin, 25*(12A), 6038–6044.

Akkucuk, U., & Sekercioglu, C. H. (2016). NGOs For Environmental Sustainability: The Case Of Kuzeydoga Foundation. *Fresenius Environmental Bulletin, 25*(12A), 6038–6044.

Aktan, C. C., & Vural, İ. Y. (2002). *Yoksulluk: Terminoloji, Temel Kavramlar ve Ölçüm Yöntemleri, Yoksullukla Mücadele Stratejileri* (C. C. Aktan, Ed.). Ankara: Hak-İş Konfederasyonu Yayınları. Retrieved from http://www.canaktan.org/ekonomi/yoksulluk/birinci-bol/aktan-vural-yoksulluk.pdf

Alagöz, A. Z., & Kocasoy, G. (2008). Improvement and modification of the routing system for the health-care waste collection and transportation in Istanbul. *Waste Management, 28*(8), 1461–1471. doi:10.1016/j.wasman.2007.08.024 PMID:17949966

Ali, M., Wang, W., Chaudhry, N., & Geng, Y. (2017). Hospital waste management in developing countries: A mini review. *Waste Management & Research, 35*(6), 581–592. doi:10.1177/0734242X17691344 PMID:28566033

Al-Momani, K., Noor, M., & Azila, N. (2009). E-service quality, ease of use, usability and enjoyment as antecedents of e-CRM performance: An empirical investigation in Jordan mobile phone services. *The Asian Journal of Technology Management, 2*(2), 50–64.

Alonso-Almeida, M. M. (2018). *El nuevo materialismo del siglo XXI: Luces y sombras*. Barcelona: Real Academia Europea de Doctores.

Alonso-Almeida, M. M., Bagur-Femenias, L., Llach, J., & Perramon, J. (2018). Sustainability in small tourist businesses: The link between initiatives and performance. *Current Issues in Tourism*, *21*(1), 1–20. doi:10.1080/13683500.2015.1066764

Alonso-Almeida, M. M., Rocafort, A., & Borrajo, F. (2016). Shedding light on eco-innovation in tourism: A critical analysis. *Sustainability*, *8*(12), 1262–1280. doi:10.3390u8121262

Alqahtani, A. Y., & Gupta, S. M. (2017a). One-dimensional renewable warranty management within sustainable supply chain. *Resources*, *6*(2), 16, 1-26. doi:10.3390/resources6020016

Alqahtani, A. Y., & Gupta, S. M. (2017b). Optimizing two-dimensional renewable warranty policies for sensor embedded remanufactured products. *Journal of Industrial Engineering & Management*, *10*(2), 145-187. doi:10.3926/jiem.2187

Alti, A. (2003). How Sensitive Is Investment to Cash Flow When Financing Is Frictionless? *The Journal of Finance*, *58*(2), 707–722. doi:10.1111/1540-6261.00542

Aman, A. L., Harun, A., & Hussein, Z. (2012). The influence of environmental knowledge and concern on green purchase intention the role of attitude as a mediating variable. *British Journal of Arts and Social Sciences*, *7*(2), 145–167.

Amin, R., Gul, R., & Mehrab, A. (2013). Hospital waste management. *The Professional Medical Journal*, *20*(6), 988–994.

Andretta, A. (2014). Key enablers for the future of Smart Cities. *Philips Lighting*. Retrieved from https://www.theclimategroup.org/sites/default/files/archive/files/Dubai-Philips---Business-Case-1.pdf

Angelsen, A., & Sven, W. (2006). Poverty and Inequality: Economic Growth is Better Than its Reputation. In D. Banik (Ed.), Poverty, Politics and Development: Interdisciplinary Perspectives. Fagbokforlaget.

Anselmsson, J., Johansson, U., & Persson, N. (2007). Understanding price premium for grocery products: A conceptual model of customer-based brand equity. *Journal of Product and Brand Management*, *16*(6), 401–414. doi:10.1108/10610420710823762

Anttonen, M., Lammi, M., Mykkänen, J., & Repo, P. (2018). Circular Economy in the Triple Helix of Innovation Systems. *Sustainability*, *10*(8), 2646–2660. doi:10.3390u10082646

Apple. (2016, February 16). *A Message to Our Customers*. Retrieved from https://www.apple.com/customer-letter/

Arabsheybani, A., Paydar, M. M., & Safaei, A. S. (2018). An integrated fuzzy MOORA method and FMEA technique for sustainable supplier selection considering quantity discounts and supplier's risk. *Journal of Cleaner Production*, *190*, 577–591. doi:10.1016/j.jclepro.2018.04.167

Arellano, M., & Bond, S. (1991). Some Tests of Specification for Panel Data: Monte Carlo Evidence and an Application to Employment Equations. *The Review of Economic Studies*, *58*(2), 277. doi:10.2307/2297968

Arnould, E. J., & Price, L. L. (2000). Authenticating acts and authoritative performances: Questing for self and community. in S. Ratneshwar, D. G. Mick, and C. Huffman (Eds.), The Why of Consumption: Contemporary Perspectives on Consumer Motives, Goals, and Desires pp. (140–163). London, UK: Routledge.

Arslan-Ayaydin, Ö., Florackis, C., & Ozkan, A. (2014). Financial flexibility, corporate investment and performance: Evidence from financial crises. *Review of Quantitative Finance and Accounting*, *42*(2), 211–250. doi:10.100711156-012-0340-x

Aryee, S., Walumbwa, F. O., Seidu, E. Y., & Otaye, L. E. (2016). Developing and leveraging human capital resource to promote service quality: Testing a theory of performance. *Journal of Management*, *42*(2), 480–499. doi:10.1177/0149206312471394

Atasu, A., Guide, V. D. R. Jr, & Van Wassenhove, L. N. (2010). So what if remanufacturing cannibalizes my new product sales? *California Management Review*, *52*(2), 56–76. doi:10.1525/cmr.2010.52.2.56

Atasu, A., Sarvary, M., & Van Wassenhove, L. N. (2008). Remanufacturing as a marketing strategy. *Management Science*, *54*(10), 1731–1746. doi:10.1287/mnsc.1080.0893

Attri, V. N. (2016). An emerging new development paradigm of the blue economy in IORA;A policy framework for the future. *IORA*. Retrieved August 8, 2018 from http://www.iora.int/media/23839/the-blue-economy-and-iora-2016.pdf

Auto Recycing Nederland. (2018). Retrieved July 2, 2018, from https://arn.nl/en/over-arn/

Automotive Parts Remanufacturers Association. (n.d.). Europe. Retrieved from https://apra.org/page/Europe

Aydemir, İ. (2017). Türkiye'de çevre bilinci kapsamında tıbbi atık üretim süreçleri ve yönetimi. *Bingöl Üniversitesi Sosyal Bilimler Enstitüsü Dergisi*, *7*(13), 295–311. doi:10.29029/busbed.310594

Badri, M. A., Abdulla, M., & Al-Madani, A. (2005). Information technology center service quality: Assessment and application of SERVQUAL. *International Journal of Quality & Reliability Management*, *22*(8), 819–848. doi:10.1108/02656710510617247

Bagur-Femenias, L., Llach, J., & Alonso-Almeida, M. M. (2013). Is the adoption of environmental practices a strategical decision for small service companies? An empirical approach. *Management Decision*, *51*(1), 41–62. doi:10.1108/00251741311291300

Bakırtaş, T., & Kandemir, O. (2012). Türkiye'de Yetersiz Eğitim ve Yoksulluk İlişkisi: İller Bazında Ekonometrik Bir Analiz. Uluslararası İstanbul Finans Kongresi. Okan Üniversitesi.

Baldauf, A., Cravens, K. S., & Binder, G. (2003). Performance consequences of brand equity management: Evidence from organizations in the value chain. *Journal of Product and Brand Management*, *12*(4), 220–236. doi:10.1108/10610420310485032

Baltagi, B. H., Feng, Q., & Kao, C. (2012). A Lagrange Multiplier Test for Cross-Sectional Dependence in a Fixed Effects Panel Data Model. *Journal of Econometrics*, *170*(1), 164–177. doi:10.1016/j.jeconom.2012.04.004

Bancel, F., & Mittoo, U. R. (2004). Cross-country determinants of capital structure choice: A survey of European firms. *Financial Management*, 103–132.

Barrington, L. (2015, November 23). *Inadequate dirty money regulation 'leaves UK open to terror funds': report*. Retrieved from reuters.com http://www.reuters.com/article/2015/11/23/us-britain-moneylaundering-idUSKBN0TC00520151123#pDBJT cbu5AoZk8hO.97

Basel Committee on Banking Supervision. (2003). *The compliance function in banks*. Bank for international settlements. Retrieved from https://www.bis.org/publ/bcbs103.pdf

Basfirinci, C., & Mitra, A. (2015). A cross cultural investigation of airlines service quality through integration of Servqual and the Kano model. *Journal of Air Transport Management*, *42*, 239–248. doi:10.1016/j.jairtraman.2014.11.005

Bastič, M., & Gojčič, S. (2012). Measurement scale for eco-component of hotel service quality. *International Journal of Hospitality Management*, *31*(3), 1012–1020. doi:10.1016/j.ijhm.2011.12.007

Batista, M. V., & Martins, E. F. (2009). Identification and evaluation of reverse logistics channels: A study on the revaluation of pet bottles. *Proceedings of National Meeting of Production Engineering.*

BCG. (2009, January). Capturing the green advantage for consumer companies. Retrieved from https://www.bcg.com/documents/file15407.pdf

Bekaert, G., & Harvey, C. R. (2003). Emerging markets finance. *Journal of Empirical Finance, 10*(1–2), 3–55. doi:10.1016/S0927-5398(02)00054-3

Berezina, K., Cobanoglu, C., Miller, B. L., & Kwansa, F. A. (2012). The impact of information security breach on hotel guest perception of service quality, satisfaction, revisit intentions and word-of-mouth. *International Journal of Contemporary Hospitality Management, 24*(7), 991–1010. doi:10.1108/09596111211258883

Berglund, M., Van Laarhoven, P., Sharman, G., & Wandel, S. (1999). Third-party logistics: Is there a future? *International Journal of Logistics Management, 10*(1), 59–70. doi:10.1108/09574099910805932

Bianchini, A., Pellegrini, M., Rossi, J., & Saccani, C. (2018). *A new productive model of circular economy enhanced by digital transformation in the Fourth Industrial Revolution-An integrated framework and real case studies. XXIII Summer School "Francesco Turco"*. Industrial Systems Engineering.

Biebuyck, C. (2014). The risks of insider trading. *Economía, 16*(July). Retrieved from http://economia.icaew.com/finance/july-2014/the-risks-of-insider-trading

Biegelman, M. T. (2008). *Building a world-class compliance program: Best practices and strategies for success*. John Wiley & Sons. doi:10.1002/9781118268193

Biswas, A., & Roy, M. (2015). Leveraging factors for sustained green consumption behavior based on consumption value perceptions: Testing the structural model. *Journal of Cleaner Production, 95*, 332–340. doi:10.1016/j.jclepro.2015.02.042

Blundell, R., & Bond, S. (1998). Initial conditions and moment restrictions in dynamic panel data models. *Journal of Econometrics, 87*(1), 115–143. doi:10.1016/S0304-4076(98)00009-8

Bocken, N., Miller, K., Weissbrod, I., Holgado, M., & Evans, S. (2018). *Slowing resource loops in the Circular Economy: an experimentation approach in fashion retail*. Available in https://www.researchgate.net/profile/Nancy_Bocken/publication/326587900_Slowing_resource_loops_in_the_Circular_Economy_an_experimentation_approach_in_fashion_retail/links/5b58270b0f7e9bc79a60aeeb/Slowing-resource-loops-in-the-Circular-Economy-an-experimentation-approach-in-fashion-retail.pdf

Bocken, N. M. P., Short, S. W., Rana, P., & Evans, S. (2014). A literature and practice review to develop sustainable business model archetypes. *Journal of Cleaner Production, 65*, 42–56. doi:10.1016/j.jclepro.2013.11.039

Boiten, V. J., Han, L.-C. S., & Tyler, D. (n.d.). *Circular economy stakeholder perspectives: Textile collection strategies to support material circularity*. Available in http://resyntex.eu/images/downloads/ValrieJBoiten_Textile _collection_strategies.pdf

BP. (2015). *Energy Outlook Global Insights 2035*. Retrieved from https://www.bp.com/content/dam/bp/pdf/energy-economics/energy-outlook-2015/bp-energy-outlook-2035-booklet.pdf

Braga, S. Jr, Merlo, E. M., & Nagano, M. S. (2008). A comparative study of reverse logistics practices in midsize retail. *Proceedings of Symposium on Production, Logistics and International Operations Management*.

Brauers, W. K., & Zavadskas, E. K. (2006). The MOORA method and its application to privatization in a transition economy. *Control and Cybernetics, 35*, 445–469.

Brazil. (2010). *Federal Law 12,305, of August 2, 2010. Institutes the National Policy on Solid Waste. Official Gazette*. Brasília, DF: Federative Republic of Brazil, Executive Branch.

Breusch, T. S., & Pagan, A. R. (1980). The Lagrange Multiplier Test and İts Applications to Model Specification in Econometrics. *The Review of Economic Studies, 47*(1), 239–253. doi:10.2307/2297111

Brounen, D., de Jong, A., & Koedijk, K. C. G. (2004). *Corporate Finance in Europe Confronting Theory with Practice*. doi:10.2139srn.559415

Brown, J. R., & Petersen, B. C. (2009). Why has the investment-cash flow sensitivity declined so sharply? Rising R&D and equity market developments. *Journal of Banking & Finance*, *33*(5), 971–984. doi:10.1016/j.jbankfin.2008.10.009

Business Commitment to Recycling (CEMPRE). (2015). *Cempre review 2015: An Overview of Recycling in Brazil*. Retrieved from http://cempre.org.br/artigo-publicacao/artigos

Byington, C. S., Watson, M., & Edwards, D. (2004). Data-driven neural network methodology to remaining life predictions for aircraft actuator components. In *Aerospace Conference* (vol. 6, pp. 3581-3589). IEEE. 10.1109/AERO.2004.1368175

Byoun, S. (2007). *Financial Flexibility, Leverage, and Firm Size*. Hankamer School of Business: Baylor University.

Byoun, S. (2011). *Financial Flexibility and Capital Structure Decision*. SSRN Electronic Journal; doi:10.2139srn.1108850

Callefi, M., Barbosa, W. P., & Ramos, D. V. (2017). The role of reverse logistics for companies: Fundamentals and importance. *R. Gest. Industr*, *13*(4), 171–187.

Camacho-Otero, J., Pettersen, I. N., & Boks, C. (2017). Consumer and user acceptance in the circular economy: what are researchers missing? In *PLATE: Product Lifetimes And The Environment*. TU Delft.

Camacho-Otero, J., Pettersen, I. N., & Boks, C. (2017). Consumer and user acceptance in the circular economy: what are researchers missing? In C. A. Bakker & R. Mugge (Eds.), *PLATE: Product Lifetimes and The Environment – Research in Design Series* (Vol. 9, pp. 65–69). Netherlands: Delft University of Technology and IOS Press.

Caniato, F., Caridi, M., Crippa, L., & Moretto, A. (2012). Environmental sustainability in fashion supply chains: An exploratory case based research. *International Journal of Production Economics*, *135*(2), 659–670. doi:10.1016/j.ijpe.2011.06.001

Cansaran, D. D. (2010). *Çevre-sağlık ilişkisi ekseninde tıbbi atık yönetimi (Yayınlanmamış doktora tezi)*. Ankara: Ankara Üniversitesi Sosyal Bilimler Enstitüsü.

Caribbean Development Bank. (2018). Financing the blue economy. *A Caribbean Development Opportunity*. Retrieved August 13, 2018 from, http://issuu.com/caribank/docs/financing_the_blue_economy-_a_carib?e=21431045/61831833

Carter, C. R., & Ellram, L. M. (1998). Reverse Logistics: A review of the literature and framework for future research. *International Journal of Business Logistics*, *19*(3), 85–103.

Cesaro, A., & Belgiorno, V. (2017). Sustainability of medical waste management in different sized health care facilities. *Waste and Biomass Valorization*, *8*(5), 1819–1827. doi:10.100712649-016-9730-y

Chakraborty, S. (2011). Applications of the MOORA method for decision making in manufacturing environment. *International Journal of Advanced Manufacturing Technology*, *54*(9-12), 1155–1166. doi:10.100700170-010-2972-0

Chang, B., Chang, C. W., & Wu, C. H. (2011). Fuzzy DEMATEL method for developing supplier selection criteria. *Expert Systems with Applications*, *38*(3), 1850–1858. doi:10.1016/j.eswa.2010.07.114

Chang, M., Jang, H. B., Li, Y. M., & Kim, D. (2017). The relationship between the efficiency, service quality and customer satisfaction for state-owned commercial banks in China. *Sustainability*, *9*(12), 2163. doi:10.3390u9122163

Chapman, J. (2015). *Emotionally Durable Design: Objects, Experiences and Empathy*. London: Routledge. doi:10.4324/9781315738802

Charonis, G. (2012). Degrowth, steady state economics and the circular economy: three distinct yet increasingly converging alternative discourses to economic growth for achieving environmental sustainability and social equity. *World Economic Association Sustainability Conference 2012*. Retrieved from http://sustainabilityconference2012.worldeconomicsassociation.org/wp-content/uploads/WEASustainabilityConference2012_Charonis_Alternative-Discoursesto-Economic-Growth.pdf

Chartier, Y., Emmanuel, J., Pieper, U., Prüss, A., Rushbrook, P., Stringer, R., ... Zghondi, R. (Eds.). (2014). *Safe management of wastes from health-care activities* (2nd ed.). Geneva: World Health Organization Press.

Chatterjee, A., Ghosh, C., & Bandyopadhyay, S. (2009). Assessing students' rating in higher education: A SERVQUAL approach. *Total Quality Management, 20*(10), 1095–1109. doi:10.1080/14783360903247114

Chaudhary, R., & Bisai, S. (2018). Factors influencing green purchase behavior of millennials in India. *Management of Environmental Quality, 29*(5), 798–812. doi:10.1108/MEQ-02-2018-0023

Chung, C. J., & Wee, H. M. (2008). Green-component life-cycle value on design and reverse manufacturing in some-closed supply chain. *International Journal of Production Economics, 113*(2), 528–545. doi:10.1016/j.ijpe.2007.10.020

Cleary, S. (1999). The Relationship between Firm Investment and Financial Status. *The Journal of Finance, 54*(2), 673–692. doi:10.1111/0022-1082.00121

Cocca, S., & Ganz, W. (2015). Requirements for developing green services. *Service Industries Journal, 35*(4), 179–196. doi:10.1080/02642069.2014.990002

Commonwealth Secretariat. (2016). The blue economy and small states. *Commonwealth Blue Economy Series*. Retrieved August 15, 2018 from http://www.cpahq.org/cpahq/Cpadocs/The%20Blue%20Economy%20and%20Small%20States.pdf

Conduct risk. (n.d.). In *Market supervision update, 57*. Australian Securities and Investment Commission. Retrieved from https://asic.gov.au/about-asic/corporate-publications/newsletters/asic-market-supervision-update/asic-market-supervision-update-previous-issues/market-supervison-update-issue-57/

Corrado, M., & Ross, M. (1990). Green Issues in Britain and the Value of Green Research Data. In *Esomar Annual Congress: Environmental Issues in the 90's* (pp. 347-369).

Curry, A., & Sinclair, E. (2002). Assessing the quality of physiotherapy services using SERVQUAL. *International Journal of Health Care Quality Assurance, 15*(5), 197–205. doi:10.1108/09526860210437412

D'Souza, C. (2004). Ecolabel programmes: A stakeholder (consumer) perspective. *Corporate Communications, 9*(3), 179–188. doi:10.1108/13563280410551105

Dabholkar, P. A. (2015). How to improve perceived service quality by increasing customer participation. In *Proceedings of the 1990 academy of marketing science (AMS) annual conference* (pp. 483-487). Springer. 10.1007/978-3-319-13254-9_97

Dahlquist, M. (2014). *Does Economic Growth reduce Poverty? An Empirical Analysis of the Relationship between Poverty and Economic Growth across Low- and Middle-income Countries, illustrated by the Case of Brazil*. Södertörn University. Retrieved from http://www.diva-portal.org/smash/get/diva2:747531/FULLTEXT01.p

Dandume, M. Y. (2014). Financial Sector Development, Economic Growth and Poverty Reduction: New Evidence From Nigeria. Çankırı Karatekin University. *Journal of the Faculty of Economics and Administrative Sciences, 4*(2), 2–22.

Data Privacy Day: A call for better privacy practices. (2016). Retrieved from https://www.trendmicro.com/vinfo/us/security/news/online-privacy/data-privacy-day-a-call-for-better-privacy-practices

Data Privacy Day: Why data privacy awareness is important. (2015). Retrieved from https://www.trendmicro.com/vinfo/us/security/news/online-privacy/data-privacy-day-why-data-privacy-is-important

Davis, D., & Donald, F. (2001). Challenges for economic policy in sustainable management of marine natural resources. *Ecological Economics*, *36*(2), 223–236. doi:10.1016/S0921-8009(00)00251-2

De Brito, M. P., & Dekker, R. (2003). *A Framework for Reverse Logistics*. Retrieved July 18, 2018, from https://repub.eur.nl/pub/354/ERS-2003-045-LIS.pdf

De Brito, M. P., Carbone, V., & Blanquart, C. M. (2008). Towards a sustainable fashion retail supply chain in Europe: Organisation and performance. *International Journal of Production Economics*, *114*(2), 534–553. doi:10.1016/j.ijpe.2007.06.012

De Faria, H. Jr, Costa, J. G. S., & Olivas, J. L. M. (2015). A review of monitoring methods for predictive maintenance of electric power transformers based on dissolved gas analysis. *Renewable & Sustainable Energy Reviews*, *46*, 201–209. doi:10.1016/j.rser.2015.02.052

De Jong, A., Verbeek, M., & Verwijmeren, P. (2012). Des Financial Flexibility Reduce Investment Distortions? *Journal of Financial Research*, *35*(2), 243–259. doi:10.1111/j.1475-6803.2012.01316.x

de Souza Barbosa, A., Shayani, R. A., & de Oliveira, M. A. G. (2018). A multi-criteria decision analysis method for regulatory evaluation of electricity distribution service quality. *Utilities Policy*, *53*, 38–48. doi:10.1016/j.jup.2018.06.002

DeAngelo, H., & DeAngelo, L. (2007). *Capital Structure, Payout Policy, and Financial Flexibility*. SSRN Electronic Journal; doi:10.2139srn.916093

DeAngelo, H., DeAngelo, L., & Whited, T. M. (2011). Capital structure dynamics and transitory debt. *Journal of Financial Economics*, *99*(2), 235–261. doi:10.1016/j.jfineco.2010.09.005

Deb, S., & Ahmed, M. A. (2018). Determining the service quality of the city bus service based on users' perceptions and expectations. *Travel Behaviour and Society*, *12*, 1–10. doi:10.1016/j.tbs.2018.02.008

Defee, C. C., Esper, T., & Mollenkopf, D. (2009). Leveraging closed-loop orientation and leadership for environmental sustainaibility. *Supply Chain Management*, *14*(2), 87–98. doi:10.1108/13598540910941957

Delone, W. H., & McLean, E. R. (2003). The DeLone and McLean model of information systems success: A ten-year update. *Journal of Management Information Systems*, *19*(4), 9–30. doi:10.1080/07421222.2003.11045748

Demajorovic, J., & Massote, B. (2017). Packaging Sector Agreement: Evaluation In Light Of Extended Producer Responsibility. *Journal of Business Administration*, *57*(5), 470–482. doi:10.15900034-759020170505

Demir, F. (2009). Volatility of Short-term Capital Flows and Private Investment in Emerging Markets. *The Journal of Development Studies*, *45*(5), 672–692. doi:10.1080/00220380802582379

Deng, N. Q., Liu, L. Q., & Deng, Y. Z. (2018). Estimating the effects of restructuring on the technical and service-quality efficiency of electricity companies in China. *Utilities Policy*, *50*, 91–100. doi:10.1016/j.jup.2017.11.002

Denis, D. J. (2011). Financial flexibility and corporate liquidity. *Journal of Corporate Finance*, *17*(3), 667–674. doi:10.1016/j.jcorpfin.2011.03.006

Denis, D. J., & McKeon, S. B. (2012). Debt Financing and Financial Flexibility Evidence from Proactive Leverage Increases. *Review of Financial Studies*, *25*(6), 1897–1929. doi:10.1093/rfs/hhs005

Department for International Development. (2008). Growth: Building Jobs and Prosperity in Developing Countries. London: Department for International Development.

Dhar, R. L. (2015). Service quality and the training of employees: The mediating role of organizational commitment. *Tourism Management*, *46*, 419–430. doi:10.1016/j.tourman.2014.08.001

Dholakia, U. M., Bagozzi, R. P., & Pearo, L. K. (2004). A social influence model of consumer participation in network-and small-group-based virtual communities. *International Journal of Research in Marketing*, *21*(3), 241–263. doi:10.1016/j.ijresmar.2003.12.004

Dincer, H., Hacioglu, U., & Yuksel, S. (2016). Balanced scorecard-based performance assessment of Turkish banking sector with analytic network process. *International Journal of Decision Sciences & Applications-IJDSA*, *1*(1), 1–21.

Dinçer, H., Hacıoğlu, Ü., & Yüksel, S. (2017). Balanced scorecard based performance measurement of European airlines using a hybrid multicriteria decision making approach under the fuzzy environment. *Journal of Air Transport Management*, *63*, 17–33. doi:10.1016/j.jairtraman.2017.05.005

Dinçer, H., Yuksel, S., & Bozaykut-Buk, T. (2018). Evaluation of Financial and Economic Effects on Green Supply Chain Management With Multi-Criteria Decision-Making Approach: Evidence From Companies Listed in BIST. In *Handbook of Research on Supply Chain Management for Sustainable Development* (pp. 144–175). IGI Global. doi:10.4018/978-1-5225-5757-9.ch009

DiPietro, B. (2014). Difference Between Compliance, Ethics: interview with M. McMillan. *Risk & Compliance Journal*. Retrieved from: http://blogs.wsj.com/riskandcompliance/2014/06/30/the-difference-between-compliance-and-ethics/

Doğan, E. (2014). *Türkiye'de Yoksulluğun Ölçülmesi*. TC Kalkınma Bakanlığı Bölgesel Gelişme ve Yapısal Uyum Genel Müdürlüğü, Uzmanlık Tezi, Yayın.

Dowlatshahi, S. (2000). Developing a theory of reverse logistics. *Interfaces*, *30*(3), 143–155. doi:10.1287/inte.30.3.143.11670

Dulman, M. T., & Gupta, S. M. (2015). Disassembling and Remanufacturing End-of-Life Sensor Embedded Cell Phones. *Innovation and Supply Chain Management*, *9*(4), 111–117. doi:10.14327/iscm.9.111

Dulman, M. T., & Gupta, S. M. (2016). *Use of sensors for collection of end-of-life products. In Proceedings for the Northeast Region Decision Sciences Institute* (pp. 577–582). NEDSI.

Dulman, M. T., & Gupta, S. M. (2018a). Evaluation of Maintenance and EOL Operation Performance of Sensor-Embedded Laptops. *Logistics*, *2*(1), 3. doi:10.3390/logistics2010003

Dulman, M. T., & Gupta, S. M. (2018b). Maintenance and Remanufacturing Strategy: Using Sensors to Predict the Status of Wind Turbines. *Journal of Remanufacturing*. 8(3), 131-152.

Dunlap, R., & Jones, R. (2002). Environmental concern: Conceptual and measurement issues. In R. Dunlap & W. Michelson (Eds.), *Handbook of Environmental Sociology*. London: Greenwood.

Durif, F., Boivin, C., & Julien, C. (2010). In search of a green product definition. *Innovative Marketing*, *6*(1), 25–33.

EBRD. (2014). *Turkish Sustainable Energy Finance Facility (TURSEFF)*. Retrieved from Retrieved from https://www-cif.climateinvestmentfunds.org/sites/default/files/knowledge-documents/turseff_case_study_jan_2014_0.pdf

EBRD. (2015). https://www.ebrd.com/work-with-us/procurement/pn-46442.html

ECOALF. (2018). *Re-Born Fabrics*. Available in: https://ecoalf.com/gb/recycled-fabrics/

Efthymiou, K., Papakostas, N., Mourtzis, D., & Chryssolouris, G. (2012). On a predictive maintenance platform for production systems. *Procedia CIRP*, *3*, 221–226. doi:10.1016/j.procir.2012.07.039

Ekström, K. M., & Salomonson, N. (2014). Reuse and recycling of clothing and textiles—A network approach. *Journal of Macromarketing*, *34*(3), 383–399. doi:10.1177/0276146714529658

Elzinga, R., & Boon, W. (2018). *Consumer behaviour in a circular economy: Testing consumer willingness to participate in circular business models* (Master's thesis). Canon Europe and the University of Utrecht.

Emirmahmutoglu, F., & Kose, N. (2011). Testing for Granger Causality in Heterogeneous Mixed Panels. *Economic Modelling*, *28*(3), 870–876. doi:10.1016/j.econmod.2010.10.018

Energy Research Centre of the Netherlands. (2017).Retrieved from https://www.ecn.nl

English, S., & Hammond, S. (2015). *The Cost of compliance*. Thomson Reuters. Retrieved from https://thegrcbluebook.com/wp-content/uploads/2015/05/Cost-of-Compliance-2015-Thomson-Reuters.pdf

Epelbaum, M. (2004). *The influence of environmental management on competitiveness and business success* (Unpublished master dissertation). Polytechnic School, University of São Paulo, SP.

Erdoğan, S. (2015). The effect of capital structure on profitability: an empirical analysis. In Handbook of Research on Developing Sustainable Value in Economics, Finance, and Marketing (pp. 307-323). Hershey, PA: IGI Global.

Erdoğan, Ö. (2018). Tıbbi atık yönetimi. In A. Başustaoğlu & A. Z. Avcı (Eds.), *Hemşirelik uygulamalarında klinik mikrobiyoloji ve enfeksiyon hastalıkları*. Ankara: Hipokrat Kitabevi.

Erkal, G., Akıncı, M., & Yılmaz, Ö. (2015). Yoksulluk, Gelir Eşitsizliği ve Ekonomik Büyüme İlişkisi: Seçilmiş Doğu Avrupa ve Latin Amerika Ülkeleri İçin Ampirik Bir Analiz. *TISK Academy/TISK Akademi*, *10*(19), 66-87.

Ernst&Young & Boston College Center for Corporate Citizenship. (2016). *Value of Sustainability Reporting*. Retrieved from https://www.ey.com/Publication/vwLUAssets/EY_-_Value_of_sustainability_reporting/%24FILE/EY-Value-of-Sustainability-Reporting.pdf

Ernst&Young & Global Reporting Initiative. (2014). *Sustainability reporting – the time is now*. Retrieved from https://www.ey.com/Publication/vwLUAssets/EY-Sustainability-reporting-the-time-is-now/$FILE/EY-Sustainability-reporting-the-time-is-now.pdf

Ernst&Young & GreenBiz. (2013). *2013 Six growing trends in corporate sustainability*. Retrieved from http://www.ey.com/Publication/vwLUAssets/Six_growing_trends_in_corporate_sustainability_2013/$FILE/Six_growing_trends_in_corporate_sustainability_2013.pdf

Ethics (2014). In *BBC Ethics guide online*. Retrieved from http://www.bbc.co.uk/ethics/introduction/intro_1.shtml#h1

EU Directive 2014/95/EU of 22 October, 2014.

EU Directorate-General for Internal Market, Industry, Entrepreneurship and SMEs. (2017). *SMEs, resource efficiency and green markets, FL456 Eurobarometer report*. Retrieved from http://ec.europa.eu/commfrontoffice/publicopinion/index.cfm/survey/getsurveydetail/instruments/flash/surveyky/2151

EU. (2014). *What is Horizon2020*. Retrieved from https://ec.europa.eu/programmes/horizon2020/what-horizon-2020

EU. (2015). *Framework conditions to support emerging industries and clusters in the area of circular economy, European Cluster Observatory Case Study*. Retrieved from http://ec.europa.eu/DocsRoom/documents/16266/attachments/1/translations/en/renditions/native

EU. (2017a). *Circular Economy: Commission delivers on its promises, offers guidance on recovery of energy from waste and works with EIB to boost investment*. Retrieved from http://europa.eu/rapid/press-release_IP-17-104_en.htm

EU. (2017b). *Parliamentary Questions*. Retrieved from http://www.europarl.europa.eu/sides/getAllAnswers.do?reference=E-2017-002428&language=EN

EU. (2017c). *Launch of Horizon 2020 Work Programme for Research & Innovation 2018-2020*. EU.

EU. (2017d). *Research on advanced tools and technological development*. Retrieved from http://ec.europa.eu/research/participants/portal/desktop/en/opportunities/h2020/topics/lc-sc3-es-6-2019.html

EU. (2017e). *Review of Waste Policy and Legislation*. Retrieved from http://ec.europa.eu/environment/waste/target_review.htm

EU. (2018a). *Circular Economy, Implementation of the Circular Economy Action Plan*. Retrieved from http://ec.europa.eu/environment/circular-economy/index_en.htm

EU. (2018b). *Energy, Climate and Environment*. Retrieved from http://ec.europa.eu/environment/integration/energy/index_en.htm

EU. (2018c). *Horizon2020 Energy Info Day*. Retrieved from https://ec.europa.eu/inea/en/news-events/events/horizon-2020-energy-info-day

Euromonitor. (2018a). *Turkey: Country Profile*. Retrieved from https://www.euromonitor.com

Euromonitor. (2018b). *Turkey's Currency Crash Worsens Outlook for the Economy*. Retrieved from https://www.euromonitor.com

Euromonitor. (2018c). *Income and Expenditure: Turkey*. Retrieved from https://www.euromonitor.com

European Commission. (2017, June). Sustainable blue economy productive seas and oceans. *Research & Innovation Projects for Policy*. Retrieved August 15, 2018 from https://ec.europa.eu/info/sites/info/files/bluegrowth_p4p-report_2017.pdf

European Commission. (2018). *Introducing the sustainable blue economy finance principles*. Retrieved 16 August, 2018 from https://ec.europa.eu/maritimeaffairs/sites/maritimeaffairs/files/introducing-sustainable-blue-economy-finance-principles_en.pdf

European Parliament. (2014). Directive 2014/57/EU of 16 April 2014 of the European Parliament and of the Council on criminal sanctions for market abuse (market abuse directive).

European Parliament. (2014). Regulation (EU) of 16 April 2014 No 596/2014 of the European Parliament and of the Council on market abuse (market abuse regulation).

European Parliament. (2016). *Circular economy package: Four legislative proposals on waste*. Retrieved from http://www.europarl.europa.eu/EPRS/EPRS-Briefing-573936-Circular-economy-package-FINAL.pdf

European Parliament. (2018). *Circular economy package: Four legislative proposals on waste*. Retrieved from http://www.europarl.europa.eu/thinktank/en/document.html?reference=EPRS_BRI(2018)614766

Eurostat. (2018a). *People at risk of poverty or social exclusion*. Retrieved from http://ec.europa.eu/eurostat/tgm/table.do?tab=table&init=1&plugin=1&language=en&pcode=tipslc10

Eurostat. (2018b). *Total General Government Expenditure, Percentage of GDP*. Retrieved from http://appsso.eurostat.ec.europa.eu/nui/submitViewTableAction.do

Fahey, B. (2016, August 24). *Culture of compliance: progress to the next level?* Educational seminar at MTS, Moscow, Russia.

Faisal, M. N. (2010). Sustainable supply chains: A study of interaction among the enablers. *Business Process Management Journal, 16*(3), 508–529. doi:10.1108/14637151011049476

Fama, E. F., & French, K. R. (2005). Financing decisions: Who issues stock? *Journal of Financial Economics, 76*(3), 549–582. doi:10.1016/j.jfineco.2004.10.003

FAO. (n.d.). *Blue growth initiative.* Retrieved August 18, 2018 from http://www.fao.org/3/a-i7862e.pdf

Farquhar, P. H. (1989). Managing brand equity. *Marketing research, 1*(3).

Farrant, L., Olsen, S. I., & Wangel, A. (2010). Environmental benefits from reusing clothes. *The International Journal of Life Cycle Assessment, 15*(7), 726–736. doi:10.100711367-010-0197-y

Faulkender, M., Flannery, M. J., Hankins, K. W., & Smith, J. M. (2012). Cash flows and leverage adjustments. *Journal of Financial Economics, 103*(3), 632–646. doi:10.1016/j.jfineco.2011.10.013

Ferrando, A., Marchica, M.-T., & Mura, R. (2017). Financial Flexibility and Investment Ability Across the Euro Area and the UK: Financial Flexibility and Investment Ability. *European Financial Management, 23*(1), 87–126. doi:10.1111/eufm.12091

Financial Actions Task Force. (n.d.). *What is money laundering?* Retrieved from http://www.fatf-gafi.org/faq/money-laundering/

Fishbein, M., & Ajzen, I. (1975). *Belief, attitude, intention and behavior: an introduction to theory and research.* Reading, MA: Addison-Wesley.

Fisher, R. J., & Price, L. L. (1992). An investigation into the social context of early adoption behavior. *The Journal of Consumer Research, 19*(3), 477–486. doi:10.1086/209317

Fitch Ratings. (2018a). *Turkey Moves Insufficient to Restore Policy Credibility.* Retrieved from https://www.fitchratings.com

Fitch Ratings. (2018b). *Turkey Faces Lower Growth, Lengthy Forced Adjustment.* Retrieved from https://www.fitchratings.com

Flannery, M. J., & Rangan, K. P. (2006). Partial adjustment toward target capital structures. *Journal of Financial Economics, 79*(3), 469–506. doi:10.1016/j.jfineco.2005.03.004

Fleischmann, M., Bloemhof-Ruwaard, J. M., Dekker, R., Van Der Laan, E., Van Nunen, J. A., & Van Wassenhove, L. N. (1997). *Quantitative models for reverse Logistics: A review* (pp. 1–21). Fontainebleau, France: INSEAD.

Fleischmann, M., Krikke, H. R., Dekker, R., & Flapper, S. D. P. (2000). A characterisation of logistics networks for product recovery. *Omega, 28*(6), 653–666. doi:10.1016/S0305-0483(00)00022-0

Fletcher, K. (2013). *Sustainable fashion and textiles: design journeys.* Routledge.

Fodness, D., Pitegoff, B. E., & Truly Sautter, E. (1993). From customer to competitor: Consumer cooption in the service sector. *Journal of Services Marketing, 7*(3), 18–25. doi:10.1108/08876049310044529

Ford, J. B., Paparoidamis, N., & Chumpitaz, R. (2015). Service quality, customer satisfaction, value and loyalty: An empirical investigation of the airline services industry. In *The Sustainable Global Marketplace* (pp. 187–187). Cham: Springer. doi:10.1007/978-3-319-10873-5_98

Fornell, C., & Larcker, D. F. (1981). Evaluating structural equation models with unobservable variables and measurement error. *JMR, Journal of Marketing Research, 18*(1), 39–50. doi:10.2307/3151312

Franke, C., Basdere, B., Ciupek, M., & Seliger, S. (2006). Remanufacturing of mobile phones—capacity, program and facility adaptation planning. *Omega, 34*(6), 562–570. doi:10.1016/j.omega.2005.01.016

Frank, M. Z., & Goyal, V. K. (2008). *Profits and Capital Structure*. SSRN Electronic Journal; doi:10.2139srn.1104886

Gadenne, D., Sharma, B., Kerr, D., & Smith, T. (2011). The influence of consumers' environmental beliefs and attitudes on energy saving behaviours. *Energy Policy, 39*(12), 7684–7694. doi:10.1016/j.enpol.2011.09.002

Gamba, A., & Triantis, A. (2008). The Value of Financial Flexibility. *The Journal of Finance, 63*(5), 2263–2296. doi:10.1111/j.1540-6261.2008.01397.x

Gao, Q., Shi, Y., Mo, D., Nie, J., Yang, M., Rozelle, S., & Sylvia, S. (2018). Medical waste management in three areas of rural China. *PLoS One, 13*(7), 1–13. doi:10.1371/journal.pone.0200889 PMID:30028841

Gaur, J., Amini, M., Banerjee, P., & Gupta, R. (2015). Drivers of consumer purchase intentions for remanufactured products: A study of Indian consumers relocated to the USA. *Qualitative Market Research, 18*(1), 30–47. doi:10.1108/QMR-01-2014-0001

Geissdoerfer, M., Savaget, P., Bocken, N., & Hultink, E. J. (2017). The Circular Economy – A new sustainability paradigm? *Journal of Cleaner Production, 143*, 757–768. doi:10.1016/j.jclepro.2016.12.048

Gencer, Y. G. (2017). Supply chain management in retailing business. *Ethics and sustainability in global supply chain management*, 197-210.

Gencer, Y. G., & Akkucuk, U. (2016). Product Recalls as an Important Category of Reverse Logistics. *DEStech Transactions on Environment, Energy and Earth Sciences.*

Gencer, Y. G., & Akkucuk, U. (2016). Reverse Logistics: Automobile Recalls and Other Conditions. In U. Akkucuk (Ed.), Handbook of Research on Waste Management Techniques for Sustainability (pp. 125-154). Hershey, PA: IGI Global.

Gencer, Y. G. (2016). Mystery of recycling: Glass and aluminum examples. In *Handbook of research on waste management techniques for sustainability* (pp. 172–191). IGI Global. doi:10.4018/978-1-4666-9723-2.ch009

Gencer, Y. G., & Akkucuk, U. (2016). Reverse Logistics: Automobile Recalls and Other Conditions. In U. Akkucuk (Ed.), *Handbook of Research on Waste Management Techniques for Sustainability* (pp. 125–154). IGI Global. doi:10.4018/978-1-4666-9723-2.ch007

Gencer, Y. G., & Akkucuk, U. (2017). Measuring Quality in Automobile Aftersales: AutoSERVQUAL Scale. *Amfiteatru Economic, 19*(44), 110.

Geng, Y., & Doberstein, B. (2008). Developing the circular economy in China: Challenges and opportunities for achieving'leapfrog development'. *International Journal of Sustainable Development and World Ecology, 15*(3), 231–239. doi:10.3843/SusDev.15.3:6

Georgiadis, P., & Athanasiou, E. (2010). The impact of two-product joint lifecycles on capacity planning of remanufacturing networks. *European Journal of Operational Research, 202*(2), 420–433. doi:10.1016/j.ejor.2009.05.022

Georgiadis, P., Vlachos, D., & Tagaras, G. (2006). The impact of product lifecycle on capacity planning of closed-loop supply chains with remanufacturing. *Production and Operations Management, 15*(4), 514–527. doi:10.1111/j.1937-5956.2006.tb00160.x

Gerner-Beuerle, C., Paech, P., & Schuster, E. P. (2013). *Study on Director's duty and liability*. London School of Economics. Retrieved from http://ec.europa.eu/internal_market/company/docs/board/2013-study-analysis_en.pdf

Gharakhani, D. (2012). The evaluation of supplier selection criteria by fuzzy DEMATEL method. *Journal of Basic and Applied Scientific Research*, *2*(4), 3215–3224.

Ghisellini, P., Cialani, C., & Ulgiati, S. (2016). A review on circular economy: the expected transition to a balanced interplay of environmental and economic systems. *Journal of Cleaner Production, 114*, 1-22. Retrieved from https://www.sciencedirect.com/science/article/pii/S0959652615012287

Ghisellini, P., Cialani, C., & Ulgiati, S. (2016). A review on circular economy: The expected transition to a balanced interplay of environmental and economic systems. *Journal of Cleaner Production*, *114*, 11–32. doi:10.1016/j.jclepro.2015.09.007

Ghorabaee, M. K., Amiri, M., Zavadskas, E. K., Turskis, Z., & Antucheviciene, J. (2017). A new hybrid simulation-based assignment approach for evaluating airlines with multiple service quality criteria. *Journal of Air Transport Management*, *63*, 45–60. doi:10.1016/j.jairtraman.2017.05.008

Giovine, H., & Sacomano, J. B. (2007). Reverse logistics as an instrument for improving the environment: A case study on the recycling plant for household appliances of matsushita. *Proceeding of National Meeting of Production Engineering*.

Global Reporting Initiative. (n.d.). *About Sustainability Reporting*. Retrieved from https://www.globalreporting.org/information/sustainability-reporting/Pages/default.aspx

Global Reporting Initiative. (n.d.). *Benefits of reporting*. Retrieved from https://www.globalreporting.org/information/sustainability-reporting/Pages/reporting-benefits.aspx

Gonçalves-Dias, S., & Teodósio, A. (2011). Perspectives of analysis of corporate environmentalism beyond demonization and sanctification. *Journal of Social and Environmental Management, 5*(2), 3-17.

Goodson, S. (2016, May 6). Stop acting like auditors! *Paper presented at International Academic Forum 2016: Professional and Academic Innovation in Internal Auditing*, Istanbul, Bogazici University.

Govindan, K., Khodaverdi, R., & Vafadarnikjoo, A. (2015). Intuitionistic fuzzy based DEMATEL method for developing green practices and performances in a green supply chain. *Expert Systems with Applications*, *42*(20), 7207–7220. doi:10.1016/j.eswa.2015.04.030

Govindan, K., & Soleimani, H. (2017). A review of reverse logistics and closed-loop supply chains: A Journal of Cleaner Production focus. *Journal of Cleaner Production*, *142*, 371–384. doi:10.1016/j.jclepro.2016.03.126

Govindan, K., Soleimani, H., & Kannan, D. (2015). Reverse logistics and closed-loop supply chain: A comprehensive review to explore the future. *European Journal of Operational Research*, *240*(3), 603–626. doi:10.1016/j.ejor.2014.07.012

Graham, J. R., & Harvey, C. R. (2001). The theory and practice of corporate finance: Evidence from the field. *Journal of Financial Economics*, *60*(2–3), 187–243. doi:10.1016/S0304-405X(01)00044-7

Granger, C. W. (1969). Investigating Causal Relations by Econometric Models and Cross-Spectral Methods. *Econometrica*, *37*(3), 424–438. doi:10.2307/1912791

Greenland, S., Coshall, J., & Combe, I. (2006). Evaluating service quality and consumer satisfaction in emerging markets. *International Journal of Consumer Studies*, *30*(6), 582–590. doi:10.1111/j.1470-6431.2005.00484.x

Greenwald, G., & McLaughlin, J. (2016, March 1). Apple Wins Major Court Victory Against FBI in a Case Similar to San Bernardino. *The Intercept*. Retrieved from https://theintercept.com/2016/02/29/apple-wins-major-court-victory-in-its-battle-against-fbi-in-a-case-similar-to-san-bernardino/

Greer, I., & Hauptmeier, M. (2016). Management whipsawing: The staging of labor competition under globalization. *Industrial & Labor Relations Review*, *69*(1), 29–52. doi:10.1177/0019793915602254

Griskevicius, V., Tybur, J. M., & Van den Bergh, B. (2010). Going green to be seen: Status, reputation, and conspicuous conservation. *Journal of Personality and Social Psychology, 98*(3), 392–404. doi:10.1037/a0017346 PMID:20175620

Gu, H., & Ryan, C. (2008). Chinese clientele at Chinese hotels—preferences and satisfaction. *International Journal of Hospitality Management, 27*(3), 337–345. doi:10.1016/j.ijhm.2007.10.005

Guide, V. D. R., Harrison, T. P., & Wassenhove, L. (2003b). The challenge of closed-loop supply chains. *Interfaces, 33*(6), 3–6. doi:10.1287/inte.33.6.3.25182

Guide, V. D. R., Jayaraman, V., & Linton, J. (2003a). Building contingency planning for closed-loop supply chains with product recovery. *Journal of Operations Management, 21*(3), 259–279. doi:10.1016/S0272-6963(02)00110-9

Guide, V. D. R. Jr, Jayaraman, V., Srivastava, R., & Benton, W. C. (2000). Supply-chain management for recoverable manufacturing systems. *Interfaces, 30*(3), 125–142. doi:10.1287/inte.30.3.125.11656

Guide, V. D. R. Jr, & Li, J. (2010). The potential for cannibalization of new products sales by remanufactured products. *Decision Sciences, 41*(3), 547–572. doi:10.1111/j.1540-5915.2010.00280.x

Guide, V. D. R. Jr, & Spencer, M. S. (1997). Rough-cut capacity planning for remanufacturing firms. *Production Planning and Control, 8*(3), 237–244. doi:10.1080/095372897235299

Guide, V. D. R. Jr, Srivastava, R., & Spencer, M. S. (1997). An evaluation of capacity planning techniques in a remanufacturing environment. *International Journal of Production Research, 35*(1), 67–82. doi:10.1080/002075497195984

Guide, V. D. R. Jr, & Van Wassenhove, L. N. (2001). Managing product returns for remanufacturing. *Production and Operations Management, 10*(2), 142–155. doi:10.1111/j.1937-5956.2001.tb00075.x

Guide, V. D. R. Jr, & Van Wassenhove, L. N. (2009). The evolution of closed-loop supply chain research. *Operations Research, 57*(1), 10–18. doi:10.1287/opre.1080.0628

Gungor, A., & Gupta, S. M. (1999). Issues in environmentally conscious manufacturing and product recovery: A survey. *Computers & Industrial Engineering, 36*(4), 811–853. doi:10.1016/S0360-8352(99)00167-9

Guo, K., & Stepanyan, V. (2011). Determinants of bank credit in emerging market economies. *International Monetary Fund.*

Gupta, S. M., & Ilgin, M. A. (2018). *Multiple Criteria Decision Making Applications in Environmentally Conscious Manufacturing and Product Recovery.* Boca Raton, FL: CRC Press.

Gurău, C., & Ranchhod, A. (2005). International green marketing: A comparative study of British and Romanian firms. *International Marketing Review, 22*(5), 547–561. doi:10.1108/02651330510624381

Güvez, H., Dege, M., & Eren, T. (2012). Medical waste collection with vehicle routing problem in Kırıkkale. *Uluslararası Mühendislik Araştırma ve Geliştirme Dergisi, 4*(1), 41–45.

H & M. (2018). *Sustentability Report 2017 Summary.* Available in https://about.hm.com/content/dam/hmgroup/countrysites/es/documents/Executive%20Summary%20SPAIN%20FINAL.pdf

Hair, J. F., Black, W. C., Babin, B. J., Anderson, R. E., & Tatham, R. L. (2006). *Multivariate data analysis* (Vol. 6).

Hair, F. J., Ringle, C. M., & Sarstedt, M. (2011). PLS-SEM: Indeed a silver bullet. *Journal of Marketing Theory and Practice, 19*(2), 139–152. doi:10.2753/MTP1069-6679190202

Hair, J. F. Jr, Hult, G. T. M., Ringle, C., & Sarstedt, M. (2014a). *A primer on partial least squares structural equation modeling (PLS-SEM).* Sage Publications.

Hair, J.F., Jr., Sarstedt, M., Hopkins, L., & Kuppelwieser, V.G. (2014b). Partial least squares structural equation modeling (PLS-SEM) An emerging tool in business research. *European Business Review*, *26*(2), 106–121. doi:10.1108/EBR-10-2013-0128

Han, H., & Kim, Y. (2010). An investigation of green hotel customers' decision formation: Developing an extended model of the theory of planned behavior. *International Journal of Hospitality Management*, *29*(4), 659–668. doi:10.1016/j.ijhm.2010.01.001

Hanning, J., & Connett, D. (2015, July 4). London is now the global money-laundering centre for the drug trade, says crime expert. *Independent*. Retrieved from http://www.independent.co.uk

Hapsari, R., Clemes, M., & Dean, D. (2016). The mediating role of perceived value on the relationship between service quality and customer satisfaction: Evidence from Indonesian airline passengers. *Procedia Economics and Finance*, *35*, 388–395. doi:10.1016/S2212-5671(16)00048-4

Haque, O. S., Freitas, J. D., Bursztajn, H. J., Cosgrove, L., Gopal, A. A., & Paul, R. … Wolfman, S. (2013). *The ethics of pharmaceutical industry influence in medicine*. Ministry of Education, Israel. Retrieved from http://medlaw.haifa.ac.il/index/main/4/EthicsofPharmaceutical.pdf

Hartmann, P., Apaolaza Ibáñez, V., & Forcada Sainz, F. J. (2005). Green branding effects on attitude: Functional versus emotional positioning strategies. *Marketing Intelligence & Planning*, *23*(1), 9–29. doi:10.1108/02634500510577447

Hartmann, P., & Apaolaza-Ibáñez, V. (2012). Consumer attitude and purchase intention toward green energy brands: The roles of psychological benefits and environmental concern. *Journal of Business Research*, *65*(9), 1254–1263. doi:10.1016/j.jbusres.2011.11.001

Hashemian, H. M. (2011). Wireless sensors for predictive maintenance of rotating equipment in research reactors. *Annals of Nuclear Energy*, *38*(2), 665–680. doi:10.1016/j.anucene.2010.09.012

Hassan, M. M., Ahmed, S. A., Rahman, K. A., & Biswas, T. K. (2008). Pattern of medical waste management: Existing scenario in Dhaka City, Bangladesh. *BMC Public Health*, *8*(36). PMID:18221548

Hazen, B. T., Boone, C. A., Wang, Y., & Khor, K. S. (2017). Perceived quality of remanufactured products: Construct and measure development. *Journal of Cleaner Production*, *142*, 716–726. doi:10.1016/j.jclepro.2016.05.099

Hazen, B. T., Overstreet, R. E., Jones-Farmer, L. A., & Field, H. S. (2012). The role of ambiguity tolerance in consumer perception of remanufactured products. *International Journal of Production Economics*, *135*(2), 781–790. doi:10.1016/j.ijpe.2011.10.011

Healy, J. (n.d.). Why the blue economy matters? Ireland as a marine hub. *KPMG*. Retrieved from https://home.kpmg.com/ie/en/home/insights/2018/03/blue-economy.html

He, P., Lü, F., Zhang, H., & Shao, L. (2013). Recent developments in the area of waste as a resource, with particular reference to the circular economy as a guiding principle, in waste as a resource. In R. E. Hester & R. M. Harrison (Eds.), *Issues in Environmental Science and Technology No 37*. The Royal Society of Chemistry.

Herzog, M. A., Marwala, T., & Heyns, P. S. (2009). Machine and component residual life estimation through the application of neural networks. *Reliability Engineering & System Safety*, *94*(2), 479–489. doi:10.1016/j.ress.2008.05.008

Holme, R., & Watts, P. (2000, January). *Corporate Social Responsibility: making good business sense*. Retrieved from http://www.ceads.org.ar/downloads/Making%20good%20business%20sense.pdf

Hossain, M. S., Santhanam, A., Norulaini, N. A. N., & Omar, A. K. M. (2011). Clinical solid waste management practices and its impact on human health and environment – A review. *Waste Management (New York, N.Y.), 31*(4), 754–766. doi:10.1016/j.wasman.2010.11.008 PMID:21186116

Hsu, C. L., Chang, C. Y., & Yansritakul, C. (2017). Exploring purchase intention of green skincare products using the theory of planned behavior: Testing the moderating effects of country of origin and price sensitivity. *Journal of Retailing and Consumer Services, 34*, 145–152. doi:10.1016/j.jretconser.2016.10.006

Huang, H. C., Chang, Y. T., Yeh, C. Y., & Liao, C. W. (2014). Promote the price promotion: The effects of price promotions on customer evaluations in coffee chain stores. *International Journal of Contemporary Hospitality Management, 26*(7), 1065–1082. doi:10.1108/IJCHM-05-2013-0204

Huang, Y., Yang, L., Tang, T., Gao, Z., & Cao, F. (2017). Joint train scheduling optimization with service quality and energy efficiency in urban rail transit networks. *Energy, 138*, 1124–1147. doi:10.1016/j.energy.2017.07.117

Hu, H., & Zhang, J. (2013). The evaluation system for cloud service quality based on servqual. In *Proceedings of the 2012 International Conference on Information Technology and Software Engineering* (pp. 577-584). Springer. 10.1007/978-3-642-34528-9_60

Human Development Report. (2016). United Nations Development Programme. Retrieved from http://hdr.undp.org/en/2016-report

Humayun, A., & Zafar, N. (2014). Pakistan's 'blue economy' potential and prospects. *Polish Perspectives, 11*(1), 57–76. doi:10.13169/polipers.11.1.0057

Hussain, R., Al Nasser, A., & Hussain, Y. K. (2015). Service quality and customer satisfaction of a UAE-based airline: An empirical investigation. *Journal of Air Transport Management, 42*, 167–175. doi:10.1016/j.jairtraman.2014.10.001

Hu, T. L., Sheu, J. B., & Haung, K. H. (2002). A reverse logistics cost minimization model for the treatment of hazardous wastes. *Transportation Research Part E, Logistics and Transportation Review, 38*(6), 457–473. doi:10.1016/S1366-5545(02)00020-0

Ibáñez, V. A., Hartmann, P., & Calvo, P. Z. (2006). Antecedents of customer loyalty in residential energy markets: Service quality, satisfaction, trust and switching costs. *Service Industries Journal, 26*(6), 633–650. doi:10.1080/02642060600850717

IEA. (2016). *Turkey 2016 Preview*. IEA.

Ilgin, M. A., & Gupta, S. M. (2010a). Environmentally conscious manufacturing and product recovery (ECMPRO): A review of the state of the art. *Journal of Environmental Management, 91*(3), 563–591. doi:10.1016/j.jenvman.2009.09.037 PMID:19853369

Ilgin, M. A., & Gupta, S. M. (2010b). Comparison of economic benefits of sensor embedded products and conventional products in a multi-product disassembly line. *Computers & Industrial Engineering, 59*(4), 748–763. doi:10.1016/j.cie.2010.07.031

Ilgin, M. A., & Gupta, S. M. (2011a). Evaluating the impact of sensor-embedded products on the performance of an air conditioner disassembly line. *International Journal of Advanced Manufacturing Technology, 53*(9-12), 1199–1216. doi:10.100700170-010-2891-0

Ilgin, M. A., & Gupta, S. M. (2011b). Performance improvement potential of sensor embedded products in environmental supply chains. *Resources, Conservation and Recycling, 55*(6), 580–592. doi:10.1016/j.resconrec.2010.05.001

Ilgin, M. A., & Gupta, S. M. (2011c). Recovery of sensor embedded washing machines using a multi-kanban controlled disassembly line. *Robotics and Computer-integrated Manufacturing, 27*(2), 318–334. doi:10.1016/j.rcim.2010.07.016

Ilgin, M. A., Gupta, S. M., & Battaïa, O. (2015). Use of MCDM techniques in environmentally conscious manufacturing and product recovery: State of the art. *Journal of Manufacturing Systems*, *37*, 746–758. doi:10.1016/j.jmsy.2015.04.010

Ilgin, M. A., Gupta, S. M., & Nakashima, K. (2011). Coping with disassembly yield uncertainty in remanufacturing using sensor embedded products. *Journal of Remanufacturing*, *1*(1), 1–14. doi:10.1186/2210-4690-1-7

Ilgin, M. A., Ondemir, O., & Gupta, S. M. (2014). An approach to quantify the financial benefit of embedding sensors into products for end-of-life management: A case study. *Production Planning and Control*, *25*(1), 26–43. doi:10.1080/09537287.2012.655801

ILOS. (2012). *Brazilian Panorama of Reverse Logistics of Post-Consumer Waste*. Paper presentation by Gisela Sousa, Mega Session: XVIII International Logistics Forum. Available at http://www.ilos.com.br/web/tag/residuos/

INDITEX. (2017). *Annual Report 2016*. Available in http://static.inditex.com/annual_report_2016/en/our-priorities/commitment-to-the-excellence-of-our-products/towards-a-circular-economy.php

INDITEX. (2018). *Annual Report 2017*. Retrieved from https://static.inditex.com/annual_report_2017/en

Insa, E., Zamorano, M., & López, R. (2010). Critical review of medical waste legislation in spain. *Resources, Conservation and Recycling*, *54*(12), 1048–1059. doi:10.1016/j.resconrec.2010.06.005

International compliance Association. (n.d.). *What is compliance?* Retrieved from http://www.int-comp.org/careers/a-career-in-compliance/what-is-compliance/

International Federation of Accountants. (2013). *ISAE 3000 (Revised), Assurance Engagements Other than Audits or Reviews of Historical Financial Information*. Author.

International Federation of Pharmaceutical Manufacturers & Associations. (2012). *Code of Practice*. Retrieved from http://www.ifpma.org/wp-content/uploads/2016/01/IFPMA_Code_of_Practice_2012_new_logo.pdf

International Organization for Standardization (2010). *ISO 26000:2010. Guidance to social responsibility*. ISO.

IPEA. (2010). *Research Report on Payment for Urban Environmental Services for Solid Waste Management*. IPEA. Available at: http://www.ipea.gov.br/portal/images/stories/PDFs/100514_relatpsau.pdf

Irajpour, A., Golsefid-Alavi, M., Hajimirza, M., & Soleimani-Nezhad, N. (2012). Evaluation of the most effective criteria in green supply chain management in automotive industries using the Fuzzy DEMATEL Method. *Journal of Basic and Applied Scientific Research*, *2*(9), 8952–8961.

ISO. (2014). ISO 19600 Compliance management systems – Guidelines.

Jain, S. K., & Gupta, G. (2004). Measuring service quality: SERVQUAL vs. SERVPERF scales. *Vikalpa*, *29*(2), 25–38. doi:10.1177/0256090920040203

Jaiswal, D., & Kant, R. (2018). Green purchasing behaviour: A conceptual framework and empirical investigation of Indian consumers. *Journal of Retailing and Consumer Services*, *41*, 60–69. doi:10.1016/j.jretconser.2017.11.008

Jamshidi, M. (2011). Reverse Logistics. In R. Z. Farahani, S. Rezapour, & L. Karder (Eds.), *Logistics Operations and management: Concepts and Models* (pp. 247–256). Elsevier. doi:10.1016/B978-0-12-385202-1.00013-X

Jensen, N. (2018). 8 steps to solve the ocean's plastic problem. *WEF*. Retrieved August 19, 2018 from https://www.weforum.org/agenda/2018/03/8-steps-to-solve-the-oceans-plastic-problem/

Jeong, J. S., & Ramírez-Gómez, Á. (2018). Optimizing the location of a biomass plant with a fuzzy-DEcision-MAking Trial and Evaluation Laboratory (F-DEMATEL) and multi-criteria spatial decision assessment for renewable energy management and long-term sustainability. *Journal of Cleaner Production, 182*, 509–520. doi:10.1016/j.jclepro.2017.12.072

Jernick, G. A., Suganthi, L., & Iniyan, S. (2018). Development and validation of multi-dimensional wind turbine service quality scale for measuring operations and maintenance service quality in wind energy sector. *International Journal of Productivity and Quality Management, 23*(1), 31–54. doi:10.1504/IJPQM.2018.088607

Jha, R., Biswal, B., & Biswal, U. D. (2001). *An Empirical Analysis of the Impact of Public Expenditures on Education and Health on Poverty in Indian States.* Working Papers 998. Queen's University, Department of Economics.

Jiménez-Parra, B., Rubio, S., & Vicente-Molina, M. A. (2014). Key drivers in the behavior of potential consumers of remanufactured products: A study on laptops in Spain. *Journal of Cleaner Production, 85*, 488–496. doi:10.1016/j.jclepro.2014.05.047

Jindal, A., & Sangwan, K. S. (2014). Closed loop supply chain network design and optimisation using fuzzy mixed integer linear programming model. *International Journal of Production Research, 52*(14), 4156–4173. doi:10.1080/00207543.2013.861948

Júnior, A. H. (2018). Reverse Logistics and Solid Waste: Challenges for the National Waste Policy (PNRS) in Brazil. In Handbook of Research on Supply Chain Management for Sustainable Development. IGI Global. DOI: 10.4018 / 978-1-5225-5757-9.ch015

Kalafatis, S. P., Pollard, M., East, R., & Tsogas, M. H. (1999). Green marketing and Ajzen's theory of planned behaviour: A cross-market examination. *Journal of Consumer Marketing, 16*(5), 441–460. doi:10.1108/07363769910289550

Kanchanapibul, M., Lacka, E., Wang, X., & Chan, H. K. (2014). An empirical investigation of green purchase behaviour among the young generation. *Journal of Cleaner Production, 66*, 528–536. doi:10.1016/j.jclepro.2013.10.062

Kant Hvass, K. (2016). *Weaving a path from waste to value: Exploring fashion industry business models and the circular economy.* Copenhagen Business School.

Kaplan, H. J. (2014, December 4). Corporate Criminal Liability for Insider Trading. Retrieved from https://www.americanbar.org/content/dam/aba/administrative/litigation/materials/2014/2014_sac/2014_sac/corporate_criminal_liability.authcheckdam.pdf

Kara, A. (n.d.). Yeni İletişim Ortamlarinda Pazarlama Faaliyetlerinin Kullanimi İle İlgili İçerik Analizi: Türk Organik Tarim Sektörü Örnek Olayi. *İşletme Ekonomi ve Yönetim Araştırmaları Dergisi, 1*(1), 17-33.

Kara, S., Mazhar, M., Kaebernick, H., & Ahmed, A. (2005). Determining the reuse potential of components based on life cycle data. *CIRP Annals-Manufacturing Technology, 54*(1), 1–4. doi:10.1016/S0007-8506(07)60036-5

Karaşan, A., & Kahraman, C. (2017). A novel intuitionistic fuzzy DEMATEL–ANP–TOPSIS integrated methodology for freight village location selection. *Journal of Intelligent & Fuzzy Systems*, 1-18.

Kazancoglu, Y., Kazancoglu, I., & Sagnak, M. (2018). Fuzzy DEMATEL-based green supply chain management performance: Application in cement industry. *Industrial Management & Data Systems, 118*(2), 412–431. doi:10.1108/IMDS-03-2017-0121

Kazemi, N., Modak, N. M., & Govindan, K. (2018). A review of reverse logistics and closed loop supply chain management studies published in IJPR: A bibliometric and content analysis. *International Journal of Production Research*, 1–24. doi:10.1080/00207543.2018.1471244

Kelton, D. W., Sadowski, R. P., & Sadowski, D. A. (2007). *Simulation with arena.* New York: McGraw-Hill.

Kennedy-Glans, D., & Dr. Schulz, B. (2005). *Corporate Integrity: a toolkit for managing beyond compliance*. Mississauga, Ontario: John Wiley & Sons, Canada, Ltd.

Keskin, G. A. (2015). Using integrated fuzzy DEMATEL and fuzzy C: Means algorithm for supplier evaluation and selection. *International Journal of Production Research*, *53*(12), 3586–3602. doi:10.1080/00207543.2014.980461

Kessel, M. (2014). Restoring the pharmaceutical industry's reputation. *Nature Biotechnology Journal, 32*, 983–990. Retrieved from http://www.nature.com/nbt/journal/v32/n10/full/nbt.3036.html

Khor, K.S., & Udin, Z.M. (2012). Impact of reverse logistics product disposition towards business performance in Malaysian E&E companies. *Journal of Supply Chain and Customer Relationship Management*. doi:10.5171/2012.699469

Khor, K. S., & Hazen, B. T. (2017). Remanufactured products purchase intentions and behaviour: Evidence from Malaysia. *International Journal of Production Research*, *55*(8), 2149–2162. doi:10.1080/00207543.2016.1194534

Kiki, R. A., Subagiarta, I. W.& Viphindrartin, S. (2015). Determinan Kemiskinan Di Kabupaten Jember Tahun 2003-2013. *Artikel Ilmiah Mahasiswa*.

Killi, A., Rapp, M. S., & Schmid, T. (2011). *Can Financial Flexibility Explain the Debt Conservatism Puzzle? Cross-Country Evidence from Listed Firms*. doi:10.2139srn.1814182

Kilponen, A. (2016). The blue economy and ocean health: part 2 - blue economy and decision-support frameworks. *OHI*. Retrieved August 6, 2018 from http://www.oceanhealthindex.org/news/blue-economy-and-decision-support-frameworks

Kilponen, A., & Mosher, L. (2017). The blue economy and ocean health: part 4: Working together for a successful blue economy. *Ocean Health Index*. Retrieved August 29, 2018 from http://www.oceanhealthindex.org/news/the-blue-economy-and-ocean-health-part-4

Kim, Y., & Choi, S. M. (2005). Antecedents of green purchase behavior: an examination of collectivism, environmental concern, and pce. In G. Menon & A. R. Rao (Eds.), *NA - Advances in Consumer Research* (Vol. 32, pp. 592–599). Duluth, MN: Association for Consumer Research.

King, A. M., & Burgess, S. C. (2005). The development of a remanufacturing platform design: A strategic response to the Directive on Waste Electrical and Electronic Equipment. *Proceedings of the Institution of Mechanical Engineers. Part B, Journal of Engineering Manufacture*, *219*(8), 623–631. doi:10.1243/095440505X32526

Kirchherr, J., Reike, D., & Hekkert, M. (2017). Conceptualizing the circular economy: An analysis of 114 definitions. *Resources, Conservation and Recycling*, *127*, 221–232. doi:10.1016/j.resconrec.2017.09.005

Kleine, R. E. III, Kleine, S. S., & Kernan, J. B. (1993). Mundane consumption and the self: A social-identity perspective. *Journal of Consumer Psychology*, *2*(3), 209–235. doi:10.1016/S1057-7408(08)80015-0

Koc, E. (2006). Total quality management and business excellence in services: The implications of all-inclusive pricing system on internal and external customer satisfaction in the Turkish tourism market. *Total Quality Management & Business Excellence*, *17*(7), 857–877. doi:10.1080/14783360600595252

Kónya, L. (2006). Exports and Growth: Granger Causality Analysis on OECD Countries With a Panel Data Approach. *Economic Modelling*, *23*(6), 978–992. doi:10.1016/j.econmod.2006.04.008

Kopicki, R., Berg, M., & Legg, L. L. (1993). *Reuse and recycling: reverse logistics opportunities*. Oak Brook, IL: Council of Logistics Management.

Korhonen, J., Nuur, C., Feldman, A., & Birkie, S. E. (2018, February). Circular economy as an essentially contested concept. *Journal of Cleaner Production*, *175*, 20. doi:10.1016/j.jclepro.2017.12.111

Korhoner, J., Honkasalo, A., & Seppala, J. (2018). Circular Economy: The Concept and its Limitations. *Ecological Economics*, *143*, 37–46. doi:10.1016/j.ecolecon.2017.06.041

Kotchen, M. J., & Reiling, S. D. (2000). Environmental attitudes, motivations, and contingent valuation of nonuse values: A case study involving endangered species. *Ecological Economics*, *32*(1), 93–107. doi:10.1016/S0921-8009(99)00069-5

Kouthouris, C., & Alexandris, K. (2005). Can service quality predict customer satisfaction and behavioral intentions in the sport tourism industry? An application of the SERVQUAL model in an outdoors setting. *Journal of Sport & Tourism*, *10*(2), 101–111. doi:10.1080/14775080500223165

KPMG Advisory N.V., Global Reporting Initiative, The Centre for Corporate Governance in Africa and United Nations Environment Programme. (2013). *Carrots and Sticks. Sustainability reporting policies worldwide – today's best practice, tomorrow's trends.* Retrieved from https://www.globalreporting.org/resourcelibrary/Carrots-and-Sticks.pdf

KPMG. (2013). *The KPMG Survey on Corporate Social Responsibility report.* Retrieved from https://assets.kpmg.com/content/dam/kpmg/pdf/2015/08/kpmg-survey-of-corporate-responsibility-reporting-2013.pdf

KPMG. (2015). *Current of change. The KPMG Survey on Corporate Social Responsibility report.* Retrieved from https://home.kpmg.com/content/dam/kpmg/pdf/2015/12/KPMG-survey-of-CR-reporting-2015.pdf

Krikke, H.R., Tsoulfas, G., Pappis, C., & Bloemhof-Ruwaard, J. (2001). *Design principles for closed loop supply chains: Optimizing economic, logistic and environmental performance.* Erasmus Research Institute of Management (ERIM).

Krikke, H., Blanc, L., & van de Velde, S. (2004). Product modularity and the design of closed-loop supply chains. *California Management Review*, *46*(2), 23–39. doi:10.2307/41166208

Kroon, L., & Vrijens, G. (1995). Returnable containers: An example of reverse logistics. *International Journal of Physical Distribution & Logistics Management*, *25*(2), 56–68. doi:10.1108/09600039510083934

Kulkarni, R. (2018). Innovative financing and regional dialogue are central for a thriving 'blue economy'. *UNDP*. Retrieved August 15, 2018 from http://www.undp.org/content/undp/en/home/blog/2018/Innovative-financing-and-regional-dialogue-are-central-for-a-thriving-blue-economy.html

Kulviwat, S., Bruner, G. C. II, & Al-Shuridah, O. (2009). The role of social influence on adoption of high tech innovations: The moderating effect of public/private consumption. *Journal of Business Research*, *62*(7), 706–712. doi:10.1016/j.jbusres.2007.04.014

Kumar, M., Tat Kee, F., & Taap Manshor, A. (2009). Determining the relative importance of critical factors in delivering service quality of banks: An application of dominance analysis in SERVQUAL model. *Managing Service Quality: An International Journal*, *19*(2), 211–228. doi:10.1108/09604520910943198

Kumar, P., & Ghodeswar, B. M. (2015). Factors affecting consumers' green product purchase decisions. *Marketing Intelligence & Planning*, *33*(3), 330–347. doi:10.1108/MIP-03-2014-0068

Kumar, S., & Malegeant, P. (2006). Strategic alliance in a closed-loop supply Chain, a case of manufacturer and Eco-Non-Profit Organization. *Technovation*, *26*(10), 1127–1135. doi:10.1016/j.technovation.2005.08.002

Kumar, S., & Putnam, V. (2008). Cradle to cradle: Reverse logistics strategies and opportunities across three industry sectors. *International Journal of Production Economics*, *115*(2), 305–315. doi:10.1016/j.ijpe.2007.11.015

Kurita, K., & Kurosaki, T. (2011). Dynamics of Growth, Poverty and İnequality: A Panel Analysis of Regional Data From Thailand and the Philippines. *Asian Economic Journal*, *25*(1), 3–33. doi:10.1111/j.1467-8381.2011.02046.x

Lakhal, S. Y., Sidibe, H., & Mida, S. (2008). Comparing conventional and certified organic cotton supply chains: The case of Mali. *International Journal of Agricultural Resources, Governance and Ecology*, *7*(3), 243–255. doi:10.1504/IJARGE.2008.018328

Lazaro, C. (1993). Green marketing: Looking beyond the quick fix. *Business Marketing Digest*, *18*(4), 67–74.

Lee, J. E., & Severt, D. (2017). The role of hospitality service quality in third places for the elderly: An exploratory study. *Cornell Hospitality Quarterly*, *58*(2), 214–221. doi:10.1177/1938965516686110

Lee, K. (2008). Opportunities for green marketing: Young consumers. *Marketing Intelligence & Planning*, *26*(6), 573–586. doi:10.1108/02634500810902839

Lee, K. (2009). Gender differences in Hong Kong adolescent consumers' green purchasing behavior. *Journal of Consumer Marketing*, *26*(2), 87–96. doi:10.1108/07363760910940456

Lee, W. H., & Cheng, C. C. (2018). Less is more: A new insight for measuring service quality of green hotels. *International Journal of Hospitality Management*, *68*, 32–40. doi:10.1016/j.ijhm.2017.09.005

Leite, P. R. (2009). *Reverse logistics: environment and competitiveness* (2nd ed.). São Paulo: Prentice Hall.

Lemmon, M. L., Roberts, M. R., & Zender, J. F. (2008). Back to the Beginning: Persistence and the Cross-Section of Corporate Capital Structure. *The Journal of Finance*, *63*(4), 1575–1608. doi:10.1111/j.1540-6261.2008.01369.x

Liao, B. F., Li, B. Y., & Cheng, J. S. (2015). A warranty model for remanufactured products. *Journal of Industrial and Production Engineering*, *32*(8), 551–558. doi:10.1080/21681015.2015.1090490

Liao, Z., & Cheung, M. T. (2008). Measuring consumer satisfaction in internet banking: A core framework. *Communications of the ACM*, *51*(4), 47–51. doi:10.1145/1330311.1330322

Lieder, M., & Rashid, A. (2016). Towards circular economy implementation: A comprehensive review in context of manufacturing industry. *Journal of Cleaner Production*, *115*, 36–51. doi:10.1016/j.jclepro.2015.12.042

Li, H., & Suomi, R. (2009). A proposed scale for measuring e-service quality. *International Journal of u-and e-Service. Science and Technology*, *2*(1), 1–10.

Lingán, J., & Wyman, L. (2013). *Exploring Civil Society Perspectives on Sustainability Reporting and Sustainability Reporting Policies, Working Paper*. Retrieved from http://citeseerx.ist.psu.edu/viewdoc/download?doi=10.1.1.737.1793&rep=rep1&type=pdf

Lin, R. J. (2013). Using fuzzy DEMATEL to evaluate the green supply chain management practices. *Journal of Cleaner Production*, *40*, 32–39. doi:10.1016/j.jclepro.2011.06.010

Macagno, T. (2013). A Model for Managing Corporate Sustainability. *Business and Society Review*, *118*(2), 223–252. doi:10.1111/basr.12009

MacArthur, E. (2013). Towards the Circular Economy Vol. 2: Opportunities for the Consumer Goods Sector. *Ellen MacArthur Foundation*. Retrieved from https://www.ellenmacarthurfoundation.org/publications/towards-the-circular-economy-vol-2-opportunities-for-the-consumer-goods-sector

Maichum, K., Parichatnon, S., & Peng, K. C. (2016). Application of the extended theory of planned behavior model to investigate purchase intention of green products among Thai consumers. *Sustainability*, *8*(10), 1077.

Maichum, K., Parichatnon, S., & Peng, K. C. (2017). Factors affecting on purchase intention towards green products: A case study of young consumers in Thailand. *International Journal of Social Science and Humanity*, *7*(5), 330–335.

Mair, C., & Stern, T. (2017). Cascading Utilization of Wood: A Matter of Circular Economy? *Current Forestry Reports*, *3*(4), 281–295. doi:10.100740725-017-0067-y

Malhotra, N. K., Ulgado, F. M., Agarwal, J., Shainesh, G., & Wu, L. (2005). Dimensions of service quality in developed and developing economies: Multi-country cross-cultural comparisons. *International Marketing Review*, *22*(3), 256–278. doi:10.1108/02651330510602204

Malviya, R. K., & Kant, R. (2014, December). Identifying critical success factors for green supply chain management implementation using fuzzy DEMATEL method. In *Industrial Engineering and Engineering Management (IEEM), 2014 IEEE International Conference on* (pp. 214-218). IEEE.

Mandal, U. K., & Sarkar, B. (2012). Selection of best intelligent manufacturing system (ims) under fuzzy moora conflicting mcdm environment. *International Journal of Emerging Technology and Advanced Engineering*, *2*(9), 301–310.

Mansell, W. (2016, March 21). *Tim Cook On Apple Vs. FBI: We Did Not Expect To Be 'At Odds With Our Own Government*. Retrieved from https://www.player.one/tim-cook-apple-vs-fbi-we-did-not-expect-be-odds-our-own-government-521018

Marchica, M.-T., & Mura, R. (2010). Financial Flexibility, Investment Ability, and Firm Value: Evidence from Firms with Spare Debt Capacity. *Financial Management*, *39*(4), 1339–1365. doi:10.1111/j.1755-053X.2010.01115.x

Maria, E. A., & ... (2018). What is blue growth? The semantics of "sustainable development" of marine environments. *Marine Policy*, *87*, 177–179. doi:10.1016/j.marpol.2017.10.019

Marković, S., Lončarić, D., & Lončarić, D. (2014). Service quality and customer satisfaction in the health care industry-towards health tourism market. *Tourism and Hospitality Management*, *20*(2), 155–170.

Mat Said, A., Ahmadun, F. L. R., Hj. Paim, L., & Masud, J. (2003). Environmental concerns, knowledge and practices gap among Malaysian teachers. *International Journal of Sustainability in Higher Education*, *4*(4), 305–313. doi:10.1108/14676370310497534

Matawale, C. R., Datta, S., & Mahapatra, S. S. (2016). Supplier selection in agile supply chain: Application potential of FMLMCDM approach in comparison with Fuzzy-TOPSIS and Fuzzy-MOORA. *Benchmarking: An International Journal*, *23*(7), 2027–2060. doi:10.1108/BIJ-07-2015-0067

Mavi, R. K., Goh, M., & Zarbakhshnia, N. (2017). Sustainable third-party reverse logistic provider selection with fuzzy SWARA and fuzzy MOORA in plastic industry. *International Journal of Advanced Manufacturing Technology*, *91*(5-8), 2401–2418. doi:10.100700170-016-9880-x

Mavi, R. K., & Shahabi, H. (2015). Using fuzzy DEMATEL for evaluating supplier selection criteria in manufacturing industries. *International Journal of Logistics Systems and Management*, *22*(1), 15–42. doi:10.1504/IJLSM.2015.070889

McCoskey, S., & Kao, C. (1998). A Residual-Based Test of The Null of Cointegration in Panel Data. *Econometric Reviews*, *17*(1), 57–84. doi:10.1080/07474939808800403

McPherson, H. (2014a, September 6). *Data Privacy—Essential for Corporate Social Responsibility*. https://www.isaca.org/Journal/Blog/Lists/Posts/Post.aspx?ID=237

McPherson, H. (2014b). Data Privacy—Protecting This Asset Is a Priority. *ISACA Journal, 3*. Retrieved from https://www.isaca.org/Journal/archives/2014/Volume-3/Pages/JOnline-Data-Privacy-Protecting-This-Asset-Is-a-Priority.aspx

McWilliams, A., Siegel, D. S., & Wright, P. M. (2006, March). *Corporate Social Responsibility: International Perspectives*. Rensselaer Working papers in economics, 0604. Rensselaer Polytechnic Institute, Department of Economics. Retrieved from http://www.economics.rpi.edu/workingpapers/rpi0604.pdf

Mehregan, M. R., Hashemi, S. H., Karimi, A., & Merikhi, B. (2014). Analysis of interactions among sustainability supplier selection criteria using ISM and fuzzy DEMATEL. *International Journal of Applied Decision Sciences*, *7*(3), 270–294. doi:10.1504/IJADS.2014.063226

Mei, L. B., Christiani, V. S., & Leite, P. R. (2011). The reverse logistics in the return of used cooking oil. *Proceedings of Anpad National Meeting*.

Mentink, B. (2014). *Circular business model innovation: a process framework and a tool for business model innovation in a circular economy* [Master's Thesis]. Delft University of Technology & Leiden University, Leiden, The Netherlands.

Merkert, R., & Assaf, A. G. (2015). Using DEA models to jointly estimate service quality perception and profitability–Evidence from international airports. *Transportation Research Part A, Policy and Practice*, *75*, 42–50. doi:10.1016/j.tra.2015.03.008

Meyer, R. (2007). Management of waste from health care institutions. *CLEAN – Soil, Air, Water (Basel)*, *35*(5), 508–510.

Michaud, C., & Llerena, D. (2006). An economic perspective on remanufactured products: Industrial and consumption challenges for life cycle engineering. In *Proceedings of LCE2006* (pp. 543–548).

Michaud, C., & Llerena, D. (2011). Green consumer behaviour: An experimental analysis of willingness to pay for remanufactured products. *Business Strategy and the Environment*, *20*(6), 408–420.

Miguez, E. C., Mendonça, F. M., & Valle, R. (2007). *Environmental, social and financial impacts of a reverse logistics policy adopted by a television factory - a case study* (Special Edition). Produção Online. doi:10.14488/1676-1901.v7i4.54

Miller, C. R., & Sarder, M. D. (2012). Public Works Policy Implications of Sustainable Reverse Logistics Operations. *Public Works Management & Policy*, *17*(1), 68–82. doi:10.1177/1087724X11429044

Minahan, T. (1998). Manufactures take aim at the end of the supply chain. *Purchasing*, *124*(6), 111–112.

Min, H., Ko, H. J., & Ko, C. S. (2006). A genetic algorithm approach to developing the multi-echelon reverse logistics network for product returns. *Omega*, *34*(1), 56–69. doi:10.1016/j.omega.2004.07.025

Mirahsani, Z. (2016). The Relationship Between Health Expenditures and Human Development İndex. *Journal of Research & Health, 6*(3), 373-377. DOI: . doi:10.7508/jrh.2016.03.011

Mirmousa, S., & Dehnavi, H. D. (2016). Development of criteria of selecting the supplier by using the fuzzy DEMATEL method. *Procedia: Social and Behavioral Sciences*, *230*, 281–289. doi:10.1016/j.sbspro.2016.09.036

Modak, N. M., Modak, N., Panda, S., & Sana, S. S. (2018). Analyzing structure of two-echelon closed-loop supply chain for pricing, quality and recycling management. *Journal of Cleaner Production*, *171*, 512–528. doi:10.1016/j.jclepro.2017.10.033

Mohammad, M. I., Gambo, Y. L., & Omirin, M. M. (2012). Assessing facilities management service in postgraduate hostel using servqual technique. *Journal of Emerging Trends in Economics and Management Science*, *3*(3), 252.

Mohd Suki, N. (2016). Green product purchase intention: Impact of green brands, attitude, and knowledge. *British Food Journal*, *118*(12), 2893–2910. doi:10.1108/BFJ-06-2016-0295

Moody's. (2018a). *Moody's downgrades Turkey's ratings to Ba3 and assigns negative outlook.* Retrieved from https://www.moodys.com

Moody's. (2018b). *Moody's downgrades 20 financial institutions in Turkey.* Retrieved from https://www.moodys.com

Moody's. (2018c). *Moody's lowers Turkey's country ceiling on foreign currency bank deposits to B2*. Retrieved from https://www.moodys.com

Moody's. (2018d). *Government of Turkey: Despite credit-supportive objectives, New Economic Plan falls short of addressing some of Turkey's key credit challenges.* Retrieved from https://www.moodys.com

Moody's. (2018e). *Sector In-Depth: Sovereigns – G-20: Policy banks pose limited fiscal risk and provide upside from business cycle smoothing for those with fiscal space.* Retrieved from https://www.moodys.com

Morillo, R., & Spalding, M. (2017). A sustainable blue economy. *Rockefeller & Co.* Retrieved August 14, 2018 from https://www.rockco.com/documents/FG/rockefeller/SI-docs/586666_RockCo-Blue_Economy_FINAL_WEB.pdf

Morrissey, O. (n.d.). *Dirk Willem te Velde and Adrian Hewitt, Defining International Public Goods: Conceptual Issues.* Retrieved from https://www.earthsummit2002.org/es/issues/

MOSS. (n.d.). *How does the Circular Economy differ to the Blue Economy?* Retrieved from http://www.moss.org.au/How-does-the-Circular-Economy-differ-to-the-Blue-Economy

Mostafa, M. M. (2009). Shades of green: A psychographic segmentation of the green consumer in Kuwait using self-organizing maps. *Expert Systems with Applications*, *36*(8), 11030–11038. doi:10.1016/j.eswa.2009.02.088

Murray, A., Skene, K., & Haynes, K. (2017). The circular economy: An interdisciplinary exploration of the concept and application in global context. *Journal of Business Ethics*, *140*(3), 369–380. doi:10.100710551-015-2693-2

Mutlu, A. (2002). *Çevre ekonomisi politikalari uygulamalar ve Türkiye*. Istanbul: Marmara university public finance research and administration publications.

Naik, C. K., Gantasala, S. B., & Prabhakar, G. V. (2010). SERVQUAL, customer satisfaction and behavioural intentions in retailing. *European Journal of Soil Science*, *17*(2), 200–213.

Nándori, E. S. (2010). The Effect of Economic Growth on Poverty in Eastern Europe. *Zarządzanie Publiczne*, *1-2*(9-10), 37-44.

Negash, S., Ryan, T., & Igbaria, M. (2003). Quality and effectiveness in web-based customer support systems. *Information & Management*, *40*(8), 757–768. doi:10.1016/S0378-7206(02)00101-5

Newman, K. (2001). Interrogating SERVQUAL: A critical assessment of service quality measurement in a high street retail bank. *International Journal of Bank Marketing*, *19*(3), 126–139. doi:10.1108/02652320110388559

Ng, P. F., Butt, M. M., Khong, K. W., & Ong, F. S. (2014). Antecedents of green brand equity: An integrated approach. *Journal of Business Ethics*, *121*(2), 203–215. doi:10.100710551-013-1689-z

Nguyen, T. N., Lobo, A., & Nguyen, B. K. (2017). Young consumers' green purchase behaviour in an emerging market. *Journal of Strategic Marketing*, 1–18.

Njong, A. M. (2010). The Effects of Educational Attainment on Poverty Reduction in Cameroon. *International Journal of Educational Administration and Policy Studies*, *2*(1), 1-8.

Norton, A. (2016). Towards an inclusive blue economy. *IIED*. Retrieved August 10, 2018 from https://www.iied.org/towards-inclusive-blue-economy

Nosratabadi, H. E., Pourdarab, S., & Nadali, A. (2011). Credit Risk Assessment of Bank Customers using DEMATEL and Fuzzy Expert System. *Economics and Finance Research*, *4*, 255–259.

NØW Turkey, (2015). *Waste into resources: EBRD moving towards a Circular economy with the near zero waste – NØW.* Retrieved from http://www.now-turkey.org/uploads/Pdf/bb2_sTkki8cHZqBwjKwRAtMvPxE23L9xHFnk.pdf

NØW Turkey. (2016). Retrieved from http://www.now-turkey.org

Nyborg, K., Howarth, R. B., & Brekke, K. A. (2006). Green consumers and public policy: On socially contingent moral motivation. *Resource and Energy Economics*, *28*(4), 351–366. doi:10.1016/j.reseneeco.2006.03.001

O'Neill, M., Palmer, A., & Charters, S. (2002). Wine production as a service experience–the effects of service quality on wine sales. *Journal of Services Marketing*, *16*(4), 342–362. doi:10.1108/08876040210433239

OECD. (2016). *The Ocean Economy in 2030.* Paris: OECD Publishing. Retrieved August 5, 2018 from doi:10.1787/9789264251724-en

OECD. (2017a). Greening the ocean economy, summary report. *OECD.* Retrieved August 8, 2018 from http://www.oecd.org/greengrowth/GGSD_2017_Summary%20Report_WEB.pdf

OECD. (2017b). Policy instruments for the environment (PINE). Retrieved from http://www.oecd.org/environment/tools-evaluation/PINE_database_brochure.pdf

OECD. (2018). *Health spending (indicator).* Retrieved from https://data.oecd.org/healthres/health-spending.htm

OECD. (n.d.). *OECD dac blended finance principles for unlocking commercial finance for the sustainable development goals.* Retrieved August 10, 2018 from http://www.oecd.org/dac/financing-sustainable-development/development-finance-topics/OECD-Blended-Finance-Principles.pdf

Oflac, B. S., & Gocer, A. (2015). A study on young consumers' perceived environmental knowledge levels and approach towards eco-labelled products. *Gazi University Journal of Faculty of Economics and Administrative Sciences*, *17*(2), 216–228.

Okay, E. (2015). Creative Energy Alternatives: Cheap and Future Energy for Turkey. In Handbook of Research on Developing Sustainable Value in Economics, Finance, and Marketing (pp. 157-178). IGI Global.

Okay, E. (2016). Towards Smart Cities in Turkey? Transitioning from Waste to Creative, Clean and Cheap Eco-Energy. In Handbook of Research on Waste Management Techniques for Sustainability, (pp. 277-303). IGI Global. doi:10.4018/978-1-4666-9723-2.ch015

Okay, E. (2017). A New Barrier for the Future of Energy Market in Turkey: Internal Capital Adequacy Assessment Process (ICAAP). In Ethics and Sustainability in Global Supply Chain Management. (pp. 178-196). IGI Global.

Okay, E. (2018). Investment on Heat Pumps: Geothermal Green Solutions for Turkey Lowering Energy Costs. In Handbook of Research on Supply Chain Management for Sustainable Development, (pp. 194-217). IGI Global.

Okay, E., Okay, N., & Akman, U. (2008). Views on Turkey's impending ESCO market: Is it promising? *Energy Policy*, *36*, 1821–1824. doi:10.1016/j.enpol.2008.02.024

Okay, E., Okay, N., & Akman, U. (2012). Turkey chapter. In P. Langlois & S. J. Hansen (Eds.), *World ESCO Outlook* (pp. 396–403). The Fairmont Press.

Oliveira, A. D., Santana, E. M., & Silva, S. C. (2009). Reverse Logistics of Returnable Packaging: An alternative for reducing costs for sustainable development. *Proceedings of National Meeting of Production Engineering.*

Ondemir, O., & Gupta, S. M. (2012). Optimal management of reverse supply chains with sensor-embedded end-of-life products. In K. D. Lawrence & G. Kleinman (Eds.), *Applications of Management Science* (pp. 109–129). Emerald Group Publishing Limited. doi:10.1108/S0276-8976(2012)0000015009

Ondemir, O., & Gupta, S. M. (2013a). Advanced remanufacturing-to-order and disassembly-to-order system under demand/decision uncertainty. In S. M. Gupta (Ed.), *Reverse supply chains: Issues and analysis* (pp. 203–228). Boca Raton, FL: CRC Press. doi:10.1201/b13749-9

Ondemir, O., & Gupta, S. M. (2013b). Quality assurance in remanufacturing with sensor embedded products. In Y. Nikolaidis (Ed.), *Quality Management in Reverse Logistics* (pp. 95–112). London: Springer. doi:10.1007/978-1-4471-4537-0_6

Ondemir, O., & Gupta, S. M. (2014a). A multi-criteria decision making model for advanced repair-to-order and disassembly-to-order system. *European Journal of Operational Research, 233*(2), 408–419. doi:10.1016/j.ejor.2013.09.003

Ondemir, O., & Gupta, S. M. (2014b). Quality management in product recovery using the Internet of Things: An optimization approach. *Computers in Industry, 65*(3), 491–504. doi:10.1016/j.compind.2013.11.006

Ondemir, O., Ilgin, M. A., & Gupta, S. M. (2012). Optimal end-of-life management in closed-loop supply chains using RFID and sensors. *IEEE Transactions on Industrial Informatics, 8*(3), 719–728. doi:10.1109/TII.2011.2166767

Organization for Economic and Co-operation Development. (2011). *OECD Guidelines for multinational enterprises.* Retrieved from OECD Library. doi:10.1787/9789264115415-

Örgev, C., & Utku, A. Ç. (2017). Sağlık kurumlarında atık kovalarının tıbbi atık yönetimine göre mikrobiyolojik değerlendirilmesi. *Sakarya Üniversitesi Fen Bilimleri Dergisi, 21*(3), 294–301.

Osterwalder, A., & Pigneur, Y. (2010). *Business model generation: a handbook for visionaries, game changers, and challengers*. John Wiley & Sons.

Ottman, J. A. (1992). Sometimes consumers will pay more to go green. *Marketing news, 26*(6), 16.

Ottman, J. A., Stafford, E. R., & Hartman, C. L. (2006). Avoiding green marketing myopia: Ways to improve consumer appeal for environmentally preferable products. *Environment, 48*(5), 22–36. doi:10.3200/ENVT.48.5.22-36

Overland, J. R. (2015). *The criminal liability of corporations for insider trading in Australia: Proposals for reform* [Doctoral dissertation]. Retrieved from http://hdl.handle.net/1885/96475

Ozaki, R., & Sevastyanova, K. (2011). Going hybrid: An analysis of consumer purchase motivations. *Energy Policy, 39*(5), 2217–2227. doi:10.1016/j.enpol.2010.04.024

Özbek, A. (2013). Analitik Ağ Süreci Yaklaşimiyla Üçüncü Parti Lojistik (3pl) Firma Seçimi. *Atatürk Üniversitesi İktisadi ve İdari Bilimler Dergisi, 27*(1).

Özcan, S. (2008). Küçük ve Orta Büyüklükteki İşletmelerde Lojistik Yönetiminin Önemi/The Importance of Logistics Management in Small And Medium Sized Enterprises. *Mustafa Kemal Üniversitesi Sosyal Bilimler Enstitüsü Dergisi, 5*(10).

Ozder, A., Teker, B., Eker, H. H., Altındis, S., Kocaakman, M., & Karabay, O. (2013). Medical waste management training for healthcare managers - a necessity? *Journal of Environmental Health Science & Engineering, 11*(1), 1–8. doi:10.1186/2052-336X-11-20 PMID:24499642

Özerol, İ. H. (2005). Tıbbi atık stratejileri nelerdir? EN/ISO normları nelerdir? Avrupa'da birlik? ABD'nin yaklaşımı? Ülkemizde durum? In *Ulusal Sterilizasyon Dezenfeksiyon Kongresi* (pp. 434-472).

Özsoy, C. (2012). Kalkınma Ekonomisinin Anlam ve İçeriği. In İktisadi Kalkınma (pp. 2-26) Eskişehir: Anadolu Üniversitesi Yayınları.

Palese, B., & Usai, A. (2018). The relative importance of service quality dimensions in e-commerce experiences. *International Journal of Information Management, 40*, 132–140. doi:10.1016/j.ijinfomgt.2018.02.001

Parasuraman, A., Zeithaml, V. A., & Berry, L. L. (1988). Servqual: A multiple-item scale for measuring consumer perc. *Journal of Retailing*, *64*(1), 12.

Patientview. (2015). The corporate reputation of pharma in 2014 — the patient perspective and how the corporate reputation of pharma companies has changed over the past four years. Retrieved from http://www.patient-view.com/uploads/6/5/7/9/6579846/patientview_11-2-2015_press_release_corp_rep_global.pdf

Patil, P. G., Virdin, J., Diez, S.M., Roberts, J., & Singh, A. (2016). *Toward a blue economy: a promise for sustainable growth in the Caribbean; An overview*. The World Bank. Retrieved April 17, 2018 from https://openknowledge.worldbank.org/bitstream/handle/10986/25061/Demystifying0t0the0Caribbean0Region.pdf?sequence=4

Paul, J., Modi, A., & Patel, J. (2016). Predicting green product consumption using theory of planned behavior and reasoned action. *Journal of Retailing and Consumer Services*, *29*, 123–134. doi:10.1016/j.jretconser.2015.11.006

Pauly, D. A. (2018). Vision for marine fisheries in a global blue economy. *Marine Policy*, *87*, 371–374. doi:10.1016/j.marpol.2017.11.010

Peattie, K., & Peattie, S. (2009). Social marketing: A pathway to consumption reduction? *Journal of Business Research*, *62*(2), 260–268. doi:10.1016/j.jbusres.2008.01.033

Peattie, K., & Ratnayaka, M. (1992). Responding to the green movement. *Industrial Marketing Management*, *21*(2), 103–110. doi:10.1016/0019-8501(92)90004-D

Pedroni, P. (2000). Full Modified OLS for Heterogeneous Cointegrated Panels. *Advances in Econometrics*, *15*, 93–130. doi:10.1016/S0731-9053(00)15004-2

PEMSEA. (2015). *Blue economy for business in east Asia towards an integrated understanding of blue economy*. Retrieved November 5, 2018 from http://www.pemsea.org/sites/default/files/PEMSEA%20Blue%20Economy%20Report%20 11.10.15.pdf

Perçin, S. (2018). Evaluating airline service quality using a combined fuzzy decision-making approach. *Journal of Air Transport Management*, *68*, 48–60. doi:10.1016/j.jairtraman.2017.07.004

Pereira, R. D. A., Pavanelli, G., & Souza, M. T. S. (2008). A Study of the Reverse Channels in a Cardboard Packaging Company. *Proceedings of National Meeting of Production Engineering*.

Pérez-Domínguez, L., Alvarado-Iniesta, A., Rodríguez-Borbón, I., & Vergara-Villegas, O. (2015). Intuitionistic fuzzy MOORA for supplier selection. *Dyna (Bilbao)*, *82*(191), 34–41. doi:10.15446/dyna.v82n191.51143

Pesaran, M. H. (2004). *General Diagnostic Tests for Cross Section Dependence in Panels*. CESifo Working Paper Series, 1229.

Pesaran, M. H. (2007). A Simple Panel Unit Root Test in the Presence of Cross-Section Dependence. *Journal of Applied Econometrics*, *22*(2), 265–312. doi:10.1002/jae.951

Pesaran, M. H., Ullah, A., & Yamagata, T. (2008). A Bias-Adjusted LM Test of Error Cross-Section İndependence. *The Econometrics Journal*, *11*(1), 105–127. doi:10.1111/j.1368-423X.2007.00227.x

Pesaran, M. H., & Yamagata, T. (2008). Testing Slope Homogeneity in Large Panels. *Journal of Econometrics*, *142*(1), 50–93. doi:10.1016/j.jeconom.2007.05.010

Petrocelli, T. (2005, December 9). *The changing face of data protection*. Retrieved from http://www.informit.com/articles/article.aspx?p=422303&seqNum=3

Phadke, M. S. (1989). *Quality engineering robust design*. Upper Saddle River, NJ: Prentice Hall.

Pigou, A. C. (1920). *The Economics of Welfare*. London: Macmillan.

Pinna, R., & Carrus, P. P. (2012). Reverse Logistics and the Role of Fourth Party Logistics Provider. In A. Groznik (Ed.), Path ways to Supply Chain Excellence (pp. 90-114). In Tech.

Polonsky, M. J. (1995). A stakeholder theory approach to designing environmental marketing strategy. *Journal of Business and Industrial Marketing*, *10*(3), 29–46. doi:10.1108/08858629510096201

Polonsky, M. J. (2011). Transformative green marketing: Impediments and opportunities. *Journal of Business Research*, *64*(12), 1311–1319. doi:10.1016/j.jbusres.2011.01.016

Potgieter, B. C., Botha, J. H., & Lew, C. (2005, July). Evidence that use of the ITIL framework is effective. *18th Annual conference of the national advisory committee on computing qualifications*, 160-167.

Pratt, K., Lenaghan, M., & Mitchard, E. (2016). Material flows accounting for Scotland shows the merits of a circular economy and the folly of territorial carbon reporting. *Carbon Balance and Management*. Retrieved from https://link.springer.com/article/10.1186/s13021-016-0063-8

Preston, F., & Lehne, J. (2017). *A Wider Circle? The Circular Economy in Developing Countries*. Chatam House.

Przychodzen, J., & Przychodzen, W. (2013). Corporate sustainability and shareholder wealth. *Journal of Environmental Planning and Management*, *56*(4), 474–493. doi:10.1080/09640568.2012.685927

Rajan, R. G., & Zingales, L. (1995). What Do We Know about Capital Structure? Some Evidence from International Data. *The Journal of Finance*, *50*(5), 1421–1460. doi:10.1111/j.1540-6261.1995.tb05184.x

Rapp, M. S., Schmid, T., & Urban, D. (2014). The value of financial flexibility and corporate financial policy. *Journal of Corporate Finance*, *29*, 288–302. doi:10.1016/j.jcorpfin.2014.08.004

Raut, R. D., Bhasin, H. V., & Kamble, S. S. (2011). Evaluation of supplier selection criteria by combination of AHP and fuzzy DEMATEL method. *International Journal of Business Innovation and Research*, *5*(4), 359–392. doi:10.1504/IJBIR.2011.041056

Razmi, S. M. J. & E. Abbasian & S. Mohammadi (2012). Investigating the Effect of Government Health Expenditure on HDI in Iran. *Journal of Knowledge Management, Economics and Information Technology*, (5).

Renewable Energy Policy Network for 21st Century. (2017). *Renewables 2013 Global Status Report*. Retrieved from http://www.ren21.net/gsr

Rettie, R., Burchell, K., & Barnham, C. (2014). Social normalisation: Using marketing to make green normal. *Journal of Consumer Behaviour*, *13*(1), 9–17. doi:10.1002/cb.1439

Rex, E., & Baumann, H. (2007). Beyond ecolabels: What green marketing can learn from conventional marketing. *Journal of Cleaner Production*, *15*(6), 567–576. doi:10.1016/j.jclepro.2006.05.013

Riman, H., Bassey, J., Ibi, E., & Edu, B. (2010). *Poverty, Health Expenditure, and Health Status: A Long Term Perspective with Evidence from Nigeria*. Retrieved from http://ssrn.com/abstract=1540303

Ringle, C. M., Wende, S., and Becker, J.-M. (2015). SmartPLS 3.

Rod, M., Ashill, N. J., Shao, J., & Carruthers, J. (2009). An examination of the relationship between service quality dimensions, overall internet banking service quality and customer satisfaction: A New Zealand study. *Marketing Intelligence & Planning*, *27*(1), 103–126. doi:10.1108/02634500910928344

Rodriguez, J. P., & Perez, C. R. (2002). Advanced sensor for optimal orientation and predictive maintenance of high power wind generators. In *Industrial Electronics Society, IEEE 2002 28th Annual Conference of the* (Vol. 3, pp. 2167-2172). IEEE.

Rodríguez-Antón, J. M., & Alonso-Almeida, M. M. (2018). *La estrategia española de Economía circular y su adecuación al Plan de Acción de la UE para la Economía circular.* Comunicación presentada en el 25th APDR Congress, Lisboa, Portugal.

Rodriguez-Antón, J. M., & Alonso-Almeida, M. M. (2018). Organización y dirección de empresas hoteleras. Ed. Sintesis.

Rogers, D. S., Lambert, D. M., Croxton, K. L., & Garcia-Dastugue, S. (2002). The Returns management process. *International Journal of Logistics Management, 13*(2), 1–18. doi:10.1108/09574090210806397

Rogers, D. S., & Tibben-Lembke, R. (1998). *Going Backwards: Reverse Logistics Trends and Practices.* Reno: Reverse Logistics Executive Council.

Rogers, D. S., & Tibben-Lembke, R. S. (1998). *Going backwards: reverse logistics trends and practices.* Pittsburgh, PA: Reverse Logistics Executive Council.

Rogers, D. S., & Tibben-Lembke, R. S. (2001). An examination of reverse logistics practices. *Journal of Business Logistics, 22*(2), 29–148. doi:10.1002/j.2158-1592.2001.tb00007.x

Rogers, D., & Tibben-Lembke, R. S. (1999). *Going Backwards: Reverse logistics Trends and practices.* Pittsburgh, PA: RLEC Press.

Rouse, M. (n.d.). *Definition of a conduct risk.* Retrieved from http://searchcompliance.techtarget.com/definition/conduct-risk

Ruan, J. J., Li, J., & Xu, Z. M. (2011). An environmentally friendly recovery production line of waste toner cartridges. *Journal of Hazardous Materials, 185*(2–3), 696–702. doi:10.1016/j.jhazmat.2010.09.074 PMID:20956056

Samuelson, P. A. (1954). The Pure Theory of Public Expenditure. *The Review of Economics and Statistics, 36*(4), 387–389. doi:10.2307/1925895

Şantaş, F. (2017). Yoksulluğun Sağlık Statüsü ve Sağlık Hizmetleri Kullanımı İle İlişkisi. *Igdir University Journal of Social Sciences*, (13), 545-591.

Saracoglu, B. O. (2017). Location selection factors of small hydropower plant investments powered by SAW, grey WPM and fuzzy DEMATEL based on human natural language perception. *International Journal of Renewable Energy Technology, 8*(1), 1–23. doi:10.1504/IJRET.2017.10001528

Sarbanes-Oxley Act of 2002, Pub. L. No. 107-204, 116 Stat. 745 (2002).

Sarkaria, M. S., & Shiwani. (2016). Education and Poverty Relationship in Punjab. *IRA-International Journal of Management & Social Sciences, 4*(2), 394-416. Retrieved from https://research-advances.org/index.php/RAJMSS/article/download/437/460

Sarkis, J. (2003). A strategic decision framework for green supply chain management. *Journal of Cleaner Production, 11*(4), 397–409. doi:10.1016/S0959-6526(02)00062-8

Sarkis, J., & Zhu, Q. (2017). Environmental Sustainability and Production: Taking the Road Less Travelled. *International Journal of Production Research, 56*(1-2), 743–759. doi:10.1080/00207543.2017.1365182

Sarstedt, M., Ringle, C. M., Smith, D., Reams, R., & Hair, J. F. Jr. (2014). Partial least squares structural equation modeling (PLS-SEM): A useful tool for family business researchers. *Journal of Family Business Strategy, 5*(1), 105–115. doi:10.1016/j.jfbs.2014.01.002

Sasikumar, P., & Kannan, G. (2008). Issues in reverse supply chains, part I: End-of-life product recovery and inventory management-an overview. *International Journal of Sustainable Engineering*, *1*(3), 154–172. doi:10.1080/19397030802433860

Sawyer, L. (2004). *Sawyer's words of wisdom*. The IIA Research Foundation.

Scarlett, A. M. (2011). Investors be aware: Assessing shareholder derivative litigation in India and China. *University of Pennsylvania Journal of International Law*, *33*(1), 173–237. Retrieved from https://www.law.upenn.edu/journals/jil/articles/volume33/issue1/Scarlett33U.Pa.J.Int'lL.173(2011).pdf

Schatzki, T. R. (1996). *Social practices: A Wittgensteinian approach to human activity and the social*. Cambridge University Press. doi:10.1017/CBO9780511527470

Schultz, P. W. (2000). New environmental theories: Empathizing with nature: The effects of perspective taking on concern for environmental issues. *The Journal of Social Issues*, *56*(3), 391–406. doi:10.1111/0022-4537.00174

Sellitto, M. A. (2013). Coprocessing of rice husks and waste tires and reverse logistics in the manufacture of cement. *Environment and Society*, *16*(1), 141–162. doi:10.1590/S1414-753X2013000100009

Sen, S., Gürhan-Canli, Z., & Morwitz, V. (2001). Withholding consumption: A social dilemma perspective on consumer boycotts. *The Journal of Consumer Research*, *28*(3), 399–417. doi:10.1086/323729

Setyawan, A., Noermijati, N., Sunaryo, S., & Aisjah, S. (2018). Green product buying intentions among young consumers: Extending the application of theory of planned behavior. *Problems and Perspectives in Management*, *16*(2), 145–154. doi:10.21511/ppm.16(2).2018.13

Shaoshuai, F., Wenxiao, S., Nan, W., & Yan, L. (2011). MODM-based evaluation model of service quality in the Internet of Things. *Procedia Environmental Sciences*, *11*, 63–69. doi:10.1016/j.proenv.2011.12.011

Shen, B., Price, L., Wang, J., & Li, M. (2012) *China's Approaches to Financing Sustainable Development: Policies, Practices, and Issues*. Ernest Orlando Lawrence Berkeley National Laboratory. Retrieved from http://china.lbl.gov/sites/all/files/lbl-5579e-green-finance-wiresjune-2012.pdf

Shiffman, M. A. (1999). Medical waste regulations. *The American Journal of Cosmetic Surgery*, *16*(4), 321–321. doi:10.1177/074880689901600408

Shih, D. H., Lu, C. M., Lee, C. H., Cai, S. Y., Wu, K. J., & Tseng, M. L. (2018). Eco-Innovation in Circular Agri-Business. *Sustainability*, *10*(4), 1140–1153. doi:10.3390u10041140

Sigala, M. (2004). The ASP-Qual model: Measuring ASP service quality in Greece. *Managing Service Quality: An International Journal*, *14*(1), 103–114. doi:10.1108/09604520410513703

Sigala, M. (2009). E-service quality and Web 2.0: Expanding quality models to include customer participation and inter-customer support. *Service Industries Journal*, *29*(10), 1341–1358. doi:10.1080/02642060903026239

Silva, L. A., Pimenta, H., & Campos, L. (2013). Reverse logistics of electronic waste in the IT sector: Reality, perspectives and challenges of the city of Natal-RN. *Produção. Online (Bergheim)*, *13*(2), 544–576.

Singh, H., Saufi, R. A., Tasnim, R., & Hussin, M. (2017). The relationship between employee job satisfaction, perceived customer satisfaction, service quality, and profitability in luxury hotels in Kuala Lumpur. *Prabandhan: Indian Journal of Management*, *10*(1), 26–39. doi:10.17010/pijom/2017/v10i1/109101

SINIR. (2015). *Sectoral agreement on packaging in general*. Retrieved from http://www.sinir.gov.br/web/guest/packages-in-general

Sirgy, M. J. (1982). Self-concept in consumer behavior: A critical review. *The Journal of Consumer Research*, *9*(3), 287–300. doi:10.1086/208924

Si, X. S., Wang, W., Hu, C. H., & Zhou, D. H. (2011). Remaining useful life estimation–A review on the statistical data driven approaches. *European Journal of Operational Research*, *213*(1), 1–14. doi:10.1016/j.ejor.2010.11.018

Skinner, D. C. (2006). Director responsibilities and liability exposure in the era of Sarbanes-Oxley. *The Practical Lawyer, June*. Retrieved from https://files.apks.com/practica_lawyer_skinner.pdf

Skjøtt-Larsen, T. (1999). Interorganisational relations from a supply chain management point of view. *Logistik management, 1*(2), 96-108.

Snezhko, S. (2015). Time to step up… . *INCOMPLIANCE, 19*, 26-28.

Srivastava, S. K. (2007). Green supply-chain management: A state-of-the-art literature review. *International Journal of Management Reviews*, *9*(1), 53–80. doi:10.1111/j.1468-2370.2007.00202.x

Srivastava, S. K. (2008). Network design for reverse logistics. *Omega*, *36*(4), 535–548. doi:10.1016/j.omega.2006.11.012

Standards and Poor's Ratings. (2018). *Turkey Long-Term Foreign Currency Rating Lowered To 'B+' On Implications Of Extreme Lira Volatility; Outlook Stable.* Retrieved from http://www.standardandpoors.com

Stanujkić, D., Đorđević, B., & Đorđević, M. (2013). Comparative analysis of some prominent MCDM methods: A case of ranking Serbian banks. *Serbian Journal of Management*, *8*(2), 213–241. doi:10.5937jm8-3774

Stilgherrian. (2014, November 7). *Customer data protection is a corporate social responsibility.* Retrieved from https://www.zdnet.com/article/customer-data-protection-is-a-corporate-social-responsibility/

Stock, J. R. (1992). *Reverse logistics.* Oak Brook, IL: Council of Logistics Management.

Studnicki, J. (1992). The management of hospital medical waste: How to increase efficiency through a medical waste audit. *Hospital Topics*, *70*(2), 11–17. doi:10.1080/00185868.1992.10543687 PMID:10119174

Su, B., Heshmati, A., & Geng, Y. (2012). A Review of the Circular Economy in China: Moving from Rhetoric to Implementation. *Journal of Cleaner Production*, *42*. Retrieved from https://www.sciencedirect.com/science/article/pii/S0959652612006117

Su, B., Heshmati, A., Geng, Y., & Yu, X. (2013). A review of the circular economy in China: Moving from rhetoric to implementation. *Journal of Cleaner Production*, *42*, 215–227. doi:10.1016/j.jclepro.2012.11.020

Suki, N. M. (2013). Green awareness effects on consumers' purchasing decision: Some insights from Malaysia. *International Journal of Asia-Pacific Studies*, *9*(2), 49–63.

Sustainable Energy for All Forum. (2018). Retrieved from http://www.seforallforum.org/about

Sustainable Energy for All. (2014). *Achieving Universal Energy Access.* Retrieved from http://www.se4all.org/sites/default/files/l/2014/12/fp_se4all_access.pdf

Sustainable Energy for All. (2017). *Energy Efficiency.* Retrieved from http://www.se4all.org/about-us_our-ambition_energy-efficiency

Szita, K. T. (2017). The application of life cycle assessment in circular economy. *Hungarian Agricultural Engineering*, *31*(31), 5–9. doi:10.17676/HAE.2017.31.5

T.C. Çevre ve Orman Bakanlığı Çevre Yönetimi Genel Müdürlüğü. (2008). Güvenli Atık Yönetimi.

T.C. Çevre ve Orman Bakanlığı. (2005). Tıbbi Atıkların Kontrolü Yönetmeliği.

Talbot, S., Lefebvre, E., & Lefebvre, L.-A. (2007). Closed-loop supply chain activities and derived benefits in manufacturing SMEs. *Journal of Manufacturing Technology Management, 18*(6), 627–658. doi:10.1108/17410380710763831

Taylan Dortyol, I., Varinli, I., & Kitapci, O. (2014). How do international tourists perceive hotel quality? An exploratory study of service quality in Antalya tourism region. *International Journal of Contemporary Hospitality Management, 26*(3), 470–495. doi:10.1108/IJCHM-11-2012-0211

Tenório, F., Silva, D., & Dacorso, E. (2014). Innovation And Decision-Making Process In Reverse Logistics: A Bibliometric Analysis. *Produção Online, Florianópolis, 14*(2), 593–616.

The Economist & Intelligence Unit. (2015). *The blue economy growth, opportunity and a sustainable ocean economy. An economist intelligence unit briefing paper for the World ocean summit 2015*. Retrieved March 27, 2018 from https://www.eiuperspectives.economist.com/sites/default/files/images/Blue%20Economy_briefing%20paper_WOS2015.pdf

The European Remanufacturing Network. http://www.remanufacturing.eu/about-remanufacturing.php

The International Integrated Reporting Council. (2013). *The International <IR> framework*. Retrieved from http://integratedreporting.org/wp-content/uploads/2015/03/13-12-08-THE-INTERNATIONAL-IR-FRAMEWORK-2-1.pdf

The International Integrated Reporting Council. (2015). *Creating value. Value to investors*. Retrieved from http://integratedreporting.org/wp-content/uploads/2015/04/Creating-Value-Investors.pdf

The Library of Economics and Liberty. (n.d.). *Arthur Cecil Pigou*. Retrieved August 22, 2018 from http://www.econlib.org/library/Enc/bios/Pigou.html

The Securities and Exchange Act of 1934, Pub. L. No. 73-291, §1, 46 Stat. 881 (1934).

Thierry, M., Salomon, M., Nunen, V. J., & Wasenhove, L. V. (1995). Strategic issues in product recovery management. *California Management Review, 37*(2), 114–135. doi:10.2307/41165792

Thompson, J. H. (2013). A Global Comparison of Insider Trading Regulations. *International Journal of Accounting and Financial Reporting, 3*(1), 1. doi:10.5296/ijafr.v3i1.3269

Tibben-Lembke, R. S., & Rogers, D. S. (2002). Differences between forward and reverse logistics in a retail environment. *Supply Chain Management, 7*(5), 271–282. doi:10.1108/13598540210447719

Tıbbi Atıkların Kontrolü Yönetmeliği. (2017). 25.01.2017 tarih ve 29959 sayı ile Resmi Gazete.

Toda, H. Y., & Yamamoto, T. (1995). Statistical İnference in Vector Autoregressions With Possibly İntegrated Processes. *Journal of Econometrics, 66*(1-2), 225–250. doi:10.1016/0304-4076(94)01616-8

Toffel, M. W. (2004). Strategic management of product recovery. *California Management Review, 46*(2), 120–141. doi:10.2307/41166214

Torres, F., Gil, P., Puente, S. T., Pomares, J., & Aracil, R. (2004). Automatic PC disassembly for component recovery. *International Journal of Advanced Manufacturing Technology, 23*(1-2), 39–46. doi:10.100700170-003-1590-5

Transparency International UK. (2015). *Don't look, won't find: weaknesses in the supervision of the UK's anti-money laundering rules*. Retrieved from http://www.transparency.org.uk/publications/dont-look-wont-find-weaknesses-in-the-supervision-of-the-uks-anti-money-laundering-rules/

Transparency International. (2014). *Transparency in corporate reporting: Assessing the World's Largest Companies*. Retrieved from https://www.transparency.org/whatwedo/publication/transparency_in_corporate_reporting_assessing_worlds_largest_companies_2014

Transparency International. (2015). *Transparency in corporate reporting: Assessing the World's Largest Telecommunications Companies*. Retrieved from http://www.transparency.org/whatwedo/publication/transparency_in_corporate_reporting_assessing_the_worlds_largest_telecommun

Trevino, L. K., & Nelson, K. A. (2010). *Managing Business Ethics: straight talk about how to do right*. U.S.: J. Wiley & Sons Inc.

Trevino, L. K., & Weaver, G. R. (2003). *Managing ethics in business organizations: a social scientific perspective on business ethics*. Stanford University Press.

Tsang, N. K., Lee, L. Y. S., & Qu, H. (2015). Service quality research on China's hospitality and tourism industry. *International Journal of Contemporary Hospitality Management*, *27*(3), 473–497. doi:10.1108/IJCHM-01-2014-0048

Tseng, M. L., Tan, K. H., Geng, Y., & Govindan, K. (2016). Sustainable consumption and production in emerging markets. *International Journal of Production Economics*, *181*(2), 257–261. doi:10.1016/j.ijpe.2016.09.016

Turkey Business Council for Sustainable Development. (2018). Retrieved from http://www.skdturkiye.org

Turoń, K., & Czech, P. (2017). Circular Economy in the Transport Industry in Terms of Corporate Social Responsibility Concept. *Journal of Corporate Responsibility and Leadership*, *3*(4), 83–94. doi:10.12775/JCRL.2016.025

Tzeng, G. H., Chiang, C. H., & Li, C. W. (2007). Evaluating intertwined effects in e-learning programs: A novel hybrid MCDM model based on factor analysis and DEMATEL. *Expert Systems with Applications*, *32*(4), 1028–1044. doi:10.1016/j.eswa.2006.02.004

U.S. Securities and Exchange Commission site. (n.d.). Insider trading. Retrieved from https://www.sec.gov/answers/insider.htm

UN. (2012). *Green Economy In Action: Articles and Excerpts that Illustrate Green Economy and Sustainable Development Efforts (Development Programme)*. Retrieved from http://www.undp.org/content/undp/en/home/librarypage/environment-energy/integrating_environmentintodevelopment/green-economy-in-action

UN. (2015). *The Sustainable Development Agenda: 17 Goals to Transform Our World*. Retrieved from https://www.un.org/sustainabledevelopment/development-agenda/

UN. (2017). *First steps to a safer future: Introducing The United Nations Framework Convention on Climate Change*. Retrieved from http://unfccc.int/essential_background/convention/items/6036.php

UN. (2017, June). *Exploring the potential of the blue economy*. Retrieved August 22, 2018 from https://www.un.org/development/desa/en/news/sustainable/exploring-potential-of-blue-economy.html

Unilever. (2017, January) Report shows a third of consumers prefer sustainable brands. Retrieved from https://www.unilever.com/news/Press-releases/2017/report-shows-a-third-of-consumers-prefer-sustainable-brands.html

United Nations Global Compact. (n.d.). *Guide to corporate sustainability. Shaping a sustainable future*. Retrieved from https://www.unglobalcompact.org/docs/publications/UN_Global_Compact_Guide_to_Corporate_Sustainability.pdf

United Nations Global Compact. (n.d.). *The Communication on progress in brief*. Retrieved from https://www.unglobalcompact.org/participation/report/cop

United Nations Office on Drugs and Crime. (2011). *Estimating illicit financial flows resulting from drug trafficking and other transnational organized crime*. Retrieved from http://www.unodc.org/documents/data-and-analysis/Studies/Illicit_financial_flows_2011_web.pdf

United Nations. (2003). *UN Guidelines for Consumer Protection*. Retrieved from http://www.un.org/esa/sustdev/publications/consumption_en.pdf

United States Business Council for Sustainable Development. (2017). *Circular Change: Turkey Materials Marketplace.* Retrieved from http://www.circularchange.com/wp-content/uploads/2017/05/Astrid-Motta-2.pdf

United States Department of Justice. (n.d.) *U.S. Attorney Manual.* Title 9: Criminal, 9-28.000 Principles of Federal Prosecution of Business Organizations, 9-28.800 Corporate Compliance Programs [Abstract]. Retrieved from https://www.justice.gov/usam/united-states-attorneys-manual

Untachai, S. (2013). Modeling service quality in hospital as a second order factor, Thailand. *Procedia: Social and Behavioral Sciences*, *88*, 118–133. doi:10.1016/j.sbspro.2013.08.487

Vadde, S., Kamarthi, S., Gupta, S. M., & Zeid, I. (2008). Product life cycle monitoring via embedded sensors. In S. M. Gupta & A. J. D. Lambert (Eds.), *Environment conscious manufacturing* (pp. 91–103). Boca Raton, FL: CRC Press.

Vafadarnikjoo, A., Mobin, M., Allahi, S., & Rastegari, A. (2015, January). A hybrid approach of intuitionistic fuzzy set theory and DEMATEL method to prioritize selection criteria of bank branches locations. In *Proceedings of the International Annual Conference of the American Society for Engineering Management.* (p. 1). American Society for Engineering Management (ASEM).

Vafadarnikjoo, A. (2014). Corrigendum to "Using fuzzy DEMATEL to evaluate the green supply chain management practices. *Journal of Cleaner Production*, *82*, 232. doi:10.1016/j.jclepro.2014.06.065

Vafadarnikjoo, A., Mishra, N., Govindan, K., & Chalvatzis, K. (2018). Assessment of Consumers' Motivations to Purchase a Remanufactured Product by Applying Fuzzy Delphi Method and Single Valued Neutrosophic Sets. *Journal of Cleaner Production*, *196*, 230–244. doi:10.1016/j.jclepro.2018.06.037

Van Loon, P., Delagarde, C., & Van Wassenhove, L. N. (2017). The role of second-hand markets in circular business: A simple model for leasing versus selling consumer products. *International Journal of Production Research*, 1–14.

Van Weelden. (2016). Paving the way towards circular consumption: Exploring consumer acceptance of refurbished mobile phones in the Dutch market. *Journal of Cleaner Production*, *113*, 743–754.

Vargo, S. L., & Lusch, R. F. (2008). Service-dominant logic: Continuing the evolution. *Journal of the Academy of Marketing Science*, *36*(1), 1–10. doi:10.100711747-007-0069-6

Verschoor, C. C. (2004, October 1). Does Superior Governance Still Lead to Better Financial Performance? *Strategic Finance*, *86*, 13–14.

Vicente-Molina, M. A., Fernández-Sáinz, A., & Izagirre-Olaizola, J. (2013). Environmental knowledge and other variables affecting pro-environmental behaviour: Comparison of university students from emerging and advanced countries. *Journal of Cleaner Production*, *61*, 130–138. doi:10.1016/j.jclepro.2013.05.015

Vigolo, V., & Cassia, F. (2015, August). Brand Reputation and Service Quality in the Italian Energy Market: A business-to-Business Perspective. *Toulon-Verona Conference Excellence in Services.*

Vijay Kumar, E., Chaturvedi, S. K., & Deshpandé, A. W. (2009). Maintenance of industrial equipment: Degree of certainty with fuzzy modelling using predictive maintenance. *International Journal of Quality & Reliability Management*, *26*(2), 196–211. doi:10.1108/02656710910928824

Vlachos, D., Georgiadis, P., & Iakovou, E. (2007). A system dynamics model for dynamic capacity planning of remanufacturing in closed-loop supply chains. *Computers & Operations Research, 34*(2), 367–394. doi:10.1016/j.cor.2005.03.005

Walingo, M. K. (2006). The Role of Education in Agricultural Projects For Food Security and Poverty Reduction in Kenya. *Review of Education, 52*, 287–304.

Walker, P. (2017). *UK considers tax on single-use plastics to tackle ocean pollution.* Retrieved June 10, 2018 from https://www.theguardian.com/environment/2017/nov/18/uk-considers-tax-on-single-use-plastics-to-tackle-ocean-pollution

Wang, P., & Kuah, A. T. (2018). Green Marketing Cradle-to-Cradle: Remanufactured Products in Asian Markets. *Thunderbird International Business Review, 60*(5), 783–795. doi:10.1002/tie.21925

Wang, Y., & Hazen, B. T. (2016). Consumer product knowledge and intention to purchase remanufactured products. *International Journal of Production Economics, 181*, 460–469. doi:10.1016/j.ijpe.2015.08.031

Wang, Y., Hazen, B. T., & Mollenkopf, D. A. (2018). Consumer value considerations and adoption of remanufactured products in closed-loop supply chains. *Industrial Management & Data Systems, 118*(2), 480–498. doi:10.1108/IMDS-10-2016-0437

Wang, Y., Huscroft, J. R., Hazen, B. T., & Zhang, M. (2018). Green information, green certification and consumer perceptions of remanufctured automobile parts. *Resources, Conservation and Recycling, 128*, 187–196. doi:10.1016/j.resconrec.2016.07.015

Wang, Y., Wiegerinck, V., Krikke, H., & Zhang, H. (2013). Understanding the purchase intention towards remanufactured product in closed-loop supply chains: An empirical study in China. *International Journal of Physical Distribution & Logistics Management, 43*(10), 866–888. doi:10.1108/IJPDLM-01-2013-0011

Wanzenried, G. (2006). Capital Structure Dynamics in the UK and Continental Europe. *European Journal of Finance, 12*(8), 693–716. doi:10.1080/13518470500460178

Wastling, T., Charnley, F., & Moreno, M. (2018). Design for Circular Behaviour: Considering Users in a Circular Economy. *Sustainability, 10*(6), 1743. doi:10.3390u10061743

Webster, K. (2017). *The circular economy: A wealth of flows.* Isle of Wight: Ellen MacArthur Foundation Publishing.

Wesseler, J., & Drabik, D. (2016). Prices matter: Analysis of food and energy competition relative to land resources in the European Union. *NJAS Wageningen Journal of Life Sciences, 77*, 19–24. doi:10.1016/j.njas.2016.03.009

Westerlund, J., & Edgerton, D. L. (2007). A Panel Bootstrap Cointegration Test. *Economics Letters, 97*(3), 185–190. doi:10.1016/j.econlet.2007.03.003

Weziak-Bialowolska, D., & Dijkstra, L. (2014). Regional Human Poverty Index Poverty in the regions of the European. *JRC Science and Policy Report.* doi:10.2788/10063

Whalen, K. A., Berlin, C., Ekberg, J., Barletta, I., & Hammersberg, P. (2018). 'All they do is win': Lessons learned from use of a serious game for Circular Economy education. *Resources, Conservation and Recycling, 135*, 335–345. doi:10.1016/j.resconrec.2017.06.021

Widiastuti, A. (2010). *Analisis Faktor-Faktor Yang Mempengaruhi Kemiskinan Di Jawa Tengah Tahun 2004-2008* (Doctoral dissertation). Universitas Diponegoro.

Wilkins, H., Merrilees, B., & Herington, C. (2007). Towards an understanding of total service quality in hotels. *International Journal of Hospitality Management, 26*(4), 840–853. doi:10.1016/j.ijhm.2006.07.006

Windfeld, E. S., & Brooks, M. S. L. (2015). Medical waste management – A review. *Journal of Environmental Management*, *163*, 98–108. doi:10.1016/j.jenvman.2015.08.013 PMID:26301686

Wong Ooi Mei, A., Dean, A. M., & White, C. J. (1999). Analysing service quality in the hospitality industry. *Managing Service Quality: An International Journal*, *9*(2), 136–143. doi:10.1108/09604529910257920

Wong, V., Turner, W., & Stoneman, P. (1996). Marketing Strategies and Market Prospects for Environmentally-Friendly Consumer Products 1. *British Journal of Management*, *7*(3), 263–281. doi:10.1111/j.1467-8551.1996.tb00119.x

Woolridge, A. C., Ward, G. D., Phillips, P. S., Collins, M., & Gandy, S. (2006). Life cycle assessment for reuse/recycling of donated waste textiles compared to use of virgin material: An UK energy saving perspective. *Resources, Conservation and Recycling*, *46*(1), 94–103. doi:10.1016/j.resconrec.2005.06.006

World Bank Group & UN. (2017). *The potential of the blue economy*. Retrieved June 10, 2018 from, https://openknowledge.worldbank.org/bitstream/handle/10986/26843/115545.pdf?sequence=1&isAllowed=y

World Bank. (1995). *Development in Practice: Priorities and Strategies for Education*. Washington, DC: World Bank. Retrieved from http://siteresources.worldbank.org/EDUCATION/Resources/278200-1099079877269/547664-1099080118171/Priorities_and_Strategies_for_Ed_WB_Review.pdf

World Bank. (1999). *Education Sector Strategy*. The World Bank. Retrieved from http://siteresources.worldbank.org/EDUCATION/Resources/ESSU/education_strategy_1999.pdf

World Bank. (2017, June). *What is the blue economy?* Retrieved August 22, 2018 from http://www.worldbank.org/en/news/infographic/2017/06/06/blue-economy

World Bank. (2018a). *Measuring Poverty*. Retrieved from Retrieved from http://www.worldbank.org/en/topic/measuringpoverty#1

World Bank. (2018b). *GDP per capita growth (annual %)*. Retrieved from http://databank.worldbank.org/data/reports.aspx?source=2&series=NY.GDP.PCAP.KD.ZG&country=

World Business Council for Sustainable Development. (2018). *Energy & Circular Economy*. Retrieved from https://www.wbcsd.org/Programs/Energy-Circular-Economy

World Health Organization. (2004). *The İmpact of Health Expenditure on Households and Options for Alternative Financing* (No. EM/RC51/R. 6). Retrieved from www.who.int/health_financing/documents/emrc51-4-healthexpenditureimpact.pdf

World Health Organization. (2007). *Working for Health. An İntroduction to the World Health Organization*. Retrieved from http://www.who.int/about/brochure_en.pdf

World Health Organization. (2014). *Household air pollution and health, Fact sheet No. 292, March 2014*. Retrieved from http://www.who.int/mediacentre/factsheets/fs292/en/

World Health Organization. (2018). *Global Health Observatory (GHO) Data*. Retrieved from http://www.who.int/gho/health_financing/health_expenditure/en/

Wu, P. H., & Liao, J. F. (2016). Service-oriented organizational citizenship behavior, perceived service quality and customer satisfaction in hospitality industry. *Journal of Applied Sciences (Faisalabad)*, *16*(1), 18–24. doi:10.3923/jas.2016.18.24

Wu, W. W., & Lee, Y. T. (2007). Developing global managers' competencies using the fuzzy DEMATEL method. *Expert Systems with Applications*, *32*(2), 499–507. doi:10.1016/j.eswa.2005.12.005

WWF. (n.d.). *Principles for a sustainable blue economy*. Retrieved August 10, 2018 from http://ocean.panda.org.s3.amazonaws.com/media/Principles+for+a+Blue+Economy+Brochure+LR.pdf

Yadav, R., & Pathak, G. S. (2016). Young consumers' intention towards buying green products in a developing nation: Extending the theory of planned behavior. *Journal of Cleaner Production*, *135*, 732–739. doi:10.1016/j.jclepro.2016.06.120

Yadav, R., & Pathak, G. S. (2017). Determinants of consumers' green purchase behavior in a developing nation: Applying and extending the theory of planned behavior. *Ecological Economics*, *134*, 114–122. doi:10.1016/j.ecolecon.2016.12.019

Yeh, T. M., & Huang, Y. L. (2014). Factors in determining wind farm location: Integrating GQM, fuzzy DEMATEL, and ANP. *Renewable Energy*, *66*, 159–169. doi:10.1016/j.renene.2013.12.003

Ye, Q., Li, H., Wang, Z., & Law, R. (2014). The influence of hotel price on perceived service quality and value in e-tourism: An empirical investigation based on online traveler reviews. *Journal of Hospitality & Tourism Research (Washington, D.C.)*, *38*(1), 23–39. doi:10.1177/1096348012442540

Yevmenyeva, A. (2013). Insider violations in EU. What can bring to justice. *Arbitration practice, 5*. Retrieved from http://pravorf.ru/upload/pravorf.ru-ins2.pdf

Yıldız, M. S., & Aksoy, S. (2015). *Analitik Hiyerarşi Prosesi ile Personel Seçimi Üzerine Bir Çalışma*. Abant İzzet Baysal Üniversitesi Sosyal Bilimler Enstitüsü Dergisi.

Yilmaz, K. G., & Belbag, S. (2016). Prediction of consumer behavior regarding purchasing remanufactured products: a logistics regression model. *International Journal of Business and Social Research*, 6(2), 01-10.

Yoo, B., Donthu, N., & Lee, S. (2000). An examination of selected marketing mix elements and brand equity. *Journal of the Academy of Marketing Science*, *28*(2), 195–211. doi:10.1177/0092070300282002

Yousapronpaiboon, K. (2014). SERVQUAL: Measuring higher education service quality in Thailand. *Procedia: Social and Behavioral Sciences*, *116*, 1088–1095. doi:10.1016/j.sbspro.2014.01.350

Youssef, F. N. (1996). Health care quality in NHS hospitals. *International Journal of Health Care Quality Assurance*, *9*(1), 15–28. doi:10.1108/09526869610109125 PMID:10156537

Yüksel, S., Dinçer, H., & Emir, Ş. (2017). Comparing the performance of Turkish deposit banks by using DEMATEL, Grey Relational Analysis (GRA) and MOORA approaches. *World Journal of Applied Economics*, *3*(2), 26–47. doi:10.22440/wjae.3.2.2

Yung, K., Li, D. D., & Jian, Y. (2015). The value of corporate financial flexibility in emerging countries. *Journal of Multinational Financial Management*, *32–33*, 25–41. doi:10.1016/j.mulfin.2015.07.001

Zavareh, F. B., Ariff, M. S. M., Jusoh, A., Zakuan, N., Bahari, A. Z., & Ashourian, M. (2012). E-service quality dimensions and their effects on e-customer satisfaction in internet banking services. *Procedia: Social and Behavioral Sciences*, *40*, 441–445. doi:10.1016/j.sbspro.2012.03.213

Zellner, A. (1962). An Efficient Method of Estimating Seemingly Unrelated Regressions and Tests for Aggregation Bias. *Journal of the American Statistical Association*, *57*(298), 348–368. doi:10.1080/01621459.1962.10480664

Zhang, C. T., & Ren, M. L. (2006). Closed-loop supply chain coordination strategy for the remanufacture of patented products under competitive demand. *Applied Mathematical Modelling*, *40*(13-14), 6243–6255. doi:10.1016/j.apm.2016.02.006

Zhijun, F., & Nailing, Y. (2007). Putting a circular economy into practice in China. *Sustainability Science*, *2*(1), 95–101. doi:10.100711625-006-0018-1

Zhu, Q., & Sarkis, J. (2006). An inter-sectoral comparison of green supply chain management in China: Drivers and practices. *Journal of Cleaner Production*, *14*(5), 472–486. doi:10.1016/j.jclepro.2005.01.003

Zhu, Q., Sarkis, J., & Lai, K. H. (2008). Confirmation of a measurement model for green supply chain management practices implementation. *International Journal of Production Economics*, *111*(2), 261–273. doi:10.1016/j.ijpe.2006.11.029

About the Contributors

Ulas Akkucuk is an Associate Professor of Quantitative Methods at Bogazici University Department of Management, Istanbul-Turkey. Dr. Akkucuk has a BS in Industrial Engineering from Bilkent University (1997), an MBA from Bogazici University (2000) and a PhD in Management Science and Information Systems from Rutgers University (2004). His research interests lie in the methodological development of multivariate techniques such as Clustering and Multidimensional Scaling and novel applications into fields including global competitiveness, CRM and technology management and environmental management. He has taught Statistics, CRM & Data Mining, and Global Aspects of Management courses, among others, at both graduate and undergraduate levels. He is associate editor and editorial board member of International Journal of Research in Business and Social Science (IJRBS) and has been an ad hoc reviewer for journals such as Journal of Multivariate Analysis, Bogazici Journal and International Journal of Business Economics and Management. He has edited four books the first entitled "Developing Sustainable Value in Marketing Finance and Economics" which was published by IGI Global in 2015, the second one "Handbook of Research on Waste Management Techniques for Sustainability" was published in 2016. The last one "Ethics and Sustainability in Global Supply Chain Management" came to fruition in 2017 and was subsequently indexed in both SCOPUS and Web of Science. The final book entitled "Handbook of Research on Supply Chain Management for Sustainable Development" was published recently in 2018. This title was also indexed in SCOPUS. He is a member of the Classification Society (CS), Society for the Study of Business and Finance (SSBF) and Turkish National Committee on Solid Waste Management (TNCSW).

* * *

María del Mar Alonso-Almeida is Lecturer of Business Administration. Her research interests focus on the corporate governance and sustainability in organisations. She has written several articles and has participated as co-author in two books about sustainability from the strategic, operational and practical perspective. In addition, she is interested in the study of the operations that affect these companies, as well as in the analysis of their organizational structures and the role of women in sustainability development.

Murat Burucuoglu received the BE degree in business administration from the Selcuk University, Turkey, in 2009, an MBA from Karamanoglu Mehmetbey University, in 2011. He received a PhD degree in business administration from Ondokuz Mayis University, Samsun, Turkey, in 2016. Dr. Burucuoglu currently an Assistant Professor in the Department of International Trade and Logistics. He has taught Marketing Management, Warehouse Management, Reverse Logistics courses. His main areas of research interest are consumer behavior and logistics management.

Ali Coskun is currently an Assistant Professor of Accounting and Information Management at Boğaziçi University in Istanbul, Turkey. He is also the Director of the Center for Applied Research in Finance (CARF) and Vice Director of Sustainable Development and Cleaner Production Center at the same university. During the period 2012 – 2015, he served as the Acting Director of Center for Innovation and Competition Based Development Studies at Boğaziçi University. Since 2012 he is the independent board member at Garanti Factoring, a subsidiary of BVBA. He is also serving as a board member of FO-DER, a non-governmental organization established to promote financial literacy in Turkey. Dr. Çoşkun received his Ph.D. in Accounting and Information Management from University of Texas at Dallas. He has an M.A. degree in Accounting and Information Management from the same university and an MBA degree from Boğaziçi University. He holds a B.S. in Industrial Engineering from Istanbul Technical University.

Hasan Dinçer is an Associate Professor of finance at Istanbul Medipol University, Faculty of Economics and Administrative Sciences, Istanbul-Turkey. Dr. Dinçer has BAs in Financial Markets and Investment Management at Marmara University. He received PhD in Finance and Banking with his thesis entitled "The Effect of Changes on the Competitive Strategies of New Service Development in the Banking Sector". He has work experience in finance sector as portfolio specialist and his major academic studies focusing on financial instruments, performance evaluation, and economics. He is the executive editor of the International Journal of Finance and Banking Studies (IJFBS) and the founder member of the Society for the Study of Business and Finance (SSBF).

Mehmet Talha Dulman received his BS degree from the Department of Industrial Engineering, Istanbul Technical University (ITU), Istanbul, Turkey in 2011. He received his MS degree from Mechanical and Industrial Engineering (MIE) Department, Northeastern University, Boston, MA, in May 2014 with a GPA of 4.00. He received his PhD degree in Industrial Engineering from Northeastern University in August 2017. While completing his PhD, he fulfilled the role of teaching assistant on several courses including logistics, warehousing and scheduling, and network analysis and advanced optimization. He also worked as a research assistant on vehicle routing and forecasting projects for Deliv, a company that provides same-day delivery. His research interests include closed-loop supply chains, environmental issues in manufacturing, vehicle routing problems, demand forecasting, and network optimization. He has co-authored several papers that have been published in conference proceedings and journals.

Evrim Erdogan received the BA degree in business administration from the Karadeniz Teknik University, Turkey, in 2001 and the MBA and Ph.D. degrees in marketing from Bulent Ecevit University, in 2006 and 2012, Turkey, respectively. She is currently an Assistant Professor in the Department of Business Administration, Ondokuz Mayis University. She has taught Principles of Marketing, Marketing Management, Service Marketing, E-Marketing courses. Her main areas of research interest are consumer behavior and digital marketing.

Seda Erdogan holds her PhD (Finance) degree from Bogazici University Department of Management. She holds her MSc (Finance) degree from Cass Business School - City University (UK) and her BA degree from Bogazici University. She is currently a lecturer in finance at Bilgi University. Previously, she worked as a research assistant at Bogazici University for six years and also in Corporate Bank and Credit Risk Departments at Citibank for eight years. Ms. Erdogan is an academic fellow of IIA-Turkey (member of ECIIA and IIA). Her research focuses on corporate finance, capital structure and emerging markets.

Yasin Galip Gencer is currently an assistant professor in Yalova University. He worked on a thesis with his advisor Dr. Ulas Akkucuk, in the Operations Management & Information Systems – PhD program in Boğaziçi University. Before joining this PhD program, he graduated from the Management Department and also has an MBA degree from Bogazici University. He is lecturing in Yalova University in the Department of International Trade and Finance as well. Furthermore, he also has a Leadership Communication certificate from Harvard Business School and has engaged in many business ventures in a family run company specializing in automotive and household appliance sales. Besides extensive business experience, he has also studied in Universiteit de Maastricht within the scope of an Erasmus exchange program. He has participated in a number of international conferences and published in proceedings volumes. His research interests are in forecasting automotive demand, determination of productivity and quality in the automotive sales and service sector.

Surendra M. Gupta, Ph.D., is a Professor of Mechanical and Industrial Engineering and the Director of the Laboratory for Responsible Manufacturing at Northeastern University in Boston, Massachusetts, USA. He received his BE in Electronics Engineering from Birla Institute of Technology and Science, MBA from Bryant University, and MSIE and Ph.D. in Industrial Engineering from Purdue University. He is a registered professional engineer in the State of Massachusetts, USA. Dr. Gupta's research interests span the areas of Production/Manufacturing Systems and Operations Research. He is mostly interested in Environmentally Conscious Manufacturing, Reverse and Closed-Loop Supply Chains, Disassembly Modeling and Remanufacturing. He has authored or coauthored twelve books and over 600 technical papers published in edited books, journals and international conference proceedings. His publications have received over 11,800 citations (with an h-index of 54) from researchers all over the world in journals, proceedings, books, and dissertations. He has traveled to all seven continents viz., Africa, Antarctica, Asia, Australia, Europe, North America and South America and presented his work at international conferences on six continents. Dr. Gupta has taught over 150 courses in such areas as operations research, inventory theory, queuing theory, engineering economy, supply chain management, and production planning and control. Among the many recognitions received, he is the recipient of outstanding research award and outstanding industrial engineering professor award (in recognition of teaching excellence) from Northeastern University as well as a national outstanding doctoral dissertation advisor award.

Hermes de Andrade Júnior, PhD. Professor, graduated in international relations, with master's degree in Sociology and PhD in Public Health (ENSP/FIOCRUZ). Member of transdisciplinary professorship, journalist, musician and environmental activist. One of the creators of the society of friends of the environmental protection area of Leme hill, in Rio de Janeiro. (SOAPA-Leme) and the Working Group on Intercultural Communication of the Society of Communication Researchers of Portugal (SOPCOM), Senior Researcher at the Center for Philosophical and Humanistic Studies of the Catholic University (CEFH / FFCS / UC) in Braga, Portugal.

Asli Kuscu has 9 years of multicultural work experience in marketing and sales in multinational companies. After completing her PhD in Marketing at Bogazici University, Turkey, Asli is currently working as an assistant professor in marketing at Yeditepe University Business Administration Department, teaching marketing courses and supervising MBA and PhD students. Her research interests and previous publications cover consumer-brand relationships and interactive marketing.

Esin Okay is a Professor in the Department of Banking and Finance at Istanbul Commerce University (ICU) since 2002. She is currently the Head of Department and serves on the board of Finance Institute. Okay was recently the director of the Center for Applied Research of International Creative Economy, Creative Industries and Creative Cities and the Center for Applied Research of Economics and Finance respectively at ICU. She received her BA in Business Administration and completed her PhD at the Institute of Banking and Insurance, respectively from the Marmara University. Prior to commencing her PhD thesis, she worked for Global Securities Inc. in Istanbul for 5 years, as a dealer and lastly the founding Deputy of Institutional Investment Department. Okay teaches undergraduate and graduate programs in the areas of finance, majorly risk management. Esin Okay has refereed papers, books and a book chapter in a widely recognized "World ESCO Outlook". In recent years, she has focused on energy finance as her papers appeared in journals of Social Science Index and received citations. Okay is a member of Professional Risk Managers' International Association (PRMIA). She also participates in sports, creative endavours and projects at ICU.

Omer Faruk Ozturk was born in Afyonkarahisar in 1981. He graduated from the Department of Economics at Erciyes University Faculty of Economics and Administrative Sciences. Completing his master's degree in Economics at Usak University Social Sciences Institute and his Ph.D. degree in the joint Public FInance program of Usak University-Afyon Kocatepe University, the author still serves as a faculty member in the Department of Public Finance at Usak University Faculty of Economics and Administrative Sciences.

Fatih Pınarbaşı is Research Assistant of marketing in İstanbul Medipol University. He has a BS in Management from Marmara University (2012. He got his master degree from the business administration in Yıldız Technical University (2017). At the same time, he got another master degree from Marmara University in 2017 with the major of marketing. His master thesis are "The role of retro-brand experience in repurchase intention and brand loyalty" and "Sensemaking of career with mind map technique: A research on business students". He is also a PhD candidate in business administration in Yıldız Technical University. His research interests lie in marketing, digital marketing and financial marketing.

José Miguel Rodríguez-Antón is Professor of Business Administration at Universidad Autónoma de Madrid (UAM), Spain, and Honorary and Visitor Professor of several European and American universities. Dr. Rodríguez-Antón is the founder and director of the Research Group on Tourism Business Management and President of the Tourism Studies Commission of the Spanish Association of Accounting and Business Administration (AECA).

Mahmut Unsal Sasmaz completed his undergraduate and graduate education at Usak University and his Ph.D. degree at Public Finance from Dumlupinar University Institute of Social Sciences. He is currently working as an Assistant Professor in Faculty of Economics and Administrative Sciences in Usak University. His major research interests are financial incentives, fiscal policy and environmental policy.

lknur Sayan worked as a manager in various management levels in the health sector for 23 years. Contributed in carrying out TS-EN-ISO 9000 Quality Assurance System activities, and establishing and improving ISO 10002: 2004, OHSAS 18001: 2007, ISO 9001: 2008, 14001: 2004 Environmental Management Systems. Improvement and development of hospitals are among the activities she has carried out. As private sector experience, she held administrative manager positions in the hospital management of Academic Hospital and Istanbul Aydın University Faculty of Dentistry. Her fields of interest are Total Quality in Health, Logistics and Procurement Management in Hospitals, Management Ethics, Business Management, Management Organization, Strategic Management in Health Institutions, Human Resources Management, and Organizational Behavior. She completed her masters degrees in Nursing Management at Marmara University Institute of Health Sciences and in Health Management at Bahçeşehir University Institute of Social Sciences. She earned her Ph.D. in Business Administration from İstanbul Aydın University and is currently a lecturer at İstanbul Kent University.

Gamze Yıldız Şeren was born in 1987. She is from Elazığ, Turkey. She is assistant professor Dr at Namık Kemal University, Faculty of Economics and Administrative Sciences, Public Finance Department Tekirdag-Turkey. She received undergraduate degree from Marmara University, Faculty of Economics and Administrative Sciences, Department of Public Finance (2008). She holds master's degree (MA) in Public Economics from Marmara University (2011) and Ph.D in Public Finance from Marmara University. Her doctorate thesis is on gender responsive budgeting. Her main research fields focus on public finance, tax law, budgeting and gender.

Bülent Sezen is a Professor of Operations Management at Gebze Technical University. He graduated from Department of Industrial Engineering in İstanbul Technical University. He received his MSc degree from Industrial Engineering Department in Virginia Tech/USA. His PhD is from Gebze Institute of Technology in Department of Business Administration. His research areas include Operations Management, Logistics and Supply Chain Management.

Svetlana Snezhko is a compliance professional. Currently she is a Leading compliance manager of one of the largest Russian Telecom operators. She has six years of experience in the telecommunications industry, implementing and maintaining compliance management systems in accordance with international standards, coordinating various compliance programs, and in particular, specializing in anti-corruption compliance (in accordance with FCPA, UK BA and Russian legislation). Among other professional interests are corporate social responsibility, sustainability factors and non-financial reporting. Svetlana is a post-graduate of MSU (Lomonosov Moscow State University), holding a Ph.D. in Sociology of management and an ICA (International Compliance Association) graduate with Int. Dip (comp), and has publications in periodicals, including articles on compliance issues.

Yunus Yayla was born in Kocaeli/Karamursel in 1989. He graduated from Uludağ University Faculty of Economics and Administrative Sciences Department of Finance in 2013. He graduated from Usak University Institute of Social Sciences Department of Public Finance in 2018. He is currently pursuing his PhD student in the Department of Public Finance at Sakarya University Institute of Social Sciences.

Sibel Yildiz Çankaya is assistant professor in the Department of Business Administration at Abant Izzet Baysal University. She graduated from the Department of Business Administration and also has an MBA degree from Bolu Abant Izzet Baysal University. She earned her Ph.D. degree from the Gebze Technical University. Her research interests focus on supply chain management.

Serhat Yüksel is Associate Professor of finance in İstanbul Medipol University. Before this position, he worked as a senior internal auditor for seven years in Finansbank, Istanbul-Turkey and 1 year in Konya Food and Agriculture University as an assistant professor. Dr. Yüksel has a BS in Business Administration (in English) from Yeditepe University (2006) with full scholarship. He got his master degree from the economics in Boğaziçi University (2008). He also has a PhD in Banking from Marmara University (2015). His research interests lie in banking, finance and financial crisis. He has more than 70 publications (books, book chapters, scientific articles, etc.).

Index

www.ingramcontent.com/pod-product-compliance
Lightning Source LLC
LaVergne TN
LVHW062141300926
849161LV00010B/2591